Beckett Great Sports Heroes

Joe Montana

By the staff of Beckett Publications

House of Collectibles • New York

Published by: House of Collectibles
201 East 50th Street
New York, NY 10022

Distributed by Ballantine Books, a division of Random House, Inc., New York,
and simultaneously in Canada by Random House of Canada Limited, Toronto.

Manufactured in the United States of America

ISBN: 0-876-37981-1

Cover design by Michaelis/Carpelis Design Associates

Cover photo by Focus on Sports, Inc.

First Edition: October 1995

10   9   8   7   6   5   4   3   2   1

No Finer Niner

Joe Montana's consistent excellence in the clutch leaves a legacy that will be difficult to match

In many ways he was Your Average Joe: physically unremarkable, self-effacing, deferential. But on NFL Sundays, particulary those denoted by a Roman numeral, he was anything but ordinary.

Joe Montana was as far from ordinary as his Western Pennsylvania roots were from the stubbornly idiosyncratic city by the bay that embraced him like a native son. His unparalleled skill at not merely rising to the occasion but *always* rising to the occasion marks him as one of the greatest clutch performers in the history of sport. Other athletes have shined in the spotlight, sure. Some more than once. But every time?

Four times he reached pro football's ultimate game, and four times he performed impeccably, even heroically. In delivering four world championships to the 49ers, Joe also transformed the franchise from an object of ridicule to an object of envy. Along the way, he captivated NFL fandom with an uncanny ability to engineer comebacks, captured and unified the hearts of a self-doubting city and compiled a record of achievement that is unlikely to be surpassed — ever.

What greater legacy can an athlete leave? This outwardly ordinary Joe forever will be remembered as anything but.

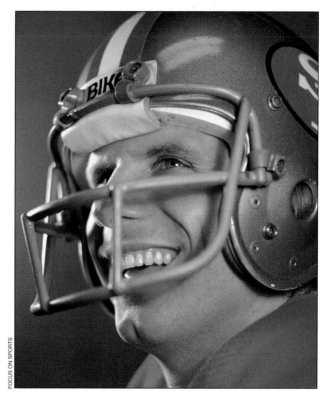

The winning aura exuded and embodied by Joe Montana enlivened a franchise and an entire city.

Gary Santaniello
Gary Santaniello
Senior Editor

CONTENTS

6 Joe's Place Joe's heroic comebacks and Super Bowl triumphs cemented his standing as a civic icon. •By Gary Swan

14 King of the Hill If winning is the key criterion, Montana reigns as one of the best quarterbacks ever. •By Rick Gosselin

22 Passage to Glory This extraordinary Joe left an indelible mark on San Francisco, the 49ers, and pro football. •By Ira Miller

28 Final Chapter After parting with the 49ers, Joe made winning another Super Bowl his Chief concern. •By Rick Dean

32 Quality Time Retirement will allow Joe more time to devote to his family and off-the-field endeavors. •By Nancy Gay

38 Big-Game Hunter Joe Cool's trophy case boasts four world championship rings and three Super Bowl MVP awards. Four NFL insiders detail how Montana bagged these sacred prizes.
•By Ira Miller, Gary Swan, Howard Balzer and Nancy Gay

48 Striking Gold Joe's Rookie Card lit up the hobby sky for eight years before the football card explosion of 1989, but collectors continue to treat Joe like an ultrahyped draft pick. •By Pete Williams

56 Comprehensive Card Checklist Montana's card collection is a championship-caliber keepsake.

60 Digging Deeper Think you've collected every piece of Montana memorabilia? Do we have a surprise for you. •By Mike Antonucci

64 Strokes of Genius Joe's ingeniousness on the gridiron made him an ideal subject for sports artists.

74 Common Threads Five relationships that left indelible imprints on Joe Montana's career. •By Gary Swan

86 "Cheer, Cheer For Old Notre Dame" Football's ultimate classroom in South Bend, Ind., taught Joe much more than just the X's and O's. •By Bill Moor

94 Passed Over Need some proof that it's tough to predict a winner? Just ask the teams who passed on Joe — some more than once — in the '79 draft. •By Will Pry

98 Portrait of a Winner Our photo essay provides a behind the scenes look at Joe through the years.

108 The Comeback Kid Regardless of the score, the weather, the opponent or his health, Montana always found a way to beat the odds. •By Dave Spadaro

118 Miracle Worker Watching Joe conduct his Sunday sermons was a religious experience for the men on the other side of the pulpit. •By Len Pasquarelli

124 Beckett Remembers Since the inception of Beckett Football Card Monthly, Beckett always has been a first-string

Joe's place

Joe Montana's cool under fire and Super Bowl heroics cemented his status as a civic treasure

By Gary Swan

"Joe brought to San Francisco excitement, pride, but more importantly, renewed dignity. He brought San Francisco back to being the nation's premier city. . . . This was a city in great distress, but then came Joe Montana."

— Former 49ers coach Bill Walsh, on the occasion of Montana's public retirement ceremony, April 18, 1995, in downtown San Francisco.

Joe Montana, whose comeback heroics thrilled football fans for years, rarely receives credit for a turnaround he inspired of far greater proportions off the field — San Francisco's own come-from-behind triumph.

As Walsh stood in front of 50,000 Montana fans who'd gathered to say goodbye on April 18, the former head coach helped put Joe's contributions into the proper historical context.

"[Joe] did more than any one person to change the city of San Francisco," said Walsh, drawing applause from a lineup of dignitaries that included the city's political and business leaders.

The task that Montana initially faced wasn't easy. When he arrived on the dismal 49ers landscape in 1979, San Francisco was a sports backwater. It was known as the city great athletes "came from" but a city where they rarely stayed. San Francisco never had risen above mediocrity as a professional sports entity. A single NBA championship was all it had, courtesy of the 1974-75 Warriors who wore the amorphous Golden State, rather than the city's name, on their uniforms.

Sure, the A's and Raiders had climbed the heights of their respected sports, but in the heart of a San Francisco native the eight-mile long Bay Bridge might well have been a bridge to nowhere. San Franciscans had looked long at Oakland as lacking the charm and refinements that made their city special the world over. They took a dim view of the Raiders' blue collar, bandit image.

Montana's magic, which produced four Super Bowl championships in the

Joe's peerless performances under pressure endeared him to San Franciscans, who gave him a rousing sendoff upon his retirement in April.

1980s, changed the city's sports scenery. His heroic exploits forced people around the country to change the way they viewed San Francisco. And, perhaps most importantly, Joe provided a welcome psychological boost to the city at a time when it sorely needed one.

Montana, the boyish looking third-round draft pick slipped unnoticed into town in 1979 — during one of the darkest chapters in San Francisco political and economic history.

Tragedies such as the Jim Jones massacre in Jonestown, Guyana, a group based in the city, and political rioting in the streets of San Francisco attracted television coverage for all the wrong reasons.

Economically, the city had taken a backseat to its rival West Coast cities. Once the business hub of California, San Francisco long had been eclipsed by

PETER READ MILLER / SPORTS ILLUSTRATED

When Joe looks back on his 16 magical years in the NFL, he'll see a legacy that spans two cities, two uniform numbers and too many fond memories to recall. Doubtlessly his legions of fans will feel the same way.

Los Angeles. And the city watched economic vitality drain south to San Jose and its Silicon Valley, which attracted some of the Bay Area's best and brightest executives. Corporations were beating a path to the suburbs, where the cost of doing business was much less.

At the same time, the city's internal critics lamented the rise of super skyscrapers that dominated a new downtown landscape. The city's tailspin was chronicled by the media heralding San Francisco's supposed demise. Old "Baghdad-by-the-Bay" epitomized everything going wrong around the country.

Oh yeah, San Francisco's NFL team was horrible, too. The 49ers Montana joined were a down-in-the-dumps outfit, coming off a 2-14 season in 1978, which was matched in Joe's rookie season of 1979. Their new, young owner — Ed DeBartolo Jr. of Youngstown, Ohio — had not endeared himself to San Franciscans after making brash comments on his way into town.

Montana made dramatic comebacks look easy, but lifting the spirits of the city up presented no simple task. After all, San Francisco's home field is Candlestick Park, a frigid concrete wind tunnel the city built to lure the football Giants from New York. The stadium's blustery

PETER READ MILLER / SPORTS ILLUSTRATED

reputation was sealed when pitcher Stu Miller was blown off the mound during an All-Star Game. The 49ers previously played at Kezar Stadium, a creaky, oversized high school field that required a steel barrier over the players' tunnel as protection from the flying beer bottles that rained down as the losses piled up.

When DeBartolo hired Joe Thomas as his general manager and Pete Mc-Culley and Fred O'Connor as his first two head coaches, the team went from bad to worse. In 1978, three coaches were hired and fired in less than 12 months. Luckily for DeBartolo, he hit pay dirt with the third guy — a relatively obscure assistant coach named Walsh.

Montana started slow. He showed up at camp with unkempt frizzy hair and a fu manchu mustache. Joe's rookie resume boasts one start in a losing cause. As fans at the civic sendoff chanted, "We love you, Joe," Walsh reminded them, "You weren't saying that in 1979. You were saying to me, 'Where did you get this guy who looks like a Swedish placekicker?'"

But in 1980, his second season, Montana provided the first hints of his ability to rally a team, starting seven of the last 10 games and throwing 15 touchdown passes and nine interceptions. Most importantly, Walsh knew he'd found the quarterback for his system. The young man responded with a team passing percentage record — nearly 65 percent.

Then in 1981, behind Montana's stalwart leadership, and with the help of All-Pros such as Ronnie Lott and Dwight Hicks, the 49ers in one magical season went from doormats to world champions, beginning a successful reign of 12 straight seasons of 10 victories or more.

San Franciscans stood together for their 49ers on that Sunday afternoon in

Joe's body took a pounding during his two seasons in Kansas City, but he always relished the opportunity to again rise to an occasion.

1981 when Montana capped the winning touchdown drive in the NFC championship game against Dallas. Joe's fearless rollout and desperation heave off his back foot found a leaping Dwight Clark along the backline of the end zone — a defining moment worthy of its own nickname. The Catch became the most celebrated event in San Francisco sports history — making the Super Bowl XVI triumph over Cincinnati two weeks later practically a foregone conclusion.

The civic celebration that greeted the 49ers upon their return from that Super Bowl in Pontiac, Mich., was the largest in the city's history. More than 500,000 people participated from all parts of northern California, joining in on the euphoria on Jan. 25, 1982. The blowout became the party to end all parties, bigger than the celebration that followed the surrender of Japan to end World War II. People were hanging out of their cars, kissing policemen, hugging each other, producing an event that unified the whole city.

And at the center of this celebration stood Montana — the most loved man in the city. Joe's popularity grew because his personal style matched that of the city's — understated, graceful and self-effacing. It's the same kinship the city felt for another beloved local hero, the Yankee Clipper Joe DiMaggio, a native San Franciscan.

But Montana, as he led the 49ers to other Super Bowl victories in 1985, 1989 and 1990, earned special consideration because he played all but the last two seasons of his pro football career by the Bay. Joe was cool, gracious and humble, and though he didn't possess Joe Namath's gift of gab and attraction to the bright lights and big city, San Francisco didn't care. Namath was New York. And no one in San Francisco envied New York.

Around the country, people thought of the 49ers in terms of Joe, and of San Francisco as an extension of the 49ers. Tourism reached new heights. Downtown office space became rare once again. Coincidence? Probably. But the city's problems took a backseat in the national spotlight to the accomplishments of its football team and its splendid quarterback.

The fact that 50,000 people showed up on a workday last April to see Montana's final farewell underscores his enduring popularity that never diminished in the two seasons he played in Kansas City. The trade to the Cheifs in April 1993 presented the only way out of an uncomfortable situation for Joe and the 49ers. But so revered was Montana that some fans scrapped their allegiance to the team for allegiance to the player.

Steve Young, with two NFL passing titles under his belt by the time Montana was traded, was the unfortunate victim of the Homeric status accorded Montana. It was as if any acknowledgment of Young's accomplishments would demean Montana's legend. It took a victory in Super Bowl XXIX and Young's fourth straight passing title before Steve could quiet the uproar in some quarters about the 49ers allowing Montana to leave for K.C.

In many ways, the master passed the torch to the student, but one thing remains clear: Young may have rented San Francisco, but Joe will always own it.   •

Gary Swan covered Joe Montana for the San Francisco Chronicle.

Super Statistics

Joe Montana's near-perfect performances on pro football's biggest stage resulted in four world championships in nine years for the 49ers

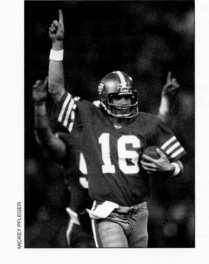

MICKEY PFLEGER

Super Bowl	Opponent	Score	Comp.	Att.	Yards	TD	Int.
SB XVI*	Cincinnati	26-21	14	22	157	1	0
SB XIX*	Miami	38-16	24	35	331	3	0
SB XXIII	Cincinnati	20-16	23	36	357	2	0
SB XXIV*	Denver	55-10	22	29	297	5	0
Totals			**83**	**122**	**1142**	**11**	**0**

*Named Most Valuable Player

By Rick Gosselin

king
of the
hill

If winning is the key criterion, Joe Montana reigns as one of the best quarterbacks ever

ou certainly can argue that Joe Montana is the best quarter-back ever to play in the NFL. He's the only quarterback in history to sport 40,000 career passing yards and four Super Bowl championships. His marriage of statistics with team success presents a powerful argument, indeed.

But you also can contend that Sammy Baugh is the greatest quarterback ever. Or Otto Graham. Or Johnny Unitas. Baugh led the NFL in passing a record six times. Graham took the Cleveland Browns to the championship game in all 10 of his seasons. And Unitas threw touchdown passes in 47 consecutive games from 1956 to 1960. That's the NFL equivalent to Joe DiMaggio's 56-game hitting streak.

Baugh, Graham and Unitas are in the Hall of Fame. All were selected to the NFL's 75th anniversary team along with Montana. You can argue into the night about their respective degrees of accomplishment. But to label one the greatest?

"I don't think you can say anyone is ever the best in a team sport," Graham says. "So much depends on your teammates. You have to have a sporting chance with your receivers, blockers. . . .You can put people in the top category. But nothing is as clear-cut in a team sport as it would be in,

say, track where one person can run the fastest or jump the highest. [In football], you need help around you.

"Take Joe Montana and put him with the Tampa Bay Bucs and I've got news for you — people wouldn't know much about him," he adds. "He'd be lying flat on his back most of the time, and he wouldn't be half as good as he is right now. The same with Steve Young. If you put me with the 49ers, I'd be pretty darn good. Take any of them. Sid Luckman, Roger Staubach, Unitas."

In fact, five years from now, people may argue as to whether Montana was even the greatest quarterback in 49ers history. Young, invisible early in his career as a quarterback for the Bucs, is thundering down the stretch of his NFL career.

Young took over for Montana as quarterback of the 49ers in 1991 at the age of 30 and has compiled a four-season run that rivals any in NFL history.

He has won a record four consecutive NFL passing titles. He has been league MVP twice and Super Bowl MVP once. Young passed for a personal-best 4,023 yards in 1993 and 35 touchdowns in 1994. Both efforts broke Montana club records. Young's passing efficiency rating of 112.8 in 1994 broke Montana's NFL single-season record, and Steve also unseated Montana as pro football's all-time leading passer along the way. Young's career rating is now 96.8, Montana's 92.3.

"If Steve Young performs a few more years like this last one, all four of us on that all-time team would be in second place," Graham says. "He'd be in first place all by himself."

But for now, the argument of Montana's supremacy remains as strong as any. And Young is the first to admit that.

"I watched him for a number of years and a lot of times just shook my head in disbelief," says Young, who spent four years on the sideline as Montana's backup. "No doubt, he's the best I've seen with my eyes. I learned this offense from him, and obviously I try to emulate a lot of things he did."

Known more for his golden arm than his mobility, Joe's attempts to scramble out of the pocket proved to be quite futile — as well as painful — later in his career.

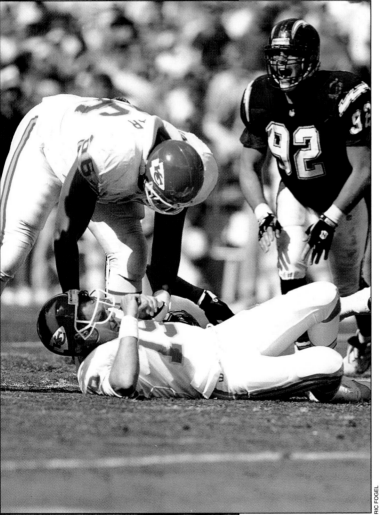

MICKEY PFLEGER

there's a lot to emulate. When Montana retired after the 1994 season, just two quarterbacks in history had completed more passes than his 3,409. Just three had thrown more touchdown passes (273) or tossed for more yards (40,551). But sheer numbers don't do Joe's career justice. His persona and ability to seize the moment truly set him apart from his peers.

Not since Graham has the NFL witnessed a winner of Montana's caliber. Graham won seven championships in his 10 seasons, four in the old All-American Football Conference and three in the NFL. Montana took his team to seven conference championship games (six with the 49ers and one with the Chiefs) in his 12 seasons as an NFL starter. Joe won four of those games and went on to win the Super Bowl each time. In three of those Super Bowls, he earned MVP honors. Montana won 70 percent of his career starts in the regular season and 69 percent of his starts in the postseason. Quite simply, he refused to lose.

Montana won 132 games in his career, including 31 with fourth-quarter rallies. His two greatest comebacks occurred in the same calendar year — 1989. The first came in Super Bowl XXIII against Cincinnati, the second in a September game against Philadelphia.

Trailing, 16-13, with 3:20 remaining in the Super Bowl, Montana drove the 49ers 92 yards in 11 plays for the winning touchdown. Montana completed eight of nine passes in that drive, climaxed by his 10-yard touchdown strike to John Taylor with 34 seconds left. It was Montana at his finest — he passed for 357 yards and two touchdowns with no interceptions to sink the Bengals. Yet it was the only Super Bowl Montana played in that he was not selected as the MVP.

The regular season game against Philadelphia may have lacked the theater of the Super Bowl comeback, but it certainly didn't lack the theatrics. The vaunted Eagles defensive front that included Reggie White and Jerome Brown hounded and pounded Montana that day, sacking him to the Veterans Stadium turf eight times. But Montana kept getting up and passed for 428 yards and five touchdowns to deliver the 49ers a 38-28 victory. He threw four touchdown passes in the fourth quarter, including three in the final seven minutes to rally the 49ers from a 28-17 deficit.

But, as Graham points out, having a great supporting cast goes a long way in winning crucial battles. Montana came to be surrounded by greatness in San Francisco with the likes of Jerry Rice, Dwight Clark, Roger Craig and Randy Cross in his huddle. Rice is surely bound for the Hall of Fame, and Clark, Craig and Cross were Pro Bowl regulars who also have strong

With solid protection from his offensive line, Joe consistently carved up secondaries with a feathery-soft passing touch.

chances to be enshrined in Canton someday.

When Montana left the 49ers, he left that great supporting cast. He was traded to the Kansas City Chiefs at his request in 1993. Instead of handing off to Craig, he was handing off to Kimble Anders. Instead of passing to Rice, he was passing to Willie Davis. Yet an aging Montana still was able to weave his magic in his new, less talented surroundings. He passed Kansas City to a division title in 1993, the first such crown by the Chiefs since 1971. He also steered them to the AFC championship game, their first appearance in a league or conference title game since 1969. The AFC coaches and players paid homage to Montana by voting him to his eighth Pro Bowl.

"If the success of a leader of any team is defined in victories, then Joe Montana and the teams he has been associated with would be recognized as simply the best," Kansas City coach Marty Schottenheimer says.

Montana reminded everyone of his powerful presence on the field in the second game of the 1994 season when he faced a unique opponent — his former team. In the eagerly awaited showdown game against the man who took his job and the team that traded him, Montana outdueled Young as the Chiefs upset the 49ers, 24-17. It was one of the just three losses San Francisco suffered last season on the way to its record fifth Super Bowl championship.

"The man was made to be a quarterback," says Craig, who traveled to Kansas City that day to see Montana extract his revenge. "He's a warrior. There's nothing he can't do."

Is Montana the greatest quarterback ever? Who knows. But as countless opponents have discovered throughout the years, it doesn't pay to bet against him. •

Rick Gosselin covers the NFL for The Dallas Morning News.

Be it in 49ers togs or a Chiefs uniform, Joe regularly wreaked havoc on opposing teams whenever he would drop back into his trademark passing stance.

"Every player has something to prove every year. You can't rely on what you've done in the past. It just won't hold up. Anyone who wants to be successful has to treat it that way."

PASSAGE TO GLORY

Joe Montana's arrival in San Francisco
barely caused a tremor.
His departure shook the city to its core.
In between, a legend was forged.

By Ira Miller

MICHAEL ZAGARIS

On the day Joe Montana held his farewell press conference at the 49ers' headquarters in Santa Clara — about 50 miles south of San Francisco — dozens of fans staged a vigil on the sidewalk just outside the building.

They carried signs and banners. They wore their 49ers caps and T-shirts. They hooted and hollered for their hero.

Say it ain't so, Joe. Say you're not leaving us.

But Joe, their Joe, was leaving. He was embarking on a new, albeit uncertain, beginning in Kansas City. San Francisco and all that Joe accomplished there was in his rearview mirror.

For the countless Bay Area fans who grew up believing No. 16 was a cross

Most of Joe's former teammates were in grade school when the Fu Manchu look was en vogue.

between Superman and James Bond, the reaction was predictable. It was as if Chinatown or the Golden Gate Bridge suddenly were being transported to Missouri.

The fascination with Montana goes far beyond four Super Bowl victories and a plethora of pro football records. It goes beyond a rather unprepossessing body and spindly legs that make Joe look, outside a football uniform, well, rather ordinary.

It goes to the man's determination — his heart. It goes to his uncanny ability to fight back from injury and adversity, at times refusing even to acknowledge nagging ailments.

In 1986, Montana politely refused advice to retire following serious back surgery, instead returning to the gridiron just eight weeks later.

Eight years later, Joe finally did retire, but on his terms — not those dictated by injuries such as his two-year fight back from major elbow surgery which would have felled mere mortals.

It goes to his quiet nature, a shyness almost. For all his success, Montana never particularly enjoyed being thrust into the limelight.

It goes to his grit. With Joe Montana at quarterback, a game was never lost until the final gun sounds. In that unwillingness to accept defeat, fans could see a metaphor for their own lives. Here was an ordinary looking fellow who performed extraordinary feats on the football field. Why couldn't they do the same in real life?

Perhaps most of all, it goes to his cool. Only Joe Cool had the presence of mind in the heat of battle — with a Super Bowl on the line — to look up in the stands, see actor John Candy (now deceased) and point him out to relax his troops.

Combine all that with a winning smile and matinee-idol looks, and the attraction to Joe is easily understood.

None of this would mean much, of course, if

"Pressure comes from the desire to succeed, or not to fail. If you don't really care about what happens to you, then you don't feel pressure. But anyone out here who says he doesn't feel pressure is crazy. They've felt it in some form or another or they wouldn't be in the position they are in."

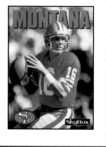

Montana couldn't play. But boy, could he play.

His name graces every short list of football's greatest quarterbacks. Has any quarterback — or any athlete, for that matter — been more relaxed, more poised or tougher under the most difficult of circumstances?

Not likely.

Sixty minutes in January. Winner take all. The ultimate pressure cooker. Reputations and millions of dollars on the line. And in four Super Bowls, Montana made nary a mistake.

Baseball's Don Larsen once pitched a perfect game in the World Series — the only one ever. Montana pitched four perfect games in the Super Bowl. Joe completed more than two-thirds of his passes, with better than one in eight completions going for a touchdown. He didn't throw an interception. He averaged more than nine yards for every attempt, boasting an out-of-this-world 127.8 quarterback rating. And don't forget his 5.6-yard per carry rushing average and two running touchdowns.

Oh, by the way, Montana also was selected as the MVP in three Super Bowls, something no other player has accomplished. Yet, it was the Super Bowl in which he didn't walk home with the MVP hardware where Joe wrote his ticket to football immortality.

Super Bowl XXIII (January 1989) will be remembered forever as the stage for Montana's 92-yard, game-winning march in the last three minutes to beat the Cincinnati Bengals.

"The Drive."

You know, like "The Catch," another unforgettable Montana freeze frame.

Joe's first huddle on The Drive was in the shadow of his own goalpost, just eight yards in front of the 49ers' end zone. Three minutes, 10 seconds flashed on the clock at Joe Robbie Stadium. Tensions were high. But before Joe put his first brush stroke on this masterpiece in the making, he decided to scope out the crowd.

What?!

"I knew what we were going to do," Montana remembers. "I was getting tired standing there. You only add to the pressure if you say, 'Oh, my God, what am I going to do? What if I miss a pass?' I had no business to discuss, and I thought pointing out John Candy might relax everyone."

The funny thing is, no one had a clue how good Montana would be when the

49ers drafted him at the end of the third round in 1979.

Of course, you never plan on any draft choice becoming the best ever. But in Montana's case, many questioned whether he'd even be a capable NFL quarterback.

Joe looked too fragile, and his arm wasn't strong enough, or so went the arguments. Teams such as the Chicago Bears and Green

Bay Packers, both desperate for quarterbacks, passed on Montana. Then, Bill Walsh, about to begin his first season as the 49ers' head coach, chose Joe after 81 other players, including three quarterbacks (Jack Thompson, Phil Simms and Steve Fuller), had been selected.

No one could have predicted the era Montana was poised to launch, and for good reason. The 49ers were in such sad shape that Walsh couldn't even entice an outsider to join the organization as general manager, despite offering the job to several people. "One of them said, 'I smell a

Some in-depth chalktalk in the locker room at halftime enabled Montana to speak volumes on the field.

MICHAEL ZAGARIS

The Genius, Bill Walsh (far left) and the owner, Eddie DeBartolo deserve their slice of the NFL's most cherished prize. But it's always been Joe and his family who've been treated like royalty.

rat,' " Walsh remembers.

"That's how bad the organization had gotten," Walsh adds. "It was so bad that people didn't want to work here."

Montana, though, was just glad to be gainfully employed in the NFL. He was eager to learn Walsh's complicated offense.

The pair developed a mutually beneficial relationship until it cooled shortly before Walsh left the 49ers. Montana believed Walsh was trying to phase him out too soon. The two men grew closer in more recent times, such as when Montana sought Walsh's advice when the 49ers committed to Steve Young as their No. 1 quarterback.

"I must say that he's shown more dedication or more courage or more persistence in playing than I thought anyone could," Walsh says. "I haven't seen a man like that, who thrived on playing, because he's reached all of the tangible goals you can reach.

"A lot of people would let down, or find a way to step away, but [that didn't] even distract him. He just kept right on going.

"Typically," Walsh adds, "someone who's won four Super Bowls, or someone who's won every major award there is in sports, would be less motivated and would have gotten more into show business, or more into public appearances and things. Joe [was] the other way. Joe [saw] less and less of the public and [became] more focused on football. He just absolutely loved to play."

Montana was both defined and consumed by football, though his life at home with wife, Jennifer, and four children appears happy and relatively normal. Joe's retirement allowed him to spend more time with his family at their new wine-country estate, as well as explore other professional options.

Part of his plan involves working as a football analyst for NBC's NFL coverage, which will allow viewers to hear his insights into the game — insights that few other players in any era enjoyed. He also will pursue his passion for auto racing, although it's doubtful he'll be behind the wheel of a race car at the Indianapolis 500.

One item of business that did not drive Montana to retirement was his health. Even though his knees plagued him during his Kansas City days, Joe says he did not retire for physical reasons.

"It's not so much my body," he told reporters the day he announced his retirement. "It just came up on me all of a sudden. I'm just not as fired up, not as excited about working out."

Jennifer would have been happy if Joe had retired following his 1986 back surgery.

"I think [going to Kansas City] was a good change for me. One thing that happens when you're in one place for a while, you get settled in and you lose a little bit. I think I got my spark back. As much as I [missed] it back [in San Francisco], career-wise, this was a boost."

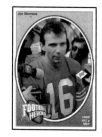

"My wife [was] ready for me to go anytime," Montana says. "She loved and hated Sundays. She loved to watch and she knew I enjoyed it, but she hated the thought of something happening physically."

There's tremendous irony in this.

Montana didn't really become an icon until a couple of years after the back surgery. Had he retired at the time he underwent the surgery for the ruptured disc, he would have been remembered as a terrific quarterback who won two Super Bowls and turned around a franchise. But he wouldn't be as revered as he is today.

That's partially because of his unprecedented recovery. He returned to action less than two months after the operation.

But it's also due to the fact that, in 1988, Montana resisted Walsh's attempted phase-out. Actually, he did more than resist, he re-established himself as the 49ers' quarterback before winning two more Super Bowls and playing the best football of his career.

The crux of his comeback came after a 1988 game at Phoenix in which the 49ers led, 23-0, in the third quarter with Young at quarterback. San Francisco lost, 24-23.

If the 49ers had won that game, it would have marked two victories in a row for Young.

Maybe Young would

"The on-field expectations I have of myself are higher than anyone's. Those are easy to live up to. Off the field is more difficult. You might have a fence [holding a crowd back], and you try to go over and sign some autographs, but you end up seeing little kids smashed against the fence by people who have no respect. A kid gets hurt, and you end up feeling twice as bad."

have remained the starting quarterback.

Maybe Walsh would have remained the coach following the season instead of stepping down.

Maybe the 49ers wouldn't have won the next two Super Bowls.

Maybe Montana would have been traded then.

Stop! Wait just a second. That's not what happened.

Montana returned to the lineup after missing two games because, to use Walsh's explanation, Joe was "fatigued" and needed rest. Still, the 49ers lost the following week to the Raiders. Then Walsh and owner Ed DeBartolo Jr. held a series of private meetings that led to Walsh's decision to retire after the season.

And the 49ers, led by

Montana, embarked on the greatest tear in franchise history. They won 34 of their next 37 games, and captured back-to-back Super Bowl titles.

During that stretch, from November 1988 to November 1990, Montana played at the highest level of his career.

Joe missed three of the 37 games due to injury. The 49ers won 31 of the 34 games Montana played in, and the team scored an average 29.4 points. Montana's *average* game during that period: 31.5 attempts, 21.1 completions, 270 yards, 2.1 touchdowns, 0.7 interceptions. His quarterback rating stood at 108.7.

Even by Montana's standards, it was excellent. It's 16.4 points above his career rating, which is the second highest of all time.

"It took him from being the best of the last few years to being the

Before being introduced to record-setting receiver Jerry Rice, Joe's favorite target was dependable Dwight Clark, who just happened to be his best friend.

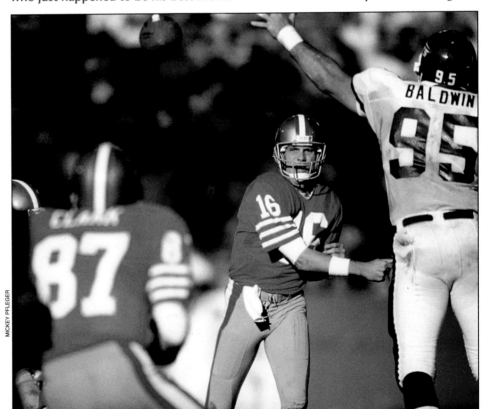

N o, it didn't turn out exactly the way everyone had hoped it would.

The Kansas City Chiefs did not become immediate Super Bowl champions upon acquiring Joe Montana, which was their hope in trading for him in April 1993. Montana consequently did not acquire the fifth Super Bowl ring he coveted — one that would have distanced him from the only other quarterback with a ring collection to match, Pittsburgh's Terry Bradshaw.

None of that should suggest, however, that Joe Montana's career-ending, two-season stint in Kansas City — the postscript of his storybook 16-season NFL career — was anything but a noble, worthy venture.

Joe, you see, got almost everything he wanted. Cheated out of two years by the arm surgery that stole his 1991 and '92 seasons, Montana wanted that time back.

And he knew he wouldn't get it in San Francisco where Steve Young had so capably replaced the 49ers' living legend.

So at age 36, Montana moved to Kansas City with a renewed interest — no, with a renewed *passion* — for the game that had been his entire life, but which he'd recently taken for granted.

"When you hear so many people say, 'You'll never throw again, you'll never play again,' it makes you want to go out and perform the way you used to perform," Montana said in explaining his rediscovered enthusiasm at his first Chiefs training camp.

There were no guarantees this new venture would be successful, no assurances that Joe Montana could be, well, Joe Montana again.

"Montana put his whole reputation on the line when he went to Kansas City," notes former quarterback and TNT football analyst Pat Haden.

FINAL CHAPTER

After parting with the 49ers, Montana made winning another Super Bowl his Chief concern

By Rick Dean

MIKE POWELL / ALLSPORT USA

Joe didn't win a fifth Super Bowl ring with the Chiefs, but he did provide fans with excitement, drama and, finally, a heartfelt goodbye during his two years in Kansas City.

"I will forever respect him for that. The easiest thing for him to have done would have been to sit on the bench in San Francisco behind Steve Young, be the crowd favorite and make a zillion dollars. But he chose a very different course, a very risky one."

The Chiefs and all of Kansas City will never regret his choice.

Injuries forced him to miss five games and kept him from finishing two others in the first season of his last chance. Still, there were many moments of Montana Magic in 1993.

In a first-round playoff game against Pittsburgh, Joe threw a fourth-down touchdown pass with less than two minutes left to tie a game Kansas City eventually won in overtime. A week later in a conference semi-final at Houston, Montana threw three fourth-quarter touchdown passes to rally KC from a 13-7 deficit to a 28-20 victory.

But the magic ran out on an appropriately dreary day in Buffalo. One game shy of the fifth Super Bowl he dreamed of, Montana was pounded into the frozen turf of Rich Stadium and knocked out of the AFC championship game. The Bills won, 30-13, ending Montana's quest.

The magic moments were fewer in 1994. There was Joe's Revenge in the much-anticipated Week 2 game against San Francisco, which the Chiefs won, 24-17, in Arrowhead Stadium. And there was a memorable 75-yard drive in the final two minutes of a Monday night game in Denver.

The Chiefs took a big step back in a 9-7 regular season, then took another in losing a first-round playoff game in Miami. Montana and Dan Marino hooked up in a classic shootout on New Year's Eve, but Joe's 26-of-37, 314-yard performance wasn't enough to prevent a 27-17 Miami victory in what became Montana's final game.

He didn't go out a winner. But he went out like a champion.

"He didn't go out with a whimper, he went out with a bang," Haden says. "He raised the level of people around him in Kansas City just as he did in San Francisco."

Montana retired with nothing but good feelings about his valiant effort in Kansas City and about the people with whom he spent his final two seasons.

Despite published reports that he was unhappy with the demanding workout schedule of Chiefs coach Marty Schottenheimer and did not believe Kansas City was capable of reaching the Super Bowl, Montana said goodbye with a heartfelt thank you to the Chiefs on April 19 — one day after confirming his retirement in San Francisco.

"I thank Marty for all the memories," Montana said to a wet-eyed Schottenheimer. "Even though we fell a little short, we had a lot of fun along the way.

"I thought that just having the opportunity to play again would be enough," Joe added. "But once I got here and saw the organization, saw the talent and determination on the football team, everyone realized we had a very good team. I wish we could have won another Super Bowl for the Chiefs."

Running back Marcus Allen, who will join Montana in the Hall of Fame someday, best put the quarterback's two-year Kansas City career in perspective.

"We were fortunate to have played with a quarterback of his caliber for two years," Allen says. "He's given us a lot, a great deal of energy and magic. But now it's time to let him do the things he wants to do — spend time with his family, watch his kids grow up. In the big picture, that's the most important thing. It's time we say thanks and let him go."   •

Rick Dean covers the Chiefs for the Topeka (Kan.) Capital Journal.

Playing quarterback well at any level takes a healthy supply of confidence and a strong dose of cockiness.

But regardless of how big the heads or bank accounts of NFL quarerbacks become, one man made them stop in their tracks. Ask any NFL signal caller which quarterback he admired most and the answer invariably was Joe Montana.

Steve Young, the man who paced the sidelines in Montana's Golden Gate-sized shadow, considers Joe a special breed.

"He's been as successful as anyone who's ever played the game," Young says. "I got to witness the personal side. Under tremendous pressure, he was always levelheaded about everything. I admired him for that."

Everyone who's ever played the game swoons over Joe's four Super Bowl rings and three Super Bowl MVP trophies. Some attempt to emulate his style: quick drop, thorough field scan and dartlike release. All marvel at his courage and determination.

"Obviously, he has had a lot of influence on me," says Packers young gun Brett Favre, who watched Montana game films during the off-season to learn how to better run coach Mike Holmgren's offense.

Holmgren, a former offensive coordinator in San Francisco, installed the 49ers' system in Green Bay a few years back.

"I used to watch him play on television and I noticed how he was always so calm," Favre says. "I used to think that he would win

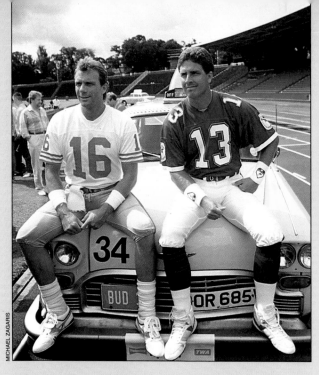

MICHAEL ZAGARIS

Both Montana and Marino will arrive in Canton in style, but as Dan the Man readily admits, he'd trade his trunkload of passing records for one of Joe's precious gems without a second thought.

every game. He just had that look about him."

Former Redskins quarterback Mark Rypien, a Super Bowl MVP himself, also has tried to follow Montana's blueprints.

"Joe Montana is everything a quarterback should be," Rypien says. "He's a winner, first of all, and that's the most important thing. He rallied the rest of the team around him."

Even for the man who can do it all, Montana represents the complete package.

"Joe's the man," Philadelphia Eagles quarterback Randall Cunningham says. "I appreciated him early in my career, and I appreciate him even more now. I watched him and saw who he saw on the field. I saw

how smart he is. When I was hurt [sidelined in 1991 with a knee injury], it made me realize that you don't have to do everything yourself. He understands that everybody has to do his job to make it all work.

"I came back and wanted to be a little more like Joe Montana. He's great. Plus, he's got all those rings, and that's what we're in the game for."

Miami Dolphins top gunner and fellow Western Pennsylvania product Dan Marino caught a glint of the fire in Montana's eyes when he faced him in Super Bowl XIX (January 1985).

"Joe took a lot of hits and had a lot of lumps [in the past couple of few seasons]," Marino says, "but he still had that fire burning. That can sometimes make the difference. You saw it in his eyes and you saw it when he was on the field during a big game. He wanted to make the big play. He won Super Bowls. He did it over and over."

For the 1993 No. 1 draft pick, New England Patriots quarterback Drew Bledsoe, Montana always has represented everything that was good about pro football.

"I grew up watching him," Bledsoe says. "He had the poise every quarterback wishes he had. I've always thought of him a a thinking-man's quarterback. He might not be the best athlete, but he has always won in the end. That's what counts."

And that's what it takes to be a master craftsman. •

Dave Spadaro covers the NFL for Eagles Digest.

MASTER CRAFTSMAN

Even the most skilled
NFL quarterbacks considered
Joe Montana a cut above

By Dave Spadaro

best in the game ever, and it also put him on a rock that was untouchable," says linebacker Matt Millen, the only man to play on Super Bowl winners for three different franchises, including the 49ers in 1989.

"In the two previous years, he was on shaky ground because the future was Steve Young, and [Joe] was an old quarterback," Millen adds. "Then he went on the next two years and did some things that nobody had seen done, flawlessly. Steve became a guy who just had to wait his time until the master finished."

There's no doubt this

> "There are two sides of Joe, the one people see on the field and the one we see at home. Dwight Clark once told me, 'You'd never recognize Joe out there.' I've asked Joe, 'What do you feel when you are under all that pressure? How can you stay so calm?' He says, 'I really don't know.' What makes him comfortable is his home and his kids and everyday life, not being put on a pedestal, not being called a hero every five minutes."
>
> — Jennifer Montana

period of Montana's career was special. It included a comeback against Philadelphia when he got up off the mat after eight sacks to engineer a victory by throwing four touchdown passes in the fourth quarter. It included a six-touchdown outburst against Atlanta, a Super Bowl nailbiter and a Super Bowl laugher. It included six playoff victories in which he threw 19 TDs and surrendered only one interception.

It's clear that even without this post-November 1988 period, Montana still would be considered great. But those games, those achievements, paved the road to legendary status.

"All those San Francisco fans who can't believe that Joe Montana left, would never have known he was gone if we were back in 1988 again, and that [collapse in Phoenix] never had taken place," Millen says. "They beat Phoenix, Steve Young's in. Joe Montana had a great career, but now, 'We have another guy.'

"I can't speak for the pre-'65 era, but in post-'65, there's nobody close to him," Millen adds. "How do you gauge it? Super Bowl victories? He's at the top. Come-from-behind victories? He's at the top. The ability to make something out of nothing? He's at the top. Every criteria you put on the guy, he's at the top."

It's always been the desire to compete that's pushed Joe Montana to those lofty heights. That insatiable desire combined with his immeasurable grit made him a true American legend, one the Bay Area will have trouble living without. Kansas City owned his body during his final few seasons, but as the old song goes, he left his heart in … well, you know the rest.   •

Ira Miller covers the 49ers for the San Francisco Chronicle.

THE BEST EVER?

Joe Montana finished No. 2 all time in overall passing efficiency, as determined by the league's quarterback rating system. Here's how 15 of the best pro quarterbacks, from various eras, stack up against Montana.

Player	Career	Att.	Comp.	Pct.	Yards	TDs	Int.	Rating
Joe Montana	1979-94	5,391	3,409	63.2	40,551	273	139	92.3
Dan Marino	1983-94	6,049	3,604	59.6	45,173	328	185	88.2
Roger Staubach	1969-79	2,958	1,685	57.0	22,700	153	109	83.4
Sonny Jurgensen	1957-74	4,262	2,433	57.1	32,224	255	189	82.6
Bart Starr	1956-71	3,149	1,808	57.4	24,718	152	138	80.5
Fran Tarkenton	1961-78	6,467	3,686	57.0	47,003	342	266	80.4
Johnny Unitas	1956-73	5,186	2,830	54.6	40,239	290	253	78.2
Otto Graham	1950-55	1,565	872	55.7	13,499	88	94	78.2
Bob Griese	1967-80	3,429	1,926	56.2	25,092	192	172	77.1
Norm Van Brocklin	1949-60	2,895	1,553	53.6	23,611	173	178	75.1
Sid Luckman	1939-50	1,744	904	51.8	14,683	139	131	75.0
Y.A. Tittle	1950-64	3,817	2,118	55.2	28,339	212	221	73.6
Sammy Baugh	1937-52	2,995	1,693	56.5	21,886	186	203	72.2
Terry Bradshaw	1970-83	3,901	2,025	51.9	27,989	212	210	70.9
Joe Namath	1965-77	3,762	1,886	50.1	27,663	173	220	65.5
Bob Waterfield	1945-52	1,617	814	50.3	11,849	98	128	61.6

Quality
Time

Retirement will allow Joe more time to devote to his family and off-field endeavors

By Kevin Lynch

A white limousine barrels through sheets of rain and rolls to a stop in front of the San Francisco 49ers' training complex. Two small boys bolt from the backseat and race into the lobby, oblivious to the pelting drops turning their white shirts transparent and their khaki trousers dark. Once inside, their enthusiasm quickly dissolves into awe.

From behind a grey locker room door, Joe Montana emerges. The kids' eyes grow as round as coffee can lids, as if a cartoon character had come alive and now stood right in front of them.

The two boys are brothers from the Midwest, both struggling with serious kidney disorders. Their parents (who linger in the background) had heard of the Make-A-Wish Foundation, a

genielike charity that grants dreams to disadvantaged and seriously ill children.

Montana takes the two boys through the grey doors into the locker room. Later, they re-emerge with the same reverent gaze and autographed footballs tucked under their arms. After many well wishes and thank you's, the boys stagger back and pile into the limousine. That spring afternoon in 1991 undoubtedly has played in their minds a thousand times.

The scene provides a rare glimpse into Montana's off-field persona. On the field, Joe's so well-known he fits in like part of the family. He was a player who transcended team loyalties. His wondrous and frightfully frequent comebacks, and his impeccable Super Bowl performances, were unforgettable.

But off the field, Montana is as elusive as he was

on it. With so many fans and media yearning for a chunk of his time, Joe often retreated for the sake of his own sanity. But one thing is certain: Montana's great love is his family.

They're the owners of all four of his Super Bowl rings, which he won while playing for the 49ers from 1979 to 1992. He has four children, one to go with each ring: Alexandra (9), Jennifer (7), Nathaniel (4) and Nicholas (2). He and his wife, Jennifer, a local television personality, often spend weekends carting their active brood to youth leagues — soccer matches and softball games.

Jennifer is using the first free summer Joe has experienced in 16 years (he spent his last two with the Kansas City Chiefs) to plan a string of family vacations, including one voyage to Europe.

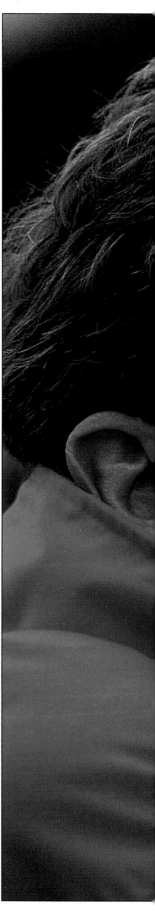

Montana retired at the end of last season, so his time away from football is in its infant stage. Still, a three-day slice out of the Joe Montana schedule book in early June provides an indication of what life will be like from now on.

On Thursday, Montana is whisked away to an unknown location to promote Franklin Mutual Funds.

On Friday, it's back home to his estate south of San Francisco for a day accompanying Jennifer as Mr. Mom.

On Saturday, the family

After 16 seasons of accommodating his fans, Joe cherishes those peaceful moments in which he ponders his retirement years with wife Jennifer.

spends the day and night in the resort beach town of Santa Cruz. Sunday it's back home, where Joe and Jennifer greet house guests. It may not sound like strenuous stuff, but when an associate calls to ask Joe how things are going, he breathlessly responds "busy."

Montana probably relishes the pace. He's notoriously hyper. When he was traded to the Chiefs, Montana allowed a journalist from the *San Francisco Examiner* a day-long interview at his Atherton, Calif., home. Around sunset, everyone adjourned to the backyard, where Montana wasn't content with simply participating in idle chatter.

Those pesky leaves littering the porch just had to be swept, and that's exactly what Montana did.

And despite his attempts to shield himself from the public at large, Montana still has to make large down payments for the price of his fame. A short junket to the grocery store can turn into a odyssey lasting hours. While Joe still was with the 49ers, Jennifer said their oldest daughter (a 4-year-old or so then) would wait patiently in the car while Montana was detained in the store by autograph hounds.

"What's he doing in there?" Jennifer would blurt out.

Alexandra would then pipe up and say, "Signing, Mommy."

Constantly being thrust into the public eye is how Montana will maintain the lifestyle he's achieved. The down payments for fame are going to get bigger, which is one of the crosses he'll bear in football retirement.

Montana has delved right into his post-football life. In the two months since his announcement, Montana has signed with NBC Sports as a football analyst, become a promoter for an IndyCar race team, received an airplane as a gift from Jennifer, and worked on his golf game.

The theme emerging in Montana's young retirement is "speed." Early in his career with the 49ers, he went to auto racing school and instantly became hooked. The Niners vehemently discouraged this passion for speed, and Montana complied. But now that he's retired, he wants to jump right in again.

He has an agreement to become part of an IndyCar racing team sponsored by Target Inc. Montana was sighted at the Indianapolis 500 this year. As for racing himself, Montana probably won't take part. He says he bought a red Ferrari a few years ago that rarely makes it out of the garage. He's afraid it will get scratched.

When it comes to speed, Montana doesn't fool around — he loves flying. Jennifer

says the hobby will keep her husband sane.

"When he's in the air, that's the only time he has that same glow as when he was playing football," Jennifer says. "His eyes get really big, and they sparkle when he talks about side winds and things like that. It will never make up for playing in the game, but it help ease the emptiness."

The 10-game gig as a studio analyst on NFL game days also may alleviate the sting of not playing. Montana was signed by NBC to do six regular season games and four playoff contests. He'll take a seat next to former Bears coach Mike Ditka.

"I look forward to sitting next to Ditka," Montana declares, "because when he wears those sweaters, I can only look good."

It's hard to imagine Montana not looking good no matter what he's doing, whether it's spending time with family, engaging in promotions or playing golf. As for the rest of Montana's time, he'll probably just say it's up in the air. •

Kevin Lynch covered Joe Montana for the 49ers Report.

Big-Game Hunter

When Lamar Hunt coined the phrase "Super Bowl" as a catchy name for the NFL vs. AFL championship game, he probably never thought he was giving birth to an American icon. After all, the first so-called Super Bowl featured a lopsided score and about 22,000 no-shows.

Today, the games still aren't much more competitive, except on rare occasions. But as for the hype surrounding the event, well, let's just say we've come a long way since 1967.

A worldwide television audience estimated at 750 million watches the Super Bowl, 2,500 journalists cover the event and the only way John Q. Public can afford a ticket to this game of games is if he's either a) A recent lottery winner or b) Married to the head coach's daughter.

The Super Bowl has become the greatest show on Earth, a stage on which every NFL player dreams of someday performing. In the 29 Super Bowls, there have been many outstanding efforts turned in by the game's leading men: Bart Starr, Joe Namath, Roger Staubach, Terry Bradshaw, Troy Aikman and Steve Young among them. We've also witnessed several one-game wonders — previous unknowns such as Max McGee, Jim O'Brien and Timmy Smith — who chose the Super Bowl as their chance to steal the spotlight, if only for a day.

But in the annals of pro football history, no other name has grabbed hold of these sacred 60 minutes in January quite like Joe Montana.

For Joe, a three-time Super Bowl MVP winner who owns a 4-0 Super Bowl record, this game has served as his personal walkway into sports immortality. Come along as four veteran pro football scribes detail how each Super Bowl triumph has fed the Montana legend.   •

Start Your Engines

By Ira Miller, who covered Super Bowl XVI for the **San Francisco Chronicle.**

Joe Montana was almost late for his date with destiny. The 49ers' team bus got stuck in traffic en route to Super Bowl XVI (January 1982) in Pontiac, Mich. To keep Montana and the rest of the players loose during this bumper-to-bumper headache on the highway, third-year head coach Bill Walsh joked that the team's equipment managers, who already were at the stadium, would be suiting up for the opening kickoff.

Unfortunately for the Cincinnati Bengals, the traffic cleared and No. 16 made it to his first big dance on time.

Each week during the '81 campaign, the 49ers seemed to accomplish something they hadn't done before, whether it was beat a particular team, win in a particular stadium or display some unforeseen facet of their game plan. The team was special.

At the time, Montana was just 25 years old and in his first season as a starter in the NFL. He led the NFC in passing during the regular season, but his reputation entering the Silverdome on Jan. 24, 1982, still was based mostly on his career with Notre Dame, not with the 49ers.

Nonetheless, the 49ers were so starved for sports heroes that Montana mania shot shock-waves throughout the Bay Area. *The San Francisco Chronicle* conducted a write-in nickname poll for Montana that attracted 10,000 suggestions. Joe chose "Big Sky," but the nickname that eventually caught on was "Joe Cool." It was perfect.

Montana's cool under pressure was a factor often during the 1981 season as the 49ers won eight games by a touchdown or less, including three consecutive three-point victories at midseason and the NFC championship game against Dallas, in which Montana hit Dwight Clark for the winning touchdown (a.k.a. "The Catch") with 51 seconds remaining.

As fans began to realize the 49ers were for real, Montana took center stage in the media spotlight. In this first go-round, he actually seemed somewhat affected by his popularity.

During the playoffs, for example, the 49ers set up a media interview area in a building adjacent to their headquarters. Late each afternoon, players dutifully trooped there to meet the press. Most barely stayed long enough to say, "Hi, Mom." Montana, however, wouldn't leave. It wasn't unusual to see Joe standing on the lawn, conducting an interview in darkness with the only lights coming from a television camera. In later years, Montana would shy away from the bright lights. But at this time, the spotlight was new and still invigorating.

Super Bowl XVI still is remembered largely for a third quarter goal-line stand by the 49ers' defense, led by rookie Ronnie Lott, and the place-kicking of Ray Wersching, who tied a Super Bowl record with four field goals. Wersching also perfectly executed Walsh's unusual orders to squib the kickoffs to prevent returns. Four Bengals returns failed to reach the 20.

But Montana was voted the game's MVP after completing 14 of 22 passes for 157 yards. He ran one yard for the 49ers' first touchdown and passed 11 yards to Earl Cooper for the other. San Francisco won, 26-21, after leading, 20-0, at halftime.

"Montana will be the great quarterback of the future," Walsh predicted after the game. "He is one of the coolest competitors of all time, and he has just started."

After the game, the 49ers' hotel turned into one gigantic party. But Joe was nowhere to be found. He'd retreated to his room to order a room service dinner. Maybe he knew there would be many more post-Super Bowl parties to attend. Three years later in his backyard of Palo Alto, Calif., Montana would celebrate his second. Since he was within walking distance, even traffic wouldn't slow him down this time. •

A traffic jam delayed Joe's entrance to the Silverdome, but once he arrived, the Bengals were nothing more than a speed bump

Stealing the Show

By Gary Swan, who covered Super Bowl XIX for the San Francisco Chronicle.

Super Bowl XIX at Stanford Stadium was billed as the Marino vs. Montana matchup. Capital "M" for Miami Dolphins quarterback Dan Marino, small "m" for San Francisco quarterback Joe Montana.

Marino was a 23-year-old gunslinger whose quick release and pinpoint accuracy had registered passing numbers in '84 never before seen: 48 touchdowns and 5,084 yards. He was called "the quarterback of the future."

On the other sideline stood Montana, five years older with neither a release nor arm that measured up to Dan the Man. Joe was the afterthought, the other guy the media reached for when they needed someone to serve as Marino's foil.

Then they played the game.

Montana carved up a porous Dolphins defense for 331 yards (24-of-35) and three touchdowns. He ran for another. Marino, who usually thrives on high-scoring affairs, couldn't keep up. His passes fell short, his receivers dropped balls, his blockers missed assignments. The NFL's quarterback of the future was gunned down in the street by the NFL's quarterback of the decade.

"Marino may be the best thrower in the league, but Joe Montana is the best quarterback," 49ers guard Randy Cross said after the 38-16 slaughter.

"Joe's best game ever," added 49ers receiver Dwight Clark.

Montana was said to be in a slump coming into the game. He'd thrown five interceptions in the previous two playoff games against the Giants and Bears. When it came time to play for the ring, though, Joe turned it up a notch. He set a Super Bowl record for passing yards and personally outrushed the Dolphins 59 yards to 25 yards. Each time Montana scrambled out of the pocket, it was a stake in the Dolphins' heart. Three runs set up touchdowns, another set up a field goal and another, a 6-yard scamper into the end zone, gave the 49ers a commanding 21-10 lead in the second quarter.

As he crossed the goal line, Joe Cool nearly got caught up in the heat of the moment. Holding the ball aloft for a fleeting second, he quickly pulled it back down.

"I wanted to spike the ball," he remembers. "Then I thought, 'Oh what the heck. There's no need.'"

No need, indeed.

The 49ers compiled 537 total yards, which topped the Super Bowl yardage record by more than 100 yards. Even humble Joe had to concede it was a near-perfect outing.

"Putting everything together, running the ball and throwing the ball, it was tough to beat that one," Montana admits.

The public agreed. Joe was a surprise Super Bowl guest in 1982 thanks to "The Catch" in the NFC title game. His subsequent Super Bowl victory was credited as much to Bill Walsh's brilliance as it was to Montana's execution.

This time, after beating the powerful Marino into submission, Montana began taking on a special glow . . . the radiance of a legend in the making.

"Some people wither when a big moment arrives," columnist Lowell Cohn wrote in the *San Francisco Chronicle*. "Montana grabs it by the throat. If there is a better quarterback out there, let him come forward." Dave Anderson of the *New York Times* fed the Superman image: "Joe Montana performed as if he were Krypton's quarterback."

The Dolphins had no kryptonite, and the man with nerves of steel had his second Super Bowl ring. But Montana's greatest January adventure still awaited, 2,300 miles and four years away in, of all places, Miami.

●

Marino was supposed to be the star attraction, but Montana took center stage with a near-flawless performance

His Finest Hour

By Howard Balzer, who covered Super Bowl XXIII for **The Sporting News.**

It took Joe Montana fewer than three minutes to show the world why he deserves to be called the best ever

In a little less than three minutes in Miami (2:36 to be exact), Joe Montana forever set himself apart from every other quarterback who's ever crouched behind center. His pressure-packed, game-winning drive against the Cincinnati Bengals in Super Bowl XXIII (January 1989) held the football world spellbound.

Montana entered Miami's Joe Robbie Stadium sporting two Super Bowl rings, but lacking the contentment such expensive jewelry should bring. Joe had endured a season with its share of downsides: He'd squabbled with head coach Bill Walsh over playing time (rising star Steve Young was inserted into several regular season games), the 49ers had stumbled out of the blocks to a 6-5 start and Joe's trusty receiver Jerry Rice was hobbled by an ankle injury. By season's end, Montana found himself in an unusual position. As unbelievable as it sounds, he needed to prove himself all over again.

With Rice healthy and Montana finally set as the quarterback, the 49ers won four of their last five games and then defeated Minnesota and Chicago on their way to the Super Bowl.

Preparations for the matchup came amid riots in Miami's Overtown section and rumors that this would be Walsh's swan song. The 49ers also knew this game would be no cakewalk since the Bengals deployed a similar offensive style (sixth-year Cincinnati head coach Sam Wyche was an assistant in San Francisco under Walsh) as well as solid team defense.

Despite losing linchpin nose tackle Tim Krumrie in the first quarter, the Bengals' defense refused to break, allowing Montana to move the ball, but effectively keeping him out of the end zone. The 49ers could muster only one field goal in the first half. In fact, they didn't score their first touchdown until 57 seconds into the fourth quarter when Montana connected with Rice on a 14-yard scoring play. That touchdown came just 1:31 after Stanford Jennings had given Cincinnati a 13-6 lead on a 93-yard kickoff return. The score remained tied until Jim Breech gave the Bengals a 16-13 lead with a 40-yard field goal. When the 49ers took over on their 8-yard line with 3:10 left in the game, the stage was set.

Joe entered the huddle, told his teammates, "Let's go, be tough," and proceeded to take the 49ers on a 92-yard ride no one ever will forget.

Like the master he is, Montana moved the ball around, hitting Rice three times for 51 total yards, running back Roger Craig three for 29, tight end John Frank once for 7 and receiver John Taylor for the winning TD of 10 yards.

Tackle Bubba Paris remembers, "We were functioning like a machine."

Montana's only incompletion of the drive came at the Bengals' 35 at a time when he later revealed he was hyperventilating. "I probably should have called time-out," Montana admits. "From all the yelling I was doing, I was getting pretty excited, and I started to have a hard time catching my breath. That never happened before. But I went ahead anyway."

On the winning play, Montana again exhibited remarkable poise.

"We broke the huddle," Craig says, "I saw Tom [Rathman] line up on the left, and that wasn't the time to argue, so I just lined up on the right. The fact that I was on the wrong side didn't affect Joe. He is so smooth, it's incredible. He looked at me first, just as he's supposed to, despite the fact that I was on the wrong side. I was double-covered, so he went to the next guy."

That was Taylor, and the rest is history.

In 156 seconds on Jan. 22, 1989, Montana directed the most memorable Super Bowl drive ever. He was bigger than life. Three fingers now garnered rings. His pinky ring was on layaway. The pickup date was Jan. 28, 1990, in New Orleans. •

Exclamation Point

By Nancy Gay, who covered Super Bowl XXIV for the **San Jose Mercury News.**

Joe Montana turned to the first page of his playbook to write his fourth Super Bowl best seller.

Using the post pattern, one of the most commonly run routes in any playbook, Montana carved up the Denver Broncos' secondary for five touchdowns — three to receiver Jerry Rice — and the 49ers claimed their record-tying fourth Super Bowl.

Just 12 months earlier in Miami, Montana had authored his most memorable Super Bowl chapter with a historic 92-yard march to glory.

San Francisco's 55-10 thrashing of Denver in Super Bowl XXIV (January 1990) at the Superdome in New Orleans couldn't match the previous thriller, but it did serve as the perfect exclamation point for the Team and Quarterback of the '80s.

The victory tied the Pittsburgh Steelers — the Team of the '70s — for Super Bowl triumphs, and Joltin' Joe walked home with his unprecedented third Super Bowl MVP, one better than Steelers quarterback Terry Bradshaw.

"Each Super Bowl becomes more precious," Montana said afterward. "The more, the merrier. They are all sweet, and this was the sweetest yet. It was so much fun, we couldn't wait to get back onto the field."

The image of Montana with his arms raised in celebration following yet another 49ers touchdown probably still sends chills down the spines of Broncos safeties Dennis Smith and Steve Atwater, who commented before the game that they would "punish" 49ers receivers.

Harkening back to sandlot simplicity, Montana told his receivers to run toward the goal post and he'd hit them in stride. No tricks. No short-passing attack that had been the 49ers' trademark. Just run up the middle of the field and catch the ball. The results were remarkable. Not only did the 49ers score 27 first-half points, but Joe barely broke a sweat. He connected on touchdown passes of 20, 38, 28, 35 and 7 yards. Said Broncos quarterback John Elway, "We couldn't stop the bleeding."

Like a club fighter stepping into the ring with the heavyweight champ, Denver never made it out of the first round. By the time Montana rolled right, pump-faked left and connected with Rice for a 38-yard knockout blow with :34 left in the first half, the Broncos were down for the count.

"Joe Montana does an outstanding job of looking off safeties," said rookie 49ers head coach George Seifert, who took over for Bill Walsh before the 1989 season. "This might have been his best game at that."

The 49ers entered the Superdome on a roll like no other team in history. They had outscored their playoff opponents — the Vikings and Rams — by 45 points, 71-26, and Joe had not thrown an interception in 54 postseason attempts.

Still, 49ers equipment manager Bronco Hinek thought Joe needed an extra incentive. Hinek placed a framed picture of Montana's three children in his locker stall. The young Montanas were wearing Super Bowl rings. An engraved plate attached to the frame said, "OK, Daddy, the next ring is yours."

Montana responded with a near-flawless performance. He completed 22 of 29 for 297 yards to bring his amazing Super Bowl totals to 83 of 122 for 1,142 yards and 11 touchdowns — all Super Bowl records.

In Super Bowl XVI against Cincinnati, Joe was a surprise guest. In Super Bowl XIX against the Dolphins, he upstaged the star attraction. In Super Bowl XXIII again facing the Bengals, he engineered a storybook drive. After authoring the destruction of the Broncos in Super Bowl XXIV, he was headed for the Hall of Fame.

Ultimately, it would be Joe's final Super Bowl chapter. But no one has written a more impressive book. ●

Montana authored an immortal performance in destroying Denver, 55-10, and writing his name into Super Bowl history books

STRIKING GOLD

Four Super Bowl diamonds have turned Joe Montana into a card collector's mother lode

•

By Pete Williams

Joe Montana spent his 16-year career transcending the game of football. Even collectors who knew little about the NFL became aware of the Notre Dame and San Francisco 49ers quarterback through his four Super Bowl victories and countless miracle comebacks.

So it comes as no surprise that Montana not only led the football card boom of 1989, but managed to sustain his collecting popularity in a hobby long dominated by baseball and now head-over-heels in love with basketball.

Baseball, with its rich history and tradition, still is the No. 1 sport for cards. Basketball, thanks to the NBA's shrewd marketing

BRAD NEWTON

and the likes of Michael Jordan, Charles Barkley and Shaquille O'Neal, currently is a strong No. 2.

Football players, meanwhile, have struggled to gain such notoriety. With shorter careers played in relative anonymity behind facemasks and pads, few gridiron greats can even dream of transcending their sport in the manner of, say, Jordan or Nolan Ryan.

Montana is the NFL's exception to the rule. And why not? No athlete, amateur or pro, shone more brightly than Joe did in the 1980s. From his early days buried

on the Notre Dame depth chart to his impossible 49ers comebacks, Montana has been an inspiration for millions of armchair quarterbacks, not to mention idolizing collectors.

By the time Pro Set and Score's debut NFL products revitalized the dormant football card hobby in 1989, Joe already was a living legend.

The 1989 Score set, in fact, initiated a numerical tribute to Montana. It leads off with him as card #1, and he retained the top spot until 1992, when Barry Sanders became the first card.

"We try to put the player who was the most dominant in the league as the first guy in the set," Score representative Julie Haddon says. "For those three years, Montana was the No. 1 player, so it was only logical that he be the No. 1 card."

While countless converted baseball card collectors frantically pieced together the 1989 Pro Set and Score sets, many also set their sights on the Rookie Cards of the NFL's surefire future Hall of Famers.

The RCs of Walter Payton (1976 Topps #148), Steve Largent (1977 Topps #177) and Montana (1981 Topps #216) leaped in status from afterthoughts to three of the hobby's undisputed glamour cards — almost overnight.

It just goes to prove that looks aren't everything. When Topps produced Joe's debut issue, the company had no competition in the football card market. As a result, they didn't feel it was necessary to pay the NFL's asking price to print the

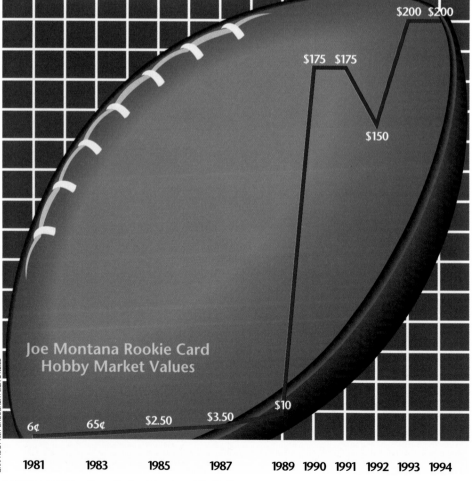

Joe Montana Rookie Card Hobby Market Values

$200 $200
$175 $175
$150
$10
6¢   65¢ $2.50 $3.50

1981   1983   1985   1987   1989 1990 1991 1992 1993 1994

GRAPHS BY AMY BROUGHER / LISA O'NEILL

* All Prices Are Taken From *The Sport Americana Price Guide*

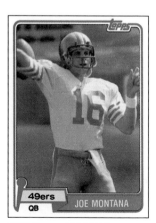

49ers
QB   JOE MONTANA

1981 Topps RC #216

helmet logos. The result is a card photo that leaves plenty to be desired. After fielding numerous collector complaints, Topps decided to spend the extra money for the licensing fees for its 1982 set.

Cardboard Chronicle

Although Joe was sidelined for long stretches by serious back and elbow injuries, his name never lost its magic with collectors. And even during Joe's final two seasons, which he spent as a Kansas City Chief, collectors lined up to grab yet another piece of his golden career.

There's certainly much to choose from. From game-used helmets and jerseys to limited edition card sets to signed lithographs to advertising and promotional material to all types of autographed items, Montana has been marketed through every avenue imaginable.

It's unlikely anyone has appeared on more football cards than Montana. Beginning with his RC and reaching to the slew of different cards produced in 1994 alone, Montana's career has been well-chronicled on cardboard.

One of the more interesting — and pricey — Montana cards is his 1991 Action Packed 24K Gold #40G, a popular and scarce insert. Montana even had an

insert set all to himself as the subject of Upper Deck's first Football Heroes set in 1991.

As Joe strides into retirement, his 1982 Topps (#488) and 1983 Topps (#169), a double print, have become even more important issues.

Montana, who also serves as a spokesperson for Upper Deck, was one of several key athletes who helped start Upper Deck Authenticated, the joint venture of Upper Deck and McNall Sports and Entertainment created to market autographed memorabilia.

When Upper Deck received a license to produce football cards for the 1991 season, company president Richard McWilliam turned to his favorite player to help promote the cards.

"He's the best quarterback ever to play the game," McWilliam says. "But more importantly, he has a great personality and is one of the most recognizable people in the U.S. He's just as marketable as anyone in professional sports and he's been a tremendous asset to us."

Howard Bauer of Chapel Hill Collection in

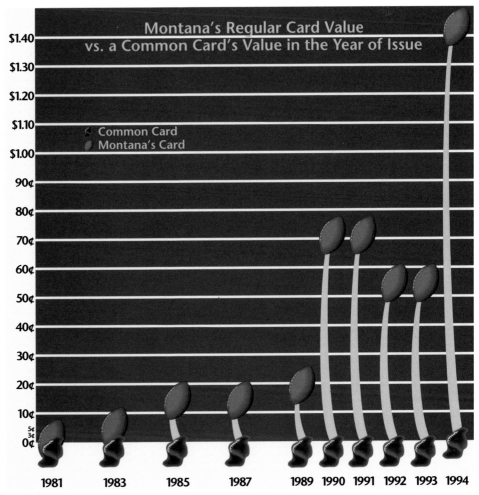

* All Prices Are Taken From *The Sport Americana Price Guide*

Greensburg, Pa., credits Montana's mass appeal to the Super Bowl wins.

"There was renewed interest in him because he went to Kansas City," Bauer said. "Other people like Dan Marino and Jerry Rice might be close, but there isn't a football player as big as Joe right now."

The bigger they are, the harder it is to find something of that player that no other collector has. That's why it's not surprising to hear about several of Joe's Notre Dame No. 3 jerseys surfacing,

or that die-hard hobbyists have sought out his high school yearbook from Ringgold High in Monongahela, Pa.

"You've reached that upper level of collectibility when people start going after your high school yearbook," said Duane Garrett, who as president of San Francisco-based Richard Wolffers Auctions has seen just about every piece of Montana equipment imaginable. "Among current [football] players, he [was] far and away the most sought after. Maybe his luster will

fade, but I doubt it."

Through the years, Montana has done numerous private signings. Before joining Upper Deck Authenticated, he had a similar arrangement to provide signed memorabilia to the Score Board Inc. of Cherry Hill, N.J.

Collectors even have a remote chance of pulling a Montana signature out of certain football packs. Joe signed 2,500 individually numbered 1991 Upper Deck Heroes checklist cards (#9), which feature Vernon Wells' artwork. The special cards, differentiated from regular cards with diamond-shaped holograms instead of the accustomed football-shaped holograms, were randomly inserted into 1991 Upper Deck low series packs.

Montana's highly prized autograph also can be found in 1992 Pro Line foil (not jumbo) packs. Joe, along with almost every player in the set, signed about 1,000 cards for random insertion in packs. The signed cards are identical to the corre-

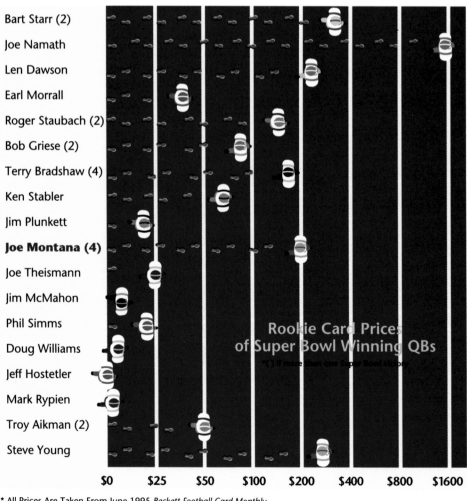

Bart Starr (2)
Joe Namath
Len Dawson
Earl Morrall
Roger Staubach (2)
Bob Griese (2)
Terry Bradshaw (4)
Ken Stabler
Jim Plunkett
Joe Montana (4)
Joe Theismann
Jim McMahon
Phil Simms
Doug Williams
Jeff Hostetler
Mark Rypien
Troy Aikman (2)
Steve Young

$0 $25 $50 $100 $200 $400 $800 $1600

Rookie Card Prices of Super Bowl Winning QBs
() if more than one Super Bowl victory

* All Prices Are Taken From June 1995 *Beckett Football Card Monthly*

1990 Pro Set #24

sponding regular-issue cards except they are un-numbered and embossed with a "CERTIFIED NFL" logo in one corner.

Just the Beginning

It didn't take long for Montana to make an impact on Kansas and Missouri. Although Montana will be remembered forever as a 49er, he became as popular in Kansas City as steak, barbecue and George Brett. His No. 19 jersey — the sum of his familiar San Francisco No. 16 and his collegiate No. 3 — became a hot seller in local sport-ing goods stores almost as soon as Montana stepped off the plane.

No football player, past or present, rivals Montana in terms of long-term col-lectibility. Although Marino has comparable career numbers, he has yet to win a Super Bowl, much less four. To find someone in Montana's class, you have to go back to Montana's child-hood hero, Joe Namath, another product of the quarterback-fertile Western Pennsylvania area. But Broadway Joe finished his career long before the sports memorabilia hobby exploded in the 1980s.

"Montana's definitely No. 1," Michael Lupo, a Las Vegas sports memorabilia dealer, says. "Marino's just as charismatic a guy, but he's never won the big one."

With growing interest in oddball sports memora-bilia, such as advertising pieces, oversized cards and collectibles other than the traditional trifecta of equip-ment, autographs and cards, Montana's items have become even more popular.

He worked with ac-tress/model/wife Jennifer (who has an immensely popular card and corre-

TOP 10 MOST SOUGHT AFTER
Joe Montana Cards

The bulk of this alphabetical listing was compiled using *The Football Card Price Guide*, by Dr. James Beckett, and the rest represents current market value. As with all cards listed in a Beckett® Price Guide, these prices are not absolute fixed values.

- 1994 Playoff Contenders Back to Back Montana/Marino #1 $350
- 1991 Upper Deck Autographed Card $300
- 1994 SP All-Pro Holoview Die Cuts #PB17 $260
- 1991 Action Packed 24K Gold #40G $160
- 1994 Finest Refractors #172 $160
- 1993 Stadium Club First Day Issue #440 $125
- 1995 Pinnacle Zenith Z-Team #ZT5 $125
- 1987 English 49ers #16
- 1994 Select Canton Bound #CB3 $80
- 1981 MSA Holsum Bread Disc $75

Hobbyists on Joe

"Collectors saw Montana as the premier field general. Other QBs like [John] Elway are secondary because they haven't proven they can win the big one."

— Mike Lawrence, Tukwila, Wash.

•

sponding autographed insert card of her own in 1991 Pro Line) in the 1980s on a series of television and print ads for Schick razors. Other advertising pieces abound, including Hanes active wear and Pepsi display items.

Montana also has been involved in promotions for Sasson, Sanka, Ocean Spray, L.A. Gear, Tiger Balm (a gel for muscle soreness) and Power Burst sports drink.

With so many collectibles available, some hobbyists focus their efforts on one player, often to the point of being an obsession.

While this phenomenon is most common in baseball, Montana ranks right up there with almost any star of the diamond.

"A lot of people are looking for out-of-the-ordinary items, and Montana, with all of his advertising gigs, has as much oddball material as anyone," Lupo says. "It seems like many collectors are trying to assemble a scrapbook of one player, which is what collecting was supposed to be about anyway."

Larry Bobbe, a San Francisco hobbyist, may have the largest collection of Montana memorabilia in the country. Bobbe has more than 200 magazines with Montana on the cover, ranging from his many *Sports Illustrated* covers to a 1985 appearance on the front of *PC World*.

Although the final chapter of Montana's storybook career did not turn out as his fans may have wanted, his picture still was splashed on the front of even more magazines and '95 cards. It's the one constant in the Montana collection.   •

Pete Williams writes a collectibles column for USA Today.

Joe Montana's
COMPREHENSIVE CARD CHECKLIST

All card #'s correspond to our football card price guides.

•

1989 Pro Set #381

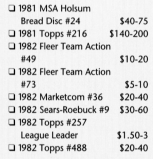

1981 Topps RC #216

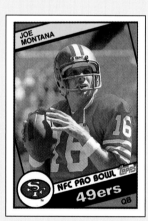

1984 Topps #358

❏ 1981 MSA Holsum Bread Disc #24	$40-75
❏ 1981 Topps #216	$140-200
❏ 1982 Fleer Team Action #49	$10-20
❏ 1982 Fleer Team Action #73	$5-10
❏ 1982 Marketcom #36	$20-40
❏ 1982 Sears-Roebuck #9	$30-60
❏ 1982 Topps #257 League Leader	$1.50-3
❏ 1982 Topps #488	$20-40
❏ 1982 Topps #489 In Action	$6-12
❏ 1982 Topps Coming Soon Sticker #5 Super Bowl	$1.25-2.50
❏ 1982 Topps Coming Soon Sticker #9 Super Bowl	$1.25-2.50
❏ 1982 Topps Sticker #5 Super Bowl	$1.50-3

❏ 1982 Topps Sticker #9 Super Bowl	$1.25-2.50
❏ 1982 Topps Sticker #70 League Leader	$1.25-2.50
❏ 1982 Topps Sticker #113	$1-2
❏ 1983 7-Eleven Coin #6	$4.50-9
❏ 1983 Topps #4 Record Breaker	$2-4
❏ 1983 Topps #169	$7.50-15
❏ 1983 Topps Sticker #265 League Leader	.75-1.50
❏ 1983 Topps Sticker #305	.75-1.50
❏ 1983 Topps Sticker Insert #21	$2.50-5
❏ 1984 49ers Police #5 Multiplayer	$5-10
❏ 1984 7-Eleven Coin #W2	$3.75-7.50
❏ 1984 Topps #358	$5-10
❏ 1984 Topps #359 Instant Replay	$2.50-5
❏ 1984 Topps Glossy Send-In #13	$2.50-5
❏ 1984 Topps Sticker #60	.60-1.25
❏ 1985 Fleer Team Action #75 Multiplayer	$2.50-5
❏ 1985 Fleer Team Action #86	$1.75-3.50
❏ 1985 49ers Police #10	$4-8
❏ 1985 49ers Smokey #2	$6.50-12.50
❏ 1985 Topps #148 Team Leader	.50-1.25
❏ 1985 Topps #157	$4-8
❏ 1985 Topps #192 League Leader	$6-12
❏ 1985 Topps Box Bottom #M	$2.50-5
❏ 1985 Topps Glossy Insert #7	$2.50-5
❏ 1985 Topps Coming	

Soon Sticker #210	$1-2
❏ 1985 Topps Sticker #210	.60-1.25
❏ 1986 DairyPak Carton #1	$7.50-15
❏ 1986 Fleer Team Action #73	$2-4
❏ 1986 McDonald's 49ers #16	$4-8
❏ 1986 McDonald's All-Stars #16	$1.50-3
❏ 1986 Topps #156	$3.50-7
❏ 1986 Topps #225 League Leader	.40-1.00
❏ 1986 Topps Sticker #61	.60-1.25
❏ 1987 English 49ers #16	$45-90
❏ 1987 Fleer Team Action #83	$1-2
❏ 1987 Topps #112	$2.50-5
❏ 1987 Topps American/ UK #29	$5-10

❏ 1987 Topps Box Bottom #H	$2-4
❏ 1987 Topps Sticker #60	.75-1.50
❏ 1987 Wheaties #12	$7.50-15
❏ 1988 Fleer Team Action #65	$1-2
❏ 1988 Fleer Team Action #70	$1-2
❏ 1988 Football Sticker Book #16	$1.50-3
❏ 1988 49ers Police #11	$4.50-9
❏ 1988 49ers Smokey #20	$10-20

❏ 1988 Kenner Starting Lineup #117	$125-200
❏ 1988 Panini Sticker #219	$1.25-2.50
❏ 1988 Panini Sticker #406	$1.25-2.50
❏ 1988 Topps #4 Record Breaker	.40-1.00
❏ 1988 Topps #38	.60-1.50
❏ 1988 Topps #215 League Leader	.20-.50
❏ 1988 Topps Sticker #64	.35-.75
❏ 1988 Topps Sticker Back #6	.50-1.00
❏ 1989 Franchise #157	$10-20
❏ 1989 Kenner Starting Lineup #106	$70-110
❏ 1989 King Disc #21	$4.50-9
❏ 1989 Panini Sticker #157	$1-2
❏ 1989 Parker Brothers Talking Football #31	$10-20
❏ 1989 Pro Set #381	.60-1.50
❏ 1989 Pro Set GTE SB Album #381	$5-10
❏ 1989 Score Promos #1	$20-35
❏ 1989 Score #1	$1.75-3.50
❏ 1989 Score #274 Playoff	.30-.75
❏ 1989 Score #275 Super Bowl Multiplayer	$1.50-3
❏ 1989 Score #279 Multiplayer	$1.50-3
❏ 1989 Score #329 Record Breaker	.60-1.50
❏ 1989 Star-Cal Decal #29	$5-10

- ❏ 1989 Topps #1 Super Bowl .15-.40
- ❏ 1989 Topps #6
  Team Leader .10-.30
- ❏ 1989 Topps #12 .60-1.50
- ❏ 1989 Topps American/UK
  #20 $3-6
- ❏ 1989 TV-4 Quarterback #18 $2-4
- ❏ 1990 Action
  Packed #246 $1.50-3
- ❏ 1990 Action Packed
  All-Madden #1 $2-4
- ❏ 1990 Fleer #10A .40-1.00
- ❏ 1990 Fleer #10B .40-1.00
- ❏ 1990 Fleer #397
  Multiplayer .30-.75
- ❏ 1990 Fleer All-Pro #1 $1.50-3
- ❏ 1990 49ers SF Examiner
  #13 $3-6
- ❏ 1990 Kenner Starting Lineup
  #23 $25-40
- ❏ 1990 Kenner Starting Lineup
  #101 $15-25
- ❏ 1990 Knudsen Bookmark
  #3 $5-10
- ❏ 1990 Notre Dame Promos
  #3 $1.50-3
- ❏ 1990 Notre Dame 200
  #1 .60-1.25
- ❏ 1990 Notre Dame 200
  #40 .60-1.25

1990 Score #1

- ❏ 1990 Notre Dame 200
  #170 .60-1.25
- ❏ 1990 Notre Dame Greats
  #5 $2-4
- ❏ 1990 Panini Sticker
  #196 All-Pro .50-1.00
- ❏ 1990 Panini Sticker #357 $1-2
- ❏ 1990 Pro Set #2A
  Player of the Year .20-.50
- ❏ 1990 Pro Set #2B
  Player of the Year .20-.50
- ❏ 1990 Pro Set #8
  League Leader .20-.50
- ❏ 1990 Pro Set #293 .40-1.00
- ❏ 1990 Pro Set #408
  Pro Bowl .20-.50
- ❏ 1990 Pro Set Super
  Bowl MVP #16 .50-1.00

- ❏ 1990 Pro Set Super
  Bowl MVP #19 .50-1.00
- ❏ 1990 Pro Set Super
  Bowl MVP #24 .50-1.00
- ❏ 1990 Pro Set FACT
  Cincinnati #2
  Playerof the Year $12.50-25
- ❏ 1990 Pro Set FACT
  Cincinnati #8
  League Leader $12.50-25
- ❏ 1990 Pro Set FACT
  Cincinnati #293 $15-30
- ❏ 1990 Pro Set Pro
  Bowl 106 #293 .50-1.00
- ❏ 1990 Pro Set Super
  Bowl 160 #33 .20-.50
- ❏ 1990 Pro Set SuperBowl
  Binder #2 $1.75-3.50
- ❏ 1990 Score #1 .40-1.00
- ❏ 1990 Score #311 Hot Gun .20-.50
- ❏ 1990 Score #582 All Pro .20-.50
- ❏ 1990 Score #594
  Record Breaker .20-.50
- ❏ 1990 Score Hot Card #1 $4-8
- ❏ 1990 Score 100 Hottest #2 .75-1.50
- ❏ 1989 Star-Cal Decal #79 $4.50-9
- ❏ 1989 Star-Cal Decal #80
  All Star $4.50-9
- ❏ 1990 Topps #1
  Record Breaker .20-.50
- ❏ 1990 Topps #13 .40-1.00
- ❏ 1990 Topps #229
  League Leader .08-.25
- ❏ 1990 Topps #515 Team Leader
  Multiplayer .08-.25
- ❏ 1990 Topps Tiffany #1
  Record Breaker $1.25-2.50
- ❏ 1990 Topps Tiffany #13 $2.50-5
- ❏ 1990 Topps Tiffany #229
  League Leader .75-1.50
- ❏ 1990 Topps Tiffany #515
  Team Leader Multiplayer .75-1.50
- ❏ 1990 Topps Box
  Bottom #C .60-1.25
- ❏ 1991 Action Packed #247 $1.25-2.50
- ❏ 1991 Action Packed
  24K Gold #40 $90-160
- ❏ 1991 Arena Hologram * #1 $1-2
- ❏ 1991 Bowman #479 .40-1.00
- ❏ 1991 Fleer #360 .40-1.00
- ❏ 1991 Fleer #408
  League Leader .20-.50
- ❏ 1991 Fleer Pro-Visions #1 .75-2.00
- ❏ 1991 Fleer Stars
  N Stripes #108 $1.25-2.50
- ❏ 1991 Kenner Starting
  Lineup #17 $15-25
- ❏ 1991 Kenner Starting Lineup
  Headline Collection #4 $18-30
- ❏ 1991 Knudsen
  Bookmark #15 $3.75-7.50
- ❏ 1991 NFL Experience #25 $1.50-3

- ❏ 1991 Pacific Prototype #1 $45-90
- ❏ 1991 Pacific #464 .40-1.00
- ❏ 1991 Pacific Picks
  The Pros Gold #10 $9-18
- ❏ 1991 Pacific Picks
  the Pros Silver #10 $9-18
- ❏ 1991 Pacific Flash Card #66 .75-1.50
- ❏ 1991 Pinnacle Promo Panel
  #2 Multiplayer #2 $4-8
- ❏ 1991 Pinnacle #66 $2.50-5
- ❏ 1991 Pro Set #3
  Player of the Year .20-.50
- ❏ 1991 Pro Set #387
  Pro Bowl .20-.50

1991 Bowman #479

- ❏ 1991 Pro Set #653 .40-1.00
- ❏ 1991 Pro Set FACT Mobil
  #3 $7.50-15
- ❏ 1991 Pro Set
  CinderellaStory #8 $1.25-2.50
- ❏ 1991 Pro Set
  Platinum #139 .40-1.00
- ❏ 1991 Pro Set
  Spanish #221 .50-1.00
- ❏ 1991 Pro Set Super
  Pro Comic #3 .50-1.00
- ❏ 1991 Score Prototype #1 $3-6
- ❏ 1991 Score #1 .40-1.00
- ❏ 1991 Score #620
  Team MVP .20-.50
- ❏ 1991 Stadium Club #327 $3.50-7
- ❏ 1991 Stadium Club
  Super Bowl XXVI #327 $20-40
- ❏ 1991 Topps #73 .40-1.00
- ❏ 1991 Ultra #251 .40-1.00
- ❏ 1991 Ultra Performances
  #4 $5-10
- ❏ 1991 Upper Deck Promo
  #1 $2-4
- ❏ 1991 Upper Deck
  #35 Multiplayer .20-.50
- ❏ 1991 Upper Deck #54 .40-1.00
- ❏ 1991 Upper Deck
  Heroes Set (10) $6-12
- ❏ 1991 Upper Deck Heroes
  Autographed $150-300
- ❏ 1991 Upper Deck Heroes
  Box Bottom Set $3-6

- ❏ 1992 Action Packed
  Rookie Update #60 $2-4
- ❏ 1992 All World #182 .50-1.25
- ❏ 1992-3 Intimidator
  Bio Sheets #18 $6-12
- ❏ 1992 Breyer Bookmark #10 $5-10
- ❏ 1992 Collector'sEdge #250 $2-4
- ❏ 1992 49ers FBI #31 $5-10
- ❏ 1992 GameDay National
  #25 $4.50-9
- ❏ 1992 GameDay #5 $1.50-3
- ❏ 1992 Kenner
  Starting Lineup #14 $15-25
- ❏ 1992 Kenner Starting
  Lineup Headline
  Collection #1 $12-24
- ❏ 1992 Newsport #20 $20-40
- ❏ 1992 Power #16 .50-1.25
- ❏ 1992 Pro Line
  Portraits #329 .60-1.50
- ❏ 1992 Pro Line Portraits
  Autograph #329 $75-150
- ❏ 1992 Pro Line Quarterback
  Gold #14 $1-2
- ❏ 1992 Pro Set #649 .50-1.25
- ❏ 1992 Pro Set HOF 2000 #6 $5-10
- ❏ 1992 SkyBox Impact #227 .50-1.25
- ❏ 1992 SkyBoxPrimetime #16 $1.75-3.50
- ❏ 1992 SkyBox Primetime
  Poster Cards #M6 $6-12
- ❏ 1992 Sports Collectors
  Expo Promo #1 $2.50-5
- ❏ 1992 Stadium Club #650 $6-12
- ❏ 1992 Topps #719 .50-1.25
- ❏ 1992 Topps Gold #719 $2.50-5
- ❏ 1992 Upper Deck #560 .50-1.25
- ❏ 1992 Upper Deck Gold
  #G36 .50-1.25

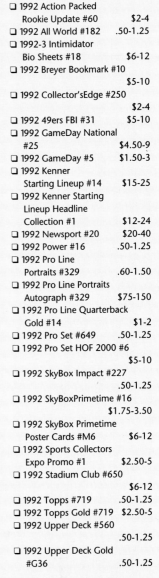

1992 All-World #182

- ❏ 1992 Upper Deck
  NFL Experience #1 .75-1.50
- ❏ 1992 Upper Deck
  NFL Experience Gold #1 $3.75-7.50

❑ 1992 Upper Deck SCD
Commemorative
Sheet #6 Multiplayer $5-10
❑ 1992 Wild Card Field Force
#1 $1.50-3
❑ 1992 Wild Card Field Force
Gold #1 $6-12
❑ 1992 Wild Card Field Force
Silver #1 $3-6
❑ 1992 Wild Card Stat Smasher
#SS11 $4-8
❑ 1993 Action Packed #23 $2-4
❑ 1993 Action Packed #216 $2-4
❑ 1993 Action Packed
All-Madden #25 $1.25-2.50
❑ 1993 Action Packed
All-Madden 24K Gold
#5 $50-100
❑ 1993 Action Packed
Monday Night Football
#11 $1.25-2.50
❑ 1993 Action Packed
Monday Night Football
24K Gold #11 $75-150
❑ 1993 Bowman #200 $3.50-7
❑ 1993 Classic Tonx
Montana #96   .50-1.00
❑ 1993 Collector's Edge #282
                         .60-1.50
❑ 1993 Collector's Edge
Rookies FX #4 $1.50-3
❑ 1993 Collector's Edge
Rookies FX Gold #4 $12.50-25
❑ 1993 Fleer #475   .60-1.50
❑ 1993 GameDay #36 $1.75-3.50
❑ 1993 GameDay
Gamebreakers #5 $3-6
❑ 1993 Kenner Starting Lineup
#15 $30-50
❑ 1993 McDonald's GameDay
#39 Multiplayer $1.50-3

1993 Pro Set #198

❑ 1993 Pacific #412   .50-1.25
❑ 1993 Pacific Gold
PrismInserts #13 $20-40
❑ 1993 Pacific Silver Prism
Inserts Circular #13 $5-10
❑ 1993 Pacific Silver Prism
Inserts Triangular #13 $7-14
❑ 1993 Pacific Prisms #42 $5-10
❑ 1993 Pacific Triple Folders #6
                         $2-4

❑ 1993 Pacific Triple Folders
Rookies/Superstars #14 $2-4
❑ 1993 Pinnacle #277 $1.75-3.50
❑ 1993 Pinnacle Team Pinnacle
#1 Multiplayer $75-125
❑ 1993 Playoff #8 $2.50-5
❑ 1993 Playoff Club #PC1
                         $12.50-25
❑ 1993 Playoff
Contenders #20 $1.75-3.50
❑ 1993 Power #200   .50-1.25
❑ 1993 Power Gold #200 $2-4

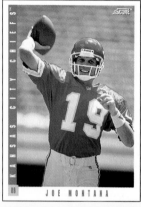

1993 Score #253

❑ 1993 Power Moves #PM10
                         .75-2.00
❑ 1993 Power Moves Gold
#PM10 $2-4
❑ 1993 Power Update Moves
#10   .75-2.00
❑ 1993 Power Update Moves
Gold #10 $3-6
❑ 1993 ProLine Live #124 .50-1.25
❑ 1993 ProLine Live
Autograph #124 $100-200
❑ 1993 ProLine Live Profiles
#559-567   .25-.60 Each
❑ 1993 Pro Set #198   .60-1.50
❑ 1993 Pro Set College
Connections #8 Multiplayer
                         $8-16
❑ 1993 Score #253   .60-1.50
❑ 1993 Select #155 $5-10
❑ 1993 SkyBox #48 $1.75-3.50
❑ 1993 SkyBox Impact #139
                         .60-1.50
❑ 1993 SkyBox Impact
Colors #139 $2.50-5
❑ 1993 SkyBox Impact
Update #6 $2.50-4
❑ 1993 SP Promo #19 $2-4
❑ 1993 SP #122 $7.50-15
❑ 1993 Stadium Club #250
Members Choice   .75-2.00
❑ 1993 Stadium Club #440
                         $1.75-3.50
❑ 1993 Stadium Club
First Day Issue #250
Members Choice $40-75
❑ 1993 Stadium Club
First Day Issue #440 $75-125
❑ 1993 Stadium Club
Members Only #250

Members Choice $5-10
❑ 1993 Stadium Club
Members Only #440 $9-18
❑ 1993 Stadium Club
Super Teams Division
Winners #440 $4.50-9
❑ 1993 Stadium Club
Super Teams Super Bowls
#250 Members Choice $3-6
❑ 1993 Stadium Club Super
Teams Super Bowls #440 $5-10
❑ 1993 Stadium Club
Master Photos II #10 $3-6
❑ 1993 Topps #200   .60-1.50
❑ 1993 Topps Gold #200
                         $3.75-7.50
❑ 1993 Topps FantaSports
#15 $3.75-7.50
❑ 1993 Ultra #203 $2-4
❑ 1993 Ultra Touchdown
Kings $15-25
❑ 1993 Upper Deck #460 .60-1.50
❑ 1993 Upper Deck Box
Bottom   .50-1.00
❑ 1993 Upper Deck
Team Chiefs #KC15 $1.25-2.50
❑ 1993 Upper Deck Team
Chiefs #KC25 Checklist
                         .75-1.50
❑ 1993 Upper Deck Miller Lite
SB #3 Multiplayer $3-6
❑ 1993 Upper Deck Miller Lite
SB #5 Multiplayer $3.75-7.50
❑ 1993 Wild Card #67   .50-1.25
❑ 1993 Wild Card
Superchrome #67 $2-4
❑ 1993 Wild Card
Field Force #44 $1.25-2.50
❑ 1993 Wild Card
Field Force #44 Gold $2.50-5
❑ 1993 Wild Card
Field Force #44 Silver $2-4
❑ 1993 Wild Card Field Force
Superchrome #3 $2.50-5
❑ 1993 Wild Card Field Force/
Red Hot Rookies Back to Back
#7 Multiplayer $2.50-5
❑ 1993 Wild Card
Stat Smashers #62 $2.50-5
❑ 1993 Wild Card Stat
Smashers Gold #62 $3.75-7.50
❑ 1994 Action Packed #49 $2-4
❑ 1994 Action Packed
Fantasy Forecast #31 $2-4
❑ 1994 Action Packed
Monday Night Football
#50 $1-2
❑ 1994 Action Packed
All-Madden #11 $1-2
❑ 1994 Action Packed
All-Madden 24K #11G $25-50
❑ 1994 Bowman $2-4
❑ 1994 Classic Images #16
                         $2.50-5
❑ 1994 Classic NFL
Experience #43   .60-1.50
❑ 1994 Collector's Choice
Prototype #19 $1.50-3
❑ 1994 Collector's Choice #36
Images of 93   .30-.75
❑ 1994 Collector's Choice #47

1993 SP #122

Traditions of Excellence .30-.75
❑ 1994 Collector'sChoice #70
                         .60-1.50
❑ 1994 Collector's Choice #384
Checklist   .08-.25
❑ 1994 Collector's Choice Gold
#36 Images of 934 $25-50
❑ 1994 Collector's Choice Gold
#47 Traditions of Excellence
                         $25-50
❑ 1994 Collector's Choice Gold
#70 $45-90
❑ 1994 Collector's Choice Gold
#384 Checklist $1.50-3
❑ 1994 Collector's Choice Silver
#36 Images of 93 $1.50-3
❑ 1994 Collector's Choice Silver
#47 Traditions of Excellence
                         $1.50-3
❑ 1994 Collector's Choice Silver
#70 $3-6
❑ 1994 Collector's Choice Silver
#384 Checklist   .20-.50

1993 Ultra #203

❑ 1994 Collector's Choice Crash
the Game #8 Blue $4.50-9
❑ 1994 Collector's Choice Crash
the Game #8 Green $4.50-9
❑ 1994 Collector's Choice Crash
the Game #8 Redemption
Bronze $1-2
❑ 1994 Collector's Choice

- Crash the Game #8
  Redemption Gold $2-4
- 1994 Collector's Choice Crash
  the Game #8 Redemption
  Silver $1.50-3
- 1994 Collector's Choice Then
  and Now #3 Multiplayer
                          $1-2.50
- 1994 Collector's Choice Then
  and Now #4 Multiplayer $2-4
- 1994 Collector's Choice Then
  and Now #8 Header $1-2.50
- 1994 Collector's Edge #94
                          $1.25-2.50
- 1994 Collector's Edge Gold
  #94 $3-6

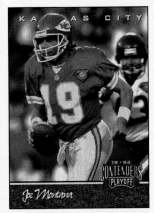

1994 Playoff Contenders #25

- 1994 Collector's Edge
  Silver #94 $2.50-5
- 1994 Collector's Edge
  Pop Warner #94 $2.50-5
- 1994 Collector's Edge Pop
  Warner 22K Gold #94 $10-20
- 1994 Collector's Edge
  Boss Squad #2 $2.50-5
- 1994 Collector's Edge Boss
  Squad Silver #2 $3.75-7.50
- 1994 Collector's Edge
  FX #2 $6-12
- 1994 Collector's Edge FX
  #2 Gold Shield $35-70
- 1994 Collector's Edge FX
  #2 Silver Shield $35-70
- 1994 Collector's Edge FX
  #2 Gold Back $35-70
- 1994 Collector's Edge FX
  #2 Silver Back $4.50-9
- 1994 Collector's Edge FX
  #2 White Back $4.50-9
- 1994 Collector's Edge FX
  #2 Gold Letters $35-70
- 1994 Collector's Edge FX
  #2 Red Letters $3-6
- 1994 Collector's Edge FX
  #2 Silver Letters $6-12
- 1994 Excalibur #33 $2-4
- 1994 Excalibur 22K Gold
  #15 $7.50-15
- 1994 Finest #172 $9-18
- 1994 Finest Refractor #172
                          $90-160
- 1994 Fleer #226   .60-1.50

- 1994 Fleer All-Pro #7 $2.50-5
- 1994 Fleer Living Legends
  #3 $20-35
- 1994 Fleer Pro-Visions #7
                          .75-2.00
- 1994 Fleer Pro-Visions Jumbo
  #7 $5-10
- 1994 Fleer Scoring Machines
  #10 $20-40
- 1994 Fleer FACT Shell #14
                          $1-2
- 1994 GameDay #194 $1.50-3
- 1994 GameDay
  Gamebreakers #7 $2-4
- 1994 Kenner Starting
  Lineup #18 $18-30
- 1994 NFL Back-to-School
  #10 $2.50-5
- 1994 Pacific #55   .60-1.50
- 1994 Pacific Gems of the
  Crown #21 $10-20
- 1994 Pacific Marquee
  Prisms #20 $2-4
- 1994 Pacific Marquee
  Prisms Gold #20   15-30
- 1994 Pacific Prisms #79 $8-16
- 1994 Pacific Prisms Gold
  #79 $40-80
- 1994 Pacific Triple
  Folders #16 $1-2
- 1994 Pacific Triple Folders
  Rookies/Superstars #19 $5-10
- 1994 Pinnacle #102
                          $1.25-2.50
- 1994 Pinnacle Trophy
  Collection #102 $30-60
- 1994 Pinnacle Performers
  #PP11 $7-14
- 1994 Pinnacle Team Pinnacle
  Dufex #1 Multiplayer $50-100
- 1994 Pinnacle Team Pinnacle
  Non-Dufex #1 Multiplayer
                          $50-100
- 1994 Pinnacle Canton
  Bound #8 $1.25-2.50
- 1994 Playoff #1 $2-4
- 1994 Playoff Contenders
  #25 $2.25-4.50
- 1994 Playoff Contenders
  Back-to-Back #1 Multiplayer
                          $250-350
- 1994 Playoff Contenders

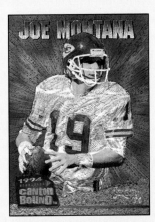

1994 Select Canton Bound

- Throwbacks #14 $25-50
- 1994 ProLine Live #61   .60-1.50
- 1994 ProLine Live
  Autographed #61 $100-175
- 1994 ProLine Live MVP
  Sweepstakes #16 $20-40
- 1994 ProLine Live
  Spotlight #PB15 $1.25-2.5
- 1994 Score #67   .60-1.50
- 1994 Score Gold #67
                          $3.75-7.50
- 1994 Select #79 $2-4
- 1994 Select Canton Bound
                          $45-80
- 1994 SkyBox #75 $1.50-3
- 1994 SkyBox
  Inside the Numbers #8 $5-10
- 1994 SkyBox Revolution
  #R9 $15-30
- 1994 SkyBox SkyTech Stars
  #ST6 $8-16
- 1994 SkyBox Impact
  #122   .60-1.50
- 1994 SkyBox Impact
  Ultimate Impact #U4 $7-14
- 1994 SP #88 $3-6
- 1994 SP Die Cuts #88 $9-18
- 1994 SP All-Pro Holoviews
  #PB17 $15-30
- 1994 SP All-Pro Holoviews
  Die-Cut #PB17 $175-260
- 1994 Sportflics #123 $2-4
- 1994 Sportflics
  #176 Starflics $1.25-2.50
- 1994 Sportflics
  Artist Proofs #123 $40-80
- 1994 Sportflics Artist Proofs
  #176 Starflics $25-50
- 1994 Sportflics
  Head-to-Head #9 $30-60
- 1994 Stadium Club #160
                          $1.50-3
- 1994 Stadium Club #615
                          $1.25-2.50
- 1994 Stadium Club First Day
  Issue #160 $35-70
- 1994 Stadium Club First Day
  Issue #615 $40-80
- 1994 Stadium Club Members
  Only #160 $7.50-15
- 1994 Stadium Club Members
  Only #615 $6-12
- 1994 Stadium Club
  Bowman's Best #BK17 $8-16
- 1994 Stadium Club
  Bowman's Best Refractors
  #BK17 $40-80
- 1994 Stadium Club Super
  Teams #13 $4-8
- 1994 Topps #520   .60-1.50
- 1994 Topps Special
  Effects #520 $7.50-15
- 1994 Ultra #145 $1.5-3
- 1994 Ultra Achievement
  Award #4 $1.50-3
- 1994 Ultra Achievement
  Award Jumbo #4 $4.50-9
- 1994 Ultra Flair
  Hot Numbers #8 $3-6
- 1994 Ultra Touchdown
  Kings #3 $18-35

- 1994 U.S. Playing Cards
  Ditka's Picks #1D   .35-.75
- 1994 Upper Deck #133
                          $1.25-2.50
- 1994 Upper Deck
  Electric Gold #133 $75-125
- 1994 Upper Deck Electric
  Silver #133 $6.50-12.50
- 1994 Upper Deck Predictor
  Award Winner #HP4 $5-10
- 1994 Upper Deck Predictor
  League Leader #RP4 $4-8
- 1994 Upper Deck 24K Gold
                          $60-120
- 1995 Classic NFL Experience
  #43   .50-1.25

**1995 Pinnacle Zenith Z-Team
#ZT5**

- 1995 Classic NFL Experience
  Gold #43 $2-4
- 1995 Classic NFL Experience
  Super Bowl Game #A3
                          $1.25-2.50
- 1995 Classic NFL
  ExperienceThrowbacks
  #T13 $12-22
- 1995 Finest #90 $8-16
- 1995 Finest Refractors
  #90 $90-150
- 1995 Pinnacle Zenith
  #Z79   6-12
- 1995 Pinnacle Zenith
  Second Season #SS4 $10-20
- 1995 Pinnacle Zenith
  Z-Team #ZT5 $75-125

Racing Cards:
- 1995 Upper Deck #135
  Championship Pit Crew
                          .50-1.25
- 1995 Upper Deck Gold
  Signature #135 Championship
  Pit Crew $30-60
- 1995 Upper Deck Silver
  Signature #135 Championship
  Pit Crew $2-4

Jennifer Montana:
- 1991 Pro Line Portraits
  Wives #SC1   .10-.30
- 1991 Pro Line Portraits
  Wives Autographs #1 $40-75

DIGGING

The "ultimate" Joe Montana collectible, says 49ers worshiper Jim Daveggio, would be one of the quarterback's four Super Bowl rings.

Impossible, right?

Right. But Daveggio, a 58-year-old Californian whose home includes a "49ers room," settled for what he believes is an authentic salesman's sample of one of Montana's rings. He paid more than $5,000 for it, and then refitted the piece with real diamonds.

That's the kind of ingenuity and passion Montana can inspire in some fans.

In fact, Joe's admirers are some of the most devoted in all of sports, accumulating all kinds of Montana memorabilia from photos to pins to

KEEPER

Most football collections are founded on Joe Montana. With so much Montana memorabilia on the market, from game-worn jerseys to autographed programs, collectors have plenty to build upon . . . for a price.

•

statues to plates and beyond.

At the top of many wish lists, of course, is game-used Montana equipment. But little is available — little that can be authenticated anyway.

Bronco Hinek, the 49ers' equipment manager, says there was a time when he sold some game-worn Montana jerseys to collectors. They were club property, and he decided to use the proceeds to buy various team supplies. He stopped when management told him it wanted to avoid developing an image as a "storefront."

Hinek, who wrote letters of authenticity for the jerseys that were sold, says about a half-dozen found their way into private collections. With so few in circulation, he notes, a buyer

should be extremely cautious when a seller claims a Montana jersey is game-used.

Although Hinek can't account for every jersey from memory, he says Montana and team owner Edward DeBartolo Jr. have key jerseys from Super Bowls and championship games. Collectors should be especially wary of anyone claiming to have a special jersey such as one of these.

At Any Cost

If you have your heart set on owning one of Joe's game-used shirts, you'd better start saving now. Andy Imperato, a Long Island, N.Y., jersey expert, says a genuine game-used Montana jersey will cost anywhere from $3,500 to $5,000. He also warns of counterfeits.

"It's so easy to buy a replica jersey and fake the rips and tears that come with game use," Imperato says. "I wouldn't spend that kind of money unless the jersey came with some verification of authenticity."

Budgetary constraints will prevent most Montana collectors from worrying about fake jerseys. For the average Joe, a game program or football signed by Montana would be the cornerstone of their collection.

Fans wandering around big city card shops or shows shouldn't have any trouble adding exciting Montana treasures to their troves . . . at least if spending a little cash isn't a problem.

Although Joe's a fairly prolific signer, considering his stature in the game and

By Mike Antonucci

in the hobby, autographed Montana material isn't cheap. Demand, and his absence from the card show circuit, keeps prices fairly high.

If you're looking for a Montana-signed 8-by-10 glossy photo, be prepared to part with $25-$40. An autographed *Sports Illustrated* or *Beckett Football Card Monthly* cover will set you back $50-$75. A signed Super Bowl pennant or hat will be in that ballpark, too. Want to add an autographed football to your collection? An official one can be yours for $200-$250. An unofficial white-panel ball costs slightly less.

As the demands on his time have changed, so has Montana's autograph. Examples of Joe's signature from the early '80s show his name spelled out completely and legibly. Most recent autographs, however, aren't as well-executed, and may include only a letter or two from his first and last names (usually the "J" and "M"), followed by an unidentifiable squiggle.

Understandably, most serious collectors would be willing to pay a premium for an earlier version.

"These days, there are so many athletes who have funky signatures, so his autograph doesn't seem to detract people," autograph expert Mark Jordan of Bedford, Texas, says. "To me, the signature definitely doesn't say Joe Montana. But if you're a Joe Montana fan, you will want it

no matter what it looks like.

"When they were winning Super Bowls, he was the most popular guy around," Jordan adds. "He rarely did card shows because there was always more demand than supply. His autograph is out there in pretty good supply right now."

Joe Cool Authenticated

Collectors in smaller towns, or those with bigger budgets, have another avenue for acquiring Montana items. Joe joined other sporting legends such as Mickey Mantle, Wayne Gretzky and Larry Bird when he signed an exclusive marketing agreement with Upper Deck Authenticated.

The deal, which precludes Montana from any other for-profit signings (meaning no more card show appearances), allows collectors the chance to purchase a variety of certified, authentic autographed items. Among those offered in the company's latest catalog are official replica jerseys ($299) and helmets ($399), framed magazine covers ($199), autographed footballs ($249) and Upper Deck card blowups ($99.95).

Although some of these prices are more than the going market rate (official helmets, for example, can be found for as little as $250), UDA issues a certificate of authenticity with each pur-

chase, guaranteeing that the signature is legitimate. Should you ever want to resell a UDA-purchased Montana item, this may help to preserve its value.

In spite of the UDA agreement, autograph hounds needn't worry about Joe altering his in-person signing habits. Montana can still sign material without going through Upper Deck, but it has to be informal (through his mail or at the field), for charity (Upper Deck coordinates some of that) or as part of a promotional event for one of the other businesses that use him as a spokesman.

Robert Hemphill of National Sports Distributors points out that Montana has been an approachable and courteous signer throughout his career.

"I've never heard anything bad about him at all when it comes to signing, either in person or through the mail," says Hemphill, whose company had regular private signings with Montana before the UDA deal. "He's a little shy, but he's always been a class act."

Although Hemphill's company deals in all kinds of autographed memorabilia, it specializes in lithographs by sports artist and regular *Beckett* contributor Dan Smith.

Hemphill says that Smith's first piece featuring Montana, titled "The Huddle," could be purchased in 1986 for $60. Nine years later, that same lithograph will cost a collector anywhere from $2,700 to $3,200.

Three others, "MVP," "Standup Joe" and "Passing Through the Decade," sell for $1,000 to $1,200. The most recent work, "Tribute," is a more affordable $395 to $450.

Numbers such as those make it obvious that Montana is clearly the key figure in the current football memorabilia market. Indeed, he is the player in the NFL when it comes to marketing clout.

According to a 1993 report in *The Sports Marketing Letter*, Montana is tied for fourth with golfer Greg Norman on its spokesperson earnings list. Basketball superstar Michael Jordan rated No.1 followed by golf giants Arnold Palmer and Jack Nicklaus.

The report estimates that Montana's contract with Upper Deck alone pays a guaranteed $1 million to $1.5 million and may include incentives, depending on how much merchandise is sold each year. Upper Deck doesn't discuss the terms of Montana's deal, but confirms that Montana ranks No. 1 in sales among the dozen or so athletes under exclusive contract.

Although Montana's dollar rankings are impressive, they don't always convey the near frenzy he can generate among fans. Former Upper Deck

spokesperson Marje Bennett recalls the response to a promotion the company held in conjunction with a Macy's department store in San Francisco. The first 650 people to spend $149 or more on Montana items in the store were invited to an event with the quarterback. It took only one week to fill the guest list.

Joe's one of the few players to appear in all seven football sets of Kenner's popular Starting Lineup plastic figurines, which are packaged with special standard-size cards. This summer, hobbyists were able to get their hands on the latest Montana figure, which was distributed at four Kenner conventions across the United States.

Ed Weinberg, a vice president at Richard Wolffers Auctions Inc. in San Francisco, says that the secret to Montana's appeal goes beyond his legendary on-field record. His collectibles attract enormous attention because Montana has a "nice guy" personality that people admire as much as his playing achievements.

"Joe Montana," Weinberg says, "is like a god here."

Quite a statement, and yet it's probably too conservative. Montana's reputation long ago made him a national idol, which is the kind of hero Upper Deck wanted as the nucleus of its football marketing.

"Montana was the leader in his field as well as on the

When Joe's star quality first shined, his penmanship was neat and easy to read. Today, autograph seekers are lucky if they can make out a "J" or an "M."

AP / WIDE WORLD PHOTOS

field," Bennetts says. "The research on his popularity showed the kind of following he has."

In a way, there's actually something surprising about that statement. Did they really need research to check out Joe Montana's popularity?

Regardless, UDA got its man, and collectors continue to reaffirm that choice. Joe may collect Steve Young, as he says in the Upper Deck commercial, but everyone else is busy collecting the man with the state on his back and all those pretty rings on his fingers. •

Mike Antonucci is a freelance writer in San Jose, Calif.

<u>Hobbyists on Joe</u>

"Here's an average, likeable guy who's earned every penny of his paycheck. Although he could have simply lived off of his fame, he just keeps driving harder."
— *Larry Nyeste, Columbus, Ohio*

strokes
for a
genius

Joe Montana's ingeniousness on the gridiron, as well as his
numerous moments of triumph, made him an ideal subject
for sports artists. As we see from their efforts, anything
Joe is associated with only burnishes his image further.

vince chiaramonte

dan smith

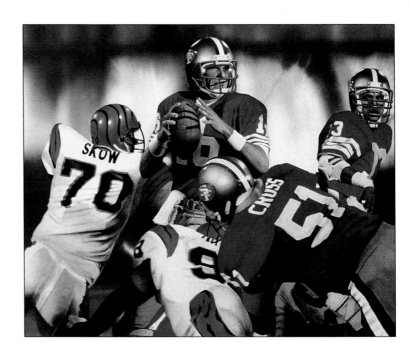

eric franchimon

dan smith

steve cusano

dan smith

anthony douglas

ed anzilotti

eric franchimon

eric franchimon

dan smith

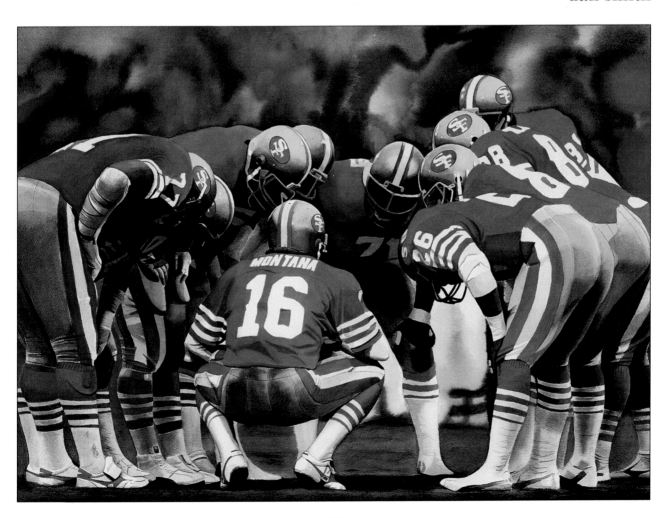

george humes

amy chenier

james fiorentino

COMMON THREADS

Five relationships
left indelible imprints on
Joe Montana's career

By Gary Swan

Joe Montana crossed paths with many people during his 16

seasons in the NFL, but of just a select few can it be said that they

truly influenced his career. Each association had its own unique

characteristics and circumstances. Some were close in nature,

some flourished solely on the professional level and some were

more complicated than others. The following pages spotlight five

key relationships in Montana's celebrated career.

JOE MONTANA & DWIGHT CLARK

INDELIBLY LINKED AS the passer and receiver in one of NFL's most famous plays, Joe Montana and Dwight Clark symbolized the youth and promise of the 49ers' first Super Bowl team.

They were the best of friends, these 1979 draft picks — Montana the third-rounder out of Notre Dame, Clark the tenth-rounder from Clemson. No one suspected when these fun-loving rookies became training-camp roommates that one would become perhaps the best quarterback ever to play the game, and the other would become the 49ers' all-time reception (506) and reception yardage (6,750) leader until Jerry Rice came along.

Ultimately, they will be best remembered as partners in The Catch, which ended the Dallas Cowboys' reign over the NFL in the 1981 NFC title game and subsequently launched the decade of the 49ers in the '80s.

"If it wasn't for [head coach] Bill Walsh and Joe Montana and this offense, I never would have been heard of," Clark says. "But I could read coverages and catch passes between five and 15 yards. As far as being one of the best of all time, no way. I'm not in that category."

Walsh spotted Clark while on a scouting trip to see Clemson quarterback Steve Fuller. In the NFL, Clark played on guts and inspiration, and forever was trying to overcome feeling like an underdog who had no right to be in the league. When his knees were injured, a common occurrence toward the end of his career, Clark would go to Montana's house, where the two buddies lifted weights in the basement. Clark would lament that his career might be finished, and Montana would reply that he came back from an injury, and he would swear that Dwight could, too.

Clark also performed well as Montana's alter ego during press interview sessions. What was Joe thinking about when he threw that game-winning pass? Montana himself would get bogged down in a technical answer, displaying no emotion. Sometimes it was better to ask Clark what he thought was going through Joe's mind. Clark could take what he knew and put it into the con-

text of the game and season, thereby embellishing the aura around Montana far better than Joe could himself.

Clark retired before the 1988 season, leaving the job of Montana's primary receiver in Rice's capable hands. He and Montana drifted apart as Clark became an Ed DeBartolo Jr.-devoted member of 49ers management in his position as coordinator of football operations and player personnel. Clark hurt Montana when he said he hoped Montana would retire at a time when Joe said he couldn't stomach retirement. "[It's] just because it's so hard for me to watch him play out there. I kept flinching," Clark said. "It just seemed like he would get hit one of these times and not be able to get up."

When Montana called it quits in April, he didn't invite many of the 49ers' establishment to his public retirement ceremony. The wounds over the trade to Kansas City were too fresh. But he invited Clark, who proudly stood front and center with his old friend and former roommate.   •

JOE MONTANA & BILL WALSH

GEORGE ROSE / ALLSPORT USA

IT'S A TWIST on the age-old question — which came first: the chicken or the egg? In San Francisco, it went like this: Was it Bill Walsh's system or Joe Montana's precision that created the 49ers' success story? You could argue either way, but the safest thing to say is that both coach and player needed each other.

Walsh always had achieved success with his offense, whether as an assistant at Cincinnati and San Diego, or as head coach at Stanford, but he'd never won a championship. At the outset with the 49ers, Walsh had Steve DeBerg as his quarterback, and DeBerg was good enough to set what at the time were club passing records. But Walsh knew he never would win a championship with DeBerg.

Meanwhile, Montana had displayed flashes of brilliance at Notre Dame, but he wasn't highly rated by pro scouts. Walsh liked Montana's agility and accuracy, and he was impressed by Montana's ability to rally a team, as he had demonstrated in Notre Dame's legendary comeback in the 1979 Cotton Bowl against Houston. Walsh believed that, with work, Montana could develop the consistency to become a top-flight quarterback.

Montana's cool head and sense of timing, of course, made him the perfect quarterback to run Walsh's complicated passing offense — simply, he was the right man in the right place at the right time. If he'd gone to a team that required the quarterback to throw deep with regularity, such as the Raiders, Montana's career may have turned out differently. But together, Walsh and Montana thrived. Together, they won three Super Bowls in an eight-year span, and Montana added a fourth without Walsh but with the same system.

One of Walsh's strengths as a personnel evaluator was knowing when players were near the end of their careers and phasing them out before their downslide led to loses. Walsh had helped make Montana a legend, but his relationship with the quarterback became strained when Steve Young arrived in 1987 and began to receive

playing time not only when Montana was hurt — which was quite often — but also at the end of games Montana had started.

In November 1990, Montana said he was afraid to leave a game with an injury for fear he'd be replaced permanently by Young. He said the threat was making him play tentatively. Walsh tried to reassure Montana that the starting job was his — for the moment. But Walsh didn't disagree with the notion that the end of Montana's career hovered on the horizon.

Walsh retired following San Francisco's 1988 Super Bowl victory, and it took his successor, George Seifert, until 1992 to proclaim Young his quarter-back. By that time, Montana had missed more than an entire season because of his elbow surgery. Walsh would have pulled the trigger much faster, oblivious to the anger and resentment it would have prompted from Montana, and saved the 49ers' organization from the inevitable division into a Montana camp and a Young camp.　　•

JOE MONTANA & ED DEBARTOLO

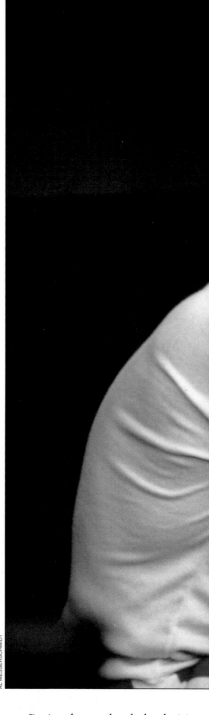

ED DEBARTOLO HIMSELF says it now: He was too close to Joe Montana. The lines between player and owner definitely were blurred in their case. And sometimes that created problems for others in 49ers management.

"I basically grew up in this franchise as an owner as he matured as a quarterback, and our friendship developed," DeBartolo told reporters on the day Montana was traded to Kansas City in 1993. "I'm not saying that's the greatest thing that can happen for an owner to become as close to a person as I became to Joe Montana, because it's very difficult in times such as this or in times of a retirement to be able to mentally do the right thing.

"This is really a tough business, and this is the hardest part of this business. It really makes me not want to be an owner," DeBartolo said, his voice shaking with sincere, heartfelt emotion.

DeBartolo bought the 49ers in 1977, when he was 30 years old. He was like an older brother to Montana, Dwight Clark, Roger Craig and the young group of players who won the franchise's first Super Bowl following the 1981 season. They partied together, and DeBartolo enjoyed the easy camaraderie with his players. But Montana was the one he was closest to, perhaps for the obvious reason that Montana was the key figure in San Francisco's first four Super Bowl victories.

How close? Montana spent the weekend at DeBartolo's home before he was traded to the Chiefs in 1993. DeBartolo would do anything to keep him — but he couldn't get around the knotty problem of Montana wanting to be starting quarterback even though he'd missed two seasons following his elbow surgery and Steve Young had capably taken over.

During that weekend, the decision was made to proclaim Montana the team's designated starter at quarterback. Head coach George Seifert was left holding the bag on that one — having to explain why Steve Young, the NFL passing leader in 1991 and 1992 and six years younger and healthier than Montana, now had to sit on the

bench. Montana himself realized how farcical that would have been and rejected the plan, setting in motion the trade to Kansas City that seemed to DeBartolo "like sending someone away to school."

DeBartolo and Montana stayed friends even after the trade. Montana asked NFL Films to put together a going-away tape, which consisted of sentimental shots of Montana and DeBartolo together during the 49ers' glory years. Steve Sabol, president of NFL Films, said it was "the first time in our 30-year history that any player ever made that request or ever even thought of something like that. A lot of players have called us and requested things about themselves, but never a player who called and said he wanted to give something to his owner."

Said DeBartolo, "I don't think I'll ever have a relationship with anybody with this organization for as long as I own this team — which is going to be a long time — that I have with Joe Montana."

•

JOE MONTANA & STEVE YOUNG

FROM THE START, Joe Montana and Steve Young mixed like oil and water.

Head coach Bill Walsh acquired Young from Tampa Bay in 1987 and immediately all but anointed him Montana's successor. Montana did not take well to the pretender to his throne, who had thrown 13 interceptions and just eight touchdowns as the Bucs starter in 1986.

Walsh found more playing time for Young in the 1988 Super Bowl season while making veiled suggestions that Montana's time to step aside might be fast approaching. Walsh was a master at spotting when a player's ability was on the wane. But this time, he underestimated Montana and created a rift between his No. 1 quarterback and the backup. Joe, after all, had another Super Bowl in him in 1989, and fell a Roger Craig fumble short of going for the "threepeat" in 1990.

Montana's insecurity worsened when George Seifert took over as head coach. Young was growing impatient for his shot and complained to Seifert. Montana saw this as whining and back-stabbing. He rallied the veterans on the team around him and, at one point, Young had trouble finding someone to eat lunch with in the locker room. In training camp in 1991, Young told reporters that maybe he needed to get away from the 49ers to get on with his career.

Montana and Young were as different as two guys with adjoining lockers could be. Montana liked his good times. He and Dwight Clark could bend training camp curfew with the best of them. It became the 49ers' way, along with winning on Sunday. Montana engineered 26 fourth-quarter 49ers comebacks — the most famous being the last-minute drive to beat Cincinnati in Super Bowl XXIII. He calmed his

teammates by entering the huddle on that fateful drive, which began 90 yards from the end zone, looking up into the stands and observing, "Hey, isn't that John Candy up there?" As tackle Harris Barton said later, "How could we doubt that we would score when the quarterback is that in control?"

No one would confuse Young with a

party animal. A direct descendant of Mormon leader Brigham Young, he lived a temperate and frugal life that was easy to poke fun at. And when he got into a game, he was so eager to do well that he invariably would overthrow his first few passes, hanging his receivers up in the air for punishing hits.

After Montana tore his elbow mid-way through training camp in 1991, he offered Young little help in running the offense. Hurt by the quarterback transition, the 49ers missed the playoffs for the second time in nine years. In 1992, Young led the 49ers to the NFL title game, where they fell to the Cowboys. By that time, more than a few players wondered why Montana stayed as far away from Young along the sideline as he could, offering no encouragement or advice as he came off the field.

Scenes such as that spoke volumes about the relationship between the two — or, more precisely, the lack of one. Still, because of their curious history together, they'll be forever linked in 49ers lore.   •

JOE MONTANA & JERRY RICE

JOE MONTANA FIRING downfield to Jerry Rice is the stuff of 49ers legend. In the six seasons they played together — 1985-1990 — they hooked up for 55 scoring passes during the regular season, plus another 13 in the postseason, including three in a 55-10 rout of Denver in Super Bowl XXIV.

Montana's uncanny accuracy and Rice's deft moves were the perfect combination in an NFL where defensive backs have to provide receivers a five-yard cushion at the line of scrimmage. Rice's precision in running his routes, honed by a work ethic that amazed teammates, found its mirror image in a quarterback such as Montana, who could spot four receivers amid the chaos of moving bodies and deliver a perfectly thrown pass to his target.

The most prosperous season for the Montana-to-Rice partnership was 1987, Rice's third season in the league.

It was a strike year, and the real 49ers played just 12 games. Rice caught at least one touchdown pass from Montana in each game and 22 in all, five more than his second-best season, 1989. Rice caught fire late that season: three touchdowns against Tampa Bay, three the next week against Cleveland and three more two weeks later against the Bears. He totaled 14 touchdowns in the last six weeks of the season — his best surge toward ultimately breaking Jim Brown's NFL career touchdown record in 1994. Rice never had a streak like that again with Montana, even including his NFL record five-touchdown game against Atlanta in 1990, when Falcons defensive back Charles "Toast" Dimry earned his nickname.

Rice experienced a tough rookie year in 1985. He dropped a few passes early in the season, but Montana kept throwing his way, and Rice never forgot

it. He finished his rookie campaign with 49 catches for 927 yards, which provided the impetus for his breakout season with Montana in 1986.

By 1991, Rice ranked among the 49ers' veterans most wanting Montana to come back from his elbow surgery and replace Steve Young. He complained openly that Young was not in sync with

him, and he didn't like the way Young threw the ball high, exposing Rice to wicked hits from defenders. Even after the 1992 season, two years since Montana threw him a pass and two years during which Young had won the NFL passing titles, Rice still wanted Montana back — and maybe for the starting job.

"I would like for Joe to return," Rice said at the time. "Knowing Joe, he's still competitive. If he feels like he can come back next year and compete for the job, then maybe he can."

It took until last season, Young's fourth as the No. 1 quarterback, for Rice to acknowledge that Young could do a passable imitation of Joe. By that time, Young had thrown 60 touchdown passes to Rice, surpassing Montana's total by five.

But nothing can surpass the special relationship Montana and Rice forged during their six glorious seasons together. •

Gary Swan is a sportswriter for the San Francisco Chronicle.

OLD NOTRE DAME"

Montana scored high marks in Comebacks 101 and aced his final exam by winning a national championship. But making the grade as quarterback for the Fighting Irish took more hard work than Joe ever imagined.

Joe Montana trotted onto the field at Purdue and into the huddle, serving as much as a curiosity as he was a concern for Boilermaker fans. Yet he was the last hope for the Fighting Irish, even though it had been almost two years since he had last quarterbacked in a game for them.

Something stirred on the Notre Dame side of the field. Someone in the stands mentioned The Comeback Kid.

The Comeback Kid? Oh, yeah, at least the nickname was coming back. Joe once had been a last-minute magician.

Had been — which sounds a lot like "has-been."

As an unpredictable sophomore in 1975, Montana had come off the bench to turn some heads and toss some touchdowns while leading the Irish to come-from-behind victories against North Carolina and Air Force.

The Comeback Kid, they called him.

But where was he coming back from now? And what was rustier, the nickname or his arm?

After all, this was the third game of the 1977 season. This was after he missed the last part of 1975 with a broken finger. This was after he missed all of 1976 with a separated shoulder.

But with 11 minutes to go and Notre Dame losing to Purdue, 24-14, head coach Dan Devine looked over to one of his assistants and barked, "Get Montana in there!"

Rated as the nation's preseason No. 1 pick, Notre Dame already had been upset by Ole Miss the previous week. Now the Irish were on the verge of dipping to 1-2 and all the way out of the polls.

"When you come off the bench, something is usually going wrong," Montana said after that game. "There's not time for pressure."

Even so, Montana's first pass of the game, a roll-out intended for Ken

BY BILL MOOR

MacAfee, was nearly picked off by Purdue defensive end James Larkins. Montana just rolled his eyes and returned to the huddle, same look, same voice, same Joe. He apparently needed only that one pass to shake off two years of rust from his golden arm.

He completed nine of his next 13 passes to lead the Irish on three scoring drives and to a rousing 31-24 victory over Purdue.

The Comeback Kid was back.

Using that game as his springboard, Montana embarked on a college career that rivaled that of any Notre Dame alum.

He directed the Irish to nine more victories in 1977, including a convincing 38-10 triumph over top-ranked Texas in the Cotton Bowl that earned Notre Dame the national championship.

In his final season (his fifth at the school because of a redshirt season), Montana led the Irish to a 9-3 record, punctuated by one of the most amazing comebacks in collegiate history. If the Heisman Trophy ballots were cast after New Year's Day, Montana likely would have won by a landslide.

On the last play of the 1979 Cotton Bowl, the last pass of his collegiate career, Montana threw the winning touchdown to Kris Haines. It was a fantastic finish — and a fitting one.

After all, comebacks were Joe's trademark at Notre Dame. Yet after the Purdue victory in 1977, consistency became an even more crucial part of his development.

"After Joe came back and started

A small-town boy trapped on a big-time campus, Montana couldn't help but come down with a bad case of homesickness during his freshman year.

playing again after his injuries, I don't think I can ever remember him having a bad practice," Devine recalls.

Notre Dame fans, spoiled for years by Fighting Irish standouts such as Paul Hornung, John Huarte, Rocky Bleier and Terry Hanratty, cared only about the bottom line — winning. Joe knew exactly how to please that demanding crowd in the most dramatic fashion.

• In 1975, Montana staged two memorable comebacks. He brought the Irish back from a 14-6 fourth quarter deficit against North Carolina to win 21-14. The clincher came with 1:03 re-

maining. Against Air Force, Montana faced a 20-point hill to climb and reached the top with 3:23 left to play. Notre Dame won, 31-30.

• In 1977, Joe's performance against Purdue is remembered most, but he also brought the Irish back from a 17-7 deficit against Clemson. Montana directed a pair of fourth quarter touchdown drives to upend the Tigers in front of their home fans in Death Valley, 21-17.

• In 1978 against Pitt, Montana led the Irish to three touchdowns in the final quarter for a 26-17 victory after trailing 17-7. Later that season, Joe put

When Montana finally won the starting spot, he did everything possible to gain the respect of his teammates, even if that meant getting caught in the middle of some violent collisions.

on a show against archrival USC, only to be turned away by a last-second field goal by the Trojans.

• Joe's heroics on Jan. 1, 1979, were icing on his comeback cake. In his final collegiate game, Montana shook off an acute chill that had lowered his body temperature to 96 degrees before leading the Irish back from a 34-12 deficit.

It's no wonder then that few doubted he'd reach his goal when he walked into a huddle on Jan. 22, 1989, with 3:10 left to play and a Super Bowl winning touchdown merely 92 yards away.

"The guy was phenomenal," says Vagas Ferguson, a tailback in Montana's Irish backfield who played four seasons in the NFL. "He would come into a huddle and say just a few words and put a calm into everything. Here he'd be standing in front of all those big linemen with a presence I've never felt before."

Montana treated the huddle as his boardroom. And he was always the chairman.

"In the huddle, all eyes would turn to Joe," fullback and close friend Steve Orsini says. "And he would thrive on it."

School of Hard Knocks

Notre Dame had known about Montana long before his freshman year in 1974. Former Irish backfield coach Tom Pagna recalls the time that he and Hanratty rested on a hill and watched this skinny kid throw passes to Bleier long after a football camp's last session had ended.

"Who is that kid throwing to Rocky?" Hanratty remembers asking. "He looks pretty good."

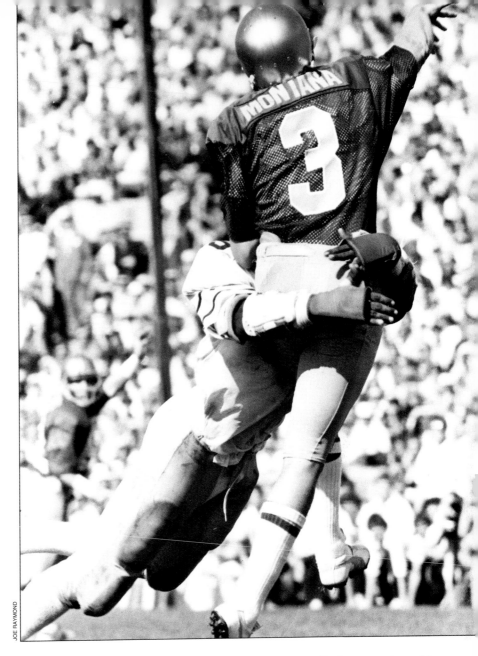

JOE RAYMOND

"His name is Montana," Pagna replied. "Joe Montana."

"Sounds like a gunslinger," Hanratty said.

A few years later, that kid — still skinny — from Monongahela, Pa., came to Notre Dame with the intent of following Hanratty's footsteps into the pros. Joe had long idolized Hanratty, whose roots also were buried deep in Western Pennsylvania soil.

Joe's desire to play pro sports probably was the main reason he turned down a scholarship offer from North Carolina State to play basketball. Although he was a tal-

ented basketball player at Ringgold High School, he realized that at 6-2, a promising pro roundball career would be tough to come by. So he turned his sights toward football and Notre Dame instead.

But with Tom Clements already penciled in as the starter and six other freshmen quarterbacks on the depth chart, Montana was nothing more than a junior varsity backup his first season. He played all of 17 seconds under head coach Ara Parseghian. The NFL seemed light years away.

Joe was homesick, writing and call-

ROOTS OF A CHAMPION

After facing the intense pressures of playing quarterback in the high school hotbed of Western Pennsylvania, Montana was ready for anything

BY VIC KETCHMAN

They were long-time rivals, two high schools with unmatched athletic traditions, and neither wanted to surrender its identity.

The small towns of Donora and Monongahela sit along the west bank of the Monongahela River, about 25 miles downstream from Pittsburgh.

Donora is famous for St. Louis Cardinals Hall of Famer Stan Musial, former Cincinnati Reds star outfielder Ken Griffey Sr. and NFL standout Deacon Dan Towler.

Monongahela has churned out former Vikings placekicker Fred Cox and some guy named Montana.

In 1969, the towns' high schools began a state-mandated merger that was as unpopular to both as each had always been to the other.

The early years of the merger into the Ringgold School District were difficult. It was Ringgold by name only, as Donora High and Monongahela High continued to operate while plans were made to build a new, joint high school. Meanwhile, Ringgold was a name that had meaning

only on the athletic field, where the schools joined forces.

Joe Montana did what no school board or city council ever could. He took two opposites and made them attract. He merged two towns into one heartbeat on Friday nights.

Beginning in 1973, Montana put Ringgold High School on the map. The school would never have an identity problem again. More importantly, the district's two towns embrace Montana with equal affection and pride.

"Joe was the pioneer for the new name," says Ringgold athletic director Paul Zolak, an assistant football coach in '73.

"Donora and Monongahela were bitter rivals. To put them together under

When Monongahela's hometown hero inked with fabled Notre Dame, he joined a long list of Western Pennsylvania QBs such as Joe Namath, Johnny Unitas, Terry Hanratty and Johnny Lujack who went on to star on a bigger stage.

one roof was difficult, not so much for the kids, but for their parents and grandparents. It took them a long time to say the word 'Ringgold,' " says Zolak, whose son Scott, now a quarterback for the New England Patriots, was a ball boy for the Ringgold team during Montana's senior year.

"Joe is the greatest ambassador we have. Ringgold and Joe are synonymous," Zolak says.

Zolak also serves as the district's PR man, and no one knows better how to use Montana's magical name to promote Ringgold High.

In 1990, Zolak put together a testimonial dinner for Montana, who was fresh off of his fourth Super Bowl triumph and third Super Bowl MVP Award.

"We only charged $20 a ticket. That's where we messed up, but we wanted to make it a family affair. We sold out 1,000 tickets in three hours," Zolak recalls of the event that brought to town 49ers owner Eddie DeBartolo Jr., team president Carmen Policy, head coach George Seifert and former 49ers wide receiver and one of Joe's closest friends, Dwight Clark.

While in town, Montana

COURTESY OF ELINOR JOHNSON

GREAT DAY FOR THE IRISH — Ringgold's Joe Montana (seated, center) signs letter of intent to enroll at Notre Dame University on a football scholarship. His parents (seated), Mr. and Mrs. Joseph Montana of Park Avenue, Montana, grin their approval as Montana's two coaches, Fran LaMendola (left), basketball, and Chuck Abramski, football, look on. (Staff photo by Bob Gardner)

Joe enjoyed a stellar high school football career, although his sour relationship with his coach spoiled some of the fun.

COURTESY OF ELINOR JOHNSON

agreed to tour Ringgold's schools. Needless to say, many in the area adopted the 49ers as their team.

"People would've rather seen him stay with the 49ers and finish out his career," Zolak says. "It's going to be unusual seeing him wearing No. 19 instead of No. 16."

Jolt of Reality

Joe wore No. 13 in high school. Ironically, he almost wore out his welcome at Ringgold.

Montana was his hometown's star athlete before he put on a high school uniform. He was clearly the most gifted kid in town, certain to be added to the long list of quarterback luminaries from Western Pennsylvania.

But Joe faced even more pressures than simply living up to echoes from the past. He and his Ringgold High football coach, Chuck Abramski, never saw eye to eye. Abramski, the ultimate taskmaster, demanded his players be tough, dedicated totally to the team concept. Montana didn't always measure up to Abramski's hard-nosed philosophy.

"We don't speak," Abramski says of his rela-

tionship with Montana, which was so stormy the summer of Joe's junior year that he actually quit the Ringgold team and worked out a couple of days at another Western Pennsylvania high school. Joe's father considered moving the family.

The story goes like this: On the second day of working out with the Butler High football team, a Butler defensive end who didn't like the idea of a newcomer taking the starting quarterback's job knocked Montana out cold. The following day, Joe was back at Ringgold, where he was a frustrated second-stringer.

Abramski wasn't stubborn enough to keep Montana on the bench for long, though.

"I made the comment before his senior year that Joe was the best quarterback in the country, and that Joe was further along than Namath or Hanratty, and people laughed at me," Abramski says.

What always had bothered Abramski was that he felt Montana was less than totally dedicated. Abramski says Joe more or less refused to play both ways (offense and defense)

and wouldn't participate in off-season conditioning programs.

You see, football wasn't Montana's only passion. He also loved and excelled on the hardwood. In fact, Joe came close to signing a basketball scholarship to attend North Carolina State, the reigning NCAA champions.

An old-school coach like Abramski didn't have much patience for players skipping football workouts to participate in frivolous endeavors such as basketball.

Abramski finally softened and Montana became Ringgold's starting quarterback a couple of games into his junior season. In his first start, Joe threw four touchdown passes.

The following year, Montana reached the star status many, including Abramski, had predicted for him. He was regarded as the best high school quarterback in the country, led Ringgold to a 7-3 record and accepted a scholarship to Notre Dame. Picking the Fighting Irish was an easy choice for Montana, since he grew up idolizing Notre Dame great Terry Hanratty.

Sadly, the relationship

between Montana and his high school coach never improved.

"They never really buried the hatchet," Zolak says.

Nonetheless, Montana's tense football career at Ringgold surely hardened him for the adversity that was to come.

"Maybe it taught him how to work a little harder, how to deal with adversity, and it may have taught him endurance," Zolak says of Joe's high school football days.

Maybe Joe taught Abramski something, too.

"I love Joe Montana. I'm so proud," says Abramski, now retired from coaching and selling real estate in Monongahela. There's an obvious pain to the words. The type of pain that comes from years of wishing the relationship had worked out differently.

Now, as the premier quarterback in pro football history enters uncharted territory in Kansas City, he again will call upon his well-developed high school root system for support. •

Vic Ketchman covers the Pittsburgh Steelers for the Standard-Observer *in Irwin, Pa.*

JOE MONTANA'S COLLEGE STATISTICS

1975

Game	Att.	Comp.	Int.	Yds.	TDs.	Result
Boston College	DNP					
Purdue	1	0	1	0	0	W 17-0
Northwestern	11	6	0	80	1	W 31-7
Michigan State *	5	2	1	19	0	L 10-3
North Carolina	4	3	0	129	1	W 21-14
Air Force	18	7	3	134	1	W 31-30
USC *	11	3	2	25	0	L 24-17
Navy *	16	7	1	120	1	W 31-10
Georgia Tech	DNP - broken finger					
Pittsburgh	DNP - broken finger					
Miami	DNP - broken finger					
TOTALS	**66**	**28**	**8**	**507**	**4**	

1976

Missed Season Due to Injury

1977

Game	Att.	Comp.	Int.	Yds.	TDs.	Result
Pittsburgh	DNP					
Mississippi	DNP					
Purdue	14	9	0	154	1	W 31-24
Michigan State *	23	8	3	105	0	W 16-6
Army *	17	8	1	109	0	W 24-0
USC *	24	13	1	167	2	W 49-19
Navy *	24	11	2	260	1	W 43-10
Georgia Tech *	25	15	0	273	3	W 69-14
Clemson *	21	9	0	172	0	W 21-17
Air Force *	15	11	1	172	1	W 49-0
Miami *	26	15	0	192	3	W 48-10
TOTALS	**189**	**99**	**8**	**1,604**	**11**	
Texas (Cotton Bowl) *	25	10	1	111	1	W 38-10

1978

Game	Att.	Comp.	Int.	Yds.	TDs.	Result
Missouri *	28	13	2	151	0	L 3-0
Michigan *	29	16	2	192	1	L 28-14
Purdue *	11	7	2	95	0	W 10-16
Michigan State *	12	6	0	149	0	W 29-25
Pittsburgh *	25	15	0	218	2	W 26-17
Air Force *	24	13	0	193	2	W 38-15
Miami *	20	12	1	175	0	W 20-0
Navy *	26	14	1	145	1	W 27-7
Tennessee *	25	11	0	144	0	W 31-14
Georgia Tech *	19	14	0	190	2	W 38-21
USC *	41	20	1	358	2	L 27-25
TOTALS*	**260**	**141**	**9**	**2,010**	**10**	
Houston (Cotton Bowl) *	34	13	3	163	1	W 35-34

* games started

ing his parents whenever he could.

He was swallowed up by a campus that boasted a population bigger than his hometown. His grades suffered. He thought seriously about quitting.

Montana went home at Christmas and got married to his high school sweetheart. The marriage didn't last through his college career.

"My first impression of Joe was that he was very immature both mentally and physically," says Devine, who took over the Irish before Montana's sophomore year. "He was such a skinny kid, who had hardly lifted any weights in high school. We had no reason to be very excited about him."

Even so, there was an undeniable confidence in the soft-spoken Montana and a competitive spirit that burned deeply.

"They say that Joe wasn't a very good practice player and at times that was true," Orsini says. "But once you started to keep score and pulled out the first-down chains, he was a different man."

Devine quickly noticed that, too.

"In all this immaturity, there also was an air of confidence," he remembers. "At one point, I went home and told my wife, 'Joe Montana is going to start some games for us, I believe.' She said, 'Who's Joe Montana?' I said, 'He's the guy who's going to make sure our kids get fed the next four years.'"

It didn't quite work out that way, although Montana did show plenty of promise his sophomore season. After taking over for an injured Rick Slager in the Northwestern game, Montana led the Irish to victory. But he was mediocre in his first start against Michigan State. Then came a

Montana's fancy footwork, a talent he honed at Notre Dame, immediately caught the 49ers' undivided attention.

A driving sleet storm that blew into Dallas on New Year's Day 1979 caused many fans not to use their Cotton Bowl tickets. What a shame.

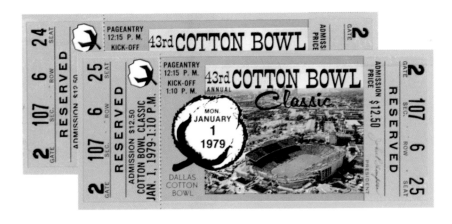

loss to USC with him at the helm. The following week against Navy, Joe broke his finger. He was so eager to return to the lineup that he removed his cast and began throwing during the team's road trip to Pitt.

"That's the only real problem we had," Devine says. "I didn't let him go on a road trip after that. If he was going to learn the hard way, then I was going to be his teacher." Montana missed the remaining three games, and the Irish finished at 8-3.

But the harsh lessons were just beginning for Joe.

During an early September practice, massive defensive end Willie Fry crashed into Montana. Joe got up, but

his throwing arm hung from a separated shoulder. The 1976 season was a wash. The Irish again finished 8-3, a Gator Bowl appearance their prize.

But 1977 was supposed to be different. Most preseason polls had ranked Notre Dame No. 1, with quarterback listed as the team's only major concern.

"I got the word in the spring [of '77] from one of the trainers that Joe wasn't properly rehabilitating his shoulder," Devine recalls. "At that point, we

didn't have him figured too much in our plans."

Devine reserved Joe a space on the bench for the first two games.

"I think most of the players thought he would be starting," Ferguson says. "We knew what he could do. But he was so humble, he wouldn't say anything."

It was another in a long line of lessons Montana learned in college, one he's used to his advantage throughout his pro career. Joe never took rehab lightly again.

In December 1978, Montana walked across the stage to pick up his diploma — a business administration degree with an emphasis in marketing. His on-field graduation exercises began that fall afternoon against Purdue. Boilermaker fans still don't know what hit them.

"Before the draft, I told some pro people that if they wanted a winner then draft Joe Montana," Devine says. "I guess I was right about that."

In the third round of the 1979 draft, Montana's name became the 82nd removed from the board. He was going to a team coming off of a 2-14 season to play for a coach with some unusual ideas about running an offense. Joe himself couldn't have prepared a better final exam. •

Bill Moor is a sportswriter for the South Bend Tribune. *He covered Joe in each of Montana's five years at Notre Dame.*

JOE RAYMOND

Passed

Need some proof that it's tough to identify a winner? Just ask the teams who passed up Joe Montana — some more than once — in the '79 draft.

By Will Pry

Over

The league passed on Joe Montana 81 times during the 1979 NFL draft. Yeah, that's right, 81 times.

Sixteen years and four Super Bowl rings later, Montana's selection in the third round — No. 82 overall — reads like a misprint.

The list of players picked before Montana more closely resembles a pro football "who's he?" than a "who's who." The draft that year was so peculiar that the No. 1 overall pick, linebacker Tom Cousineau, turned down his selection by the Buffalo Bills to begin a three-year stint in the Canadian Football League.

Three quarterbacks were among the 81 players chosen before Montana.

The Cincinnati Bengals spent their first of two first-round picks, No. 3 overall, on Washington State's Jack Thompson. The New York Giants used their top choice on Phil Simms, taking the Morehead State standout with the seventh pick.

Kansas City, where Montana ended

As we approached the 1979 season, we expected Steve DeBerg to be our quarterback of the future. We had every reason to think he would be. We entered that year's draft looking for the best thrower we could find who would compete with him for the job and bring another dimension to it.

My offensive coordinator, Sam Wyche, and I probably looked at a dozen guys. As the draft grew nearer and nearer, it became very evident that some of these guys, like Phil Simms, were going to be picked before we selected. We hadn't seen Joe Montana. He wasn't avoiding us, but he was never quite available. Then about three or four days before the draft, Sam and I flew to Los Angeles where Joe was.

The minute I saw Joe drop back, I said, "Oh, we've got something." His feet were beautiful. The first thing I noticed was how nimble and quick he was on his feet. He looked like Joe Namath.

When Sam and I got on the plane, we knew that Joe would be our guy, and that it was going to work out great because there just wasn't much interest in Joe in the NFL. People were saying a sixth- or seventh-round pick was the highest he would go.

Joe wasn't a real outgoing guy to start with, but he was just right for us. He learned quickly. Meanwhile, Steve did pretty well. But Joe could really move, so we designed plays that would fit him.

Joe had about 10 plays his rookie year that were really good, but in his second year he began to demonstrate himself. I remember his first start against Detroit. We split Charlie Young out and threw a slant, and Joe threw it 20 yards over his head. It soared into the stands, and I said, "Geez!" But by the time the year was over, he was great.

Because of his performances, he became a leader. Dan Fouts was a great leader at San Diego. The players didn't like Dan at all when they were losing. They hated him because he was so strong and so demanding of them. With Joe, it was just performance. He got along beautifully with everybody. He wasn't cliquish. He was popular as well as a great performer. With his maturity, he naturally became a standard bearer and leader. More importantly, it's just how he played the game that did it.

He never came over to the bench with a blank stare. He might have been mad at himself, but he never showed it.

Joe has to be considered the best quarterback who ever played. He has to be considered one of the best players who ever played, maybe THE best player. When you go through other positions, it's tough to quarrel with some of them. For the man who handles the ball, he would have to be the best.

Discovering a Gem

The 49ers unearthed the steal
of the 1979 NFL draft
when they picked Joe Montana,
who former head coach Bill Walsh
now calls the greatest QB ever

By Bill Walsh

(as told to Mark Soltau)

and may never see again. It was a combination of spontaneity, intuition, intense competitive ability and a certain serene poise that others don't have. He's possessed that all of his career. I'm sure he had that when he was 10 years old.

Part of the reason his teammates performed is because they knew he could do it. For people to say he was the greatest player ever to play, you have to have a great group of supporting players. Joe did, but he always was the difference.

I think the system was a major factor in Joe being able to live up to his potential. It was always there — it's not as though we made him a player. But the system enhanced him and gave him a vehicle to really take advantage of [his ability].

His ability to perform in the clutch was a combination of everything. His teammates had to come through, too, but Joe has an intuitive sense as an athlete that I haven't seen before,

When we drafted Joe Montana, I never thought of him in terms of greatness. The only guys I felt would do what he's done were Jerry Rice and Ronnie Lott. In Joe's case, you couldn't conceive of it. •

Bill Walsh coached the 49ers for 10 seasons and currently is the head coach at Stanford University. Mark Soltau covers Stanford for the San Francisco Examiner.

Walsh's system, Montana's talent: A winning mix.

AL MESSERSCHMIDT

his career 16 years later, grabbed Clemson product Steve Fuller with its second pick, the 23rd of the first round.

Of the three quarterbacks chosen ahead of Montana, only Simms lived up to first-round expectations.

Thompson spent his first four seasons in Cincinnati, backing up longtime Bengal Ken Anderson. After not attempting a single pass in 1982, Thompson departed for Tampa Bay in '83.

In 1984, journeyman quarterback Steve DeBerg replaced Thompson, who again was relegated to a backup role. Thompson concluded his NFL career after just 52 pass attempts in '84.

In a small twist of irony, DeBerg found his way to Tampa by way of Denver after being replaced by Montana as the 49ers' starter.

Fuller showed some promise in his first two seasons under center with the Chiefs but never returned to full stride after a knee injury in 1981. Fuller's second season (1980) later proved to be his best.

His 1983 campaign with the Rams preceded three quiet seasons in Chicago, where Fuller backed up Jim McMahon. After sitting out 1987 with a shoulder injury, his career ended with a whimper in San Diego in 1988.

Simms, meanwhile, managed to piece together a prolific passing portfolio. The owner of 19 Giants records, Simms guided New York to victory in Super Bowl XXI and earned MVP honors.

Things rapidly raced downhill from there.

After being injured late in the 1990 season, Simms watched backup Jeff Hostetler lead the Giants to their second Super Bowl title, winning, 20-19, over Buffalo in Super Bowl XXV. Late the next season, Hostetler went down with an injury, allowing Simms to reclaim his starting position.

Simms held that spot until four games into the 1992 season, when he and Hostetler switched places again after yet another injury. Simms returned to the top of his game in 1993 under new coach Dan Reeves, as he powered the Giants to an 11-5 record and an NFC playoff berth.

Despite a solid 16-game performance in 1993, the Giants released Simms prior to the '94 season.

Although Joe Montana may not have been a first-rounder, on draft day, he certainly reminds fans of the folly of dismissing third-round draft choices •

Will Pry is an assistant editor at Beckett Publications.

Sprinting to Canton

From his early days as a Ringgold Ram, to his glorious career at Notre Dame and on to the biggest stage of all in the Super Bowl, Joltin' Joe always gave fans reason to cheer.

JOE MONTANA: PORTRAIT

SCOTT CUNNINGHAM

Gunslinger's Stare

The Comeback Kid was quicker on the draw than Ken Anderson, Dan Marino, Boomer Esiason and John Elway. Now, with those four Super Bowl notches in his belt, is there a quarterback in the land brave enough to call him out into the street?

MICHAEL ZAGARIS

"OK, Let's Go, Be Tough"

That was the only rah-rah speech Montana gave to his troops when the 49ers entered the huddle with 3:10 to play at their own 8-yard line, trailing Cincinnati by three. "As soon as I looked into Joe's eyes," receiver Jerry Rice recalls of "The Drive" in Super Bowl XXIII, "I knew we were going to win that game."

Cuts Like a Knife

As Montana discovered throughout nearly two full seasons of inactivity, some scars heal faster than others. This one, the result of tendon surgery to Joe's golden right elbow, was only skin deep. Others, such as wounds from the media, cut a bit deeper.

MICHAEL ZAGARIS

Experience Wins Out

Although this unique art card of "Little Joe" (part of the 1992 NFL Experience set) paints the league's greatest quarterback as a small fry, Montana has illustrated time and time again that he measures up in the biggest of games.

Buddy System

Best friends Montana and Dwight Clark hooked up for one of the most memorable touchdowns in NFL history when Clark hauled in "The Catch" in the 1981 NFC title game. Fittingly, the pair joined forces again for this 1984 San Francisco 49ers Police card (#5) promoting teamwork. Before Super Bowl XXIII, Joe hung his buddy's old jersey No. 87 next to the adjoining locker for good luck. It worked.

RON VESELY

Slim Chance

Tagged as "skinny" by most NFL scouts, Montana was muscled out of the first two rounds of the 1979 draft by quarterbacks Jack Thompson (picked third overall by the Cincinnati Bengals), Phil Simms (picked seventh overall by the New York Giants) and Steve Fuller (picked 23rd overall by the Kansas City Chiefs). The 49ers figured Joe would be healthy competition for incumbent Steve DeBerg. Soon, Montana won the starting job, and several scouts probably lost theirs.

MICHAEL ZAGARIS

Mr. January

Seconds after the final gun sounded on the 49ers' 55-10 destruction of Denver in Super Bowl XXIV, No. 16 was surrounded by a media procession fit for a king. Meanwhile, the Broncos' No. 7 (star quarterback John Elway, upper right) became just another face in the crowd.

COURTESY OF ELINOR JOHNSON

Lifelong Lessons

Joe once tried to quit his youth football team and join the Boy Scouts. While his father didn't mind the decision, he convinced his son to finish out the season. "He didn't want me to quit on my teammates," Joe remembers.

Welcome to Joe, Mont., pop. 22

Voter turnout wasn't a problem for Ismay, Mont., when the town proposed changing its name to Joe for the 1993 football season.

The results: 21-0, one citizen out of town. There's been no word on whether the volunteer fire department will repaint its truck.

Lucky Charm

Joe "Montanalow," as he was called by many of his college teammates because of his likeness to pop crooner Barry Manilow, sat behind seven quarterbacks on the Notre Dame depth chart his freshman season. By the time he graduated, his name stood atop the illustrious Irish honor roll.

Cover Boy

The National Sports Daily isn't around anymore, but don't blame Joe for its circulation downfall. For more than a decade now, his lovable mug, captured on this special 1990 National Sports Card Collectors Convention promo issue, has been a key selling point for every major sports publication.

Calm Before the Storm

Joe gathers his thoughts in the 49ers' locker room minutes before taking the field for Super Bowl XXIII. Former San Francisco teammate Tim McKyer, who played with Montana from 1986 through '89, lends an interesting perspective on Joe Cool: "He's like Lazarus. You roll back the stone, Joe limps out, throws off the bandages — and then he throws for 300 yards."

Hearty Welcome

An eatery in River Falls, Wisc., capitalized on Joe's popularity by naming a burger after him on the occasion of his first training camp with the Chiefs.

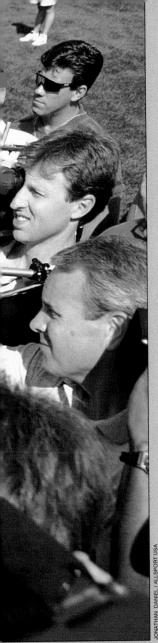

The Man to See

Once he began collecting Super Bowl rings, Joe Montana began attracting the attention of virtually everyone with access to a notebook, tape recorder or minicam. Though not known as a particularly quotable subject, he nevertheless was asked about every topic imaginable — some more than once. And when Joe was traded to Kansas City in 1993, he found himself answering many of the same questions — and a few new ones — for a new audience.

The Last Goodbye

For the previous two seasons Joe had worn the uniform of a team from another city, yet thousands of fans attended his farewell to football press conference in San Francisco last April. Montana may have finished his career as a Chief, but to San Franciscans he forever will be a 49er.

By Dave Spadaro

the
COMEBACK
kid

No matter how great the

deficit, how big the game

or how many obstacles stand in his

path, Joe Montana always finds a

way to beat the final gun

The counting has ceased. Joe Montana concluded his football career with a grand total of 38 fourth-quarter comebacks. The list boasts 31 in the NFL, six at Notre Dame and one more in the Big 33 Pennsylvania-Ohio high school all-star game.

No one knows for sure if that's a record, but let's just say that Montana's nickname, "The Comeback Kid," suits him.

His latest and greatest comeback had nothing to do

MICKEY PFLEGER

AL MESSERSCHMIDT

with cheering crowds, teary-eyed defensive backs and last-second heroics, though. This time, Joe battled an enemy many fans thought might finally get the best of him. Father Time was the clock he fought. An injury to his throwing elbow was the defense in his way.

But Montana made it

back, in a new city, wearing a new uniform and atop the NFL. Was there ever really any doubt?

"No, I've wanted to come back and play ever since I was injured. I always thought I'd come back and play in the NFL again," Montana said shortly after being introduced as the Kansas City

Chiefs' new quarterback.

Montana was back, smiling, shaking hands and talking of team goals like winning the AFC West and getting the Chiefs into the Super Bowl. You just never could count him out.

Montana's comeback was two years in the making. It was two years fill-

ed with suspense and speculation.

"I learned a long time ago never to doubt Joe," 49ers wide receiver Jerry Rice said at the time. "If he says he's coming back, he's coming back. The game needs him, and he definitely needs the game."

From Mike Brantley, his favorite target in junior high and high school, to Vagas Ferguson, his running back at Notre Dame, to Rice, his Hall of Fame counterpart by the Bay, teammates always had complete faith in The Comeback Kid.

"You just never felt like you were out of a game with Joe at the helm," says Ferguson, who still has trouble believing he was part of the 1979 Cotton Bowl comeback against Houston. "No matter how bad we played for three quarters, if Joe was in the game, we still had a chance in the fourth."

Case in point: Facing a 21-10 fourth-quarter deficit against an Eagles defense that already had sacked him eight times, Montana somehow mustered up enough energy to fight back. He threw four touchdowns in that final period — a 70-yarder to John Taylor, an 8-yarder to

MICKEY PFLEGER

Always cool under pressure, Montana often waited until the last possible second before releasing the ball.

Joe's knack for regrouping at halftime allowed him to lead some of the game's most remarkable comebacks.

Tom Rathman, a 25-yarder to Brent Jones and a 33-yarder to Rice. His fourth-quarter stat line read: 11 completions in 12 attempts for 227 yards. He also rushed for 19 yards. San Francisco 38, shell-shocked Philadelphia 28.

"I think we relaxed on them," former Eagles defensive end Reggie White said afterward. "You think we would have learned. You can't relax on Joe Montana. We had him beat up. We kept knocking him down. But he just got back up and beat us. It hurts. He doesn't quit."

That's the theme of Montana's football career. He never gave up.

Joe's first pro comeback remains a regular season record. Trailing New Orleans, 35-7, Montana rallied the 49ers and tied the score at 35 by the end of regulation. San Francisco won in overtime, 38-35. For the Saints, Dec. 7, 1980, is a date that will live in infamy.

"Joe Montana is the guy I want with the ball in the fourth quarter," former 49ers head coach Bill Walsh had said. "He never loses his cool. He is always so poised and he knows exactly what he has to do to win games.

MICHAEL ZAGARIS

Joe Montana's NFL Comebacks

Date	Opponent	End of 3rd Quarter Score	Final Score
Dec. 7, 1980	New Orleans	21-35	38-35 (OT)
Nov. 1, 1981	at Pittsburgh	10-14	17-14
Nov. 22, 1981*	at L.A. Rams	27-24	33-31
Jan. 10, 1982#	Dallas	21-27	28-27
Dec. 2, 1982*	at L.A. Rams	20-17	30-24
Dec. 26, 1982	at Kansas City	9-10	26-13
Sept. 25, 1983	Atlanta	17-20	24-20
Oct. 23, 1983	at L.A. Rams	17-28	45-35
Dec. 31, 1983##	Detroit	17-23	24-23
Sept. 2, 1984	at Detroit	17-20	30-27
Nov. 4, 1984	Cincinnati	10-17	23-17
Dec. 15, 1985	at New Orleans	17-19	31-19
Dec. 14, 1986	at New England	16-17	29-24
Sept. 20, 1987	at Cincinnati	20-26	27-26
Oct. 18, 1987	St. Louis	21-28	34-28
Oct. 25, 1987	at New Orleans	17-19	24-22
Sept. 11, 1988	at N.Y. Giants	13-17	20-17
Oct. 16, 1988	at L.A. Rams	17-21	24-21
Jan. 22, 1989**	Cincinnati	6-13	20-16
Sept. 17, 1989	at Tampa Bay	6-9	20-16
Sept. 24, 1989	at Philadelphia	10-21	38-28
Nov. 6, 1989	at New Orleans	10-17	24-20
Dec. 11, 1989	at L.A. Rams	10-24	30-27
Sept. 10, 1990*	at New Orleans	10-9	13-12
Oct. 7, 1990	at Houston	14-21	24-21
Dec. 10, 1990*	at Cincinnati	14-10	20-17 (OT)
Oct. 17, 1993	at San Diego	7-10	17-14
Jan. 8, 1994+	Pittsburgh	10-17	27-24 (OT)
Jan. 16, 1994++	at Houston	7-10	28-20
Oct. 17, 1994	at Denver	21-21	31-28
Nov. 20, 1994	Cleveland	10-13	20-13

* - Team fell behind during fourth quarter
** - Super Bowl XXIII
\# - NFC Championship game

- NFC Divisional playoff game
+ - AFC Wild Card game
++ - AFC Divisional playoff game

the Drive

Montana calmly marched the team of the decade to its third Super Bowl title and vaulted himself to legendary status

If "The Drive" had taken a wrong turn, Joe Montana still would be regarded as a great NFL quarterback. He still would be headed for the Pro Football Hall of Fame in five years. He still would be everyone's football hero.

The Drive, his 19th come-from-behind victory as a pro, simply elevated an already well-respected superstar to a higher level, one few athletes ever reach.

Ironically, Montana's super effort (23 of 36, including eight of nine on The Drive, for a Super Bowl-record 357 yards) didn't earn him the Super Bowl XXIII MVP Award. All-world receiver Jerry Rice won that honor. But Joe's most famous comeback definitely stole the show.

The Cincinnati Bengals had played their hearts out. Despite losing their inspirational leader, nose tackle Tim Krumrie, to a broken leg in the first quarter, the Bengals were magnificent. They'd played the perfect game. And with just 3:20 to play at Joe Robbie Stadium, it looked as though they'd beaten football's team of the decade.

Jim Breech's 40-yard field goal gave Cincinnati a 16-13 lead. Enter Montana, stage left.

"Let me put it this way," says Bengals head coach Sam Wyche, who was Montana's quarterback coach in San Francisco, "I knew that there was too much time and too much Joe Montana left to be celebrating after we took the lead. I knew we had some football in front of us."

Bengals wide receiver Cris Collinsworth shared his coach's belief. When teammates started celebrating on the sideline after Breech's kick, he turned to them and said, "Have you seen who's quarterbacking San Francisco?"

— *Dave Spadaro*

Play by Play

THE KICKOFF Breech's kickoff was high, and Del Rodgers caught it on the San Francisco 7-yard line. His 15-yard return was nullified by a holding penalty. Montana set up at the 8.

Right tackle Harris Barton remembers Montana's first words before entering the huddle.

"He said, 'Hey check it out.' I said, 'Check what out?' He said, 'There in the stands, standing near the exit ramp, there's John Candy.' I looked. I grabbed John Frank, our tight end. 'Hey, John,' I said. 'There's John Candy.' Then I got a hold of myself. What the hell was I doing? Fifteen seconds later, we're in the huddle and Joe's clapping his hands and saying, 'Hey, you guys want it? Let's go.' "

PLAY #1 On first down, Montana, who called every play on The Drive himself, completed a pass to running back Roger Craig for eight yards, giving the offense some breathing room.

PLAY #2 From the 16, Montana dropped back quickly and zipped a pass good for seven yards and a first down to Frank.

PLAY #3 On first down from the 23, Montana hit Jerry Rice for seven yards.

PLAY #4 Craig then carried for one yard. Montana faced his first major crisis — third-and-2.

"We knew it was two-down territory," Montana said later. "We expected the Bengals to be more worried about giving up a deep ball, and we were confident we could get Roger Craig through a hole."

PLAY #5 That was the call — Craig on the right side. He gained four yards to the 35. First down with 1:54 left.

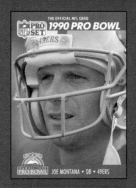

PLAY #6 Montana again found Rice. This time, it was a connection worth 17 yards, and the 49ers crossed into Bengals territory.

PLAY #7 Craig caught Montana's swing pass and highstepped his way 13 more yards.

PLAY #8 That's when Montana got into trouble. He'd been yelling so much, calling signals so loudly, he began hyperventilating. He couldn't catch his breath.

"He signaled to me that he wanted a timeout," 49ers head coach Bill Walsh recalls. "He didn't know if he could go on. I waved it off. I didn't realize what was happening to him. He came up to the line, and the next pass he threw went over Jerry Rice's head. It was his only incomplete pass of The Drive. Later he said he threw it away because he didn't want to risk an interception."

PLAY #9 On second down, the 49ers' Randy Cross was flagged for being illegally downfield, nullifying a 10-yard pickup by Craig and moving San Francisco back to the Bengals' 45.

PLAY #10 Undaunted, Montana threw a strike to Rice cutting across the middle. Rice, who caught 11 passes for a Super Bowl-record 215 yards, broke free to the Bengals' 18. It was the longest pickup of The Drive.

PLAY #11 Montana then went back to Craig over the middle for eight yards to the 10. Montana signaled for his team's second time-out with 39 seconds left.

PLAY #12 Montana called for "20 halfback, curl, X-up." Craig was the intended receiver out of the backfield. But when the team broke the huddle, fullback Tom Rathman lined up where Craig was supposed to be. Montana noticed, but continued with the normal snap count.

Joe looked first to Craig, as planned, but Roger was blanketed. Calmly, Montana found receiver John Taylor, who was running a post route. Taylor caught the bullet pass. Touchdown.

"Joe is amazing," Taylor says. "We knew if we got open he'd get it to us. He's always like that. We knew we had a chance, sure. As long as you've got Joe Montana, you've got a chance. He's the best."

AL MESSERSCHMIDT

Regardless of how Montana left the field, opponents knew he'd return with a vengeance.

"I can't tell you how many times we were in trouble and he bailed us out. He has the complete confidence of everyone on his team. Anybody who plays with Joe believes in him. You have to. His confidence rubs off on you. It's infectious."

Walsh caught the fever along with 75,000 others on Jan. 22, 1989, at Joe Robbie Stadium in Miami as Montana led the 49ers 92 yards in the final three minutes to win Super Bowl XXIII. Despite hyperventilating during "The Drive," Montana kept his cool and carried San Francisco to the title.

"He told me that as he was coming to the line he felt himself getting his breath back," Walsh remembers. "He didn't panic. Now you take your strutting quarterback, and he couldn't function like that. But the thing was that Joe functioned in a clearheaded manner, even in distress. He didn't lose it. It's like the soldier taking two in the belly and still finishing the charge."

Pushed to the Limit

Perhaps Montana was so good at coming back on the field because he had to work so hard off of it. The road to Canton for Montana is littered with countless full-speed, helmet-to-helmet hits and lengthy rehab stints. At 37, and with nothing to prove, there was only one reason to return.

"Football is in my blood," Joe once said. "I love to play. I've really missed being out there in the heat of the battle. There's nothing better

for me. That's why I'm here."

Joe was born to play quarterback. He learned to throw a football about the same time he learned to walk. Growing up in Monongahela, Pa., a coal-and steel-mining town in which football was the primary language spoken, and playing in the shadows of Pennsylvania legends Johnny Unitas, George Blanda and Joe Namath, only made Montana push harder to succeed.

Eighty-one choices were made before the 49ers selected Joe in the third round of the 1979 draft. Many scouts felt his arm was too weak, his body too frail to excel in the pros. One by one, teams passed on Montana. The Giants picked Phil Simms out of Morehead State. The Chiefs chose Steve Fuller out of Clemson. The Bears, in dire need of a dependable quarterback, instead grabbed a running

back — Willie McClendon out of Georgia.

More pushing. More reasons never to give up.

Montana found a home with the 49ers and in Walsh's intricate offense. For the better part of a decade, no defense stopped him. In fact, the only thing ever to get in Joe's way was Joe.

Montana first encountered physical problems in 1986, when he injured his back in the opening game against Tampa Bay. An examination revealed that Montana had "a congenital spinal stenosis associated with an acute rupture of the L5-S1 disc." In other words, he was supposed to be out for quite some time. After he underwent surgery, most wrote him off until '87.

Miraculously, Montana returned late in the '86 season to lead the 49ers to the playoffs. But this fairy tale ended with a thump. In one of the most memorable NFL head-on collisions, the Giants' Jim Burt crashed into Montana, knocking Joe out of the game with a concussion. But the back held.

"A good, clean hit," Montana called it. "I didn't know where I was. It was a tough way to end a tough season."

But the '86 season had nothing on the last two years. Constant pain in his throwing arm caused Joe to return to the doctor's office early in 1991. He was

The date was Jan. 10, 1982. The place was Candlestick Park, hard by the Bay in San Francisco. The occasion was the NFC championship game. The Dallas Cowboys were making their fifth NFC title appearance in seven years, meeting the young upstarts from San Francisco, who were looking for the 32-year-old franchise's first conference crown.

Dallas led, 27-21, with 58 seconds remaining. The ball was on the Dallas 6-yard line. It was third-and-goal. The play was called "sprint-right option," with wide receiver Freddie Solomon as Joe Montana's primary target. His "X" receiver, or second choice, was Dwight Clark.

The Cowboys' Dennis Thurman lined up on Solomon; Everson Walls on Clark. That Walls, a rookie from Grambling, was even in the stadium that January day was remarkable. He had signed a free agent contract before the '81 season and was the longest of long shots to make the team. Now, here he was, in the biggest game of his life about to see his career flash before his eyes.

"It was historic," Everson says of The Catch. "You can't deny Montana or Clark . . . or myself. What I always tell people is, it was really an honor to play in that game and to play as well as I did [Walls had two interceptions and a fumble recovery] and to be remembered in that game. It's just not an honor to be remembered in that aspect because it overshadowed everything that I have done — not only everything that I did in that game, but everything that I've done throughout my career."

As the play dictated, Montana rolled right and immediately searched for Solomon. With three Cowboys defenders — Ed "Too Tall" Jones, D.D. Lewis and Larry Bethea — closing in for the kill, Montana lofted a pass off his back foot high into the back of the end zone. Many still believe Joe was just trying to throw it away to avoid the sack. Walls only remembers the result.

"I didn't know what was going

The Catch was a culmination of an 89-yard drive keyed by running plays, not passes. It began with 4:54 to play and ended with 51 seconds remaining.

on behind me," Walls says. "But me and Dwight were back there just kind of playing around in the back of the end zone. He was going this way, that way. This way, that way. He must have gone back and forth about three times. And then, you know — he had a view of it, and I had my back toward [the play]. So he just kept his feet moving.

"And there really wasn't much to it until the ball came, and then that's when he had the jump on me. He was able to react before I could. The guy just reached so high, it was ridiculous."

Forever an NFL freeze-frame, Dwight nearly leaping out of every television set, the bottom third of the ball coming to rest in just his fingertips and his feet coming down in the end zone for what turned out to be the official kickoff of the 49ers' dynasty.

"On the touchdown play, my concentration level was never so high," Montana recalls of the play that was voted by the NFL as being one of the 10 most exciting of all time.

"I remember pump-faking to get those guys chasing me off the ground, just like when I was playing basketball with my dad. I remember trying to get the ball to Dwight high, so no one else could get it. I never saw the catch. I heard the roar."

Before The Catch, Montana was just, well, some ordinary Joe, a third-round draft choice in 1979 from Notre Dame. This was his first full season to start. The Cowboys knew what Joe could do especially since he had riddled them for 279 yards and two touchdowns in a 45-14 regular season victory.

"You could tell he was good," Walls says, "but you didn't know whether he was going to be one of those guys who was just going to be a good quarterback and couldn't lead his team to victory, or whether he was going to be a leader.

"Well, that game pretty much solidified it."

That game. That play. The Catch.

The ball used in The Catch currently resides in a special place in Clark's Redwood City restaurant, along with some photographs of the play. One of the photos is signed by Walls.

It reads, "To Dwight, you were out, Everson."

Mickey Spagnola is a freelance writer in Dallas.

the Catch

No one ever will forget the historic play in the 1981 NFC title game that most regard as the starting point for the Montana legend — especially not the man who was its victim

By Mickey Spagnola

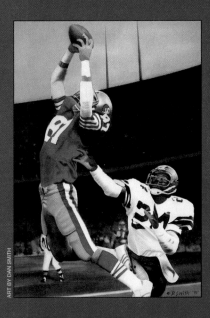

ART BY DAN SMITH

It was almost an afterthought, but Notre Dame team doctor Les Bodnar tucked the can of chicken soup in his bag just in case.

Bodnar was heading to the 1979 Cotton Bowl in Dallas with the Fighting Irish football team and he remembered that one of the offensive linemen had been sick. His youngest daughter had put the can of soup in his Christmas stocking along with the usual apples and oranges.

A week later, it proved the perfect medicine for Irish quarterback Joe Montana. Teeth chattering and chilled to the bone after playing in arctic conditions, Montana sat out the third quarter in the locker room while out on the frozen field his team was getting badly beaten by Houston.

After battling the flu earlier in the week, Montana's body temperature had dropped to about 96 degrees on a day when the windchill factor had fallen to 10 degrees below zero. The Cotton Bowl, like the rest of Dallas, took a direct hit from a New Year's Eve ice storm. It was no place for a sick man to play out heroics. Bodnar, who had warmed the soup on a Bunsen burner in the locker room, had Montana sip it slowly to regain his strength.

Meanwhile, the Cougars were in the process of finishing off a string of 34 unanswered points after the Irish had quickly grabbed a 12-0 lead.

"We were told that Joe wasn't coming back in the second half, and we thought it was over," Irish center Dave Huffman remembers.

Montana had other ideas. "I was coming back no matter what," he says.

With 4:40 left in the third quarter, Montana was back on the sidelines. He arrived just in time to see Houston take a 34-12 lead and most of the announced crowd of 32,500 head for the warmth of their cars.

The chicken soup may have warmed up Montana, but could he bring out the hot hand that the Irish so desperately needed? In the first half, he'd completed just six of 15 passes with two interceptions in the unbearable conditions.

He threw his third interception of the game just before the third quarter ended. Then he was picked off once more — this time with the wind at his back — with 13:36 remaining in the game. In fact, he completed only one of his first 11 passes after returning to action.

But just his presence may have given the Irish the hope — if not the heat — they needed.

"When Joe came back to the field, I started thinking this was a fairy tale," former Notre Dame split end Kris Haines says. "I thought how he had done it so many times before. This time, though, it had to be a miracle."

Finally, the Irish scored with 7:25 left in the game — and they did it without Montana even touching the ball. Two freshman defenders supplied the heroics as Tony Belden blocked a Houston punt and Steve Cichny ran it back 33 yards for the score. Montana's two-point conversion made the score 34-20.

After the Irish defense held, Montana directed a five-play, 51-yard drive, taking the ball the final two yards himself. Montana and Haines hooked up on the two-point conversion. Suddenly, it was 34-28 with 4:15 remaining.

With 2:25 left, Notre Dame got the ball back. Montana found Haines for six yards and Pete Holohan for 14 more. Joe then scrambled for 16 yards to the Houston 20. But as he evaded one tackler, he was hit from behind and fumbled away the football. The Cougars recovered with 2:05 to play.

"After I fumbled, I was afraid that was it. But then I realized we had some time-outs left, and I also remembered the defense was playing fantastic," Montana recalls. "I didn't want to lose this game on that fumble."

Thanks to the Irish de-

Soup of the Day

Fighting frigid conditions and a nasty flu bug, Joe Cool needed some chicken soup to warm his body and heat up the Irish in the 1979 Cotton Bowl

By Bill Moor

AP WIDE WORLD PHOTOS

The few hardy souls who toughed it out on New Year's Day 1979 in Dallas saw football history when senior flanker Kris Haines hauled in Montana's last and most noteworthy collegiate pass.

ense, he didn't. On fourth-and-inches from their own 29, Cougars head coach Bill Yeoman decided to gamble. Instead of punting into a stiff wind, Houston went for the first. Notre Dame freshman Joe Gramke stuffed the play and gave the Irish one more chance.

Montana had 28 seconds to move his team 29 yards with no time-outs.

• Play #1: Joe scrambled 11 yards around right end. First down on the Houston 18. Eleven seconds remained.

• Play #2: Montana hit Haines on a sideline pattern for 10 yards and another first down. Six seconds remained, the ball sat on the Houston 8. The Cougars called time-out.

• Play #3: Montana looked for Haines on a quick turnout, but he couldn't shake his defender. Montana threw the ball away. Two seconds remained.

Montana looked over at the bench and actually smiled. Then he returned to the huddle. "He said, 'OK, guys, same play,' " Ferguson recalls. "Then he took his finger to diagram how Kris was going to go in the corner again. 'I almost had you last time,' he said."

• Play #4: Haines ran the exact route he had on the previous play and got some daylight on his defender. With no time on the clock, Montana rolled right and found his favorite receiver, who made a diving catch in the corner of the end zone.

"Joe had to throw it low and outside," Haines says, "and he threw it where it had to be. It was so clutch."

An illegal procedure penalty on the ensuing point after attempt made Joe Unis' kick a little more challenging. But Unis, a walk-on from Dallas, converted, and Notre Dame's sideline celebrated. Irish 35, Cougars 34.

Montana, just 13-of-34 with four interceptions, had pulled off one of the most amazing comebacks in sports history. He fought off the flu, finger-numbing cold and the Houston Cougars all in 12 minutes of football. Of course, he had some help from the Notre Dame defense and a doctor with the right medicine. Needless to say, chicken was the soup of the day. •

Bill Moor is sports editor of the South Bend Tribune.

SCORING SUMMARY 1979 COTTON BOWL (DALLAS, TEXAS)

Notre Dame	12	0	0	23	35
Houston	7	13	14	0	34

Attendance: 32,500   Temperature: 20 degrees

SCORING PLAYS
1st Quarter (6:55) Notre Dame — Joe Montana 3 run (Joe Unis kick failed)
1st Quarter (4:40) Notre Dame — Pete Buchanan 1 run (Montana pass failed)
1st Quarter (:17) Houston — Willis Adams 15 pass from Danny Davis (Kenny Hatfield kick)
2nd Quarter (6:27) Houston — Randy Love 1 run (Hatfield kick)
2nd Quarter (3:00) Houston — FG 21 Hatfield
2nd Quarter (:03) Houston — FG 34 Hatfield
3rd Quarter (6:29) Houston — Davis 2 run (Hatfield kick)
3rd Quarter (4:40) Houston — Davis 5 run (Hatfield kick)
4th Quarter (7:25) Notre Dame — Steve Cichy 33 blocked punt return (Vagas Ferguson pass from Montana)
4th Quarter (4:15) Notre Dame — Montana 2 run (Kris Haines pass from Montana)
4th Quarter (:00) Notre Dame — Haines 8 pass from Montana (Unis kick)

placed on injured reserve on Aug. 27 with what the 49ers described as tendinitis. Or so they hoped. Montana threw on the sideline, but the pain only grew worse.

Finally, the diagnosis: a torn tendon in his right elbow. Surgery and rest were required.

Two years of watching Steve Young direct the 49ers. Two years of answering the same questions from fans and the media. Two years of working with physical therapists. Two years of pain. And for what?

On a Monday night, Dec. 28, 1992, against Detroit, that answer came through loud and clear. Montana made his triumphant return in the 49ers' regular season finale. The Candlestick Park crowd, which had stayed despite a steady rain to see their man, went into a frenzy.

"It felt great. It felt won-

Jim Burt's hit on Montana in the 1986 playoffs was like a freight train hitting a grocery cart, but Joe's surgically repaired back withstood the punishment.

derful," says Joe of his warm reception. "It sent shivers up and down my spine to be back on the field and hearing the fans."

Montana gave the crowd its money's worth. He showered the Detroit Lions for 126 yards (15 of 21) and two touchdowns. Plus, he ran three times for 28 yards. Great stuff. The stuff of legends.

Rice said about Joe's return to the game. "I missed Joe. He's the ultimate pro."

After coming back in a new town in a new conference, Montana proved he's the same old Joe — a fierce competitor no one ever could count out. •

Dave Spadaro covers the NFL for Eagles Digest.

Defenders who've been brought to their knees by Montana's favorite Sunday sermons rejoiced upon word of Joe's retirement

MIRACLE WORKER

By Len Pasquarelli

For years now, fire-and-brimstone tel-evangelist Oral Roberts has nudged his millions of followers out of their Sunday morning inertia and into a virtual frenzy with the energizing ex-hortation, "Expect a miracle!"

Joe Montana's congregation of the past knows the battle cry well. For the better part of 12 NFL campaigns with the San Francisco 49ers, before his right elbow demanded the surgi-cal repairs that sidelined him for all but two quar-ters of the 1991 and '92 seasons, Montana was the Miracle Worker, a player whose mere presence on the field could stir the troops from their lethargy.

Whether it be his last-second lob to Dwight Clark in the 1981 NFC title game against Dallas, or his last-minute, short-post laser beam to John Taylor to steal a Super Bowl XXIII crown from the clutches of the Cincinnati Bengals, or simply any of the other 30-plus late-game rallies he authored, Montana was the league's surest bet when the game was on the line and the score-board clock was moving inexorably toward 0:00.

Born into a new career in Kansas City, Joe Montana faced an uphill climb. At the age of 37, he fought off the residual effects of the scalpel

SUPER BOWL STATS XVI

San Francisco 26
Cincinnati 21
Pontiac Silverdome
Detroit, Mich.
Jan. 24, 1982
Attendance: 81,270

Score by Periods
49ers   7 13 0   6 - 26
Bengals 0   0 7 14 - 21

Scoring
49ers — Joe Montana
1 run (Ray Wersching kick).

49ers — Earl Cooper
11 pass from Montana
(Wersching kick).

49ers — Field goal
Wersching 22.

49ers — Field goal
Wersching 26.

Bengals — Ken Anderson
5 run (Jim Breech kick).

Bengals — Dan Ross
4 pass from Anderson
(Breech kick).

49ers — Field goal
Wersching 40.

49ers — Field goal
Wersching 23.

Bengals — Ross 3 pass
from Anderson (Breech
kick).

Passing
San Francisco, Joe Montana
Atts. Comp. Yds. Int. TD
22   14   157   0   1

Cincinnati, Ken Anderson
Atts. Comp. Yds. Int. TD
34   25   300   2   2

and the sedentary football existence to which he'd been relegated of late. Those who have stared across the line of scrimmage at him and suffered the painful consequences of his cliffhanger brilliance feared he could become that player again.

Indeed, there was no greater endorsement for Chiefs management than the fact that league defenders roundly supported the deal K.C. made to acquire Montana from the 49ers. There's no greater honor for Montana than the fact that those same men still speak with the same degree of fear and respect they held for him before he became the league's greatest curiosity.

Give Montana the ball again with two minutes left, a couple of time-outs at his disposal and 75 yards between him and the end zone, and the specter is still enough to send chills up the backs of defenders who too often have seen him trample the odds.

"If you looked up the scores of the games he played against us during the years," says Scott Case, Atlanta Falcons nine-season veteran safety, "a lot of them are one-sided, and you wouldn't think it was the old 'Miracle Joe' many times. But the guy definitely has a magic about him, a great feel for the game. There were times you hated to go out there against him because it was like he had ESP or something, almost like he was in your huddle. He'd invariably know what you were doing in coverages, sometimes better than you did. It was scary.

"They can say what they want about his arm now, but the

Since Montana took his first pro snap from center as a starter in 1981, defensive coordinators have lost sleep, lost hair and lost their jobs trying to wipe the smile off Joe's face.

mental side of it . . . you don't just lose that overnight. And besides, Joe never had the strongest arm anyway. The thing was, he was going to beat you with his brain. Sooner or later, he was going to find a weakness and exploit the hell out of it. That's just how he worked."

Killing Them Softly

Montana was nothing if not workmanlike. In the possession offense perfected a decade and a half ago by Bill Walsh (and installed during Joe's first Chiefs training camp by first-year offensive coordinator Paul Hackett), the goal was to

FIRE STARTER
(Montana's Regular Season Record as a Starter)

Team	W	L	Team	W	L
Atlanta	14	5	Miami	0	2
Buffalo	3	2	Minnesota	3	2
Chicago	3	3	New England	4	0
Cincinnati	4	0	New Orleans	15	2
Cleveland	4	1	N.Y. Giants	4	1
Dallas	4	0	N.Y. Jets	1	1
Denver	1	5	Philadelphia	1	1
Detroit	1	3	Phoenix/ St. Louis	4	1
Green Bay	3	1	Pittsburgh	2	2
Houston	5	0	San Diego	3	3
Indianapolis	1	0	San Francisco	1	0
Kansas City	2	0	Seattle	5	1
L.A. Raiders	4	2	Tampa Bay	7	1
L.A. Rams	12	8	Washington	5	1
			Totals	**116**	**48**

TOM DiPACE

San Francisco 38
Miami 16
Stanford Stadium
Palo Alto, Calif.
Jan. 20, 1985
Attendance: 84,059

Score by Periods

Dolphins 10 6 0 0 - 16
49ers   7 21 10 0 - 38

Scoring

Dolphins — Field goal
Uwe von Schamann 37.

49ers — Earl Monroe
33 pass from Joe Montana
(Ray Wersching kick).

Dolphins — Dave Johnson
2 pass from Dan Marino
(von Schamann kick).

49ers — Roger Craig
8 pass from Montana
(Wersching kick).

49ers — Montana 6 run
(Wersching kick).

49ers — Craig 2 run
(Wersching kick).

Miami — Field goal
von Schamann 31.

Miami — Field goal
von Schamann 30.

49ers — Field goal
Wersching 27.

49ers — Craig 16 pass
from Montana (Wersching
kick).

Passing

Miami, Dan Marino

Atts.	Comp.	Yds.	Int.	TD
50	29	318	2	1

San Francisco, Joe Montana

Atts.	Comp.	Yds.	Int.	TD
35	24	331	0	3

force defenders to make basic plays. Throw a 3-yard pass, the offense reasons, and if a safety misses the first tackle, it's a 12-yard gain. Play the percentages, dump the ball off, execute the most basic of offensive endeavors, and then dare the opposition to do the same on their side of the ball.

A Frankenstein-like creation of Walsh, the once-robotic Montana was a guy who learned by rote that something is always better than nothing at all. Yet, unlike some of the dink-dink-dink quarterbacks of the past (Ken Anderson comes to mind), opposition players did not hold Montana in disdain. Why? Probably because, with the chips on the table, he could have made every pass he needed to make.

"Just when you think you've got Joe, that he can't get the ball there, boom, he does it," said Tampa Bay defensive back Jerry Gray prior to Joe's retirement. "He sets you up so well for things. He might be thinking three, four plays ahead, and almost nobody does that. Or maybe even sometimes a series ahead.

"What complements that, though, is that he's so competitive, he can overcome whatever physical limitations he's got," Gray continued. "In terms of arm strength, he's probably not among the greatest. And people like to say, 'Well, a lot of his 60-yard touchdowns were really 10-yard passes that Jerry [Rice] broke loose on.' But you know what? He beat us deep a lot of times."

In San Francisco's 1992 regular season finale against Detroit, Montana rarely even looked deep against the Lions. Montana admitted that while the game was a meaningless one to his teammates (who already had clinched home-field advantage for the playoffs), it was a game in which his future was at

Known more for precision than power, Montana always had the ability to catch a secondary napping with one decisive strike.

stake. Despite a brilliant performance that had the fans in Candlestick Park mentally turning back the clock, Montana never really gunned the ball. Instead, he dissected the Lions slowly and skillfully — and left some of the younger defenders in awe.

PRO LOG

(Montana's Regular Season Statistics)

Year	G-S	Att.	Comp.	Yds.	Pct.	TD	Int.	LG	Rating
'79	16/1	23	13	96	56.5	1	0	18	80.9
'80	16/7	273	176	1,795	64.5	15	9	71	87.8
'81	16/16	488	311	3,656	63.7	19	12	58	88.2
'82	9/9	346	213	2,613	61.6	17	11	55	87.9
'83	16/16	515	332	3,910	64.5	26	12	77	94.6
'84	16/15	432	279	3,630	64.6	28	10	80	102.9
'85	15/15	494	303	3,653	61.3	27	13	66	91.3
'86	8/8	307	191	2,236	62.2	8	9	48	80.7
'87	13/11	398	266	3,054	66.8	31	13	57	102.1
'88	14/13	397	238	2,981	59.9	18	10	96	87.9
'89	13/13	386	271	3,521	70.2	26	8	95	112.4
'90	15/15	520	321	3,944	61.7	26	16	78	89.0
'91	Did Not Play								
'92	1/0	21	15	126	71.4	2	0	17	118.4
'93	11/11	298	181	2,144	60.7	13	7	50	87.4
'94	14/14	493	299	3,283	60.6	16	9	57	83.6
Totals	192/164	5,391	3,409	40,551	64.4	273	139	96	92.3

San Francisco 20
Cincinnati 16
Joe Robbie Stadium
Miami, Fla.
Jan. 22, 1989
Attendance: 75,129

Score by Periods

Bengals 0 3 10 3 - 16
49ers 3 0 3 14 - 20

Scoring

49ers — Field goal Mike Cofer 41.

Bengals — Field goal Jim Breech 34.

Bengals — Field goal Breech 43.

49ers — Field goal Cofer 32.

Bengals — Stanford Jennings 93 kickoff return (Breech kick).

49ers — Jerry Rice 14 pass from Joe Montana (Cofer kick).

Bengals — Field goal Breech 40.

49ers — John Taylor 10 pass from Montana (Cofer kick).

Passing

Cincinnati, Boomer Esiason

Atts.	Comp.	Yds.	Int.	TD
25	11	144	1	0

San Francisco, Joe Montana

Atts.	Comp.	Yds.	Int.	TD
36	23	357	0	2

"When he walks onto the field, you just know that it's all business with him," Detroit safety Bennie Blades said. "He doesn't [swagger] or strut or anything, but he's got a certain air of confidence that lets you know who's in charge. I'm sure it's evident in their huddle, because 10 or 12 yards away, on our side of the line, we could feel it. You know, it's just there."

New Orleans Saints defensive lineman Frank Warren had his own perspective. "[Montana] is the bossman, that's it, pure and simple," Warren said. "He's not a guy who screams and hollers, but he commands respect just because of who he is, where he's been, what he's been through. And, you know what? He's a tough son of a gun."

No Pain, No Gain

Despite Montana's miraculous comeback from a career-threatening back surgery in 1986 — he still suffers from stenosis, the medical term for an abnormally narrow spinal column — and his ability to overcome a myriad of other injuries, his physical toughness often was overlooked by some.

Montana displayed a raw courage and grit that garnered him plenty of respect from defenders who watched him pick himself up, dust himself off, then proceed to destroy even their best defensive game plans.

Detroit linebacker Pat Swilling, who spent the first seven seasons of his NFL career chasing Montana for the New Orleans Saints, knew the pattern well.

"You can knock Joe down and, if he feels the pain, he doesn't let on," Swilling says. "He'll say something like, 'Hey, good play, man,' and go back in the huddle and act like nothing ever happened. Unless he's really, really hurt — the kind of hurt that puts you out of a game — Joe doesn't show the pain. He's not going to let you know that you got to him, that's all. He's not going to

TARGET PRACTICE

(Montana's 273 Regular Season TD Targets)

Jerry Rice	55	Keith Cash	3
Dwight Clark	41	Ron Heller	3
Freddie Solomon	29	Eason Ramson	3
Roger Craig	15	Mike Sherrard	3
John Taylor	15	Joe Valerio	3
Russ Francis	12	Lake Dawson	2
Mike Wilson	12	Kimble Anders	1
Brent Jones	9	Bob Bruer	1
Earl Cooper	8	Lenvil Elliot	1
Willie Davis	8	Tracy Greene	1
John Frank	8	Jonathan Hayes	1
Wendell Tyler	6	Amp Lee	1
Charlie Young	6	Guy McIntyre	1
J.J. Birden	5	Carl Monroe	1
Jeff Moore	4	Ricky Patton	1
Renaldo Nehemiah	4	Bill Ring	1
Tom Rathman	4	Harry Sydney	1
Marcus Allen	3	Derrick Walker	1

let his teammates see it. That's just not his manner. You're not going to see a sign of weakness in Joe, not even in his eyes."

Longtime Atlanta Falcons defensive end Tim Green agrees that Montana's darting eyes were the mirror to a soul that simply would not give in at any time, no matter the circumstances.

"A lot of times, you'll just beat the hell out of a quarterback, and he'll give in," Green says. "You can look in his eyes and see almost a fear, like he doesn't want to be out here anymore. You never see that with Joe. He just thrives on the competition, the ebb and flow of the game. He's smart enough to know that once in a while, you're going to nail him. But he's also smart enough, and good enough, to know that in the end, he's probably going to get back at you."

The critics of the Kansas City trade pointed out that perhaps Montana would have been better served being dealt to a team where he would have

PRIME TIME PERFORMER

(Montana's Postseason Passing Statistics)

Year	G-S	Att.	Comp.	Yds.	Pct.	TD	Int.	LG	Rating
'81	3-3	88	56	747	63.6	6	4	58	94.4
'83	2-2	79	45	548	57.0	4	2	76	85.1
'84	3-3	108	67	873	62.0	7	5	40	89.9
'85	1-1	47	26	296	66.3	0	1	36	65.7
'86	1-1	15	8	98	53.3	0	2	24	34.2
'87	1-1	26	12	109	46.2	0	1	33	42.0
'88	3-3	90	56	823	62.2	8	1	61	117.0
'89	3-3	83	65	800	78.3	11	0	72	146.4
'90	2-2	57	40	464	70.2	3	1	61	104.7
'92	Did Not Play								
'93	3-3	104	59	700	56.7	4	3	41	78.2
'94	1-1	37	26	314	70.3	2	1	57	102.8

SUPER BOWL STATS XXIV

San Francisco 55
Denver 10
Louisiana Superdome
New Orleans, La.
Jan. 28, 1990
Attendance: 72,919

Score by Periods
49ers   13 14 14 14 - 55
Broncos   3 0 7 0 - 10

Scoring
49ers — Jerry Rice 20 pass from Joe Montana (Mike Cofer kick).

Broncos — Field goal David Treadwell 42.

49ers — Brent Jones 7 pass from Montana (kick failed).

49ers — Tom Rathman 1 run (Cofer kick).

49ers — Rice 38 pass from Montana (Cofer kick).

49ers — Rice 28 pass from Montana (Cofer kick).

49ers — John Taylor 35 pass from Montana (Cofer kick).

Broncos — John Elway 3 run (Treadwell kick).

49ers — Rathman 3 run (Cofer kick).

49ers — Craig 1 run (Cofer kick).

Passing

San Francisco, Joe Montana

Atts.	Comp.	Yds.	Int.	TD
29	22	297	0	5

San Francisco, Steve Young

Atts.	Comp.	Yds.	Int.	TD
3	2	20	0	0

Denver, John Elway

Atts.	Comp.	Yds.	Int.	TD
26	10	108	2	0

Denver, Gary Kubiak

Atts.	Comp.	Yds.	Int.	TD
3	1	28	0	0

Timex has the perfect spokesman in Montana, who took a licking from some of the NFL's best hitmen throughout the years, yet continued to perform like precision clockwork.

BRUCE L. SCHWARTZMAN

been the final piece of a well-planned puzzle. With the Chiefs, a team revamping their offense, he didn't quite fit that description.

But that thought hadn't occurred to many who've faced him in the past.

"Joe's always been so opportunistic that you assume he'll do OK," former Chicago Bears linebacker Mike Singletary says. "Somehow, he'll get people to adapt to him. He'll make it work, mostly because he's always made it work. I mean, he's Joe Montana, right? Somewhere between his brain and his arm, he'll get it done."

His brain and his brawn aside, an indescribable aura surrounds Joe — one players around the league will hate to see disappear.

"From my own standpoint," Atlanta Falcons tailback Eric Dickerson says, "I know for a fact that it's getting near the end [of my career]. But I also know that I'll realize when it's done. As an athlete, unless you're just lying to yourself, you know when it's time to bow out. And Joe obviously doesn't think it's time yet. That's good, I think. Nobody wants to see a career end the way Joe's would have. He'll go out as a competitor, which he always has been. And when he leaves, it'll be the end of a golden time."

For two more seasons, the golden era continued. And few players around the league were surprised that Montana hadn't displayed a penchant for ending it. It would have been easy, they point out, to take his four Super Bowl rings and his passing records and walk away — the final memory of him being a guy with a gimpy right elbow. But that wouldn't have been Joe Montana.

"He doesn't need that money and he doesn't need the [adulation]," Green says. "But Joe still needs the game, and it's tremendous to know that, after everything he's been through, he still retains that fire. Some people in his position, it would have been easy to throw it in and retire. I'm sure he came close to that a few times. But the stuff that makes him Joe Montana is what's bringing him back — and probably what'll make him Joe Montana again."

Although Chiefs fans did not receive the miracle they had hoped for, Montana's magic renewed their faith in the abilities of "The Miracle Worker." •

Len Pasquarelli covers the Falcons for the Atlanta Constitution-Journal.

BECKETT

Joe Montana didn't invent the Super Bowl. It only seems that way. Montana's three Super Bowl MVP trophies and four Super Bowl rings prove that he's conquered one of the sports world's most demanding tests.

Joe didn't invent the football card hobby, either. But without this likable golden boy to help lead the way downfield, the hobby wouldn't have scored as quickly and as often as it has.

Joe has been a vital part of the Beckett Publications game plan since the inaugural issue of *Beckett Football Card Monthly* (December 1989, issue #1). In a special feature examining the chances current players had at being elected to the Pro Football Hall of Fame, Montana, as would be expected, fared extremely well.

When we chose the front cover subject for *BFCM* #2 (January/February 1990), Joltin' Joe was an obvious pick, as was his popular 1981 Topps RC #216, which accompanied the photo. Joe returned to the front cover just seven issues — and another Super Bowl ring — later on *BFCM* #9 (December 1990).

Injuries forced Montana backstage for much of the next two seasons, but like a fine wine, Joe only grew more attractive with age. Soon after the Kansas City Chiefs acquired the 37-year-old living legend from San Francisco, *Beckett*® responded by showing curious readers just how Montana looked in his new bright-red threads on the front cover of *BFCM* #40 (July 1993).

Every football fan can remember something special about Joe Montana's brilliant gridiron career. *Beckett*® Remembers provides several exciting option plays.

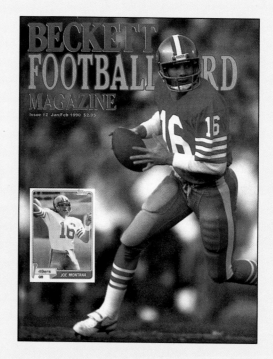

It's no coincidence that *BFCM*'s January/February 1990 issue (#2) features the Super Bowl king himself, Joe Montana.

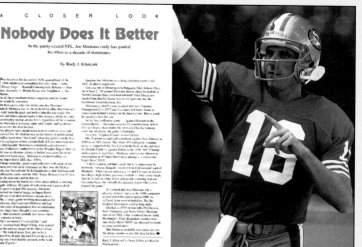

The headline says all you need to know about the focus of our "Closer Look" in issue #2 (January/February 1990).

REMEMBERS

The consummate team player, Joe was a perfect fit into the 49ers' championship puzzle. Our unique "Closer Look" in issue #6 (September 1990) shows readers how those pieces go together.

BFCM took readers inside one of Joe's board meetings in issue #8 (November 1990).

BFCM #9 (December 1990) gives readers a nose tackle's perspective of the greatest quarterback in pro football history.

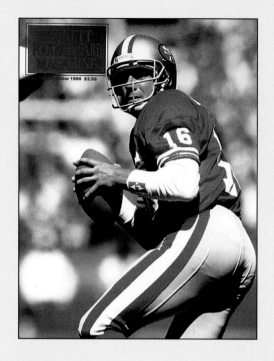

When *BFCM* #13 (April 1991) decided to dissect the NFL's most dangerous quarterback/receiver duos, picking Montana and Jerry Rice to kick off this feature was easy.

Our "Deeper Look" in issue #30 (September 1992) examines Joe's bouts with adversity and whether he'll again be able to conjure his magical formula and come back strong. The answer appears in the story on the next page.

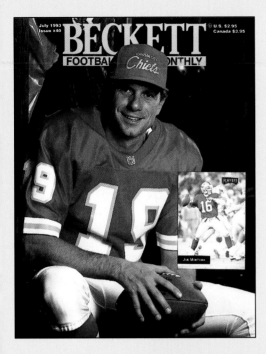

Joe's first Chiefs training camp was hectic, but he some-how found the time to pose for our midsummer classic cover shot (issue #40, July 1993).

Montana sporting a Chiefs helmet might have taken some getting used to, but readers were more comfortable with the idea after reading our "Closer Look" in issue #40.

BECKETT GREAT SPORTS HEROES

DON'T MISS THE WHOLE NEW LINEUP!

They are household names, and their performance on the court or field has made them legends. Just a mention of these extraordinary athletes brings to mind the epitome of grace under pressure, courage, persistence, and the highest levels of sportsmanship.

Beckett Publications and House of Collectibles are proud to celebrate the top sports heroes of yesterday, today, and tomorrow with the continuing series of Beckett Great Sports Heroes.

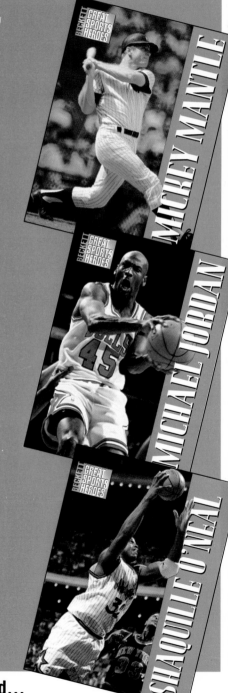

Introduction to Relational Databases and SQL Programming

Introduction to Relational Databases and SQL Programming

Christopher Allen
Simon Chatwin
Catherine Creary

Technology Education

Burr Ridge, IL Dubuque, IA Emeryville, CA New York San Francisco
Bangkok Bogotá Caracas Lisbon London Madrid Mexico City
Milan New Delhi Seoul Singapore Sydney Taipei Toronto

Technology Education

1333 Burr Ridge Parkway
Burr Ridge, Illinois 60527
U.S.A.

Introduction to Relational Databases and SQL Programming

1 2 3 4 5 6 7 8 9 0 QPD QPD 0 1 9 8 7 6 5 4 3

Book p/n 0-07-222925-X and CD1 P/N# 0-07-222926-8,
CD2 P/N# 0-07-222927-6, and CD3 P/N# 0-07-222928-4
parts of
ISBN 0-07-222924-1

This book was composed with Corel Ventura™ Publisher.

Sponsoring Editor
Christopher C. Johnson

Developmental Editor
Pamela Woolf

Senior Project Editor
LeeAnn Pickrell

Technical Editor
Douglas Shook

Copy Editor
Margaret Berson

Proofreader
Stefany Otis

Indexer
Karin Arrigoni

Illustrators
Kathleen Edwards,
Melinda Lytle,
Michael Mueller, Jackie Sieben

Composition
Carie Abrew, Tabitha Cagan

Series Design
John Walker, Peter F. Hancik

Cover Series Design
Jeff Weeks

Cover Photograph
Ken Davies/Masterfile

■ About the Authors

Christopher Allen has provided data expertise to organizations such as IBM, Microsoft, Amgen, the California Institute of Technology, the Department of Justice, Universal Studios, and Dell over the last 20 years. He has designed and built hundreds of custom applications, and has taught over a thousand computer classes for professionals. He is an Oracle Certified Professional DBA and Application Developer. This is his tenth book on computer topics.

Simon Chatwin always wanted to be an engineer, to make stuff! He graduated from Cambridge University, England, with a degree in Electrical Sciences and went to work in electronic engineering, designing industrial instruments. After a pause for an MBA, he worked as a management consultant for a while, then gradually migrated into the world of data analysis and computing. He wrote software in the Hollywood entertainment industry for a few years (yearning for a lunch invite with Sharon Stone while working on the back-office systems for animation companies).

He has been designing databases since 1987 with DB3 and now works as a Data Architect for a large biotech company. As time permits he sails, attempts fine carpentry, sells his wife's pottery at art fairs, and lives in a round house on a hill in the California sunshine. And he did get to have brunch with Ms. Stone, but that's another story...

Catherine Creary is an independent technical trainer, database administrator, and author, and currently holds a Bachelor of Education, MCT, MCSE, MCSA, and MCDBA. She has over 15 years of experience in the field of education. Catherine has extensive experience in computer training, including development of adult education computer courses and curriculum design. In addition to being the author of numerous training courses, such as Digital Think, Catherine is an Exchange 2000 columnist for OutlookExchange.com, and author of McGraw-Hill/Osborne's *Network+ Lab Manual, MCSE Windows XP Professional Lab Manual*, and *Introduction to Unix and Linux Lab Manual*.

■ About the Technical Editor

Douglas Shook
Clinical Associate Professor Ph.D.
University of Southern California.

Douglas Shook specializes in the design, implementation, and management of information technology, with particular focus on data management, data modeling, and information technology architecture. His primary teaching responsibilities at the Marshall School include MBA core classes on managing information systems and graduate and undergraduate elective courses in computer-based business systems, data modeling, and database design/implementation.

■ About the Peer Reviewers

Bill McClure
DeVry Institute of Technology
Irving, TX

Lewis Pulpisher
Central Carolina Community College
Sanford, NC

Mariana Hentea
Purdue University
Hammond, IN

Carl Dudley
Staffordshire University
United Kingdom

■ Acknowledgments

Thanks to Chris Johnson, Pamela Woolf, LeeAnn Pickrell, and Margaret Berson for making the production process as painless as possible. A special thanks to Simon Chatwin for adding his elegant thinking to this project, as well as to Doug Shook for valuable editorial input along the way.

Lastly I thank my wife Grace, who shouldered a lot of extra responsibilities during the months this was being written. She did this with the long-term vision, depth of character, and positive outlook that are truly befitting of her name.

—Christopher Allen

Thanks to Chris Johnson and Chris Allen for persuading me into this project, Pamela Woolf for trying to keep us on schedule, and the folks at Oracle for making a database guy's life so interesting.

—Simon Chatwin

Thanks go to Todd Jackson—Database Administrator Extraordinaire. Thanks to Letham Burns and Dean Karayanis for your endless support. Thanks to the team at McGraw-Hill—Chris Johnson, Athena Honore, Pamela Woolf, and LeeAnn Pickrell.

Thanks also to Christopher and Simon for their data modeling expertise, and to the technical expertise of Doug Shook.

—Catherine Creary

■ *For Grace and Zachary*
—Christopher Allen

■ *For Leslie, who brings beauty into my life; For Charlie, who rescued me in my deepest despair; For Jeremy and Clare who make me envious with Edward, Dominic, and Lucy*
—Simon Chatwin

■ *To Todd Jackson— your SQL expertise and friendship will keep us in business in the years ahead*
—Catherine Creary

About This Book

Important Database Management Skills

Databases are often referred to as the king of applications because they are so integral to all information systems. Database technology is used by every type of business, non-profit organization, or government agency, from groceries, restaurants, and hospitals to banks, automakers, and online bookstores. To take advantage of the opportunities, however, you need to understand how to work with databases. This book is designed to build a solid foundation for success by introducing fundamental database concepts and giving you essential computer skills.

Step-by-Step exercises put concepts into practice.

Clapham Specialty Store case study puts concepts in a real-world context.

Inside Information sidebars provide tips and techniques from experienced database professionals.

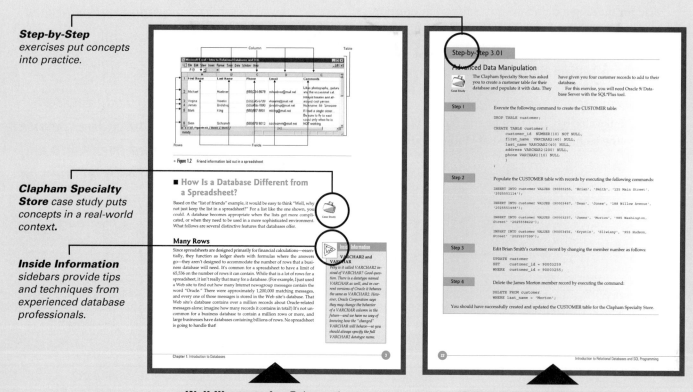

Well Illustrated — Enhanced illustrations, figures, tables, and code examples bring technical subjects to life.

Offers Practical Experience — Step-by-Step tutorials and lab assignments develop essential hands-on skills and puts concepts in a real-world context.

Proven Learning Method Keeps You on Track

Introduction to Relational Databases and SQL Programming is structured to give you a practical working knowledge of essential database skills and technologies. The book's active learning methodology guides you beyond mere recall and through thought-provoking case studies, laboratory exercises, and sidebars, which help you to develop critical-thinking, diagnostic, and communication skills.

Effective Learning Tools

This pedagogically rich book makes learning easy and enjoyable and helps you develop the skills and critical-thinking abilities that will enable you to adapt to different job situations and troubleshoot problems. Christopher Allen, Simon Chatwin, and Catherine Creary leverage their years of database design experience to explain concepts in a clear and direct way that makes this book interesting, motivational, and fun.

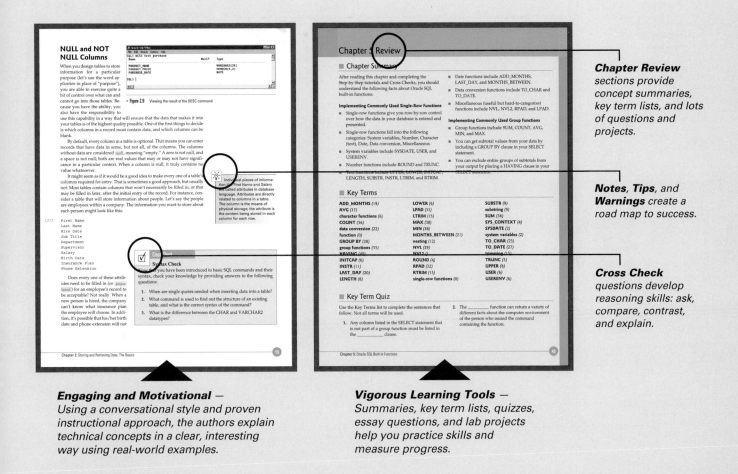

Chapter Review sections provide concept summaries, key term lists, and lots of questions and projects.

Notes, Tips, and **Warnings** create a road map to success.

Cross Check questions develop reasoning skills: ask, compare, contrast, and explain.

Engaging and Motivational — Using a conversational style and proven instructional approach, the authors explain technical concepts in a clear, interesting way using real-world examples.

Vigorous Learning Tools — Summaries, key term lists, quizzes, essay questions, and lab projects help you practice skills and measure progress.

Each chapter includes:

- **Learning Objectives** that set measurable goals for chapter-by-chapter progress
- **Figures, Illustrations, Tables,** and **Code** examples that give you a clear picture of the technology
- **Step-by-Step Tutorials** that teach you to perform essential tasks and procedures hands-on
- **Cross Check** and **Inside Information** sidebars that encourage you to practice and apply concepts in real-world settings

- **Notes, Tips,** and **Warnings** that guide you through difficult areas
- **Chapter Summaries** and **Key Term Lists** that provide you with an easy way to review important concepts and vocabulary
- **Challenging End-of-Chapter Tests** that include vocabulary-building exercises, multiple-choice questions, essay questions, and on-the-job lab projects

CONTENTS AT A GLANCE

Chapter 1 ■ Introducing Relational Databases 1

Chapter 2 ■ Storing and Retrieving Data: The Basics 16

Chapter 3 ■ Performing Advanced Data Manipulation 52

Chapter 4 ■ Controlling SQL*Plus 80

Chapter 5 ■ Oracle SQL Built-in Functions 104

Chapter 6 ■ Indexes, Joins, and Subqueries 152

Chapter 7 ■ Creating a Program with PL/SQL 188

Chapter 8 ■ Reading a Data Model 230

Chapter 9 ■ Basics of Designing a Database's Structure 246

Chapter 10 ■ Normalization 272

Chapter 11 ■ Analyzing Data Quality Issues 294

Chapter 12 ■ Other Useful Oracle Techniques 338

Appendix ■ On the CD-ROMs 370

■ Glossary 373

■ Index 385

CONTENTS

Introduction xvii

Chapter 1
■ Introducing Relational Databases 1

What Exactly Is a Database?   1
   Tables   1
   Rows/Records   2
   Columns/Fields   2
How Is a Database Different
   from a Spreadsheet?   3
   Many Rows   3
   Many Users Simultaneously   4
   Security   4
   Relational Abilities   5
   Constraints to Ensure Data Quality   6
   Case Study—Clapham Specialty Store . . .   6
   Designing Your First Database   7
How Will Knowing This Help You?   8
   When Developing Software   8
   When Doing Database Administration   8
   When Doing Business Analysis   8
   If You Just Want to Know How
     to Use Databases Better   9
History of SQL   9
Chapter 1 Review   11

Chapter 2
■ Storing and Retrieving Data: The Basics 16

Prepare to Work with a Database   17
   Creating a Table   17
   Inserting Records   18
   Selecting Records   18
   Dropping a Table   18
Creating Tables   20
   Guidelines for Naming Tables and Columns . .   21
   Creating a More Involved Table   24
   Determining a Table's Structure   30
   NULL and NOT NULL Columns   31
Inserting Data—Additional Techniques   32
   How to Insert Records Containing
     NULL Values   32

Creating and Populating a Table   35
How to Insert Data That Contains
   Apostrophes   37
Viewing Data from a Table—Additional
   Techniques   37
   Selecting Specific Columns   38
   Changing Column Order   38
   Performing Math Using Data in a Table . . .   39
   Connecting Two or More Pieces
     of Text Together   41
   Assigning Aliases to Columns   42
   Changing the Data Values You View   43
Chapter 2 Review   45

Chapter 3
■ Performing Advanced Data Manipulation 52

SQL Command Categories   53
   Data Definition   53
   Data Manipulation   53
   Data Control   53
   Data Retrieval   54
   Transaction Control   54
Limiting Which Records You Select   54
   Filtering Records Based on Numbers   55
   Filtering Records Based on Text   59
   Filtering Records Based on Dates   60
Viewing Records in a Different Order   62
   Sorting on Individual Columns   63
   Sorting on Multiple Columns   63
Showing Only Unique Values   64
Selecting from the DUAL Table   66
Modifying Data in a Table   67
Removing Records from a Table   68
   Deleting Rows Matching Specific Criteria . .   68
   Deleting All Rows   68
Transaction Control   69
   Undoing DML Transactions   69
   Making Data Available to Others   72
   Implicit and Explicit COMMITs   73
   Performing Advanced Data Manipulation . .   74
Chapter 3 Review   75

Chapter 4
■ Controlling SQL*Plus 80

Editing Prior Commands 81
   Using a Text Editor 81
   Using the EDIT Command 82
   Line-Level Editing 83
Copying and Pasting 85
   Using Your Mouse to Edit Text 86
Clearing the SQL*Plus Screen 87
Customizing the SQL*Plus Environment 87
   *Customizing Using the SQL*Plus Menu* . . . 87
   Customizing Using Commands 89
Saving Environment Customizations 89
Producing More Readable Output 90
   *Formatting Numbers in SQL*Plus* 90
   *Formatting Text in SQL*Plus* 91
   Formatting Column Headings
     *in SQL*Plus* 92
Spooling Output to Disk 94
SQL Script Files 95
   Creating a Script File 95
   Running a Script File 96
   Using Variables In Script Files 96
Chapter 4 Review 99

Chapter 5
■ Oracle SQL Built-in Functions 104

Implementing Commonly Used Single-Row
   Functions 105
   System Variables 106
   Number Functions 108
   Text Functions 110
   Using Single-Row Functions 120
   Date 121
   Data Conversion 126
   Other Functions 132
Implementing Commonly Used
   Group Functions 139
   Grouping Data via the GROUP BY Clause . . 142
   Including and Excluding Grouped Rows
     via the HAVING Clause 143
   Using Group Functions 145
Chapter 5 Review 147

Chapter 6
■ Indexes, Joins, and Subqueries 152

Creating the Test Tables 153
Indexes 155
   Indexes in Databases 155
   How to Create Indexes 156

Types of Indexes 157
   B-Tree Indexes 157
   Bitmap Indexes 159
   Bitmap Versus B-Tree Indexes 160
   Function-Based Indexes 160
When to Use Indexes 161
Relationships Between Tables 162
   Creating an Index 163
   Writing SELECT Statements to Display
     Data from More Than One Table 164
   Types of Joins 167
   Set Operators 173
Writing Subqueries 177
   What Is a Subquery? 177
   Types of Problems Subqueries Can Solve . . . 177
   Single-Row Subqueries 177
   Multirow Subqueries 179
   Multicolumn Subqueries 180
   Correlated Subqueries 181
Chapter 6 Review 183

Chapter 7
■ Creating a Program with PL/SQL 188

What Is PL/SQL? 189
   Describing PL/SQL 192
   Who's Who in SQL, PL/SQL,
     *and SQL*Plus* 193
   Stored Procedures, Functions,
     and Triggers 194
   Stored Procedures and SQL Scripts 196
Structure of a PL/SQL Block 196
   Header Section 197
   Declaration Section 197
   Execution Section 198
   Exception Section 198
Creating a Simple PL/SQL Procedure 199
   Calling Procedures and Functions 200
PL/SQL Variables and Constants 201
   Declaring PL/SQL Variables 202
   Declaring PL/SQL Constants 202
   Assigning Values to Variables 203
   Using Variables 204
Control Structures in PL/SQL 205
   IF Statement 206
   Loops 208
   Cursors 210
   Nested Loops and Cursor Example 215
Error Handling 217
   Exceptions 217
   System-Defined Exceptions 218
   Programmer-Defined Exceptions 220
   Creating a Programmer-Defined Exception . . 221
Chapter 7 Review 223

Chapter 8
■ Reading a Data Model 230

Overview of Data Model Design 231
   Purpose and Benefits of Models 231
   Relational Integrity: Quality Data 232
Types of Data Models 233
   Conceptual Model 233
   Logical Data Model 234
   Physical Data Model 234
Reading an Entity Relationship Diagram 236
   Entities 236
   Attributes 237
   Relationships 238
   Cardinality and Optionality Notations . . . 240
   Reading an Entity Relationship Diagram . . . 241
Chapter 8 Review 242

Chapter 9
■ Basics of Designing a Database's Structure 246

The Business Specification: Let the Data Tell You
   Where It Goes 247
Selecting the Database's Grain 247
Entities and Attributes 248
Identifying Records Reliably: Primary Keys . . . 251
   Why Do You Need a Primary Key? 251
   Composite Primary Keys 251
   Natural Primary Keys vs. Surrogate
      Primary Keys 252
   Relationships: Referring to Data
      in Other Tables 254
Common Data Model Standards 255
   Crow's Foot (IE) 256
   IDEF1X 256
Relationships: Cardinality and Optionality . . . 258
   One-to-Many 258
   Many-to-Many 259
   One-to-One 260
   Optionality 261
   Dependency: Identifying Relationships . . . 263
   Recursive vs. Binary 264
Modeling Multiple Categories:
   Supertype and Subtypes 264
   Creating Basic Data Models 265
   Categories, Supertypes, and Subtypes 265
   Implementing Super/Subtypes
      in a Physical Model 267
Chapter 9 Review 268

Chapter 10
■ Normalization 272

The Process of Normalization 273
Dependency 273
   Dependents and Determinants 273
The First Three Normal Forms 275
   First Normal Form: Eliminate
      Repeating Groups 275
   Second Normal Form: Eliminate
      Redundant Data 277
   Third Normal Form: Eliminate Attributes Not
      Dependent on the Primary Key 278
Apply the Normal Forms
   to a Database Model 279
The Fourth and Fifth Normal Forms 279
   Fourth Normal Form: Isolate Independent
      Multiple Relationships 280
   Fifth Normal Form: Isolate Semantically
      Related Multiple Relationships 282
The Rules You Really Need 283
Anomalies in the Data 283
   Normalizing the Data 284
   Insert 285
   Delete 285
   Update 285
   A Tax on Being Law-Abiding 286
Moving from Logical to Physical Models 286
   Choosing Your Engine 286
   Changing Terminology 287
   Translating Super- and Subtypes 287
Chapter 10 Review 289

Chapter 11
■ Analyzing Data Quality Issues 294

Datatypes and Missing Data: Quality Basics . . 295
   Handling Missing Values 295
   Apples and Oranges: Defining Datatypes . . . 296
   Choosing a Datatype 298
   Creating a Table and Inserting Data 299
   Converting Datatypes: Weak and
      Strong Typing 301
Data Domains: Sanity Checks 301
   Domains as Sets of Values 301
Column and Table Constraints 302
   Column Constraints 303
   Table Constraints 305
Primary Key Constraints and Indexes 307
   Uniqueness and How to Enforce It 307
   Alternate Keys 310
   Other Indexes 311

Foreign Key Constraints:
   Values from Other Tables 312
     Adding the Constraint 313
     Implementing Cardinality and Optionality . . 314
     Cascading Effects 316
     Cascade Delete on a Recursive Relationship . . 319
     The Cascades That Don't 321
     Creating the Movie Database 322
Declarative Relational Integrity: Pros and Cons 326
     Declaring Foreign Key Constraints 327
     Triggers and Procedural Code 327
Naming Constraints: Make It Easy for the
   Programmers 329
     Naming Tables and Columns 330
     Naming Check Constraints 330
     Naming Foreign Key Constraints 330
     Naming Indexes 331
Chapter 11 Review 332

Chapter 12
■ Other Useful Oracle Techniques 338

Transferring Data Between Tables 339
     Transferring Data Using INSERT 342
     Creating a New Table Based
       on an Existing One 343
Renaming Tables 344
Altering a Table's Structure 345
     Adding Columns 345

     Changing Column Datatypes 345
     Changing NULL Options 346
Views 348
     Creating a View 349
     Updateable Views 350
     Dropping Views 351
     Top N Analysis 352
     Creating a View on a Table 353
Other Database Objects 358
     Sequences 358
     Synonyms 362
Chapter 12 Review 365

Appendix
■ On the CD-ROMs 370

About Oracle 9*i* Standard Edition
   for Windows 370
     System Requirements 370
     Registering with the Oracle
       Technology Network 371
     *Installing Oracle 9*i* Standard Edition* 372

■ Glossary 373

■ Index 385

INTRODUCTION

Most programmers think about database design only in terms of the application they are writing that moment. It really isn't their fault; that is usually how programming is taught. But designing how the data will be stored requires a longer-term perspective. A well-designed database can be reused by future applications, year after year, because it reflects the *business* it is designed to serve, not just a particular application the business uses at the moment.

Good real-world database design requires common sense, substantial programming experience, understanding of design compromises—and most of all, thinking about business information in an unusually methodical way.

This book shows how to design and build databases that are flexible, ready for future growth, and well-matched to the needs of the business for which they are built. The book is filled with examples demonstrating not only *how* to use a particular technique, but also *why*. Its exercises mirror the kinds of tasks you'll be asked to accomplish when you design and build databases and SQL queries of your own.

We've done our best to make the writing reasonably interesting to read, so your flame of interest in this fascinating topic stays burning. If you have ideas about how this book could be better, send them to **plsql101@yahoo.com**. We'll do our best to remember that you're doing us a favor by giving positive *or* negative feedback. You can also write there to get the scripts used in this book.

All the best in your design and programming endeavors.

Introducing Relational Databases

"Knowledge is power."
—FRANCIS BACON

In this chapter, you will learn how to

- **Identify the basic parts of a database**
- **Describe the difference between a database and a spreadsheet**
- **Explain the practical benefits of databases and Structured Query Language (SQL)**
- **Trace the history of SQL**

Welcome to the wonderful world of databases. "Huh?" you might say to yourself. "What's so wonderful about databases?" The answer lies not with databases themselves, but with what they contain: information. Information that can make your life easier, transform a mountain of chaos into a manageable chunk of order, and help you discover things you would never have the time to find out otherwise. When you learn how to use databases knowledgeably, you learn how to control the way you receive information. More and more, this fundamental skill is becoming the difference between getting the answers you need and not.

■ What Exactly Is a Database?

Stripped down to its most basic form, a `database` is a list of information, or a set of lists that work together. A database program is a sophisticated list manager.

Databases are a regular part of just about everyone's life. For example, a telephone book is a paper representation of a database. It provides you with specific pieces of information about people, and it sorts that information into an order designed to help you find what you want quickly. If the telephone book contains business listings, the information there will be sorted by business type, and within each business type, it will be sorted by name.

You probably have an address book—it's a database too. So is your checkbook register. If your local television provider has a channel that shows what's playing on each channel, that information is coming from a database.

You have probably used databases on the Internet, too. If you have looked for a book or CD using a Web site, the information that came back to you was pulled from a database. Online auction sites are large databases containing information about buyers, sellers, items, bids, and feedback. Internet search engines such as AltaVista and Yahoo! are enormous databases containing key information about millions of Web pages.

Tables

Databases are always designed to store a particular type of information. For instance, in the case of a telephone book, the information is about people and about businesses. A database would generally store such information by having one `table` containing all the information about people, and another table containing the information about businesses. Each of these tables would look a lot like a spreadsheet, with individual columns for each type of information being stored (name, address, number, and so on) and a row for each person or business. For instance, a simple EMPLOYEE table might look like this:

```
EMPLOYEE_ID   FIRST_NAME      LAST_NAME         SALARY    HIRE_DATE
-----------   ------------    ---------------   --------  ---------
       1024   Scott           Campbell            63000   17-FEB-03
       2048   Linda           Hammond             68000   15-JAN-04
       3072   Dave            Anthony             69000   11-APR-05
       4096   Tiff            Berlin              66000   24-DEC-06
```

The most important thing to remember about a table is this: *It stores information about **one** type of thing*. A table about people will not store information about lawnmowers! A table about school classes will not store information about the people who take those classes. If a database needs to store information about more than one type of thing—and it almost always will—it does so by using more than one table. For example, to properly track school classes, a database would have (at the very least) a table for faculty, another one for classes, a third one for classrooms, and a fourth one for students. Keeping the different types of information separate allows a database to store information very efficiently and in a highly organized (and therefore easy-to-use) manner.

Rows/Records

The simple employee table shown earlier contains information about four people. Each person's information is on a line of its own. Each line is called a `row`, and the data it contains is called a `record`. Each row will contain the information for one—and only one—of the items defined by the table's name. For instance, in an EMPLOYEE table, each row contains information for only one employee. Similarly, each employee's information is stored on just one row. You design the table so that it only takes one row to hold all of the information specific to each of whatever the table's name says it holds. (You'll be doing this yourself very soon.)

Columns/Fields

Each row contains several pieces of information. In the employee example, those pieces included Employee_ID, First_Name, and so on. In a table, each of these pieces of information is stored in a `column`. The junction point of a row and a column—for instance, a particular person's first name—is called a `field`. A field contains a single piece of information about something—for instance, a telephone number for one person.

Let's think about a concrete example. Imagine that you want to put information for five of your friends onto 3" × 5" index cards. Each friend will get his or her own index card, so you'll use a total of five cards. By doing this, you're creating a small database. It's a physical database, as opposed to one on a computer, but it's a database nonetheless, and the concepts of tables, records, and fields still apply. Figure 1.1 shows the relationships between the index cards and these terms.

Now let's say you've put the information for the same five friends into a spreadsheet. Figure 1.2 shows how the terms you've just learned would apply to that situation.

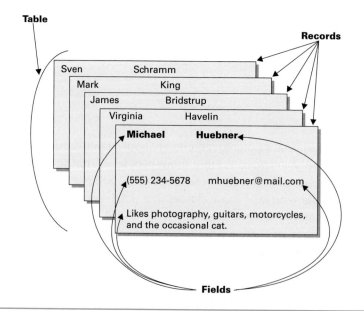

● Figure 1.1   Friend information laid out on index cards

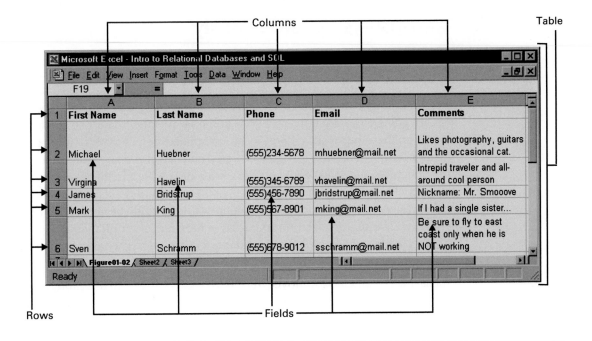

	A	B	C	D	E
1	**First Name**	**Last Name**	**Phone**	**Email**	**Comments**
2	Michael	Huebner	(555)234-5678	mhuebner@mail.net	Likes photography, guitars and the occasional cat.
3	Virgina	Havelin	(555)345-6789	vhavelin@mail.net	Intrepid traveler and all-around cool person
4	James	Bridstrup	(555)456-7890	jbridstrup@mail.net	Nickname: Mr. Smooove
5	Mark	King	(555)567-8901	mking@mail.net	If I had a single sister...
6	Sven	Schramm	(555)678-9012	sschramm@mail.net	Be sure to fly to east coast only when he is NOT working

Rows — Fields

● **Figure 1.2**   Friend information laid out in a spreadsheet

■ How Is a Database Different from a Spreadsheet?

Based on the "list of friends" example, it would be easy to think "Well, why not just keep the list in a spreadsheet?" For a list like the one shown, you could. A database becomes appropriate when the lists get more complicated, or when they need to be used in a more sophisticated environment. What follows are several distinctive features that databases offer.

Many Rows

Since spreadsheets are designed primarily for financial calculations—essentially, they function as ledger sheets with formulas where the answers go—they aren't designed to accommodate the number of rows that a business database will need. It's common for a spreadsheet to have a limit of 65,536 on the number of rows it can contain. While that is a lot of rows for a spreadsheet, it isn't really that many for a database. (For example, we just used a Web site to find out how many Internet newsgroup messages contain the word "Oracle." There were approximately 1,200,000 matching messages, and every one of those messages is stored in the Web site's database. That Web site's database contains over a million records about Oracle-related messages alone; imagine how many records it contains in total!) It's not uncommon for a business database to contain a million rows or more, and large businesses have databases containing billions of rows. No spreadsheet is going to handle that!

Many Users Simultaneously

Because databases are at the core of many businesses, it's essential that they allow lots of people to access the same data simultaneously. To understand why, imagine a retail store chain that has a hundred computerized cash registers distributed among its stores. On a busy sale day, many of those registers are going to be doing transactions at the same time. If you had to wait for all of the other transactions to be completed before yours could go through, you would probably get frustrated and leave, and so would a lot of other people—and sales would suffer. On a bigger scale, airline reservation systems can deal with thousands of requests every second—if each of those had to wait for all the others, the reservation system would be very slow and annoying. The ability to accommodate large numbers of simultaneous users is one of the key characteristics of a database. A well-designed database can answer requests from thousands—or even millions—of users simultaneously and still provide satisfactory performance.

Security

Databases contain some of the most sensitive information in a business: salaries, customer information, and project schedules, for instance. If this information were to be deleted, changed, or revealed to coworkers or competitors, it could cause problems ranging from embarrassment to failure of the business itself. Because of this, databases have extremely robust security systems. You won't find any passwords stored in easily snooped text files in a database system; everything is encrypted, including the information sent between the database and a user's computer when he or she logs in.

Even valid users of a database don't necessarily get access to everything the database contains. Users can be given privileges (the ability to select, insert, update, or delete records) to specific tables, and not to others. A privilege for a specific database object such as a table or sequence is known as an object privilege . A system privilege is a privilege for an action anywhere in the database—for example, inserting data into any table. When assigning privileges, it's even possible to make some columns within a table visible to all users, and other columns visible to only a select group. In addition, a database can be instructed to filter a table's rows so that some users see only certain rows, while other users see all rows.

A database's security features go even further. In addition to controlling who can see what information, a database allows you to specify who can insert new information, update existing information, or delete information. This helps ensure that people who have no business reason to change or delete information, for instance, cannot do so accidentally (or not so accidentally).

When business information is translated into a relational database system, it is entered into the database tables in the form of data. Data is basically information that can be transmitted or processed. For example, the number 3994 by itself is simply data that means nothing if it is not placed in the correct context. It is simply raw data. Once this number is associated with a table name, such as EMPLOYEE, and a column name, such as Employee_Number, it becomes useful information that can be processed by the database system.

In a large database system—say, one with 1,000 users or more—managing all of these different kinds of privileges would quickly become impossible if they had to be set on a user-by-user basis. Fortunately, databases like Oracle allow you to gather a specific set of privileges into something called a `role` . That way, whenever users are added to the database, they are assigned one or more roles, and those roles carry the privileges the users can exercise. This works well because businesses generally have specific job descriptions, and the privileges each user will need relate directly to his or her job description. An accounting clerk will need the ability to enter data from bills, but perhaps only the accounting managers will have the ability to change data once it's been entered. Similarly, perhaps only accounting executives can do anything at all with the company's salary data. Each of these three job descriptions would be a good candidate for a database role. For instance, an "accounting clerk" role would be assigned to all of the accounting clerks. Security roles help ensure that everyone has exactly the privileges they need. Roles also make it very easy to assign a new privilege to a group: You just add the privilege to that group's role, and the job is done.

Relational Abilities

Since a database employs separate tables to store different types of data—remember the example of a school's database having individual tables for faculty, classes, classrooms, and students—there must be a way to connect records in one table with relevant records in the other tables. Databases accommodate this by letting you define `relationships` between the tables.

For example, let's consider an order-entry system. The core of this type of system is the business's inventory, so there will always be a table containing information about products. The PRODUCT table will store each piece of information pertaining to an inventory item, including description, manufacturer, price, and quantity currently in stock. The PRODUCT table will also store a unique identifier for each product, as a way of unquestionably identifying one product as opposed to another. Let's say for the sake of discussion that in the PRODUCT table, the unique identifier is the Stock Keeping Unit (SKU).

Now that we have a table in which to store products, we need another table in which to store orders for those products. Each row in the ORDER table will store the date, time, location, and total order value. The ORDER table must also identify what product the order is for, and it can do this simply by storing the product's SKU as part of the order record. Here's where the relationship comes in: *The only product information an order contains is the product's SKU.* The product's description, price, and other information are not stored in the ORDER table. Why? It would waste space, among other reasons, because each product's description, price, and so on are already available in the PRODUCT table. The only requirement to making this work is that the database must be told that an order's SKU is the unique identifier in the PRODUCT table. Once it knows that, the database can join information from both tables, and present the combined information on a single line, as if it came from one table.

A database that employs this technique of relating records in separate tables is called a `relational database` . It's not uncommon for business databases to contain tables that have relationships to dozens of other tables.

There are many reasons for doing this, and they will be discussed in depth in Chapter 6. The opposite of this approach is a single large table that repeats information every time it is needed. This type of table is called a flat file, indicating that it is two-dimensional—just rows and columns, no related tables.

Constraints to Ensure Data Quality

Sometimes the data stored in a database comes directly from other machines: automated sensors, timers, or counters. Most of the data in a database, though, is entered by people. And people make mistakes. (Not you, of course, but you probably know others who do.) When designing a database, it's easy to define constraints identifying conditions that data in a particular field must meet before the database accepts the record. The constraint defines what must be true about the data in order for it to be accepted. These constraints can be very simple—like ensuring that a price is a positive number—or more involved, like ensuring that an SKU entered into an order actually exists in the PRODUCT table, or requiring that certain fields in a record be entered if other fields contain specific values. By automating these types of quality-control functions, the database helps guarantee that the data it contains is clean.

Case Study

Case Study—Clapham Specialty Store

The Clapham Specialty Store, a small grocery and delicatessen, has been purchased recently by a new owner, John Balfour, who would like to expand the store and improve its profits. The store sells general groceries, wines and liquors, has a small deli counter, and is open from 5:00 AM to 12:00 AM. Many of the customers are repeat customers who stop in to buy products they forgot to buy at the supermarket.

The store sells approximately 3,000 different products, ranging from toilet cleaner to two-ounce jars of caviar to liverwurst and champagne. Products are displayed on aisles, which are grouped by department. When the products are delivered, employees record their cost, quantity, SKU, package size, and purchase date before stocking the items. The store has three cash registers, one of them by the deli counter, and employs between three and seven people, depending on the time of day and how busy the store is. At each register, the cashier logs in to the register at the start of their shift and logs out at the end. Each employee's name, address, and social security number is recorded. Employees are paid hourly and receive their checks on a weekly basis.

As a convenience, the store offers a local delivery service for registered customers; walk-ins must sign up to receive deliveries by recording their name, address, and phone number. Each sale is identified by a Till Receipt No and a

 Cross Check

Tables

All right, so we covered a lot of stuff so far. Take a moment to check your knowledge by answering the following questions:

1. What is the most significant characteristic of a table?

2. Define the following terms: row, record, column, field, table, database, and constraint.

3. What are the key features that make a database suitable for storing large amounts of data?

timestamp (date and time) and consists of the sale items with a quantity and price recorded for each product.

John, the new owner, wants to know which products sell the most and which are the most profitable. He is also interested in knowing whether it is worth keeping the store open for such long hours, since the employees not only have to be paid more for late-night work but also fewer sales are made.

John can find the cost of goods from the accounts system. What he needs to know is the sale item profit from a point of sale system (POS) that records what has been sold, to whom it has been sold, for how much, and when it was sold. Also, he needs to be able to record which sales are deliveries and the cost of delivery trips.

Step-by-Step 1.01

Designing Your First Database

Case Study

The Clapham Specialty Store needs to create a simple system for tracking their customers. In this tutorial, you will design a simple database that will do exactly that. Later, you will create the database using the Oracle software that comes with this book.

For this exercise, you will need the following materials:

- Four blank sheets of paper or index cards
- Two differently colored pens or pencils

Step 1

Gather four blank sheets of paper. The sheets can be any size—index cards will work as well as 8.5" × 11" sheets. On each sheet, write the first name, last name, phone number, and address of a friend or associate (you will do this for a total of four people—one per sheet).

Step 2

After you have written the information onto the sheets, lay the sheets on a table—separately, so that they do not touch each other.

Step 3

Move the sheets right next to each other, so they form a grid that is two sheets wide and two sheets high. In this arrangement, each sheet will touch two other sheets. Tape the sheets together in this arrangement.

Step 4

Take a pen that is a different color and on the top-left sheet, circle each item that would be stored in a database field. Write the word **Fields** at the bottom of the sheet, and draw arrows to each of the circled fields.

Step 5

Next, put a rectangle around each item in the four-sheet grid that would relate to a row in a database. Write the word **Rows** in the center of the four-sheet grid, and draw arrows from the word to each square.

Step 6

Finally, write **Address column** on the four-sheet grid wherever you have some space. Then draw one long line that connects that phrase to every item in the grid that would be stored in a table's Mailing_Address column.

You should successfully have mapped out the rows and columns that could be used in a database table to track Clapham Specialty Store customers.

■ How Will Knowing This Help You?

Everybody is busy these days, and if you are reading this book, you are probably busier than most. It's reasonable that you will want to know how something is going to help you before investing the time to learn it. What follows is a list of the ways that learning about databases and Structured Query Language (SQL) can help you in different situations.

When Developing Software

Whether you develop programs using Java, C++, or Oracle's own Forms Developer product, the chances are high that at some point you will need to write some SQL code to interact with a database directly. Many developers stumble through this, making mistakes that cost them time and performance. Investing the time to learn SQL properly will pay for itself many times over. The documentation supplied with Oracle includes sections dedicated to interacting with Oracle via Java, C, C++, and COBOL.

When Doing Database Administration

It's impossible to be an Oracle database administrator (DBA) without knowing SQL, and very difficult without knowing Oracle's SQL superset named PL/SQL. This is because many of the tasks that are generally done by a DBA are accomplished using SQL, and quite a few require the programming capabilities of PL/SQL, as well. While Oracle does provide a number of software programs enabling administrators to perform tasks using a nice graphical user interface (GUI), these tools have their fair share of bugs. In addition, some tasks can just be done faster when using SQL directly, and in some database installations, connections to databases are accomplished using text-based terminals that cannot run the pretty GUI tools. The importance of SQL is reflected in the fact that Oracle's own DBA certification program, which consists of five separate exams, devotes the entire first exam to SQL and PL/SQL.

When Doing Business Analysis

Being able to slice and dice huge mounds of data into the information you need is an essential part of a business analyst's job. Lots of people do this by getting an extract of their company's database, putting it in a spreadsheet, and manually creating the analyses they need. This approach is flexible, but it can be time-consuming. Some companies also provide their analysts with software tools designed to make data analysis quick and easy. But even these tools don't provide every imaginable way of looking at the information; they provide the subsets that their designers think are the most likely to be used. The chances are good that you will want to look at the data in some way that the tool doesn't support. Often a single SQL query can provide the information you need.

If You Just Want to Know
How to Use Databases Better

In the Silicon Valley area of California one of the local newspapers contains *two* sets of movie listings, one sorted by geographic area, and the other sorted by movie title. So if you wanted to find out what was showing near you, you would use one listing; if you wanted to find out where a specific movie was playing, you would use the other. This simple, powerful idea made the listings a real pleasure to use. It was probably thought up by someone with database experience, someone who was familiar with the idea that the content of the data and how it is displayed are two different things.

These days, practically everything is built around a database. If you understand how databases work, you understand how a lot of businesses function. This can be extremely useful. For instance, if you call a company's customer service department but don't have your customer number with you, you might think to ask "What else can you search on to find my record?" When you use a Web search site to locate information, you will get the results you want much more quickly if you understand how databases interpret search terms. (You can also amaze your friends with how quickly you can find relevant information using search sites. The only trick you need: educated decisions about what to enter as search criteria.) Understanding databases is becoming a lot like being able to do basic math quickly in your head: It isn't essential, but it sure comes in handy a lot.

■ History of SQL

A little bit of history is useful to give perspective, and the history of SQL parallels the history of relational databases. In 1969, Dr. Edgar F. Codd published an IBM Research Report with the catchy title *Derivability, Redundancy, and Consistency of Relations Stored in Large Data Banks*. This paper described an approach to structuring databases with related tables, which was quite different than the flat-file approach used by databases at the time. The paper was stamped with IBM's Limited Distribution Notice, so it wasn't widely read. Codd revised the concepts and published them in a 1970 article named "A Relational Model of Data for Large Shared Data Banks" in the journal of the Association of Computer Machinery. The relational model described by Codd was used in a prototype relational database management system (RDBMS) called System R in 1974. Describing the system's query language in a November 1976 article in the *IBM Journal of R&D*, IBM used the name Structured English QUEry Language (SEQUEL). The language and its name evolved, becoming Structured Query Language (SQL), pronounced either "sequel" or "S-Q-L." The first commercially available version of SQL was released in 1979 by Oracle Corporation (although the company's name was Relational Software, Inc. at the time).

In 1986, the American National Standards Institute (ANSI) stepped in and published a formal SQL standard, which it identified as ANSI X3.135-1986. The International Standards Organization (ISO) picked up this standard the following year and published it as ISO 9075-1987. The specification was expanded in 1992, 1999, and 2001. The current specification is in nine parts, named ANSI/ISO/IEC 9075-1:1999 through 9075-9-2001, and can be found online at www.iso.org.

SQL is an industry-standard language for querying databases. Many database companies modify it a bit to suit their needs, but the core SQL functions remain essentially unchanged. This is good news for database users and developers, because the time invested in learning SQL will reap benefits for years to come, across software revision after software revision, and even to other products.

The bottom line is: SQL is a versatile and essential tool for anyone who works with databases regularly.

Chapter 1 Review

■ Chapter Summary

After reading this chapter and completing the Step-by-Step tutorial and Cross Check, you should understand the following facts about databases and SQL:

Identify the Basic Parts of a Database

■ Stripped down to its most basic form, a database is a list of information, or a set of lists that work together. A database program is a sophisticated list manager.

■ Familiar databases include telephone books, checkbook registers, and Web sites providing online auctions, ordering, and searching.

■ Databases are always designed to store a particular type of information. For instance, in the case of a telephone book, the information is about people and about organizations.

■ A database would generally store such information by having one table containing all the information specific to people, and another table containing the information specific to organizations.

■ Each of these tables would look a lot like a spreadsheet, with individual columns for each type of data being stored (name, address, number, and so on) and a row for each person or business.

■ The most important thing to remember about a table is this: *It stores information about **one** type of thing*. If a database needs to store information about more than one type of thing—and it almost always will—it does so by using more than one table. Keeping the different types of information separate allows a database to store information very efficiently, and in a highly organized (and therefore easy-to-use) manner.

■ Each line in a table contains information about one instance of whatever the table is designed to store. Each line is called a row, and the data it contains is called a record. You design the table so that it only takes one row to hold all of the information that is specific to each item the table contains.

■ Each row contains several pieces of information. In a table, each piece of information is stored in its own column.

■ The junction point of a row and a column—for instance, a particular person's first name—is called a field. A field contains a single piece of information about something—for example, the last name for one person.

Describe the Difference Between a Database and a Spreadsheet

■ While a table in a database stores data in rows and columns like a spreadsheet, there are many characteristics that make a database more appropriate when the data gets more complicated, or when it needs to be used in a more sophisticated environment.

■ A database can handle billions of rows of data.

■ With a database, your data can be available to thousands of users simultaneously.

■ A database helps you keep your data safe by providing security based on privileges to objects.

■ In a database you can create relationships between separate tables. Doing this results in a relational database.

■ A database enables you to constrain the content of incoming data to ensure quality information.

Explain the Practical Benefits of Databases and Structured Query Language (SQL)

■ When developing software, it's likely you will need to interact with databases by writing SQL commands to insert, select, update, and delete data within programs you write using languages such as Java and C++.

■ SQL is an essential skill if you're planning to be an Oracle DBA, because many DBA tasks are executed using SQL commands.

■ When doing business analysis, knowing SQL enables you to interact directly with the database, slicing and dicing its information the way you want, without being limited by predesigned queries created by someone else.

Trace the History of SQL

- SQL is based on concepts pioneered by Dr. Edgar F. Codd and first published in 1969.

- SQL has become the de facto standard language for interacting with all major database programs.

■ Key Terms

column *(2)*	privilege *(4)*	Structured Query Language (SQL) *(9)*
constraint *(6)*	record *(2)*	system privilege *(4)*
database *(1)*	relational database *(5)*	table *(1)*
field *(2)*	relationship *(5)*	
flat file *(6)*	role *(5)*	
object privilege *(4)*	row *(2)*	

■ Key Term Quiz

Use the Key Terms list to complete the sentences that follow. Not all terms will be used.

1. A system that allows multiple tables to refer to each other is called a(n) _____.

2. When one table refers to another table, a(n) _____ is created between them.

3. A table that does not reference any other tables can be called a(n) _____.

4. Each row in a table represents one _____ of data.

5. A database can limit what data it accepts, allowing in only those values you specify. You can make this happen by creating a(n) _____.

■ Matching Definition Quiz

Relate each term on the left with the appropriate description on the right.

Term		Description	
1.	Row	a.	Stores all information about one type of thing (for instance, people or products)
2.	Record	b.	Contains a single piece of information about something
3.	Column	c.	One line in a table
4.	Field	d.	Collection of one type of information stored in a table (for instance, all of the phone numbers or all of the last names)
5.	Table	e.	Data contained in a table row

■ Multiple-Choice Quiz

1. Which of the following are examples of databases that you're likely to encounter in daily life? (More than one answer may apply.)

   a. Front page news

   b. Telephone books

   c. Checkbook registers

   d. Web sites providing online auctions, ordering, and searching

   e. Ads with sale prices

   f. Movie listings

2. What is the most significant characteristic of a table?

   a. It has rows and columns.

   b. It can be related to other tables.

   c. It stores information about one type of thing.

   d. It contains records and fields.

3. Which of the following statements apply to roles in a database? (Choose all that apply.)

   a. Oracle allows you to gather a specific set of privileges into a role.

   b. Roles are limited to 32 users per role.

   c. When users are added to the database, they are assigned one or more roles, and those roles carry the privileges the users can exercise.

   d. Once users are assigned to any role, they are given complete access to all database tables.

4. Which of the following are reasons why a database is the best choice for working with large quantities of business data? (More than one answer may apply.)

   a. Can handle billions of rows

   b. Runs only on PCs

   c. Can accommodate thousands of simultaneous users

   d. Provides object-specific security

   e. Can relate many tables together

   f. Allows you to define constraints defining conditions that data must satisfy before it is accepted into the database

5. Whose work pioneered relational database theory?

   a. E. F. Skinner

   b. Edgar Winter

   c. E. F. Codd

   d. Edgar Piece

6. Which of the following statements are true regarding rows? (Choose all that apply.)

   a. The data contained in a row is called a record.

   b. Each row will contain the information for one—and only one—of the items defined by the table's name.

   c. A row is a juncture point between a record and a column.

   d. A database table can have a maximum of 65,536 rows.

7. Which of the following statements are true regarding constraints? (Choose all that apply.)

   a. Constraints can be used to ensure data quality.

   b. A constraint may require that certain fields in a record be entered if other fields contain specific values.

   c. Certain constraints define what must be true about data in order for it to be accepted into a column.

   d. When designing a database, you can define constraints identifying conditions that data in a particular field must meet before the database accepts the record.

8. Which of the following statements are true regarding SQL? (Choose all that apply.)

   a. SQL is based on concepts pioneered by Dr. Edgar F. Codd and first published in 1969.

   b. SQL is an essential skill if you're planning to be an Oracle DBA, because many DBA tasks are executed using SQL commands.

   c. SQL enables you to interact directly with the database, slicing and dicing its information the way you want, without being limited by predesigned queries created by someone else.

   d. SQL has become the de facto standard language for interacting with all major database programs.

9. Which of the following statements are true regarding databases? (Choose all that apply.)

   a. A database helps you keep your data safe by providing object-specific security.

   b. With a database, your data can be available to thousands of users simultaneously.

   c. A database can handle only a limited number of rows of data.

   d. A database enables you to constrain the content of incoming data to ensure quality information.

10. Which of the following statements is true regarding a flat file? (Choose all that apply.)

   a. Flat files are limited to 65,536 rows.

   b. A flat file is a single large table that repeats information every time it is needed.

c. Each line of a flat file contains information about one instance of whatever the file is designed to store.

d. A flat file is two-dimensional——just rows and columns, no related tables.

11. Which of the following terms refer to *structural* components of a database, as opposed to the *content* stored within a database? (More than one answer may apply.)

   a. Record

   b. Column

   c. Table

   d. Constraint

12. Which of the following activities is likely to benefit from knowing how databases work? (More than one answer may apply.)

   a. Swimming

   b. Searching for something on the Internet

   c. Shopping at a computer store

   d. Writing a custom computer program

   e. Analyzing business data

13. Which of the following activities is likely to benefit from knowing SQL? (More than one answer may apply.)

   a. Soccer

   b. Searching for something on the Internet

   c. Shopping at a computer store

   d. Writing a custom computer program

   e. Analyzing business data

14. A specific database object such as a table or sequence is known as a(n):

   a. System privilege

   b. Role

   c. Object privilege

   d. Table privilege

   e. Sequence privilege

15. Which of the following statements are true regarding security roles? (Choose all that apply.)

   a. Roles help ensure that everyone has exactly the privileges they need.

   b. Roles carry the privileges the users can exercise.

   c. Roles also make it easy to assign a new privilege to a group.

   d. Becoming a member of a role allows users to upgrade their user privileges.

   e. Becoming a member of a role allows users to assign privileges to other users.

■ Essay Quiz

1. Describe at least two areas in your own life where it would be useful to know more about databases.

2. In your own words, describe at least two situations in which it would make sense to keep a list in a spreadsheet, and at least two other situations in which a database would make more sense.

3. There are many places in daily life where we interact with databases. Describe at least three situations where you have used a database in the last week. Try to think of examples that happened *away* from your own computer.

4. Think of your favorite Internet search tool. Now write which features of the tool you like the most, as well as which features you think should be added to the tool to make it more useful.

Lab Projects

• Lab Project 1.1

This lab involves you noticing day-to-day uses of databases. You will need the following:

- Paper, or other item to take notes with
- An area to walk around for 30 minutes

Then do the following:

1. Walk around for half an hour, noting everything you see that could or should rely on a database to hold its information. For

example, the "card catalog" at a library, or the bus schedule at a bus stop. (Note: If you use a Personal Digital Assistant [PDA] to take your notes, look around inside the PDA too, and don't stop at the Address Book.)

• Lab Project 1.2

One of the best ways to see how well you understand a concept is to try to explain it, in plain language, to someone not familiar with the subject. This process often helps you deepen your own understanding of the subject, as you strive to think up examples and descriptions that will make sense to your audience.

You will need the following materials:

- A curious associate who does not yet understand the concept of databases. Ideally, this should be someone *not* familiar with computer science.

- A little bit of uninterrupted time.

Then do the following:

1. Explain the concept of databases to your associate. Use everything at your disposal to help illustrate the concept. Continue this until they understand.

2. Write a paragraph describing the experience, what you did to explain the concept, and what examples and/or tools you used.

Storing and Retrieving Data: The Basics

"Data is what distinguishes the dilettante from the artist."
—GEORGE V. HIGGINS

In this chapter, you will learn how to

- **Prepare to work with a database**
- **Create a table**
- **Insert data into a table**
- **View data from a table**

This chapter starts with a quick exercise in which you will create a table, insert records into it, view those records, and then delete the table. This exercise is deliberately kept quick and simple; it's like testing the temperature of a lake before jumping in. Next, you will take an extended tour of these activities, learning many details about creating versatile tables, inserting various types of data into them, and viewing the information they contain in a myriad of ways.

■ Prepare to Work with a Database

In this section, you will do a quick exercise to see, in a basic way, what a database does. This will be a very simple exercise; databases can do infinitely more than what you will see in the next few pages. The purpose of this step is to give you some of the "big picture" about how basic database techniques fit together. That framework will help you later in the chapter: As you learn more detailed techniques, you can put them into the context of the "big picture."

To perform the steps that follow, you need to be running SQL*Plus, the program supplied by Oracle that lets you communicate with a database. To do that, you will need to have been given a user ID, password, and database name by your instructor, and shown how to start SQL*Plus on your own computer system.

Assuming you have been given the necessary information and now have SQL*Plus showing a SQL> prompt, let's proceed.

Explaining how to install an Oracle database and configure SQL*Plus is beyond the scope of this book. If you would like to learn more about it, check out your Oracle documentation.

Creating a Table

As you will recall from the first chapter, a table is constructed something like a spreadsheet: It is made up of columns, and you place rows of data into it. Before you can add the rows of data, you must define the columns that make up the table. You do this with the `CREATE TABLE` command.

For example, our company, the Clapham Specialty Store, wants to keep track of its regular customers. Therefore, we would create a table named TEST_CUSTOMER that could contain the data associated with each customer.

Case Study

To see how this command works, enter the following code at the SQL> prompt:

```
CREATE TABLE test_customer (
     customer_id  NUMBER(10),
     first_name   VARCHAR2(10),
     last_name    VARCHAR2(10),
     address      VARCHAR2(20),
     phone        VARCHAR2(10)
     )
;
```

After you have typed this command, press the ENTER key. Your screen should look like the one shown in Figure 2.1.

This response from SQL*Plus tells you that the command was successful. (If you see any other response, check the spelling in your command and try again.) You now have a table in Oracle! The structure of the command you used to create the table is discussed in detail later in this chapter. For now, let's proceed directly to using the table by entering some records into it.

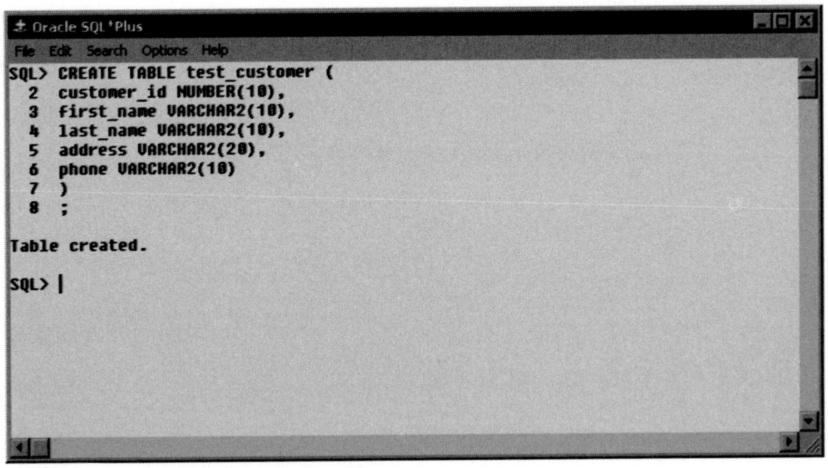

```
± Oracle SQL*Plus
File  Edit  Search  Options  Help
SQL> CREATE TABLE test_customer (
  2  customer_id NUMBER(10),
  3  first_name VARCHAR2(10),
  4  last_name VARCHAR2(10),
  5  address VARCHAR2(20),
  6  phone VARCHAR2(10)
  7  )
  8  ;

Table created.

SQL>
```

● **Figure 2.1** Creating a table

Inserting Records

Case Study

The Clapham Specialty Store has several regular customers. Now that you have created the structure of the TEST_CUSTOMER table, let's look at adding name and address information to the table. To place records in a table, use the **INSERT** command. In SQL*Plus, type the following line at the SQL> prompt:

```
INSERT INTO test_customer
VALUES (1234567890, 'George', 'Prayias', '123 Main Street', '555-1222')
;
```

After you have typed this command, press the ENTER key. You should see a response similar to the one shown in Figure 2.2.

Your table now contains its first record. How do you see this record? Read on.

Throughout the textbook you will create and work with tables that are named with a "test" prefix when learning SQL commands. This "test" prefix will distinguish the tables from all Clapham Specialty Store database tables that you will create when completing the Step-by-Step exercises and Lab Projects for each chapter. The tables that you create through these exercises will build the Clapham Specialty Store database.

Selecting Records

To see the records you have inserted into your table, use the **SELECT** command:

```
SELECT *
FROM test_customer
;
```

In response, you should see the record you entered, as shown in Figure 2.3.

Dropping a Table

To complete this first foray into the world of databases, you will drop the table you created.

To drop your table, use the **DROP** command:

```
DROP TABLE test_customer;
```

Your screen should show the response depicted in Figure 2.4.

From this point on, the text will not tell you to press the ENTER key after every command. It will simply instruct you to enter one or more lines of SQL commands. Press the ENTER key after every line in order for SQL*Plus to accept the commands.

```
Oracle SQL*Plus
File  Edit  Search  Options  Help
SQL> CREATE TABLE test_customer (
  2    customer_id NUMBER(10),
  3    first_name VARCHAR2(10),
  4    last_name VARCHAR2(10),
  5    address VARCHAR2(20),
  6    phone VARCHAR2(10)
  7  )
  8  ;

Table created.

SQL> INSERT INTO test_customer
  2    VALUES (1234567890, 'George', 'Prayias', '123 Main Street', '555-1222')
  3  ;

1 row created.

SQL>
```

● **Figure 2.2**   Inserting a record into a table

Introduction to Relational Databases and SQL Programming

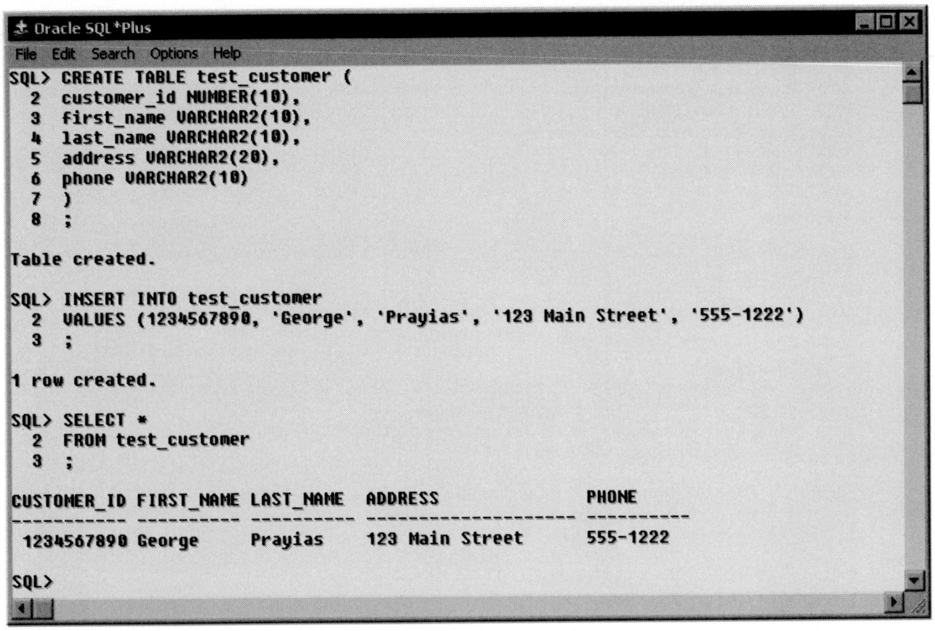

• **Figure 2.3** Viewing table data using a SELECT statement

This response tells you that the command succeeded. You can double-check this by trying to select records from the table, using the command that follows:

```
SELECT *
FROM test_customer;
```

You should see a display similar to the one shown in Figure 2.5. With this command, you are attempting to select records from a table that doesn't exist. In response, Oracle displays four lines of text. The first response line repeats the portion of your command where Oracle encountered a problem. (Since your command was only one line long, that is the line shown.) The second response line places an asterisk (*) beneath the spot in the command line where Oracle started getting confused. The third response line announces that there was an error, and the fourth response line tells you what that error is—in this case, that the table you have named (TEST_CUSTOMER) doesn't exist.

Dropping a table is a serious step! It is not reversible! Only use this command when you are absolutely certain you do not need the records the table contains.

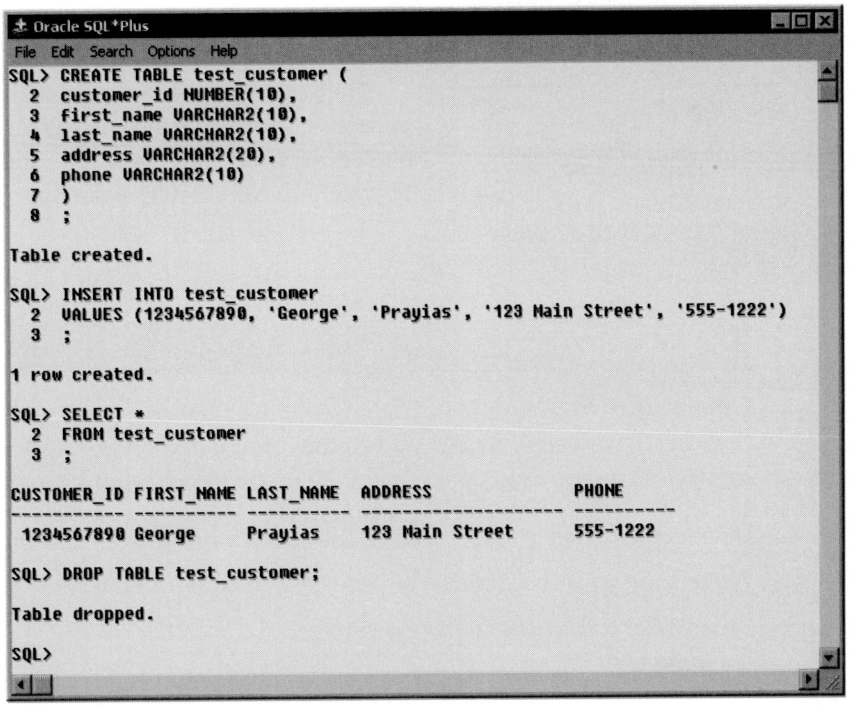

• **Figure 2.4** Dropping a table from a database

```
Oracle SQL*Plus                                                    _ □ X
File  Edit  Search  Options  Help
SQL> CREATE TABLE test_customer (
  2  customer_id NUMBER(10),
  3  first_name VARCHAR2(10),
  4  last_name VARCHAR2(10),
  5  address VARCHAR2(20),
  6  phone VARCHAR2(10)
  7  )
  8  ;

Table created.

SQL> INSERT INTO test_customer
  2  VALUES (1234567890, 'George', 'Prayias', '123 Main Street', '555-1222')
  3  ;

1 row created.

SQL> SELECT *
  2  FROM test_customer
  3  ;

CUSTOMER_ID FIRST_NAME LAST_NAME  ADDRESS               PHONE
----------- ---------- ---------- -------------------- ----------
 1234567890 George      Prayias    123 Main Street       555-1222

SQL> DROP TABLE test_customer;

Table dropped.

SQL> SELECT *
  2  FROM test_customer
  3  ;
FROM test_customer
     *
ERROR at line 2:
ORA-00942: table or view does not exist

SQL>
```

● **Figure 2.5** Selecting data from a nonexistent table

In order to maintain security, users need specific privileges or authorization to CREATE or DROP tables, as well as INSERT, UPDATE, or DELETE data from a table.

The steps you just took demonstrated the most basic functions of a table: to receive, store, and supply information. Good job! You're done with the book now. Okay, not really. The steps you have taken show just a tiny part of what you can do with a database. To learn more, read on.

☑ Cross Check

Basic SQL Statements

Now that you have been introduced to basic SQL commands, check your knowledge by providing answers to the following questions:

1. What is the correct command for creating a table?

2. What is the correct command for inserting data into a table?

3. What is the correct command for viewing all data in a database table?

■ Creating Tables

Databases are all about storing data, and data is stored in tables. To make a database useful, you need to know how to create tables that are somewhat more sophisticated than the one you created in the prior exercise. You need to know how to create tables that

- Store various types of data, such as text, numbers, and dates

- Enforce length limits on the data entered

- Require important columns to contain data before the record can be stored

- Ensure that the values being entered in specific columns fall within a reasonable range

- Relate in a sensible way to data stored in other tables

In this section you will learn how to create tables satisfying the first three of these points. The last two points will be covered in Chapter 11.

Guidelines for Naming Tables and Columns

There are certain guidelines you must follow regarding the names you give tables and columns. Some of them are hard-and-fast rules, while others are recommendations that will keep your tables from looking as if a novice created them.

Rules

The following rules are true for any table or column. Do your best to memorize these *now* to save yourself some head scratching later when you inadvertently try to specify a name that violates one or more of the rules. (It's a good idea to put a copy of these rules on a piece of paper that you can refer to while practicing your SQL commands.)

- The maximum length of a table or column name is 30 characters.

- Table or column names can include letters, numbers, and the underscore character (_). (There are a couple of other special characters that can be used if you employ an inconvenient workaround, but using them would be nothing but trouble, so you should stick with letters, numbers, and the underscore character.)

- Table or column names must start with an alphabetic character. A name can include numbers or underscores, but must start with a letter.

- Uppercase and lowercase characters are treated the same in table and column names.

- A table or column name cannot contain spaces.

- Tables in Oracle are assigned to users; by default, they are assigned to whatever user created them. Every one of a user's tables must have a name that is different than all the other tables the user owns. In other words, a user cannot have two tables with the same name. (It is okay for different users to create tables with the same names, however.) Within a table, all the columns must have unique names.

- Certain words represent commands and parameters to Oracle itself, and therefore cannot be used to name a table or column. You probably won't memorize all these words, but it's good to get an idea of what they are. The restricted words are shown in Table 2.1.

 Speaking of table names, one way to ensure that a table name never matches an Oracle reserved word is to preface every table's name with an abbreviation denoting the system the table is part of. For instance, in an Accounts Payable system, each table's name could begin with "AP_".

ACCESS	COMMENT	ENFORCE	INSTANCE
ACCOUNT	COMMIT	ENTRY	INSTANCES
ACTIVATE	COMMITTED	ESCAPE	INSTEAD
ADD	COMPATIBILITY	ESTIMATE	INT
ADMIN	COMPILE	EVENTS	INTEGER
AFTER	COMPLETE	EXCEPTIONS	INTERMEDIATE
ALL	COMPOSITE_LIMIT	EXCHANGE	INTERSECT
ALL_ROWS	COMPRESS	EXCLUDING	INTO
ALLOCATE	COMPUTE	EXCLUSIVE	IS
ALTER	CONNECT	EXECUTE	ISOLATION
ANALYZE	CONNECT_TIME	EXEMPT	ISOLATION_LEVEL
AND	CONSTRAINT	EXISTS	KEEP
ANY	CONSTRAINTS	EXPIRE	KEY
ARCHIVE	CONTENTS	EXPLAIN	KILL
ARCHIVELOG	CONTINUE	EXTENT	LAYER
ARRAY	CONTROLFILE	EXTENTS	LESS
AS	CONVERT	EXTERNALLY	LEVEL
ASC	COST	FAILED_LOGIN_ATTEMPTS	LIBRARY
AT	COUNT	FALSE	LIKE
AUDIT	CPU_PER_CALL	FAST	LIMIT
AUTHENTICATED	CPU_PER_SESSION	FILE	LINK
AUTHORIZATION	CREATE	FIRST_ROWS	LIST
AUTOEXTEND	CURRENT	FLAGGER	LOB
AUTOMATIC	CURRENT_SCHEMA	FLOAT	LOCAL
BACKUP	CURRENT_USER	FLUSH	LOCK
BECOME	CURSOR	FOR	LOG
BEFORE	CYCLE	FORCE	LOGFILE
BEGIN	DANGLING	FOREIGN	LOGGING
BETWEEN	DATABASE	FREELIST	LOGICAL_READS_PER_
BFILE	DATAFILE	FREELISTS	LOGICAL_READS_PER_CALL
BITMAP	DATAFILES	FROM	LONG
BLOB	DATAOBJNO	FULL	MANAGE
BLOCK	DATE	FUNCTION	MASTER
BODY	DBA	GLOBAL	MAX
BY	DEALLOCATE	GLOBAL_NAME	MAXARCHLOGS
CACHE	DEBUG	GLOBALLY	MAXDATAFILES
CACHE_INSTANCES	DEC	GRANT	MAXEXTENTS
CANCEL	DECIMAL	GROUP	MAXINSTANCES
CASCADE	DECLARE	GROUPS	MAXLOGFILES
CAST	DEFAULT	HASH	MAXLOGHISTORY
CFILE	DEFERRABLE	HASHKEYS	MAXLOGMEMBERS
CHAINED	DEFERRED	HAVING	MAXSIZE
CHANGE	DEGREE	HEADER	MAXTRANS
CHAR	DELETE	HEAP	MAXVALUE
CHAR_CS	DEREF	IDENTIFIED	MEMBER
CHARACTER	DESC	IDLE_TIME	MIN
CHECK	DIRECTORY	IF	MINEXTENTS
CHECKPOINT	DISABLE	IMMEDIATE	MINIMUM
CHOOSE	DISCONNECT	IN	MINUS
CHUNK	DISMOUNT	INCLUDING	MINVALUE
CLEAR	DISTINCT	INCREMENT	MODE
CLOB	DISTRIBUTED	IND_PARTITION	MODIFY
CLONE	DML	INDEX	MOUNT
CLOSE	DOUBLE	INDEXED	MOVE
CLOSED_CACHED_OPEN_	DROP	INDEXES	MTS_DISPATCHERS
CURSORS	DUMP	INDICATOR	MULTISET
CLUSTER	EACH	INITIAL	NATIONAL
COALESCE	ELSE	INITIALLY	NCHAR
COLUMN	ENABLE	INITRANS	NCHAR_CS
COLUMNS	END	INSERT	NCLOB

NEEDED	PACKAGE	ROLE	TABLE
NESTED	PARALLEL	ROLES	TABLES
NETWORK	PARTITION	ROLLBACK	TABLESPACE
NEW	PASSWORD	ROW	TABLESPACE_NO
NEXT	PASSWORD_LIFE_TIME	ROWID	TABNO
NLS_CHARACTERSET	PASSWORD_LOCK_TIME	ROWLABEL	TEMPORARY
NLS_CALENDAR	PASSWORD_REUSE_MAX	ROWNUM	THAN
NLS_ISO_CURRENCY	PASSWORD_REUSE_TIME	ROWS	THE
NLS_LANGUAGE	PASSWORD_VERIFY_ FUNCTION	RULE	THEN
NLS_NUMERIC_ CHARACTERS	PASSWORD_GRACE_TIME	SAMPLE	THREAD
		SAVEPOINT	TIME
NLS_SORT	PCTFREE	SCAN_INSTANCES	TIMESTAMP
NLS_TERRITORY	PCTINCREASE	SCHEMA	TO
NOARCHIVELOG	PCTTHRESHOLD	SCN	TOPLEVEL
NOAUDIT	PCTUSED	SCOPE	TRACE
NOCACHE	PCTVERSION	SD_ALL	TRACING
NOCOMPRESS	PERCENT	SD_INHIBIT	TRANSACTION
NOCYCLE	PERMANENT	SD_SHOW	TRANSITIONAL
NOFORCE	PLAN	SEG_BLOCK	TRIGGER
NOLOGGING	PLSQL_DEBUG	SEG_FILE	TRIGGERS
NOMAXVALUE	POST_TRANSACTION	SEGMENT	TRUE
NOMINVALUE	PRECISION	SELECT	TRUNCATE
NONE	PRESERVE	SEQUENCE	TX
NOORDER	PRIMARY	SERIALIZABLE	TYPE
NOOVERIDE	PRIOR	SESSION	UBA
NOPARALLEL	PRIVATE	SESSION_CACHED_ CURSORS	UID
NORESETLOGS	PRIVATE_SGA		UNARCHIVED
NOREVERSE	PRIVILEGE	SESSIONS_PER_USER	UNDER
NORMAL	PRIVILEGES	SET	UNDO
NOS_SPECIAL_CHARS	PROCEDURE	SHARE	UNION
NOSORT	PROFILE	SHARED	UNIQUE
NOT	PUBLIC	SHARED_POOL	UNLIMITED
NOTHING	PURGE	SHRINK	UNLOCK
NOWAIT	QUEUE	SIZE	UNRECOVERABLE
NULL	QUOTA	SKIM_UNUSABLE_INDEXES	UNTIL
NUMBER	RANGE	SMALLINT	UNUSABLE
NUMERIC	RAW	SNAPSHOT	UNUSED
NVARCHAR2	RBA	SOME	UPDATABLE
OBJECT	READ	SORT	UPDATE
OBJNO	REAL	SPECIFICATION	USAGE
OBJNO_REUSE	REBUILD	SPLIT	USE
OF	RECOVER	SQL_TRACE	USER
OFF	RECOVERABLE	SQLCODE	USING
OFFLINE	RECOVERY	SQLERROR	VALIDATE
OID	REF	STANDBY	VALIDATION
OIDINDEX	REFERENCES	START	VALUE
OLD	REFERENCING	STATEMENT_ID	VALUES
ON	REFRESH	STATISTICS	VARCHAR
ONLINE	RENAME	STOP	VARCHAR2
ONLY	REPLACE	STORAGE	VARRAY
OPCODE	RESET	STORE	VARYING
OPEN	RESETLOGS	STRUCTURE	VIEW
OPTIMAL	RESIZE	SUCCESSFUL	WHEN
OPTIMIZER_GOAL	RESOURCE	SUM	WHENEVER
OPTION	RESTRICTED	SWITCH	WHERE
OR	RETURN	SYNONYM	WITH
ORDER	RETURNING	SYSDATE	WITHOUT
ORGANIZATION	REUSE	SYSDBA	WORK
OVERFLOW	REVERSE	SYSOPER	WRITE
OWN	REVOKE	SYSTEM	XID

Recommendations

Now that you have practiced creating tables with SQL statements, and have learned the rules for tables and columns, let's take a look at some recommendations for naming tables. The following items are good to keep in mind when designing your tables:

- Table names should be singular, not plural. You know the PRODUCT table is going to contain records for multiple products. So does everyone else, so you don't need to indicate that in the table's name. Keep the name singular so that when you are looking at a diagram showing the database's tables (discussed in Chapter 12), you can move from table to table, saying things like "A PRODUCT is referenced by a PURCHASE ORDER…"

- Don't include the word TABLE or DATA in a table name. Experienced users understand that an object storing information in a database is a table, and that tables store data. You don't need to remind them by putting TABLE or DATA in the tables' names.

Creating a More Involved Table

When creating a table, you have to tell Oracle the datatype and length for each column. Oracle tables can store all kinds of data, including text, numbers, dates, pictures, sound files, and other items. Oracle has specific features related to each kind of data. By far the most common types of data in a table are text, numbers, and dates. What follows are examples of how to specify each of these common **datatypes**, along with explanations of the features that differentiate one datatype from another.

How Oracle Stores Text

As a basis for this topic, it's important to be clear about what a database considers to be text. It might seem obvious, but it isn't always, because some text columns are meant to store nothing but numbers.

A text column can store letters, numbers, spaces, and special characters—anything you can type on the keyboard. When a number is entered into a text column, it is still text; it's just text that happens to display as a number character. Numbers in text columns cannot be added, averaged, or subjected to any other mathematical operation. (However, there are functions enabling you to convert numbers in text columns to numbers for math purposes… but we'll save that for later.)

So why would you ever put a number in a text column, if you can't do math with it? Because there are situations where numbers are used for things other than math. Telephone numbers, for instance. Consider this phone number:

(800) 555-1212

It consists of numbers and symbols, which could be interpreted in a mathematical way—but doing so wouldn't make any sense. The same is true for zip codes (12345-6789) and Social Security numbers (123-45-6789). In each of these cases, the data is made up of numbers and math symbols, but is never

When you want to store numbers in a table, how can you decide whether to use a number or text column? Ask yourself whether you will ever be adding the numbers, averaging them, or performing any other mathematical operations on them. If so, use a number column. If not, it's probably better to use a text column. Numeric columns should always be used where possible (when the data does not contain any non-numeric characters), as they provide performance benefits and maximize the use of space.

intended to be added, subtracted, and so on. This type of data is best stored in a text column.

Oracle offers a number of different ways to store text, and each is appropriate for a different type of use. The most straightforward text datatype is the one you used when creating the table in the previous exercise; that datatype is called CHAR (short for "character"). When you define a CHAR column for a table, you also specify the maximum number of characters the column can hold. You accomplish this using a command constructed like the one that follows (don't enter this one yet—it is only an example):

```
CREATE TABLE table_name (column_name CHAR(n));
```

This simple example shows the language you would use to create a table with one CHAR column. Note that three locations in the example are italicized: the table name, the column name, and the number of characters the column can hold. When italics are used in an example command like this, they indicate locations where you would put in your own information, rather than typing exactly what is in the italicized text. In this case, the italics indicate where you would place your own table name, column name, and column length into the command. Examples like this that show how a command is constructed are demonstrating the command's syntax .

The column's length is indicated with the character "n." In the world of databases, "n" is used to represent a location in which a number will be placed. You fill in the number that is appropriate for your application.

The other column datatype for storing text is VARCHAR2 (variable-length character). Like CHAR, the VARCHAR2 datatype stores text, numbers, and special characters. So how is it different? When a CHAR column is designed to store, say, ten characters of text, it stores ten characters of text even if the data entered doesn't consume all of those characters. A CHAR column will pad the end of the data with spaces until it is the full length of the column. So the name "George", a Clapham Specialty Store customer, entered into a CHAR(10) column would actually be stored as "George" with four spaces following it. Since there is no point in storing additional spaces in a column whose contents will vary in length, CHAR columns are best suited for columns where the length of the text is known to be fixed, such as abbreviations for states, countries, or gender.

In contrast, a VARCHAR2 stores only as many characters as are typed. A VARCHAR2(10) column storing "George" would only store six characters of data. The VARCHAR2 datatype is best suited for columns where the length of the text cannot be precisely predicted for each record, which describes most text columns stored in a database, such as names, descriptions, and so on.

To try out these two text datatypes, enter the following code into SQL*Plus:

```
CREATE TABLE test_customer_2(
    name    VARCHAR2(20),
    gender  CHAR(1)
    )
;
```

It is possible to define a CHAR column without specifying its length. If you do, a default length of 1 will be assigned. However, it is considered sloppy technique to define a column without specifying its length explicitly. Be sure to specify the column's length in all situations, even if that length is 1.

Inside Information

VARCHAR2 and VARCHAR
Why is it called VARCHAR2 instead of VARCHAR? Good question. There is a datatype named VARCHAR as well, and in current versions of Oracle it behaves the same as VARCHAR2. However, Oracle Corporation says they may change the behavior of a VARCHAR column in the future—and we have no way of knowing how the "changed" VARCHAR will behave—so you should always specify the full VARCHAR2 datatype name.

Inside Information

Stringing Along

In computer terminology, a piece of text is called a string, which is a short way of saying "a string of characters." People who work with data a lot often use the terms "text" and "string" interchangeably. Another common term is ASCII, which stands for American Standard Code for Information Interchange. (It's pronounced "as-key.") ASCII is an agreed-upon standard for the computer values that represent text, numbers, the special characters on your keyboard, and a few special codes for controlling devices like printers. It's the "lowest common denominator" standard for transferring information between computers. In standard daily use, "ASCII" is used to indicate that a file essentially contains just text—no formatting, margins, boldface, or underlining. For instance, a Microsoft Word .doc file is not ASCII—there are additional codes included reflecting margins, formatting, and other display characteristics—but if you use Word's File | Save As command to save the file with a type of Text Only, the resulting file will be ASCII. ASCII files can be opened in any word processor or text editon.

```
INSERT INTO test_customer_2
VALUES ('Dean', 'M')
;
INSERT INTO test_customer_2
VALUES ('Cathy', 'F')
;

SELECT *
FROM test_customer_2
;

DROP TABLE test_customer_2;
```

When you are done, your SQL*Plus screen should look similar to the one shown in Figure 2.6.

There is also another column datatype designed to store text: LONG. The LONG datatype can store up to 2,147,483,647 characters (two gigabytes) of text, also known as a string of characters. This immense capacity comes at a price, however: The LONG datatype has many restrictions on how it can be used. Using this datatype is outside the scope of an introductory book, but if you need that type of storage, you can find out everything you need to know by checking Oracle's online documentation.

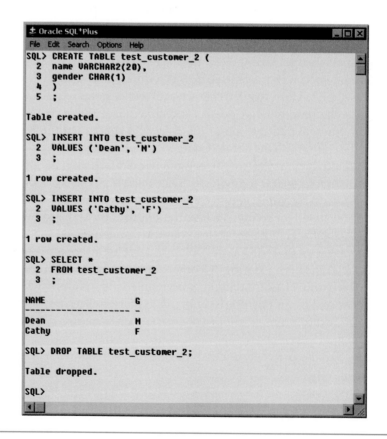

● **Figure 2.6**   Working with CHAR and VARCHAR2 datatypes

Introduction to Relational Databases and SQL Programming

How Oracle Stores Numbers

To define columns that will store numbers within a table, you use the NUMBER column datatype. When defining a NUMBER column, you also specify how many digits the column will need to store. This specification can be in two parts: the total number of digits the column can store, before a value's decimal point, and the number of digits it can store after the decimal point.

For instance, let's say you want to create a table that stores prices for products. All product prices are less than $100. Enter the following commands now to see how creating and using such a table would work:

```
CREATE TABLE test_product (
    product_name  VARCHAR2(25),
    product_price NUMBER(4,2)
    )
;

INSERT INTO test_product
VALUES ('Product Name 1', 1)
;
INSERT INTO test_product
VALUES ('Product Name 2', 2.5)
;
INSERT INTO test_product
VALUES ('Product Name 3', 50.75)
;
INSERT INTO test_product
VALUES ('Product Name 4', 99.99)
;

SELECT *
FROM test_product
;

DROP TABLE test_product;
```

When you are through, your screen should look similar to Figure 2.7.

As you probably noticed, the syntax of the NUMBER datatype is as follows:

```
NUMBER(total_number_of_digits,
digits_after_a_decimal_point)
```

The NUMBER datatype can store truly huge numbers: the largest value it can store is 999,999,999,999,999,999,999,999,999,999, 990,000,000,000,000,000,000,000,000,000,000, 000,000,000,000,000,000,000,000,000,000,000, 000,000,000,000,000,000. It can even store as many as 127 digits after a decimal place. This kind of industrial-strength capacity is one of the things that separates serious databases like Oracle from standard office productivity products such as spreadsheets.

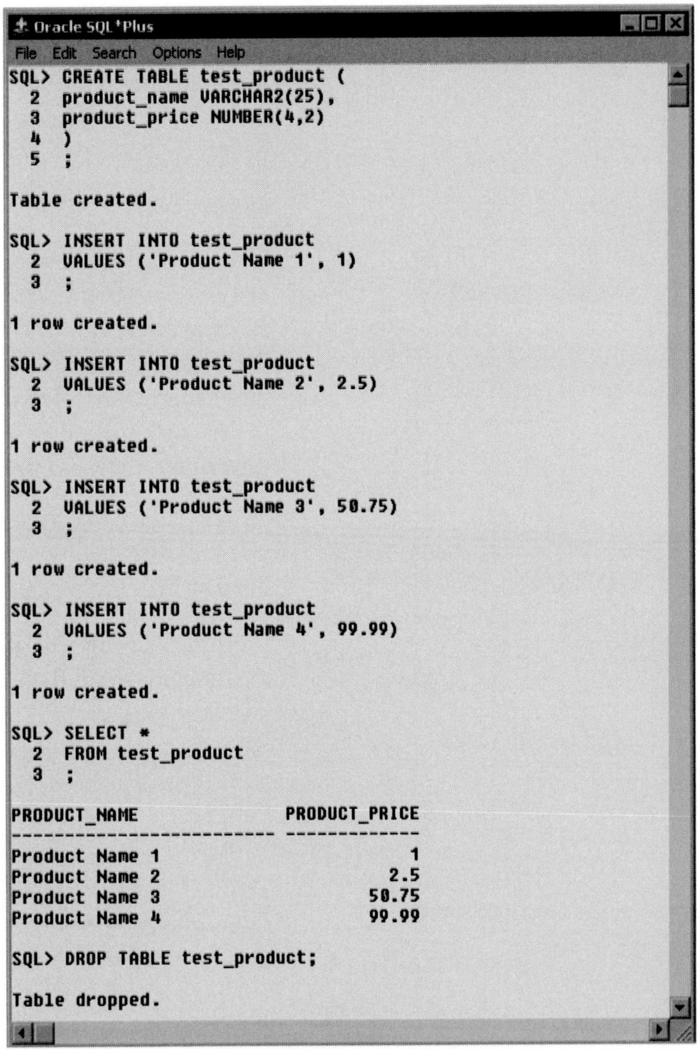

Figure 2.7 Working with the NUMBER datatype

How Oracle Stores Dates

Dates present an interesting problem for computers. For instance, consider a list of dates like the ones that follow:

```
January 15, 2002
February 15, 2002
March 15, 2002
```

You could store this list in a text column, but the dates will not sort properly because text columns sort from left to right, and the "F" that begins February falls before the "J" for January and the "M" for March. To get around this problem, you might use numbers to represent the months, instead of month names. This would result in the following list:

```
01-15-2002
02-15-2002
03-15-2002
```

This would sort the months properly. If the dates within each month were different, this approach would handle that too, since the day-of-the-month characters follow the month characters. However, if the years are different, this approach has a problem. Consider this variation on the list:

```
01-15-2010
02-15-2005
03-15-2000
```

If these are stored in a text column and then sorted, they will sort into exactly the order shown, because text columns sort from left to right. As soon as Oracle sees that the second record's first two characters are "02," it's going to put it after the record whose first two characters are "01," no matter what characters follow.

A workaround to this problem would be to put the year first. This approach would make the list look as follows:

```
2010-01-15
2005-02-15
2000-03-15
```

From the standpoint of sorting, this would work quite well. With the characters being read from left to right, a sorted version of the list would look like this:

```
2000-03-15
2005-02-15
2010-01-15
```

That's a very nice solution, as long as all you need to do with dates is sort them into the proper chronological order. However, lots of business situations require you to do more with dates than just sort them.

Case Study

Let's take a look at our company, the Clapham Specialty Store. Their accounting department may want to know what receivables are due during the next 15 days, and which customers are more than 30 days late in paying their bill. John, the owner, may need to know how this period's sales compare with the same period last year.

This type of work requires the ability to compare two dates and count how many days (or weeks, months, or years) separate them. This is called date math .

You can't do date math with dates stored as text because the text representations have no intrinsic value as dates. They're just strings of text characters that we, as humans, have agreed to interpret as dates. What's needed for date math is a means of converting dates into numbers. Since most date math involves counting days, the most useful approach would be one in which each day has a unique number, and tomorrow's number will be one higher than today's. That way, if you subtract an earlier date from a later one, the difference will be the number of days between the two.

With humans being clever and all, an approach to keeping track of days in this manner already exists: Julian dates . When a system uses Julian dates, it specifies a starting date as day 1; the next day is called day 2, and so on. Since each subsequent day increments the count by one, this type of calendar is ideally suited for date math. Oracle supports Julian dates, and its starting date is January 1, 4712 BC. Oracle automatically handles the conversion of dates between the visual format we can understand (for example, '08-MAY-2004') and the Julian date equivalent. You just insert dates using a familiar text representation, and Oracle converts them to their Julian equivalent behind the scenes. When you select those dates back out from the table, they appear in the familiar form of days, months, and years. You never have to look at dates in their Julian form.

To get a taste of how dates work in Oracle, enter the commands that follow:

```
CREATE TABLE test_purchase (
    product_name  VARCHAR2(25),
    product_price NUMBER(4,2),
    purchase_date DATE
    )
;

INSERT INTO test_purchase VALUES
    ('Product Name 1', 1, '5-NOV-2000')
;
INSERT INTO test_purchase VALUES
    ('Product Name 2', 2.5, '29-JUN-2001')
;
  INSERT INTO test_purchase
VALUES
    ('Product Name 4', 99.99, '31-AUG-2003')
;

SELECT *
FROM test_purchase
;
```

After completing this exercise, your screen should look like the one shown in Figure 2.8.

Julian dates have other benefits in addition to accommodating date math. For instance, if someone tries to insert the date February 29, 2002 into an Oracle date column, Oracle will prevent the insert from succeeding, because it recognizes that 2002 is not a leap year and therefore does

 Dates must be surrounded by single quotes in SQL statements, just like text strings.

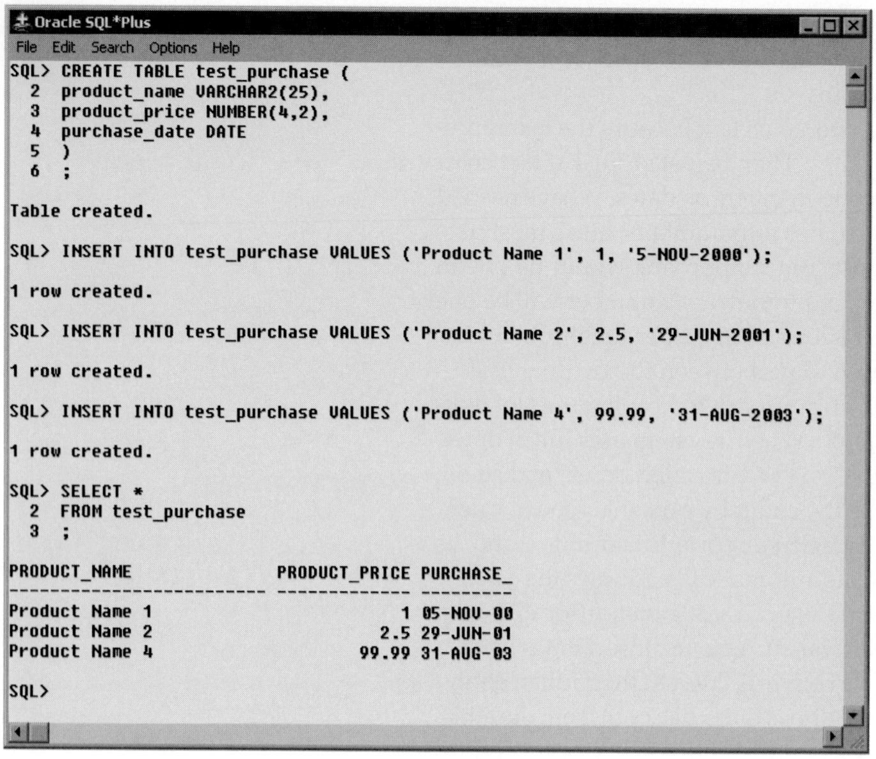

```
± Oracle SQL*Plus                                              _ □ X
 File  Edit  Search  Options  Help
SQL> CREATE TABLE test_purchase (
  2    product_name VARCHAR2(25),
  3    product_price NUMBER(4,2),
  4    purchase_date DATE
  5    )
  6  ;

Table created.

SQL> INSERT INTO test_purchase VALUES ('Product Name 1', 1, '5-NOV-2000');

1 row created.

SQL> INSERT INTO test_purchase VALUES ('Product Name 2', 2.5, '29-JUN-2001');

1 row created.

SQL> INSERT INTO test_purchase VALUES ('Product Name 4', 99.99, '31-AUG-2003');

1 row created.

SQL> SELECT *
  2    FROM test_purchase
  3  ;

PRODUCT_NAME                 PRODUCT_PRICE PURCHASE_
---------------------------  ------------- ---------
Product Name 1                           1 05-NOV-00
Product Name 2                         2.5 29-JUN-01
Product Name 4                       99.99 31-AUG-03

SQL>
```

not have a February 29. In addition, Julian dates can store time values. Time is stored as a decimal value following the integer that represents the date (or following 0 if the value is solely a time, with no date component). For instance, if a given day's Julian date value is 54321, then noon on that day would be stored as 54321.5 (the .5 shows that half of the day has gone by—the portion of the day necessary to reach noon). Oracle would store 6:00 A.M. on that same day as 54321.25, and 6:00 P.M. would be 54321.75. Other times would be stored as values that aren't nearly so tidy; for instance, 3:16 P.M. would add .636111111 to the day's Julian value.

● **Figure 2.8**   Working with the DATE datatype

Determining a Table's Structure

When you create your own table, you know what its structure is… for a while. Then other things take up that space in your memory and you forget. Moreover, if someone else created the table, you won't know what its structure is at all. What you need is a way to find out the structure of an existing table. You probably won't be surprised to learn that Oracle provides a command that does just that. The command is DESCRIBE, which can be shortened to DESC. Its syntax is as follows:

DESC *table_name*

   This is one of the few commands that does not need to end with a semicolon. However, including it doesn't hurt anything, so you may want to include the semicolon just to reinforce the habit.

   To see how the DESC command works, enter the following command:

DESC test_purchase

The display you see in response should look like the one shown in Figure 2.9. The DESC command's output consists of three columns: NAME, NULL?, and TYPE. The NAME column lists each of the table's columns by name, in the order that the columns appear in the table. The NULL? column's purpose will be explained in the next paragraph, and the TYPE column shows the datatype and length for each of the table's columns.

NULL and NOT NULL Columns

When you design tables to store information for a particular purpose (let's use the word *application* in place of "purpose"), you are able to exercise quite a bit of control over what can and cannot go into those tables. Because you have the ability, you also have the responsibility to use this capability in a way that will ensure that the data that makes it into your tables is of the highest quality possible. One of the first things to decide is which columns in a record must contain data, and which columns can be blank.

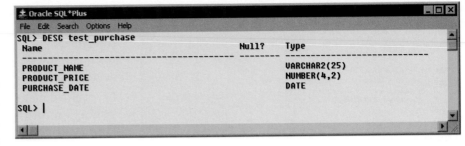

● **Figure 2.9**   Viewing the result of the DESC command

By default, every column in a table is optional. That means you can enter records that have data in some, but not all, of the columns. The columns without data are considered NULL, meaning "empty." A zero is not NULL, and a space is not NULL; both are real values that may or may not have significance in a particular context. When a column is NULL, it truly contains no value whatsoever.

It might seem as if it would be a good idea to make every one of a table's columns required for entry. That is sometimes a good approach, but usually not: Most tables contain columns that won't necessarily be filled in, or that may be filled in later, after the initial entry of the record. For instance, consider a table that will store information about people. Let's say the people are employees within a company. The information you want to store about each person might look like this:

```
First Name
Last Name
Hire Date
Job Title
Department
Supervisor
Salary
Birth Date
Insurance Plan
Phone Extension
```

Does every one of these attributes need to be filled in (or populated) for an employee's record to be acceptable? Not really. When a new person is hired, the company can't know what insurance plan the employee will choose. In addition, it's possible that his/her birth date and phone extension will not

> Individual pieces of information like First Name and Salary are called attributes in database language. Attributes are directly related to columns in a table. The column is the means of physical storage; the attribute is the content being stored in each column for each row.

 Cross Check

Syntax Check

Now that you have been introduced to basic SQL commands and their syntax, check your knowledge by providing answers to the following questions:

1. When are single quotes needed when inserting data into a table?

2. What command is used to find out the structure of an existing table, and what is the correct syntax of the command?

3. What is the difference between the CHAR and VARCHAR2 datatypes?

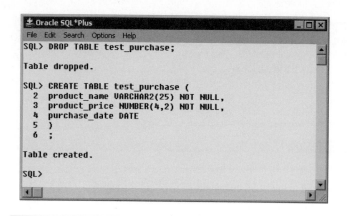

● Figure 2.10 Using the NOT NULL constraint on a column forces every record in the table to contain a value for that column.

be immediately known. Requiring that these columns contain data in order for a record to be accepted would make the table unusable for its intended purpose.

On the other hand, it would be a very good idea to require data in some of the other columns. For instance, a record without a First Name, Last Name, Hire Date, and Salary is not likely to be usable, so those columns should be required.

You can specify which columns are required when you issue a CREATE TABLE command. (You can also change an existing table; that will be covered in Chapter 3.) Within the command, you identify a column as required by placing the words "NOT NULL" after the column's name and datatype. To see this in action, enter the following commands into SQL*Plus:

```
DROP TABLE test_purchase;

CREATE TABLE test_purchase (
    product_name  VARCHAR2(25) NOT NULL,
    product_price NUMBER(4,2)  NOT NULL,
    purchase_date DATE
    )
;
```

When you are done, your screen should look similar to Figure 2.10. To test the results of defining a column as NOT NULL, you need to know how to insert a record that does not contain data for every column in the table.

■ Inserting Data—Additional Techniques

This section provides tips you will find useful—perhaps even essential—for entering data in a wide variety of situations.

How to Insert Records Containing NULL Values

Earlier in the chapter you learned that a NULL value is an empty attribute—for instance, a blank birthday in a personnel record. You will probably run into a variety of situations that call for inserting records with NULL values in certain columns. There are two ways to accomplish this.

The first technique is to just use the word "NULL" in the INSERT statement wherever you would have specified a value. For instance, in the most recent table you created (TEST_PURCHASE), the Product_Name and Product_Price are required, but the Purchase_Date is not. Therefore, you could insert a record that populates just the first two attributes by entering the following commands:

```
INSERT INTO test_purchase
VALUES ('Product Name 1', 1, NULL)
;


SELECT *
FROM test_purchase
;
```

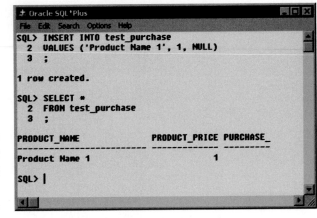

Your screen should now look similar to the one shown in Figure 2.11. Notice that when SQL*Plus displays your record in response to the SELECT command, the record's third column is blank.

Now that you know how to insert records with NULL values, it is time to check whether the NOT NULL settings you defined for the table's first two columns are working. How can you check this? By trying to insert a record that omits values in either or both of the required columns. To be thorough, you should test all three variations: missing the product name, missing the product price, and missing both. Enter the following commands to perform these tests:

• **Figure 2.11**   Inserting a NULL value using the word NULL

```
INSERT INTO test_purchase
VALUES
     (NULL, 2.5, '29-JUN-2001')
;
INSERT INTO test_purchase
VALUES
     ('Product Name 3', null, '10-DEC-2002')
;
INSERT INTO test_purchase
VALUES
     (NULL, NULL, '31-AUG-2003')
;


SELECT *
FROM test_purchase
;
```

The results of these commands should look similar to what you see in Figure 2.12. Each of the INSERT commands produced an Oracle error message reminding you in its friendly way that you can't insert NULL values into columns created as NOT NULL.

The second technique for inserting NULL values into a table produces exactly the same results as using NULL in your list of inserted values; it just achieves that result in a different way.

The technique uses a variation of the INSERT command syntax. In this variation, you explicitly name every column you are inserting data into. In all of your INSERT commands up to this point, you have not stated which columns you were inserting into; you just specified the values to be inserted. When you write INSERT commands in that way, Oracle makes two assumptions: You are inserting values into every column the table has, and the values you specify are in the same order as the columns in the table. By explicitly

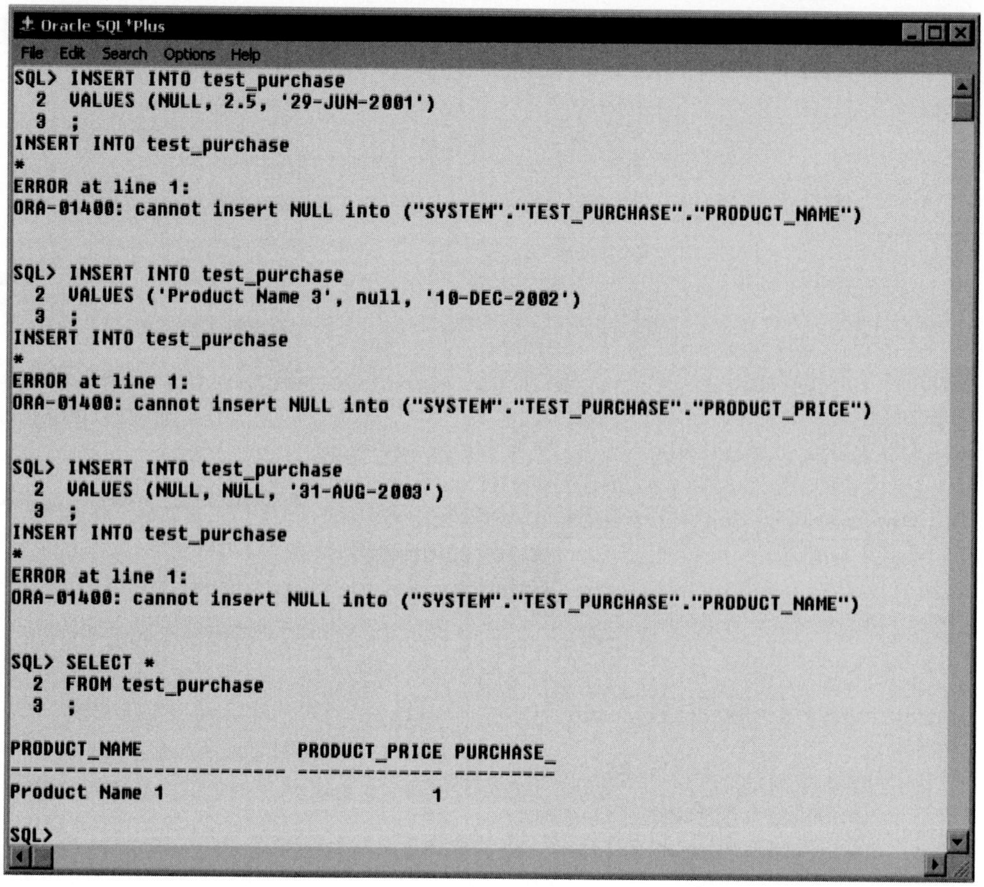

```
Oracle SQL *Plus                                                                    _ □ X
File  Edit  Search  Options  Help
SQL> INSERT INTO test_purchase
  2   VALUES (NULL, 2.5, '29-JUN-2001')
  3  ;
INSERT INTO test_purchase
*
ERROR at line 1:
ORA-01400: cannot insert NULL into ("SYSTEM"."TEST_PURCHASE"."PRODUCT_NAME")


SQL> INSERT INTO test_purchase
  2   VALUES ('Product Name 3', null, '10-DEC-2002')
  3  ;
INSERT INTO test_purchase
*
ERROR at line 1:
ORA-01400: cannot insert NULL into ("SYSTEM"."TEST_PURCHASE"."PRODUCT_PRICE")


SQL> INSERT INTO test_purchase
  2   VALUES (NULL, NULL, '31-AUG-2003')
  3  ;
INSERT INTO test_purchase
*
ERROR at line 1:
ORA-01400: cannot insert NULL into ("SYSTEM"."TEST_PURCHASE"."PRODUCT_NAME")


SQL> SELECT *
  2   FROM test_purchase
  3  ;

PRODUCT_NAME                     PRODUCT_PRICE PURCHASE_
-------------------------------- ------------- ---------
Product Name 1                               1

SQL>
```

● **Figure 2.12**   Viewing the results of the NOT NULL constraint on a column

stating which columns you are populating, and in what order, you override both of those assumptions, and give yourself the ability to skip columns altogether.

To see this in action, enter the following commands:

```
INSERT INTO test_purchase (product_name, product_price)
    VALUES ('Product Name 2', 2.5)
;
INSERT INTO test_purchase (product_name, product_price)
    VALUES ('Product Name 3', 50.75)
;
INSERT INTO test_purchase (product_price, product_name)
    VALUES (99.99, 'Product Name 4')
;

SELECT *
FROM test_purchase
;
```

The results you see should be similar to those shown in Figure 2.13.

Notice that in the last of the INSERT commands you just performed, the columns are named in reverse order. It doesn't matter what order you specify

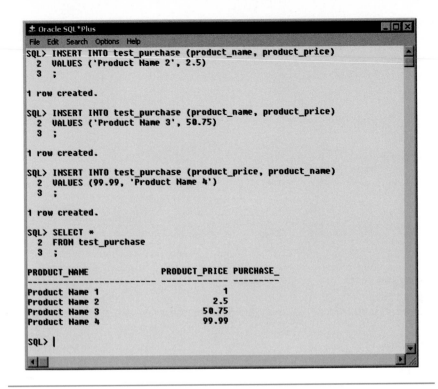

```
Oracle SQL*Plus
File  Edit  Search  Options  Help
SQL> INSERT INTO test_purchase (product_name, product_price)
  2  VALUES ('Product Name 2', 2.5)
  3  ;

1 row created.

SQL> INSERT INTO test_purchase (product_name, product_price)
  2  VALUES ('Product Name 3', 50.75)
  3  ;

1 row created.

SQL> INSERT INTO test_purchase (product_price, product_name)
  2  VALUES (99.99, 'Product Name 4')
  3  ;

1 row created.

SQL> SELECT *
  2  FROM test_purchase
  3  ;

PRODUCT_NAME              PRODUCT_PRICE PURCHASE_
------------------------  ------------- ---------
Product Name 1                        1
Product Name 2                      2.5
Product Name 3                    50.75
Product Name 4                    99.99

SQL>
```

● **Figure 2.13**   Explicitly stating column names when inserting values ensures that the correct values are entered into the correct columns.

the columns in, as long as the values are provided in the same order as the columns are named. Generally, you will want to specify the columns in the order in which they occur in the table—but it's good to know how to change the INSERT command's column order if you need to.

Step-by-Step 2.01

Creating and Populating a Table

Case Study

John at the Clapham Specialty Store has asked you to create a table in the database to keep track of all employees who work at his store.

For this exercise, you will need Oracle9*i* Database Server with the SQL*Plus tool.

Step 1

Using the SQL*Plus tool, at the SQL> prompt, type the following code to create the EMPLOYEE table definition:

```
CREATE TABLE employee
(       employee_id        NUMBER(10) NOT NULL,
        supervisor_id      NUMBER(10) NULL,
        job_type           VARCHAR2(20) NOT NULL,
        first_name         VARCHAR2(40) NULL,
        last_name          VARCHAR2(40) NOT NULL,
```

```
            social_security_number CHAR(11)NOT NULL,
            pay_rate                  NUMBER(8,2) NULL
)
;
```

Step 2

Insert the following data into the EMPLOYEE table:

```
INSERT INTO employee
VALUES(100, NULL, 'Owner', 'John', 'Balfour', '123-45-6789', NULL)
;

INSERT INTO employee
VALUES(102, 100, 'Floor Manager', 'Dean', 'Karayanis', '111-23-4532', 20.00)
;

INSERT INTO employee
VALUES(103, 100, 'Register Clerk', 'Krystin', 'DeLuca', '125-95-2396', 10.00)
;

INSERT INTO employee
VALUES(104, 100, 'Register Clerk', 'Keith', 'Doherty', '100-38-8572', 11.00)
;

INSERT INTO employee
VALUES(105, 101, 'Delivery', 'Brian', 'Doherty', '493-23-1256', 9.50)
;

INSERT INTO employee
VALUES(106, 101, 'Delivery', 'Joel', 'Morton', '14-235-9832', 9.50)
;
```

Step 3

Verify that the data was successfully placed in the EMPLOYEE table by executing the following command:

```
SELECT *
FROM employee
;
```

Step 4

Attempt to add the following record to the EMPLOYEE table to verify that the NOT NULL constraints on the columns are working correctly:

```
INSERT INTO employee
VALUES (NULL, 100, 'Register Clerk', 'Jennifer', 'Smith', NULL, 11.00)
;
```

Did you receive an error message? Remember that the Employee_ID and Social_Security_ Number columns were defined to not accept NULL values.

You should have successfully created and populated an EMPLOYEE table in the Clapham Specialty Store database. This will help John keep track of employees and their related pay rates, job types, and supervisors.

How to Insert Data That Contains Apostrophes

At some time or another, you will probably need to insert records with text that contains apostrophes. This presents a bit of a problem, since Oracle interprets apostrophes as the beginning or end of a text string. If you try to just place an apostrophe in the middle of a piece of text and then insert it, Oracle will think that the text string ends when it reaches the apostrophe, and when it discovers that more text follows the apostrophe, it will get thoroughly confused. If you would like to see this in action, enter the following command:

```
INSERT INTO test_purchase
VALUES
    ('Fifth Product's Name', 25, '05-MAY-2003')
;
```

In response, Oracle will display the error message shown in Figure 2.14. Clearly, this approach does not work. To make it work, you have to do two things: execute a SET SCAN OFF command before the INSERT, and place two apostrophes in a row at the location in the text string where you want the single apostrophe to be inserted. The resulting commands look like this:

```
SET SCAN OFF

INSERT INTO test_purchase
VALUES
    ('Fifth Product''s Name', 25, '05-MAY-2003')
;

SET SCAN ON
```

Enter those commands, and then check how well they worked by entering this one:

```
SELECT *
FROM test_purchase
;
```

You should see your newly inserted record, as reflected in Figure 2.15.

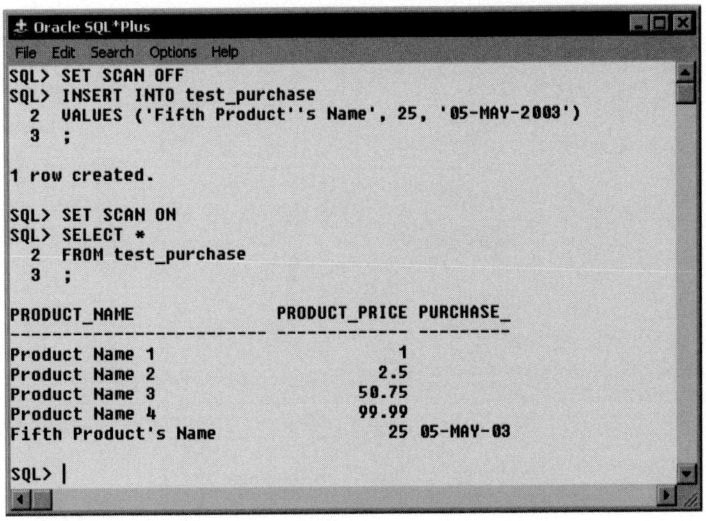

■ Viewing Data from a Table—Additional Techniques

Now that you know how to do basic SELECT commands, it's time to learn some more sophisticated techniques for viewing data in a table. In this section, you will learn how to select

● **Figure 2.14** Incorrectly using an apostrophe in a text string produces an error message.

● **Figure 2.15** Correct use of an apostrophe in a text string

Chapter 2: Storing and Retrieving Data: The Basics

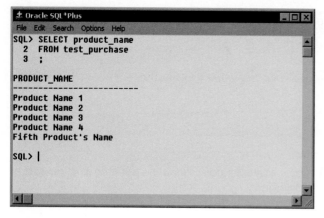

● **Figure 2.16**   Viewing a single column from a database table

specific columns out of a table, change the order in which selected columns are displayed, perform math using data in a table, connect text strings together, and change the names assigned to columns. Ready? Of course you are.

Selecting Specific Columns

As your tables get larger, it's likely that sometime you will want to view some, but not all, of the columns in a table. It's easy to do; you just name the columns you want in your SELECT statement, rather than specifying all of them using the "*" character, as you have done up to this point. To try out this technique, enter the following command to select just the first column from the table you created earlier:

```
SELECT product_name
FROM test_purchase
;
```

In response, you should see a display like the one shown in Figure 2.16. To practice this technique further, take a moment now to execute SELECT commands for each of the other columns in the table.

To choose more than one column, name each column you want, and place a comma between each name. For instance, to choose the first and third columns from your TEST_PURCHASE table, enter the following command:

```
SELECT product_name, purchase_date
FROM test_purchase
;
```

Changing Column Order

Now that you know how to choose specific columns from a table, it's very easy to change the order in which those columns are shown. In your SELECT command, you just name the columns in the order you want them to appear.

For instance, to see the columns from the TEST_PURCHASE table with the last column first and the first column last, enter this command:

```
SELECT purchase_date, product_price, product_name
FROM    test_purchase
;
```

In response, you should see output matching Figure 2.17. To help become familiar with this technique, take some time now to select records from your TEST_PURCHASE table in varying column arrangements.

● **Figure 2.17**   Viewing varied column arrangements from a database table

Performing Math Using Data in a Table

There are many reasons why you might want to perform math operations using data stored in a table. For instance, at the Clapham Specialty Store, John might want to see what the price of a CD rental would be if he increased it by 7 percent. Or he might want to calculate the amount an item costs including local tax, even if the tax isn't stored in the table. This is easy to do using SQL. You simply write SELECT statements that include the math operations.

Case Study

For instance, let's say you wanted to see what the prices in the TEST_PURCHASE table would look like if they were increased by 15 percent. Type in the following command to accomplish this:

```
SELECT product_name, product_price * 1.15
FROM test_purchase
;
```

The results you see from this command should match what is shown in Figure 2.18.

Math Operators

The technical name for math symbols is operators . The plus sign is an operator, for instance; so is the minus sign. Oracle supports standard four-function math: addition, subtraction, multiplication, and division. As you saw in the last example, multiplication is identified with the asterisk character (*). Division results from the / character, while addition and subtraction are produced by the + and – characters, respectively. To try each of these out in a way that is reasonably relevant to real-life work, we need to create a new table that has two number columns. The following set of commands will do this, as well as demonstrate the math operators.

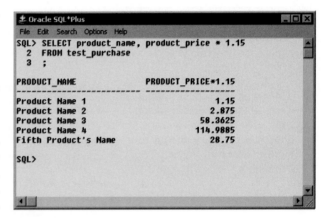

● **Figure 2.18** Performing math in a SELECT statement

```
DROP TABLE test_purchase;

CREATE TABLE test_purchase (
     product_name   VARCHAR2(25),
     product_price  NUMBER(4,2),
     sales_tax      NUMBER(4,2),
     purchase_date  DATE,
     salesperson    VARCHAR2(3)
     )
;

INSERT INTO test_purchase
VALUES
     ('Product Name 1', 1, .08, '5-NOV-2000', 'AB')
;
INSERT INTO test_purchase
VALUES
     ('Product Name 2', 2.5, .21, '29-JUN-2001', 'CD')
;
```

```
INSERT INTO test_purchase
VALUES
    ('Product Name 3', 50.75, 4.19, '10-DEC-2002', 'EF')
;
INSERT INTO test_purchase
VALUES
    ('Product Name 4', 99.99, 8.25, '31-AUG-2003', 'GH')
;

SELECT product_name, product_price + sales_tax
FROM test_purchase
;
SELECT product_name, 100 - product_price
FROM test_purchase
;
SELECT product_name, sales_tax / product_price
FROM test_purchase
;
```

This exercise demonstrates inserting dates with only two digits specifying the year. This is necessary in some versions of Oracle7, which do not like seeing a four-digit year under normal circumstances. If you are using Oracle8 or later, it is always a good idea to specify the full four digits of a year in any SQL command.

The results of the three SELECT commands should look similar to what is shown in Figure 2.19.

What Is an Expression?

Within the world of Oracle, the term **expression** is used to denote a variety of things. For our purposes, it refers to the portion of a command that consists of one or more column names, NULL, a value you have entered yourself (like the ".05" in the previous batch of commands, which would also be called a **constant** because its value is fixed), or a combination of any of those

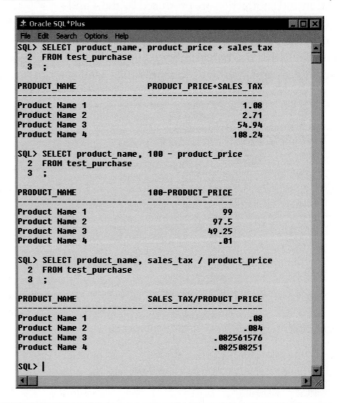

• **Figure 2.19** Using math operators to obtain results

Introduction to Relational Databases and SQL Programming

things connected by math operators. For instance, consider the following command:

```
SELECT product_name, product_price * 2 + 10
FROM test_purchase
;
```

In the preceding command, PRODUCT_NAME is an expression, and PRODUCT_PRICE * 2 + 10 is another expression.

Looking at that example, you might wonder: "How does Oracle handle a situation where an expression contains more than one math operator?" That brings us to the topic of operator precedence .

Operator Precedence

When an expression contains more than one math operator, Oracle does have a method to decide the order in which to perform the operations. Multiplication, division, and any numbers appearing in parentheses are done first and from left to right. Once these calculations are completed, addition and subtraction are done next, also left to right.

However, many people forget which math operators are calculated first, if they ever knew at all. Because of this, it's a good idea to identify calculation precedence explicitly in your statements by using parentheses. Surround the portion of the expression you want executed first in a pair of parentheses, and there will never be any question how the expression will be calculated.

For instance, a clearer way to write the preceding example would be as follows:

```
SELECT product_name, (product_price * 2) + 10
FROM test_purchase
;
```

Connecting Two or More Pieces of Text Together

There are many, many situations in the world of databases where it is desirable to display the contents of two or more text columns together in one connected string of text, while continuing to store the text pieces in separate columns. For instance, a mailing label has a person's last name following their first name, and the city, state, and zip code (or equivalents for your country) are all on the same line—but are stored in separate columns in the table. Connecting two pieces of text is called concatenation .

In Oracle SELECT statements, you can indicate that two columns should be concatenated by putting two vertical bars (||) between the column names. For instance, the following command would concatenate the contents of the Product_Name and Salesperson columns:

```
SELECT product_name || salesperson
FROM test_purchase
;
```

However, this command's output would be hard to read, because the salesperson's initials would follow the product name immediately; there would be no space between them. A more readable variation would be to insert between the columns a fixed string of text written to support and clarify the data that will be on either side. To separate the fixed text from the data that will surround it, it often makes sense to place a space before the fixed text, and another space after it. As is the case with other text in SQL commands, the fixed text string will be surrounded with single quotes. Type in the following command to see how this works:

```
SELECT product_name || ' was sold by ' || salesperson
FROM    test_purchase
;
```

The results of this command should match what you see in Figure 2.20.

When you include fixed text in a command, the fixed text is called a literal. This means that it will be reproduced character for character, and not interpreted as the name of a table, column, or other object.

Assigning Aliases to Columns

You may have noticed in the last command that the column's header has gotten out of hand. By default, column headers are the column names. However, when you execute a SELECT statement that includes concatenated columns, the entire expression that generates the concatenated output is displayed as the column's header. This is usually unattractive and rarely helpful. SQL lets you define what will be placed at the top of a column in a SELECT statement. It's easy: After the column name (or expression), you just type the text you want displayed at the top of the output column.

To see this in action, enter the following variation on the previous SELECT command:

```
SELECT product_name || ' was sold by ' || salesperson SOLDBY
FROM    test_purchase
;
```

The surrogate name you specify for the column is called a column alias. This particular column alias, SOLDBY, gives a more readable column name, but it's still a little clumsy. If you surround the alias in double quotes, you can include spaces in it, and use lowercase letters, too. (You have to use double quotes here so Oracle will not try to interpret the column

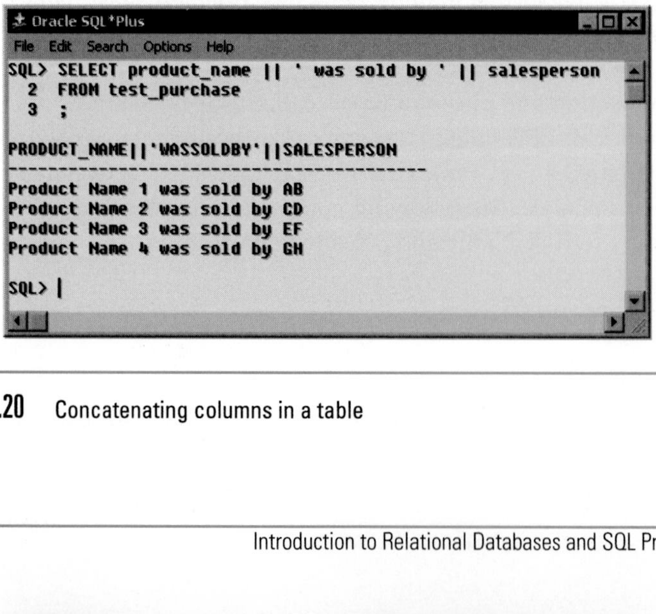

```
± Oracle SQL*Plus                                          _ |□| X
File  Edit  Search  Options  Help
SQL> SELECT product_name || ' was sold by ' || salesperson  ▲
  2  FROM test_purchase
  3  ;

PRODUCT_NAME||'WASSOLDBY'||SALESPERSON
-------------------------------------------
Product Name 1 was sold by AB
Product Name 2 was sold by CD
Product Name 3 was sold by EF
Product Name 4 was sold by GH

SQL> |                                                      ▼
 ◄|                                                       ►|
```

● **Figure 2.20**   Concatenating columns in a table

alias as a column name to select.) You can see this work by entering the following command:

```
SELECT product_name || ' was sold by ' || salesperson "Sold By"
FROM   test_purchase
;
```

Your display should look similar to the one shown in Figure 2.21.

SQL also supports the use of the AS keyword. The AS keyword is used before the column alias name as shown in the following statement:

```
SELECT product_name AS product
FROM test_purchase
;
```

The result of this statement will indicate the Product_Name column with a title of PRODUCT, as column headings appear in uppercase by default. The AS keyword is used to show the distinction between the current column name, indicated when the table was created, and the alias that you want displayed on the screen when viewing the column heading and table data. The AS keyword is optional indicating column alias names. The result of the preceding query would be the same if the AS keyword were not used.

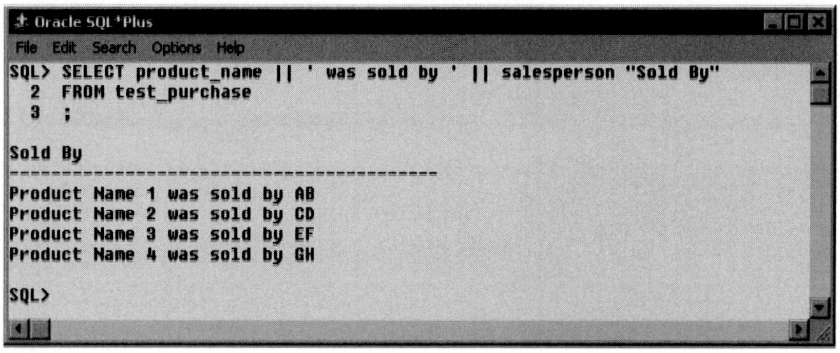

Figure 2.21 Specifying a column alias

Step-by-Step 2.02

Changing the Data Values You View

Case Study

The Clapham Specialty Store is considering having a sale and decreasing the cost of all items by 8 percent. They are interested in creating an item table that would contain the item identification number, the original item cost that the Clapham Specialty Store paid for the item, and the current item price that they are charging customers. They would like to use the table data to test the price decrease. They wish to delete this table after testing the price decrease as it will not be needed in the database for future reference.

For this exercise, you will need Oracle9*i* Database Server with the SQL*Plus tool.

Step 1

Using the SQL*Plus tool, at the SQL> prompt, type the following code to create the ITEM table definition:

```
CREATE TABLE item(
     item_no NUMBER(3) NOT NULL,
     item_cost NUMBER(8,2)  NOT NULL,
     item_price NUMBER(8,2) NOT NULL
     )
;
```

Step 2

Insert the following data into the ITEM table:

```
INSERT INTO item
VALUES (101, 8.00, 12.50)
;

INSERT INTO item
VALUES (102, 2.50, 4.99)
;

INSERT INTO item
VALUES (103, 1.25, 1.40)
;
```

Step 3

Execute the following command to view the data in the ITEM table:

```
SELECT *
FROM item
;
```

Step 4

Execute the following command to view the proposed price decreases for all items in the ITEM table:

```
SELECT item_no, item_price * .92
FROM item
;
```

Step 5

Calculate whether or not the price decrease still nets a profit for each item in the ITEM table by subtracting the original item costs from newly generated sale prices that you calculated in the previous step:

```
SELECT item_no,
       item_cost,
       item_price * .92,
       item_price * .92 - item_cost
FROM item
;
```

Step 6

Drop the ITEM table by executing the following command:

```
DROP TABLE item;
```

You should have successfully created an ITEM table, calculated the results of a proposed 8 percent price decrease on all items in the table, and deleted the table from the database.

Chapter 2 Review

■ Chapter Summary

After reading this chapter and completing the Step-by-Step tutorial and Cross Checks, you should understand the following facts about databases and SQL tables:

Prepare to Work with a Database

- SQL*Plus is the program supplied by Oracle that lets you communicate with a database.

- Tables are created using the CREATE TABLE command.

- Records are inserted into tables using the INSERT INTO command.

- Table data can be viewed by executing the SELECT FROM statement.

- Tables can be removed from the database with the DROP TABLE command.

Create a Table

- The maximum length of a table or column name is 30 characters.

- Table or column names can include letters, numbers, and the underscore character (_).

- Table or column names must start with an alphabetic character. A name can include numbers or underscores, but must start with a letter.

- Uppercase and lowercase characters are treated the same in table and column names.

- A table or column name cannot contain spaces.

- Tables in Oracle are assigned to users; by default, they are assigned to whichever user created them. Every one of a user's tables must have a name that is different than all the other tables the user owns.

- Within a table, all of the columns must have unique names.

- Certain words represent commands and parameters to Oracle itself, and therefore cannot be used to name a table or column.

- It is recommended that table names should be singular, not plural.

- Table names should be unique in a database.

- The words TABLE or DATA should not be included in a table name.

- When creating a table, you have to tell Oracle the datatype and length for each column.

- CREATE TABLE commands can include NOT NULL specifications for any or all columns, causing Oracle to require inserted or updated records to contain values in those columns before the records will be accepted.

Insert Data into a Table

- Oracle tables can store all kinds of data, including text, numbers, dates, pictures, and sound files.

- Text columns can store letters, numbers, spaces, and special characters—anything you can type on the keyboard.

- Numbers in text columns cannot be added, averaged, or subjected to any other mathematical operation.

- There are two main types of text columns: fixed length (CHAR) and variable length (VARCHAR2).

- A text value is commonly referred to as a "string." When referring to strings in SQL commands, you must always surround the string in single quotes.

- When creating a number column, you simply specify the maximum number of digits it can hold, along with the number of digits it will use before and after the decimal.

- Oracle provides a DATE datatype that stores both dates and times. To store dates, Oracle converts familiar-looking dates (which are also surrounded by single quotes) into their Julian equivalents—but you never have to specify dates as Julian values.

- The DATE datatype stores time values as decimal amounts representing how much of a day has passed at the time being stored.

- Oracle can perform date math, giving the ability to calculate how far apart two dates or times are, or to add or subtract seconds, minutes, hours, days, weeks, months, and/or years to/from a starting date or time.

- The DESC command is used to see the structure of an existing table.

- When adding or changing data in tables whose columns *do* accept NULLs, you can bypass entering a value in a column by specifying NULL in that column's location in the SQL statement.

- You can skip columns in INSERT commands by naming every column you care about in the command, and simply not naming the column you do not intend to insert data into.

- To insert data containing apostrophes using the SQL*Plus program, precede your INSERT command with a SET SCAN OFF command. Once you have finished inserting data containing apostrophes, issue a SET SCAN ON command to return things to normal.

View Data from a Table

- You can specify which of a table's columns you wish to view by naming the columns you want in your SELECT statement, rather than specifying all of them using the "*" character.

- If you would like to see columns in a different order, name them in the order you want them when writing your SELECT command.

- To perform math using data stored in a table, write the math operators into your SELECT statement, with the column name you care about included as a math variable.

- When writing math formulas, you must pay attention to operator precedence, that is, the order in which Oracle performs operations if the formula contains more than one math operator.

- Multiplication, division, and any operations appearing in parentheses are done first and from left to right. Once these calculations are done, addition and subtraction are done next, also left to right.

- The best way to handle operator precedence is to specify it explicitly in your statements by using parentheses; surround the portion of the expression you want executed first in a pair of parentheses, and there will never be any question of how the expression will be calculated.

- When you want to add text instead of numbers—that is, concatenate text from two columns together—you can do so by placing two vertical bars (| |) between the column names in your SELECT statement.

- If you wish to place a space between the two pieces of text, you can do so by using | |' '| | between the column names.

Key Terms

AS *(43)*

column alias *(42)*

concatenation *(41)*

constant *(40)*

CREATE TABLE *(17)*

datatype *(24)*

date math *(29)*

DROP *(18)*

expression *(40)*

INSERT *(18)*

Julian dates *(29)*

literal *(42)*

NULL *(31)*

operator precedence *(41)*

operators *(39)*

populated *(31)*

SELECT *(18)*

string *(26)*

syntax *(25)*

Key Term Quiz

Use the Key Terms list to complete the sentences that follow. Not all terms will be used.

1. _____ is an indicator that data does not exist and the value is not known at all.

2. A surrogate name assigned to a column in SQL commands is known as a(n) _____.

3. A piece of command or program construct that, when executed, results in one or more values is a(n) _____.

4. Performing arithmetic operations with dates—for example, finding the number of days between two dates—is known as _____.

5. The operation of joining two pieces of text to make a single piece of text is _____.

Matching Definition Quiz

Relate each term on the left with the appropriate description on the right.

Term	Description
1. Literal	a. The technical name for mathematical operation symbols, such as the plus sign and minus sign
2. Datatype	b. Fixed text in a command or program that does not change and is interpreted literally, instead of as a name for a variable
3. Populated	c. Type of data—for example, NUMBER, CHAR, and so on
4. String	d. When a valid data value is stored in an attribute or a field
5. Operators	e. Text characters

Multiple-Choice Quiz

1. What is the correct syntax for creating a table containing two columns?

   a.
   ```
   CREATE TABLE table_name
     column_name_1 datatype,
     column_name_2 datatype
   ;
   ```

   b.
   ```
   CREATE TABLE table_name
       FROM column_name_1 datatype,
             column_name_2 datatype
   ;
   ```

   c.
   ```
   CREATE TABLE table_name (
     column_name_1 datatype,
     column_name_2 datatype
   )
   ;
   ```

   d.
   ```
   CREATE TABLE table_name (
     column name 1 datatype,
     column name 2 datatype
   )
   ;
   ```

   e.
   ```
   CREATE table_name TABLE(
     column_name_1 datatype,
     column_name_2 datatype
   )
   ;
   ```

2. What is a datatype?

   a. Hard-coded information typed directly into a SQL command

   b. The method Oracle uses to store dates

   c. A declaration of whether a column will store text, numbers, dates, or other types of information

   d. A type of computer terminal, used before personal computers, that relied on the presence of a mainframe computer

   e. A SQL command used to determine whether data in a table is text, numbers, or any other type of information

3. Which of the following is *not* a benefit of using Julian dates?

   a. Date math

   b. Validity checking

   c. Proper sorting

   d. Faster operation

   e. Ability to store times

4. On which line will the following command fail?

   ```
   SELECT first_name ||
          " " ||
          last_name
          "Full Name"
   FROM   test_person
   ;
   ```

   a. 1

   b. 2

   c. 3

   d. 4

   e. 5

   f. The command will succeed.

5. Which of the following are *not* operators you can use in a math formula within a SQL statement? (Choose all that apply.)

   a. +

   b. (

c.]

d. *

e. {

6. What is the proper syntax for assigning a column alias?

    a. SELECT *column_name* ALIAS *alias_name*
FROM *table_name*;

    b. SELECT *column_name alias_name*
FROM *table_name*;

    c. SELECT *alias_name*
FROM *table_name*;

    d. ASSIGN *alias_name* TO *column_name*;

    e. ASSIGN *alias_name* TO *column_name* FOR
table_name

7. What is the maximum number of characters allowed in a table or column name?

    a. 7

    b. 14

    c. 15

    d. 20

    e. 30

8. The DESC command is used to

    a. View all table data

    b. Sort number values of a table in descending order

    c. Describe the contents of a database table

    d. Describe the structure of a database table

    e. Delete a table from the database

9. To perform math using data stored in a table, it is best to

    a. Write the math operators into the table names you care about, as math variables

    b. Write the math operators into the column names you care about, as math variables

    c. Write the math operators into your CREATE TABLE statement, with the column name you care about included as a math variable

    d. Write the math operators into your INSERT INTO statement, with the column name you care about included as a math variable

    e. Write the math operators into your SELECT statement; with the column name you care about included as a math variable

10. The best way to handle operator precedence is to

    a. Specify it explicitly in your statements by using multiplication and division operators first, before addition and subtraction operators.

    b. Specify it explicitly in your statements by using only multiplication and division operators within parentheses, and addition and subtraction operators between parentheses.

    c. Specify it explicitly in your statements by using parentheses; surround the portion of the expression you want executed first in a pair of parentheses, and there will never be any question of how the expression will be calculated.

    d. Specify it explicitly in your statements by using only the minimum number of operators necessary to complete the calculation.

    e. Specify it explicitly in your statements by using parentheses; surround the leftmost portion of the expression in parentheses.

11. If you would like to view table columns in a specific order

    a. Name them in the order you want them when writing your SELECT statement

    b. Name them in the order you want them when writing your CREATE TABLE statement

    c. Name them in the order you want them when inserting data into your table

    d. Number the columns when creating them in the database tables

    e. Name them in alphabetical order when writing your CREATE TABLE statement

12. You can skip columns in INSERT commands by

    a. Naming every column you care about in the CREATE TABLE command

    b. Naming every column you care about in the INSERT command, and simply not naming the column you do not intend to insert data into

c. Using column aliases for columns that you do not wish to insert data

d. Only naming columns that have NOT NULL constraints

e. Only naming columns for which you will enter non-NULL values

13. Which of the following statement or statements are false regarding column names? (Choose all that apply.)

a. Column names must start with an alphabetic character. A name can include numbers or underscores, but must start with a letter.

b. Column names can include letters, numbers, and the underscore character (_).

c. The maximum length of a column name is 20 characters.

d. Certain words represent commands and parameters to Oracle itself, and therefore cannot be used to name a column.

e. Column names must contain all uppercase characters.

14. Which of the following statement or statements are true regarding NULL values? (Choose all that apply.)

a. The columns without data are considered NULL, meaning "empty."

b. CREATE TABLE commands can include NOT NULL specifications for any or all columns, causing Oracle to require inserted or updated records to contain values in those columns before the records will be accepted.

c. When adding or changing data in tables whose columns *do* accept NULLs, you can bypass entering a value in a column by specifying NULL in that column's location in the SQL statement.

d. A NOT NULL specification for a column in a CREATE TABLE command specifies that this column not be shown in the output of a SELECT statement.

e. A NULL specification when inserting data indicates that this column not be shown in the output of a SELECT statement.

15. Which of the following statements are true regarding numbers in SQL commands? (Choose all that apply.)

a. The correct format for using numbers in SQL statements is

NUMBER(*total_number_of_digits, digits_after_a_decimal_point*)

b. Numbers in text columns cannot be added, averaged, or subjected to any other mathematical operation.

c. Numbers must be surrounded by single quotes in an INSERT INTO statement.

d. When creating a number column, you simply specify the maximum number of digits it can hold, along with the number of decimal places its numbers will need.

e. Numbers must be surrounded by single quotes when inside parentheses.

■ Essay Quiz

1. Provide an example of a situation in the world of databases where it is desirable to display the contents of two or more text columns together in one connected string of text, while continuing to store the text pieces in separate columns.

2. How are tables assigned to users in Oracle by default?

3. What types of data can be stored in Oracle tables?

4. What must you do if you wish to place a space between two column names that you are concatenating?

5. In what order are math calculations computed in a SQL statement?

Lab Projects

Lab Project 2.1

Case Study

The Clapham Specialty Store requires a database table in which to record their products as they arrive in the store before they place them on the shelves to be sold. They would like you to create and populate this table according to the following specifications:

- **Columns** SKU (max. 20 characters), Name (max. 80 characters), Package_Size (max. 20 characters), Cost (8-digit number plus 2 characters after the decimal), Location_ID (10-digit number), Quantity_In_Stock (3-digit number), Last_Purchased (date)

- **NULL constraints** All columns allow NULL values except the SKU column

- **Data** 2340588D, Quart of whole milk, 12 quarts per flat, 1.00, 9835138899, 240, August 3, 2003

- 2340548D, 1 Pound of Butter, 30 pounds, 1.25, 9835134839, 240, August 4, 2003

- 2340878P, Romaine Lettuce, 50 heads, .50, 9835138300, 241, August 9, 2003

- 2340392P, Iceberg Lettuce, 20 heads, .30, 98351388301, 241, August 8, 2003

- 2340244P, Red Lettuce, 10 heads, .60, 9835138302, 242, August 7, 2003

- 2340313P, Turnips, 20 indiv., .65, 9835138200, 241, August 8, 2003

- 2340922P, Eggplant, 15 indiv., .60, 9835138204, 241, August 7, 2003

- 2340399P, Red Peppers, 25 indiv., .28, 9835138205, 241, August 5, 2003

- 2340993P, Green Peppers, 25 indiv., .25, 9835138206, 241, August 4, 2003

- 2340235P, Lemons, 50 indiv., .10, 9835138220, 241, August 4, 2003

You will need the Oracle9*i* Database Server with the SQL*Plus tool. Then follow these steps:

1. Create a PRODUCT table according to the preceding specifications.

2. Populate the PRODUCT table with the indicated data.

Lab Project 2.2

Case Study

The Clapham Specialty Store requires a database table in which to record the location where they will place the products in their store. They would like you to create and populate this LOCATION table according to the following specifications:

- A 10-digit location ID must be indicated for each record in the table.

- The department name can be up to 40 characters in length and may or may not be indicated for each record in the table.

- The 3-digit aisle number may or may not be indicated for each record in the table.

- The one-character abbreviation for the left or right side of each aisle may or may not be indicated for each record in the table.

- The shelf name can be up to 10 characters in length and may or may not be indicated for each record in the table.

They have provided you with the following location information for the store:

- There is one designated store location for each department.

- There are eight designated store departments: produce, baked goods, deli, frozen goods, dry goods, dairy, household goods, wines and liquors.

- There are ten aisles.

- There are two sides to every aisle.

- There are three shelves on every aisle, except for aisles in the produce department, where a single shelf is used.

You will need Oracle9*i* Database Server with the SQL*Plus tool. Then do the following:

① Create a LOCATION table according to the preceding specifications.

② Populate the LOCATION table with the following data records:

Columns: Location_ID, Department, Aisle, Side, Shelf
Records: 1234567890, produce, 1, R, single
1234567891, produce, 1, L, single
1234567892, dairy, 2, L, upper
1234567893, dairy, 2, L, middle
1234567894, dairy, 2, L, lower
1234567895, dairy, 2, R, upper
1234567896, dairy, 2, R, middle
1234567897, dairy, 2, R, lower
1234567898, dairy, 3, L, upper
1234567899, dairy, 3, L, middle
1234567800, dairy, 3, L, lower

③ Concatenate the columns in the table so that the results read as follows:

Department is located in aisle number *Aisle* and has the location id of *Location ID*

④ Display the contents of the location table with the following column aliases:

Location_ID—Location Number
Department—Department Name
Aisle—Aisle Name
Side—Aisle Side
Shelf—Shelf Location

Performing Advanced Data Manipulation

"We live in a world of things, and our only connection with them is that we know how to manipulate or to consume them."

—ERICH FROMM (1900–1980), U.S. PSYCHOLOGIST

In this chapter, you will learn how to

- **List the SQL command categories**
- **Limit which table records you select**
- **View records in a different order**
- **Show only unique values**
- **Select from the DUAL table**
- **Modify data in a table**
- **Remove records from a table**
- **Maintain transaction control**

In the previous chapter you stepped out of the realm of theory and were introduced to writing SQL statements through creating tables, inserting records into tables, viewing those records, and then deleting the tables. You learned how Oracle stores text, numbers, and dates in database tables. You performed mathematical calculations, concatenated text, worked with expressions and operators, and viewed the results of NULL and NOT NULL values. You also worked with columns directly—learning how to select specific columns, change the order of columns, and assign aliases to columns.

In this chapter, you will explore more sophisticated ways to work with data. You will learn how to limit selected records to only those satisfying criteria you specify, how to sort records into whatever order you want, and how to make Oracle perform real-time calculations (like a calculator). In addition, you will learn how to change data already in a table, delete data from a table, select unique values from a table, and undo DML operations such as INSERT, UPDATE, and DELETE. You'll have an opportunity to put all this into practice when you work with the case study company, Clapham Specialty Store. Sounds useful, eh? You bet it is.

■ SQL Command Categories

SQL commands fall into functional groups that help make them easy to remember. These groups include

- Data definition
- Data manipulation
- Data control
- Data retrieval
- Transaction control

You've already worked with a few of these commands in the previous chapter and will continue throughout the book. Here's an overview of the categories of commands you will learn to use.

Data Definition

Oracle and all major database programs are database platforms—meaning that they provide an environment that supports working with tables very well, but they don't provide any tables already created for your use. You get to define what data will be stored and in what configuration. SQL provides a collection of commands for these purposes: CREATE, ALTER, DROP, RENAME, and TRUNCATE. These commands fall into a group called Data Definition Language (DDL).

Data Manipulation

Okay, you learned how to create some tables. What's the next step? Putting data into them. SQL provides an INSERT command enabling you to add data to tables. After the data has been inserted, you can change it using the UPDATE command, or remove it using the DELETE command.

This category of commands is called SQL's Data Manipulation Language (DML).

Data Control

Remember the security features discussed in Chapter 1? (I'm sure you do, but if anyone reading over your shoulder doesn't remember it, it's in the section titled "How Is a Database Different from a Spreadsheet?") You can let some users use particular tables while other users cannot by assigning users privileges for specific tables or activities. An object privilege allows a user to perform specified actions on a table (or on other database objects, which will be covered in other parts of this book).

An example of an object privilege would be the ability to insert records into an EMPLOYEE table. In contrast, a system privilege enables a user to perform a particular type of action anywhere in the database. An example of a system privilege would be the ability to insert records into *any* table in the database.

Database objects include items such as tables, table columns, table relationships, constraints, stored procedures, and triggers. These objects will be discussed in detail throughout the textbook.

Database privileges are assigned and removed using the SQL commands GRANT and REVOKE. These commands fall into the category of Data Control Language (DCL).

Data Retrieval

The whole point of putting information into a database is getting it out again in a controlled fashion. There is just one command in this category—SELECT—but it has a wealth of parameters that provide *a lot* of flexibility. The SELECT command is the command you're likely to use more than any other, especially if you plan to use SQL from another programming language like Java or C++.

Transaction Control

Oracle's SQL provides an undo capability enabling you to cancel any recent DML commands before they are applied to the database. (Quick quiz: What commands are DML commands? If you need a reminder, take another look at the section titled "SQL Command Categories," earlier in this chapter.) After performing one or more DML commands, you can either issue a COMMIT command to save your changes to the database, or issue a ROLLBACK command to undo them.

The undo capability provides multiple levels, too: You can reverse just the last DML transaction, or the last several, or whatever level you need. Taking advantage of this multiple-level redo takes a little more forethought than it does in your favorite word processor, however. If you want to be able to undo to intermediate points, you have to mark those points by issuing a SAVEPOINT command at whatever point you want to be able to roll back to.

■ Limiting Which Records You Select

One of the most common functions you will perform when selecting records is getting a specific subset of the records in a table. The subset you want will change constantly in order to answer questions like "Which customers haven't heard from me for more than two weeks?" or "What products have sold more than 100 units in the last 30 days?" Filtering records in this fashion is accomplished by adding a clause to your SELECT statement. The clause is WHERE, and you follow it with a statement of whatever conditions must be true about records in order for them to be shown. The syntax is as follows:

```
SELECT columns FROM table_name WHERE condition(s);
```

As an example, a condition could be that a person's last contact date is more than two weeks ago. Or it could be that a product's sale date is 30 or fewer days before today, and that the total quantity sold is greater than 100. Let's go through some exercises to show how this is done. To give you something to work with, let's create the TEST_PRODUCT table with a few more columns, and place records in it using the following commands:

```
DROP TABLE test_product;

CREATE TABLE test_product (
     product_name      VARCHAR2(25),
     product_price     NUMBER(4,2),
     quantity_on_hand  NUMBER(5,0),
     last_stock_date   DATE
     )
;


INSERT INTO test_product VALUES
     ('Small Widget', 99, 1, '15-JAN-2003');
INSERT INTO test_product VALUES
     ('Medium Wodget', 75, 1000, '15-JAN-2002');
INSERT INTO test_product VALUES
     ('Chrome Phoobar', 50, 100, '15-JAN-2003');
INSERT INTO test_product VALUES
     ('Round Chrome Snaphoo', 25, 10000, null);
```

Filtering Records Based on Numbers

There are several ways you can filter records based on values in columns. You can tell Oracle to show you only records that have a specific value in a column, or to show records with values above or below an amount you specify, or to show records with values between a certain range.

Selecting Records Based on a Single Value

To select all the records from your test table that have a quantity of 1, enter the following command:

```
SELECT *
FROM test_product
WHERE quantity_on_hand = 1;
```

The display you get in response should look like Figure 3.1. Take a moment now and practice this technique by selecting records whose price equals 25.

The next step is to select records containing values above or below a specific amount. For instance, to find products that may need to be restocked, you could enter the following command:

```
SELECT *
FROM test_product
WHERE quantity_on_hand < 500;
```

Enter this command now, and compare your results with those shown in Figure 3.2. The preceding command excludes records whose Quantity_On_Hand is exactly 500. If you want to select

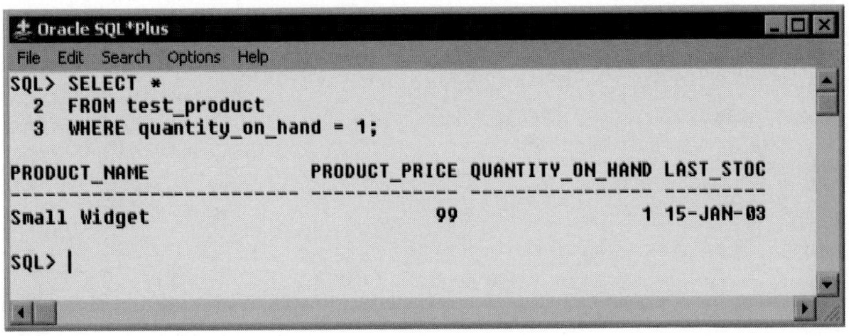

> The SELECT statement with the WHERE condition is one of the most common statements executed when searching for or filtering database information. As you'll see later on in the chapter, it can be expanded with additional clauses.

• **Figure 3.1**   Selecting records with values matching a specific number

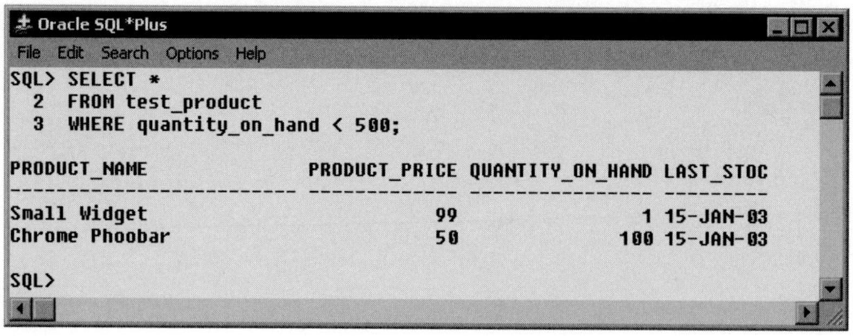

● **Figure 3.2**   Selecting records with values below a specific number

records that are less than or equal to a specific value, you can do so by adding an equal sign after the less-than sign. Try entering the following pair of commands to see the impact of this variation:

```
SELECT *
FROM test_product
WHERE quantity_on_hand < 1000;
```

```
SELECT *
FROM test_product
WHERE quantity_on_hand <= 1000;
```

The results from these two commands, shown in Figure 3.3, demonstrate the effect of adding the equal sign after the less-than sign. The first command, which specifies only records with a quantity on hand less than 1000, does not include the record for the *Medium Wodget* because that record's quantity on hand is exactly 1000, not less. The second command, by specifying that the values can be less than or equal to 1000, causes the record for the *Medium Wodget* to be included.

Extending this technique a bit further, you can select records containing values above a specific amount by using the greater-than sign instead of the less-than sign. Try out the following pair of commands to see this in action:

```
SELECT * FROM test_product
WHERE quantity_on_hand > 1000;
```

```
SELECT * FROM test_product
WHERE quantity_on_hand >= 1000;
```

Selecting Records Based on a Range of Values

The next step is selecting records containing values that fall within a range. To define the range, you simply specify a bottom limit and a top limit. To do this, you will learn a new technique: how to designate two separate conditions that must both be satisfied in order for a record to make it through the filter. It's easy, really: You just connect the two conditions with the word "AND." Try out the following code to see how this works:

```
SELECT * FROM test_product
WHERE   product_price >= 50
        AND
        product_price <= 100;
```

Using AND between two criteria is the classic way to define a range of acceptable values. The AND operator requires both conditions in the statement to be TRUE. It works with practically

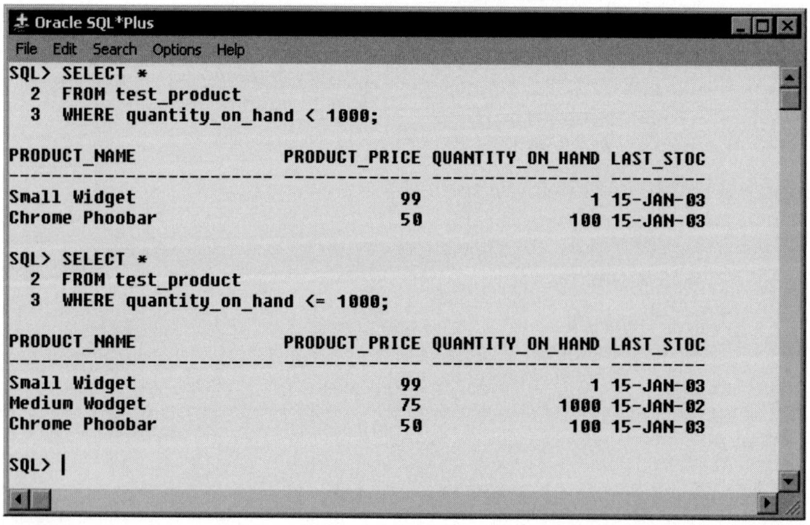

● **Figure 3.3**   Selecting records with values below or equal to a specific number

every database in existence. Oracle offers an alternative way to achieve the same result that is less traditional but easier to read: the BETWEEN clause. Using BETWEEN, the preceding code could be rewritten as follows:

```
SELECT * FROM test_product
WHERE   product_price BETWEEN 50 AND 100;
```

For practice purposes, create a series of SELECT statements now to determine whether the BETWEEN clause is exclusive or inclusive (that is, if the selected records include values that exactly match either of the numbers defined after the BETWEEN).

Excluding Records

What if you need to *exclude* a specific range from the selected records? No problem—just reverse the greater-than and less-than signs, and use OR instead of AND to connect the two conditions. This is shown in the following command:

```
SELECT * FROM test_product
WHERE   product_price < 50
        or
        product_price > 100
;
```

You can also use the BETWEEN clause to exclude a range of values; just precede it with the modifier "NOT." For example:

```
SELECT * FROM test_product
WHERE   product_price NOT BETWEEN 50 AND 100;
```

The preceding example shows how to exclude a range of values from the records selected. If you just want to exclude one specific value, there is an easier way. By using the operators "<>" in your comparison, you state that records must be greater than or less than the value you specify, which is just another way of saying the records must be "not equal to" the value you define. To see how this approach works, enter the following command:

```
SELECT * FROM test_product
WHERE   Product_Price <> 99;
```

This traditional technique is understood by many different databases. Oracle also offers another way to produce the same result: using "!=" instead of "<>". Placing the exclamation point in front of the equal sign changes the meaning from "is equal to" to "is not equal to." To see how this works, enter the following commands:

```
SELECT * FROM test_product
WHERE   product_price = 99;
```

```
SELECT * FROM test_product
WHERE   product_price != 99;
```

As the last few commands demonstrate, using "<>" or "!=" instead of "=" for individual values causes Oracle to display exactly the records it would filter out if a "=" was used instead. You might be surprised how often this is useful.

Selecting Records Based on a Group of Acceptable Values

There may be times when you want to select records containing any of a group of values—for instance, every product whose color is either red *or* green *or* white. You can use the OR operator for this purpose. The OR operator requires either condition in the statement to be true for any record to be selected. Examine the following command (don't try to enter this one—it is for example purposes only):

```
SELECT * FROM product
WHERE   COLOR = 'Red'
        OR
        COLOR = 'Green'
        OR
        COLOR = 'White'
;
```

However, this approach will quickly get tedious if you have large number values that can be matched. Instead, you can get the same result more easily by using the IN function, as demonstrated with this code (also an example only):

```
SELECT * FROM product
WHERE   COLOR IN ('Red', 'Green', 'White')
;
```

Note that the IN function is followed by an opening parenthesis, a list of acceptable values separated by commas, and then a closing parenthesis. Now let's look at how to apply the IN function to the TEST_PRODUCT table you have built. Enter the following command to see how it works:

```
SELECT * FROM test_product
WHERE   product_price IN (50, 99);
```

Order of Precedence

You've learned that using the AND operator requires both conditions in the statement to be TRUE. You've also learned that using the OR operator requires either condition in the statement to be true for any record to be selected. But what if you were to use both the AND and OR operators in the same statement? How does Oracle evaluate the statement to determine what operator has precedence? Enter the following command to see how this works:

```
SELECT product_name, product_price, quantity_on_hand
FROM test_product
WHERE product_name = 'Small Widget'
      OR product_name = 'Medium Wodget'
      AND product_price > 80
;
```

As you can see, there are two conditions to the statement. The first condition is that the Product_Name is Medium Wodget and the Product_Price is greater than 80. The second condition is that the Product_Name is Small Widget. When dealing with operator precedence, Oracle evaluates AND operators before OR operators. Therefore, Oracle reads the SELECT statement as "The product name is Medium Wodget AND the product price is greater than 80, OR the product name is Small Widget." The result set would include only the product named Small Widget, as the table does not contain a record for a product named Medium Wodget that has a price greater than 80.

If you want to affect the order of precedence, you can use the addition of parentheses to your SELECT statement. For example:

```
SELECT product_name, product_price, quantity_on_hand
FROM test_product
WHERE (product_name = 'Small Widget'
       OR
       product_name = 'Medium Wodget'
       )
       AND product_price > 80
;
```

Now the first condition of the SELECT statement is that the product name is Small Widget or Medium Wodget. The second condition of the statement is that the product price is greater than 80. So as you can see, you can force the priority of the operator precedence to filter the result set to your liking.

Filtering Records Based on Text

Now that you know how to create WHERE clause expressions evaluating numbers, it's easy to apply the same techniques to evaluating text columns. To find records containing values that match a specific text string, simply include a WHERE clause stating that the appropriate column equals the text string (which must be surrounded by single quotes, as all text is in SQL commands). Try the following command to see this in action:

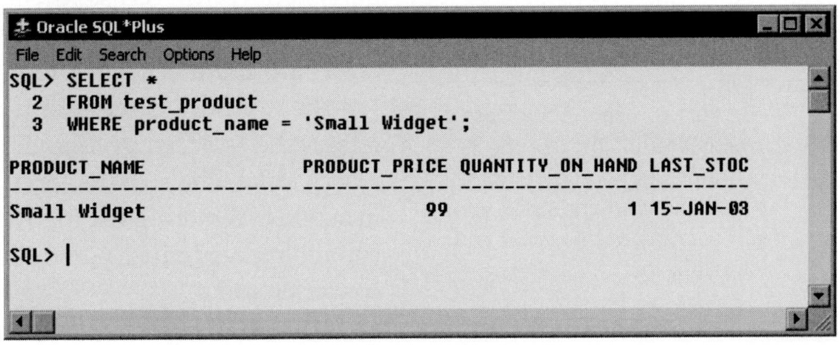

● **Figure 3.4**   Selecting records matching an explicit string

```
SELECT *
FROM    test_product
WHERE   product_name ='Small Widget';
```

In response, you should get a display matching the one shown in Figure 3.4.

You can also specify a list of values to match by employing the IN function. The following command demonstrates this technique:

```
SELECT *
FROM    test_product
WHERE   product_name IN ('Small Widget', 'Round Chrome Snaphoo');
```

Using Wildcards

When searching text, it is often useful to be able to find a small bit of text anywhere within a column—for instance, to find all records that contain the word "Chrome" anywhere within the product name, such as "Chrome

Phoobar" or "Round Chrome Snaphoo." You can accomplish this by using wildcards to represent the portion of text that can vary. For instance, to find every record in your TEST_ PRODUCT table whose product name starts with "Chrome," use the following command:

```
SELECT * FROM test_product
WHERE   product_name LIKE 'Chrome%';
```

Note that the word "Chrome" is followed by a percent sign (%). The percent sign is the wildcard character, and when it follows a text string, it means "anything can follow this text string, and it will still be a match."

You may have noticed, however, that the previous example did not return every record that has the word "Chrome" in its product name. That's because in the other record containing "Chrome" there is text before the word "Chrome" as well as after. To include both records in your results, place percent sign wildcards before *and* after the word "Chrome," as demonstrated in the following command:

```
SELECT * FROM test_product
WHERE   product_name LIKE '%Chrome%';
```

The results of the previous two commands should look like Figure 3.5. One important fact to point out here is that while the Oracle commands themselves are not case-sensitive—you will get the same result from SELECT, select, or SeLeCt—the text you put between single quotes for comparison purposes *is* case-sensitive. Searching for "Chrome" will not return records containing the word "chrome" or "CHROME." You will learn about a way around this in Chapter 5.

The % wildcard represents any amount of text—any number of characters can be replaced by a single % wildcard. There is also a wildcard that replaces just a single character: the underscore (_). You can see this wildcard in action by entering the following command, which retrieves every record containing a product name that contains the letter "W" followed by any character and a "d":

```
SELECT * FROM test_product
WHERE   product_name LIKE '%W_d%';
```

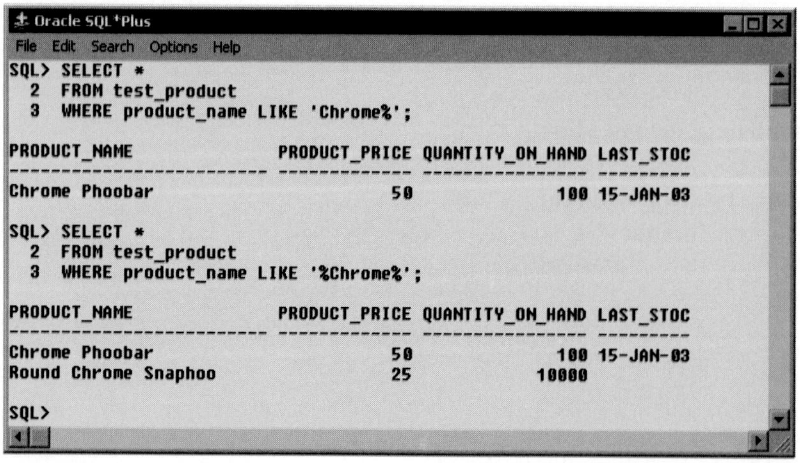

> Be sure to use the wildcards correctly. If you confuse the % and underscore (_) characters, the data that will appear in your result set may not be what you are looking for.

Figure 3.5   Using wildcards to find text

Filtering Records Based on Dates

Selecting records based on the dates they contain works very similarly to selecting based on numbers. Since the values you're comparing are dates, however, you will need to remember to surround any date you specify with single quotes, just as you did when you inserted them. For example, to find every record in your TEST_PRODUCT table whose stock date is January 15, 2003, enter the following command:

```
SELECT * FROM test_product
WHERE  last_stock_date = '15-JAN-2003';
```

The results you see should match those shown in Figure 3.6. You can also specify years using two digits, as demonstrated in this command:

```
SELECT * FROM test_product
WHERE  last_stock_date = '15-JAN-03';
```

If you want to find records containing dates before or after a specific date, you can do so using the familiar greater-than and less-than signs, as demonstrated in this code:

```
SELECT * FROM test_product
WHERE  last_stock_date > '31-DEC-2002';
```

You can also use the BETWEEN clause to find dates that fall within a range, as shown in the following command:

```
SELECT * FROM test_product
WHERE  last_stock_date BETWEEN '01-JAN-2003' and '31-DEC-2003';
```

By adding the NOT clause, you can identify a range to be excluded rather than included:

```
SELECT * FROM test_product
WHERE  last_stock_date NOT BETWEEN '01-JAN-2003' and '31-DEC-2003';
```

Selecting Records Based on NULL Values

You may have noticed that even though the last two commands contain exactly opposite criteria, their combined outputs do not show every record in the database. How could there be a record that does not match either criterion, when one criterion is the opposite of the other? This situation arises when the database contains records with NULL values in a column named in the WHERE clause. A NULL value does not match any criterion, except one that checks for a NULL value. You can check for a NULL value by placing IS NULL in your WHERE clause, as shown in this command:

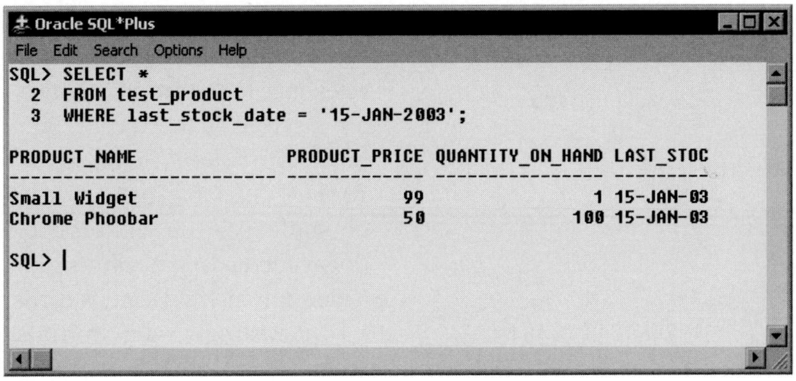

• **Figure 3.6**   Filtering records based on date

```
SELECT * FROM test_product
WHERE  last_stock_date IS NULL;
```

To find records that contain data in a specific column, use IS NOT NULL, as shown in this code:

```
SELECT * FROM test_product
WHERE  last_stock_date IS NOT NULL;
```

Try both of the previous commands, and compare the output you get with that shown in Figure 3.7.

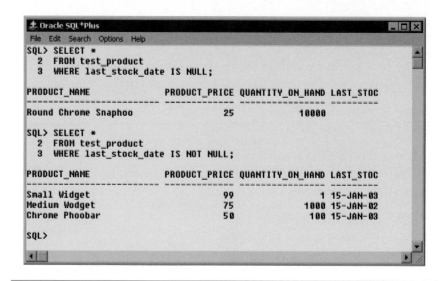

```
Oracle SQL*Plus                                          _ □ ×
File  Edit  Search  Options  Help
SQL> SELECT *
  2  FROM test_product
  3  WHERE last_stock_date IS NULL;

PRODUCT_NAME                PRODUCT_PRICE QUANTITY_ON_HAND LAST_STOC
--------------------------- ------------- ---------------- ---------
Round Chrome Snaphoo                   25            10000

SQL> SELECT *
  2  FROM test_product
  3  WHERE last_stock_date IS NOT NULL;

PRODUCT_NAME                PRODUCT_PRICE QUANTITY_ON_HAND LAST_STOC
--------------------------- ------------- ---------------- ---------
Small Widget                           99                1 15-JAN-03
Medium Wodget                          75             1000 15-JAN-02
Chrome Phoobar                         50              100 15-JAN-03

SQL>
```

● **Figure 3.7**   Filtering for NULL values

The parameters IS NULL and IS NOT NULL work in expressions evaluating numbers and text, too; in fact, they work for any type of column.

■ Viewing Records in a Different Order

Most of the time, the order in which data is inserted into a table bears little relevance to the order in which you want to view it. For instance, purchases are inserted as they occur, but you may want to see them later in order by product or store. Similarly, a company's employees are entered into its EMPLOYEE table in the order the people are hired, but when you view a list of employees you will probably want to see them sorted by name and/or department. To get results like these, you need to know how to control the order in which selected records are displayed.

Interestingly, you won't actually change the order of records within whatever table they're stored. At least not very often—doing so is a tedious, time-consuming task that few applications benefit from. Instead, you just change the order in which they're shown to you. Oracle fulfills this request by sorting a copy of the selected records before displaying them, and then displaying the sorted copy. This allows you (and thousands of other people connected to the database) to display records in any order you want without constantly rewriting tables with newly re-sorted versions.

 Cross Check

Filtering Records

Now that you've been introduced to filtering records, take a moment to check your knowledge by answering the following questions:

1. How can you filter records containing dates before or after a specific date?

2. What does the % wildcard represent?

Introduction to Relational Databases and SQL Programming

Sorting on Individual Columns

To change the order in which records are displayed, you just add an ORDER BY clause to your SELECT command. In the ORDER BY clause, you identify one or more columns that Oracle should sort the records by. The ORDER BY clause's syntax is as follows:

```
SELECT * FROM table_name ORDER BY column_to_sort_by;
```

To see this in action, enter the following command:

```
SELECT * FROM test_product ORDER BY product_price;
```

In response, you should see a display similar to the one shown in Figure 3.8. Experiment with this technique further now by writing a SELECT command that sorts records by their Quantity_On_Hand.

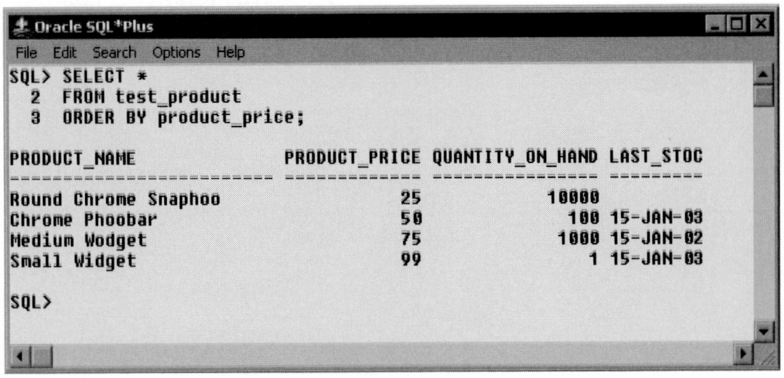

Sorting on Multiple Columns

If you sort your TEST_PRODUCT table by the Last_Stock_Date column, you will see that a problem becomes evident: Two of the table's records contain the same last stock date. How will Oracle know what order to place those records in? You can control it by specifying a second sort column in your SELECT command's ORDER BY clause.

Figure 3.8 Sorting records by a single column

To see this in action, you will write a command that sorts product records by stock date, and within a given stock date, by product name. The command is as follows:

```
SELECT * FROM test_product
ORDER BY last_stock_date, product_name;
```

The results you see from this command should match what is shown in Figure 3.9. Note that to define two sort columns; you simply separate the column

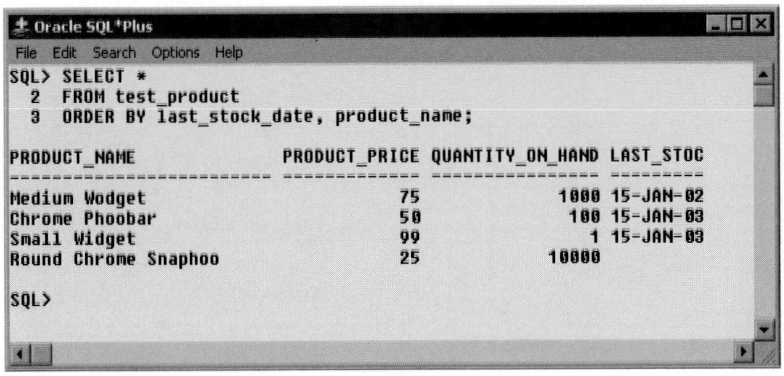

Figure 3.9 Sorting records by two columns

When you specify two or more sort columns in an ORDER BY clause, the columns are not treated equally. The first column you name is the primary sort column, and it will determine all sorting until it reaches two or more records that have the same value in that column. Then the second sort column is applied to those records. If any of them have identical values in the second sort column, Oracle looks to see if you have defined a third sort column, and so on.

names with a comma. This is the same method you used to separate column names when you wanted to select specific columns from a table.

In fact, let's combine the two techniques: selecting columns by name, and sorting records by column. In the previous exercise, the records were sorted based on the rightmost column shown. That can easily confuse someone else looking at the data, because they will probably look at the first column, see that it isn't in order, and assume that the records are in no order whatsoever. Generally, you want the order of columns to reflect the order the records are sorted in: the leftmost column is the primary sort key, the next column is the secondary sort key (if a secondary sort key is needed), and so on. You can easily make this happen with the TEST_PRODUCT table. Try out the following command as an example:

```
SELECT    last_stock_date,
          product_name,
          product_price,
          quantity_on_hand
FROM      test_product
ORDER BY  last_stock_date,
          product_name
;
```

Your results should match those shown in Figure 3.10.

You can also sort columns in descending order, so that larger values are on top. While this is rarely useful for text columns, it is often handy for number or date columns. For instance, you could find the highest-priced products in your TEST_PRODUCT table by entering the following command:

```
SELECT * FROM test_product ORDER BY product_price DESC;
```

You can even sort by a column that isn't being selected. For instance, try out this command:

```
SELECT product_name FROM test_product ORDER BY quantity_on_hand;
```

As a result, you see a list of product names. But without a column showing the quantity on hand, it's impossible to tell why the product names are sorted the way they are. This is why you will usually want to include the sort column in the columns displayed and, as mentioned earlier, put those columns in the same order as the sort order.

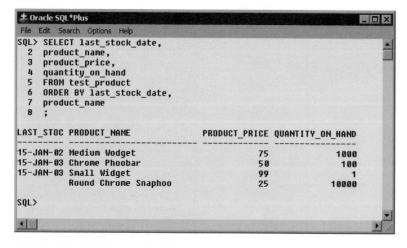

● Figure 3.10 Specifying column order to reflect sort order

■ Showing Only Unique Values

There will probably be times when you want to know what values a column contains, but you only want to see one instance of each value. For instance, if you need to know which salesperson sold products during a particular period of time, there would be no point in having the salesperson's ID shown repeatedly, once for every sale made. You just want to know who is in that group and who isn't. Therefore, you only need to see one row for every salesperson who has at least one sales record within the timeframe you have specified. This type of approach is useful for answering questions like "Who is scheduled to work next week?" and "What products sold this weekend?"

Cross Check

Changing the Order of Records

Now that you've been introduced to changing the order of records, take a moment to check your knowledge by answering the following questions:

1. When ordering records in a result by more than one column, how does Oracle know what order to place the records in?

2. How can you sort columns in descending order, so that larger values are on top?

To see this technique in action, you're going to re-create a transaction table and populate it with records. Then you will see how to get unique values out of the table. To create and populate the table, enter the following commands:

```
DROP TABLE test_purchase;

CREATE TABLE test_purchase (
    product_name  VARCHAR2(25),
    quantity      NUMBER(4,2),
    purchase_date DATE,
    salesperson   VARCHAR2(3)
    )
;

INSERT INTO test_purchase VALUES
    ('Small Widget', 1, '14-JUL-2003', 'CA');
INSERT INTO test_purchase VALUES
    ('Medium Wodget', 75, '14-JUL-2003', 'BB');
INSERT INTO test_purchase VALUES
    ('Chrome Phoobar', 2, '14-JUL-2003', 'GA');
INSERT INTO test_purchase VALUES
    ('Small Widget', 8, '15-JUL-2003', 'GA');
INSERT INTO test_purchase VALUES
    ('Medium Wodget', 20, '15-JUL-2003', 'LB');
INSERT INTO test_purchase VALUES
    ('Chrome Phoobar', 2, '16-JUL-2003', 'CA');
INSERT INTO test_purchase VALUES
    ('Round Snaphoo', 25, '16-JUL-2003', 'LB');
INSERT INTO test_purchase VALUES
    ('Chrome Phoobar', 2, '17-JUL-2003', 'BB');
```

Selecting unique values from a table is similar to selecting a regular list of values; you just add the modifier DISTINCT to the SELECT command, as shown in the following pair of commands:

```
SELECT     product_name
FROM       test_purchase
ORDER BY product_name;

SELECT DISTINCT product_name
FROM            test_purchase
ORDER BY        product_name;
```

The DISTINCT and UNIQUE modifiers produce identical results. Because DISTINCT tends to be more common, it is used throughout this book.

After you have entered both of these commands, compare the results you get with those shown in Figure 3.11.

You can also get the same results by using the modifier UNIQUE instead of DISTINCT, as shown in the following command:

```
SELECT UNIQUE product_name
FROM           test_purchase
ORDER BY       product_name;
```

Selecting unique values is especially useful when you limit the records to those matching a criterion that is important to you. For instance, to see who made sales during the first half of July, you could use the following command:

```
SELECT DISTINCT salesperson
FROM           test_purchase
WHERE          purchase_date BETWEEN '01-JUL-2003' AND '15-JUL-2003'
ORDER BY       salesperson;
```

■ Selecting from the DUAL Table

In Chapter 2 you saw that it was possible to perform math on values stored in a database by defining the equation in your SELECT statement. The examples you tried in that chapter included the following (which will not work now, by the way, because the table they refer to no longer has a Sales_Tax column):

```
SELECT product_name, product_price + sales_tax FROM test_purchase;
SELECT product_name, 100 - product_price FROM test_purchase;
SELECT product_name, sales_tax / product_price FROM test_purchase;
```

Inside Information

The DUAL Table

DUAL is a table automatically created by Oracle when it is installed. It has one column, DUMMY, defined to be VARCHAR2(1), and contains one row with a value 'X'. DUAL is in the schema of the user SYS, but is accessible by the name DUAL to all users. Selecting from the DUAL table is useful for computing a constant expression with the SELECT statement. Because DUAL has only one row, the constant is returned only once.

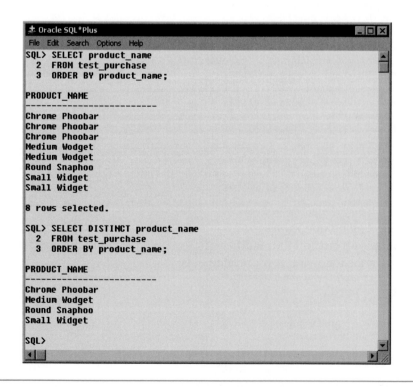

• **Figure 3.11**   Selecting unique values from a table

You can take this one step further and have the SELECT statement specify all of the values that should be used in the calculation, meaning that no values are derived from the table at all. To see this in action, try this command, which calculates the result of increasing the value 18 by 5 percent:

```
SELECT 18*1.05 FROM test_purchase;
```

As your display will undoubtedly show, the answer is getting calculated, all right—calculated once for every record in the table. Wouldn't it be convenient if there was a table setup that you knew would always have just one record? Well, the folks who designed Oracle thought about that, too, and in response they designed Oracle's installation process to create a table called DUAL that is available to all users.

To see how DUAL is constructed, enter the following commands:

```
DESC DUAL;
SELECT * FROM DUAL;
```

As you can see, the DUAL table contains one column (named DUMMY) and one row (whose value is simply X). The DUAL table's data is never meant to be used directly. Instead, the DUAL table is provided to support on-the-fly queries like the one you just did. Try it out by entering the following command:

```
SELECT 18*1.05 FROM DUAL;
```

In response, you should see just one instance of the answer of 18.9 displayed, as shown in Figure 3.12.

Cross Check

Working with Unique Values

Now that you've been introduced to unique values, take a moment to check your knowledge by answering the following questions:

1. List the two modifiers that are used to select unique values from a table.

2. Indicate the proper syntax for a command that selects a unique product name from the products table and order the results by the product name.

It is very important that you include a WHERE condition in your UPDATE command. If you do not include a WHERE condition, every record in the table will be updated!

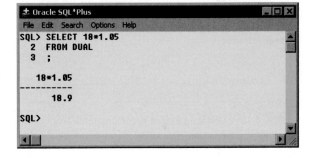

● **Figure 3.12**   Selecting values from DUAL

■ Modifying Data in a Table

It's very easy to change data in an Oracle table. The command to perform this operation is UPDATE, and its syntax is as follows:

```
UPDATE table_name SET column_name = new_value WHERE condition;
```

For instance, to change all products named "Small Widget" to "Large Widget" in your TEST_PURCHASE table, enter the following command:

```
SELECT * FROM test_purchase;

UPDATE test_purchase
SET    product_name = 'Large Widget'
WHERE  product_name = 'Small Widget';

SELECT * FROM test_purchase;
```

Now select all the records in the TEST_PURCHASE table. Your display should match Figure 3.13.

```
+ Oracle SQL*Plus                                    _ [] X
File  Edit  Search  Options  Help
SQL> SELECT *
  2  FROM test_purchase
  3  ;

PRODUCT_NAME               QUANTITY PURCHASE_ SAL
------------------------- ---------- --------- ---
Small Widget                      1 14-JUL-03 CA
Medium Wodget                    75 14-JUL-03 BB
Chrome Phoobar                    2 14-JUL-03 GA
Small Widget                      8 15-JUL-03 GA
Medium Wodget                    20 15-JUL-03 LB
Chrome Phoobar                    2 16-JUL-03 CA
Round Snaphoo                    25 16-JUL-03 LB
Chrome Phoobar                    2 17-JUL-03 BB

8 rows selected.

SQL> UPDATE test_purchase
  2  SET product_name = 'Large Widget'
  3  WHERE product_name = 'Small Widget'
  4  ;

2 rows updated.

SQL> SELECT *
  2  FROM test_purchase
  3  ;

PRODUCT_NAME               QUANTITY PURCHASE_ SAL
------------------------- ---------- --------- ---
Large Widget                      1 14-JUL-03 CA
Medium Wodget                    75 14-JUL-03 BB
Chrome Phoobar                    2 14-JUL-03 GA
Large Widget                      8 15-JUL-03 GA
Medium Wodget                    20 15-JUL-03 LB
Chrome Phoobar                    2 16-JUL-03 CA
Round Snaphoo                    25 16-JUL-03 LB
Chrome Phoobar                    2 17-JUL-03 BB

8 rows selected.

SQL> |
```

• **Figure 3.13** Updating data in specific records

■ Removing Records from a Table

The last of the fundamental skills you need while working with tables is the ability to delete records. The DELETE command uses the following syntax:

```
DELETE FROM table_name WHERE condition
```

The DELETE command is easy to use—maybe too easy. Be sure you're thinking about the condition(s) you specify when using this command!

Deleting Rows Matching Specific Criteria

Let's start our experimentation with this command by deleting the newest records in your TEST_PURCHASE table. Enter the following command to remove all records whose purchase date is later than July 15, 2003:

```
SELECT * FROM test_purchase;

DELETE FROM test_purchase
WHERE purchase_date > '15-JUL-2003';

SELECT * FROM test_purchase;
```

Your results should match those shown in Figure 3.14.

You can delete records using any column or columns in your condition clause. For instance, try the following command to delete the "Large Widget" records:

```
DELETE FROM test_purchase
WHERE product_name = 'Large Widget';
```

Select all the records once again, and you will see that the only remaining records are those in which wodgets or phoobars were purchased July 15 or earlier.

Deleting All Rows

The final variation of deleting records is deleting all rows from a table. There are two ways to do this: using the DELETE command without specifying a WHERE condition, and using an entirely new command: TRUNCATE .

Deleting Records Without Specifying Criteria

The syntax for deleting all records in a table is as follows:

```
DELETE FROM table_name;
```

While this command is easy to read and understand, it has a major drawback: Even though it says that every record should be deleted, it still forces Oracle to read every row before deleting it, as it would if you had included a WHERE condition. This can be extremely time-consuming, wasting both your time and server resources. If you want to delete all records in a table, a more efficient method is to use the TRUNCATE command.

Truncating a Table

The advantage offered by the TRUNCATE command is speed. When Oracle executes this command, it does not evaluate the existing records within a table; it basically chops them off. In addition to speed, this command provides the added benefit of automatically freeing up the table space that the truncated records previously occupied. This is an advantage in that a DELETE does not release space.

The syntax of the command is

```
TRUNCATE TABLE table_name;
```

To see this in action, truncate your TEST_PURCHASE table and then view its contents, using the commands that follow:

```
TRUNCATE TABLE test_purchase;
SELECT * FROM test_purchase;
```

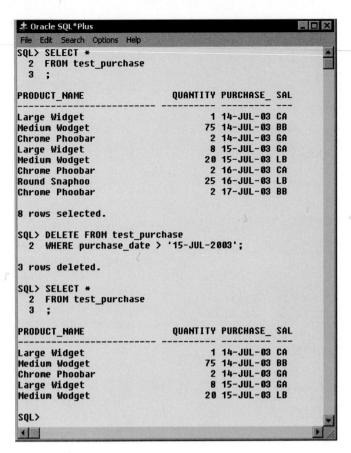

● **Figure 3.14**   Deleting records based on date

 The TRUNCATE command is not reversible! Use it only when you really mean it!

■ Transaction Control

So far in this chapter, you have created and dropped tables, inserted and deleted records, and generally done whatever you wanted, without having to think about how your actions may impact others. In real life you will be working with tables containing data that other people care about, and the changes you make will impact other users. To work responsibly, you need to understand how Oracle applies the changes you make. One of the immediate benefits of this is that you learn how to use Oracle's "undo" facility.

Undoing DML Transactions

When you insert, update, or delete data in a table, Oracle does not actually apply those changes to the table immediately. It appears to you that the changes are applied right away; if you do a SELECT command, the changes you made are reflected in the output. But those changes are being held in temporary storage, and will only be applied to the actual table in response to one of several different catalysts. You'll see what those catalysts are soon; for now, let's see how things work *before* one of those catalysts has occurred.

If you have just started reading in this chapter and don't yet have a TEST_PURCHASE table to practice with, create one now using the following command:

```
CREATE TABLE test_purchase (
    product_name   VARCHAR2(25),
    quantity       NUMBER(4,2),
    purchase_date  DATE,
    salesperson    VARCHAR2(3)
    )
;
```

Oracle's undo capability comes via the ROLLBACK command. When you roll back one or more transactions, you request that the Oracle Database Management System not apply them to the database. To see this in action, enter the following commands:

```
INSERT INTO test_purchase VALUES
    ('Small Widget', 1, '14-JUL-2003', 'CA');
INSERT INTO test_purchase VALUES
    ('Medium Wodget', 75, '14-JUL-2003', 'BB');

SELECT * FROM test_purchase;

ROLLBACK;

SELECT * FROM test_purchase;
```

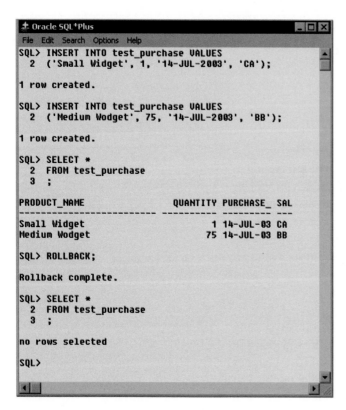

• **Figure 3.15**   Rolling back data changes

Compare your results with those shown in Figure 3.15. The important part of this exercise is that your first SELECT returned records, while the second SELECT did not. The ROLLBACK command you issued removed the records from your local storage, and kept them from ever being written to the database table for permanent storage. The net result is as if you never entered those two records.

The ability demonstrated by the ROLLBACK command is a useful undo mechanism, and it isn't limited to just one level of undo. By pairing ROLLBACK with another command, SAVEPOINT, you may specify any number of points to which a ROLLBACK command can return. The syntax of the SAVEPOINT command is as follows:

```
SAVEPOINT savepoint_name;
```

Why would you need multiple return points? Flexibility. If you have a large batch of commands to execute, you can put a savepoint after the end of each logical group of commands, and if the next group of commands is unsatisfactory for any reason, you can still roll back to the most recent savepoint and apply your changes up to that point in the database.

To see this in action, you'll enter a series of records and place a separate savepoint after each one. Then you will roll back to each savepoint, and see how that affects the records returned to you by SELECT statements. The commands to do this are as follows:

```
INSERT INTO test_purchase VALUES
    ('Small Widget', 1, '14-JUL-2003', 'CA');
SAVEPOINT a;
INSERT INTO test_purchase VALUES
    ('Medium Wodget', 75, '14-JUL-2003', 'BB');
SAVEPOINT sp_2;
INSERT INTO test_purchase VALUES
    ('Chrome Phoobar', 2, '14-JUL-2003', 'GA');
SAVEPOINT third;
INSERT INTO test_purchase VALUES
    ('Small Widget', 8, '15-JUL-2003', 'GA');
SAVEPOINT final_sp;
INSERT INTO test_purchase VALUES
    ('Medium Wodget', 20, '15-JUL-2003', 'LB');
SELECT * FROM test_purchase;
ROLLBACK TO final_sp;
SELECT * FROM test_purchase;
ROLLBACK TO third;
SELECT * FROM test_purchase;
ROLLBACK TO sp_2;
SELECT * FROM test_purchase;
ROLLBACK TO a;
SELECT * FROM test_purchase;
ROLLBACK;
SELECT * FROM test_purchase;
```

Notice that the savepoint names in the preceding example don't really follow a methodical pattern. Actually, each name is an example of what could be a methodical pattern if it were applied to every savepoint name in the session. Savepoint names are just labels, so they can be anything you want. It is up to you to select savepoint names that make it obvious what data each savepoint covers. Savepoint names follow conventions similar to those for tables and columns: a maximum length of 30 characters, and the first character must be a letter.

Now that you know how to undo changes, you're ready to learn how to make changes permanent. The command to do this is COMMIT. Because the COMMIT command causes Oracle to write your changes to the database table—which renders rollbacks impossible—any savepoints present at the time of the commit are cleared. To see this in action, enter the following commands:

```
INSERT INTO test_purchase VALUES
    ('Small Widget', 1, '14-JUL-2003', 'CA');
SAVEPOINT A;
INSERT INTO test_purchase VALUES
    ('Medium Wodget', 75, '14-JUL-2003', 'BB');
SAVEPOINT B;
INSERT INTO test_purchase VALUES
    ('Chrome Phoobar', 2, '14-JUL-2003', 'GA');
SAVEPOINT C;
INSERT INTO test_purchase VALUES
    ('Small Widget', 8, '15-JUL-2003', 'GA');
SAVEPOINT D;
INSERT INTO test_purchase VALUES
    ('Medium Wodget', 20, '15-JUL-2003', 'LB');
```

```
COMMIT;

ROLLBACK TO D;

SELECT * FROM test_purchase;
```

Your results should match those shown in Figure 3.16. Notice that Oracle complains about the ROLLBACK command, telling you it's never heard of a savepoint named "d," even though you created one. Oracle has forgotten about your savepoint because they were all cleared when the data changes were committed to the table.

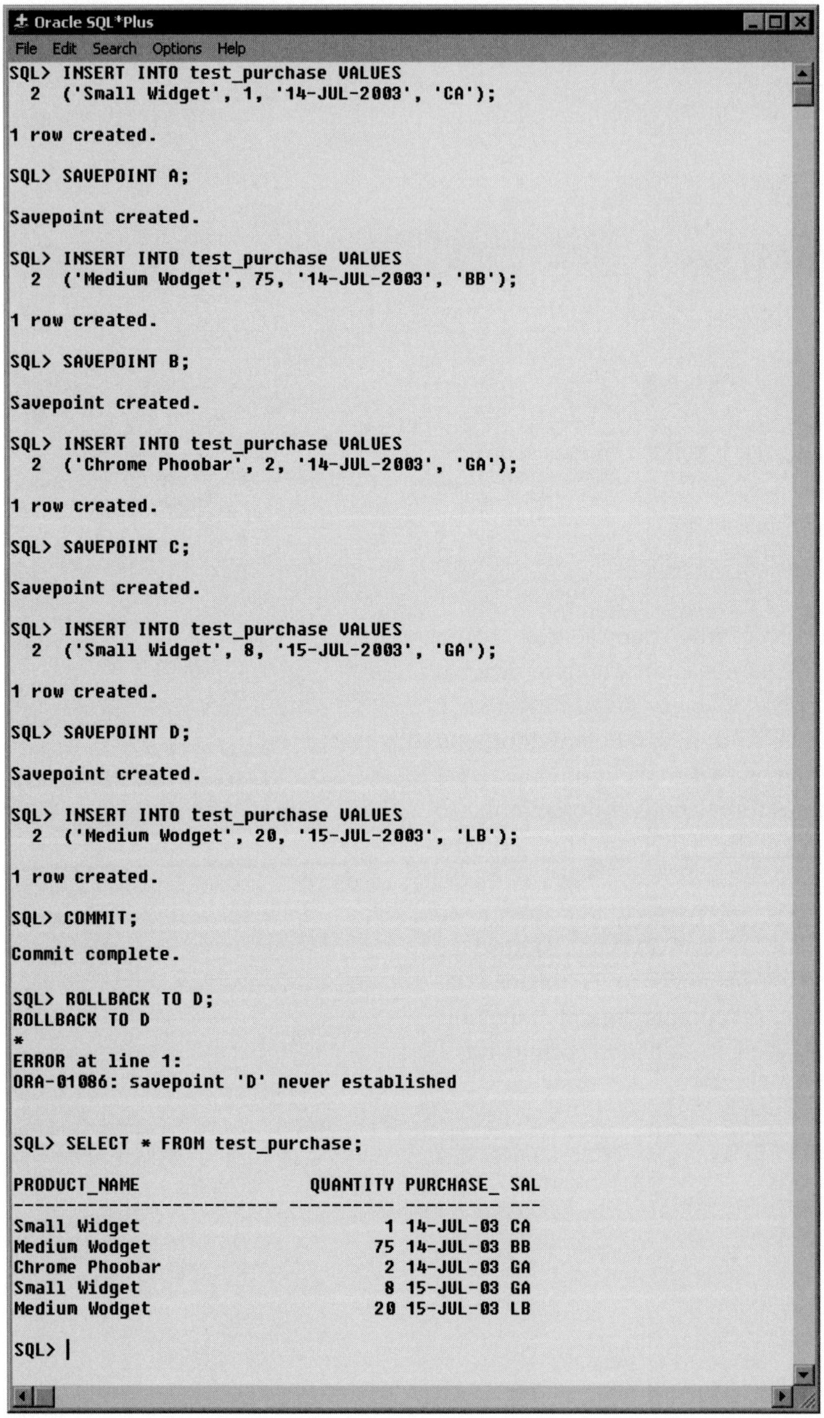

Making Data Available to Others

Because the COMMIT command causes your changes to be written to the database shared by all other users, committing your work affects the data other users see. When you issue the COMMIT command, it makes your changes visible to other users. The flip side of that fact is that the changes you make will not be visible to other users until you commit those changes—you could insert a thousand new records, change a thousand more, and then delete another thousand, and none of those changes would be reflected in other users' SELECT statements until you commit your work.

If you want to test this for yourself, you can do so by opening a second SQL*Plus window (using the same username and password you used for the first one), changing some data in your first SQL*Plus window, and looking for the results of those changes in the second SQL*Plus window. Go ahead and open a second SQL*Plus window now, and enter the commands shown in Table 3.1 in each window.

The final result for the second window should be similar to what is shown in Figure 3.17.

● **Figure 3.16** Committing changes to a table

Table 3.1	Commands to Enter in SQL* Plus Windows
Commands for First SQL*Plus Window	**Commands for Second SQL*Plus Window**
`SELECT * FROM test_purchase;`	
	`SELECT * FROM test_purchase;`

`INSERT INTO test_purchase`
`    VALUES ('Round Snaphoo', 5,`
`    '16-JUL-2003', 'CA');`	

	`SELECT * FROM test_purchase;`
`COMMIT;`	
	`SELECT * FROM test_purchase` `ORDER BY product_name;`

Implicit and Explicit COMMITs

By doing the exercises up to this point, you have performed several COMMIT commands. Entering the command explicitly, as you have, is one way to commit changes to the database—and there are other ways, too. Certain Oracle commands execute a COMMIT without waiting for you to tell them to—in other words, implicitly—before the new command is executed. To be specific, any DDL command (such as CREATE TABLE or DROP TABLE) will implicitly commit any unsaved data before executing the command's stated function. In addition, logging out of Oracle (or simply closing SQL*Plus) will automatically (implicitly) commit your changes.

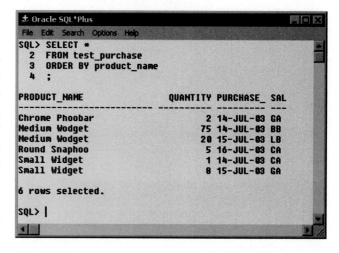

● Figure 3.17   Impact of the COMMIT command from a first database session on a second database session

☑ **Cross Check**

Explicit and Implicit COMMIT statements

Now that you've been introduced to explicit and implicit COMMIT statements, take a moment to check your knowledge by answering the following questions:

1. What type of commit is indicated by simply closing SQL*Plus without indicating the COMMIT command?

2. Will the DROP TABLE command explicitly commit the database change?

Performing Advanced Data Manipulation

Case Study

The Clapham Specialty Store has asked you to create a customer table for their database and populate it with data. They have given you four customer records to add to their database.

For this exercise, you will need Oracle 9*i* Database Server with the SQL*Plus tool.

Step 1

Execute the following command to create the CUSTOMER table:

```
DROP TABLE customer;

CREATE TABLE customer (
    customer_id  NUMBER(10) NOT NULL,
    first_name  VARCHAR2(40) NULL,
    last_name VARCHAR2(40) NULL,
    address VARCHAR2(200) NULL,
    phone VARCHAR2(10) NULL
    )
;
```

Step 2

Populate the CUSTOMER table with records by executing the following commands:

```
INSERT INTO customer VALUES (90003255, 'Brian', 'Smith', '125 Main Street',
'2025551114');

INSERT INTO customer VALUES (90003467, 'Dean', 'Jones', '188 Willow Avenue',
'2025551498');

INSERT INTO customer VALUES (90003257, 'James', 'Morton', '985 Washington
Street', '2025558422');

INSERT INTO customer VALUES (90003456, 'Krystin', 'Sliwiany', '955 Hudson
Street', '2025557399');
```

Step 3

Edit Brian Smith's customer record by changing the member number as follows:

```
UPDATE  customer
SET     customer_id = 90003259
WHERE   customer_id = 90003255;
```

Step 4

Delete the James Morton member record by executing the command:

```
DELETE FROM customer
WHERE last_name = 'Morton';
```

You should have successfully created and updated the CUSTOMER table for the Clapham Specialty Store.

Chapter 3 Review

◾ Chapter Summary

After reading this chapter and completing the Step-by-Step tutorial and Cross Checks, you should understand the following facts about advanced data manipulation:

List the SQL Command Categories

- SQL commands can be divided into categories based on the types of functions they perform.

- Data Definition Language (DDL) commands are used to define how you want your data to be stored; these commands include CREATE, ALTER, DROP, RENAME, and TRUNCATE.

- Data Manipulation Language (DML) commands enable you to work with your data; they include INSERT, UPDATE, and DELETE.

- Data Control Language (DCL) commands control who can do what within the database, with object privileges controlling access to individual database objects and system privileges providing global privileges across the entire database. DCL commands include GRANT and REVOKE.

- For data retrieval, SELECT is the sole command, but its many variations are likely to make it the most frequently used command in your arsenal.

- To control transactions, SQL provides the COMMIT command to save recent DML changes to the database; the ROLLBACK command to undo recent DML changes; and the SAVEPOINT command to let you undo some, but not all, of a string of DML commands.

Limit Which Table Records You Select

- You began by learning how to limit which records Oracle returns by including a WHERE clause in your SELECT statements.

- When filtering with a WHERE clause, you can use a variety of comparison operators in the filtering condition, including =, !=, >>, <, <<>, >>=, <, BETWEEN, IN, AND, OR, and NOT.

- When searching text, you can specify wildcards in your search string by using "_" to represent single characters, and "%" to represent multiple characters, along with the LIKE operator.

- With any datatype, you can find or avoid records with empty columns by using the IS NULL or IS NOT NULL operator in your WHERE clause.

View Records in a Different Order

- You can change the order in which records are displayed by including an ORDER BY clause.

- When you specify two or more sort columns in an ORDER BY clause, the columns are not treated equally. The first column you name is the primary sort column, and it will determine all sorting until it reaches two or more records that have the same value in that column. Then the second sort column is applied to those records.

Show Only Unique Values

- You can query for one instance of each value in a column by adding the modifier DISTINCT right after the word SELECT in your query.

- You can also get the same results by using the modifier UNIQUE instead of DISTINCT.

Select from the DUAL Table

- You can also perform real-time calculations on data that isn't even in a table by selecting values from DUAL.

- The DUAL table's data is never meant to be used directly. Instead, the DUAL table is provided to support on-the-fly queries.

Modify Data in a Table

- Employ the UPDATE command to identify the table to be updated, state what value should be assigned to what column, and then specify what condition a record must meet in order to receive the update.

- Include the WHERE condition in UPDATE statements, because if you don't, every record will be updated.

Remove Records from a Table

- Include the WHERE condition when you are removing records with the DELETE command.

- The TRUNCATE command doesn't bother reading every record in the table before deleting it.

Maintain Transaction Control

- The most significant "transaction control" command is the ROLLBACK command, which undoes any DML commands (INSERT, UPDATE, and DELETE) that have been performed since the last commit was performed.

- An explicit commit is performed whenever you issue the COMMIT command.

- An implicit commit occurs whenever you perform a DDL operation (including CREATE and DROP, among others), as well as when you exit from SQL*Plus.

- By issuing a SAVEPOINT command, you set a named marker that can later be rolled back to by using a ROLLBACK command along with the name of the desired savepoint.

Key Terms

AND (56)	**DISTINCT** (65)	**ROLLBACK** (54)
BETWEEN (57)	**DROP TABLE** (73)	**SAVEPOINT** (54)
COMMIT (54)	**DUAL** (67)	**system privilege** (53)
Data Control Language (DCL) (54)	**INSERT** (53)	**TRUNCATE** (68)
Data Definition Language (DDL) (53)	**object privilege** (53)	**UNIQUE** (66)
	OR (58)	**UPDATE** (67)
Data Manipulation Language (DML) (53)	**ORDER BY** (63)	**WHERE** (54)
	privilege (53)	**wildcard** (60)

Key Term Quiz

Use the Key Terms list to complete the sentences that follow. Not all terms will be used.

1. When you issue the _____ command, it makes your changes visible to other users.

2. The _____ command you issued removed the records from your local storage, and kept them from ever being written to the database table for permanent storage.

3. If you use the _____ command, you can roll back to the most recent point and apply your changes up to that point in the database.

4. Selecting unique values from a table is similar to selecting a regular list of values; you just add the modifier _____ to the SELECT command.

5. The _____ table is provided to support on-the-fly queries.

Matching Definition Quiz

Relate each term on the left with the appropriate description on the right.

Term		**Description**	
1.	INSERT	a.	Changes data in the table
2.	Wildcard	b.	Removes rows from the database table
3.	ORDER BY	c.	Changes the order in which records are displayed
4.	DELETE	d.	Adds new rows to the table
5.	UPDATE	e.	Used, when searching text, to represent the portion of text that can vary

Multiple-Choice Quiz

1. What is the definition of a "savepoint"?

   a. A place within a set of DML commands where you want Oracle to save data to the server so that it is visible to other users.

   b. A place where Oracle should stop processing until you tell it to continue.

   c. A place within a set of DML commands to which Oracle can return, nullifying changes made beyond that point.

   d. A parameter used to indicate when Oracle needs to back up and restore its database.

   e. A parameter used to indicate when Oracle needs to find all table data that has been saved.

2. Which of the following is a valid condition?

   a. WHERE 'Smith'

   b. WHERE 'Job_Description' = 'Manager'

   c. WHERE SaLaRy = SYSDATE

   d. WHERE LAST_NAME BETWEEN 'K' AND 9

   e. WHERE HIREDATE BETWEEN '02-JAN-02' AND '01-JAN-01'

3. Which of the following are *not* reasonable series of transaction-control commands? (Choose as many as apply.)

   a. Insert some records, COMMIT, ROLLBACK

   b. ROLLBACK, insert some records, COMMIT

   c. SAVEPOINT, insert some records, ROLLBACK, ROLLBACK, COMMIT

   d. ROLLBACK, insert some records, COMMIT, COMMIT

   e. INSERT, update some records, SAVEPOINT

4. Which of the following shows the wildcards for a single character and multiple characters, respectively?

   a. ?, *

   b. _, %

   c. ?, _

   d. ?, %

   e. %, _

5. On which line would a command using the following syntax fail?

   ```
   UPDATE table_name
   WHERE column_name = condition_to_be_met
   ```

   ```
   SET column_name = new_value
   ORDER BY column_name;
   ```

   a. 1

   b. 2

   c. 3

   d. 4

   e. The command would succeed.

6. Which of the following SQL commands fall into the category of Transaction Control?

   a. GRANT and REVOKE

   b. SELECT

   c. CREATE, ALTER, DROP, RENAME, and TRUNCATE

   d. COMMIT, ROLLBACK, and SAVEPOINT

   e. INSERT, UPDATE, and DELETE

7. The DUAL table consists of

   a. Two columns and two rows

   b. Two rows and one column

   c. Two columns and one row

   d. One column and one row

   e. Three rows and three columns

8. Which of the following statements are true regarding savepoints? (Choose all that apply.)

   a. Savepoint names must contain letters only.

   b. By pairing ROLLBACK with the SAVEPOINT command, you may specify any number of points to which a ROLLBACK command can return.

   c. The correct syntax of the SAVEPOINT command is SAVEPOINT *savepoint_name;*.

   d. Savepoint names have a maximum length of 30 characters.

   e. The first character of a savepoint name must be a letter.

9. To change data in an Oracle table, the correct command is

   a. INSERT *table_name* SET *column_name* = *new_value* WHERE *condition;*

   b. UPDATE *table_name* SET *column_name* = *new_value* WHERE *condition;*

   c. UPDATE *column_name* SET *column_name* = *new_value* WHERE *condition;*

   d. UPDATE *table_name* SET *table_name* = *new_value* WHERE *condition*;

   e. INSERT *column_name* SET *column_name* = *new_value* WHERE *condition*;

10. On which line would a command using the following syntax fail?

```
SELECT DISTINCT salesperson
FROM            test_purchase
ORDER BY        salesperson;
WHERE           purchase_date BETWEEN
'01-JUL-2003' AND '15-JUL-2003'
```

   a. 1

   b. 2

   c. 3

   d. 4

   e. The command would succeed.

11. Which of the following statements regarding the DELETE command are true? (Choose three.)

   a. The syntax for the DELETE command is DELETE FROM *table_name* WHERE *condition*.

   b. The DELETE command deletes an entire table when the WHERE condition is not mentioned.

   c. The DELETE command never presents the same results as the TRUNCATE command.

   d. You can delete records using any column or columns in your condition clause.

   e. The syntax for deleting all records in a table is as follows: DELETE FROM *table_name*;.

12. When filtering with a WHERE clause, which of the following comparison operators can be used in the filtering condition? (Choose all that apply.)

   a. =

   b. <<

   c. >

   d. !=

   e. NOT

13. How can you avoid records with empty columns? (Choose two.)

   a. By using the IS NULL operator in your WHERE clause

   b. By using the IS NOT NULL operator in your WHERE clause

   c. By using the UNIQUE modifier in your WHERE clause

   d. By using the DISTINCT modifier in your WHERE clause

   e. By ensuring that no columns are allowed to have NULL values

14. The DUAL table is

   a. Accessible to all users

   b. Accessible only to the SYS account

   c. Accessible only to the SYSTEM account

   d. Accessible only to the database designer

   e. Not accessible to any users

15. By issuing a SAVEPOINT command, you

   a. Save the contents of a table up to that point so that they can never be rolled back

   b. Set a named marker to which a subsequent rollback can take place by using a ROLLBACK command

   c. Truncate the table to where the savepoint occurs

   d. Instruct the database to remove any null columns

   e. Instruct the database to automatically provide a savepoint name

■ Essay Quiz

1. When you insert, update, or delete data in a table, does Oracle apply those changes to the table immediately?

2. What are the ways to commit data changes to a database?

3. What is the naming convention for a savepoint when inserting data to a table?

4. What is the advantage of using the TRUNCATE command to delete records from a table?

5. Why is it important to include a WHERE condition in an UPDATE command?

Lab Projects

Lab Project 3.1

Case Study

The Clapham Specialty Store requires you to search for and update records in the customer database table. They would like the result sets to be based on the following steps.

You will need the following materials:

- Oracle 9*i* Database Server with SQL*Plus tool
- Completion of Step-by-Step 3.01

Then follow these steps:

1. Search for all records in the CUSTOMER table and sort the results by the Customer_ID column with the largest value on top. Indicate the correct command.

2. Search for all records in the CUSTOMER table that do not possess the customer identification numbers 90003456 and 90003467.

Lab Project 3.2

Case Study

The Clapham Specialty Store requires you to insert new records into the CUSTOMER database table. The new member data is as follows:

Customer_ID Number: 90003246, Name: Colleen Reilly, Street: 124 Johnson Avenue, Phone number: 2017451111

Customer_ID Number: 90003247, Name: Cindy Brown, Street: 125 Johnson Avenue, Phone number: 2017451122

Customer_ID Number: 90003248, Name: Roseanne Jackson, Street: 333 Highland Avenue, Phone number: 2017451229

They have asked you to ensure that this data can be rolled back to each particular record that you have inserted.

You will need the following materials:

- Oracle 9*i* Database Server with SQL*Plus tool
- Completion of Step-by-Step 3.01 and Lab Project 3.1

Then follow these steps:

1. Populate the CUSTOMER table with the records indicated. Select all records in the table, rolled back to after the insertion of the first new record. Select all records in the table, rolled back to after the insertion of the second new record.

2. Select the unique Customer_ID records from the CUSTOMER table for the Clapham Specialty Store that have a Johnson Avenue address. Order the result set by Customer_ID.

Controlling SQL*Plus

chapter 4

"The controlling Intelligence understands its own nature, and what it does, and whereon it works."

—MARCUS AURELIUS

In this chapter, you will learn how to

- **Edit prior commands in SQL*Plus**
- **Copy and paste commands**
- **Clear the SQL*Plus screen**
- **Customize the SQL*Plus environment**
- **Save environment customizations**
- **Produce more readable input**
- **SPOOL output to disk**
- **Work with SQL script files**

This chapter presents useful techniques for getting the most out of the SQL*Plus program. You will learn how to save time and keystrokes by modifying and reusing old commands; get a "clean slate" in SQL*Plus by clearing the screen; customize the way SQL*Plus works and save those customizations so they are used automatically next time; improve the readability of data retrieved via SELECT commands; write selected data out to a disk file; and store commands in script files that can easily be rerun with very few keystrokes.

■ Editing Prior Commands

Up to this point, each time you have entered a SQL command into SQL*Plus you have had to type the command manually, even if it was similar to the prior command entered. SQL*Plus offers a variety of ways you can edit and reuse commands without having to completely retype them. We'll start with an approach that is likely to be very familiar, and then proceed to another approach that can be faster in certain situations.

Using a Text Editor

Even if you just started writing SQL commands when you began reading this book, You have probably experienced a time when you wrote a SQL command that was a few lines long, entered it, and immediately discovered a minor mistake in the command. Wouldn't it be nice to be able to edit that command—as you edit text in a word processor—and have it automatically resubmitted for execution? You can. If you type the command **EDIT** (or its abbreviation, ED) at the next SQL> prompt, SQL*Plus will open your computer's default text-editing program and automatically place your last SQL command into it. You can edit the command, have it "saved" back into SQL*Plus, and then execute the edited version of the command.

Let's step through an exercise that demonstrates how to do this. Enter the following SQL commands to create these new tables before proceeding to the Step-by-Step exercise.

```
DROP TABLE test_purchase;
CREATE TABLE test_purchase (
     product_name   VARCHAR2(25),
     salesperson    VARCHAR2(3),
     purchase_date DATE,
     quantity       NUMBER(4,2)
     )
;

INSERT INTO test_purchase VALUES
     ('Small Widget', 'CA', '14-JUL-2003', 1);
INSERT INTO test_purchase VALUES
     ('Medium Wodget', 'BB', '14-JUL-2003', 75);
INSERT INTO test_purchase VALUES
     ('Chrome Phoobar', 'GA', '14-JUL-2003', 2);
INSERT INTO test_purchase VALUES
     ('Small Widget', 'GA', '15-JUL-2003', 8);
INSERT INTO test_purchase VALUES
     ('Medium Wodget', 'LB', '15-JUL-2003', 20);
INSERT INTO test_purchase VALUES
     ('Round Snaphoo', 'CA', '16-JUL-2003', 5);

DROP TABLE test_product;
CREATE TABLE test_product (
     product_name      VARCHAR2(25),
     product_price     NUMBER(4,2),
     quantity_on_hand NUMBER(5,0),
     last_stock_date   DATE
```

```
                )
        ;

        INSERT INTO test_product VALUES
            ('Small Widget', 99, 1, '15-JAN-2003');
        INSERT INTO test_product VALUES
            ('Medium Wodget', 75, 1000, '15-JAN-2002');
        INSERT INTO test_product VALUES
            ('Chrome Phoobar', 50, 100, '15-JAN-2003');
        INSERT INTO test_product VALUES
            ('Round Chrome Snaphoo', 25, 10000, null);
```

Step-by-Step 4.01

Using the EDIT Command

For this exercise, you will need Oracle9*i* Database
Server with the SQL*Plus tool. To see how the EDIT
command works, take the following steps:

Step 1

Enter the following command. Note that it contains some misspellings.

```
SELECT    product_nmae
FROM      test_produtc
WHERE     quantity_on_hand >= 100
          AND
          last_stock_date IS NOT NULL
ORDER BY product_name;
```

Step 2

In response, SQL*Plus should display the message "ORA-00942: table or view does not exist." This is Oracle's way of telling you that it cannot find the table because the name is misspelled.

Step 3

Type **edit** and press the ENTER key. The editing program that is opened to edit your text may vary from computer to computer. Your command will have been placed into a temporary file with a name like *afiedt.buf*. The name is irrelevant because you aren't going to actually save your command to disk.

Step 4

Correct the spelling of the column name on line 1, and the spelling of the table name on line 2.

Step 5

Exit from the text-editing program (generally the File | Exit command will accomplish this). It will ask if you want to save your changes. Usually, a prompt like this means you are about to create (or update) a file on disk, but what's really going to happen is that the text-editing program will write your edited command back into SQL*Plus. Answer **Yes** to the prompt that asks about saving your changes.

You should have successfully used the EDIT command and corrected the misspelled word.

Note: When editing using the EDIT command, a text editor program will open. (On Windows systems it will be Notepad by default, while on Unix systems it's likely to be ED or VI.)

Line-Level Editing

While it is very nice to be able to edit commands in a full-screen editor, sometimes the change you want to make is so small that you could retype the entire command in less time than it would take to open a text editor, make the change, and save it.

In instances like these, you can employ a SQL*Plus feature allowing you to edit your previous command right in SQL*Plus. This approach doesn't offer the full features of a text editor, so it isn't well suited for multiline SQL commands, but it is the fastest way to make changes to short commands.

The best way to understand this approach is to try it first, and afterward read an explanation of what you saw happen. Take the steps that follow to see how this approach to editing works:

1. Enter the following command. Notice that the column name is spelled incorrectly—be sure to type it that way.

   ```
   SELECT product_nmae FROM test_product;
   ```

2. Notice that the error message displayed by SQL*Plus flags the column name Product_Nmae with an asterisk (*). This, of course, is because it is misspelled.

3. Type the following command:

   ```
   change/nmae/name
   ```

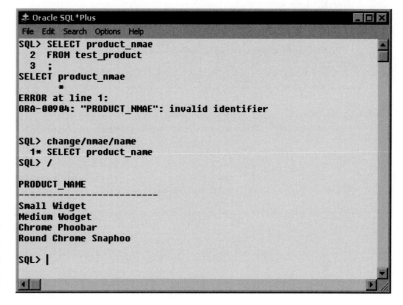

4. Press ENTER to execute the CHANGE command. Notice that SQL*Plus redisplays the command, this time with "NAME" replacing the old "NMAE" in the column name.

5. To execute the newly modified command, type a slash (/) and press ENTER. Compare the results you got with those shown in Figure 4.1.

As you can see from the preceding example, the CHANGE command allows you to replace any text string in a command with any other. CHANGE is not a SQL command; it works only within the SQL*Plus program. In the previous exercise you started the command with "CHANGE." You can also

● **Figure 4.1** Correcting a command line using the CHANGE command abbreviate this to simply "C." The long and short versions of the command do the same thing; the "C" shortcut is simply a convenience.

The syntax of the CHANGE command is as follows:

```
C[HANGE]  separator_character  old_text  [separator_character  new_text]
```

The square brackets represent portions of the command that are optional. The separator character that follows can be any character that is not a letter or a number. (In the previous exercise the separator character was the forward slash, and that is the most common character used as a separator.) After the separator character, you specify the old text that should be replaced. If you stop the command there and press ENTER, the old text will be removed and nothing will replace it. If you want to put something in place of the old text, just type the separator character again, followed by the new text to replace the old.

Take a moment now to experiment with this command. Enter a valid SQL statement, execute it, and then change it using the CHANGE command. Then enter an erroneous SQL statement and change it using the same technique.

Controlling Which Line Is Edited During Line-Level Editing

In the previous two examples, you used EDIT to modify multiple lines and CHANGE to modify single lines. The CHANGE command can also do multiline editing, but it works differently than EDIT. Instead of giving you a nice text-editing environment where you can move your cursor from line to line by just pressing arrow keys or clicking with your mouse, the CHANGE command continues to let you edit just one line at a time. To correct multiline statements with the CHANGE command, you must specify which line you want to work on before making any actual changes. You do this simply by entering the number of the line you want to change before using the CHANGE command. Entering the line number causes SQL*Plus to make that line current.

This may all seem a little abstract, because very few programs in the consumer world work this way. The best way to learn it, as usual, is to try it for yourself. Enter the following commands to do this:

Cross Check

Editing SQL Commands

Now that you've been introduced to editing, take a moment to check your knowledge by answering the following questions:

1. What does typing the command EDIT accomplish?
2. What is the function of the CHANGE command?

```
SELECT    product_nmae
FROM      test_produtc
WHERE     quantity_on_hand >= 100
          AND
          last_stock_date IS NOT NULL
ORDER BY  product_name;

1
c/ma/am
2
c/tc/ct
/
```

Compare your results now with those shown in Figure 4.2. As you can see, each time you enter a number, SQL*Plus makes that line number from

Introduction to Relational Databases and SQL Programming

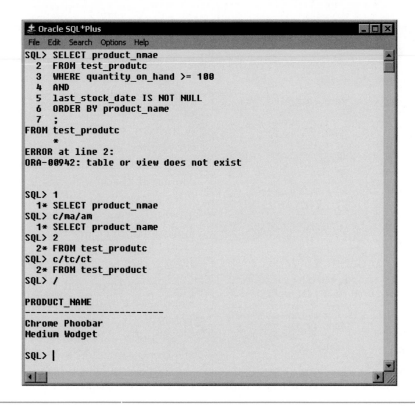

```
Oracle SQL*Plus
File  Edit  Search  Options  Help
SQL> SELECT product_nmae
  2  FROM test_produtc
  3  WHERE quantity_on_hand >= 100
  4  AND
  5  last_stock_date IS NOT NULL
  6  ORDER BY product_name
  7  ;
FROM test_produtc
     *
ERROR at line 2:
ORA-00942: table or view does not exist


SQL> 1
  1* SELECT product_nmae
SQL> c/ma/am
  1* SELECT product_name
SQL> 2
  2* FROM test_produtc
SQL> c/tc/ct
  2* FROM test_product
SQL> /

PRODUCT_NAME
-----------------------
Chrome Phoobar
Medium Wodget

SQL> |
```

● **Figure 4.2**   Using the CHANGE command for multiline editing

the prior SQL command current and allows you to modify the line using the CHANGE command.

■ Copying and Pasting

It's common to need to repeat a SQL command that you executed two, three, or even more commands ago. In these instances, the CHANGE and EDIT commands won't help you, because the command you want is no longer in SQL*Plus's command buffer. You can, however, leverage your prior typing in a different way. You can copy commands from the SQL*Plus display screen and reuse them by pasting them back in at the SQL> prompt. To see this in action, start by entering the following commands:

```
SELECT * FROM test_product;

UPDATE test_product
SET    product_name = 'Large Widget'
WHERE  product_name = 'Small Widget';
```

To check the results of your UPDATE command, you don't need to re-type the SELECT statement. You can just copy it. Move your computer's mouse so that it is just before the "S" of "SELECT." Hold down the left mouse button and drag the mouse along the entire length of the command,

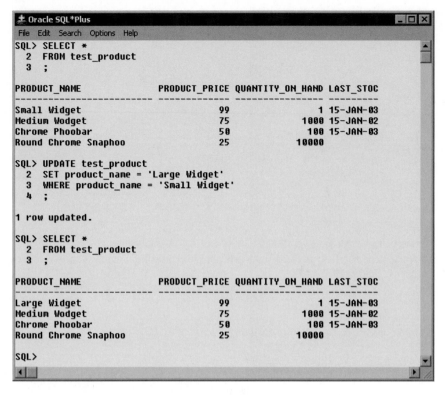

```
Oracle SQL*Plus                                          _ □ X
File  Edit  Search  Options  Help
SQL> SELECT *
  2  FROM test_product
  3  ;

PRODUCT_NAME              PRODUCT_PRICE QUANTITY_ON_HAND LAST_STOC
------------------------- ------------- ---------------- ---------
Small Widget                         99                1 15-JAN-03
Medium Wodget                        75             1000 15-JAN-02
Chrome Phoobar                       50              100 15-JAN-03
Round Chrome Snaphoo                 25            10000

SQL> UPDATE test_product
  2  SET product_name = 'Large Widget'
  3  WHERE product_name = 'Small Widget'
  4  ;

1 row updated.

SQL> SELECT *
  2  FROM test_product
  3  ;

PRODUCT_NAME              PRODUCT_PRICE QUANTITY_ON_HAND LAST_STOC
------------------------- ------------- ---------------- ---------
Large Widget                         99                1 15-JAN-03
Medium Wodget                        75             1000 15-JAN-02
Chrome Phoobar                       50              100 15-JAN-03
Round Chrome Snaphoo                 25            10000

SQL>
```

● **Figure 4.3** Results of copying and pasting a SQL command

as you would if you wanted to copy it within a word processor. When the entire command is highlighted, let go of the mouse button and open SQL*Plus's Edit menu. Select the Copy command to place a duplicate of the command into the Windows copy buffer. Then execute the menu command Edit | Paste to paste the command back into SQL*Plus. Press ENTER to cause the command to execute. Your screen should now look similar to Figure 4.3.

You can also use your operating system's standard keyboard shortcuts for the Copy and Paste commands used in this approach. For instance, if you are running SQL*Plus in a Windows environment, you can hold down the CTRL key and tap the letter "C" to copy the selected command, then use CTRL-V to paste it. There's an even quicker way, too. Try the following Step-by-Step exercise, which uses your mouse to aid in editing text.

Step-by-Step 4.02

Using Your Mouse to Edit Text

Using your mouse, make a copy of your last UPDATE command to change the product name back to its original value.

For this exercise, you will need Oracle9i Database Server with the SQL*Plus tool.

Step 1	Move your mouse pointer so it is just to the left of the "U" for "UPDATE" in the first line of the UPDATE command.
Step 2	Hold down your left mouse button. Drag the mouse over the entire first line of the original UPDATE command.
Step 3	While still holding down the left mouse button, click the right mouse button once. You will see the text you selected automatically copied to the SQL> prompt.
Step 4	Press the ENTER key to start a new line at the SQL> prompt (its prompt will be "2"). Move your mouse pointer so it is just to the left of the "S" for "SET" in the second line of the original UPDATE command.

Step 5	Hold down your left mouse button. Drag the mouse over the second line until it reaches the "L" of "Large." You want to include the single quote just before "Large," but not the "L."
Step 6	While still holding down the left mouse button, click the right mouse button once. You will see the partial command you selected automatically copied to the SQL> prompt.
Step 7	Type the word **Small** followed by a space. Select the rest of the original UPDATE command's second line and copy it using the same double-mouse-button technique you have used twice already. Press ENTER to start a new line at the SQL> prompt.
Step 8	Perform a similar treatment on the original UPDATE command's third line, changing "Small" to "Large." Press ENTER to run the command. This technique works for commands that have scrolled off the top of your SQL*Plus window, too. You can scroll up to find a command, use this technique, and the command will be pasted next to your current SQL> prompt.

■ Clearing the SQL*Plus Screen

By now you have executed dozens or perhaps hundreds of SQL commands while practicing the things you've learned in this book. At any point have you wished you could clear up the SQL*Plus screen—return it to a blank slate, to reduce the clutter? You can, and it's easy to do. Just hold down the SHIFT key, and while holding it down, tap the DELETE key. You will see the dialog box shown in Figure 4.4. Click the OK button, and your SQL*Plus screen will clear to show just a SQL> prompt.

● **Figure 4.4**   SQL*Plus dialog box for clearing the screen

■ Customizing the SQL*Plus Environment

Many facets of SQL*Plus's behavior can be modified. You won't get much benefit from changing most of the facets, but a handful of them are very handy. We'll see how to change them using the SQL*Plus menu, and then see how to change a few using commands at the SQL*Plus prompt.

Customizing Using the SQL*Plus Menu

Within SQL*Plus, execute the Options | Environment menu command. This will cause a dialog box to appear that looks like the one shown in Figure 4.5. The left half of the Environment dialog box contains a scrolling list of options, while the right half contains two settings controlling how much data SQL*Plus keeps in its scrollback buffer. By default, SQL*Plus remembers up to 100 characters of each line you type, and up to 1,000 such lines. Using the Environment dialog box, however, you can tell SQL*Plus to store up to 1,000 characters per line (occasionally useful) and up to 2,000 lines (often useful,

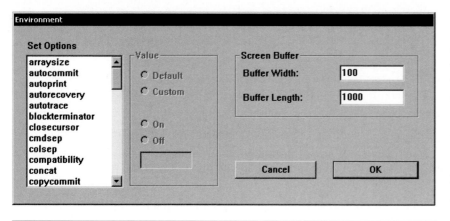

• **Figure 4.5**   SQL*Plus Environment dialog box

since the lines of data that display in response to your commands are counted too). By changing these values, you can maximize the number of prior commands and results SQL*Plus stores, making it easier to go back and find commands to copy or results to compare.

To change the buffer width and length, type **1000** into the Buffer Width field, and **2000** into the Buffer Length field.

On the left side of the Environment dialog box, two of the options in the Set Options list are useful at this time: linesize and pagesize. Linesize sets the maximum width SQL*Plus will provide for each line before wrapping. When the linesize is too small, the data you select may be wider than SQL*Plus can display on one line, in which case SQL*Plus will wrap columns to make them fit. It does make them fit, but it also makes them very difficult to read. Figure 4.6 shows an example of this problem. By setting a linesize large enough to accommodate the width of the data being displayed, you can make your listings more readable… to a point. The trade-off is that SQL*Plus doesn't scroll to the right, so any data not shown on your screen won't be viewable at all.

The linesize value is independent of the Buffer Width parameter modified earlier. Linesize controls how wide the lines can be, while Buffer Width determines how many characters of each line will be stored in memory for later retrieval. It makes sense for the two values to be the same, so that all of the data you see is being stored in the memory buffer.

To set the linesize value so it matches the Buffer Width, scroll down the Set Options list until you see the linesize option. Select it, and in the dialog box's Value box, click the Custom radio button. This will enable the value field at the bottom of the dialog box's Value box. Enter **1000** into that field. Then click the OK button to close the Environment dialog box. Making this change will help ensure that the results you get look less like Figure 4.6 and more like Figure 4.7.

Another useful option is pagesize, which controls how many lines of data SQL*Plus will display in response to a SELECT command before it repeats the column headings. The default value is quite low, causing SQL*Plus to show numerous sets of headings per screen when running on a modern high-resolution display. Changing the pagesize to 9999 modifies the display so that only the longest lists of

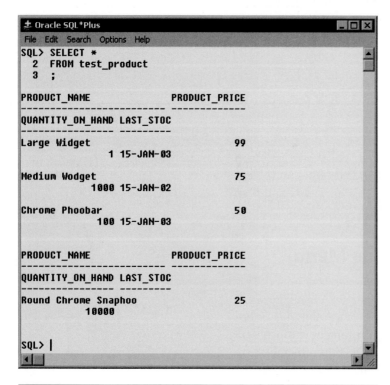

• **Figure 4.6**   Results of having data wider than the linesize

Introduction to Relational Databases and SQL Programming

data contain more than one set of headers. You can try out this setting by entering **9999** into the pagesize option's value field.

Once you are done changing values in the Environment dialog box, click the OK button to close it.

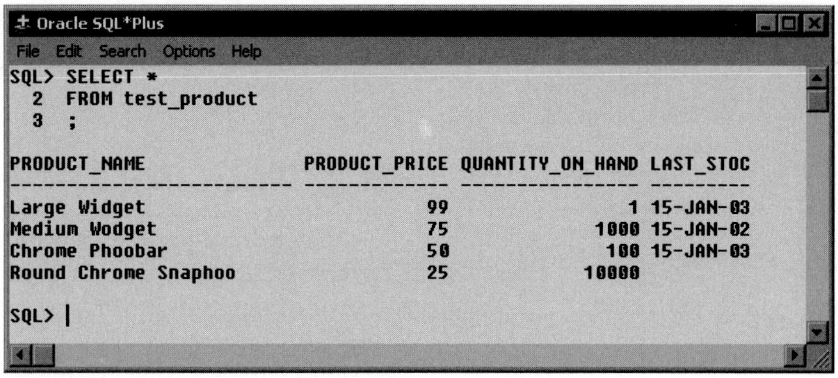

Customizing Using Commands

All of the options shown in the Environment dialog box's Set Options list can be changed from SQL*Plus. To see this in action, enter the following commands at the SQL> prompt:

```
SET LINESIZE 1000
SET PAGESIZE 9999
```

Figure 4.7 Results of setting a more accommodating linesize

■ Saving Environment Customizations

You can tell SQL*Plus to store all of its environment settings in a file that it will then read each time you start the program. This feature makes it easy to make changes that improve SQL*Plus's functionality and have those changes automatically reapplied each time you start SQL*Plus. To accomplish this, take the following steps:

1. Determine the file path of your *Oracle home*. The Oracle home is the folder WS (or *directory* in more traditional computer language) on your computer's hard disk where Oracle program files are stored. If you are using Windows NT, open the Windows Explorer program (Start | Programs | Windows NT Explorer) and look for a directory with a name like "OraNT." If you use Windows 95, 98, 2000, or later versions to run SQL*Plus, you should look for a directory whose name is similar to "ORAWIN95." If you cannot determine which directory is the Oracle home on your computer, ask your database administrator.

2. In SQL*Plus, enter the following command:

   ```
   STORE SET drive:oracle_home\LOGIN.SQL APPEND
   ```

3. Replace the *drive:oracle_home* portion of the command with the disk-drive letter and directory name of the Oracle home directory on your own computer. Note that this command does not need to end with a semicolon; that is because this command controls only the SQL*Plus program, and does not even get sent to the Oracle database.

The login.sql file, located in the DBS directory under your Oracle home, is automatically read each time SQL*Plus starts. By storing your settings in that file, you ensure that they will be reinstated each time you start SQL*Plus.

The STORE command instructs SQL*Plus to save all of your current environment settings to a disk file.

■ Producing More Readable Output

You may have noticed by now that SQL*Plus does very little to beautify the records it displays. It doesn't align decimal places in numbers, it cuts off column headings as it sees fit, and it insists on showing the entire contents of a large text column in a single row, regardless of how wide the column must become in order to do so. With a few simple commands you can improve the appearance of SQL*Plus's output dramatically.

The solution to doing all of this is the COLUMN command. Like STORE, the COLUMN command does not get sent to the Oracle database. Its only job is to affect the way your own copy of SQL*Plus displays information. As such, COLUMN commands do not need to end with a semicolon as standard SQL commands do. In addition, they stay active only as long as your SQL*Plus session lasts—if you exit SQL*Plus and then restart it, the effect is gone until you issue the COLUMN commands again.

Before you start experimenting with the COLUMN command, it would be good to add a record that needs a lot of formatting to your TEST sample tables. Enter the following code to add such a record:

```
INSERT INTO test_product VALUES (
    'Extra Huge Mega Phoobar +',
    9.95,
    1234,
    '15-JAN-2004')
;
```

Formatting Numbers in SQL*Plus

There are three things that commonly need to be done to numbers:

- Aligning their decimals
- Placing a separator between hundreds, thousands, and so on
- Placing a currency symbol with them

We'll look at each need individually, then combine them.

Aligning Decimals

The syntax of the COLUMN command to align decimals is as follows:

```
COLUMN column_name FORMAT format_code
```

If your country's standard format uses a different character than "." to denote decimals, use "D" in the COLUMN command's *format_code* argument instead of ",", and the decimal indicator from your database's national configuration will be used.

You replace the *column_name* argument with the name of the column you wish to format. You replace the *format_code* argument with a representation of how the numbers should look. The representation consists of one "9" for every digit your numbers will require, along with a "." for the decimal place.

To see the COLUMN command in action, enter the following commands:

```
SELECT * FROM test_product;


COLUMN product_price FORMAT 9999.99


SELECT * FROM test_product;
```

Your screen should now look similar to the one shown in Figure 4.8. Notice how the values in the Product_Price column started out unaligned, and then became aligned after you issued the COLUMN command.

Adding a Group Separator

A group separator is a character that separates hundreds, thousands, and so on, within a number. Your TEST_PRODUCT table has values in its Quantity_On_Hand column that could benefit from having a comma separate the hundreds from the thousands. You can achieve this result with the same COLUMN syntax you used to get decimal alignment; you just need to change

```
± Oracle SQL*Plus
File  Edit  Search  Options  Help
SQL> SELECT * FROM test_product;

PRODUCT_NAME                   PRODUCT_PRICE QUANTITY_ON_HAND LAST_STOC
------------------------------ ------------- ---------------- ---------
Small Widget                              99                1 15-JAN-03
Medium Wodget                             75             1000 15-JAN-02
Chrome Phoobar                            50              100 15-JAN-03
Round Chrome Snaphoo                      25            10000
Extra Huge Mega Phoobar+                9.95             1234 15-JAN-04

SQL> COLUMN product_price FORMAT 9999.99
SQL> SELECT * FROM test_product;

PRODUCT_NAME                   PRODUCT_PRICE QUANTITY_ON_HAND LAST_STOC
------------------------------ ------------- ---------------- ---------
Small Widget                           99.00                1 15-JAN-03
Medium Wodget                          75.00             1000 15-JAN-02
Chrome Phoobar                         50.00              100 15-JAN-03
Round Chrome Snaphoo                   25.00            10000
Extra Huge Mega Phoobar+                9.95             1234 15-JAN-04

SQL>
```

• **Figure 4.8**   Using the COLUMN command to align decimals

the format code. Enter the following commands to see how it works. In response, you'll see that the Quantity_On_Hand column now includes commas when appropriate.

```
COLUMN quantity_on_hand FORMAT 99,999


SELECT * FROM test_product;
```

Including a Currency Symbol

As you might suspect, this too is simply a variation on the format code. Try the following code to place a dollar sign ($) before each Product_Price value:

```
COLUMN product_price FORMAT $99.99


SELECT * FROM test_product;
```

Other Useful Number Format Codes

Table 4.1 contains a list of the most important format codes you can use with numbers. Take a moment now and try out each one of these codes, so you can see firsthand what they do. Be sure to try the RN code for a little bit of fun.

Formatting Text in SQL*Plus

One of the most common complaints about SQL*Plus is that it doesn't wrap the contents of large text columns. This is a valid complaint, because it

Inside Information

The COLUMN Command

Using the COLUMN command indicated the column_name *argument; however, there is no mention of which table the column is in. The COLUMN command affects all columns with the name you specify, regardless of the tables in which the columns reside. Fortunately, if two columns have the same name they probably contain similar data, so the formatting you apply to one generally makes sense for the other as well.*

Table 4.1	Number Format Codes	
Element	Example	Description
$	$9999	Places a dollar sign before the value
, (comma)	9,999	Places a comma in the position indicated
. (period)	99.99	Places a decimal point in the position indicated
MI	9999MI	Causes a minus sign (–) to be displayed after any negative value
S	S9999	Places a plus sign (+) for positive values and a minus sign (–) for negative values in position indicated
PR	9999PR	Causes negative values to be surrounded by angle brackets (<>)
D	99D99	Displays your country's decimal character in the position indicated
G	9G999	Displays your country's group separator in the position indicated
C	C999	Displays the ISO currency symbol in the position indicated
L	L999	Displays the local currency symbol in the position indicated
RN or rn	RN	Causes numbers to display as upper- or lowercase Roman numerals (limited to integers between 1 and 3,999)
0	0999	Displays one or more leading zeros
0	9990	Causes empty values to display as zeros

diminishes the program's usefulness. However, there is a simple way to make SQL*Plus wrap large text columns. It uses a variation on the COLUMN command. The syntax is as follows:

```
COLUMN column_name FORMAT Ann WORD_WRAP
```

The "A" preceding the number argument in the COLUMN command stands for "alphanumeric."

You've probably figured out that you replace *column_name* with the name of the column you want to wrap. The other argument is *nn*, which is where you place a number representing how many characters wide the wrapped column should be.

Try out the following commands to see how this works:

```
SELECT * FROM test_product;

COLUMN product_name FORMAT A10 WORD_WRAP

SELECT * FROM test_product;
```

As you can see, the product names now fit easily into a narrow space. You might be thinking, "They fit before, too." That's true. This technique works best with columns that are wider: 30, 40, 50, 100, or even several hundred characters wide. So why didn't the exercise show how it looks with wide columns? Do *you* want to type in a bunch of hundred-character-long product names? Probably not, so let's keep this exercise easy. Remember this technique, and when a situation arises where a wide column doesn't fit within the SQL*Plus screen, you'll know what to do.

Formatting Column Headings in SQL*Plus

While the techniques you've learned so far give you the ability to polish up the appearance of the records being displayed, the column headings above those records are still a mess. Besides consisting entirely of capital letters, the column names are too long to fit within the width of some of the columns—so some of the names are cut off. A variation of the COLUMN command will take care of that. The new syntax is

```
COLUMN column_name HEADING 'heading_text' JUSTIFY LEFT
```

...or...

```
COLUMN column_name HEADING 'heading_text' JUSTIFY CENTER
```

...or...

```
COLUMN column_name HEADING 'heading_text' JUSTIFY RIGHT
```

In addition to letting you control what headings are displayed above columns, this technique offers a couple of other nice benefits: You can use a mixture of upper- and lowercase characters, and you can break the headings into multiple lines. Within the *heading_text* argument, a vertical bar (|) represents a line break. You can even specify whether the headings should be justified to the column's left margin, to its center, or to its right margin.

To see this in action, try the following commands:

```
SELECT * FROM test_product;

COLUMN product_name HEADING 'Product|Name' JUSTIFY CENTER

SELECT * FROM test_product;
```

You can put all of these COLUMN command options together and use them at the same time. Try out the following commands, and then compare your results with those shown in Figure 4.9.

```
SELECT * FROM test_product;

COLUMN product_name FORMAT A10 WORD_WRAP HEADING 'Name' JUSTIFY CENTER
COLUMN product_price FORMAT $99.99 HEADING 'Price' JUSTIFY RIGHT
COLUMN quantity_on_hand FORMAT 99,999 HEADING 'On|Hand' JUSTIFY RIGHT
COLUMN last_stock_date HEADING 'Last|Stock|Date' JUSTIFY RIGHT

SELECT * FROM test_product;
```

To turn off the formatting from the COLUMN command, you can use this syntax:

```
COLUMN column_name OFF
```

For instance, to make the columns in your TEST_PRODUCT table display as they did before you applied any formatting, enter the following commands:

```
COLUMN product_name OFF
COLUMN product_price OFF
COLUMN quantity_on_hand OFF
COLUMN last_stock_date OFF

SELECT * FROM test_product;
```

```
Oracle SQL*Plus                                    _ □ X
File  Edit  Search  Options  Help
SQL> SELECT * FROM test_product;

 Product
   Name    PRODUCT_PRICE QUANTITY_ON_HAND LAST_STOC
---------- ------------- ---------------- ---------
Large           $99.00                 1 15-JAN-03
Widget

Medium          $75.00             1,000 15-JAN-02
Wodget

Chrome          $50.00               100 15-JAN-03
Phoobar

Round           $25.00            10,000
Chrome
Snaphoo

Extra Huge       $9.95             1,234 15-JAN-04
Mega
Phoobar +


SQL>
SQL> COLUMN product_name FORMAT A10 WORD_WRAP HEADING 'Name' JUSTIFY CENTER
SQL> COLUMN product_price FORMAT $99.99 HEADING 'Price' JUSTIFY RIGHT
SQL> COLUMN quantity_on_hand FORMAT 99,999 HEADING 'On|Hand' JUSTIFY RIGHT
SQL> COLUMN last_stock_date HEADING 'Last|Stock|Date' JUSTIFY RIGHT
SQL>
SQL> SELECT * FROM test_product;

                          Last
                    On   Stock
   Name    Price   Hand   Date
---------- ------ ------ --------
Large      $99.00      1 15-JAN-03
Widget

Medium     $75.00  1,000 15-JAN-02
Wodget

Chrome     $50.00    100 15-JAN-03
Phoobar

Round      $25.00 10,000
Chrome
Snaphoo

Extra Huge  $9.95  1,234 15-JAN-04
Mega
Phoobar +

SQL>
```

● **Figure 4.9**   Formatting text with a variety of COLUMN commands

For those of you running SQL*Plus on Unix, the path for the spool file will have a structure more like this:
`/u01/user/test_test.prn`

■ Spooling Output to Disk

Spooling is the process of writing information out to a file on a disk. There are times when it's handy to do this from within SQL*Plus, either to make a record of a series of commands and their results, or to store voluminous output from a single command. (If the output fits within a single SQL*Plus screen, you can simply use the mouse to select the information you want, copy it, and paste it into whatever program you want. Once the information is pasted into the destination program, you may need to apply a fixed-width font such as Courier New to it in order for its lines to align properly.)

The syntax of the SPOOL command is as follows:

```
SPOOL spool_file_name
```

The spool filename can include a file extension if you wish (such as .sql or .prn or .txt). If you do not specify one, the extension .lst will be appended to the end of the name you specify. Also, you can include a *path* as part of the spool filename; the path is the name of the disk drive and directory in which the spool file should be stored. If you do not include a path, the spool file will be stored in the BIN directory beneath your Oracle home directory.

To try the SPOOL command, enter the following commands. Note that because SPOOL controls behavior within SQL*Plus—and does not affect the Oracle server—you do not need to place a semicolon at the end of each SPOOL command.

```
SPOOL c:\test_test.prn
SELECT * FROM test_product;
SELECT * FROM test_purchase;
SPOOL OFF
```

After executing these commands, use Windows Explorer or the File Manager to navigate to the location where you stored your test_test.prn file. Open the file and you will see a complete record of everything that crossed your SQL*Plus screen.

Remember that path and filenames in Unix are case-sensitive.

■ SQL Script Files

By this time, you have learned quite a few different SQL commands, and you have typed in many lines as you experimented with those commands. In a business environment, it's common to have certain operations that get performed in exactly the same way—or almost exactly the same way—many times. Retyping the same commands over and over can get tedious quickly. Instead, you can store the commands needed to accomplish a specific task in a disk file. This has three major benefits: It saves you time by eliminating the need to retype repetitive commands; it makes the procedure finish more quickly because commands are read from the disk file much more quickly than you could type them; and it ensures that the commands are executed in exactly the same way, with perfect syntax, each time.

Creating a Script File

A script file is just a plain text file. You can create one using any text editor or word processor. (If you use a word processor, be sure to use the Save As command to save the file in a "text only" format, so it will not contain any of the word processor's formatting codes.) You can even use SQL*Plus's EDIT command to start your system's default text editor to create a new script file. To see how this works, let's use a script file to create and populate a table from the case study:

Case Study

1. In SQL*Plus, enter this command:

   ```
   EDIT c:\case_study.sql
   ```

   Choose to create a new file if prompted.

2. Within the text editor, enter the following commands into your case_study.sql file:

Unix users should modify the file path to a selected location. The same guideline will apply to subsequent exercises that involve file paths.

```
CREATE TABLE location (
    location_id NUMBER(10) NOT NULL,
    department VARCHAR2(40),
    aisle      NUMBER(3),
    side       CHAR(1),
    shelf      VARCHAR2(10)
    )
;

INSERT INTO location VALUES (1000, 'Deli', 2, 'L', 'Bottom');
INSERT INTO location VALUES (1001, 'Deli', 2, 'L', 'Middle');
INSERT INTO location VALUES (1002, 'Paper Goods', 3, 'R', 'Top');
INSERT INTO location VALUES (1003, 'Paper Goods', 3, 'L', 'Top');
INSERT INTO location VALUES (1004, 'Canned Veg', 4, 'L', 'Lower Mid');

SELECT * FROM location;

DROP TABLE location;
```

3. Exit from the text editor. When asked if you want to save the file you just created, answer Yes.

That's it! You now have a script file containing SQL commands. This particular script file contains commands that create a table, populate it with data, select data out of it, and then drop it. You would never create a script with these commands in real life, because the script is self-nullifying. However, it serves as an excellent example of the kinds of commands you can include in a script file to automate common actions.

Running a Script File

Running a script file in SQL*Plus is very easy. You simply precede the name of the file with the "at" sign (@). Enter the following command at the SQL> prompt to see this in action:

```
@c:\case_study
```

In response, you should see a screen similar to the one shown in Figure 4.10. Notice that you did not need to include the .sql file extension in the command. If you do not specify a file extension in the @ command, the extension of .sql is assumed.

Notice the screen shows only the responses to the commands—to see the commands as they execute you should use SET ECHO ON before running the script.

Using Variables in Script Files

Sometimes it is handy to be able to write a script file that can work in a variety of situations, changing what it does in each situation. You can accomplish this by using variables in your script files. A variable takes the place of a portion of your command, allowing you to "fill in" that portion when the script is run—thereby changing what the script does. (The opposite of this is information typed explicitly into the script file. This type of information is called hard-coded because it cannot be changed when the script is run.) You can build variables into your SQL scripts in two different ways: using substitution variables, and using the ACCEPT command.

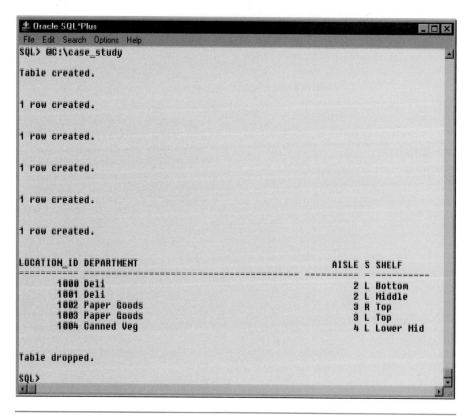

● **Figure 4.10** Running a SQL script file

Substitution Variables

Using a substitution variable is the simplest way to build a variable into your script. To see how this works, create a script file named test_test2.sql, and place within it the following commands:

```
SET VERIFY OFF

SELECT product_name, quantity, purchase_date
FROM    test_purchase
WHERE   quantity >= &minimum_quantity_sold
;

SET VERIFY ON
```

Save and run the script. You will see a brand-new prompt asking you to "Enter value for minimum_quantity_sold." The number that you type in will be placed into the script's WHERE clause as if it had been hard-coded into the script. Enter a value of **20** and see how the script performs. Then run it again (you can do that just by typing a slash (/) and pressing ENTER) and respond to the prompt with a value of **5**, to see how the script's behavior changes.

The SET VERIFY OFF and SET VERIFY ON commands in the script help improve its appearance when the script runs. Without them, SQL*Plus would insist on showing old and new values for the substitution variable before executing your SELECT command, which will confuse anyone running the script other than its creator—and will eventually annoy even its creator.

Substitution variables work just as well for text and dates, too. You must remember, though, that SQL requires text and dates to be surrounded by single quotes. Since it is unlikely that other people using your script will remember this, the best practice is to place the single quotes into the script itself. Consider the following code for an example:

```
SET VERIFY OFF

SELECT product_name, quantity, purchase_date
FROM    test_purchase
WHERE   purchase_date = '&date_you_want_to_select'
;

SET VERIFY ON
```

Notice that the substitution variable in this example is surrounded by single quotes. Those quotes will surround whatever date the user types in, thereby making a properly formatted date.

Place this code in a script file named test_test3.sql, and then run it to see how it works. (The table currently contains records whose dates are 14-JUL-03, 15-JUL-03, and 16-JUL-03.)

To sharpen your skill with this technique, create a script file that allows the user to specify two dates between which records will be selected. This will involve using the BETWEEN clause and two separate substitution variables.

The ACCEPT Command

You may have noticed that the prompt SQL*Plus displays to users when it encounters a substitution variable isn't exactly attractive. An alternative is the **ACCEPT** command, which allows you to define any prompt you want. The command's syntax is as follows:

```
accept variable_name prompt 'prompt text'
```

To see how it works, create a script named test_test4.sql and place the following commands within it:

```
SET VERIFY OFF
SET ECHO OFF

ACCEPT v_earliest_date PROMPT 'Earliest date you would like to see? (dd-mmm-yy): '
ACCEPT v_latest_date PROMPT 'Thank you. Latest date you would like to see? (dd-mmm-yy): '
SELECT product_name, quantity, purchase_date
FROM    test_purchase
WHERE   purchase_date BETWEEN '&v_earliest_date' AND '&v_latest_date'
ORDER BY product_name, quantity
;

SET VERIFY ON
SET ECHO ON
```

This script employs one more pair of new commands: **SET ECHO** OFF and SET ECHO ON. The SET ECHO commands control whether commands in the script file are shown to the user. In this case, they ensure that the user only sees the prompts from the ACCEPT commands and does not see the commands themselves.

 Cross Check

Script Files

Now that you have been introduced to script files, check your knowledge by providing answers to the following questions:

1. What tools do you need to create a script file?
2. What are the functions of the SET ECHO commands?

Chapter 4 Review

■ Chapter Summary

After reading this chapter and completing the Step-by-Step tutorial and Cross Checks, you should understand the following facts about controlling SQL*Plus:

Edit Prior Commands in SQL*Plus

- The ED or EDIT command can be used to invoke your system's default text editor.

- The CHANGE command can be used to perform line-level editing.

- To correct multiline statements with the CHANGE command, you must specify which line you want to work on before making any actual changes.

Copy and Paste Commands

- You can copy commands from the SQL*Plus display screen and reuse them by pasting them back in at the SQL> prompt.

- You can use your operating system's standard keyboard shortcuts for the Copy and Paste commands.

Clear the SQL*Plus Screen

- To clear the SQL*Plus screen, hold down the SHIFT key, and while holding it down, tap the DELETE key.

Customize the SQL*Plus Environment

- You can customize the SQL*Plus environment using the Options | Environment menu command.

- By default, SQL*Plus remembers up to 100 characters of each line you type, and up to 1,000 such lines.

- The linesize sets the maximum width SQL*Plus will provide for each line before wrapping.

- The Buffer Width determines how many characters of each line will be stored in memory for later retrieval.

- The pagesize controls how many lines of data SQL*Plus will display in response to a SELECT command before it repeats the column headings.

Save Environment Customizations

- You can tell SQL*Plus to store all of its environment settings in a file that it will then read each time you start the program.

- The STORE command instructs SQL*Plus to save all of your current environment settings to a disk file.

Produce More Readable Input

- With a few simple commands you can improve the appearance of SQL*Plus's output.

- The COLUMN command's job is to affect the way your own copy of SQL*Plus displays information from numbers to column headings.

- A group separator is a character that separates hundreds, thousands, and so on, within a number.

SPOOL Output to Disk

- Spooling is the process of writing information out to a file on a disk. Spooling can be done within SQL*Plus, either to make a record of a series of commands and their results, or to store voluminous output from a single command.

- The spool filename can include a file extension if you wish (such as .sql or .prn).

Work with SQL Script Files

- A script file is a plain text file. You can use SQL*Plus's EDIT command to start your system's default text editor to create a new script file.

- Running a script file in SQL*Plus is done by preceding the name of the file with the "at" sign (@).

- You can write a script file that can work in a variety of situations, changing what it does in each situation by using variables in your script files.

- You can build variables into your SQL scripts in two different ways: using substitution variables, and using the ACCEPT command.

- The SET VERIFY OFF and SET VERIFY ON commands in the script help improve its appearance when the script runs.

- The ACCEPT command allows you to define any prompt you want.

- SET ECHO OFF and SET ECHO ON—the SET ECHO commands control whether commands in the script file are shown to the user.

Key Terms

ACCEPT *(98)*
Buffer Width *(88)*
CHANGE *(83)*
COLUMN *(90)*
EDIT *(81)*
group separator *(91)*

hard-coded *(96)*
linesize *(88)*
pagesize *(88)*
script file *(95)*
SET ECHO *(98)*
SET VERIFY *(97)*

SPOOL *(94)*
spooling *(94)*
STORE *(90)*
variable *(96)*

Key Term Quiz

Use the Key Terms list to complete the sentences that follow. Not all terms will be used.

1. When _____ is too small, the data you select may be wider than SQL*Plus can display on one line, in which case SQL*Plus will wrap columns to make them fit.

2. The _____ command instructs SQL*Plus to save all of your current environment settings to a disk file.

3. A(n) _____ takes the place of a portion of your command, allowing you to "fill in" that portion when the script is run—thereby changing what the script does.

4. You can use the _____ command to create a disk file containing everything you see go across your SQL*Plus screen.

5. The _____ command does not get sent to the Oracle database. Its only job is to affect the way your own copy of SQL*Plus displays information.

Matching Definition Quiz

Relate each term on the left with the appropriate description on the right.

Term	Description
1. Substitution variable	a. The process of writing information out to a file on a disk
2. Spooling	b. Controls whether commands in the script file are shown to the user
3. Group separator	c. Controls how many lines of data SQL*Plus will display in response to a SELECT command before it repeats the column headings
4. SET ECHO command	d. A variable name or numeral preceded by one or two ampersands that are used in a command file to represent values to be provided when the command file is run
5. Pagesize	e. A character that separates hundreds, thousands, and so on within a number

Multiple-Choice Quiz

1. What editor is started when you execute the ED command from SQL*Plus?

   a. Oracle's internal editor

   b. Your system's default editor

   c. The EDIT program

   d. The VI program

   e. DOSEDIT

2. Which of the following commands will *not* alter the way data is displayed on your screen?

   a. COLUMN

   b. SET LINESIZE

   c. SPOOL

   d. SET PAGESIZE

   e. SET COLUMN

3. On which line will the following command fail?

```
SET VERIFY OFF
SET ECHO OFF
ACCEPT v_earliest_date PROMPT 'Earliest date?
    (dd-mmm-yy): '
ACCEPT v_latest_date PROMPT 'Latest date?
    (dd-mmm-yy): '
SELECT product_name, quantity, purchase_date
FROM test_purchase
WHERE purchase_date BETWEEN '&earliest_date'
AND '&latest_date'
ORDER BY product_name, quantity:
SET VERIFY ON
SET ECHO ON
```

   a. 1

   b. 3

   c. 5

   d. 7

   e. 9

4. The correct syntax of the CHANGE command is

   a. C[HANGE] *column_name* FORMAT A*nn* WORD_WRAP

   b. C[HANGE] *separator_character old_text* [*separator_character new_text*]

   c. CHANGE *column_name* FORMAT A*nn* WORD_WRAP

   d. C[HANGE] *old_text separator_character* [*new_text separator_character*]

   e. C[HANGE] *separator_character new_text* [*separator_character old_text*]

5. This feature of SQL*Plus determines how many characters of each line will be stored in memory for later retrieval.

   a. Linesize

   b. Pagesize

   c. Buffer Width

   d. Buffer Length

   e. Group separator

6. To run a script file, you

   a. Precede the name of the file with the "at" sign (@)

   b. Precede the name of the file with the double ampersands (&&)

   c. Precede the name of the file with a percentage sign (%)

   d. Precede the name of the file with double "at" signs (@@)

   e. Precede the name of the file with an ampersand (&)

7. The "A" preceding the number argument in the COLUMN command stands for

   a. Argument

   b. "At" sign

   c. Alphanumeric

   d. Ampersand

   e. Alternate

8. Which format code places a plus sign (+) for positive values and a minus sign (–) for negative values?

   a. MI

   b. PR

   c. G

   d. C

   e. S

9. Which format code causes numbers to display as upper- or lowercase Roman numerals (limited to integers between 1 and 3,999)?

   a. RN

   b. PR

   c. MI

   d. L

   e. C

10. Which of the following actions commonly need to be done to numbers? (Choose three.)

   a. Place a currency symbol with them

   b. Convert them to a date format

   c. Place a separator between hundreds, thousands, and so on

   d. Align their decimals

   e. Calculate their total value

11. What are the major benefits of storing the commands needed to accomplish a specific task in a disk file? (Choose three.)

   a. It prevents commands from executing the same way each time.

   b. It saves you time by eliminating the need to retype repetitive commands.

c. It makes the procedure finish more quickly because commands are read from the disk file much more quickly than you could type them.

d. It allows scripts on the disk to be run automatically when accessed.

e. It ensures that the commands are executed in exactly the same way, with perfect syntax, each time.

12. A character that separates hundreds, thousands, and so on, within a number is known as a

a. System variable

b. Variable

c. Column separator

d. Substitution variable

e. Group separator

13. This command instructs SQL*Plus to save all of your current environment settings to a disk file:

a. SAVE

b. ACCEPT

c. CHANGE

d. STORE

e. SPOOL

14. These commands control whether commands in the script file are shown to the user:

a. SPOOL

b. STORE

c. SET VERIFY

d. ACCEPT

e. SET ECHO

15. Hard-coded information is defined as

a. Information typed explicitly into the script file that cannot be changed when the script is run

b. Information that is easily changed when a script is run

c. Information that is only executed with an "at" (@) sign

d. Information that is only executed with an ampersand

e. Information that is surrounded by single quotes

■ Essay Quiz

1. What is the difference between the CHANGE and EDIT commands? Give reasons why these commands would be helpful to you when creating SQL scripts.

2. Name two ways you can clear the SQL*Plus screen. Explain why this is useful to you in your daily use of SQL*Plus.

3. What are the issues involved when setting an appropriate linesize in SQL*Plus? What is the result of an improper linesize?

4. What is the process of aligning decimals for use with numbers in SQL*Plus?

5. What is the result of not using SET VERIFY commands when running scripts?

Lab Projects

• Lab Project 4.1

Case Study

John has asked you to create a SALE_ITEM table in the Clapham Specialty Store database in order to keep track of the products that they sell at a reduced cost. He wants to be able to call up the sale item records that show the item price and item cost in dollar value format. He also wants to change the view of column headings per his request.

You will need the Oracle9*i* Database Server with the SQL*Plus tool. Then, do the following:

① Create a SALE_ITEM table according to the following SQL code:

```
CREATE TABLE sale_item (
    till_receipt_no NUMBER(10) NOT NULL,
    item_no         NUMBER(3)     NOT NULL,
    sku             VARCHAR2(20) NOT NULL,
    quantity        NUMBER(3)     NOT NULL
    item_price      NUMBER(8, 2) NOT NULL,
    item_cost       NUMBER(8, 2) NULL
    )
;
```

② Correct the mistake in the SQL code by using the EDIT command, then create the SALE_ITEM table.

③ Insert the following records to the SALE_ITEM table:

```
Till Receipt No: 8099375722, Item No: 908,
SKU: 34KK784,
Quantity: 2, Item price: 5.99 Item Cost 3.00
Till Receipt No: 8800334588, Item No: 905,
SKU: 45IE686,
Quantity: 3, Item price: 5.99, Item Cost:
3.50
```

```
Till Receipt No: 8800334580, Item No: 906,
SKU: 45IE690,
Quantity: 3, Item price: 1.99, Item Cost:
1.00
Till Receipt No: 8800334533, Item No: 907,
SKU: 45IE683,
Quantity: 2, Item price: 4.99, Item Cost:
2.00
Till Receipt No: 8800334557, Item No: 904,
SKU: 45IE693,
Quantity: 5, Item price: 5.99, Item Cost:
2.80
```

④ Select the Item_Price and Item_Cost column values from the SALE_ITEM table. Format the display so that a dollar sign ($) is placed before each item price and item cost value in the result set.

⑤ John has requested that the Till_Receipt_No, and Item_No column headings of the SALE_ITEM table be changed so that they read Till Receipt Number and Item Number in the result set.

• Lab Project 4.2

Case Study

John at the Clapham Specialty Store has asked you to create a SQL script that he can run at his convenience. John wants to know what items, if sold at a 50%-off sale price, would not net John a profit, based on the actual cost of the item that John paid to his suppliers for the items. This script is to select the SKU, item number, item price, and item cost for all items that were sold at a reduced price of 50% where the Sale_Item_Price is less than the Item_Cost. John wants to be prompted for the Item_Numbers, as he wants to run this script several times throughout the life of his business.

You will need the Oracle9i Database Server with the SQL*Plus tool.

Complete the following tasks:

① Open the text editor and create a new SQL script named sale_item.sql on your C: drive.

② Write a script that selects the SKU, item number, item price, and item cost from the SALE_ITEM table according to the requirements indicated in the lab description. Remember, John wants to be prompted for the item number when running the script, so ensure that this is added to the script.

③ Run the rental_history.sql script.

④ At the item number prompt, enter the following values separately to view the individual records: 908, 907, 906, 905, 904.

Oracle SQL Built-in Functions

"The test of a first-rate intelligence is the ability to hold two opposed ideas in the mind at the same time, and still retain the ability to function."

—F. Scott Fitzgerald

In this chapter, you will learn how to

- **Implement commonly used single-row functions**
- **Implement commonly used group functions**

This chapter contains a wealth of techniques you can use to make your Oracle applications easier to use, more powerful, and more efficient. This chapter focuses on the fascinating world of SQL functions. A function is like a mini-command you can place within a larger SQL statement. Data goes into a function looking one way, and comes out looking another way, based on the purpose the function is designed to fulfill. For instance, functions can change the way data appears (like turning a date value into the related day of the week), subtotal the data in a way you specify, or alter the content of the data (like taking one set of codes and translating them into a different set of codes). By learning to use functions, you take a major step ahead of those who have merely been exposed to SQL, and toward the group of people who really understand how to make SQL dance for them.

The functions will be presented in two groups: single-row functions and group functions. Single-row functions perform operations that could affect the display of every row in a table. In contrast, group functions are designed to give you information about subsets of your data, with the groupings defined in any way you please.

■ Implementing Commonly Used Single-Row Functions

This section introduces you to single-row functions . These functions give you row-by-row control over how the data in your database is entered and presented. The functions fall into the following categories:

- System variables
- Number
- Character (text)
- Date
- Data conversion
- Miscellaneous

If you just started reading in this chapter and have not done any of the exercises in the preceding chapters, you will need to create the TEST_PRODUCT table built in prior chapters before you can do the exercises in this chapter. You can accomplish this by entering the following SQL commands:

```
DROP TABLE test_product;
CREATE TABLE test_product (
     product_name     VARCHAR2(25),
     product_price    NUMBER(4,2),
     quantity_on_hand NUMBER(5,0),
     last_stock_date  DATE
     )
;

INSERT INTO test_product VALUES
     ('Small Widget', 99, 1, '15-JAN-2003');
INSERT INTO test_product VALUES
     ('Medium Wodget', 75, 1000, '15-JAN-2002');
INSERT INTO test_product VALUES
     ('Chrome Phoobar', 50, 100, '15-JAN-2003');
INSERT INTO test_product VALUES
     ('Round Chrome Snaphoo', 25, 10000, null);
INSERT INTO test_product VALUES
     ('Extra Huge Mega Phoobar +', 9.95, 1234,'15-JAN-2004');
```

You should also rebuild the TEST_PURCHASE table with the following commands:

```
DROP TABLE test_purchase;
CREATE TABLE test_purchase (
     product_name   VARCHAR2(25),
     quantity       NUMBER(4,2),
     purchase_date  DATE,
     salesperson    VARCHAR2(3)
     )
;
```

```
INSERT INTO test_purchase VALUES
    ('Small Widget', 1, '14-JUL-2003', 'CA');
INSERT INTO test_purchase VALUES
    ('Medium Wodget', 75, '14-JUL-2003', 'BB');
INSERT INTO test_purchase VALUES
    ('Chrome Phoobar', 2, '14-JUL-2003', 'GA');
INSERT INTO test_purchase VALUES
    ('Small Widget', 8, '15-JUL-2003', 'GA');
INSERT INTO test_purchase VALUES
    ('Medium Wodget', 20, '15-JUL-2003', 'LB');
INSERT INTO test_purchase VALUES
    ('Round Snaphoo', 5, '16-JUL-2003', 'CA');
```

System Variables

System variables are maintained by Oracle to provide you with information about the environment in which the database is running. The three system variables presented here allow you to determine the system date and time, the ID of the user executing a SQL statement, and the name of the computer from which a user is executing commands. These functions (SYSDATE, USER, USERENV) can be very useful in a variety of ways, as you will see.

SYSDATE

The SYSDATE function returns the current date and time. To be more specific, it returns the current date and time from the Oracle server's point of view, so if the server happens to be in another time zone, that time zone's information will be returned. To see the function in action, enter the following command:

```
SELECT SYSDATE FROM DUAL;
```

In response, you will see the current date appear on your screen. A more interesting way to use this command is in DML statements. For instance, you can cause the current date to be inserted into any date field by specifying SYSDATE in the INSERT statement. Try the following command to see how this works:

```
INSERT INTO test_purchase VALUES
    ('Small Widget', 10, SYSDATE, 'SH');
```

After you have entered this command, use a SELECT statement to see all the records in your TEST_PURCHASE table, and you will see that your new record has been added with today's date in the Purchase_Date column. (Actually, the value entered in that column contains both the date and the time—you will see how to display the time component of the value later in this chapter.)

Let's extend this idea a bit further by using some date math in the INSERT statement. Enter the following commands:

```
INSERT INTO test_purchase VALUES
    ('Medium Wodget', 15, sysdate-14, 'SH');
INSERT INTO test_purchase VALUES
    ('Round Snaphoo', 25, sysdate-7, 'SH');
```

```
INSERT INTO test_purchase VALUES
    ('Chrome Phoobar', 10, sysdate+7, 'SH');
```

With these commands, you can see that today's date can be manipulated simply by adding and subtracting days. For instance, by subtracting 7 from today's SYSDATE value, you get the date value for exactly a week ago.

SYSDATE is also useful when you want to view records containing dates that have a certain relationship to today. For instance, to see all the sales that occurred in the last 30 days, you could use a command like the one that follows:

```
SELECT * FROM test_purchase
WHERE  purchase_date BETWEEN (SYSDATE-30) AND SYSDATE;
```

The results you get from this command could be similar to those you see in Figure 5.1, or you could get no results at all, depending on what date you are reading this textbook and executing the command.

Take a few moments now to experiment with SYSDATE. For instance, try selecting all the records that have been entered in the last two weeks, the last six months, and the last year. When you are done, delete the records used for this SYSDATE section by issuing the following command:

> SYSDATE has a time element, so the result set may sometimes not be what you expect if the column data has also been entered using the SYSDATE function.

```
DELETE FROM test_purchase
WHERE  SALESPERSON = 'SH';
```

USER

Before explaining what the **USER** function does, we want to tell you that we won't be able to demonstrate a good use for this function until later in the book. The same is true for the USERENV function that follows. The USER and USERENV functions are both useful when you want to audit activity on a table—that is, keep track of who is inserting, updating, and deleting records. Doing that is a relatively sophisticated operation, and you will learn how to do it in a later chapter in this book.

Let's begin with the USER function. It returns the Oracle user ID of the person who issues the command containing a USER function. Try the following command to see this in action:

```
SQL> SELECT *
  2  FROM test_purchase
  3  WHERE purchase_date
  4  BETWEEN (SYSDATE-30)
  5  AND SYSDATE
  6  ;

PRODUCT_NAME                  QUANTITY PURCHASE_ SAL
----------------------------- -------- --------- ---
Small Widget                         1 14-JUL-03 CA
Medium Wodget                       75 14-JUL-03 BB
Chrome Phoobar                       2 14-JUL-03 GA
Small Widget                         8 15-JUL-03 GA
Medium Wodget                       20 15-JUL-03 LB
Round Snaphoo                        5 16-JUL-03 CA
Small Widget                        10 06-AUG-03 SH
Medium Wodget                       15 23-JUL-03 SH
Round Snaphoo                       25 30-JUL-03 SH

9 rows selected.

SQL>
```

● **Figure 5.1**   Selecting records using SYSDATE in the WHERE clause

```
SELECT USER FROM DUAL;
```

In response, you will see the name you logged in as when you started SQL*Plus. As mentioned earlier, this is nothing more than an interesting novelty at the moment, but later on it will be useful when you want Oracle to store the user ID of a person making changes to the database.

A big part of growing more valuable as a technical person is being familiar with what a system *can* do, so that when a new need arises, you know what tools are available for taking care of that need.

When exactly half is rounded to 0 decimal places, the number gets rounded up rather than down. This would mean that 1.5 rounded to 0 decimal places would result in a value of 2, rather than a value of 1.

USERENV

The USERENV function can return a variety of different facts about the computer environment of the person who issued the command containing the USERENV function. The most useful of these facts is the name of the computer the person is working on. To see this, enter the following command:

```
SELECT USERENV('TERMINAL') FROM DUAL;
```

In response, you will see your computer's name. This function, combined with the USER function you just learned, enables you to determine who took an action and from what computer. Add a SYSDATE function to the mix, and you have the beginning of a detailed audit record.

Number Functions

Number functions such as ROUND and TRUNC manipulate numeric values, changing them to suit your needs. The functions presented here provide common mathematical features. If the data you work with is mostly text-oriented, you might not see a need to know these functions. You should learn them anyway because you will undoubtedly need them at some point.

ROUND

The ROUND function rounds numbers to whatever degree of precision you specify. Its syntax is as follows:

```
ROUND(input_value, decimal_places_of_precision)
```

To use the ROUND function—and every other function that modifies a value—you "wrap" it around the value you want to modify. Since this is usually done in a SELECT statement, you accomplish this by wrapping the function around the column name containing the values to be modified.

Let's look at an example. The TEST_PRODUCT table contains prices for the products. Some of those prices are integers with no decimal values—but not all. Try this command to see the ROUND function in action:

```
SELECT product_name, product_price, ROUND(product_price, 0)
FROM   test_product;
```

The results you get should look similar to those shown in Figure 5.2. This example shows one of the most common uses for the ROUND function. Another would be rounding detailed values that contain a lot of decimal places down to dollars and cents; that would require specifying a decimal precision value of 2. You can specify any number of decimals of precision you want, but certain values make more sense than others. If you specify a negative number, the ROUND function starts rounding *before* the decimal point, resulting in numbers that are rounded to the nearest 10, 100, 1000, and so on.

The best way to see the relationship between the ROUND function's decimal places of precision and the change the function makes in the value it processes is to use it on numbers containing many decimal places. Since your test tables don't contain any records whose values have many decimal places—and it wouldn't make sense to create product records with prices like that—we'll use DUAL to demonstrate what ROUND does with such numbers. Enter the following commands to see the relationship between the

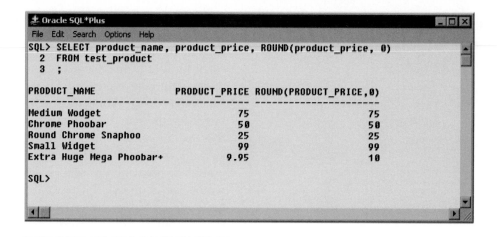

● **Figure 5.2**   The ROUND function

ROUND function's decimal places of precision and the way the function rounds the number it is given. The results are summarized in Table 5.1.

```
SELECT ROUND(1234.5678, 4) FROM DUAL;
SELECT ROUND(1234.5678, 3) FROM DUAL;
SELECT ROUND(1234.5678, 2) FROM DUAL;
SELECT ROUND(1234.5678, 1) FROM DUAL;
SELECT ROUND(1234.5678, 0) FROM DUAL;
SELECT ROUND(1234.5678, -1) FROM DUAL;
SELECT ROUND(1234.5678, -2) FROM DUAL;
SELECT ROUND(1234.5678, -3) FROM DUAL;
```

TRUNC

The `TRUNC` function truncates precision from a number. The difference between this and rounding becomes apparent when a number contains decimal values of .5 or higher. Rounding the number would cause it to move up to the next higher number, while truncating it does not. Enter the following series of commands to see how this works. The results are summarized in Table 5.2.

Table 5.1	ROUND Function Precision Results
ROUND Function	**Resulting Number**
ROUND(1234.5678, 4)	1234.5678
ROUND(1234.5678, 3)	1234.568
ROUND(1234.5678, 2)	1234.57
ROUND(1234.5678, 1)	1234.6
ROUND(1234.5678, 0)	1235
ROUND(1234.5678, -1)	1230
ROUND(1234.5678, -2)	1200
ROUND(1234.5678, -3)	1000

```
SELECT TRUNC(1234.5678, 4) FROM DUAL;
SELECT TRUNC(1234.5678, 3) FROM DUAL;
SELECT TRUNC(1234.5678, 2) FROM DUAL;
SELECT TRUNC(1234.5678, 1) FROM DUAL;
SELECT TRUNC(1234.5678, 0) FROM DUAL;
SELECT TRUNC(1234.5678, -1) FROM DUAL;
SELECT TRUNC(1234.5678, -2) FROM DUAL;
SELECT TRUNC(1234.5678, -3) FROM DUAL;
```

Let's take a look at our case study again. As you know, the Clapham Specialty Store keeps track of the price and cost of sale items in the SALE_ITEM

Case Study

Table 5.2	TRUNC Function Precision Results
TRUNC Function	**Resulting Number**
TRUNC(1234.5678, 4)	1234.5678
TRUNC(1234.5678, 3)	1234.567
TRUNC(1234.5678, 2)	1234.56
TRUNC(1234.5678, 1)	1234.5
TRUNC(1234.5678, 0)	1234
TRUNC(1234.5678, -1)	1230
TRUNC(1234.5678, -2)	1200
TRUNC(1234.5678, -3)	1000

table of their database. What if John chose to calculate the sale price of each item, but instead of rounding each number to the nearest whole dollar value, he used the TRUNC function to do so? Would the results be different than if he used the ROUND function? You bet! The result of using the TRUNC command would be that all the sale prices would be rounded down to the lower dollar value, rather than up to the higher dollar value. Item prices of $3.99 would become $3.00 rather than $4.00. This would result in a great difference in profit if John were to calculate the sum total of all sale items sold.

Text Functions

Text functions, referred to in Oracle as character functions, manipulate text strings. The most common things to do with text strings are changing their case (between uppercase, lowercase, and mixed case); separating a long string into a number of shorter substrings; and cleaning up text coming in from an external source that is padded with extra spaces. By learning the character functions that follow (UPPER, LOWER, INITCAP, SUBSTR, INSTR, LTRIM, RTRIM), you will learn how to do each of those things.

UPPER, LOWER, and INITCAP

These three functions change the case of the text you give them. Try these commands to see how they work:

```
SELECT UPPER(product_name) FROM test_product;
SELECT LOWER(product_name) FROM test_product;
SELECT INITCAP(product_name) FROM test_product;
```

The results you get from these commands should match what you see in Figure 5.3. As you may have noticed, the INITCAP function doesn't really do anything in this example, because the product names already have the first character of each word capitalized. The function's ability to clean up messy text is better demonstrated by the following command:

```
SELECT INITCAP('this TEXT hAd UNpredictABLE caSE') FROM DUAL;
```

Of the three case-changing character functions, you will probably use UPPER the most. One very handy use for it is in SELECT statements, when you are not sure what case your desired text will be in. For those instances, you just wrap an UPPER function around the name of the column you're searching, and then specify the text you want to match in uppercase letters. The opposite applies for the LOWER function. To demonstrate this technique, you need to change your test records a little, so there are records containing the same word but with different case. The following code makes this change, demonstrates how to use the

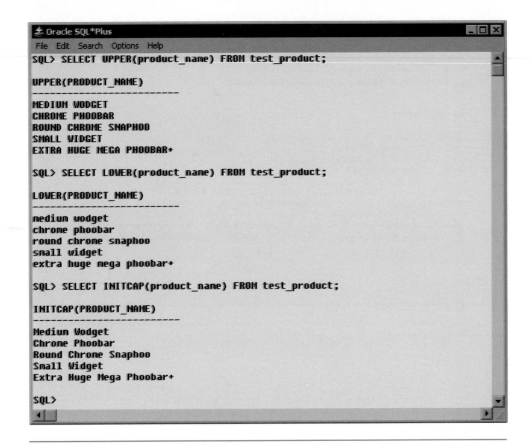

```
± Oracle SQL*Plus                                        _□ X
 File  Edit  Search  Options  Help
SQL> SELECT UPPER(product_name) FROM test_product;

UPPER(PRODUCT_NAME)
-------------------
MEDIUM WODGET
CHROME PHOOBAR
ROUND CHROME SNAPHOO
SMALL WIDGET
EXTRA HUGE MEGA PHOOBAR+

SQL> SELECT LOWER(product_name) FROM test_product;

LOWER(PRODUCT_NAME)
-------------------
medium wodget
chrome phoobar
round chrome snaphoo
small widget
extra huge mega phoobar+

SQL> SELECT INITCAP(product_name) FROM test_product;

INITCAP(PRODUCT_NAME)
-------------------
Medium Wodget
Chrome Phoobar
Round Chrome Snaphoo
Small Widget
Extra Huge Mega Phoobar+

SQL>
```

● **Figure 5.3**   Results of the UPPER, LOWER, and INITCAP functions

UPPER function to overcome the difference in case, and then changes the data back so that the case is once again the same. Enter the commands and compare the results of your SELECT command with those shown in Figure 5.4.

```
UPDATE test_product
SET    product_name = 'chrome phoobar'
WHERE  product_name = 'Chrome Phoobar';

SELECT * FROM test_product
WHERE  UPPER(product_name) LIKE '%PHOOBAR%';
```

Using the UPPER function in this way can make it a lot easier to find the text you want when you don't know the case in which it was originally entered. However, as you can see in Figure 5.4, the data displayed as a result is still inconsistent in its use of upper- and lowercase characters. The solution is to wrap an INITCAP function around the Product_Name column to clean it up. Enter the following code to see how this works:

```
SELECT INITCAP(product_name),
       product_price,
       quantity_on_hand,
       last_stock_date
FROM   test_product
WHERE  UPPER(product_name) LIKE '%PHOOBAR%';
```

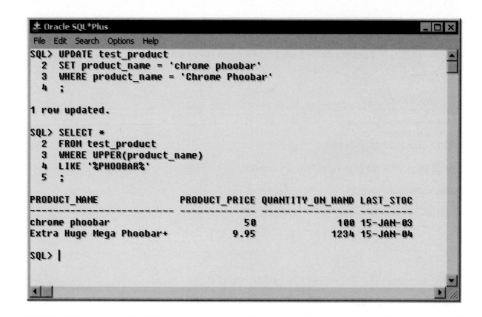

● **Figure 5.4** Using the UPPER function to simplify text searches

After you have compared the results you got with those shown in Figure 5.5, enter the following code to return your product names to the state they were in before this exercise:

```
UPDATE test_product
SET    product_name = 'Chrome Phoobar'
WHERE  product_name = 'chrome phoobar';
```

LENGTH

There are times when it is useful to determine the lengths of data stored in a database column. The LENGTH function provides this capability. Imagine, for example, that you are using a table similar to the TEST_PRODUCT table in your business, and the table feeds product names into the catalog department. They are considering using a smaller page size for the catalog, and the new page size requires them to reduce the length of product names from 25 characters to 15 characters. To help in their decision, they would like to know how many product names they would need to change. You can produce a list of the names that would need to be changed by employing the following command:

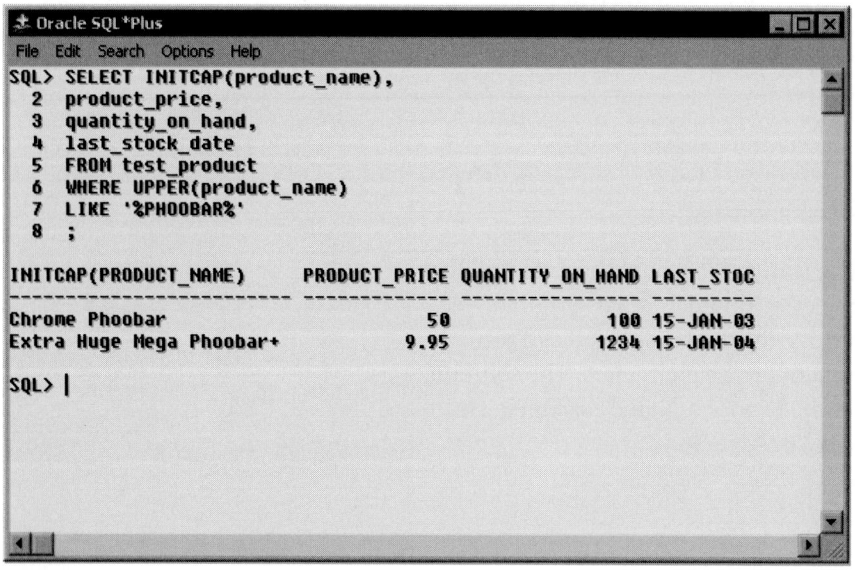

● **Figure 5.5**   Using the INITCAP function to clean up mixed-case data

```
SELECT     product_name, LENGTH(product_name) AS NAME_LENGTH
FROM       test_product
WHERE      LENGTH(product_name) >15
ORDER BY product_name;
```

This example applies the alias NAME_LENGTH to the column containing product-name lengths, in order to make the column headings more readable.

The LENGTH function is also useful for determining the size of the largest entry in a column, as well as the size of the average entry in a column. You will see how to do both of these things a bit later in this section.

SUBSTR

There will be times in your Oracle career when you encounter data with a column containing multiple bits of data that you need to separate in discrete segments. In plain language, you will need to turn a column like this:

ITEM_ID
LA-101
LA-102
LA-103
LA-104
NY-101
NY-102
NY-103
NY-104

into multiple columns like this:

MANUFACTURER LOCATION	MANUFACTURER ITEM NUMBER
LA	101
LA	102
LA	103
LA	104
NY	101
NY	102
NY	103
NY	104

Since text is referred to as a string in the computer world, a smaller portion of text derived from a larger piece of text is called a substring. In the example just shown, the strings in the Item_ID column were broken out into two substrings each. This process is called parsing strings.

Oracle provides a function named SUBSTR to do this. Whenever you want to cut strings up into substrings, you need to specify the point at which the substring should start (you can travel only forward through a string when producing a substring), as well as the length that the substring should be. For instance, in the preceding example, the first substring was the manufacturer's location. Its values start at the first character position in the Item_ID column, and extend for two characters. The next substring was the manufacturer's item number, whose values start at the fourth character position within the Item_ID and extend for three characters.

None of your current sample tables from this book contain data that calls for parsing. That means you get more practice with the CREATE TABLE command. Enter the following commands to create an appropriate table and records:

```
CREATE TABLE test_old_item (
     item_id   CHAR(20),
     item_desc CHAR(25)
     )
;


INSERT INTO test_old_item VALUES
     ('LA-101', 'Can, Small');
INSERT INTO test_old_item VALUES
     ('LA-102', 'Can, Large');
INSERT INTO test_old_item VALUES
     ('LA-103', 'Bottle, Small');
INSERT INTO test_old_item VALUES
     ('LA-104', 'Bottle, Large');
INSERT INTO test_old_item VALUES
     ('NY-101', 'Box, Small');
INSERT INTO test_old_item VALUES
     ('NY-102', 'Box, Large');
INSERT INTO test_old_item VALUES
     ('NY-103', 'Shipping Carton, Small');
INSERT INTO test_old_item VALUES
     ('NY-104', 'Shipping Carton, Large');
```

Now that you have data that can use parsing, it's time to learn the syntax of the SUBSTR command:

```
SUBSTR(source_text, starting_character_position, number_of_characters)
```

The *source_text* value will usually be the name of the column that needs to be parsed. The *starting_character_position* is the first character in the column to include, and the *number_of_characters* is the number of characters to get. To parse the item ID into a manufacturer location and item number, enter the following command:

```
SELECT SUBSTR(item_id, 1, 2) MFGR_LOCATION,
       SUBSTR(item_id, 4, 3) ITEM_NUMBER,
       item_desc
FROM   test_old_item
;
```

After you have entered this command, compare the results you get with those shown in Figure 5.6.

Parsing strings is a very common part of transferring data from one application to another, because two applications never store data in exactly the same way. Later in this chapter you will become familiar with this process by learning how to copy records from one table to another, and part of the process will include parsing the data along the way.

INSTR

Using SUBSTR as shown in the previous exercise works great when you know exactly how long each substring will be. Often, however, you will be called upon to parse strings like those in the Item_Desc column of your TEST_OLD_ITEM table—strings whose substrings vary in length. This means that not only is the length of the first substring unknown, but the starting position of the second substring can also vary. The only way to parse a string like this is to find out the location of the character (or characters) separating the items you want to parse. Oracle provides a function named INSTR that does just that.

INSTR searches for the text you specify and returns a number identifying the starting position of that text within a string. By using the number returned by INSTR to control the length of your first SUBSTR function, as well as the starting po-

```
Oracle SQL*Plus
File   Edit   Search   Options   Help
SQL> SELECT SUBSTR(item_id, 1, 2) MFGR_LOCATION,
  2    SUBSTR(item_id, 4, 3) ITEM_NUMBER,
  3    item_desc
  4    FROM test_old_item
  5    ;

MF ITE ITEM_DESC
-- --- -------------------------------
LA 101 Can, Small
LA 102 Can, Large
LA 103 Bottle, Small
LA 104 Bottle, Large
NY 101 Box, Small
NY 102 Box, Large
NY 103 Shipping Carton, Small
NY 104 Shipping Carton, Large

8 rows selected.

SQL> |
```

● **Figure 5.6**   Parsing data using the SUBSTR function

sition of the next substring, you can reliably slice and dice long strings no matter how they are divided.

The INSTR function's syntax is as follows:

```
INSTR(source_text, text_to_locate, starting_character_position)
```

The *source_text* is generally the name of the column containing the long string you want to parse. The *text_to_locate* is the text you want to find, and the *starting_character_position* specifies the character number in the source text at which you want to start searching (to start at the beginning of the text, use a *starting_character_position* value of 1).

The INSTR function can help us separate the TEST_OLD_ITEM table's Item_Desc column into two pieces. All we have to do is tell it to locate the comma that separates the item category from the item size. By using the number it returns, we can specify the proper size for the item category, as well as the starting point for the item size.

If we're going to have the INSTR function help us separate the TEST_OLD_ITEM table's Item_Desc column into two pieces, we need to understand what information the function provides for each record. Enter the following command to see the INSTR function in action:

```
SELECT item_desc,
       INSTR(item_desc,
             ',',
             1
             )
FROM   test_old_item;
```

As Figure 5.7 shows, the INSTR function returns a number identifying the location of the comma in each record's item description. We could use that number as the length of our SUBSTR function to get the item category, but if we did, the category would include the comma. Therefore we will want to subtract 1 from the INSTR function's value. The following code demonstrates how to do this:

```
SELECT item_desc,
       SUBSTR(item_desc,
              1,
              INSTR(item_desc,
                    ',',
                    1
                    )
              -1
              )
FROM   test_old_item;
```

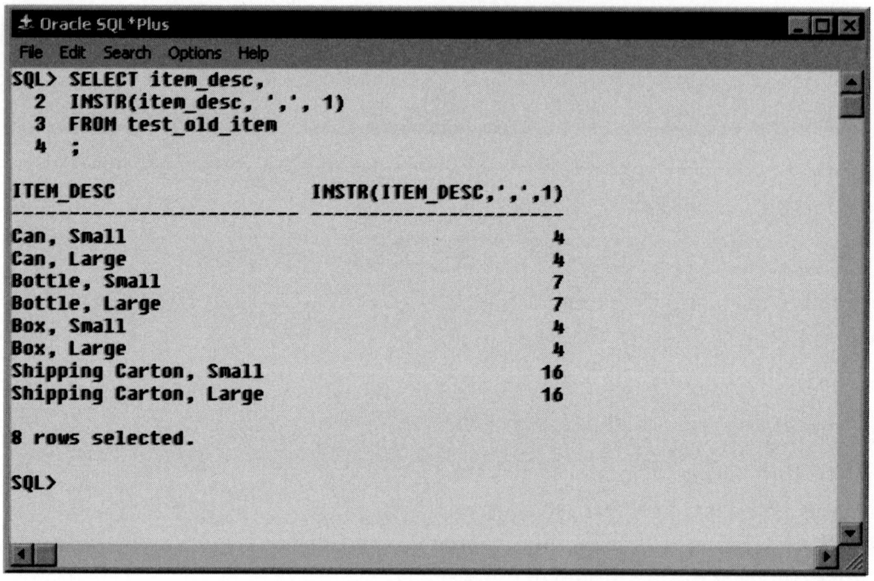

Enter the code and compare your results with those shown in Figure 5.8. As you can see, you now have a means to get a clean item category from each item record.

You have just had your first experience using one function within another one. This is called nesting functions. In a nested function, the inner function returns a value that is then used by the outer function. This is a powerful capability.

Getting back to the subject at hand, you still need to extract the item size from the Item_Desc column. The tricky part of this is the starting position for the size's SUBSTR function. Once again the INSTR function provides the solution by identifying the location of the comma preceding the size. However, that comma is located two characters before the actual start of the size, so you will want to add 2 to the value returned by the INSTR function. Enter the code that follows to get a nice clean list of each item's size:

```
SELECT item_desc,
       SUBSTR(item_desc,
              INSTR(item_desc,
                    ',',
                    1
                    ) +2,
              99
              )
FROM   test_old_item;
```

In this case, the length of the substring is not a concern, because you are extracting the last portion of text in the overall string. To signify this, the example specified a length of 99, which can help serve as a reminder that the SUBSTR function is pulling out the last text in the overall string.

• **Figure 5.7** Results of the INSTR function

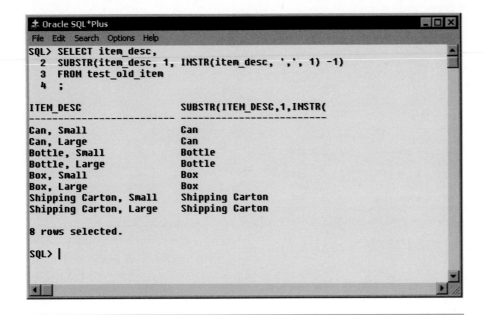

● **Figure 5.8**   Parsing a variable-length substring

Now that you have seen how to parse each item's category and size, it's time to do both in one command. The code that follows will include two SUBSTR functions: one for category, and the other for size. To help keep things clear, the example places a column alias after each SUBSTR function identifying which attribute it is producing.

```
SELECT item_desc,
       SUBSTR(item_desc,
              1,
              INSTR(item_desc,
                    ',',
                    1
                    ) -1
              )              CATEGORY,
       SUBSTR(item_desc,
              INSTR(item_desc,
                    ',',
                    1
                    ) +2,
              99
              )              ITEM_SIZE
FROM   test_old_item
;
```

The results you get from this command should match those shown in Figure 5.9.

The formatting used in the code just shown uses indenting to help clarify how the portions of each function and nested function are grouped together.

> 🔆 It's useful to use indenting when you are learning about functions, because it helps you keep clear about what part of which function you are dealing with at any given location in the command.

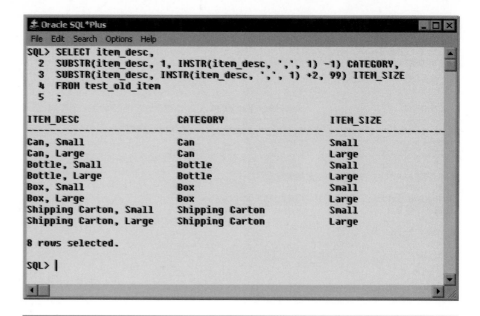

```
SQL> SELECT item_desc,
  2   SUBSTR(item_desc, 1, INSTR(item_desc, ',', 1) -1) CATEGORY,
  3   SUBSTR(item_desc, INSTR(item_desc, ',', 1) +2, 99) ITEM_SIZE
  4   FROM test_old_item
  5  ;

ITEM_DESC                    CATEGORY                 ITEM_SIZE
---------------------------  -----------------------  --------------------
Can, Small                   Can                      Small
Can, Large                   Can                      Large
Bottle, Small                Bottle                   Small
Bottle, Large                Bottle                   Large
Box, Small                   Box                      Small
Box, Large                   Box                      Large
Shipping Carton, Small       Shipping Carton          Small
Shipping Carton, Large       Shipping Carton          Large

8 rows selected.

SQL>
```

● **Figure 5.9**   Parsing multiple variable-length substrings

Oracle doesn't care how the command is formatted, and will produce identical results from the following code, which contains exactly the same command in a more compact form:

```
SELECT item_desc,
       SUBSTR(item_desc, 1, INSTR(item_desc, ',', 1) -1)  CATEGORY,
       SUBSTR(item_desc, INSTR(item_desc, ',', 1) +2, 99) ITEM_SIZE
FROM   test_old_item;
```

You will get a chance to work with substrings more a little later in the chapter, when you learn how to copy records from one table to another.

LTRIM and RTRIM

The best way to explain what these functions do is to show you the problem they solve. Enter the following code and compare your results with those in Figure 5.10.

```
SELECT 'Item  ' ||
       item_id ||
       ' is described as a ' ||
       item_desc ||
       '.'  "Item Description Sentence"
FROM   test_old_item;
```

Why is there so much space after the Item_ID and Item_Desc values? Because both columns are defined as CHAR datatypes. Remember the difference between the VARCHAR2 datatype and the CHAR datatype? VARCHAR2 is variable length, while CHAR is fixed length. This means that data stored in a CHAR column is padded with spaces to fill the data out to the column's defined length. Those spaces become a problem when you want to concatenate the column's contents with anything else. They can also be unnecessary space-wasters when importing fixed-length data from another database system into your own tables.

Functions to the rescue. The process of removing extra spaces from the beginning or end of a text string is called trimming, and Oracle provides two functions that do it: LTRIM and RTRIM. The LTRIM function removes spaces from the beginning of a string, while the RTRIM function removes spaces from the end. The syntax for both functions is essentially identical:

```
LTRIM(column_name)
RTRIM(column_name)
```

In the Item_ID and Item_Desc columns, the problem is extra spaces at the end of each entry. The RTRIM function is the answer to this problem. You just wrap an RTRIM function around each column's name, as shown in the following code:

```
Oracle SQL*Plus
File  Edit  Search  Options  Help

SQL> SELECT 'Item ' ||
  2         item_id ||
  3         ' is described as a ' ||
  4         item_desc ||
  5         '.' "Item Description Sentence"
  6  FROM   test_old_item;

Item Description Sentence
------------------------------------------------------------
Item  LA-101          is described as a Can, Small           .
Item  LA-102          is described as a Can, Large           .
Item  LA-103          is described as a Bottle, Small        .
Item  LA-104          is described as a Bottle, Large        .
Item  NY-101          is described as a Box, Small           .
Item  NY-102          is described as a Box, Large           .
Item  NY-103          is described as a Shipping Carton, Small .
Item  NY-104          is described as a Shipping Carton, Large .

8 rows selected.

SQL>
```

● **Figure 5.10**   Concatenating text from CHAR columns

```
SELECT 'Item  ' ||
       RTRIM(item_id) ||
       ' is described as a ' ||
       RTRIM(item_desc) ||
       '.'  "Item Description Sentence"
FROM   test_old_item;
```

Try this code, and compare the results with those you see in Figure 5.11.

The RTRIM and LTRIM functions can also trim characters from the right and left side of a string. The following example trims the letters "jr" from the right side of a string:

```
SELECT RTRIM('KARAYANISjr','jr')"Employee Surname"
    FROM DUAL;
```

The result set would simply show the name KARAYANIS under the Employee Surname column.

Cross Check

Text Functions

Take a moment to check your knowledge of text functions by answering the following questions:

1. What are the three functions that affect the case of text that you indicate?

2. What do you need to specify when dividing strings into substrings?

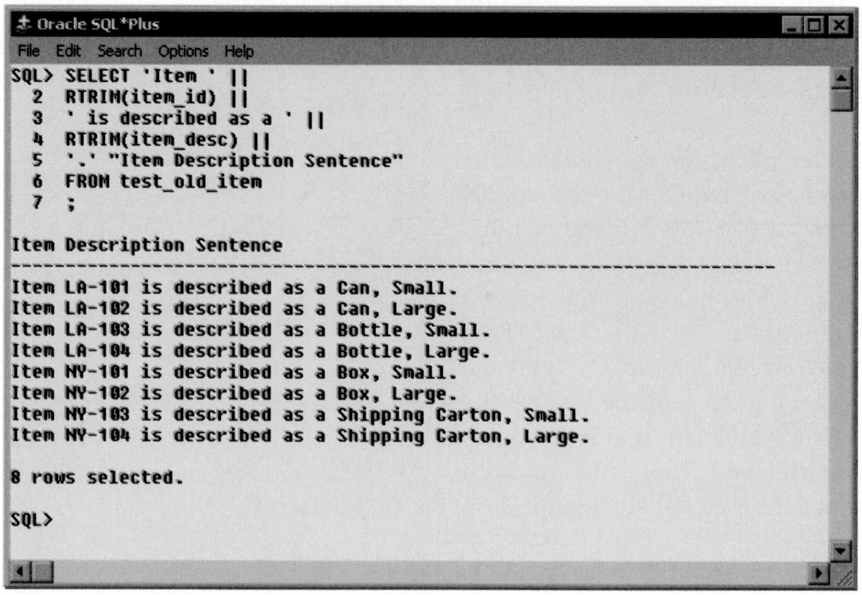

```
±- Oracle SQL*Plus                                               _ □ X
File  Edit  Search  Options  Help
SQL> SELECT 'Item ' ||
  2  RTRIM(item_id) ||
  3  ' is described as a ' ||
  4  RTRIM(item_desc) ||
  5  '.' "Item Description Sentence"
  6  FROM test_old_item
  7  ;

Item Description Sentence
-----------------------------------------------------------------
Item LA-101 is described as a Can, Small.
Item LA-102 is described as a Can, Large.
Item LA-103 is described as a Bottle, Small.
Item LA-104 is described as a Bottle, Large.
Item NY-101 is described as a Box, Small.
Item NY-102 is described as a Box, Large.
Item NY-103 is described as a Shipping Carton, Small.
Item NY-104 is described as a Shipping Carton, Large.

8 rows selected.

SQL>
```

• **Figure 5.11** Trimming fixed-length text values

Step-by-Step 5.01

Using Single-Row Functions

Greg's Organic Grocery Store wants to keep track of the products that are too old to be sold on their store shelves throughout their Canadian stores. They have stores in Winnipeg, Toronto, Calgary, and Vancouver. The problem with the current tracking system is that it places the store name and product number under one column heading called Product_Name. This data needs to be divided, and two columns, Store_Name and Product_No, need to be created with the appropriate data under each column heading for easier viewing.

The current tracking system also groups the product type and size into a heading named Product_Desc. The data in this column would also need to be divided into separate Product_Type and Product_Size columns.

For this exercise, you will need Oracle9i Database Server with the SQL*Plus tool.

Step 1

Create an OLD_PRODUCTS table as follows:

```
CREATE TABLE old_products(
      product_name CHAR(15),
      product_desc CHAR(20)
      )
;
```

Step 2

Insert the following records into the OLD_PRODUCTS table:

```
INSERT INTO old_products VALUES
      ('WPG-10', 'Jar, Small');
INSERT INTO old_products VALUES
```

```
                ('WPG-11', 'Bottle, Large');
        INSERT INTO old_products VALUES
                ('TO-12', 'Can, Small');
        INSERT INTO old_products VALUES
                ('TO-13', 'Jar, Large');
        INSERT INTO old_products VALUES
                ('CGY-14', 'Box, Small');
        INSERT INTO old_products VALUES
                ('CGY-15', 'Box, Large');
        INSERT INTO old_products VALUES
                ('VAN-16', 'Carton, Small');
        INSERT INTO old_products VALUES
                ('VAN-17', 'Carton, Large');
```

Step 3

To parse the Product_Name into a Store_Name and Product_No, enter the following command:

```
SELECT SUBSTR(product_name, 1, 3) STORE_NAME,
        SUBSTR(product_name, 5, 2) PRODUCT_NUMBER,
        product_desc
FROM    old_products
;
```

Step 4

To divide the product description for each old product into two separate columns (Product_Type and Product_Size), execute the following command:

```
SELECT product_desc,
        SUBSTR(product_desc, 1, INSTR(product_desc, ',', 1) -1) PRODUCT_TYPE,
        SUBSTR(product_desc, INSTR(product_desc, ',', 1) +2, 9)  PRODUCT_SIZE
FROM    old_products
;
```

You should have successfully completed the step-by-step instructions and divided the data into separate columns by using the SUBSTR and INSTR functions.

Date

Oracle offers a number of functions designed to make it easier to work with dates. This section will start by showing you how to combine two functions you already know to create a new result that is useful in a lot of situations. Next, you will see how to use simple functions to do date tricks that would otherwise require a *lot* of thought and coding.

SYSDATE and TRUNC

To see the problem you're about to learn how to solve, enter the following code:

```
INSERT INTO test_product VALUES
     ('Square Zinculator', 45, 1, SYSDATE);

SELECT * FROM test_product;
```

Looks fine so far, right? You see the new record for the zinculator, and all the data for it appears correct. Now enter the following command, replacing the *dd-mon-yyyy* with the current date (the one shown in your zinculator record):

```
SELECT * FROM test_product
WHERE  last_stock_date = 'dd-mon-yyyy';
```

If you enter these commands correctly, the result should be… no records displayed! Why isn't your zinculator record showing when you can see very clearly that it contains today's date? The answer, of course, is that using SYSDATE generated the date placed into the zinculator record, and SYSDATE returns more than just the current date; it also returns the current time. Even though you can't see the time component of the date value (you will learn how to see time very soon), it is still there and it keeps the record's value from matching the date value for the current day. It's like trying to match 1 and 1.4 in a column that is formatted to not show decimal places: the difference is there, even if it doesn't show.

The solution: Use the TRUNC function to make your WHERE clause ignore the time value within the last stock date. To make this happen, you must wrap the TRUNC function around the reference to the Last_Stock_Date column, as shown in the modified SELECT statement here:

```
SELECT * FROM test_product
WHERE  TRUNC(last_stock_date) = 'dd-mon-yyyy';
```

This will produce the results you expected the first time. This technique is very handy when you need to work with a table containing a column with date and time combined together.

An alternative use of the TRUNC function is to ensure that the date value stored in the database doesn't have a time component in the first place. Enter the following commands to see how this would work, and notice how the INSERT statement has a TRUNC function wrapped around its SYSDATE function:

```
DELETE FROM test_product
WHERE  product_name = 'Square Zinculator';

INSERT INTO test_product VALUES
    ('Square Zinculator', 45, 1, trunc(sysdate));

SELECT * FROM test_product
WHERE  last_stock_date = 'dd-mon-yyyy';
```

How can you decide whether to use the TRUNC function at the input stage or the output stage? It depends on the application. The time something occurs could be an important piece of information when you are recording transactions, tracking events, or storing auditing information. On the other hand, it may not be important at all if you are recording when something arrived, or identifying a follow-up date that is *nn* days from today. If you have an application that calls for automatic entry of today's date but is not concerned with time of day, you will save yourself (and others) a lot of confusion and extra work if you truncate the SYSDATE value before inserting it.

ADD_MONTHS

The ADD_MONTHS function returns a date that has the same day of the month as the original date it was provided, but is a specified number of months in the future (or the past). The function's syntax is as follows:

```
ADD_MONTHS('starting_date', number_of_months)
```

The *starting_date* can be today's date (using TRUNC(SYSDATE)), or it can be the name of a column in a table. The *number_of_months* is an integer representing the number of months you want added to or subtracted from the starting date. (If you want months subtracted, specify a negative value for the number of months.)

If you want to see the function in action, enter the following commands:

```
SELECT ADD_MONTHS(SYSDATE,1) FROM DUAL;
SELECT ADD_MONTHS(SYSDATE,12) FROM DUAL;
```

One interesting thing about the ADD_MONTHS function is that it is smart enough to understand when the day it's been given is the last day of the month and adjust accordingly. To see what that means, enter the following commands and compare your results with those in Figure 5.12.

```
SELECT ADD_MONTHS('28-NOV-00', 1) FROM DUAL;
SELECT ADD_MONTHS('29-NOV-00', 1) FROM DUAL;
SELECT ADD_MONTHS('30-NOV-00', 1) FROM DUAL;
SELECT ADD_MONTHS('31-DEC-00', -1) FROM DUAL;
```

Notice that in the last sample command, a month is subtracted from December 31. If you were to guess quickly, you might say the answer should be November 31—until you remembered that November only has 30 days. The ADD_MONTHS function is smart enough to know that and adjust accordingly. This adjustment only occurs when the starting date is the last day of a month. You can see in the preceding three sample commands that ADD_MONTHS adds precisely one month until it is given a starting date that is the last day of a month.

One example of when this would be useful might be a tickler file, where you want to record a date a month away when you will check up on something or get back in touch with someone. You can cause your INSERT or UPDATE statement to place the proper date in your table by including this in the statement:

```
ADD_MONTHS(TRUNC(SYSDATE), 1)
```

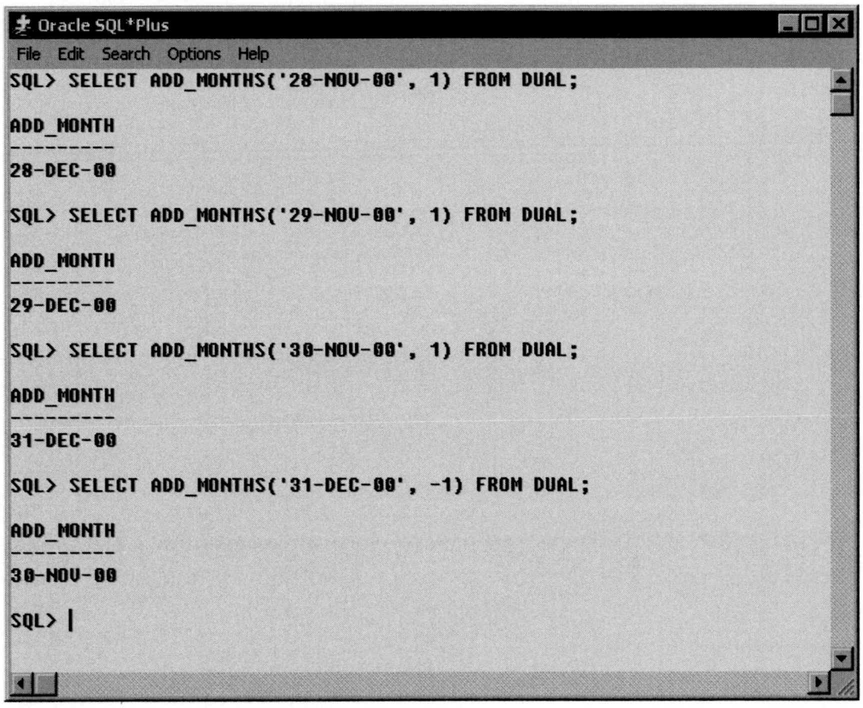

• **Figure 5.12**   Using the ADD_MONTHS function

LAST_DAY

The **LAST_DAY** function performs a simple task that would be a lot more work to have to program yourself: It returns the last day of whatever month is included in the date it is given. Its syntax is

```
LAST_DAY('date')
```

Like any other date function, it can be tested using SYSDATE as the *date* value. Try this series of commands to see the results it produces:

```
SELECT LAST_DAY(SYSDATE) FROM DUAL;
SELECT LAST_DAY('01-JAN-02') FROM DUAL;
SELECT LAST_DAY('15-JAN-02') FROM DUAL;
SELECT LAST_DAY('31-JAN-02') FROM DUAL;
```

There are a number of business situations where this type of function can be handy. For instance, in many companies a new employee's health insurance coverage begins on the first day of whatever month follows their hire date—meaning that if they started working on April 1 their insurance starts on May 1, and if they started working on April 30 their insurance still starts on May 1. Take a moment now and think: how can a date function that returns the last day of a month be modified to instead return the first day of the following month?

The answer is to simply add 1 to the value returned by the LAST_DAY function. To see this in action, you will need to create a new table that contains people and hire dates. You can do this with the following commands:

```
DROP TABLE test_person

CREATE TABLE test_person (
    person_code VARCHAR2(3),
    first_name  VARCHAR2(15),
    last_name   VARCHAR2(20),
    hire_date   DATE
    )
;

INSERT INTO test_person VALUES
    ('CA', 'Charlene', 'Atlas', '01-FEB-02');
INSERT INTO test_person VALUES
    ('GA', 'Gary', 'Anderson', '15-FEB-02');
INSERT INTO test_person VALUES
    ('BB', 'Bobby', 'Barkenhagen', '28-FEB-02');
INSERT INTO test_person VALUES
    ('LB', 'Laren', 'Baxter', '01-MAR-02');
```

Now that you have a suitable table, you can see how the LAST_DAY function can be useful for this purpose. Enter the SELECT command that follows, noting how the LAST_DAY function is used to determine the first day of the month following each person's hire date:

```
SELECT first_name,
       last_name,
       hire_date,
```

```
       LAST_DAY(hire_date)+1
INSURANCE_START_DATE
FROM   test_person;
```

When you are done, the results of your SELECT statement should look like Figure 5.13.

You can produce some very interesting results by nesting date functions together. Consider this example: each record in your TEST_PRODUCT table contains a date indicating when the item was last restocked. Let's say that in the fictional company where you're working, three months must go by before an item is restocked. To get the restock date, you could just use the ADD_MONTHS function to produce dates that are three months after the last restock date. But there's a twist—ordering only happens on the first of each month. So what you really want are dates that are three months after the last restock date, moved forward to the first day in whatever month follows. How can you accomplish this?

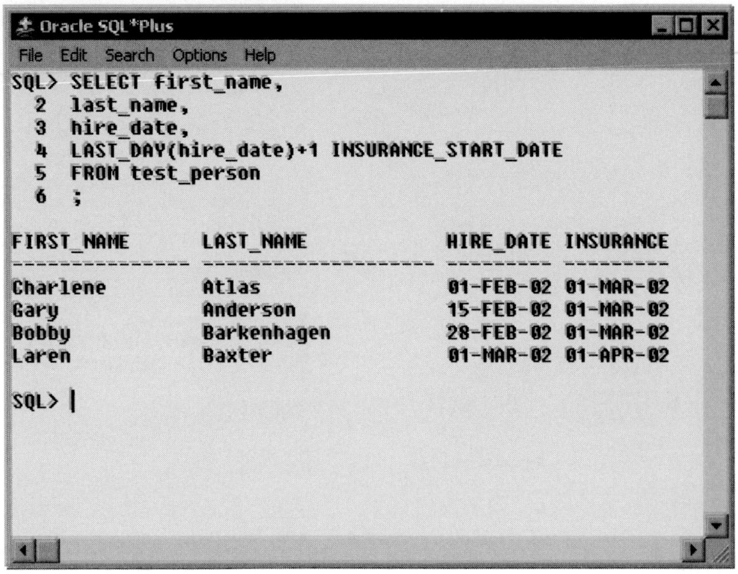

By combining the two techniques you just learned: adding a specified number of months to a date, and using the LAST_DAY function to get the last day of a month and add 1 to it. The resulting nested function syntax looks like this:

Figure 5.13   Using the LAST_DAY function to determine the first day of the following month

```
LAST_DAY(
         ADD_MONTHS(
              column_containing_restock_date,
              number_of_months_forward) )+1
```

Look at the code that follows, paying particular attention to the fourth item being selected. Note how the syntax just shown is used with the Last_Stock_Date column and the three-month interval. To make it more realistic, the example code limits the products to those whose stock is low, and it sorts the records so the product names are listed alphabetically. Enter the code now and compare your results with those shown in Figure 5.14.

```
SELECT product_name,
       quantity_on_hand,
       last_stock_date,
       LAST_DAY(ADD_MONTHS(last_stock_date, 3))+1 RESTOCK_DATE
FROM   test_product
WHERE  quantity_on_hand <= 100
ORDER BY product_name;
```

MONTHS_BETWEEN

MONTHS_BETWEEN is a simple little function that returns the number of months between any two dates. Its syntax is as follows:

```
MONTHS_BETWEEN(later_date, earlier_date)
```

This command is most useful for comparing two date columns, or for comparing one date column with today's date. For instance, if you wanted

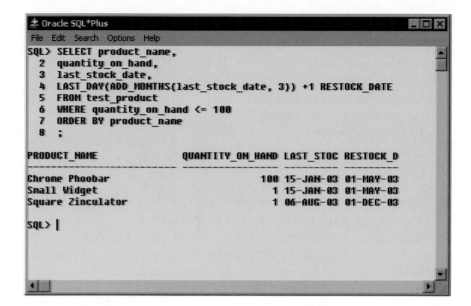

● Figure 5.14   Nesting date functions

to see how long items in your TEST_PRODUCT table have been in stock, you could do so with this command:

```
SELECT product_name,
       last_stock_date,
       MONTHS_BETWEEN(SYSDATE, last_stock_date) STOCK_MONTHS
FROM   test_product;
```

If you wanted to make the months a little bit easier to read, you could do so by wrapping a ROUND function around the MONTHS_BETWEEN function, like this:

```
SELECT product_name,
       last_stock_date,
       ROUND(MONTHS_BETWEEN(SYSDATE, last_stock_date),0) STOCK_MONTHS
FROM   test_product;
```

If you wanted to see how many months you have been on this planet, you could do so with a command like this (fill in your birthdate where it says *birthdate*, and be sure to use a four-digit year):

```
SELECT MONTHS_BETWEEN(SYSDATE, birthdate) FROM DUAL;
```

Congratulations on surviving all those months! Makes the rest of this chapter seem like a walk in the park, doesn't it?

Data Conversion

Data conversion is the label used to describe converting information from one datatype to another—usually between text and dates, times, or numbers. Within your own Oracle database there will be relatively little need for converting datatypes, but the data conversion functions will still be useful for two reasons:

- They enable you to change the way dates, times, and numbers are displayed.

- They simplify importing data from other sources.

In this section you will learn about functions designed to convert numbers, dates, times, and text.

TO_CHAR

The `TO_CHAR` function converts dates, times, or numbers to text. Its main value is giving you quite a bit of control over how dates, times, and numbers are displayed; the fact that they are text is irrelevant when they are scrolling across a SQL*Plus screen.

You may have noticed that when you select data containing numbers from a table, the numbers don't have any particular formatting applied to them; they display with however many decimals they contain, so the list is not decimal-aligned. Dates, too, have their problems: They're displayed in a way that few of us would use on a daily basis, and they do not display any time component. TO_CHAR gives you the means to correct both of these situations.

Formatting Date and Time Values The syntax for a TO_CHAR function designed to change the way dates and times are displayed is as follows:

```
TO_CHAR(input_value, format_code)
```

The *input_value* can be written directly into the TO_CHAR function, but is more commonly derived by referring to a column in a table. The *format_code* consists of one or more elements identifying how you want the function to represent portions of a date or time.

Enter the SELECT statement that follows to see a simple example of the TO_CHAR function in action:

```
SELECT TO_CHAR(SYSDATE, 'MM-DD-YYYY HH24:MI:SS') NOW
FROM DUAL;
```

As you can see from the results in SQL*Plus, the *format_code* portion of this example causes the current date to be displayed using a format that is familiar to many people, and it gives a way to (finally) see the time portion of SYSDATE. You can make up any format code you want, combining elements as your needs dictate. The elements you can use are shown in Table 5.3. Take a moment to look at the table now and, if you are like me, marvel at the incredible number of ways Oracle can display dates and times.

The DD format element that displays the day of the month has a couple of optional suffixes that add some nice cosmetic polish. You can follow the DD element with TH to have Oracle display "1ST" instead of "1" for the day (and "2ND" instead of "2", and so on). Try the following command to see how this works:

```
SELECT TO_CHAR(SYSDATE, 'MONTH DDTH')
FROM DUAL;
```

Table 5.3	TO_CHAR Date and Time Format Code Elements
Element	**Meaning**
– / , . ; : `'any text'`	Punctuation and quoted text is reproduced in the result.
AD A.D.	AD indicator with or without periods.
AM A.M.	Meridian indicator with or without periods.
BC B.C.	BC indicator with or without periods.
CC SCC	One greater than the first two digits of a four-digit year; "S" prefixes BC dates with "-". For example, '20' from '1900'.
D	Day of week (1-7).
DAY	Name of day, padded with blanks to length of nine characters.
DD	Day of month (1-31).
DDD	Day of year (1-366).
DY	Abbreviated name of day.
E	Abbreviated era name (Japanese Imperial, ROC Official, and Thai Buddha calendars).
EE	Full era name (Japanese Imperial, ROC Official, and Thai Buddha calendars).
HH	Hour of day (1-12).
HH12	Hour of day (1-12).
HH24	Hour of day (0-23).
IW	Week of year (1-52 or 1-53) based on the ISO standard.
IYYY	Four-digit year based on the ISO standard.
IYY IY I	Last three, two, or one digit(s) of ISO year.
J	Julian day; the number of days since January 1, 4712 BC. Number specified with "J" must be an integer.
MI	Minute (0-59).
MM	Month (01-12; JAN = 01).
MON	Abbreviated name of month.
MONTH	Name of month, padded with blanks to length of nine characters.
PM P.M.	Meridian indicator with or without periods.
Q	Quarter of year (1, 2, 3, 4; JAN-MAR = 1).
RM	Roman numeral month (I-XII; JAN = I).
RR	Given a year with two digits, returns a year in the next century if the year is <50 and the last two digits of the current year are >=50; returns a year in the preceding century if the year is >=50 and the last two digits of the current year are <50.
RRRR	Round year. Accepts either four-digit or two-digit input. If two-digit, provides the same return as RR. If you don't want this functionality, simply enter the four-digit year.
SS	Second (0-59).

Table 5.3	TO_CHAR Date and Time Format Code Elements (*continued*)
Element	**Meaning**
SSSSS	Seconds past midnight (0-86399).
WW	Week of year (1-53) where week 1 starts on the first day of the year and continues to the seventh day of the year.
W	Week of month (1-5) where week 1 starts on the first day of the month and ends on the seventh.
Y,YYY	Year with comma in this position.
YEAR SYEAR	Year, spelled out; "S" prefixes BC dates with "-".
YYYY SYYYY	Four-digit year; "S" prefixes BC dates with "-".
YYY YY Y	Last three, two, or one digit(s) of year.

You can also follow the DD format element with SP to have Oracle spell out the day of the month. Enter the following code for an example:

```
SELECT TO_CHAR(SYSDATE, 'MONTH DDSP')
FROM DUAL;
```

By combining these two suffixes, you can make Oracle spell out the day of the month *and* include "st", "nd", "rd", or "th" after it. The following command demonstrates this:

```
SELECT TO_CHAR(SYSDATE, 'MONTH DDSPTH')
FROM DUAL;
```

You may notice in these last three examples that the resulting date formats could use a little more cosmetic help. For instance, the MONTH format element always pads the month name to nine characters in length, so there is a lot of space between the month and the date if you are dealing with a date whose month name is short. Also, the entire result is capitalized, giving it a somewhat glaring look. You can solve these problems by using some of the other functions you have already learned. A complete list of the cosmetic problems follows:

- Month is followed by unnecessary spaces.
- Month name is all caps.
- Suffix following date is all caps (for example, "TH" instead of "th").
- When SP format code element suffix is used, spelled-out date is all caps.

Let's look at how to use the functions you've learned to solve each problem step by step. For this example, we'll correct the display of this date format:

```
SELECT TO_CHAR(SYSDATE, 'MONTH DDTH')
FROM DUAL;
```

To remove the extra spaces after the month name, you can use the RTRIM function. To do this, however, you will need to separate the month from the date that follows it. You can easily do that by selecting them as two separate items that are concatenated together. The following command shows how to separate the month name from the date. Enter it now, and you will see that the output it produces looks identical to that produced by the prior command.

```
SELECT TO_CHAR(SYSDATE, 'MONTH') ||
       ' ' ||
       TO_CHAR(SYSDATE, 'DDTH')
FROM DUAL;
```

Now it's time to get rid of the extra spaces following the month name. Wrap an RTRIM function around the TO_CHAR function that produces the month name, as shown in the code that follows:

```
SELECT RTRIM(TO_CHAR(SYSDATE, 'MONTH')) ||
       ' ' ||
       TO_CHAR(SYSDATE, 'DDTH')
FROM DUAL;
```

This produces the desired spacing. Next you want to change the capitalization of the month name, so that only its first letter is capitalized. The INITCAP function does just that. Surround the entire month-name portion of your SELECT statement with an INITCAP function, as shown in the following code:

```
SELECT INITCAP(RTRIM(TO_CHAR(SYSDATE, 'MONTH'))) ||
       ' ' ||
       TO_CHAR(SYSDATE, 'DDTH')
FROM DUAL;
```

The last change is making the date's TH element produce a lowercase suffix after the day of the month. You probably already have an idea how to do this. That's right: You place a LOWER function around the date portion of the SELECT statement, as shown in this code:

```
SELECT INITCAP(RTRIM(TO_CHAR(SYSDATE, 'MONTH'))) ||
       ' ' ||
       LOWER(TO_CHAR(SYSDATE, 'ddTH'))
FROM DUAL;
```

Using the techniques you just practiced, take a moment now to "get it into your fingers" by improving the appearance of the date displayed by this code:

```
SELECT TO_CHAR(SYSDATE, 'MONTH DDSPTH')
FROM DUAL;
```

Formatting Number Values   The TO_CHAR function can also standardize the way numbers are displayed. For instance, look at the output produced by this command:

```
SELECT * FROM test_product;
```

The product prices are not decimal-aligned, which makes them harder to read than they need to be. By placing a simple TO_CHAR function around the reference to Product_Price in your SELECT command, you can fix this problem. Try the following code to see how this works:

Introduction to Relational Databases and SQL Programming

```
SELECT product_name,
       TO_CHAR(product_price, '$9,999.00') "Price",
       quantity_on_hand,
       last_stock_date
FROM   test_product;
```

The results you get should look similar to those shown in Figure 5.15.

As was the case with date formats, number formats are made up of one or more elements that each represent a facet of the formatting being applied. Those elements are shown in Table 5.4. Take a moment to look over the number format code elements offered, and then practice your skills by producing a SELECT statement that formats your TEST_PRODUCT table's Quantity_On_Hand column so that it is more readable.

TO_DATE

The `TO_DATE` function converts text that looks like a date (and/or time) into an actual Oracle date/time value. While its primary use is for importing text files containing dates and times from other databases, it is also handy when you want to enter a date manually using a format other

```
± Oracle SQL*Plus                                    _ □ X
File  Edit  Search  Options  Help
SQL> SELECT product_name,
  2   TO_CHAR(product_price, '$9,999.00') "Price",
  3   quantity_on_hand,
  4   last_stock_date
  5   FROM test_product
  6   ;

PRODUCT_NAME              Price      QUANTITY_ON_HAND LAST_STOC
------------------------- ---------- ---------------- ---------
Medium Wodget                $75.00             1000 15-JAN-02
Chrome Phoobar               $50.00              100 15-JAN-03
Round Chrome Snaphoo         $25.00            10000
Small Widget                 $99.00                1 15-JAN-03
Extra Huge Mega Phoobar+      $9.95             1234 15-JAN-04
Square Zinculator            $45.00                1 06-AUG-03

6 rows selected.

SQL>
```

● **Figure 5.15** Using the TO_CHAR function to improve appearance of numbers

Table 5.4		**Number Format Code Elements**
Element	**Example**	**Description**
$	$9999	Places a dollar sign before the value
, (comma)	9,999	Places a comma in the position indicated
. (period)	99.99	Places a decimal point in the position indicated
MI	9999MI	Causes a "–" to be displayed after any negative value
S	S9999	Places a "+" for positive values and a "–" for negative values, in position indicated
PR	9999PR	Causes negative values to be surrounded by <angle brackets>
D	99D99	Displays your country's decimal character in the position indicated
G	9G999	Displays your country's group separator in the position indicated
C	C999	Displays the ISO currency symbol in the position indicated
L	L999	Displays the local currency symbol in the position indicated

Table 5.4	Number Format Code Elements (continued)	
Element	Example	Description
RN or rn	RN	Causes numbers to display as upper- or lowercase Roman numerals (limited to integers between 1 and 3999)
0	0999	Displays one or more leading zeros
0	9990	Causes empty values to display as zeros

than Oracle's default of DD-MON-YY, or a time. The syntax of the function is as follows:

```
TO_DATE(input_value, format_code)
```

The TO_DATE function uses a subset of the format code elements used by the TO_CHAR function. The TO_DATE function's elements are shown in Table 5.5.

To see how the TO_DATE function enables you to insert dates and times more flexibly, enter the following code and compare your results with Figure 5.16.

```
SELECT  product_name,
        product_price,
        quantity_on_hand,
        TO_CHAR(last_stock_date, 'MM-DD-YYYY HH24:MI') "Last Stocked"
FROM    test_product;

UPDATE  test_product
SET     last_stock_date = TO_DATE('December 31, 2002, 11:30 P.M.',
                                  'Month dd, YYYY, HH:MI P.M.')
WHERE   product_name LIKE '%Zinc%';

SELECT  product_name,
        product_price,
        quantity_on_hand,
        TO_CHAR(last_stock_date, 'MM-DD-YYYY HH24:MI') "Last Stocked"
FROM    test_product;
```

Other Functions

This section presents a group of SQL functions whose only common trait is that they don't fit easily into any other group. That doesn't make them any less useful, though, and every one of these functions provides a valuable service that you are likely to use over and over.

NVL

The NVL function performs a simple but useful function: Whenever it is presented with a value that is NULL, it returns a value of your choosing instead. This ability to fill in blank values automatically

Cross Check

Data Conversion

Take a moment to check your knowledge of data conversion by answering the following questions:

1. What is the syntax for a TO_CHAR function designed to change the way dates and times are displayed?

2. What are the six elements of the TO_DATE function that deal with days?

can help give your output a more finished look. The NVL function's syntax is as follows:

```
NVL(input_value, result_if_input_value_is_null)
```

Table 5.5	Date and Time Format Code Elements
Element	**Meaning**
– / , . ; : 'any text'	Punctuation and quoted text is reproduced in the result.
AD A.D.	AD indicator with or without periods.
AM A.M.	Meridian indicator with or without periods.
BC B.C.	BC indicator with or without periods.
D	Day of week (1-7).
DAY	Name of day, padded with blanks to length of nine characters.
DD	Day of month (1-31).
DDD	Day of year (1-366).
DY	Abbreviated name of day.
HH	Hour of day (1-12).
HH24	Hour of day (0-23).
J	Julian day; the number of days since January 1, 4712 BC. Number specified with "J" must be an integer.
MI	Minute (0-59).
MM	Month (01-12; JAN = 01).
MON	Abbreviated name of month.
MONTH	Name of month, padded with blanks to length of nine characters.
PM P.M.	Meridian indicator with or without periods.
RM	Roman numeral month (I-XII; JAN = I).
RR	Given a year with two digits, returns a year in the next century if the year is <50 and the last two digits of the current year are >=50; returns a year in the preceding century if the year is >=50 and the last two digits of the current year are <50.
RRRR	Round year. Accepts either four-digit or two-digit input. If two-digit, provides the same return as RR. If you don't want this functionality, simply enter the four-digit year.
SS	Seconds (0-59).
SSSSS	Seconds past midnight (0-86399).
Y,YYY	Year with comma in this position.
YYYY SYYYY	Four-digit year; "S" prefixes BC dates with "-".
YYY YY Y	Last three, two, or one digit(s) of year.

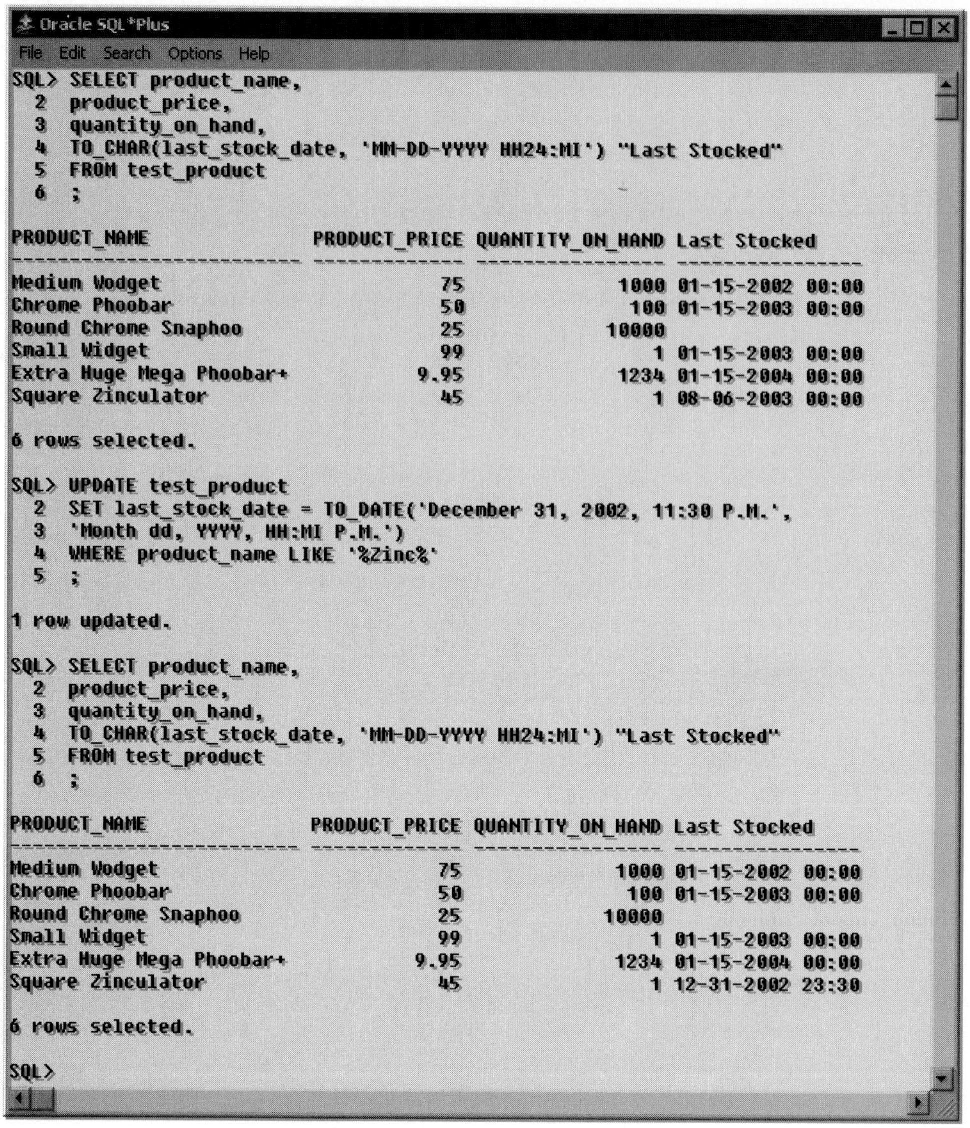

● **Figure 5.16** Using TO_DATE to insert dates and time flexibly

As is often the case with functions, the *input_value* is usually the name of a column. The *result_if_input_value_is_null* can be anything you specify: a literal (that is, hard-coded) value, a reference to another column, or any other expression you want.

Enter the following example to see the NVL function in action. Your results should match what you see in Figure 5.17.

```
SELECT  product_name,
        last_stock_date
FROM    test_product;


SELECT  product_name,
        NVL(last_stock_date, '01-JAN-2001') "Last Stocked"
FROM    test_product;
```

As you can see from the example, the NVL function replaced the Round Chrome Snaphoo's empty Last_Stock_Date value with the date specified in the NVL function. You could have had it replace the NULL value with to-day's date instead, by using this code:

```
SELECT product_name,
       NVL(last_stock_date, TRUNC(SYSDATE)) "Last Stocked"
FROM   test_product;
```

One quirk with the NVL function is that it expects the datatypes for the *input_value* and *result_if_input_value_is_null* to be the same; if the *input_value* is a date, the *result_if_input_value_is_null* should also be a date, and so on. This becomes an issue if you want the function to display the popular "N/A" whenever it finds a NULL value, because "N/A" is text. If the column it gets as an *input_value* is a text column, then everything is fine. However, if the function is checking for NULLs in a date or number column, you will need to wrap a TO_CHAR function around the *input_value* column name, so that the input value is also text. The following code demonstrates

The NVL function does not actually update any values in a table. The source data is left untouched.

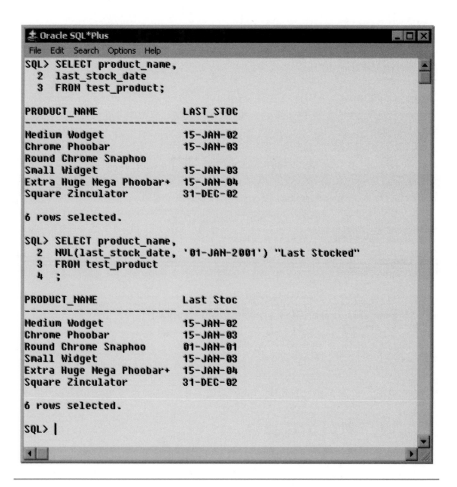

● **Figure 5.17**   NVL function filling NULL date with a default date

this: The first version of the command will fail, while the second one will succeed. Enter the code and compare your results with those shown in Figure 5.18.

```
SELECT product_name,
       NVL(last_stock_date, 'N/A') "Last Stocked"
FROM   test_product;

SELECT product_name,
       NVL(TO_CHAR(last_stock_date), 'N/A') "Last Stocked"
FROM   test_product;
```

RPAD

The RPAD function will left-justify your output by adding spaces or characters to the right in order to fill the void between data and column width. You must simply provide the name of the column and the amount of space to allocate for the column. The following example right-pads the Employee Name with dashes until it is 11 characters long:

```
SELECT RPAD('Karayanis', 11, '-') "Employee Name"
FROM DUAL;
```

The result set should be:

```
Employee Name
--------------
Karayanis--
```

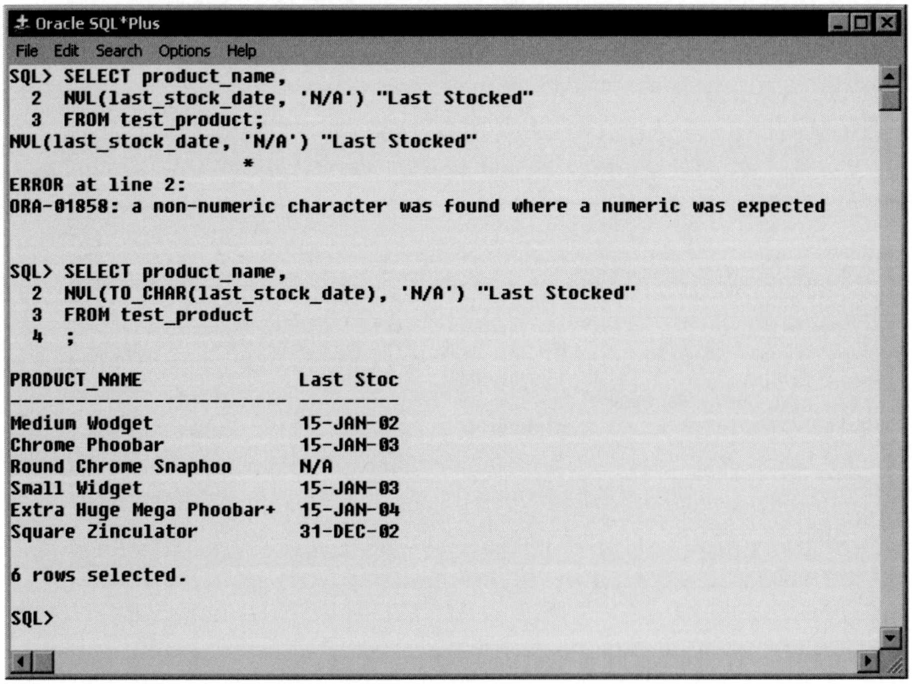

● Figure 5.18   Using the NVL function with different datatypes

LPAD

The **LPAD** function will right-justify your output by adding spaces or characters to the left of data in order to fill the void between data and the column width specified by the user. It works the same as the RPAD function and requires the same input of a column name and the amount of space to allocate for the column. The following example left-pads a string with the character "*":

```
SELECT LPAD('19.95',10,'*') "LPAD example"
FROM DUAL;
```

The result set should be

```
LPAD example
--------------
*****19.95
```

Inserting Comments in SQL Scripts

In Chapter 4 you learned how to create and run SQL script files. These files are essentially programs—simple programs at this stage, but programs nonetheless. And programs need to be documented. SQL scripts are rarely long enough to justify an external document explaining what they do, so the most common method of documenting a script file is to place comments directly within the file. When done correctly, these comments are ignored by Oracle, so you can leave them in the script file and still run the file as you normally would.

There are two types of comments. The first type is a single line long, and is good for little reminders, or to temporarily disable a portion of code you don't want to run but also don't want to delete. The second type can be as many lines long as you want, but is not quite as obvious, and therefore doesn't "jump out at you" when reading the script file. Both types have their place, and many script files incorporate both.

To create a single-line comment, you simply make the first two characters on the line a pair of dashes. Whatever follows the dashes is ignored by Oracle. Enter the following SQL lines to see this in action:

```
SELECT *
FROM test_product
;
-- This line will be ignored.  Oracle will not try to run it.
SELECT *
FROM test_purchase
;
```

The results you see should match those shown in Figure 5.19. You can use this approach for any number of lines, whether they are separate or grouped together.

If you are going to have several lines of comments in a group, however, you may want to employ the other type of comment. In this approach, you

A single-line comment can also be created by starting the line with "REM" instead of "--". This technique is used in other programming languages, and is thus familiar to programmers who are learning SQL after learning some other language. However, from a visual standpoint the "REM" does not catch your eye as easily as "--". Perhaps this is the reason that "--" is more common.

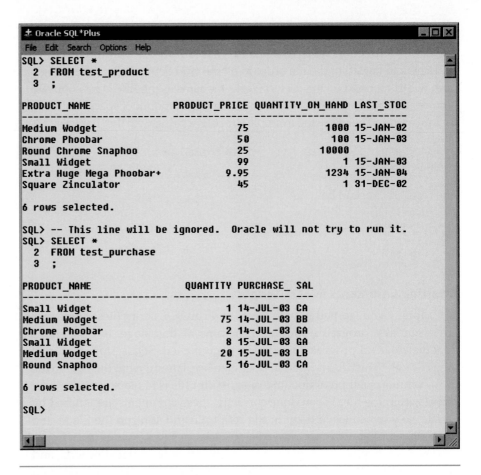

```
± Oracle SQL*Plus                                                    _ □ ✕
File  Edit  Search  Options  Help
SQL> SELECT *
  2  FROM test_product
  3  ;

PRODUCT_NAME                    PRODUCT_PRICE QUANTITY_ON_HAND LAST_STOC
------------------------------- ------------- ---------------- ---------
Medium Wodget                              75             1000 15-JAN-02
Chrome Phoobar                             50              100 15-JAN-03
Round Chrome Snaphoo                       25            10000
Small Widget                               99                1 15-JAN-03
Extra Huge Mega Phoobar+                 9.95             1234 15-JAN-04
Square Zinculator                          45                1 31-DEC-02

6 rows selected.

SQL> -- This line will be ignored.  Oracle will not try to run it.
SQL> SELECT *
  2  FROM test_purchase
  3  ;

PRODUCT_NAME                      QUANTITY PURCHASE_ SAL
------------------------------- ---------- --------- ---
Small Widget                             1 14-JUL-03 CA
Medium Wodget                           75 14-JUL-03 BB
Chrome Phoobar                           2 14-JUL-03 GA
Small Widget                             8 15-JUL-03 GA
Medium Wodget                           20 15-JUL-03 LB
Round Snaphoo                            5 16-JUL-03 CA

6 rows selected.

SQL>
```

● **Figure 5.19**   Commenting out single lines in a SQL script

place the characters "/*" at the start of the comment section, and "*/" at the end. The lines in between are ignored. Try the following code to see this:

```
/*
This script is designed to show how multiple-line commenting works.
*/

SELECT *
FROM test_product
;

SELECT *
FROM test_purchase
;
```

The results you see should match those shown in Figure 5.20.

Dashes can be used to comment out actual pieces of code from statements. For example:

```
SELECT product_name
--      product_price,
FROM test_product
;
```

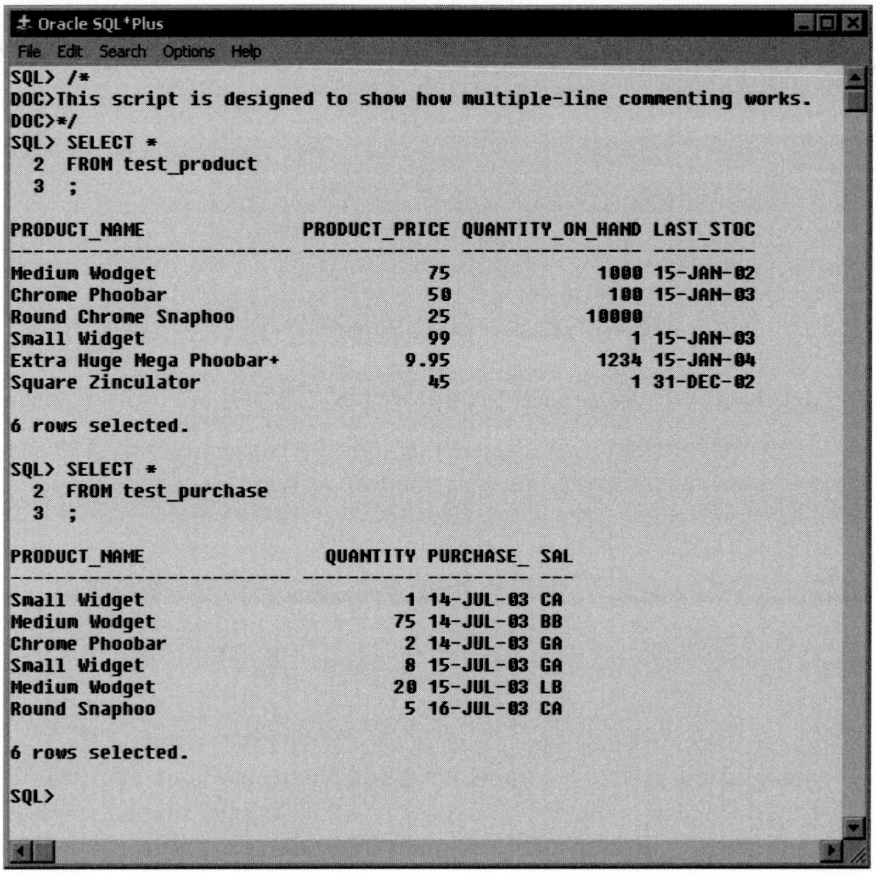

```
 Oracle SQL*Plus                                                    _ □ ✕
File  Edit  Search  Options  Help
SQL> /*
DOC>This script is designed to show how multiple-line commenting works.
DOC>*/
SQL> SELECT *
  2  FROM test_product
  3  ;

PRODUCT_NAME              PRODUCT_PRICE QUANTITY_ON_HAND LAST_STOC
------------------------  ------------- ---------------- ---------
Medium Wodget                        75             1000 15-JAN-02
Chrome Phoobar                       50              100 15-JAN-03
Round Chrome Snaphoo                 25            10000
Small Widget                         99                1 15-JAN-03
Extra Huge Mega Phoobar+           9.95             1234 15-JAN-04
Square Zinculator                    45                1 31-DEC-02

6 rows selected.

SQL> SELECT *
  2  FROM test_purchase
  3  ;

PRODUCT_NAME                 QUANTITY PURCHASE_ SAL
------------------------  ---------- --------- ---
Small Widget                       1 14-JUL-03 CA
Medium Wodget                     75 14-JUL-03 BB
Chrome Phoobar                     2 14-JUL-03 GA
Small Widget                       8 15-JUL-03 GA
Medium Wodget                     20 15-JUL-03 LB
Round Snaphoo                      5 16-JUL-03 CA

6 rows selected.

SQL>
```

● **Figure 5.20**   Commenting out groups of lines in a SQL script

This statement would only select the values from the Product_Name column of the TEST_PRODUCT table, as the Product_Price column has been commented out.

■ Implementing Commonly Used Group Functions

So far, every function you have learned was designed to work on a row-by-row basis with records. SQL also has group functions that return values useful when you are analyzing groups of records that share something in common; for instance, they are for the same product, or the same department, or the same time range. Group functions are very useful for statistical analysis.

If you define what constitutes a group, the group functions will provide you with totals, record counts, and average, smallest, and largest values within each group. If you don't define a group, the default group would be used. The default group is the entire set of records returned by the query.

This section will start by presenting the most frequently used group functions, and then it will show you how to define record groups so that the functions return statistical information for each group. Since you will not know how to group records when you're first introduced to the functions, they will return values representing the entire set of records within your table.

SUM

The **SUM** function adds values and returns the total. Enter the following SQL statements to see it in action:

```
SELECT * FROM test_purchase;
SELECT SUM(quantity) FROM test_purchase;
```

COUNT

The **COUNT** function (you guessed it) counts records. You might be surprised how often this is useful. For instance, the easiest way to find out if a table contains any records is to use a command like this one:

```
SELECT COUNT(*) FROM test_purchase;
```

You can also specify a single column for the COUNT function to count, like this:

```
SELECT COUNT(product_name) FROM test_purchase;
```

Usually, the preferred column name is the first column in the table, for reasons that will be explained in the next chapter. An even simpler way is to define a literal value instead of a column name as the COUNT function's argument, like this:

```
SELECT COUNT(1) FROM test_purchase;
```

Strictly speaking, this causes Oracle to return the value "1" for every record in the table. You could just as easily put "Hi There" in the COUNT function instead of the "1"; it doesn't matter what literal value is in the function, because the function ignores the literal value itself. It just counts the records and tells you how many it found.

One interesting facet of the COUNT function is that if you specify a column in the table whose records you are counting, the COUNT function only counts records that actually have a value in that column. You can use this to determine what percentage of records in a table are NULL in a specific column. As you enter the code that follows, notice that the first command tells the total number of records in the table; the second command produces the same number, because no records have a blank product name; the third command tells how many of the records have the Last_Stock_Date column populated; and the final command gives you the percentage of records with that column populated. This kind of information can be handy if you are determining how useful a particular column is. After entering your commands, compare your results with those shown in Figure 5.21.

```
SELECT COUNT(1)
FROM test_product;

SELECT COUNT(product_name)
FROM test_product;
```

```
SELECT COUNT(last_stock_date)
FROM test_product;
```

```
SELECT COUNT(last_stock_date) / COUNT(product_name)
"Populated Records"
FROM test_product;
```

AVG

The AVG function returns the average of the values in the column you specify. If it encounters a NULL value, it ignores the NULL. Since the function has to actually read the column values in order to do its job, there is no point in specifying "1" or any other literal value as the function's argument; you must specify a column name. For instance, to get the average price of the items in your TEST_PRODUCT table's inventory, enter the following statement:

```
SELECT AVG(product_price) FROM test_product;
```

MIN

The MIN function returns the smallest value found in the column specified in its argument. For instance, to get the price of the cheapest item in the table of products, you could issue this command:

```
SELECT MIN(product_price) FROM test_product;
```

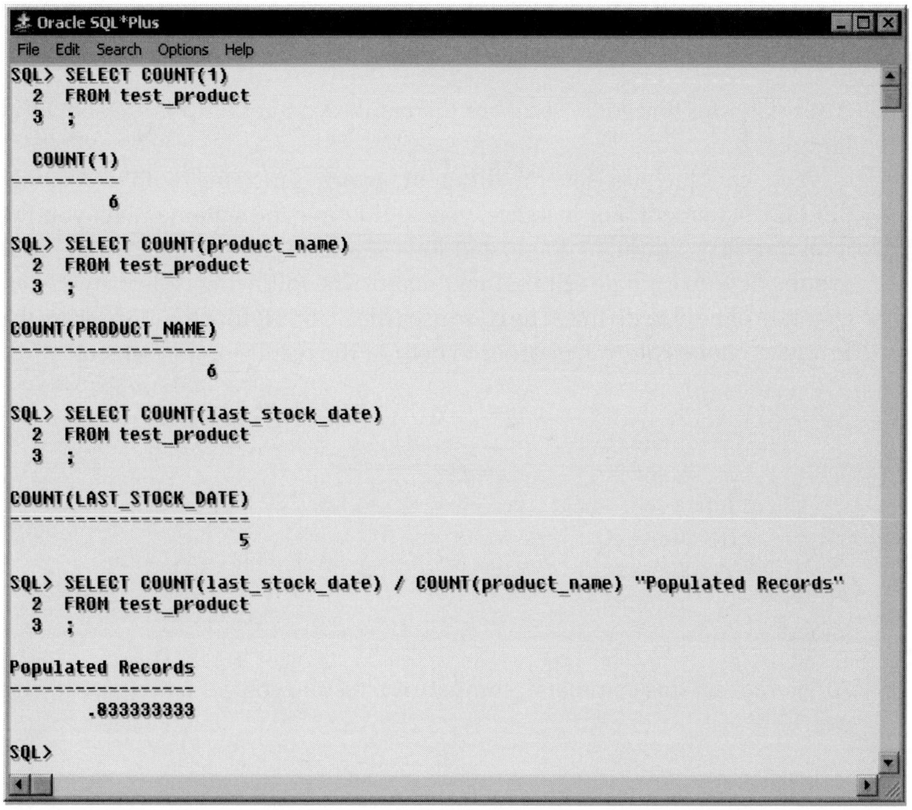

● **Figure 5.21**   Using the COUNT function

MAX

As you have probably guessed, the MAX function returns the largest value found in the column specified in its argument. For instance, to see the highest price in the table of products, you could use this command:

```
SELECT MAX(product_price) FROM test_product;
```

The MAX function has a variety of useful capabilities. For example, there may be a time in the future when you are considering reducing the length of a text column in an existing table. You would want to know how much of the column's width is actually being used, and therefore need to know the length of the longest item within that column. You can do this easily by specifying the length of the column as a MAX function's argument, as shown in the second command in this set:

```
DESC test_purchase;
SELECT MAX(LENGTH(product_name)) FROM test_purchase;
```

Grouping Data via the GROUP BY Clause

Now that you know about group functions, it's time to learn how to create groups. You accomplish this by adding the clause GROUP BY to the SELECT statement, as shown in the following example:

```
SELECT * FROM test_purchase;

SELECT product_name, SUM(quantity)
FROM    test_purchase
GROUP BY product_name;
```

 After the GROUP BY clause, you simply state what column contains the values you want the groups to be based on. Any column listed in the SELECT statement that is not part of a group function *must* be listed in the GROUP BY clause. Omission of a column will cause the statement to fail.

After entering this code, compare the results you get with those shown in Figure 5.22.

You can include several different group functions within a single SELECT statement. For instance, you could have the statement tell you the total quantity, count, average, and lowest and highest values within each group, all with a single SELECT command. The following code provides an example of how to do this. The code uses the SUBSTR function to narrow the Product_Name column, in order to help fit the results on the screen.

```
SELECT SUBSTR(product_name, 1, 15) "Product",
       SUM(quantity) "Total Sold",
       AVG(quantity) "Average",
       COUNT(quantity) "Transactions",
       MIN(quantity) "Fewest",
       MAX(quantity) "Most"
FROM    test_purchase
GROUP BY product_name;
```

After entering this command, compare the results you get with those in Figure 5.23.

Including and Excluding Grouped Rows via the HAVING Clause

You probably remember that a WHERE clause can filter which records are returned by a SELECT statement. A WHERE clause works the same way when you are grouping records: It filters individual records, keeping them from ever being factored into the calculations done by the group functions.

Once the groups are created, however, there is a new need: to be able to filter the groups themselves, based on group information. For instance, let's say that your company is running out of warehouse space, and wants to reduce the number of products it carries in stock. To support this effort, you need to produce a list of the products that are selling poorly—products that have sold fewer than five items, for example. This is where the HAVING clause comes in. It filters

```
Oracle SQL*Plus
File  Edit  Search  Options  Help
SQL> SELECT *
  2  FROM test_purchase
  3  ;

PRODUCT_NAME                 QUANTITY PURCHASE_ SAL
-------------------------- ---------- --------- ---
Small Widget                        1 14-JUL-03 CA
Medium Wodget                      75 14-JUL-03 BB
Chrome Phoobar                      2 14-JUL-03 GA
Small Widget                        8 15-JUL-03 GA
Medium Wodget                      20 15-JUL-03 LB
Round Snaphoo                       5 16-JUL-03 CA

6 rows selected.

SQL> SELECT product_name, SUM(quantity)
  2  FROM test_purchase
  3  GROUP BY product_name
  4  ;

PRODUCT_NAME                 SUM(QUANTITY)
-------------------------- -------------
Chrome Phoobar                          2
Medium Wodget                          95
Round Snaphoo                           5
Small Widget                            9

SQL>
```

● **Figure 5.22**   Using the GROUP BY clause

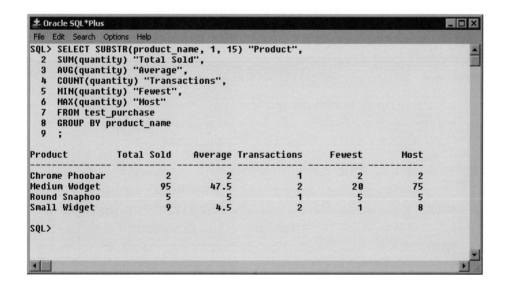

```
Oracle SQL*Plus
File  Edit  Search  Options  Help
SQL> SELECT SUBSTR(product_name, 1, 15) "Product",
  2  SUM(quantity) "Total Sold",
  3  AVG(quantity) "Average",
  4  COUNT(quantity) "Transactions",
  5  MIN(quantity) "Fewest",
  6  MAX(quantity) "Most"
  7  FROM test_purchase
  8  GROUP BY product_name
  9  ;

Product          Total Sold    Average Transactions     Fewest       Most
---------------- ---------- ---------- ------------ ---------- ----------
Chrome Phoobar            2          2            1          2          2
Medium Wodget            95       47.5            2         20         75
Round Snaphoo             5          5            1          5          5
Small Widget              9        4.5            2          1          8

SQL>
```

● **Figure 5.23**   Using multiple group functions in one SELECT statement

groups based on group values. While the WHERE clause filters records before they are grouped, the HAVING clause filters entire groups. To see this in action, enter the following code (this command is identical to the prior one, with addition of a single line at the end, so you can save time by using the EDIT command and just adding the line containing the HAVING clause):

```
SELECT SUBSTR(product_name, 1, 15) "Product",
       SUM(quantity)               "Total Sold",
       AVG(quantity)               "Average",
       COUNT(quantity)             "Transactions",
       MIN(quantity)               "Fewest",
       MAX(quantity)               "Most"
FROM   test_purchase
GROUP BY product_name
HAVING SUM(quantity) < 5
```

As you can see, this causes the SELECT statement to include only those products that have been selling poorly. What if you wanted the opposite: a list of strong-selling products, with the performers excluded? Just change the criterion in the HAVING clause, as shown in the following code:

```
SELECT SUBSTR(product_name, 1, 15) "Product",
       SUM(quantity)               "Total Sold",
       AVG(quantity)               "Average",
       COUNT(quantity)             "Transactions",
       MIN(quantity)               "Fewest",
       MAX(quantity)               "Most"
FROM   test_purchase
GROUP BY product_name
HAVING SUM(quantity) >= 5;
```

Be sure to note in the previous statement that the WHERE clause was not included in the statement. The WHERE clause cannot be used to restrict groups. The use of the WHERE clause with the GROUP BY function will cause the statement to fail. Only the HAVING clause can restrict groups.

 Cross Check

Group Functions and Groups

Take a moment to check your knowledge by answering the following questions regarding group functions and groups:

1. Why is there no point in specifying "1" or any other literal value as the function's argument when using the AVG function?

2. What is the difference between using a WHERE clause versus a HAVING clause as it pertains to groups of records?

Introduction to Relational Databases and SQL Programming

Using Group Functions

Cindy wants to display the supervisor identification number and the pay rate from the TEST_EMPLOYEE table for the lowest paid employee for that supervisor. She wants to exclude anyone whose supervisor is not known and any groups where the minimum pay rate is less than $9.00/hr. She wants the result set displayed in descending order of pay rate.

For this exercise, you will need Oracle9*i* Database Server with the SQL*Plus tool.

Step 1

Create the TEST_EMPLOYEE table according to the following command:

```
DROP TABLE test_employee;
CREATE TABLE test_employee (
        employee_id   NUMBER(10)   NOT NULL,
        supervisor_id NUMBER(10)   NULL,
        job_type      VARCHAR2(20) NOT NULL,
        first_name    VARCHAR2(40) NULL,
        last_name     VARCHAR2(40) NOT NULL,
        pay_rate      NUMBER(8,2)  NULL
        )
;
```

Step 2

Insert the following data records into the TEST_EMPLOYEE table:

```
INSERT INTO test_employee VALUES
    (123, 21, 'Sales Clerk', 'Sally', 'Smith', 9.50);
INSERT INTO test_employee VALUES
    (124, 21, 'Sales Clerk', 'Steve', 'Smith', 10.50);
INSERT INTO test_employee VALUES
    (125, 22, 'Delivery', 'Sally', 'Smith', 8.00);
INSERT INTO test_employee VALUES
    (126, 22, 'Delivery', 'Cindy', 'Jones', 11.50);
INSERT INTO test_employee VALUES
    (127, 22, 'Delivery', 'Kevin', 'Symes', 13.50);
INSERT INTO test_employee VALUES
    (128, null, 'Sales Clerk', 'Sheryl', 'McKenzie', 9.50);
```

Step 3

To select the supervisor identification number and the minimum pay rate from the employee table, type the following:

```
SELECT supervisor_id, MIN(pay_rate)
FROM test_employee
```

Step 4

To exclude any records where the supervisor is unknown, type this:

```
WHERE supervisor_id IS NOT NULL
```

Step 5	To group results by Supervisor_ID, type
	`GROUP BY supervisor_id`
Step 6	To exclude employees with pay rates below $9.00/hr, type
	`HAVING MIN(pay_rate) > 9.00`
Step 7	To order the result set by Pay_Rate, type
	`ORDER BY MIN(pay_rate) DESC;`
Step 8	To drop the TEST_EMPLOYEE table, type
	`DROP TABLE test_employee;`

You should have successfully created and updated the TEST_EMPLOYEE table and obtained the result set indicated in the step-by-step description.

Chapter 5 Review

Chapter Summary

After reading this chapter and completing the Step-by-Step tutorials and Cross Checks, you should understand the following facts about Oracle SQL built-in functions:

Implement Commonly Used Single-Row Functions

- Single-row functions give you row-by-row control over how the data in your database is entered and presented.
- Single-row functions fall into the following categories: System variables, Number, Character (text), Date, Data conversion, Miscellaneous.
- System variables include SYSDATE, USER, and USERENV.
- Number functions include ROUND and TRUNC.
- Text functions include UPPER, LOWER, INITCAP, LENGTH, SUBSTR, INSTR, LTRIM, and RTRIM.

- Date functions include ADD_MONTHS, LAST_DAY, and MONTHS_BETWEEN.
- Data conversion functions include TO_CHAR and TO_DATE.
- Miscellaneous (useful but hard-to-categorize) functions include NVL, RPAD, and LPAD.

Implement Commonly Used Group Functions

- Group functions include SUM, COUNT, AVG, MIN, and MAX.
- You can get subtotal values from your data by including a GROUP BY clause in your SELECT statement.
- You can exclude entire groups of subtotals from your output by placing a HAVING clause in your SELECT statement.

Key Terms

ADD_MONTHS *(123)*
AVG *(141)*
character function *(110)*
COUNT *(140)*
data conversion *(126)*
function *(104)*
GROUP BY *(142)*
group function *(139)*
HAVING *(144)*
INITCAP *(110)*
INSTR *(115)*
LAST_DAY *(124)*
LENGTH *(112)*

LOWER *(110)*
LPAD *(137)*
LTRIM *(119)*
MAX *(142)*
MIN *(141)*
MONTHS_BETWEEN *(125)*
nesting *(116)*
NVL *(132)*
ROUND *(108)*
RPAD *(136)*
RTRIM *(119)*
single-row function *(105)*
SUBSTR *(113)*

substring *(113)*
SUM *(140)*
SYS_CONTEXT *(108)*
SYSDATE *(106)*
system variable *(106)*
TO_CHAR *(127)*
TO_DATE *(131)*
trimming *(119)*
TRUNC *(109)*
UPPER *(110)*
USER *(107)*
USERENV *(108)*

Key Term Quiz

Use the Key Terms list to complete the sentences that follow. Not all terms will be used.

1. Any column listed in the SELECT statement that is not part of a group function must be listed in the _____ clause.

2. The _____ function can return a variety of different facts about the computer environment of the person who issued the command containing the function.

3. The _____ function returns a date that has the same day of the month as the original date it was provided, but is a specified number of months in the future or past.

4. The _____ function has the ability to fill in missing or unknown values automatically by returning a value of your choosing when presented with a NULL value.

5. The _____ function returns the largest value found in the column specified in its argument.

Matching Definition Quiz

Relate each term on the left with the appropriate description on the right.

Term

1. LTRIM
2. LAST_DAY
3. TO_DATE
4. RTRIM
5. ADD_MONTHS

Description

a. It returns the last day of whatever month is included in the date it is given.

b. It returns a date that has the same day of the month as the original date it was provided, is a specified number of months in the future or the past.

c. It removes spaces from the beginning of a string.

d. It converts text that looks like a date or time into an actual Oracle date/time value.

e. It removes spaces from the end of a string.

Multiple-Choice Quiz

1. On which line will the following command fail?

```
INSERT INTO test_product (
    product_name,
    product_price,
    quantity_on_hand,
    last_stock_date )
VALUES (
    'New Product',
    1.95,
    10,
    TO_CHAR(USER) )
;
```

   a. 1
   b. 2
   c. 7
   d. 10
   e. The command will succeed.

2. Which of the following statements is true?

   a. ROUND(4.5, 0) < TRUNC(4.5, 0)
   b. ROUND(4.1, 0) < TRUNC(4.2, 0)
   c. ROUND(8.9, 0) > TRUNC(8.9, 0)
   d. ROUND(8.9, 1) > TRUNC(8.95, 2)
   e. ROUND(5.5, 0) < TRUNC(5.5, 0)

3. What will be the result of using the ROUND function on the number 3.5 to 0 places?

   a. 3.5
   b. 3
   c. 4
   d. You will receive an error message.
   e. 3.0

4. What will be the result of the following SUBSTR function when presented with an input value of 'Psychic trance, Medium' in the Item_Desc column?

   a. Medium
   b. Psychic trance
   c. Psychic trance, Medium
   d. Medium, Psychic trance
   e. The command will fail.

5. Which of the following functions would return the last day of the year 2002?

   a. SELECT ADD_MONTHS(LAST_DAY ('14-OCT-02'), 1) FROM DUAL;
   b. SELECT ADD_MONTHS(LAST_DAY ('15-OCT-02'), –1) FROM DUAL;
   c. SELECT ADD_MONTHS(LAST_DAY ('16-OCT-02'), 2) FROM DUAL;
   d. SELECT ADD_MONTHS(LAST_DAY ('17-OCT-02'), -2) FROM DUAL;

e. SELECT ADD_MONTHS(LAST_DAY ('18-OCT-02'), 1) FROM DUAL;

6. The RTRIM and LTRIM functions are useful when dealing with

   a. Padded spaces in a CHAR column

   b. Padded spaces in a VARCHAR2 column

   c. Empty spaces in a NUMBER column

   d. NULL values in columns

   e. Decimal values in a NUMBER column

7. On which line will the following command fail?

```
SELECT SUBSTR(product_name, 1, 15) "Product",
       SUM(quantity) "Total Sold",
       AVG(quantity) "Average",
       COUNT(quantity) "Transactions",
       MIN(quantity) "Fewest",
       MAX(quantity) "Most"
FROM   test_purchase
GROUP BY product_name
WHERE SUM(quantity) >= 5;
```

   a. 1

   b. 2

   c. 3

   d. 8

   e. 9

8. Which of the following statements are true regarding the COUNT function? (Choose all that apply.)

   a. By specifying "*" as the function's column set, you inadvertently force Oracle to read the entire table before returning an answer.

   b. The COUNT function always counts all records in a table.

   c. If you specify a column in the table whose records you are counting, the COUNT function only counts records that actually have a value in that column.

   d. The COUNT function counts all records for columns with NULL values.

   e. You can define a literal value instead of a column name as the COUNT function's argument.

9. Which of the following symbols can be used to insert comments in a SQL script? (Choose all that apply.)

   a. --

   b. /* */

   c. **

   d. /-- --/

   e. REM

10. Which of the following statements are true regarding the INSTR function? (Choose all that apply.)

   a. You can use the number returned by INSTR to control the length of your first SUBSTR function, as well as the starting position of the next substring.

   b. The INSTR function always returns the end position of the first substring.

   c. INSTR searches for the text you specify and returns a number identifying the starting position of that text within a string.

   d. The INSTR function's syntax is INSTR(*source_text*, *text_to_locate*, *starting_character_position*).

   e. The INSTR function always returns the ending position of the text you specify within a string.

11. Which of the following statements are true regarding data conversion? (Choose all that apply.)

   a. Data conversion is most often done between Oracle databases.

   b. Data conversion functions simplify importing data from other sources.

   c. Data conversion is the label used to describe converting information from one datatype to another.

   d. Data conversion is usually between text and dates, times, or numbers.

   e. Data conversion functions enable you to change the way dates, times, and numbers are displayed.

12. Which of the following format code elements apply to the year portion of a date? (Choose all that apply.)
    a. YYY
    b. Y,YYY
    c. YEARS
    d. Y
    e. SYYYY

13. Which of the following number format code elements displays the local currency symbol?
    a. L
    b. G
    c. D
    d. C
    e. RN

14. Which of the following statements are true regarding the NVL function? (Choose all that apply.)

    a. The NVL function does not actually update any values in a table.
    b. Whenever it is presented with a value that is NULL, the NVL function returns a value of your choosing instead.
    c. The NVL function updates all values in a table that are indicated in the statement.
    d. The NVL function does not work when presented with a value that is NULL.
    e. The NVL function's syntax is NVL(*input_value, result_if_input_value_is_null*).

15. Single-row functions include which of the following categories? (Choose all that apply.)
    a. Count
    b. Number
    c. System variables
    d. Aggregate
    e. Data conversion

■ Essay Quiz

1. Describe a real-world scenario where the LAST_DAY and ADD_MONTHS functions may be useful.

2. What is the purpose and result of a nested function? Describe a scenario where nested functions can be useful.

3. Give an example of when you would use the GROUP BY clause and how it would aid in obtaining results of a query.

4. Give an example of when you would use the HAVING clause and how it would aid in obtaining results of a query.

5. What is the advantage of using the INSTR and SUBSTR functions together?

Lab Projects

• Lab Project 5.1

Using the TEST_PURCHASE table, you need to determine the exact minute that a product was purchased. To practice working with the TO_CHAR and TO_DATE functions, you will view and edit the way the date of purchase is displayed in the TEST_PURCHASE table that you have previously created.

You will need Oracle9*i* Database Server with the SQL*Plus tool.
Then do the following:

① View the date of purchase for all items in the TEST_PURCHASE table with a MM-DD-YYYY HH24:MI format.

② Update the date of purchase for the Round Snaphoo product name to 8:30 P.M. on May 31, 2003.

③ View the updated date of purchase for the Round Snaphoo product, and all other products in the TEST_PURCHASE table with a MM-DD-YYYY HH24:MI format.

• Lab Project 5.2

Case Study

Jon has asked you to keep a record of all employees' pay rates at the Clapham Specialty Store for accounting purposes. He has asked you to create an EMPLOYEE table from the following SQL statement:

```
DROP TABLE employee;
CREATE TABLE employee (
        employee_id            NUMBER(10)   NOT NULL,
        supervisor_id          NUMBER(10)   NULL,
        job_type               VARCHAR2(20) NOT NULL,
        first_name             VARCHAR2(40) NULL,
        last_name              VARCHAR2(40) NOT NULL,
        social_security_number CHAR(11)     NOT NULL,
        pay_rate               NUMBER(8,2)  NULL
        )
;
```

and insert the following records:

Employee ID	Supervisor ID	Job Type	First Name	Last Name	Social Security Number	Pay Rate
80009000		Manager	James	Karayanis	123-45-6789	25.00
80009001		Manager	Gus	Prayias	234-56-7890	25.00
80009002	80009000	Register Clerk	Kelly	Doherty	345-67-8901	10.00
80009003	80009000	Register Clerk	Kevin	Gleason	456-78-9012	9.75
80009004	80009000	Register Clerk	Sally	Morton	567-89-0123	10.50
80009005	80009001	Delivery	Jonah	Hirsch	678-90-1234	8.75
80009006	80009001	Delivery	Letham	Burns	789-01-2345	9.00
80009007	80009000	Register Clerk	Julie	Smith	890-12-3456	9.50
80009008	80009001	Delivery	Bernie	Piggott	901-23-4567	10.00

You will need Oracle9i Database Server with the SQL*Plus tool. Then do the following:

① Display the minimum, maximum, sum, and average pay rate of all employees (including managers), labeling the columns respectively. Round the results of the computations to the nearest whole number.

② Write a query that displays the job type, total number of employees per job type, and average pay rate for each job type. Group the results by job type.

Indexes, Joins, and Subqueries

"If you don't find it in the index, look very carefully through the entire catalogue."

—SEARS, ROEBUCK, AND CO. CONSUMER'S GUIDE, 1897

In this chapter, you will learn how to

- **Recognize what an index does**
- **Identify the types of indexes**
- **Determine when to use an index**
- **Examine relationships between tables**
- **Write SQL subqueries**

Building on the fundamental knowledge of tables, columns, and SQL that you have acquired in the previous chapters, this chapter introduces you to concepts and techniques that are squarely in the realm of database designers and administrators. The chapter starts by explaining what indexes are, and then shows you how to use them to help your database operate more quickly. After that, you will learn about relationships between tables, and how to select data from more than one table. Finally, you will see how to write queries that incorporate other queries, which can produce some pretty sophisticated results with very little code.

■ Creating the Test Tables

If you just started reading in this chapter and have not yet created the test tables used in prior chapters, you can use the following code to create them before proceeding:

```
DROP TABLE test_person;
CREATE TABLE test_person (
     person_code VARCHAR2(3),
     first_name  VARCHAR2(15),
     last_name   VARCHAR2(20),
     hire_date   DATE
     )
;

INSERT INTO test_person VALUES
     ('CA', 'Charlene', 'Atlas', '01-FEB-2002');
INSERT INTO test_person VALUES
     ('GA', 'Gary', 'Anderson', '15-FEB-2002');
INSERT INTO test_person VALUES
     ('BB', 'Bobby', 'Barkenhagen', '28-FEB-2002');
INSERT INTO test_person VALUES
     ('LB', 'Laren', 'Baxter', '01-MAR-2002');

DROP TABLE test_product;
CREATE TABLE test_product (
     product_name    VARCHAR2(25),
     product_price   NUMBER(4,2),
     quantity_on_hand NUMBER(5,0),
     last_stock_date  DATE
     )
;

INSERT INTO test_product VALUES
     ('Small Widget', 99, 1, '15-JAN-03');
INSERT INTO test_product VALUES
     ('Medium Wodget', 75, 1000, '15-JAN-02');
INSERT INTO test_product VALUES
     ('Chrome Phoobar', 50, 100, '15-JAN-03');
INSERT INTO test_product VALUES
     ('Round Chrome Snaphoo', 25, 10000, null);
INSERT INTO test_product VALUES
     ('Extra Huge Mega Phoobar +',9.95,1234,'15-JAN-04');
INSERT INTO test_product VALUES ('Square Zinculator',
     45, 1, TO_DATE('December 31, 2002, 11:30 P.M.',
                    'Month dd, YYYY, HH:MI P.M.')
     )
;

DROP TABLE test_purchase;
CREATE TABLE test_purchase (
     product_name  VARCHAR2(25),
     salesperson   VARCHAR2(3),
     purchase_date DATE,
     quantity      NUMBER(4,2)
     )
;

INSERT INTO test_purchase VALUES
     ('Small Widget', 'CA', '14-JUL-03', 1);
INSERT INTO test_purchase VALUES
```

```
                ('Medium Wodget', 'BB', '14-JUL-03', 75);
INSERT INTO test_purchase VALUES
      ('Chrome Phoobar', 'GA', '14-JUL-03', 2);
INSERT INTO test_purchase VALUES
      ('Small Widget', 'GA', '15-JUL-03', 8);
INSERT INTO test_purchase VALUES
      ('Medium Wodget', 'LB', '15-JUL-03', 20);
INSERT INTO test_purchase VALUES
      ('Round Snaphoo', 'CA', '16-JUL-03', 5);


DROP TABLE test_old_item;
CREATE TABLE test_old_item (
      item_id   CHAR(20),
      item_desc CHAR(25)
      )
;


INSERT INTO test_old_item VALUES
      ('LA-101', 'Can, Small');
INSERT INTO test_old_item VALUES
      ('LA-102', 'Can, Large');
INSERT INTO test_old_item VALUES
      ('LA-103', 'Bottle, Small');
INSERT INTO test_old_item VALUES
      ('LA-104', 'Bottle, Large');
INSERT INTO test_old_item VALUES
      ('NY-101', 'Box, Small');
INSERT INTO test_old_item VALUES
      ('NY-102', 'Box, Large');
INSERT INTO test_old_item VALUES
      ('NY-103', 'Shipping Carton, Small');
INSERT INTO test_old_item VALUES
      ('NY-104', 'Shipping Carton, Large');


DROP TABLE test_employee;
CREATE TABLE test_employee (
      employee_id             NUMBER(10)   NOT NULL,
      supervisor_id           NUMBER(10)   NULL,
      job_type                VARCHAR2(20) NOT NULL,
      first_name              VARCHAR2(40) NULL,
      last_name               VARCHAR2(40) NOT NULL,
      social_security_number  CHAR(11)     NOT NULL,
      pay_rate                NUMBER(8,2)  NULL,
      hrs_per_week            NUMBER(3)    NULL
      )
;


INSERT INTO test_employee VALUES (
80009000,null,'Manager','James','Karayanis','123-45-6789',25,40);
INSERT INTO test_employee VALUES (
80009001,null,'Manager','Gus','Prayias','234-56-7890',25,40);
INSERT INTO test_employee VALUES (
80009002,80009000,'Register Clerk','Kelly','Doherty',
'345-67-8901',10,20);
INSERT INTO test_employee VALUES (
80009003,80009000,'Register Clerk','Kevin','Gleason',
'456-78-9012',9.75,40);
INSERT INTO test_employee VALUES (
80009004,80009000,'Register Clerk','Sally','Morton',
'567-89-0123',10.5,20);
INSERT INTO test_employee VALUES (
80009005,80009001,'Delivery','Jonah','Hirsch','678-90-1234',8.75,20);
```

```
INSERT INTO test_employee VALUES (
80009006,80009001,'Delivery','Letham','Burns','789-01-2345',9,10);
INSERT INTO test_employee VALUES (
80009007,80009000,'Register Clerk','Julie','Smith',
'890-12-3456',9.5,40);
INSERT INTO test_employee VALUES (
80009008,80009001,'Delivery','Bernie','Piggott','901-23-4567',10,20);
```

■ Indexes

You are undoubtedly familiar with the concept of an index at the back of a book. In fact, the book you are reading has an index; take a moment now and look at it. What did you see? A word or two defining each subject or idea, followed by one or more page numbers. You can look a subject up in the index, find the page numbers related to that subject, and go directly to those pages. Indexes are useful because they let you find something specific within a book without having to look through every one of the book's pages.

Indexes in Databases

You can apply the same indexing concept to a table in a database. When a table contains a lot of records, it can take a long time for Oracle (or any other database program) to look through the table to locate specific records—just as it would take a long time to look at every page in a book to find pages discussing a specific topic. Oracle has an easy-to-use feature that creates a second, hidden table containing one or more important columns from the main table, along with pointers to rows in the main table. In this case, instead of page numbers, the pointers in the hidden second table—which I'm going to start calling the main table's index—will be row locations or ROWIDs. By looking in the index, Oracle knows exactly what rows to jump to in order to find a specific piece of data (as long as the data being asked for is in the columns that make up the index). Since the index is much smaller than the table it refers to—just as a book's index is much smaller than the book's complete text—finding data in a table with an index can be dramatically faster than in a table without an index because of both the size and the structure of the index.

For example, while writing this we ran a little SQL routine that inserted one million rows into a test table. Selecting records matching a specific value from this million-record table takes 18.9 seconds. After creating an index on the table, the same query takes only 0.6 seconds to finish. Adding an index to the table made it possible for the table to answer queries 31 times faster!

Figure 6.1 shows how a standard index on the TEST_PERSON table would look. In this figure, the TEST_PERSON table has been indexed, with the Person_Code column being the basis of the index. Note that the index is sorted by Person_Code, even though the table stores records in the order they were entered. An index always sorts its entries by the columns it contains. The

TEST_PERSON Table

PERSON_CODE	FIRST_NAME	LAST_NAME	HIRE_DATE
CA	Charlene	Atlas	28-Feb-04
GA	Gary	Anderson	29-May-04
BB	Bobby	Barkenhagen	28-Aug-04
LB	Laren	Baxter	27-Nov-04

PERSON_CODE Index

PERSON_CODE	ROWID
BB	3
CA	1
GA	2
LB	4

● **Figure 6.1** Table with one index

```
INSERT INTO test_employee VALUES (
80009006,80009001,'Delivery','Letham','Burns','789-01-2345',9,10);
INSERT INTO test_employee VALUES (
80009007,80009000,'Register Clerk','Julie','Smith',
'890-12-3456',9.5,40);
INSERT INTO test_employee VALUES (
80009008,80009001,'Delivery','Bernie','Piggott','901-23-4567',10,20);
```

■ Indexes

You are undoubtedly familiar with the concept of an index at the back of a book. In fact, the book you are reading has an index; take a moment now and look at it. What did you see? A word or two defining each subject or idea, followed by one or more page numbers. You can look a subject up in the index, find the page numbers related to that subject, and go directly to those pages. Indexes are useful because they let you find something specific within a book without having to look through every one of the book's pages.

Indexes in Databases

You can apply the same indexing concept to a table in a database. When a table contains a lot of records, it can take a long time for Oracle (or any other database program) to look through the table to locate specific records—just as it would take a long time to look at every page in a book to find pages discussing a specific topic. Oracle has an easy-to-use feature that creates a second, hidden table containing one or more important columns from the main table, along with pointers to rows in the main table. In this case, instead of page numbers, the pointers in the hidden second table—which I'm going to start calling the main table's index—will be row locations or ROWIDs. By looking in the index, Oracle knows exactly what rows to jump to in order to find a specific piece of data (as long as the data being asked for is in the columns that make up the index). Since the index is much smaller than the table it refers to—just as a book's index is much smaller than the book's complete text—finding data in a table with an index can be dramatically faster than in a table without an index because of both the size and the structure of the index.

For example, while writing this we ran a little SQL routine that inserted one million rows into a test table. Selecting records matching a specific value from this million-record table takes 18.9 seconds. After creating an index on the table, the same query takes only 0.6 seconds to finish. Adding an index to the table made it possible for the table to answer queries 31 times faster!

Figure 6.1 shows how a standard index on the TEST_PERSON table would look. In this figure, the TEST_PERSON table has been indexed, with the Person_Code column being the basis of the index. Note that the index is sorted by Person_Code, even though the table stores records in the order they were entered. An index always sorts its entries by the columns it contains. The

TEST_PERSON Table

PERSON_CODE	FIRST_NAME	LAST_NAME	HIRE_DATE
CA	Charlene	Atlas	28-Feb-04
GA	Gary	Anderson	29-May-04
BB	Bobby	Barkenhagen	28-Aug-04
LB	Laren	Baxter	27-Nov-04

PERSON_CODE Index

PERSON_CODE	ROWID
BB	3
CA	1
GA	2
LB	4

● **Figure 6.1**   Table with one index

TEST_PURCHASE Table

PRODUCT_NAME	QUANTITY	PURCHASE_DATE	SALESPERSON
Small Widget	1	20-Jul-05	CA
Medium Wodget	75	21-Jul-05	BB
Chrome Phoobar	2	22-Jul-05	GA
Small Widget	8	23-Jul-05	GA
Medium Wodget	20	24-Jul-05	LB
Round Snaphoo	5	25-Jul-05	CA

PRODUCT_NAME Index

PRODUCT_NAME	ROWID
Chrome Phoobar	3
Medium Wodget	2
Medium Wodget	5
Round Snaphoo	6
Small Widget	1
Small Widget	4

SALESPERSON Index

SALESPERSON	ROWID
BB	2
CA	1
CA	6
GA	3
GA	4
LB	5

● **Figure 6.2**   Table with indexes on two different columns

index's ROWID column keeps track of each row's original location in the table.

Figure 6.2 shows a similar relationship between the TEST_PURCHASE table and two indexes. That's right, a table can have more than one index. Why would you want to do that? The answer is well demonstrated by the TEST_PURCHASE table. It contains at least two columns that are likely candidates for indexes: Product_ Name and Salesperson. It's very likely that queries against the table will often be based on a particular product, and it's just as likely that other queries will often be based on salesperson. By creating a separate index for each of these columns, you generate the same improvement in access speed described earlier for a table with one index—but that improvement is available when searching by product name *or* by salesperson.

When deciding what columns to index, the following columns are often indexed:

■ Columns appearing in the WHERE clause

■ Foreign keys

■ Primary keys (Oracle automatically indexes these)

In terms of what columns *not* to index, it is not necessary to index a column used in an ORDER BY or GROUP BY statement. Strangely enough, Oracle does not generally use indexes for ordering result sets.

You should also consider the cost associated with indexing—the increased transaction processing times during online transaction processing. In general, you may want to index columns that will be used for online transaction processing only. Columns used in reports (online analytical processing) will get indexed just before the report and then get dropped after the report is run, as there is no sense in continually updating the index when it may be only used for periodic reports.

Once you have created an index on a table, Oracle automatically keeps the index synchronized with that table. Any INSERT, UPDATE, or DELETE on the table automatically changes the index as well, and any SELECT on the table will automatically be routed through an index, if one exists containing the columns needed by the SELECT statement. You can add or drop indexes without affecting the table's operations—any program that used the table before will still operate. It may operate more slowly, however. If you drop a table, any indexes associated with that table will automatically be dropped too, since an index has no purpose without its associated table.

How to Create Indexes

Creating an index is very easy. The syntax for the command is as follows:

```
CREATE INDEX index_name ON table_name  (column_name);
```

If you want the index to contain more than one column from the table, the syntax would look like this:

```
CREATE INDEX index_name ON table_name (
        first_column_name,
        second_column_name
        );
```

Applying this to your own test tables, you can create the index shown in Figure 6.1 by issuing the following command:

```
CREATE INDEX test_person_code_index
ON test_person(person_code);
```

This index would be most useful in searches referring to the Person_Code in the WHERE clause. If, on the other hand, most of your searches were going to be based on a person's first and last name, an index based on those columns would be more useful. The following command would create such an index:

```
CREATE INDEX test_person_name_index
ON test_person(last_name, first_name);
```

This is an example of a composite index (sometimes called a concatenated index). A composite index is simply an index based on more than one column in a table. It is appropriate whenever the table contains columns that are likely to be used together in a query's WHERE clause—for instance, first and last name, or city and state. In versions of Oracle before Oracle9i, the first column in the WHERE clause needed to be the same as the first column in the index for the index to help a query run more quickly. As of Oracle9i, you can place columns in the index in any order you want. In all versions, columns in a composite index do not have to be next to each other in the table they came from.

Take a moment now to practice creating indexes by writing commands to produce the two indexes shown back in Figure 6.2.

> The largest number of columns you can include in a standard Oracle index is 32 and the total number of characters in a row is limited by the particular database installation.

■ Types of Indexes

As you have probably deduced by now, an index is basically a way to summarize the locations of records based on what those records contain. The contents of a database can vary dramatically from system to system, and different kinds of content benefit from different kinds of organization. Oracle offers several different types of indexes, each using a different organizational approach. This section describes the three most common types of indexes; the others are used only in highly complicated databases and are better suited for a book on database administration.

B-Tree Indexes

The default index type in Oracle organizes records into what is called a B-tree. Figure 6.3 shows how a B-tree index organizes records.

Database Table

ROWID	LAST_NAME
1	Norton
2	Gutwirth
3	Trumble
4	Fletcher
5	Zoraster
6	Moss
7	Allen
8	Smith

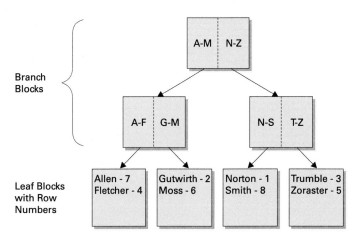

Branch Blocks

Leaf Blocks with Row Numbers

● **Figure 6.3**   How a B-tree index organizes records

In the example shown in Figure 6.3, the branch blocks split the alphabet evenly. In real life, the branch points are determined by the values in the records. For instance, if a table contained many more records whose names started with "A" than any other letter, an entire branch block might be devoted to "A," with the next branch block starting at "B."

When creating a B-tree index, Oracle analyzes the values in the column(s) being indexed and determines how to split the table into leaf blocks with equal numbers of records. It then creates layers of branch blocks enabling records in the lower leaf blocks to be located in as few steps as possible. In a B-tree index, the branch blocks do not contain any actual records but only values for indexed fields in records to help reach the leaf blocks in as few steps as possible.

The beauty of a B-tree index is that it quickly allows Oracle to identify records it does not need to read. By minimizing the amount of data that must be read—and therefore the amount of work it has to do—Oracle can return answers to you much more quickly. (The improvements listed in Table 6.1 were realized using Oracle's default index type of B-tree.) For example, consider a table that contains a billion records, and you want to see the record that has a specific ID number. The table isn't necessarily sorted by ID number, so Oracle may have to read as many as a billion records to find the one you want. If a B-tree index is defined for the table, however, Oracle can find the record in a maximum of 31 steps. Each step eliminates half of the records in the table, so Oracle can reduce the job to manageable proportions very quickly. Table 6.1 shows how quickly a B-tree index reduces the number of records involved in an operation.

Table 6.1	Number of Steps Needed for B-tree Index to Find a Specific Value
After Step	**Number of Records That Must Be Searched to Find Desired Value**
1	>1,000,000,000
2	>500,000,000
3	>250,000,000
4	>125,000,000
5	>62,500,000
6	>31,250,000
7	>15,625,000
8	>7,812,500
9	>3,906,250
10	>1,953,125
11	>976,563
12	>488,281
13	>244,141
14	>122,070
15	>61,035
16	>30,518
17	>15,259
18	>7,629
19	>3,815
20	>1,907
21	>954
22	>477

Table 6.1	Number of Steps Needed for B-tree Index to Find a Specific Value (continued)	
After Step	Number of Records That Must Be Searched to Find Desired Value
23	>238
24	>119
25	>60
26	>30
27	>15
28	>7
29	>4
30	>2
31	>1

Since a B-tree index works by dividing data into sets and subsets based on content, this type of index works best when the column being indexed contains a wide variety of values, such as names or dates. For columns that contain a narrow range of values—such as gender, for instance—a bitmap index is a better choice.

Case Study

Let's take a look at our case study company, the Clapham Specialty Store, to see how a B-tree index could be advantageous. For example, a customer named Richard wants to find a pound of unsalted butter, so he enters the store and locates the dairy aisle. Once there, he walks beside the dairy products until he reaches the shelves containing butter. He stops and then searches through the types of butter until he finds a pound of unsalted butter. This is a real-life example of a user traversing through many objects that are indexed to find an individual object.

In this example, the dairy aisle helps Richard get closer to his goal. This aisle plus the butter shelves are the branch blocks that he searches to locate the unsalted butter—the leaf block. The index is efficiently traversed to locate the desired ROWID, so it doesn't matter if a customer searches for milk or cream or salted butter; the query performance will be consistent because the leaf blocks are all at the same level, below the dairy level.

B-tree indexes perform well when doing range scans that look up a range of values. For example, if Richard wanted to find all the brands of butter, he could do so rather quickly using the same method.

Bitmap Indexes

If a B-tree index structure is optimal for indexing a column containing many unique values, then it stands to reason that a different index structure may be better suited for a column that contains only a few unique values. For example, a gender column would probably contain just three possible values: "M," "F," or "U" (for "Unknown"). Placing this small number of unique values into a B-tree index structure would not make sense, because the "divide into subgroups step by step" approach that makes the B-tree structure so useful for diverse values offers little benefit when there are only a few unique values. In this situation, using a bitmap index makes more sense. Figure 6.4 contains a somewhat simplified depiction of how a bitmap index is designed.

The term cardinality can refer to the number of unique values a column contains. A column that can contain very few unique values—like gender or any true/false column—has low cardinality. A column with many unique values—like price or name—has high cardinality.

ROWID	LAST_NAME	GENDER
1	Norton	F
2	Gutwirth	M
3	Trumble	M
4	Fletcher	M
5	Zoraster	F
6	Moss	M
7	Allen	F
8	Smith	U

Database Table

ROWID	FEMALE	MALE	UNKNOWN
1	1		
2		1	
3		1	
4		1	
5	1		
6		1	
7	1		
8			1

Bitmap Index on Gender

• **Figure 6.4** How a bitmap index organizes records

In SELECT queries in which the WHERE clause is a low-cardinality column (such as gender or any other column with only a few possible values), creating a bitmap index on that column beforehand can greatly decrease the time it takes to get your answers. The speed increase is the result of two factors: bitmap indexes can be quite small (because bits require only a fraction of the storage space needed by other datatypes that would be in a standard index), and the "1" or "0" value stored in a bitmap index can be evaluated very quickly by a computer.

The syntax for creating a bitmap index is almost identical to that for a standard index; you just add the word "BITMAP," as shown in the following example:

```
CREATE BITMAP INDEX index_name ON table_name(column_name);
```

Bitmap Versus B-Tree Indexes

We just learned that standard B-tree indexes are effective when the column being indexed contains a wide variety of values, such as names or dates, and that bitmap indexes are effective for columns that contain a narrow range of values—such as gender. But at what point do you decide to use one index or the other? When should a bitmap index be chosen over a B-tree index, or vice versa?

There is no one rule of thumb for determining when to use one index over the other, other than to choose an index, create it, and test the query performance. There are many variables, such as the number of rows, update frequency, and query composition, that must be considered when determining the performance benefits of each index.

Function-Based Indexes

Before Oracle8i, any SQL statement that contained a function or expression within the columns being searched on in the WHERE clause, could not use an index. For example, the statement

```
SELECT last_name
FROM test_employee
WHERE pay_rate * hrs_per_week > 180;
```

would not use an index. The entire table would be searched in order to retrieve the result set.

With the introduction of Oracle8i, you are now able to build both bitmap and B-tree indexes on columns containing functions or expressions. With function-based indexes , rather than indexing a column, you index the function on that column, precompute the product of the function (this can be an arithmetic expression, or an expression that contains a SQL or PL/SQL function), and store that value in the index—rather than storing the original column data. Take a look at the way function-based indexes can be created:

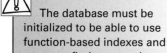

Bitmap indexes cannot be defined as unique indexes; only regular or B-tree indexes can be unique.

The database must be initialized to be able to use function-based indexes and you may find you need special privileges in the database to be able to create function-based indexes. Please consult your administrator.

Introduction to Relational Databases and SQL Programming

```
CREATE INDEX weekly_pay_rate
ON test_employee (pay_rate * hrs_per_week);
```

The product of the function will be precomputed (Pay_Rate × Hrs_Per_Week), and that value will be stored in the WEEKLY_PAY_RATE index for the EMPLOYEE table.

☑ **Cross Check**

Comparing Types of Indexes

Now that you've been introduced to indexes, take a moment to check your knowledge by answering the following questions:

1. How have function-based indexes solved the problem of functions or expressions within columns being searched in WHERE clauses of SELECT statements?

2. What types of indexes are effective when the column being indexed contains a wide variety of values?

■ When to Use Indexes

Adding indexes to a table will *not* speed up data entry via INSERT commands; in fact, the opposite is true. Why would the presence of an index make an insert take longer? Remember that an index is really a table itself. So when you add a record to a table that has an index, Oracle has to add a record to both the table and the index—in essence, Oracle has to perform *two* inserts for every record. Because of this, adding an index to a table will cause inserts to take a little more than twice as long (the time doubles for the two inserts, plus a little extra time is needed for handling the coordination between them). Adding two indexes makes inserts take three times as long, adding three indexes makes indexes take four times as long, and so on.

So the use of indexes is a trade-off. They make data entry take longer but make reading data faster. Therefore an application in which data entry must happen as quickly as possible is not a good candidate for adding indexes to tables. For example, store point-of-sale systems need their cash registers to turn around sales transactions (which, in case you haven't thought about it, are inserts into a database) as rapidly as possible. In this case, placing many indexes on the table storing transactions would be a mistake, because it would make the inserts slower. At the same time the same business could have executives who want to run queries analyzing transactions, and these queries would benefit greatly from having well-indexed tables. How do you handle these conflicting needs? In many systems, the transactions are copied out of the transaction table automatically every night, and the duplicates are placed into a well-indexed table that is used the next day for analysis. The inserts into the well-indexed table take much longer than they did for the index-free transaction table, but nobody cares because the stores are closed, no customers are waiting, and computers are doing the work.

The larger a table, the more benefit you will see from creating indexes on that table. For instance, the tables you have created so far in this book are so small that everything you do to them is essentially instantaneous. As a result, indexes on those tables will not produce a noticeable benefit. As tables get larger, the benefit increases. Using the million-record table once again as an example, Table 6.2 shows how long various DML operations took with and without an index on the table. The first row of statistics repeats the SELECT information you read earlier, while the subsequent rows show the impact of an index on UPDATE and DELETE commands. All times are measured in seconds. Look at how much faster the operations are, and imagine

The index itself will subsequently have to be updated, requiring additional time and processing. If you are updating a column for most of the records in a table, an index will degrade performance. If you are only selecting one record in a very large table for updating, the tradeoff is most likely positive.

Table 6.2	Execution Times for DML Statements With and Without an Index		
Operation	Without Index	With Index	Speed Increase
SELECT 50 records	18.9	0.6	31.5 times faster
UPDATE 50 records	19.7	0.5	39.4 times faster
DELETE 50 records	19.6	0.06	326.7 times faster

what kind of a hero you would be if you started a new job and in the first day reduced the time required for a database process from hours to minutes.

Often we do not want to index the column that is being updated; we would want an index on the column used to locate the column to be updated. For example

```
UPDATE test_product
SET quantity_on_hand = quantity_on_hand - 1
WHERE product_name = 'Small Widget';
```

Here we want the index on Product_Name, but not on Quantity_On_Hand. You should not index a column that will frequently be updated (like Quantity_On_Hand), as you would end up updating the index every time you sell or add a product, slowing down the ordering/sales transactions. It's best to avoid indexing tables with high creation rates as well as avoid indexing columns with frequent update rates.

■ Relationships Between Tables

In this section, you will learn to select information from more than one table at a time, so you can retrieve related information from multiple tables simultaneously and present it in a single spreadsheet-like list. In order to do this you will have to understand the relationship between tables in a relational database. In order for a relationship to exist between two tables, two things must be true:

- The parent table must have a column (or set of columns) that uniquely identifies every record it contains.

- The child table must have an identical column (or set of columns) to contain the values that uniquely identify the parent record.

For example, in the TEST_PRODUCT table you've been working with, each product has a product name. That value is what uniquely identifies each product record. It is called the table's **primary key**. The primary key is the main way you refer to records in a table. The primary key in the TEST_PERSON table is the person code.

There are many examples of primary keys in daily life. Walk into a store—or call your local pizza-delivery service—and if you already have an account with them, they will probably ask for your phone number to look up the account. In their database's list of people, the phone number is the primary key—the main way of uniquely identifying each person in the list. Schools assign their students ID numbers, employers assign their employees employee numbers, and mail-order catalogs ask for product numbers. All of these are primary keys for their respective tables.

Step-by-Step 6.01

Creating an Index

To practice creating, confirming, and dropping an index on the TEST_PRODUCT table, complete the following steps.

    For this exercise, you will need the following materials:

- Oracle9*i* Database Server with the SQL*Plus tool
- Completion of Lab Project 5.2

Step 1

To create an index on the TEST_PRODUCT table, execute the following command:

```
CREATE INDEX product_index
ON test_product (product_name);
```

Step 2

To confirm that an index has been created on the TEST_PRODUCT table, query the User_Indexes and User_Ind_Columns data dictionary views by executing the following commands:

```
set linesize 100
col index_name format a30
col column_name format a30

SELECT ic.index_name,
       ic.column_name,
       ic.column_position  column_position,
       ix.uniqueness
FROM   user_indexes      ix,
       user_ind_columns ic
WHERE  ic.index_name = ix.index_name
       AND
       ic.table_name = 'TEST_PRODUCT';
```

Step 3

Remove the TEST_PRODUCT index from the data dictionary by executing the following command:

```
DROP INDEX product_index;
```

You should have successfully created, confirmed the creation of, and dropped the TEST_PRODUCT table's index.

    The tables you have been working on throughout this book already have implied relationships with each other. The product names in TEST_PRODUCT are used in each record in TEST_PURCHASE, and the person codes in TEST_PERSON are referred to in TEST_PURCHASE within the Salesperson column. These types of relationships form the basis of a relational database system. They allow you to enter data in one table and then refer to that data in other tables, thereby eliminating the need to enter it again.

Parent/Child Relationships

Tables in a relational database use parent/child relationships. In a parent/child relationship, a single record in the parent table can be referred to by any number of records in the child table. In order for a parent table's primary key to be used in a relationship, it must be referred to in the child table. This is done by including a column (or set of columns) in the child table that has exactly the same datatype(s) as the parent table's primary key. When you want to create a child-table record referring to a parent-table record, you include the parent record's primary-key value(s) in the child record. For instance, to identify what product was purchased in a transaction, you must include the product's name or number— whichever is used as the primary key in the PRODUCT table—in the transaction record.

The child-table columns that contain primary-key values from a parent table are called foreign keys*. A foreign key allows a child record to refer to a parent record. For instance, in the TEST_ PURCHASE table, the Product_ Name column is a foreign key back to the TEST_PRODUCT table. Similarly, the Salesperson column in TEST_PURCHASE is a foreign key back to the TEST_ PERSON table.*

You will learn about table relationships in great detail in Chapters 8 through 11.

Writing SELECT Statements to Display Data from More Than One Table

Now that you have selected information from a single table, it's time to learn how to join together information from related tables in the database. For instance, what if you want to get a list of purchases that identifies the salespeople by name, rather than by their person code? This type of need is very common, and it's easy to fulfill. The syntax of a SELECT statement that draws from two tables is as follows:

```
SELECT  table_1_name.column_name,
        table_2_name.column_name
FROM    table_1_name,
        table_2_name
WHERE parent_table_name.primary_key = child_table_name.foreign_key
;
```

Being the perceptive reader that you are, you probably noticed that even though the SELECT statement is supposed to join data from only two tables, the example syntax I've written refers to *four* different generic table names: *table_1_name*, *table_2_name*, *parent_table_name*, and *child_table_name*. The four generic names do apply to only two tables. The reason I've used more than one generic name per table is that when you are specifying columns, you can do them in any order: the parent table's column(s) can be first, or the child table's column(s) can be first, or you can mix them—it doesn't matter, as long as you identify which table each column comes from (by preceding the column name with the name of its table and a period). However, when you write the WHERE clause of the command, it is essential that you identify the primary key column(s) in the parent table, and the foreign key column(s) in the child table. By describing the parent/child relationship in your SELECT statement, you allow Oracle to understand how information in the parent table should be linked to information in the child table.

Let's put this theory into practice by getting a list of purchases with the full names of their salespeople. You can achieve this result by entering the following command:

```
SELECT  test_purchase.product_name,
        test_person.last_name,
        test_person.first_name,
        test_purchase.quantity
FROM    test_purchase,
        test_person
WHERE   test_person.person_code = test_purchase.salesperson;
```

Compare your results with those shown in Figure 6.5.

Writing a command that combines data from more than one table into a single list is called creating a join .

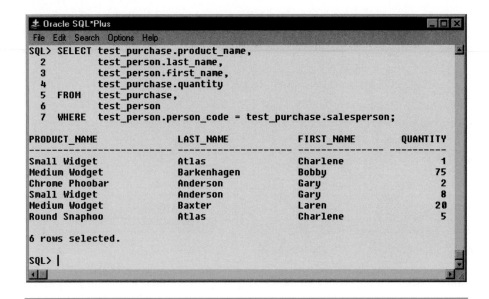

Figure 6.5 Writing a SELECT statement that joins records from two tables

To see the results of a join without a WHERE clause, enter the following code and compare your results with those shown in Figure 6.6:

```
SELECT  test_purchase.product_name,
        test_person.last_name,
        test_person.first_name,
        test_purchase.quantity
FROM    test_purchase,
        test_person;
```

With four records in the TEST_PERSON table and six records in the TEST_PURCHASE table, the join produces 24 rows of completely useless results. This type of result, created by issuing a join without a WHERE clause, is called a Cartesian product .

You can join records from many different tables into a single SELECT statement. To do so, you simply have to ensure that (a) the tables are logically related via primary-key/foreign-key relationships, and (b) you define each of those relationships in the WHERE clause of the SELECT statement.

For example, let's say you want to get a list of each purchase, the price of the product purchased, and the last name of the salesperson who made the sale. This information resides in three different tables. The code to perform this join is as follows:

 You must include a WHERE clause describing how the parent table's primary key relates to the child table's foreign key. If you do not, Oracle will join *every* record in the parent table with *every* record in the child table, creating what could be a very, very long list. (This type of mistake can slow a database to a crawl while it is processing the incorrectly written request, so it is to be avoided.)

```
SELECT  test_purchase.product_name,
        test_product.product_price,
        test_purchase.quantity,
        test_person.last_name
FROM    test_product,
        test_person,
        test_purchase
WHERE   test_product.product_name = test_purchase.product_name
  AND   test_person.person_code = test_purchase.salesperson;
```

```
Oracle SQL*Plus
File  Edit  Search  Options  Help
SQL> SELECT test_purchase.product_name,
  2         test_person.last_name,
  3         test_person.first_name,
  4         test_purchase.quantity
  5  FROM   test_purchase,
  6         test_person;

PRODUCT_NAME              LAST_NAME            FIRST_NAME       QUANTITY
------------------------- -------------------- --------------- ----------
Small Widget              Atlas                Charlene                 1
Medium Wodget             Atlas                Charlene                75
Chrome Phoobar            Atlas                Charlene                 2
Small Widget              Atlas                Charlene                 8
Medium Wodget             Atlas                Charlene                20
Round Snaphoo             Atlas                Charlene                 5
Small Widget              Anderson             Gary                     1
Medium Wodget             Anderson             Gary                    75
Chrome Phoobar            Anderson             Gary                     2
Small Widget              Anderson             Gary                     8
Medium Wodget             Anderson             Gary                    20

PRODUCT_NAME              LAST_NAME            FIRST_NAME       QUANTITY
------------------------- -------------------- --------------- ----------
Round Snaphoo             Anderson             Gary                     5
Small Widget              Barkenhagen          Bobby                    1
Medium Wodget             Barkenhagen          Bobby                   75
Chrome Phoobar            Barkenhagen          Bobby                    2
Small Widget              Barkenhagen          Bobby                    8
Medium Wodget             Barkenhagen          Bobby                   20
Round Snaphoo             Barkenhagen          Bobby                    5
Small Widget              Baxter               Laren                    1
Medium Wodget             Baxter               Laren                   75
Chrome Phoobar            Baxter               Laren                    2
Small Widget              Baxter               Laren                    8

PRODUCT_NAME              LAST_NAME            FIRST_NAME       QUANTITY
------------------------- -------------------- --------------- ----------
Medium Wodget             Baxter               Laren                   20
Round Snaphoo             Baxter               Laren                    5

24 rows selected.

SQL>
```

• **Figure 6.6** Creating a join without a WHERE clause

Enter this code now and review your results. Now try to create a SELECT statement that displays each purchase's date and quantity, the last stock date for the item purchased, and the last name of the salesperson.

You may have noticed while entering these commands that it can become tedious to enter the table names over and over. You can assign a short **table alias** to each table, and refer to the tables by their aliases throughout the command. The table alias should be less than 30 characters and should be a logical name that is meaningful to the reader. The alias goes right after the table name in the FROM section of the statement. Using this approach, the most recent command could be rewritten as follows:

```
SELECT c.product_name,
       a.product_price,
       c.quantity,
       b.last_name
```

```
FROM    test_product  a,
        test_person   b,
        test_purchase c
WHERE  a.product_name = c.product_name
  AND  b.person_code   = c.salesperson;
```

This is definitely less typing, but the command is hard to read, because you have to keep checking which table is represented by alias a, b, or c. It's much better to make each alias something that immediately reminds you what table the alias refers to, so an abbreviation of the table's name is commonly used. Since the tables in this example all have names that are very similar, it isn't possible to create one-letter aliases that intuitively remind you which table they refer to. Instead, we'll have to use a few letters for each alias. The result of this modification follows.

```
SELECT purc.product_name,
       prod.product_price,
       purc.quantity,
       pers.last_name
FROM    test_product  prod,
        test_person    pers,
        test_purchase purc
WHERE  prod.product_name = purc.product_name
  AND  pers.person_code   = purc.salesperson;
```

To save further keystrokes, you can also skip identifying the tables of any columns whose names are unique among the tables being selected from. In other words, if Oracle can look at a column name and see that it exists in only one of the tables, then you don't need to specify which table it is in. However, doing this has two undesirable results: It slows down the processing somewhat (because Oracle has to look in all tables before determining that a column can only come from one of them), and it makes the command harder to read.

Types of Joins

There are three main types of joins that we will look at in this chapter—inner joins (also known as equijoins), outer joins, and self-joins. Let's begin with inner joins.

Inner Joins

An inner join is created when the values in the columns from both tables in the join are equal. For example, let's say you have two tables—EMPLOYEE and DEPARTMENT. The EMPLOYEE table contains the Employee Number and Department Number columns. The DEPARTMENT table contains the Department Number and Location columns.

If you were searching for the employee number and location of the department that the employee works in, you may have to use an inner join to obtain the correct result set. As the EMPLOYEE table and DEPARTMENT table both have a Department Number column with identical values, the inner join could be created using the values in those identical columns.

The statement would look similar to this (remember, these tables are fictitious):

```
SELECT  employee.employee_no,
        employee.employee_dept_no,
        department.dept_no,
        dept_location
FROM    employee,
        department
WHERE employee.dept_no = department.dept_no;
```

The result set would show one table that contains the Employee_No, Dept_No, Dept_No, and Dept_Location columns from the EMPLOYEE and DEPARTMENT tables. Notice that the identical column data values are indicated separately in the following result set:

EMPNO	DEPT_NO	DEPT_NO	LOCATION
1231	23	23	NJ
2345	22	22	NY
9845	29	29	CT

Because the column names are identical in both tables, they must be prefaced by the table name in order to tell them apart.

Outer Joins

To understand the problem this topic solves, enter the following code:

```
SELECT product_name FROM test_product
ORDER BY product_name;

SELECT  prod.product_name,
        prod.product_price,
        purc.purchase_date,
        purc.quantity
FROM    test_product  prod,
        test_purchase purc
WHERE  prod.product_name = purc.product_name
ORDER BY prod.product_name;
```

Look closely at the product names in the two lists, and you will see that several product names in the first list do not show up in the second list. This is because the WHERE clause in the SELECT statement requires an exact match on the product names in both tables, and any product name that is in one table but not in the other will not be shown.

There are times when that is desirable—for instance, when you want a list of what has actually sold. However, there will be many situations where you will want (for instance) a complete list of products, along with information about transactions—and the list needs to show every product, even if there are no transactions for some of them. In order to achieve this result, you must tell Oracle that the child table may not have records to match every record in the parent table. You can do this by placing the characters **(+)**

You can also achieve inner joins by using the JOIN command, which we will discuss in an upcoming section.

Introduction to Relational Databases and SQL Programming

after the child table's name in the WHERE clause. The resulting command looks like this:

```
SELECT product_name FROM test_product
ORDER BY product_name;

SELECT prod.product_name,
       prod.product_price,
       purc.purchase_date,
       purc.quantity
FROM   test_product  prod,
       test_purchase purc
WHERE  prod.product_name = purc.product_name (+)
ORDER BY prod.product_name;
```

Enter this code, and in Figure 6.7 you will see that the listing it produces contains every product name, even if there have been no sales transactions for a product. This is called creating an **outer join** . When creating an outer join, you place the **(+)** characters after the name of one table in each of the *parent_table_name.primary_key = child_table_name.foreign_key* statements in the WHERE clause. The **(+)** characters identify which table may not have matching records for every record in the other table. In other words, you place the **(+)** characters after the table that may produce some blanks for the column being matched. Generally, you will place the **(+)** characters after the name of the child table, and not the parent table. This is because if your referential integrity is working properly (meaning you have foreign-key constraints in place), the parent table can contain records that are not matched in the child table, but the child table should never contain records that are not matched by records in the parent table.

You can also combine rows from two tables that match the join condition, plus any unmatched rows of either the left or right table by using left or right outer joins. Any rows that do not match the join condition display a NULL value in the result set.

A *left outer join* can be used to display all rows from the first-named table (the table on the left of the expression). A *right outer join* can be used to display all rows from the second-named table (the table on the right of the expression). A *full outer join* can be used to display all

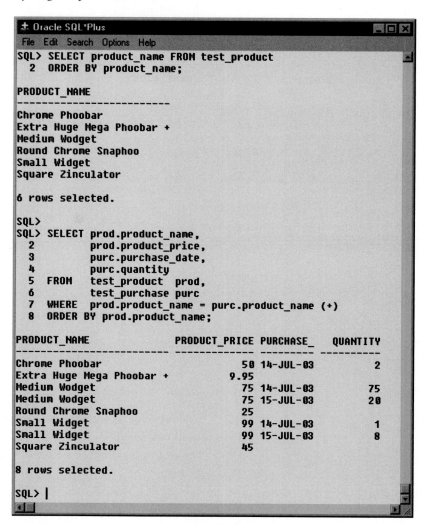

• **Figure 6.7** Two queries showing the effect of an outer join

In an upcoming section entitled JOIN, you will learn to combine tables using left, right, and full outer joins using the JOIN statement.

Case Study

rows from both tables in the join, regardless of whether the tables have any matching values.

Self-Joins

There are times when you may need to join a table to itself to get the result set you are looking for.

For example, let's take a look at our case study, the Clapham Specialty Store. The EMPLOYEE table has the following columns: Employee_ID, Supervisor_ID, Job_Type, First_Name, Last_Name, Social_Security_Number, Pay_Rate.

If you don't have these columns in your database, enter these commands to re-create the EMPLOYEE table from the case study:

```
CREATE TABLE Employee (
        Employee_ID             NUMBER(10) NOT NULL,
        Supervisor_ID           NUMBER(10) NULL,
        First_Name              VARCHAR2(20) NULL,
        Last_Name               VARCHAR2(20) NOT NULL,
        Social_Security_Number CHAR(11) NOT NULL,
        Pay_Rate                NUMBER(8,2) NULL,
        Job_Type                VARCHAR2(20) NOT NULL
);
INSERT INTO employee VALUES(100, null, 'John', 'Balfour',
 '123-45-6789', 30, 'Owner');
INSERT INTO employee VALUES(101, 100, 'Susan', 'Saronnen',
 '456-78-8912', 20, 'Register Clerk');
INSERT INTO employee VALUES(102, 100, 'Eric', 'La Sold',
 '678-90-1234', 6.75, 'Register Clerk');
INSERT INTO employee VALUES(103, 100, 'Martin', 'Murphy',
 '901-23-4567', 13.5, 'Storeman');
INSERT INTO employee VALUES(104, 103, 'Erica', 'Strange',
 '234-56-7890', 6.75, 'Delivery');
INSERT INTO employee VALUES(105, 103, 'Noah', 'Tamil',
 '567-89-0123', 9, 'Delivery');
commit;
```

If you wanted to find the name of each employee's supervisor, you would have to perform a self-join by joining the EMPLOYEE table to itself. The correct command would be

```
SELECT staff.last_name || ' works for ' ||supervisor.last_name
FROM   employee staff,
       employee supervisor
WHERE staff.supervisor_id = supervisor.employee_id;
```

The result set is shown in the following illustration.

```
 Oracle SQL*Plus                                        _ □ X
 File  Edit  Search  Options  Help
SQL> select employee_id, supervisor_id, last_name
  2  from employee;

EMPLOYEE_ID SUPERVISOR_ID LAST_NAME
----------- ------------- --------------------
        100               Balfour
        101           100 Saronnen
        102           100 La Sold
        103           100 Murphy
        104           103 Strange
        105           103 Tamil

6 rows selected.

SQL> SELECT staff.last_name || ' works for ' ||supervisor.last_name
  2  FROM   employee staff,
  3         employee supervisor
  4  WHERE staff.supervisor_id = supervisor.employee_id;

STAFF.LAST_NAME||'WORKSFOR'||SUPERVISOR.LAST_NAME
--------------------------------------------------------
Saronnen works for Balfour
La Sold works for Balfour
Murphy works for Balfour
Strange works for Murphy
Tamil works for Murphy

SQL> |
```

- Code log of employee and supervisor self-join

JOIN

Oracle9i supports the use of the JOIN keyword for joining tables together. In fact, the Oracle Corporation strongly recommends that you use this syntax to join tables. You can choose to use this syntax to replace the table expressions that you've learned so far. By using the JOIN keyword, you explicitly state that a join is being performed and which tables are to be joined and how to join them. The ON keyword is used with the JOIN keyword and it specifies which columns the tables in the join have in common. The syntax for a SELECT statement using the JOIN and ON keywords would be

```
SELECT  column_name
FROM    table_name
        [INNER | {LEFT, RIGHT, FULL} | OUTER] JOIN
        joined_table_name
        ON condition;
```

For example, instead of using the traditional Oracle outer joins syntax of

```
SELECT  prod.product_name,
        pur.salesperson
FROM    test_product prod,
        test_purchase pur
WHERE   prod.product_name(+) = pur.product_name
ORDER BY prod.product_name;
```

You can now use the JOIN statement to achieve the same results. To view an example of how the JOIN keyword is used in a right outer join, execute the following command:

```
SELECT prod.product_name,
       pur.salesperson
FROM   test_product prod
       RIGHT OUTER JOIN
       test_purchase pur
       ON prod.product_name = pur.product_name
ORDER BY prod.product_name;
```

Your results should be the same as if you used the traditional Oracle outer joins syntax as shown in Figure 6-8.

You can also use the JOIN statement to indicate a left outer join to return the names of all product names, even if no salesperson has been indicated for the purchase of the product. Notice that the Salesperson column will be

```
± Oracle SQL*Plus                                                   _ □ X
 File  Edit  Search  Options  Help
SQL> SELECT  prod.product_name,
  2          pur.salesperson
  3  FROM    test_product prod,
  4          test_purchase pur
  5  WHERE   prod.product_name(+) = pur.product_name
  6  ORDER BY prod.product_name;

PRODUCT_NAME                 SAL
-------------------------    ---
Chrome Phoobar               GA
Medium Wodget                BB
Medium Wodget                LB
Small Widget                 CA
Small Widget                 GA
                             CA

6 rows selected.

SQL> SELECT  prod.product_name,
  2          pur.salesperson
  3  FROM    test_product prod
  4          RIGHT OUTER JOIN
  5          test_purchase pur
  6          ON prod.product_name = pur.product_name
  7  ORDER BY prod.product_name;

PRODUCT_NAME                 SAL
-------------------------    ---
Chrome Phoobar               GA
Medium Wodget                LB
Medium Wodget                BB
Small Widget                 GA
Small Widget                 CA
                             CA

6 rows selected.

SQL> |
```

• **Figure 6.8**   Comparison of traditional and newer JOIN syntax

blank for products in which there was a NULL value for the salesperson after executing the following command:

```
SELECT  prod.product_name,
        pur.salesperson
FROM    test_product    prod
        LEFT OUTER JOIN
        test_purchase   pur
        ON prod.product_name = pur.product_name
ORDER BY prod.product_name;
```

To indicate a full outer join to return all rows from the TEST_PRODUCT table and all rows from the TEST_PURCHASE table, you would indicate the following command:

```
SELECT  *
FROM    test_product    prod
        FULL OUTER JOIN
        test_purchase   pur
        ON prod.product_name = pur.product_name
ORDER BY prod.product_name;
```

Set Operators

Now that you know how to make a traditional join between tables, it is time to show you some alternative types of operations. These are useful for different situations: times when you want to combine the contents of multiple tables that have similar layouts, or when you want to compare records in different tables and see which ones either are in both or are in one but not the other.

You can accomplish this by using set operators to connect two SELECT statements. There are four different set operators, and they are shown in Table 6.3.

The following illustration gives a graphical representation of the results produced by each set operator.

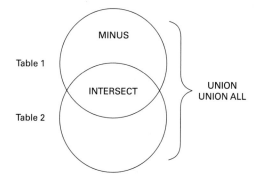

In order to see the set operators work in a way that is useful, you will need to create a new table and populate it with a few records. The following commands will give you the data you need to try the next examples.

```
CREATE TABLE test_purchase_archive (
    product_name  VARCHAR2(25),
    salesperson   VARCHAR2(3),
    purchase_date DATE,
```

```
        quantity        NUMBER(4,2)
     );

INSERT INTO test_purchase_archive VALUES
     ('Round Snaphoo', 'BB', '21-JUN-2001', 10);
INSERT INTO test_purchase_archive VALUES
     ('Large Harflinger', 'GA', '22-JUN-2001', 50);
INSERT INTO test_purchase_archive VALUES
     ('Medium Wodget', 'LB', '23-JUN-2001', 20);
INSERT INTO test_purchase_archive VALUES
     ('Small Widget', 'ZZ', '24-JUN-2002', 80);
INSERT INTO test_purchase_archive VALUES
     ('Chrome Phoobar', 'CA', '25-JUN-2002', 2);
INSERT INTO test_purchase_archive VALUES
     ('Small Widget', 'JT', '26-JUN-2002', 50);
```

Table 6.3	Set Operators
Set Operator	**Results Produced**
UNION	All rows from both SELECT statements, excluding duplicate rows
UNION ALL	All rows from both SELECT statements, with duplicate rows shown
INTERSECT	Rows that were returned by both SELECT statements
MINUS	Rows that were returned by the first SELECT statement, minus those returned by the second one

UNION

The UNION set operator performs the useful task of combining data from multiple tables into a single list. This differs from the relational techniques you used earlier in this chapter in that the UNION set operator is usually used when the *structure* of the two tables is similar or identical, but the *content* of the tables differs. The UNION set operator provides a way to easily combine the contents of such tables into one listing.

To see this in action, enter the following commands and compare your results with those shown in Figure 6.9.

```
UPDATE test_purchase
SET    product_name = 'Round Chrome Snaphoo'
WHERE  product_name = 'Round Snaphoo';

SELECT product_name FROM test_purchase
ORDER BY product_name;
SELECT product_name FROM test_purchase_archive
ORDER BY product_name;

SELECT product_name FROM test_purchase
UNION
SELECT product_name FROM test_purchase_archive
ORDER BY product_name;
```

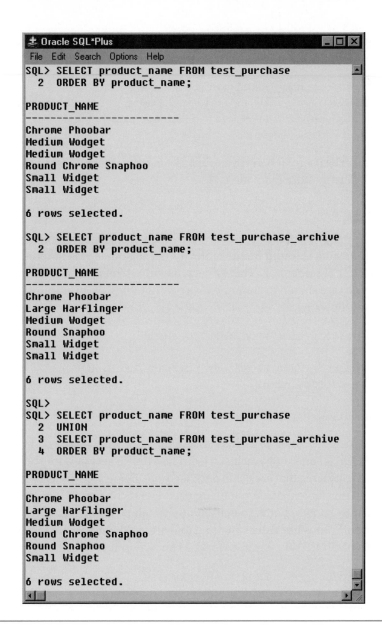

```
Oracle SQL*Plus                          _ □ X
 File  Edit  Search  Options  Help
SQL> SELECT product_name FROM test_purchase
  2   ORDER BY product_name;

PRODUCT_NAME
------------------------
Chrome Phoobar
Medium Wodget
Medium Wodget
Round Chrome Snaphoo
Small Widget
Small Widget

6 rows selected.

SQL> SELECT product_name FROM test_purchase_archive
  2   ORDER BY product_name;

PRODUCT_NAME
------------------------
Chrome Phoobar
Large Harflinger
Medium Wodget
Round Snaphoo
Small Widget
Small Widget

6 rows selected.

SQL>
SQL> SELECT product_name FROM test_purchase
  2   UNION
  3   SELECT product_name FROM test_purchase_archive
  4   ORDER BY product_name;

PRODUCT_NAME
------------------------
Chrome Phoobar
Large Harflinger
Medium Wodget
Round Chrome Snaphoo
Round Snaphoo
Small Widget

6 rows selected.
```

● **Figure 6.9**   The UNION set operator

Note that each of the tables being queried contains products the other table does not. The TEST_PURCHASE table contains a Round Chrome Snaphoo not found in the TEST_PURCHASE_ARCHIVE table, while the latter contains a Large Harflinger that is absent from the former. The list of product names produced by the UNION set operator contains both, as well as all the other products shared by both tables.

UNION ALL

The UNION ALL set operator functions similarly to the UNION set operator, except that UNION ALL causes every row to be returned, instead of just one distinct row for each unique value. UNION ALL generally will run much faster than UNION since it does not have to go back and apply an

ORDER BY and DELETE to remove the duplicate values it encounters. To see the difference this makes, enter the following command:

```
SELECT product_name FROM test_purchase
UNION ALL
SELECT product_name FROM test_purchase_archive
ORDER BY product_name;
```

This can be useful when you would like to count the number of instances of each value in more than one table.

The ORDER BY clause applies to the overall result set after applying UNION ALL; it does not apply just to the second SELECT.

INTERSECT

The INTERSECT set operator returns only the values that are present in *both* tables. If a value is found in one table but not the other, it is ignored by the INTERSECT set operator. This is very useful when you need to find out what values are shared in common by a pair of tables. An example of this set operator follows:

```
SELECT product_name FROM test_purchase
INTERSECT
SELECT product_name FROM test_purchase_archive
ORDER BY product_name;
```

MINUS

The MINUS set operator does essentially the opposite task from the INTERSECT set operator you just tried. The MINUS set operator shows you records in one table that are *not* in another table. Being able to easily uncover records in one table that are not being used in a second table is useful when you want to know what zero-activity items can be archived, or when you need to find out what values in one table are not being represented in another. The MINUS set operator works as shown in this code example:

```
SELECT product_name FROM test_purchase
MINUS
SELECT product_name FROM test_purchase_archive
ORDER BY product_name;
```

Cross Check

Joins and Set Operators

Now that you've been introduced to joins and set operators, take a moment to check your knowledge by answering the following questions:

1. What is the difference between the UNION and UNION ALL set operators?

2. What do the **(+)** characters identify in an outer join?

■ Writing Subqueries

Continuing with our theme of multiple-table operations, this section covers subqueries. Within this section you will learn what a subquery is, when to use them, and how to write them.

What Is a Subquery?

A subquery is a standard SELECT query that is nested within a SELECT, UPDATE, or DELETE command. It is used to provide data for the FROM or WHERE portions of the parent statement.

A subquery can even contain subqueries within itself. The Oracle documentation claims that you can nest subqueries to an infinite number of levels of depth. Usually a specification of "unlimited" translates to "it depends on the amount of computer resources available, but in any case it's likely to be more than you will ever use."

Types of Problems Subqueries Can Solve

A subquery enters the picture when one question must be answered before a larger question can be addressed. For instance, to find out which products are selling better than average, you must first determine what "average" is. To find out how much money has been made by your top salesperson, you first need to know who the top salesperson is. To identify products that are selling less than they did a year ago, you need to know how many were sold a year ago. These are all situations where a subquery can provide the needed information.

Single-Row Subqueries

Let's consider an example. You've discovered that the most recent shipment of Small Widgets was intercepted while on its way to you, and replaced with cheap knockoffs. You want to know what else arrived that day, so you can check those products, as well. You don't know what date the Small Widgets arrived, so you can't specify the date explicitly in the WHERE clause. You can, however, have Oracle derive that date for you and use it as if you had typed it in by hand. You'll accomplish this by telling the SELECT statement's WHERE clause that it must retrieve the last stock date for the Small Widgets itself, and then use that date to filter other product records for you. Enter the following command, and compare your results with those shown in Figure 6.10.

```
SELECT *
FROM   test_product
WHERE  last_stock_date = (
       SELECT last_stock_date
       FROM   test_product
       WHERE  product_name = 'Small Widget'
       );
```

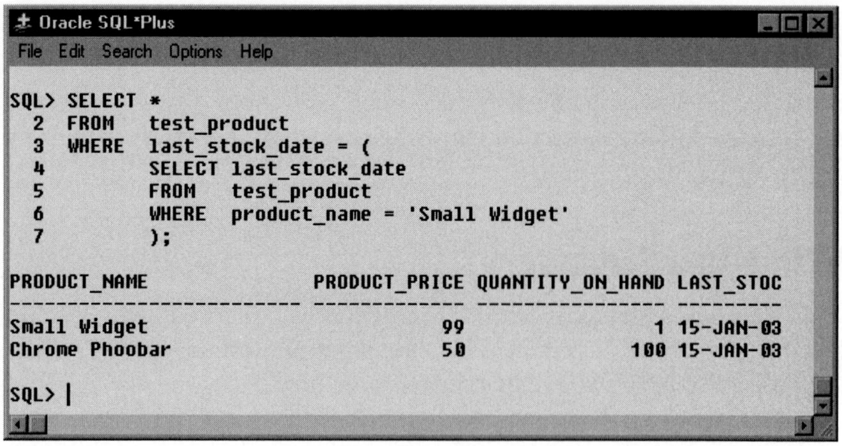

● **Figure 6.10** Subquery based on Last_Stock_Date

A key characteristic of the subqueries you just wrote is that they are capable of returning only one value. For example, when you write a subquery that finds the last stock date for a Small Widget, only a single value can be returned; the Small Widget cannot have more than one last stock date, because there's only one column set aside to store that value in the PRODUCT table. Since you can be sure that the subquery will return only one value, you can write the WHERE clause with an equal sign between the parent statement's WHERE clause and the subquery. You could not use the equal sign if the subquery had the potential for returning multiple values, because the parent statement's last stock date could never equal more than one value. This type of subquery is called a single-row subquery , because the subquery can only return one row of answers. (The parent statement can return any number of rows based on the subquery's one answer, of course.)

The subquery and the parent statement can refer to completely different tables, if you wish. For example, let's say you wanted to see all the sales made by Gary Anderson. You know the salesperson's name, but not the code that would be used to represent him or her in the PURCHASE table. (That part may not make much sense with these test tables, where the person code is simply the person's initials, but in a real database the person would most likely be represented by a number that had no obvious relation to who the person is, and would therefore be difficult to guess.) You can make the SELECT statement go and find Gary Anderson's code for you, and still show you his sales records. Enter the following code to see how to make this happen:

```
SELECT * FROM test_purchase
WHERE   salesperson = (
        SELECT person_code
        FROM   test_person
        WHERE  first_name = 'Gary' AND last_name = 'Anderson'
        );
```

As a last example of a single-row subquery, consider a situation where you want to know which of your products are the most expensive. You can accomplish this by writing a subquery that determines the average price of a product, as shown in this code:

```
SELECT *
FROM   test_product
WHERE  product_price > (
       SELECT AVG(product_price)
       FROM   test_product
       );
```

Multirow Subqueries

As you may have guessed, a multirow subquery is one in which the subquery has the potential of returning more than one row of answers. The reason you need to think about this ahead of time is that it affects what comparison operator you use: You cannot compare something using an equal sign if the subquery is going to return more than one row of answers. Instead of the equal sign, you can use the IN function for multirow subqueries.

For example, let's say you want to know which products are not selling. To do that, you can tell your subquery to get a list of all the product names in the PURCHASE table, and then provide that list back to the parent statement so those product names can be excluded from the product records returned to you. To see this in action, enter the following code and compare your results with those shown in Figure 6.11:

```
SELECT *
FROM  test_purchase
ORDER BY product_name;

SELECT *
FROM   test_product
WHERE  product_name NOT IN (
       SELECT DISTINCT product_name
       FROM   test_purchase
       )
ORDER BY product_name;
```

As mentioned earlier, you can also use subqueries in UPDATE and DELETE statements. For example, let's say you have been instructed to make a 10 percent reduction in the price of any item that has not sold. You can do that with a single UPDATE command by placing a subquery in its WHERE clause to determine which products have not sold. Enter the following code to see how this works:

```
UPDATE test_product
SET product_price  = product_price * (100 - 10)/100
WHERE  product_name NOT IN (
       SELECT DISTINCT product_name
       FROM   test_purchase
       );

SELECT * FROM  test_product;
```

```
Oracle SQL*Plus                                              _ □ ×
File  Edit  Search  Options  Help
SQL> SELECT *
  2  FROM  test_purchase
  3  ORDER BY product_name;

PRODUCT_NAME                    SAL PURCHASE_    QUANTITY
------------------------------- --- ---------- ----------
Chrome Phoobar                  GA  14-JUL-03           2
Medium Wodget                   BB  14-JUL-03          75
Medium Wodget                   LB  15-JUL-03          20
Round Chrome Snaphoo            CA  16-JUL-03           5
Small Widget                    CA  14-JUL-03           1
Small Widget                    GA  15-JUL-03           8

6 rows selected.

SQL>
SQL> SELECT *
  2  FROM  test_product
  3  WHERE  product_name NOT IN (
  4         SELECT DISTINCT product_name
  5         FROM  test_purchase
  6         )
  7  ORDER BY product_name;

PRODUCT_NAME             PRODUCT_PRICE QUANTITY_ON_HAND LAST_STOC
------------------------ ------------- ---------------- ---------
Extra Huge Mega Phoobar +         9.95             1234 15-JAN-04
Square Zinculator                   45                1 31-DEC-02

SQL>
```

• **Figure 6.11**   Using a multirow subquery to find unmatched records

Notice that after the UPDATE command has been run, the prices have been changed only on those products that were not selling. Handy, eh?

Multicolumn Subqueries

Each of the subqueries you have seen so far retrieves just a single column of data. It's possible to use subqueries that return multiple columns of data, too. To demonstrate this, the following code evaluates the product names and purchase dates in the TEST_PURCHASE table to return only the most recent purchase of each product. (When we interview people for PL/SQL jobs, we give a little quiz that includes a question that requires this technique to answer; *very* few people get it right.)

```
SELECT *
FROM   test_purchase
ORDER BY product_name, purchase_date;

SELECT *
FROM   test_purchase
WHERE  (product_name, purchase_date)
IN     (SELECT product_name, MAX(purchase_date)
        FROM   test_purchase
        GROUP BY product_name
        );
```

Correlated Subqueries

A correlated subquery is a nested SELECT statement that refers to a column from the outer SELECT statement. For example, the nested SELECT statement might include an employee number that is required to match the employee number in the outer SELECT statement.

Case Study

These subqueries can sometimes cause problems because the inner query's result set must be constructed for every row that is a possible candidate for inclusion in the outer query's result set. This can result in poorly performing queries if both result sets contain a large amount of data.

Let's take a look at our case study, the Clapham Specialty Store, to see a correlated subquery in action. If John wanted to know which employees' salaries exceed the average salary for that particular job type, he could execute the following correlated subquery:

```
SELECT job_type, last_name, pay_rate
FROM employee;

SELECT job_type,
       last_name,
       pay_rate
FROM    employee    emp
WHERE   pay_rate > (SELECT AVG(pay_rate)
                    FROM    employee
                    WHERE   emp.job_type = job_type
                    )
ORDER BY job_type;
```

The illustration shows the results from this query with only two people. The others don't show up because their Pay_Rate is *equal* to the average Pay_Rate, and our query requires we show only those whose Pay_Rate is *greater than* the average.

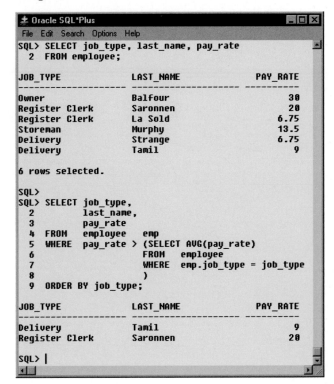

In this statement, for each FROM of the EMPLOYEE table, the outer query uses the correlated subquery to compute the average pay rate for employees working at the same job type. The correlated subquery must determine the job type for each employee, use the job type to evaluate the outer query, and then determine if that employee's pay rate is greater than the average pay rate for the employee's particular department. If the employee's pay rate *is* greater, then the result will be returned. This process must be done for every employee record in the EMPLOYEE table, sometimes resulting in a poorly performing query if there are many records in the EMPLOYEE table.

Chapter 6 Review

■ Chapter Summary

After reading this chapter and completing the Step-by-Step tutorial and Cross Checks, you should understand the following facts about indexes, joins, and subqueries:

Recognize What an Index Does

- A database index contains key information from each row in a table, along with pointers to the related rows in that table.

- You can add or drop indexes without affecting the table's operations—any program that used the table before will still operate.

Identify the Types of Indexes

- Bitmap indexes make more sense on columns that contain a small number of unique values, such as gender or any kind of yes/no column.

- For columns with low cardinality, bitmap indexes are faster than B-tree indexes.

- With function-based indexes, rather than indexing a column, you index the function on that column, precompute the product of the function (this can be an arithmetic expression, or an expression that contains a SQL or PL/SQL function), and store that value in the index—rather than storing the original column data.

Determine When to Use an Index

- Indexes improve the response time of commands that have to read a table's contents in order to perform their operations.

- Adding indexes to a table will *not* speed up data entry via INSERT commands.

- There is no one rule of thumb for determining when to use one index type over another, other than to choose an index, create it, and test the query performance.

Examine Relationships Between Tables

- In order for a relationship to exist between two tables, two things must be true: The parent table must have a column (or set of columns) that uniquely identifies every record it contains. The child table must have an identical column (or set of columns) to contain the values that uniquely identify the parent record.

- In a parent/child relationship, a single record in the parent table can be referred to by any number of records in the child table.

- Writing a command that combines data from more than one table into a single list is called creating a join.

- There are three main types of joins—inner joins (also known as equijoins), outer joins, and self-joins.

- UNION, UNION ALL, INTERSECT, and MINUS are set operators.

Write SQL Subqueries

- A subquery is a standard SELECT query that is nested within a SELECT, UPDATE, or DELETE command.

- A subquery can even contain subqueries within itself.

- A multirow subquery is one in which the subquery has the potential of returning more than one row of answers.

- It's possible to use subqueries that return multiple columns of data.

■ Key Terms

bitmap index *(159)*
branch block *(158)*
B-tree index *(157)*
Cartesian product *(165)*

composite index *(157)*
concatenated index *(157)*
correlated subquery *(181)*
foreign key *(164)*

function-based index *(160)*
inner join *(167)*
INTERSECT *(176)*
join *(164)*

JOIN *(171)*
leaf block *(158)*
MINUS *(176)*
multirow subquery *(179)*
ON *(171)*

outer join *(169)*
primary key *(162)*
range scan *(159)*
self-join *(170)*
set operator *(173)*

single-row subquery *(178)*
subquery *(177)*
table alias *(166)*
UNION *(174)*
UNION ALL *(175)*

■ Key Term Quiz

Use the Key Terms list to complete the sentences that follow. Not all terms will be used.

1. The _____ set operator performs the useful task of combining data from multiple tables into a unique single list.

2. A(n) _____ is a standard SELECT query that is nested within a SELECT, UPDATE, or DELETE command.

3. The _____ set operator returns only the values that are present in both tables.

4. A(n) _____ is one in which the subquery has the potential of returning more than one row of answers.

5. The _____ set operator causes every row to be returned, instead of just one distinct row for each unique value.

■ Matching Definition Quiz

Relate each term on the left with the appropriate description on the right.

Term		Description	
1.	Inner join	a.	A join without a WHERE clause
2.	Cartesian product	b.	Allows a child record to refer to a parent record
3.	Composite index	c.	An index based on more than one column in a table
4.	Function-based index	d.	Created when the values in the columns from both tables in the join are equal
5.	Foreign key	e.	Stores the product value of the function or expression in the index

■ Multiple-Choice Quiz

1. Which of the following is not a benefit of indexes?

   a. Faster operation during INSERT commands
   b. Faster operation during UPDATE commands
   c. Faster operation during SELECT commands
   d. Faster operation during DELETE commands

2. On which line will the following command fail?

   ```
   CREATE INDEX test_purchase_pk ON
   test_purchase (
       product_name,
       salesperson,
       purchase_date
       );
   ```

   a. 1
   b. 2

   c. 3
   d. 4
   e. The command will succeed.

3. Which of the following index types is best suited for a column with high cardinality?

   a. Composite
   b. B-tree
   c. Bitmap
   d. Function-based
   e. Unique

4. Which of the following commands would ensure that products entered into a purchase record exist in the product table?

a. CREATE INDEX *index_name* ON
table_name(column_name);

b. ALTER TABLE *table_name* MODIFY
(*column_name* NOT NULL);

c. ALTER TABLE *table_name* ADD
CONSTRAINT *constraint_name* UNIQUE
(*column_name*);

d. ALTER TABLE *table_name* ADD
CONSTRAINT *constraint_name* CHECK
(*column_name condition_to_satisfy*);

e. ALTER TABLE *table_name* ADD
CONSTRAINT *constraint_name* FOREIGN
KEY (*column_name*) REFERENCES
parent_table_name;

5. What will be the result of the following
command if table 1 contains five records and
table 2 contains ten records?

```
SELECT table_1_name.column_name_1,
       table_2_name.column_name_2
FROM   table_1_name,
       table_2_name
;
```

a. The five records from table 1 will display.

b. The ten records from table 2 will display.

c. Fifteen records will display, with data from
both tables.

d. Fifty records will display, with data from
both tables.

e. The number of records displayed will depend
on how many records in table 1 share values
with records in table 2.

6. The type of join created without issuing a
WHERE clause is known as a(n)

a. Inner join

b. Outer join

c. Self-join

d. Cartesian product

e. Equijoin

7. This set operator performs the useful task of
combining data from multiple tables into a single
list, duplicate values not shown:

a. UNION ALL

b. JOIN

c. UNION

d. INTERSECT

e. MINUS

8. This set operator returns only the values that are
present in both tables:

a. UNION ALL

b. JOIN

c. UNION

d. INTERSECT

e. MINUS

9. This set operator causes every row to be returned
from both tables, duplicate values included

a. UNION ALL

b. JOIN

c. UNION

d. INTERSECT

e. MINUS

10. This type of join could be created when the
values in the columns from both tables in the join
are equal. (Choose all that apply.)

a. Inner join

b. Outer join

c. Self-join

d. Cartesian product

e. Union

11. Which of the following index types is best suited
for a column with low cardinality?

a. Bitmap

b. B-tree

c. Function-based

d. Unique

e. Composite

12. What kind of index is created by the following
statement? (Choose all that apply.)

```
CREATE INDEX total_sal_comm on
test_employee (salary + commission);
```

a. Function-based

b. Bitmap

c. B-tree

d. Composite

e. Unique

13. What type of subquery is indicated by the following statement?

```
SELECT *
FROM    test_product
WHERE   product_name NOT IN (
        SELECT DISTINCT product_name
        FROM    test_purchase
        )
ORDER BY product_name;
```

   a. Single-row subquery

   b. Multirow subquery

   c. Multicolumn subquery

   d. Function-based subquery

   e. Single-column subquery

14. What do the **(+)** characters indicate in an outer join?

   a. The **(+)** characters identify which table may not have matching records for every record in the other table.

   b. The **(+)** characters identify which rows may not have matching records in the other table.

   c. The **(+)** characters identify which records may not have matching records in the other table.

   d. The **(+)** characters identify which tables have matching records for every other record in the other table.

   e. The **(+)** characters identify which table has matching records for every other table.

15. Which of the following statements are true regarding indexes?

   a. Once you have created an index on a table, Oracle automatically keeps the index synchronized with that table.

   b. Any SELECT on the table will automatically be routed through an index, if one exists containing the columns needed by the WHERE statement.

   c. You can add or drop indexes without affecting the table's operations—any program that used the table before will still operate.

   d. If you drop a table, any indexes associated with that table will automatically be dropped too, since an index has no purpose without its associated table.

   e. All of the above.

■ Essay Quiz

1. Explain how indexes help the search for data in Oracle database tables.

2. Describe how a B-tree index is used by Oracle.

3. Describe a scenario when indexes would be effective on a table.

4. Describe a scenario when an index would not be effective on a table.

5. What types of problems can subqueries solve?

Lab Projects

• Lab Project 6.1

Case Study

John at the Clapham Specialty Store wants you to query the database for his employees' names, numbers, and pay rate. He would like to know all the employees who earn more than the average pay rate. He also would like to know which of those employees that earn more than the average pay rate work at the same job type as the employee with the last name of Morton.

You will need the following:

■ Oracle9i Database Server with the SQL*Plus tool

■ Completion of Lab Project 5.2

1. Write a query to display the employee number, name, and pay rate for all employees at the Clapham Specialty Store who earn more than the average pay rate.

2. Write a query to display the employee number, name, and pay rate for all employees at the Clapham Specialty Store who earn more than the average pay rate and who work at the same job type as the employee with the last name of Morton.

• Lab Project 6.2

Case Study

John at the Clapham Specialty Store has asked you to display the Product_Name, Location_ID, Department, Aisle, Side, and Shelf of all products in his store. In order to do this, he has asked you to join the PRODUCT and LOCATION tables using the common column of Location_ID. He has also asked you to create a SALE table to keep track of the sales information that he has provided to you.

You will need the following materials:

- Oracle9i Database Server with the SQL*Plus tool
- Completion of Lab Projects 2.1 and 2.2

Then do the following:

1. Create a query that will display the Product_Name, Location_ID, Department, Aisle, Side, and Shelf for each product in the Clapham Specialty Store. Join the PRODUCT and LOCATION tables on the common Location_ID column to create this display.

2. Create a SALE table according to the following command:

```
CREATE TABLE sale (
    till_receipt_no NUMBER(10) NOT NULL,
    customer_id NUMBER(10) NULL,
    register_id NUMBER(10) NOT NULL,
    sale_date_time DATE NULL,
    register_clerk_id NUMBER(10) NOT NULL,
    delivery_person_id NUMBER(10) NULL
);
```

3. Insert the following data into the SALE table:

```
INSERT INTO sale VALUES (5345, 124, 2,
'10-JUL-2003',80009004, 80009005);
INSERT INTO sale VALUES (5346, 125, 2,
'10-JUL-2003',80009004, null);
INSERT INTO sale VALUES (5347, 126, 3,
'11-JUL-2003',80009007, 80009005);
INSERT INTO sale VALUES (5348, 127, 3,
'11-JUL-2003',80009007, 80009006);
```

4. Create a query that will display all data in a single list from both the SALE and CUSTOMER tables, ensuring that every row is to be returned, instead of just one distinct row for each unique value. Order all records by the Customer_ID.

5. Create a query that will display the customer last name, customer identification number, till receipt number, register identification number, and register clerk identification number from the CUSTOMER and SALE tables.

Creating a Program with PL/SQL

"Those parts of the system that you can hit with a hammer (not advised) are called hardware; those program instructions that you can only curse at are called software."

—ANONYMOUS

In this chapter, you will learn how to

- **Describe the purpose and scope of the PL/SQL language**
- **Define the structure of a PL/SQL block**
- **Create a basic PL/SQL procedure: "Hello world" application**
- **Employ PL/SQL variables and constants**
- **Write control structures**
- **Catch and respond to errors when your PL/SQL statements execute**

Storing and retrieving information is just one part of any real-life application. Even the simplest applications need to do some processing that is difficult or impossible using SQL alone. Just think of how complex the computations are when the government's share of your earnings needs to be computed every year! OK, maybe you want to think of another example instead. In any case, SQL alone isn't up to the task.

In the previous chapter you examined indexes, joins, and subqueries. You learned how to create bitmap, B-tree, and function-based indexes. You also learned how to select data from several tables using inner, outer, and self-joins as well as select data from tables using subqueries.

In this chapter you will be introduced to the basics of PL/SQL. You will learn the difference between SQL, SQL*Plus, and PL/SQL. You will also start writing simple PL/SQL procedures, as well as functions using basic PL/SQL constructs like variables, loops, and cursors. Then you will learn about the important art of handling errors in a way the user can easily understand.

■ What Is PL/SQL?

PL/SQL stands for Procedural Language/Structured Query Language . Why do we need this extension to SQL, particularly as this is just Oracle's extension?

SQL is a declarative language. The statements have no flow to them and, with certain restrictions, can be executed in any order. You may have noticed that there are no variables in SQL, only tables and columns. You cannot pass the result of one SQL statement to the next statement. You have to rewrite the statements to do it all in one big declaration. SQL does not have IF or LOOP commands, which would allow you to control the order in which programming commands are executed.

PL/SQL, on the other hand, is a procedural language that makes up for all the missing elements in SQL. It has IF and LOOP commands to control the flow of the program. It has variables to store values in and to pass values from one statement to the next. PL/SQL arose from the desire of programmers to have a language structure that was more familiar than SQL's purely declarative nature. Earlier versions of SQL were not as capable as current implementations and a procedural language was required to allow full use of the database.

 Inside Information

Procedural vs. Declarative Languages

SQL is derived from the mathematics of sets, in which order is not regarded as important (in fact, a set is defined as a collection without order). In a fully defined mathematical language it is possible to prove that any action accomplished by a procedural program can also be accomplished by a declaration in a declarative language. The proof is beyond the scope of this book, so you'll just have to trust us or look it up.

For example, say you have a table, DIGIT, with one column, Num, and 10 rows each containing a single digit. Say you want to fill a table, RANKING, with 10,000 numbers—0 to 9,999. Procedurally you can write a loop that simply counts up, saving each number as you go. It's much more fun to do this declaratively like this:

```
CREATE TABLE digit (num  NUMBER(1,0));
INSERT INTO digit VALUES (0);
INSERT INTO digit VALUES (1);
INSERT INTO digit VALUES (2);
INSERT INTO digit VALUES (3);
INSERT INTO digit VALUES (4);
INSERT INTO digit VALUES (5);
INSERT INTO digit VALUES (6);
INSERT INTO digit VALUES (7);
INSERT INTO digit VALUES (8);
INSERT INTO digit VALUES (9);
```

```
CREATE TABLE ranking (rank NUMBER(4,0));

INSERT INTO ranking (rank)
SELECT THOUSANDS.num * 1000 +
       HUNDREDS.num  * 100 +
       TENS.num      * 10 +
       ONES.num
FROM   digit THOUSANDS,
       digit HUNDREDS,
       digit TENS,
       digit ONES
WHERE  THOUSANDS.num * 1000 +
       HUNDREDS.num  * 100 +
       TENS.num      * 10 +
       ONES.num
       BETWEEN 0 AND 9999;

SELECT COUNT(1) FROM ranking;
DROP TABLE digit;
DROP TABLE ranking;
```

Since the WHERE clause does not specify any rules for joining records between THOUSANDS, HUNDREDS, TENS, and ONES, you get a useful Cartesian product resulting in all possible combinations being inserted—from a simple anonymous procedure.

If you just started reading in this chapter and have not done any of the exercises in the preceding chapters, you will need to create the sample tables built in prior chapters before you can do the exercises in this chapter. You can accomplish this by entering the following SQL commands:

```
DROP TABLE test_purchase;
DROP TABLE test_product;
DROP TABLE test_person;
DROP TABLE test_old_item;
DROP TABLE test_purchase_archive;

CREATE TABLE test_person (
    person_code VARCHAR2(3) PRIMARY KEY,
    first_name  VARCHAR2(15),
    last_name   VARCHAR2(20),
    hire_date   DATE
    )
;
CREATE INDEX test_person_name_index
ON test_person(last_name, first_name);

INSERT INTO test_person VALUES
    ('CA', 'Charlene', 'Atlas', '01-FEB-2002');
INSERT INTO test_person VALUES
    ('GA', 'Gary', 'Anderson', '15-FEB-2002');
INSERT INTO test_person VALUES
    ('BB', 'Bobby', 'Barkenhagen', '28-FEB-2002');
```

```
INSERT INTO test_person VALUES
     ('LB', 'Laren', 'Baxter', '01-MAR-2002');

CREATE TABLE test_product (
     product_name      VARCHAR2(25) PRIMARY KEY,
     product_price     NUMBER(4,2),
     quantity_on_hand NUMBER(5,0),
     last_stock_date   DATE
     )
;
INSERT INTO test_product VALUES
     ('Small Widget', 99, 1, '15-JAN-2003');
INSERT INTO test_product VALUES
     ('Medium Wodget', 75, 1000, '15-JAN-2002');
INSERT INTO test_product VALUES
     ('Chrome Phoobar', 50, 100, '15-JAN-2003');
INSERT INTO test_product VALUES
     ('Round Chrome Snaphoo', 25, 10000, null);
INSERT INTO test_product VALUES
     ('Extra Huge Mega Phoobar +',9.95,1234,'15-JAN-2004');
INSERT INTO test_product VALUES ('Square Zinculator',
     45, 1, TO_DATE('December 31, 2002, 11:30 P.M.',
                    'Month dd, YYYY, HH:MI P.M.')
     )
;


CREATE TABLE test_purchase (
     product_name   VARCHAR2(25),
     salesperson    VARCHAR2(3),
     purchase_date DATE,
     quantity       NUMBER(4,2)
     )
;
CREATE INDEX test_purchase_product
ON test_purchase(product_name);
CREATE INDEX test_purchase_salesperson
ON test_purchase(salesperson);
INSERT INTO test_purchase VALUES
     ('Small Widget', 'CA', '14-JUL-2003', 1);
INSERT INTO test_purchase VALUES
     ('Medium Wodget', 'BB', '14-JUL-2003', 75);
INSERT INTO test_purchase VALUES
     ('Chrome Phoobar', 'GA', '14-JUL-2003', 2);
INSERT INTO test_purchase VALUES
     ('Small Widget', 'GA', '15-JUL-2003', 8);
INSERT INTO test_purchase VALUES
     ('Medium Wodget', 'LB', '15-JUL-2003', 20);
INSERT INTO test_purchase VALUES
     ('Round Chrome Snaphoo', 'CA', '16-JUL-2003', 5);

UPDATE test_product
SET    product_price = product_price * .9
WHERE  product_name NOT IN (
       SELECT DISTINCT product_name
```

```
                FROM    test_purchase
                )
    ;


CREATE TABLE test_old_item (
        item_id    CHAR(20),
        item_desc CHAR(25)
        )
    ;
INSERT INTO test_old_item VALUES
        ('LA-101', 'Can, Small');
INSERT INTO test_old_item VALUES
        ('LA-102', 'Can, Large');
INSERT INTO test_old_item VALUES
        ('LA-103', 'Bottle, Small');
INSERT INTO test_old_item VALUES
        ('LA-104', 'Bottle, Large');
INSERT INTO test_old_item VALUES
        ('NY-101', 'Box, Small');
INSERT INTO test_old_item VALUES
        ('NY-102', 'Box, Large');
INSERT INTO test_old_item VALUES
        ('NY-103', 'Shipping Carton, Small');
INSERT INTO test_old_item VALUES
        ('NY-104', 'Shipping Carton, Large');


CREATE TABLE test_purchase_archive (
        product_name   VARCHAR2(25),
        salesperson    VARCHAR2(3),
        purchase_date DATE,
        quantity       NUMBER(4,2)
        )
    ;
INSERT INTO test_purchase_archive VALUES
        ('Round Snaphoo', 'BB', '21-JUN-2001', 10);
INSERT INTO test_purchase_archive VALUES
        ('Large Harflinger', 'GA', '22-JUN-2001', 50);
INSERT INTO test_purchase_archive VALUES
        ('Medium Wodget', 'LB', '23-JUN-2001', 20);
INSERT INTO test_purchase_archive VALUES
        ('Small Widget', 'ZZ', '24-JUN-2002', 80);
INSERT INTO test_purchase_archive VALUES
        ('Chrome Phoobar', 'CA', '25-JUN-2002', 2);
INSERT INTO test_purchase_archive VALUES
        ('Small Widget', 'JT', '26-JUN-2002', 50);
```

Describing PL/SQL

PL/SQL augments SQL with features such as looping, conditional branches, reusable functions, and the ability to respond to errors. For instance, let's say you need to build an application that can transfer each day's business activity into a daily summary table— PL/SQL packages can help you do this. You want to know whether you need to arrange for extra supplies for purchase orders that are really large—PL/SQL provides triggers that will notify you as soon as any order placed is found to be larger than certain limits decided by you. You can use PL/SQL stored procedures to compute your employees' performance to help you decide about bonuses. A PL/SQL function could provide certain types of calculations to a variety of other programs.

PL/SQL lets you use all the SQL data manipulation, cursor control, and transaction control commands, as well as all the SQL functions and operators. So, you can manipulate Oracle data flexibly and safely. Also, PL/SQL fully supports SQL datatypes. That reduces the need to convert data passed between your applications and the database. PL/SQL also supports dynamic SQL, an advanced programming technique that makes your applications more flexible and versatile. Your programs can build and process SQL data definition, data control, and session control statements "on the fly" at run time.

Before we proceed to learn more about some of these power tools, let's look at how PL/SQL, SQL, and SQL*Plus relate to each other.

Who's Who in SQL, PL/SQL, and SQL*Plus

Think of a restaurant. You go in and a well-trained waiter or waitress waits on you. You look through the menu and place an order. The waiter writes down your order and takes it into the kitchen. The kitchen is huge—there are many chefs and assistants. You can see a lot of food—cooked, partially cooked, and uncooked—stored in the kitchen. You can also see people with various jobs: They take the food in and out of storage, prepare a particular type of food (just soups or just salads, for instance), and so forth. Depending on what menu items you ordered, the waiter takes the order to different chefs. One chef completes some simple orders, while more complex orders may require help from assistants, or even multiple chefs. In addition, some orders are standard items—a waiter can just tell a chef "mushroom pizza"—while other orders are custom creations requiring a detailed list of exactly what ingredients you want.

Now alter this scenario a little. Think of an Oracle database as the restaurant's kitchen, with SQL*Plus serving as the waiter taking our orders—scripts, commands, or programs—to the kitchen, or database. Inside the kitchen are a master chef, PL/SQL, and an under-chef, SQL. The master chef directs the under-chef and organizes the order—the procedure—in which they work. The under-chef (SQL) can act on simple instructions directly from the waiter or can respond to the master chef (PL/SQL). Like a waiter, SQL*Plus knows what orders it can process on its own, as well as what orders to take to specific chefs. In the same way that a waiter can bring you a glass of water without having to get it from a chef, SQL*Plus can adjust the width of the lines shown on its screen without needing to go to the database.

The commands or programs you enter and execute at the SQL*Plus prompt are somewhat like your special-order pizza. For custom orders the chefs have to do some thinking each time. Just as the chef has the recipe for cheese pizza stored in his or her brain, you can have PL/SQL store "recipes" for your favorite orders. These stored PL/SQL elements are called triggers, stored functions, stored procedures, and packages. You will learn more about them soon.

Remember that some orders require more than one chef to prepare them. Most of the interesting and useful database applications you create will have SQL and PL/SQL working together, passing information back and forth between them to process a script or program. In a restaurant, after an order is prepared it goes to a waiter to be taken to your table. Similarly, when SQL and PL/SQL process commands, the results go to SQL*Plus (or a custom front-end form) to be displayed to the user.

Stored Procedures, Functions, and Triggers

PL/SQL procedures, functions, and triggers all help you build complex business logic easily and in a modular fashion (meaning piece by piece, with the pieces being reusable by other pieces). Storing these modules in the Oracle server provides two immediate benefits: They can be used over and over with predictable results, and they execute very rapidly because server operations involve little or no network traffic.

Stored Procedures

A **stored procedure** is a defined set of actions written using the PL/SQL language. When a procedure is called, it performs the actions it contains. The procedure is stored in the database, which is the reason it is called a stored procedure.

A stored procedure can execute SQL statements and manipulate data in tables. It can be called to do its job from within another PL/SQL stored procedure, stored function, or trigger. A stored procedure can also be called directly from a SQL*Plus prompt. As you read through the pages that follow, you will learn how to employ each of these methods for calling a stored procedure.

A procedure consists of two main parts: the specification and the body. The **procedure specification** contains the procedure's name and a description of its inputs and outputs. The inputs and outputs we are talking about are called the procedure's **formal parameters** or formal arguments. If a call to a procedure includes command-line parameters or other inputs, those values are called **actual parameters** or actual arguments.

Now let's take a look at some samples of procedure specifications. (Remember, the specification doesn't contain any code; it just names the procedure and defines any inputs and outputs the procedure can use.)

This simple specification contains only the procedure's name. It has no parameters:

```
run_ytd_reports
```

A value can be passed to this procedure when it is called:

```
increase_prices (increase_percent NUMBER)
```

Case Study

Let's look at our case study, the Clapham Specialty Store. If they want to run a procedure to calculate taxes on increased salaries, they may create a procedure to do so as shown in the following code. Within the procedure, the value will be addressed as INCREASE_PERCENT. Note that the value's datatype has been specified: NUMBER.

```
increase_salary_find_tax (increase_percent IN      NUMBER := 7,
                          sal                IN OUT NUMBER,
                          tax                       OUT NUMBER
                          )
```

Here we have a procedure with three formal parameters. The word IN after a parameter's name indicates that the procedure can read an incoming value from that parameter when the procedure is called. The word OUT after a parameter's name indicates that the procedure can use that parameter to send a value back to whatever called it. Having IN OUT after a parameter's name means that the parameter can bring a value into the procedure and also be used to send a value back out.

The INCREASE_PERCENT parameter in this example gets assigned a default value of 7 by including := 7 after the datatype. Because of this, if the procedure is called without specifying any increase percentage, it will increase the salary given by 7 percent and calculate the tax based on the new salary.

The procedure body is a block of PL/SQL code, which you will learn about in the next section of this chapter.

Datatypes for the procedure parameters cannot have size specifications. For instance, you can specify that a parameter is a NUMBER datatype, but not a NUMBER(10,2) datatype. You can, and must for VARCHAR2, specify the length of the variables in the procedure.

Stored Functions

A PL/SQL function is similar to a PL/SQL procedure: It has a function specification and a function body. The main difference between a procedure and a function is that a function is designed to return a value that can be used within a larger SQL statement.

For instance, think for a moment about a function designed to calculate the percentage difference between two numbers. Ignoring the code that would perform this calculation, the function specification would look like this:

```
calc_percent(value_1 NUMBER,
             value_2 NUMBER) return NUMBER
```

This function accepts two numbers as input, referring to them internally as VALUE_1 and VALUE_2. Once the body of this function is written, it could be referred to in a SQL statement in the following way:

```
INSERT INTO employee VALUES (3000, calc_percent(300, 3000));
```

Triggers

A trigger is a PL/SQL procedure that Oracle executes automatically whenever some event defined by the trigger—the triggering event —happens. You can write triggers that fire when an INSERT, UPDATE, or DELETE statement is performed on a table; when DDL statements are issued; when a user logs on or off; or when the database starts, encounters an error, or shuts down.

Triggers differ from PL/SQL procedures in four ways:

- You cannot call a trigger from within your code. Triggers are called automatically by Oracle in response to a predefined event.

Stored Procedures and SQL Scripts

While SQL scripts reside on your computer's hard disk, stored procedures reside within your Oracle database. A SQL script contains a series of SQL commands that are executed, one by one, when you invoke the script. In contrast, a stored procedure can contain flow-control commands allowing it to iterate through a particular section of code over and over, branch to another code section when particular situations occur, and respond to error conditions in a way you specify.

■ Structure of a PL/SQL Block

In this section you will learn about the PL/SQL basic block. Everything in PL/SQL that actually does work is made up of basic blocks. After learning about the basic blocks, you will see examples of complete procedures, functions, and triggers in the next section.

A PL/SQL basic block is made up of four sections: the header section, an optional declaration section, the execution section, and the optional exception section.

An anonymous block is a PL/SQL block with no header or name section, hence the term anonymous block. Anonymous blocks can be run from SQL*Plus and they can be used within PL/SQL functions, procedures, and triggers. Recall that PL/SQL procedures, functions, and triggers are all made up of basic blocks. What this means is that you can have a basic block within a basic block. You will learn more about this later in this section.

Perhaps the best way to begin to understand a basic block is to examine a sample. First type the following command so that information printed by programs can be made visible in SQL*Plus.

```
set serveroutput on
```

Now try the following sample code to create an anonymous block. Compare your results with Figure 7.1.

```
DECLARE
  num_a NUMBER := 6;
  num_b NUMBER;
BEGIN
  num_b := 0;
```

```
  num_a := num_a / num_b;
  num_b := 7;
  dbms_output.put_line(' Value of num_b ' || num_b);
EXCEPTION
  WHEN ZERO_DIVIDE
  THEN
    dbms_output.put_line('Trying to divide by zero');
    dbms_output.put_line(' Value of num_a ' || num_a);
    dbms_output.put_line(' Value of num_b ' || num_b);
END;
/
```

Header Section

The header section for a block varies based on what the block is part of. Recall that procedures, functions, triggers, and anonymous blocks are made up of basic blocks. In fact, each has one basic block that makes up its body. This body block may contain more basic blocks inside it. The header for this top-level basic block of a function, procedure, or trigger is the specification for that function, procedure, or trigger. For anonymous blocks the header contains only the keyword DECLARE. For labeled blocks the header contains the name of the label enclosed between << and >>, followed by the keyword DECLARE, as shown here:

```
<<just_a_label>>
DECLARE
```

Block labels help make it easier to read code. In a procedure using nested blocks (blocks inside other blocks), you can refer to an item in a specific block by preceding the item's name with the name of the block (for example, *block_label .item_label*).

Declaration Section

The declaration section is optional. When used, it begins after the header section and ends at the keyword BEGIN. The declaration section contains the declarations for PL/SQL variables, constants, cursors, exceptions, functions, and procedures that will be used by the execution and exception sections of the block. All variable and constant declarations must come before any function or procedure declarations within the declaration section. You will learn more about PL/SQL variables and constants in the following sections. A declaration tells PL/SQL to create a variable, constant, cursor, function, or procedure as specified in the declaration.

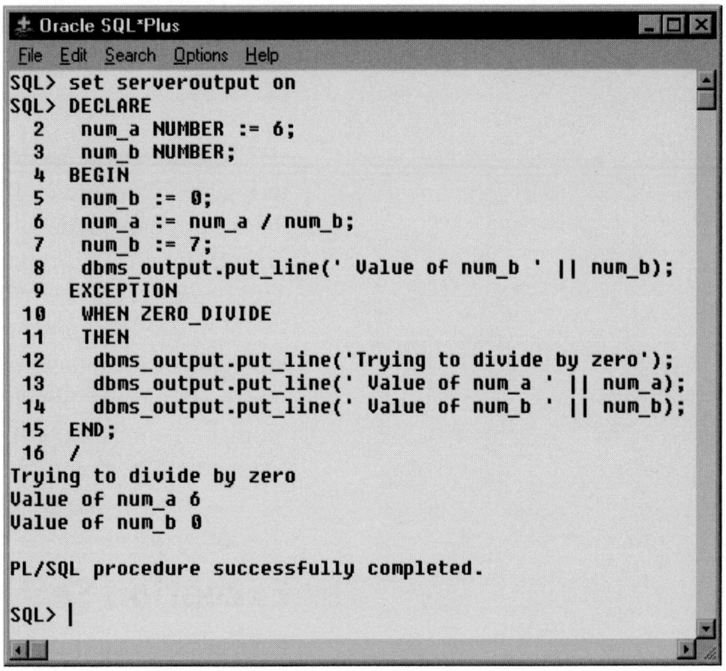

```
± Oracle SQL*Plus                              _ □ X
File  Edit  Search  Options  Help
SQL> set serveroutput on
SQL> DECLARE
  2    num_a NUMBER := 6;
  3    num_b NUMBER;
  4  BEGIN
  5    num_b := 0;
  6    num_a := num_a / num_b;
  7    num_b := 7;
  8    dbms_output.put_line(' Value of num_b ' || num_b);
  9  EXCEPTION
 10    WHEN ZERO_DIVIDE
 11    THEN
 12    dbms_output.put_line('Trying to divide by zero');
 13    dbms_output.put_line(' Value of num_a ' || num_a);
 14    dbms_output.put_line(' Value of num_b ' || num_b);
 15  END;
 16  /
Trying to divide by zero
Value of num_a 6
Value of num_b 0

PL/SQL procedure successfully completed.

SQL> |
```

• **Figure 7.1** Example of an anonymous PL/SQL block

The declaration section in the example shown in Figure 7.1 tells PL/SQL to create two number type variables called Num_a and Num_b. It also assigns a value of 6 by default to Num_a.

When a basic block has finished its run, everything declared within the declaration section stops existing. Things declared within the declaration section of a basic block can be used only within the same block. Thus, after running the example block in SQL*Plus, there is no way to pass Num_a to another PL/SQL procedure. Num_a and Num_b just go out of existence as soon as the block finishes its run. However, if you call a PL/SQL function or procedure within the execution or exception section of the block, you can pass Num_a and Num_b to them as actual parameters.

The long and short of the story is: Whatever is in the declaration section is the private property of the block—to be used by and visible only to itself. Thus what is in the declaration section of the block only lives as long as the block. In technical terms, Num_a and Num_b are said to have the scope of the block in which they are declared. The scope of the block starts at the beginning of the block's declaration section and ends at the end of its exception section.

Execution Section

The execution section starts with the keyword BEGIN and ends in one of two ways. If there is an exception section, the execution section ends with the keyword EXCEPTION. If no exception section is present, the execution section ends with the keyword END, followed optionally by the name of the function or procedure, and a semicolon. The execution section contains one or more PL/SQL statements that are executed when the block is run. The structure for the executable section is shown here:

```
BEGIN
        one or more PL/SQL statements
[exception section]
END [name of function or procedure];
```

The executable section in the example block, shown later in the chapter in Figure 7.2, contains three PL/SQL assignment statements. The assignment statement is the most commonly seen statement in PL/SQL code. The first statement assigns the value of zero to Num_b. The colon followed by an equal sign (:=) is the assignment operator. The assignment operator tells PL/SQL to compute whatever is on its right-hand side and place the result in whatever is on its left-hand side.

The second statement assigns Num_a the value of Num_a divided by Num_b. Note that after this statement is executed successfully, the value of Num_a will be changed.

The third statement assigns the value of 7 to Num_b.

Exception Section

It is possible that during the execution of PL/SQL statements in the execution section, an error will be encountered that makes it impossible to proceed with the execution. These error conditions are called exceptions. The procedure's user should be informed when an exception occurs and told why it has occurred. You may want to issue a useful error message to the user or you may want to take some corrective action and retry whatever the procedure was attempting before the error happened. You may want to roll back changes done to the database before the error occurred.

For all these situations PL/SQL helps you by providing exception-handling capabilities. Exceptions are so important for good applications that the end of this chapter has a special section where you will learn more about them. As an introduction, here is the structure for the exception section:

```
EXCEPTION
    WHEN first_exception_name
    THEN
        actions to take when this exception occurs
    WHEN second_exception_name
    THEN
        actions to take when this exception occurs
```

The exception section begins at the keyword EXCEPTION and ends at the end of the block. For each exception there is a WHEN *exception_name* statement that specifies what should be done when a specific exception occurs. Our example has three funny-looking statements that have the effect of making text display on your SQL*Plus screen. The DBMS_OUTPUT package and PUT_LINE procedure are part of the Oracle database; together they cause text to display on your SQL*PLUS screen one line at a time.

All the statements between the statement that causes the exception and the exception section will be ignored. So, in the case of the example block (Figure 7.1), the assigning of 7 to Num_b is not executed. You can verify this by looking at the value for Num_b that the example code prints out.

When a statement in the exception section deals with an exception, we refer to the action as **exception handling**.

Detecting that the error occurred and which exception best describes it and then taking appropriate steps to inform PL/SQL about it so as to make it possible for PL/SQL to find the exception section for that exception is called **raising an exception**. In the example code the exception is raised by PL/SQL on its own by detecting that there is an attempt at division by zero. PL/SQL has a predefined name for this exception—ZERO_DIVIDE.

When creating blocks of code, it is good practice to only have *one* exception handler in a procedure or function. This encourages you to separate different logical blocks into different procedures and makes your code more modular and easier to maintain.

■ Creating a Simple PL/SQL Procedure

We have all the ingredients to try out writing a complete PL/SQL procedure. You know about the basic block and you have learned about procedure specifications.

To create a simple PL/SQL procedure, type the following code:

```
CREATE PROCEDURE my_first_proc IS
  greetings VARCHAR2(20);
BEGIN
  greetings := 'Hello World';
  dbms_output.put_line(greetings);
END my_first_proc;
/
```

The syntax for creating a stored procedure is

```
CREATE PROCEDURE procedure_specification IS procedure_body
```

In our sample, the procedure specification is just the name of the procedure and the body is everything after it up to the last semicolon. For functions you will use the keyword FUNCTION instead of PROCEDURE.

```
CREATE FUNCTION function_specification IS function_body
```

The forward slash (/) tells SQL*Plus to go ahead and process the commands in the program. You can re-create the same procedure or function by changing the command CREATE to CREATE OR REPLACE. This will destroy the old definition of the procedure or function and replace it with the new one. If there is no old definition it will simply create a new one.

```
CREATE OR REPLACE PROCEDURE procedure_specification
IS procedure_body
```

Now let us see how this procedure can be called from SQL*Plus:

```
set serveroutput on
EXECUTE my_first_proc;
```

SERVEROUTPUT ON allows you to see the printed output. The command EXECUTE actually executes the procedure. You can call the procedure from within an anonymous block as follows. Compare your results with those shown in Figure 7.2.

```
BEGIN
        my_first_proc;
END;
/
```

> When a procedure is replaced, the privileges and other database objects that depend on the procedure are left in place. This can greatly reduce the work of editing a procedure.

Calling Procedures and Functions

A procedure or function may or may not have formal parameters with default values. In fact, it may not have any formal parameters at all. For each case the way the procedure or function is called is different. However, the following applies regardless of the parameters:

- The datatypes for the actual parameters must match or should be convertible by PL/SQL to the datatypes of corresponding formal parameters.

- Actual parameters must be provided for all formal parameters that do not have default values.

When calling a function without any parameters, you can just use the name with or without parentheses, like this:

```
Oracle SQL*Plus                                    _ □ ✕
File  Edit  Search  Options  Help
SQL> set serveroutput on
SQL> CREATE PROCEDURE my_first_proc
  2  IS
  3    greetings VARCHAR2(20);
  4  BEGIN
  5    greetings := 'Hello World';
  6    dbms_output.put_line(greetings);
  7  END my_first_proc;
  8  /

Procedure created.

SQL> EXECUTE my_first_proc;
Hello World

PL/SQL procedure successfully completed.

SQL> BEGIN
  2    my_first_proc;
  3  END;
  4  /
Hello World

PL/SQL procedure successfully completed.

SQL>
```

Figure 7.2   Simple "Hello World" PL/SQL procedure

```
procedure_name();
```

or

```
procedure_name;
```

The same syntax is used when dealing with a function, except a semicolon will not be used when the function is called as part of an expression.

When a procedure has formal parameters with default values and when they are all at the end of the list of formal parameters in the procedure specification, the procedure may be called without specifying values for the last few formal parameters for which default values exist. However, all the formal parameters for which actual parameters are being supplied at call time must be listed before all of the formal parameters for which no actual parameters are being supplied. The call will then look like this:

```
procedure_name(actual_param1,
               actual_param2,
               . . .
               actual_paramN);
```

N may be less than or equal to the number of formal parameters for the procedure and *N* must be greater than or equal to the number of formal parameters for which default values do not exist.

When the default-valued formal parameters are not the last parameters in the specification, or when you wish to avoid having PL/SQL figure out which actual parameter corresponds to which formal parameter using its order in the list, you can specifically tell PL/SQL which actual parameter is for which formal parameter using the following syntax:

```
procedure_name(formal_param1 => actual_param1,
               formal_param2 => actual_param2,
               . . .
               )
;
```

This is called named notation for calling functions and procedures. The earlier notation is called positional notation as the parameters are matched by their position in the list.

The same calling methods apply to functions. Functions, however, can appear within other expressions and may not have any semicolon at the end. You will see an example for named notation in the next section. It is possible to mix two notations but the positional list must precede the notational list in the call.

■ PL/SQL Variables and Constants

You have seen some examples of PL/SQL variables in previous sections. Now we will discuss them in greater detail. Variables are essentially containers with name tags. They can contain or hold information or data of different kinds. Based on the kind of data they can hold, they have different datatypes, and to distinguish them from one another they have names. Just as oil comes in a bottle and flour in a paper bag, PL/SQL will store numbers in variables of the NUMBER datatype and text in CHAR or VARCHAR2 datatype variables. Taking it a step further, imagine the refrigerator in your company's break room. It's filled with brown paper bags that contain your lunch and the lunches of your coworkers. How will you find your noontime feast among all the other bags? Right! You'd put your name on the bag. Variables are given names, too, in order to avoid confusion. Further, if your lunch consisted of only bananas, you may eat them and put the peels back into the brown paper bag. Now the contents of the bag have changed. Similarly, the contents of variables can be changed during the execution of PL/SQL statements.

Declaring PL/SQL Variables

The syntax for declaring a variable in PL/SQL is either of the following:

```
variable_name  data_type  [ [NOT NULL]  := default_value_expression];
variable_name  data_type  [ [NOT NULL] DEFAULT default_value_expression];
```

variable_name is any valid PL/SQL identifier . A valid PL/SQL identifier is

- Up to 30 characters long and has no white space of any form in it (as space or tabs).
- Made up of letters, digits 0 to 9, underscore (_), dollar ($), and pound (#) signs.
- Starts with a letter.
- Not the same as a PL/SQL or SQL reserved word, which has special meaning for PL/SQL or SQL. For example, BEGIN cannot be a variable name. BEGIN has a special meaning telling PL/SQL that here starts the beginning of a basic block execution section.

data_type is any valid SQL or PL/SQL datatype. More information on datatypes can be found in the next section.

The use of NOT NULL requires that the variable have a value and, if specified, the variable must be given a default value.

When a variable is created, it can be made to have a value specified by the default value expression. It is just a shorthand way to assign values to variables.

You already know about SQL datatypes—NUMBER, VARCHAR2, and DATE. PL/SQL shares them with SQL. PL/SQL has additional datatypes that are not in SQL. For a complete list, please refer to Oracle PL/SQL references.

Declaring PL/SQL Constants

The syntax for declaring a constant is

```
variable_name  data_type  CONSTANT  := constant_value_expression;
```

Unlike variables, constants must be given a value and that value cannot change during the life or scope of the constant. Constants are very useful for enforcing safe and disciplined code development in any application. For example, if you have a threshold to apply—say you want to give pay raises only to those people earning less than $25,460 per year—you should put this value (25460) into a constant and give it a meaningful name, such as MAX_PAY_FOR_RAISE. This would be declared:

```
max_pay_for_raise  CONSTANT NUMBER(10,2) := 25460;
```

Now, if someone wants to modify this threshold, they only have to edit it in one place in the code and they can be sure that everywhere the threshold was applied will be changed.

Assigning Values to Variables

There are three ways a variable can get its value changed. Assignment of a valid expression to it using the PL/SQL assignment operator is one. You have seen a number of examples of this kind. The syntax is

```
variable_name := expression ;
```

Second, a variable can be passed as the actual parameter corresponding to some IN OUT or OUT formal parameter when calling a PL/SQL procedure. After the procedure is finished, the value of the variable may change. The following example shows the named notation for calling procedures. Refer to Figure 7.3 for the expected output.

```
CREATE PROCEDURE hike_prices (old_price      NUMBER,
                              percent_hike   NUMBER := 5,
                              new_price OUT NUMBER)
IS
BEGIN
     new_price := old_price + old_price * percent_hike / 100;
END hike_prices;
/
```

The following procedure shows the variables changing their values:

```
DECLARE
     price_to_hike NUMBER(6,2) := 20;
     hiked_price NUMBER(6,2) := 0;
BEGIN
     dbms_output.put_line('Price before hike ' || price_to_hike);
     dbms_output.put_line('hiked_price before hike ' || hiked_price);
     hike_prices (old_price => price_to_hike,
               new_price => hiked_price);
     dbms_output.put_line('price_to_hike after hike ' || price_to_hike);
     dbms_output.put_line('hiked_price after hike ' || hiked_price);
END;
/
```

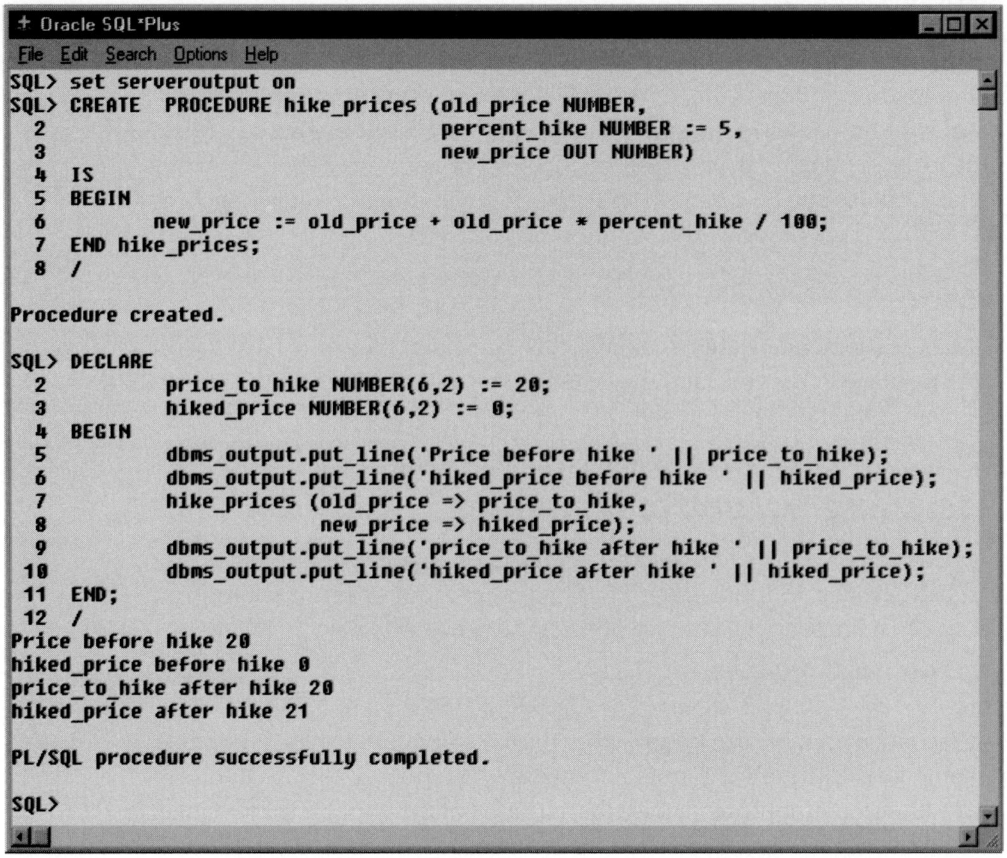

```
+ Oracle SQL*Plus                                                    _ □ X
 File  Edit  Search  Options  Help
SQL> set serveroutput on
SQL> CREATE  PROCEDURE hike_prices (old_price NUMBER,
  2                                 percent_hike NUMBER := 5,
  3                                 new_price OUT NUMBER)
  4  IS
  5  BEGIN
  6          new_price := old_price + old_price * percent_hike / 100;
  7  END hike_prices;
  8  /

Procedure created.

SQL> DECLARE
  2          price_to_hike NUMBER(6,2) := 20;
  3          hiked_price NUMBER(6,2) := 0;
  4  BEGIN
  5          dbms_output.put_line('Price before hike ' || price_to_hike);
  6          dbms_output.put_line('hiked_price before hike ' || hiked_price);
  7          hike_prices (old_price => price_to_hike,
  8                       new_price => hiked_price);
  9          dbms_output.put_line('price_to_hike after hike ' || price_to_hike);
 10          dbms_output.put_line('hiked_price after hike ' || hiked_price);
 11  END;
 12  /
Price before hike 20
hiked_price before hike 0
price_to_hike after hike 20
hiked_price after hike 21

PL/SQL procedure successfully completed.

SQL>
```

● **Figure 7.3**   Assigning values to PL/SQL variables by using them as actual parameters

The third way of changing or assigning values to variables is to read them in from a table via a SQL SELECT statement. The following code snippet demonstrates this approach. Figure 7.4 shows the results.

```
DECLARE
      product_quant           NUMBER;
BEGIN
      SELECT    quantity_on_hand
      INTO      product_quant
      FROM      test_product
      WHERE     product_name = 'Small Widget';
dbms_output.put_line ('Small Widget ' || product_quant);
END;
/
```

product_quant is assigned the value equal to the quantity of small widgets.

Using Variables

Variables are the very basic units of PL/SQL programs. They are used to hold results of computations, to return values from function calls, as actual parameters for calling functions and procedures, and so on. Variables should be used to make your application clean and easier to read, thereby creating a lower-maintenance, more efficient program.

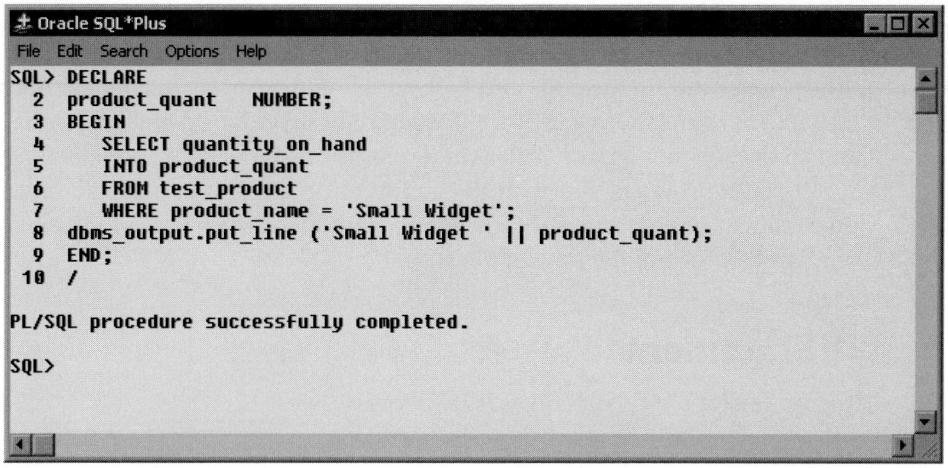

```
Oracle SQL*Plus                                          _ □ ✕
File  Edit  Search  Options  Help
SQL> DECLARE
  2    product_quant    NUMBER;
  3    BEGIN
  4      SELECT quantity_on_hand
  5      INTO product_quant
  6      FROM test_product
  7      WHERE product_name = 'Small Widget';
  8    dbms_output.put_line ('Small Widget ' || product_quant);
  9    END;
 10  /

PL/SQL procedure successfully completed.

SQL>
```

● **Figure 7.4**   Assigning values to PL/SQL variables using SQL

Suppose you want to perform a number of calculations using the current quantity of small widgets—compare it with the quantity from three months ago, or to the quantity of medium widgets. By using the variable to hold the value, you avoid the delay that would come from getting the quantity from the table again and again.

By naming variables in a way that makes sense to you, you can make your code easy to read and understand. The same principle applies when you use variables to hold the results of some very complex expressions instead of repeating the expressions in the code in multiple places.

☑ **Cross Check**

Working with PL/SQL Variables and Constants

Now that you've been introduced to PL/SQL variables and constants, take a moment to check your knowledge by answering the following questions:

1. What are PL/SQL variables used for?

2. What is the syntax for declaring a constant?

3. How is a declared constant useful?

■ Control Structures in PL/SQL

Many times you want to do one thing if something is true and something else if it is not true. For example, if a purchase order exceeds a certain dollar amount, you would like to take 5 percent off the order, or maybe 10 percent off if the order exceeds some other amount. This kind of logic may be required inside your application that prints out the final invoice for your customers. This is conditional processing of data. Based on the condition, different parts of the code need to be executed.

Recall the case where you need to compute income tax for each employee. You need to complete a function for each employee such as finding the earnings and filing status and then applying the correct formula to find the tax. The correct formula differs for each employee based on filing status and all of the other factors. This is an example of an iterative operation .

PL/SQL provides you with the ability to do conditional and iterative processing. The constructs it provides are said to cause change of program flow and so control the flow of the execution.

IF Statement

The syntax for an IF statement is as follows:

```
IF condition_1 THEN
        actions_1;
[ELSIF condition_2 THEN
        actions_2;]
...
[ELSE
        actions_last;]
END IF;
```

actions_1 to actions_last represent one or more PL/SQL statements. Each set of statements gets executed only if its corresponding condition is true. When one of the IF conditions is determined to be true, the rest of the conditions are not checked.

Enter the following example and see that your results match those shown in the top portion of Figure 7.5.

```
CREATE FUNCTION compute_discounts (order_amt NUMBER)
RETURN NUMBER
IS
-- Compute discounts on orders.
-- Input order amount. Returns discount amount (zero for wrong inputs).
        small_order_amt NUMBER := 400;
        large_order_amt NUMBER := 1000;
        small_disct NUMBER := 1;
        large_disct NUMBER := 5;
BEGIN
        IF (order_amt < large_order_amt
            AND
            order_amt >= small_order_amt)
        THEN
             RETURN (order_amt * small_disct / 100);
        ELSIF (order_amt >= large_order_amt)
        THEN
             RETURN (order_amt * large_disct / 100);
        ELSE
             RETURN(0);
        END IF;
END compute_discounts;
/
```

This function will give a 1 percent discount for orders between 400 and 1000 and a 5 percent discount on orders above 1000. It will return zero for all

```
  Oracle SQL*Plus                                                      _ □ ×
 File  Edit  Search  Options  Help
SQL> CREATE FUNCTION compute_discounts (order_amt NUMBER)
  2    RETURN NUMBER
  3    IS
  4            small_order_amt NUMBER := 400;
  5            large_order_amt NUMBER := 1000;
  6            small_disct NUMBER := 1;
  7            large_disct NUMBER := 5;
  8    BEGIN
  9            IF (order_amt < large_order_amt
 10               AND
 11               order_amt >= small_order_amt)
 12            THEN
 13                   RETURN (order_amt * small_disct / 100);
 14            ELSIF (order_amt >= large_order_amt)
 15            THEN
 16                   RETURN (order_amt * large_disct / 100);
 17            ELSE
 18                   RETURN(0);
 19            END IF;
 20    END compute_discounts;
 21    /

Function created.

SQL> DECLARE
  2            tiny NUMBER := 20;
  3            med NUMBER := 600;
  4            big NUMBER := 4550;
  5            wrong NUMBER := -35;
  6    BEGIN
  7            dbms_output.put_line (' Order        AND       Discount ');
  8            dbms_output.put_line (tiny || '   ' || compute_discounts(tiny));
  9            dbms_output.put_line (med || '   ' || compute_discounts (med));
 10            dbms_output.put_line (big || '   ' || compute_discounts (big));
 11            dbms_output.put_line (wrong || '   ' || compute_discounts (wrong));
 12    END;
 13    /
Order        AND        Discount
20  0
600  6
4550  227.5
-35  0

PL/SQL procedure successfully completed.

SQL>
```

● Figure 7.5   Example of an IF statement

other amounts including wrong values. For example, someone may try to use a negative value for *order_amt*, which is meaningless.

Observe at the start how the function is clearly documented. You should always consider all possibilities when writing your code and either clearly state in your documentation what you are going to do about error conditions or, if the conditions are severe enough, give appropriate error messages. Suppose in our case—however unimaginable it is—that this function may be called with a negative value for the *order_amt*, and we have documented what the function will do in such a case.

You can test the function by calling it in an anonymous block. Be sure you have SERVEROUTPUT on. Refer to the bottom portion of Figure 7.5 to compare the results of this example.

```
DECLARE
     tiny  NUMBER := 20;
     med   NUMBER := 600;
     big   NUMBER := 4550;
     wrong NUMBER := -35;
BEGIN
     dbms_output.put_line ('Order AND Discount ');
     dbms_output.put_line (tiny || '      ' || compute_discounts(tiny));
     dbms_output.put_line (med || '      ' || compute_discounts (med));
     dbms_output.put_line (big || '      ' || compute_discounts (big));
     dbms_output.put_line (wrong || '      ' || compute_discounts (wrong));
END;
/
```

Loops

PL/SQL provides three different iteration constructs. Each allows you to repeatedly execute a set of PL/SQL statements. You stop the repeated executions based on some condition.

LOOP

The syntax for the LOOP construct is

```
<<loop_name>>
LOOP
        statements;
        EXIT loop_name [WHEN exit_condition_expression];
        statements;
END LOOP ;
```

All the statements within the loop are executed repeatedly, and during each repetition or iteration of the loop, the exit condition expression is checked for positive value if the WHEN condition is present. If the expression is true, the execution skips all statements following the EXIT and jumps to the first statement after END LOOP within the code. No more iterations are done. If the WHEN condition is not present, the effect is to execute statements between LOOP and EXIT only once. You will obviously be doing something illogical if you are not using the WHEN condition. After all, the idea of a loop is to potentially loop through the code.

Try out this loop example and compare your results with Figure 7.6. It simply prints out the first ten numbers.

As usual, remember to set SERVEROUTPUT on to see the output.

```
DECLARE
     just_a_num NUMBER := 1;
BEGIN
     <<just_a_loop>>
     LOOP
         dbms_output.put_line(just_a_num);
```

```
        EXIT just_a_loop
        WHEN (just_a_num >= 10);
                just_a_num := just_a_num + 1;
        END LOOP;
END;
/
```

Each iteration increments the variable *just_a_num* by 1. When 10 is reached, the exit condition is satisfied and the loop is exited.

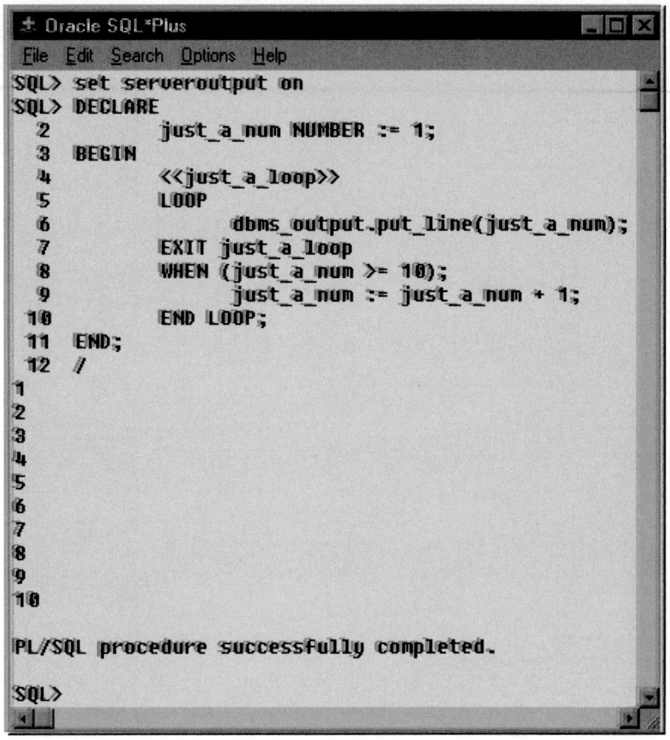

WHILE Loop

Another type of loop is the WHILE loop . A WHILE loop is well suited for situations when the number of loop iterations is not known in advance, but rather is determined by some external factor. The syntax for a WHILE loop is as follows:

```
WHILE while_condition_expression
LOOP
        statements;
END LOOP;
```

Practice creating a WHILE loop by entering the following code. Your results should match those of Figure 7.7.

```
DECLARE
        just_a_num NUMBER := 1;
BEGIN
        WHILE (just_a_num < 10)
        LOOP  dbms_output.put_line(just_a_num);
                just_a_num := just_a_num + 1;
        END LOOP;
END;
/
```

The contents of the WHILE loop will execute only if the WHILE condition is true when the WHILE loop is reached.

FOR Loop

The FOR loop uses a counter variable, also called a loop index , to count the number of iterations. The counter is incremented starting from the lower limit specified or decremented starting from the upper limit specified at the end of each iteration or loop. If it is out of the range the looping stops. The syntax for the FOR loop is as follows:

```
FOR counter IN [REVERSE] lower_bound .. upper_bound
LOOP
        statements;
END LOOP;
```

● **Figure 7.6**   Example of a simple LOOP

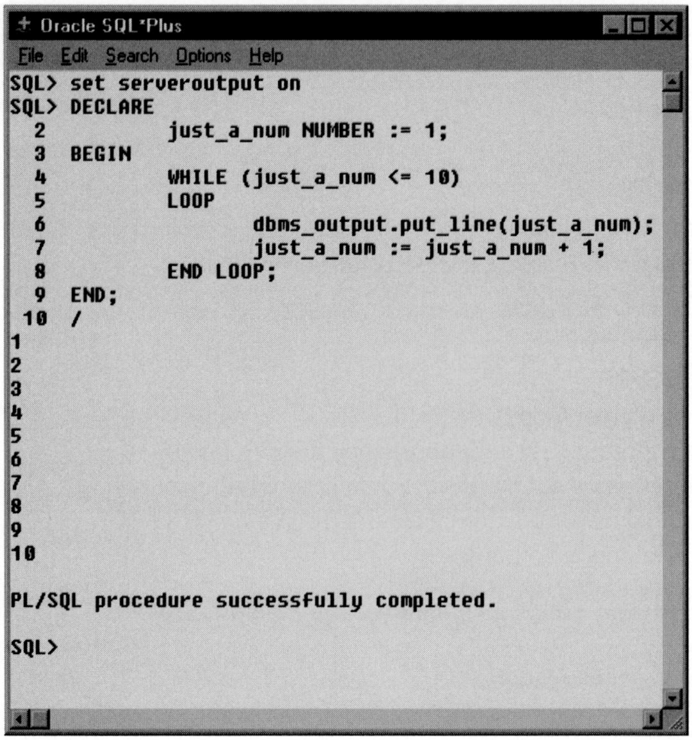

```
Oracle SQL*Plus                                    _ □ ×
File  Edit  Search  Options  Help
SQL> set serveroutput on
SQL> DECLARE
  2              just_a_num NUMBER := 1;
  3  BEGIN
  4              WHILE (just_a_num <= 10)
  5              LOOP
  6                      dbms_output.put_line(just_a_num);
  7                      just_a_num := just_a_num + 1;
  8              END LOOP;
  9  END;
 10  /
1
2
3
4
5
6
7
8
9
10

PL/SQL procedure successfully completed.

SQL>
```

• **Figure 7.7**   Example of a WHILE loop

Now create your first FOR loop using the following code. See Figure 7.8.

```
BEGIN
        FOR just_a_num IN 1..10
        LOOP
                dbms_output.put_line(just_a_num);
        END LOOP;
END;
/
```

Now for fun and experience, try using the command REVERSE in your FOR loop. Your results should show the numbers in reverse order from 10 to 1.

Case Study

Think about our case study example of the Clapham Specialty Store. How could loops help John at his store? When you have time, come up with a few situations where John may use loops to aid in the display of data from the database.

Cursors

The cursor is an extremely important PL/SQL construct. It is the heart of PL/SQL and SQL cooperation and stands for "current set of records." A cursor is a special PL/SQL element that has an associated SQL SELECT statement. Using a cursor, each row of the SQL statement associated with the cursor can be processed one at a time. A cursor is declared in the declaration

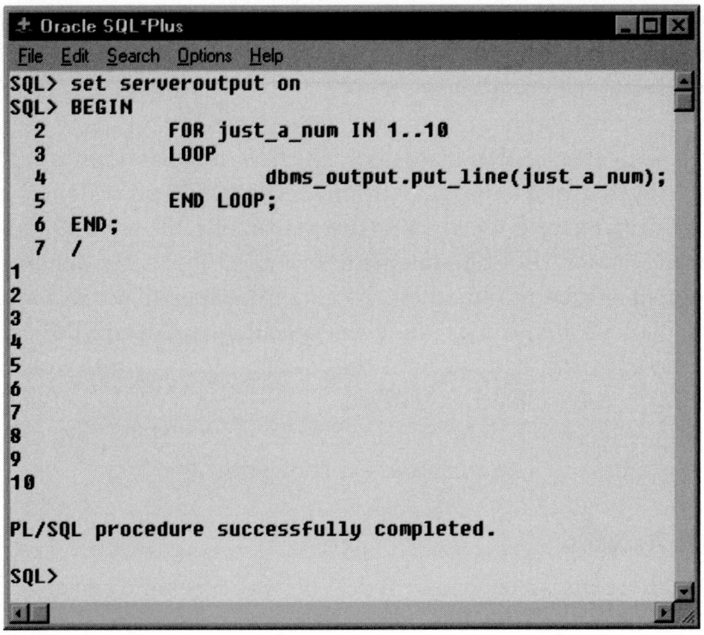

● **Figure 7.8**   Example of a FOR loop

section of a basic block. A cursor is opened using the command OPEN and rows can be fetched using the command FETCH. After all processing is done, the cursor is closed using the command CLOSE. Closing the cursor releases all of the system resources that were used while the cursor was open. You can lock the rows selected by a cursor to prevent other people from modifying them while you are using them. Closing the cursor or executing an explicit COMMIT or ROLLBACK will unlock the rows.

PL/SQL uses hidden or implicit cursors for SQL statements within PL/SQL code. In this section we will focus on explicit cursors, which simply means cursors that have been assigned a name.

We will write a simple procedure that uses a cursor to compute the commissions for all salespersons. Before we do that, however, take a look at the syntax for an explicit cursor.

Cursor Declaration and Cursor Attributes

A cursor is declared within a PL/SQL procedure in the following manner:

```
CURSOR cursor_name [( [parameter1 [, parameter2 ...])]
[RETURN return_specification]
IS
     select_statement
[FOR UPDATE
               [OF table_or_col1
                [, table_or_col2 ...]
                ]
          ]
;
```

The parameters are similar to procedure parameters but they are all IN parameters. They cannot be OUT or IN OUT because the cursor cannot modify them. The parameters are used in the WHERE clause of the cursor SELECT statement. The return specification tells what type of records will be selected by the SELECT statement. The *table_or_col* is a column name you intend to update or a table name from which you intend to delete or update rows, and it must be taken from the names of tables and columns used within the cursor SELECT statement. It is used to clearly document what may potentially be modified by the code that uses this cursor. The commands FOR UPDATE lock the rows selected by the SELECT statement when the cursor is opened, and they remain locked until you close the cursor in the ways already discussed.

A cursor has some indicators to show its state and they are called **attributes of the cursor** . The attributes are shown in Table 7.1.

PL/SQL Records

A PL/SQL record is a collection of data of basic types and can be accessed as a single unit. You access the individual fields of the record using the *record_name.field_name* notation you are already familiar with for use with table columns. Records are of three types and you can declare variables of rec- ord types. The three types of records are as follows:

- **Table-Based**   The record has fields that match the names and types of the table columns. So if a cursor selects the entire row—by using SELECT* from *some_table,* for example—the records it returns can be directly copied into the variable of the table-based record type for *some_table*.

- **Cursor-Based**   The record has fields that match in name, datatype, and order to the final list of columns in the cursor's SELECT statement.

- **Programmer-Defined**   These are records in which you define a record type.

Table 7.1	Cursor Attributes
Attribute	**Description**
cursor_name%ISOPEN	Checks if the cursor is open. It returns TRUE if the cursor *cursor_name* is already open.
cursor_name%ROWCOUNT	The number of table rows returned by the cursor SELECT statement.
cursor_name%FOUND	Checks whether the last attempt to get a record from the cursor succeeded. It returns TRUE if a record was fetched.
cursor_name%NOTFOUND	Opposite of the FOUND attribute. It returns TRUE when no more records are found.

Using OPEN, FETCH, and CLOSE Cursor

Here is the syntax for opening, fetching from, and closing a cursor:

```
OPEN cursor_name[(parameter_1, ...)];
FETCH cursor_name INTO record_var_or_list_of_var;
CLOSE cursor_name;
```

When opened, a cursor contains a set of records if the cursor's SELECT statement was successful and resulted in fetching selected rows from the database. Each **FETCH** then removes a record from the open cursor and moves the record's contents into either a PL/SQL variable—of a record type that matches the record type of the cursor record—or into a different set of PL/SQL variables such that each variable in the list matches in type with the corresponding field in the cursor record.

You will check if there are any more records left in the cursor before trying to fetch one from the cursor using the **FOUND** and **NOTFOUND** attributes of the cursor. Fetching from an empty cursor will fetch the last fetched record over and over again and will not give you any error. So make sure you use FOUND or NOTFOUND if you are using FETCH.

> You cannot use FOUND or NOTFOUND before the first FETCH of a cursor. Oracle will give an error if you do this.

The actual processing of records from a cursor usually occurs within a loop. When writing the loop, it's a good idea to start by checking whether a record has been found in the cursor. If so, the code proceeds to perform whatever processing you need; if not, the code exits from the loop. There is a more compact way to do the same where PL/SQL takes care of opening, fetching, and closing without your needing to do it—the cursor FOR loop.

Cursor FOR Loop

The syntax for the cursor FOR loop is

```
FOR cursor_record IN cursor_name LOOP
        statements;
END LOOP;
```

This cursor FOR loop continues fetching records from the cursor into the *cursor_record* record type variable. You can use *cursor_record* fields to access the data within your PL/SQL statements in the loop. When all the records are done, the loop ends. The cursor is automatically opened and closed for your convenience by PL/SQL.

You will receive an invalid cursor message if you try to fetch from a cursor that is not open. If you do not close cursors, you may end up eventually running into the maximum number of open cursors that the system allows. Note that the implicit cursors also count toward this limit.

WHERE CURRENT OF

When the cursor is opened in order to update or delete the rows it selects, you can use **WHERE CURRENT OF**

```
WHERE CURRENT OF cursor_name
```

to access the table and row corresponding to the most recently fetched record in the WHERE clause of the UPDATE or DELETE statement. For example, to

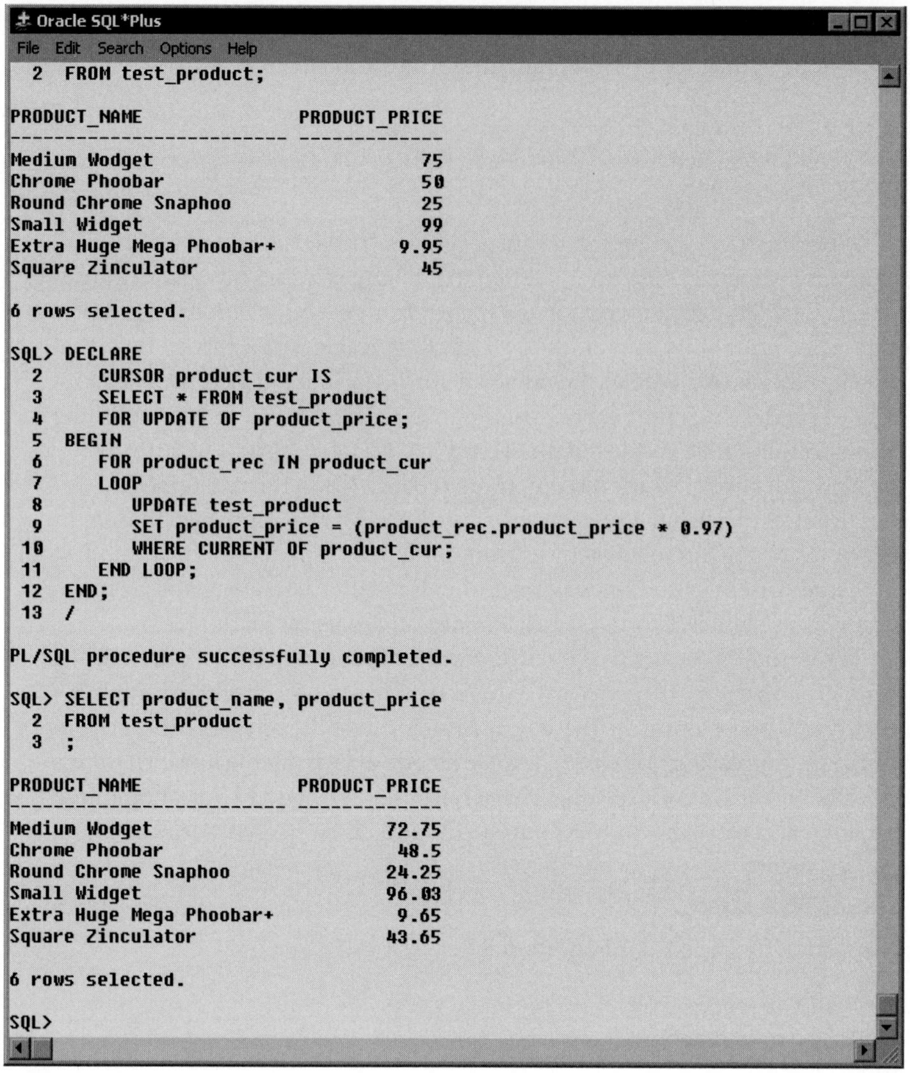

```
Oracle SQL*Plus
File  Edit  Search  Options  Help
  2  FROM test_product;

PRODUCT_NAME                  PRODUCT_PRICE
----------------------------- -------------
Medium Wodget                            75
Chrome Phoobar                           50
Round Chrome Snaphoo                     25
Small Widget                             99
Extra Huge Mega Phoobar+               9.95
Square Zinculator                        45

6 rows selected.

SQL> DECLARE
  2      CURSOR product_cur IS
  3      SELECT * FROM test_product
  4      FOR UPDATE OF product_price;
  5  BEGIN
  6      FOR product_rec IN product_cur
  7      LOOP
  8         UPDATE test_product
  9         SET product_price = (product_rec.product_price * 0.97)
 10         WHERE CURRENT OF product_cur;
 11      END LOOP;
 12  END;
 13  /

PL/SQL procedure successfully completed.

SQL> SELECT product_name, product_price
  2  FROM test_product
  3  ;

PRODUCT_NAME                  PRODUCT_PRICE
----------------------------- -------------
Medium Wodget                         72.75
Chrome Phoobar                         48.5
Round Chrome Snaphoo                  24.25
Small Widget                          96.03
Extra Huge Mega Phoobar+               9.65
Square Zinculator                     43.65

6 rows selected.

SQL>
```

• **Figure 7.9** Example of a cursor FOR loop and WHERE CURRENT OF clause

reduce the prices in the TEST_PRODUCT table by 3 percent, type the following code and check your results against those in Figure 7.9.

```
SELECT product_name, product_price
FROM   test_product;

DECLARE
     CURSOR product_cur IS
     SELECT * FROM test_product
     FOR UPDATE OF product_price;
BEGIN
     FOR product_rec IN product_cur
     LOOP
          UPDATE test_product
          SET    product_price = (product_rec.product_price * 0.97)
          WHERE  CURRENT OF product_cur;
```

```
     END LOOP;
END;
/

SELECT product_name, product_price
FROM   test_product;
```

Nested Loops and Cursor Example

The following code demonstrates complete use of cursors and loops within loops or **nested loops** . Enter the following code:

```
-- This procedure computes the commissions for salespersons.
-- It prints out the salesperson's code, his or her total sales,
-- and corresponding commission.
-- No inputs. No errors are reported and no exceptions are raised.
/* Logic: A cursor to create a join between TEST_PRODUCT and
TEST_PURCHASE on PRODUCT_NAME column is done.
The result is ordered by salesperson.
Outer loop starts with a new salesperson and inner loop
processes all rows for one salesperson.
*/
CREATE OR REPLACE PROCEDURE do_commissions IS
     commission_rate NUMBER   := 2   ;
     total_sale      NUMBER   := 0   ;
     current_person  CHAR(3) := ' ' ;
     next_person     CHAR(3)          ;
     quantity_sold   NUMBER   := 0   ;
     item_price      NUMBER   := 0   ;
     CURSOR sales_cur IS
         SELECT tab1.salesperson,
                tab1.quantity,
                tab2.product_price
         FROM   test_purchase tab1,
                test_product  tab2
         WHERE  tab1.product_name = tab2.product_name
         ORDER BY salesperson;
BEGIN
     OPEN sales_cur;
     LOOP
         FETCH sales_cur INTO
               next_person, quantity_sold, item_price;
         WHILE (next_person = current_person
                AND
                sales_cur%FOUND)
         LOOP
             total_sale :=
                   total_sale + (quantity_sold * item_price);
               FETCH sales_cur INTO
                   next_person, quantity_sold, item_price;
         END LOOP;
         IF (sales_cur%FOUND)
         THEN
               IF (current_person != next_person)
               THEN
```

 PL/SQL has two ways to mark a comment. Use two dashes (--) somewhere on the line to make everything from the dashes to the end of the line a comment. Use /* and */ to bracket a comment that covers several lines.

```
                                    IF (current_person != ' ' )
                                    THEN
                                            dbms_output.put_line
                                                (current_person ||' ' ||total_sale ||
                                                ' ' ||
                                                total_sale * commission_rate / 100);
                                    END IF;
                                    total_sale := quantity_sold * item_price;
                                    current_person := next_person;
                            END IF;
                    ELSE IF (current_person != ' ')
                    THEN
                            dbms_output.put_line(current_person ||
                                        ' ' ||
                                        total_sale ||
                                        ' ' ||
                                        total_sale * commission_rate / 100);
                    END IF;
                END IF;
                EXIT WHEN sales_cur%NOTFOUND;
                END LOOP;
                CLOSE sales_cur;
        END do_commissions;
/
```

First look at the cursor's SELECT statement. It lists, from the
TEST_PURCHASE table, the quantities of items sold. It also shows their corresponding prices from the TEST_PRODUCT table. This is achieved by creating a join. The result is ordered by salesperson so that we have all of the
records for a particular salesperson together.

Once the cursor is opened and the first row is fetched, the condition for
WHILE is checked. The first FETCH command for the current person has a
value that cannot match any salesperson code; recall that its default value is
a single space ( ). Therefore, the loop is skipped and we jump to the first IF
statement. The IF statement checks to see if the last FETCH command returned any records. If records were returned, a check is made to see whether
the *current_person* and *next_person* values match. If they don't match, we
know that the last FETCH is the start of a new salesperson and it is time to
print out the commissions for the current salesperson. Note that the first record for *current_person* is not valid; therefore, the IF check will fail and
nothing will print.

The next statement sets the value for *total_sale* to be equal to the cost for
the very first product. The statement after that stores the *next_person* value
into the *current_person* variable. Now we will be back to the first FETCH in
the loop as the loop's EXIT condition is not yet true. This FETCH may result
in the same value for *next_person* as the *current_person*, in which case we
have more than one entry for the current person in our list of sales. When
that is the case, the WHILE loop is entered and the cost for items is added to
the total sale amount. This loop will keep adding costs by fetching new records from the cursor until a new salesperson is identified. This process repeats over and over until there are no records left in the cursor. At that point,
the validity of the *current_person* is checked. If the *current_person* is valid,

then the very last IF statement prints out sales and commissions for that person; the commissions are calculated using the value in the *commission_rate* constant.

To test the procedure, enter the following commands. The first command shows the raw records in the TEST_PURCHASE table, while the second command causes the DO_COMMISSIONS procedure to subtotal the sales in those records and calculate appropriate commissions for each salesperson.

Cross Check

Working with Control Structures in PL/SQL

Now that you've been introduced to control structures in PL/SQL, take a moment to check your knowledge by answering the following questions:

1. What is a cursor and how is it used?
2. How does the cursor FOR loop work?

```
SELECT  tab1.salesperson,
        tab1.quantity,
        tab2.product_price
FROM    test_purchase tab1,
        test_product  tab2
WHERE   tab1.product_name = tab2.product_name
ORDER BY salesperson;
EXECUTE do_commissions;
```

■ Error Handling

It is important to issue user-friendly error messages when error conditions occur. Earlier in this chapter the section on basic PL/SQL blocks included a mention of exceptions; now it is time to get into more detail.

Exceptions

An exception is an error state that is activated—or raised—when a specific problem occurs. There are many different exceptions, each relating to a different type of problem. When an exception is raised, the code execution stops at the statement that raised the exception, and control is passed to the exception-handling portion of the block. If the block does not contain an executable section, PL/SQL tries to find an executable section in the enclosing basic block, which is an outer block of code surrounding the block in which the exception was raised. If the immediate enclosing block does not have an exception handler to accommodate the raised exception, then the search continues to the next enclosing block and so on until a proper exception handler is found or, if not found, execution is halted with an unhandled exception error.

The exception-handling portion of a block is the perfect opportunity to issue meaningful error messages and clean up anything that could cause confusion or trouble later. A typical cleanup could involve issuing the ROLLBACK statement if an exception is raised during a procedure that has inserted rows into a table.

Once control is passed to the exception handler, control is not returned to the statement that caused the exception. Instead, control is passed to the enclosing basic block at the point just after the enclosed block or procedure/function was called.

System-Defined Exceptions

You are familiar with the ZERO_DIVIDE exception predefined by PL/SQL. There are quite a few other system-defined exceptions that are detected and raised by PL/SQL or Oracle. Table 7.2 provides a more complete list of system-defined exceptions.

PL/SQL has two ways of showing a user information about an error. One option is the use of the command SQLCODE, which returns the error code. An error code is a negative value that usually equals the value of the corresponding ORA error that would be issued if the exception remains unhandled when an application terminates. The other option returns a text message regarding the error. Not surprisingly, this command is SQLERRM. You can use both SQLCODE and SQLERRM in the exception handler.

Not all system-defined exceptions are named.

Table 7.2	System-Defined Exceptions
System-Defined Exception	**Description**
CURSOR_ALREADY_OPEN	Tried to open an already open cursor.
DUP_VAL_ON_INDEX	Attempted to insert duplicate value in column restricted by unique index to be unique.
INVALID_CURSOR	Tried to FETCH from cursor that was not open or tried to close a cursor that was not open.
NO_DATA_FOUND	Tried to SELECT INTO when the SELECT returns no rows (as well as other conditions that are outside the scope of this book).
PROGRAM_ERROR	Internal error. Usually means you need to contact Oracle support.
STORAGE_ERROR	Program ran out of system memory.
TIME_OUT_ON_RESOURCE	A resource was not available within the allowed wait time.
TOO_MANY_ROWS	SELECT INTO in PL/SQL returns more than one row.
VALUE_ERROR	PL/SQL encountered invalid data conversions, truncations, or constraints on data.
ZERO_DIVIDE	Attempt at division by zero.
OTHERS	All other exceptions or internal errors not covered by the exceptions defined in the basic block. Used when you are not sure which named exception you are handling but you do want to handle whichever exception was raised.

Now try the previous example again, but this time use SQLCODE and SQLERRM. Enter the following code and compare your results with those shown in Figure 7.10.

```
DECLARE
    Num_a NUMBER := 6;
    Num_b NUMBER;
BEGIN
    Num_b := 0;
    Num_a := Num_a / Num_b;
    Num_b := 7;
    dbms_output.put_line(' Value of Num_b ' || Num_b);
EXCEPTION
    WHEN ZERO_DIVIDE THEN
        DECLARE
            err_num NUMBER         := SQLCODE;
            err_msg VARCHAR2(512) := SQLERRM;
        BEGIN
            dbms_output.put_line('ORA Error Number '  || err_num );
            dbms_output.put_line('ORA Error message ' || err_msg);
            dbms_output.put_line(' Value of Num_a '    || Num_a);
            dbms_output.put_line(' Value of Num_b '    || Num_b);
        END;
END;
/
```

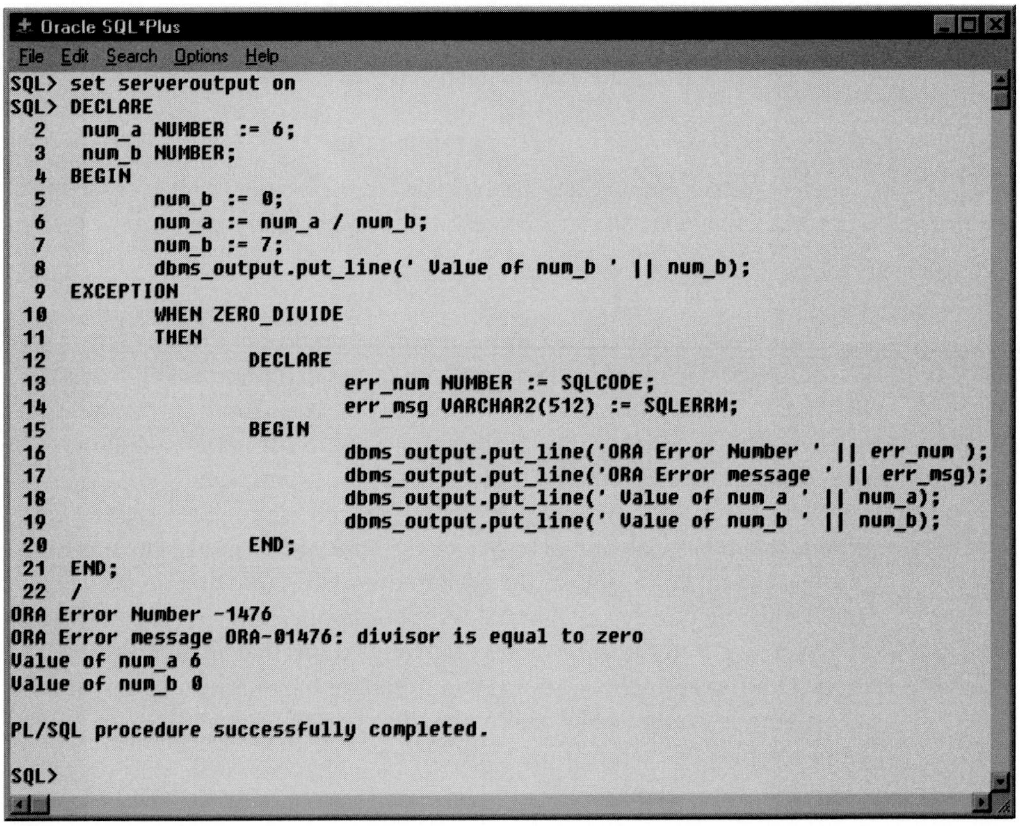

```
+ Oracle SQL*Plus                                            _ □ X
File  Edit  Search  Options  Help
SQL> set serveroutput on
SQL> DECLARE
  2    num_a NUMBER := 6;
  3    num_b NUMBER;
  4  BEGIN
  5        num_b := 0;
  6        num_a := num_a / num_b;
  7        num_b := 7;
  8        dbms_output.put_line(' Value of num_b ' || num_b);
  9  EXCEPTION
 10        WHEN ZERO_DIVIDE
 11        THEN
 12            DECLARE
 13                    err_num NUMBER := SQLCODE;
 14                    err_msg VARCHAR2(512) := SQLERRM;
 15            BEGIN
 16                    dbms_output.put_line('ORA Error Number ' || err_num );
 17                    dbms_output.put_line('ORA Error message ' || err_msg);
 18                    dbms_output.put_line(' Value of num_a ' || num_a);
 19                    dbms_output.put_line(' Value of num_b ' || num_b);
 20            END;
 21  END;
 22  /
ORA Error Number -1476
ORA Error message ORA-01476: divisor is equal to zero
Value of num_a 6
Value of num_b 0

PL/SQL procedure successfully completed.

SQL>
```

• **Figure 7.10**   Using SQLCODE and SQLERRM for system-defined exceptions

Programmer-Defined Exceptions

One handy feature of PL/SQL is that it allows you to create your own exception conditions and names. When raising and handling your own exceptions, they must be named and declared just like any other PL/SQL entity.

Here is a complete example of how to name and define your own exception. Enter the following code and compare your results with those shown in Figure 7.11.

```
set serveroutput on
DECLARE
     quantity1 NUMBER := -2;
     quantity2 NUMBER := 3;
     total NUMBER := 0;
     quantity_must_positive EXCEPTION;
     FUNCTION find_cost (quant NUMBER) RETURN NUMBER IS
     BEGIN
         IF (quant > 0)
         THEN
              RETURN(quant * 20);
         ELSE
              RAISE quantity_must_positive;
         END IF;
     END find_cost;
BEGIN
     total := find_cost (quantity2);
     total := total + find_cost(quantity1);
EXCEPTION
     WHEN quantity_must_positive
     THEN
         dbms_output.put_line('Total until now: ' || total);
         dbms_output.put_line('Tried to use negative quantity ');
END;
/
```

The exception is declared in the declaration section. Just like any other PL/SQL variable declared there, the life of the exception is valid only for this block. Since *find_cost* is also in this block or is enclosed by this block, it can use the exception name. If the same function was defined as, say, a stored function, you could not use the same exception name.

You can use your own exceptions for application-specific exception conditions that otherwise cannot be detected by the system or have no meaning for the system. For example, the system does not know that quantities ordered must be positive integer values. Your application should know this, however, and you can enforce it by catching values that are not positive integers as an exception while doing computations based on quantities. This is a very simple example, but you can imagine and will certainly come across more complex cases in real-life applications.

```
± Oracle SQL*Plus                                        ▄ □ ✕
File  Edit  Search  Options  Help
SQL> set serveroutput on
SQL> DECLARE
  2        quantity1 NUMBER := -2;
  3        quantity2 NUMBER := 3;
  4        total NUMBER := 0;
  5        quantity_must_positive EXCEPTION;
  6        FUNCTION find_cost (quant NUMBER) RETURN NUMBER IS
  7        BEGIN
  8            IF (quant > 0)
  9            THEN
 10                RETURN(quant * 20);
 11            ELSE
 12                RAISE quantity_must_positive;
 13            END IF;
 14        END find_cost;
 15  BEGIN
 16        total := find_cost (quantity2);
 17        total := total + find_cost(quantity1);
 18  EXCEPTION
 19        WHEN quantity_must_positive
 20        THEN
 21            dbms_output.put_line('Total until now: ' || total);
 22            dbms_output.put_line('Tried to use negative quantity ');
 23  END;
 24  /
Total until now: 60
Tried to use negative quantity

PL/SQL procedure successfully completed.

SQL>
```

● **Figure 7.11**   Programmer-defined exceptions

Step-by-Step 7.01

Creating a Programmer-Defined Exception

Case Study

Work through the following steps to create a programmer-defined exception that updates the package size of a product for the Clapham Specialty Store PRODUCT table. When updating the table, the user should be able to supply the SKU number for the PRODUCT and the new product package size. If the user enters a SKU that does not exist, no rows should be updated in the PRODUCT table. An exception should be raised and a message should be printed, alerting the user that an invalid product number was entered.

For this exercise, you will need Oracle9i Database Server with the SQL*Plus tool. You must enter all of the steps as one statement in order to create the programmer-defined exception. The statement will end with the END IF command in Step 3.

Step 1

Declare the name for the programmer-defined exception within the declare section by typing:

```
DECLARE
e_invalid_product        EXCEPTION;
```

where *e_invalid_product* is the name of the programmer-defined exception.

Step 2

Enter the following UPDATE statement:

```
BEGIN
    UPDATE product
    SET package_size = '&package_size'
    WHERE SKU = &sku;
    IF SQL%NOTFOUND THEN
```

Step 3

Use the RAISE statement to raise the exception explicitly within the executable section by typing:

```
RAISE e_invalid_product;
END IF;
COMMIT;
```

Step 4

Reference the exception within the corresponding exception-handling routine.

```
EXCEPTION
    WHEN e_invalid_product THEN
    DBMS_OUTPUT.PUT_LINE ('Invalid product number.') ;
END;
```

Chapter 7 Review

■ Chapter Summary

After reading this chapter and completing the Step-by-Step tutorial and Cross Checks, you should understand the following facts about PL/SQL:

Describe the Purpose and Scope of the PL/SQL Language

- PL/SQL is a powerful programming language that works hand in hand with SQL to provide the features that allow you to do sophisticated processing of information.

- PL/SQL lets you use all the SQL data manipulation, cursor control, and transaction control commands, as well as all the SQL functions and operators.

- PL/SQL fully supports SQL datatypes and dynamic SQL.

- PL/SQL procedures, functions, and triggers all help you build complex business logic easily and in a modular fashion.

Define the Structure of a PL/SQL Block

- All PL/SQL program units are made up of one or more basic blocks.

- A PL/SQL basic block is made up of four sections: the header section, an optional declaration section, the execution section, and the optional exception section.

- The header section contains identifying information for the block.

- An anonymous block is a PL/SQL block with no header or name section, hence the term anonymous block. For anonymous blocks, the header section is empty.

- The declaration section contains declarations for variables, constants, exceptions, cursors, functions, and procedures to be used within the block's execution and exception sections; if none of these are used, the declaration section will be empty.

- The execution section contains PL/SQL executable statements. The execution section is not optional and must be present to form a block.

- The exception section is used to handle error, or exception, conditions occurring within the execution section.

Create a Basic PL/SQL Procedure: "Hello World" Application

- The syntax for creating a stored procedure is CREATE PROCEDURE *procedure_specification* IS *procedure_body*.

- You can re-create the same procedure or function by changing the command CREATE to CREATE OR REPLACE.

- A procedure or function may or may not have formal parameters with default values.

Employ PL/SQL Variables and Constants

- Variables are containers with name tags and contain information or data of different kinds.

- Constants must be given a value and that value cannot change during the life or scope of the constant.

- Constants are very useful for enforcing safe and disciplined code development in large and complex applications.

Write Control Structures

- PL/SQL program flow control constructs allow you to conditionally execute a piece of code once or repeatedly.

- The IF statement allows conditional execution once.

- The LOOP, WHILE loop, and FOR loop allow for repeated execution of the same set of statements.

- Cursors are the means for PL/SQL to communicate with SQL and hence the database.

- The cursor FOR loop allows you to process rows of tables one at a time.

Catch and Respond to Errors When Your PL/SQL Statements Execute

- The exception-handling portion of a block is the perfect opportunity to issue meaningful error messages and clean up anything that could cause confusion or trouble later.

- PL/SQL has two ways of showing a user information about an error—the commands SQLCODE and SQLERRM.

- When raising and handling programmer-defined exceptions, they must be named and declared just like any other PL/SQL entity.

- Programmer-defined exceptions can be used for application-specific exception conditions that otherwise cannot be detected by the system or have no meaning for the system.

■ Key Terms

actual parameter *(194)*	FOUND *(213)*	positional notation *(201)*
anonymous block *(196)*	IF *(206)*	Procedural Language/Structured
attributes of the cursor *(212)*	implicit cursors *(211)*	Query Language *(189)*
basic block *(196)*	iteration *(208)*	procedure body *(195)*
conditional processing *(205)*	iterative operation *(206)*	procedure specification *(194)*
cursor *(210)*	LOOP *(208)*	program flow *(206)*
enclosing basic block *(217)*	loop index *(209)*	raised *(217)*
exception *(198)*	named notation *(201)*	raising an exception *(199)*
exception handler *(217)*	nested loops *(215)*	scope *(198)*
exception handling *(199)*	NOTFOUND *(213)*	stored procedure *(194)*
explicit cursors *(211)*	PL/SQL function *(193)*	trigger *(195)*
FETCH *(213)*	PL/SQL identifier *(202)*	triggering event *(195)*
FOR loop *(209)*	PL/SQL package *(192)*	WHERE CURRENT OF *(213)*
formal parameter *(194)*	PL/SQL stored procedure *(193)*	WHILE loop *(209)*

■ Key Term Quiz

Use the Key Terms list to complete the sentences that follow. Not all terms will be used.

1. _____ are error states that are activated or raised when a specific problem occurs.

2. A(n) _____ is a PL/SQL block with no header or name section.

3. _____ are actual variables or constants that are usually copied to the formal parameters of a function or procedure when a call is made.

4. A(n) _____ is an outer block of code surrounding the block in which the exception was raised.

5. The FOR loop uses a(n) _____ to count the number of iterations.

■ Matching Definition Quiz

Relate each term on the left with the appropriate description on the right.

Term		Description	
1.	Trigger	a.	Uses a counter variable to count the number of iterations
2.	FOR loop	b.	A PL/SQL procedure that gets executed automatically whenever some event defined by the procedure happens
3.	WHILE loop	c.	Cursors that have been assigned a name
4.	Stored procedure	d.	This is well suited for situations when the number of iterations is not known in advance, but rather is determined by some external factor
5.	Explicit cursors	e.	A defined set of actions written using the PL/SQL language

■ Multiple-Choice Quiz

1. Which of the following are true about PL/SQL procedures and functions? (Choose two.)

   a. There is no difference between the two.

   b. A function has a return type in its specification and must return a value specified in that type. A procedure does not have a return type in its specification and should not return any value, but it can have a return statement that simply stops its execution and returns to the caller.

   c. Both may have formal parameters of OUT or IN OUT modes but a function should not have OUT or IN OUT mode parameters.

   d. Both can be used in a WHERE clause of a SQL SELECT statement.

   e. Neither can be used in a WHERE clause of a SQL SELECT statement.

2. Which is the correct output for a run of the following code sample?

```
<<outer_block>>
DECLARE
    scope_num NUMBER := 3;
BEGIN
    DECLARE
        scope_num NUMBER := 6;
        Num_a    NUMBER :=
        outer_block.scope_num;
    BEGIN
        dbms_output.put_line(scope_num);
        dbms_output.put_line(Num_a);
    END;
    dbms_output.put_line(scope_num);
END;
/
```

   a. 6 3 3

   b. Gives error saying duplicate declaration and aborts execution

   c. 3 3 3

   d. 6 3 6

   e. 3 3 6

3. Which of the following are true about IF statements? (Choose as many as apply.)

   a. At most one set of executable statements gets executed corresponding to the condition that is TRUE. All other statements are not executed.

   b. It depends. Sometimes more than one set of statements gets executed as multiple conditions may be TRUE and then statements for each of them should get executed.

   c. You can change the logical flow of statements using conditional IF statements.

d. Conditional IF statements include IF THEN END IF and IF THEN ELSE END IF.

e. If the condition in an IF statement is FALSE or NULL, you can use the ELSE clause to carry out other actions.

4. Which of the following LOOPs will be entered at least once?

   a. Simple LOOP

   b. WHILE loop

   c. FOR loop

   d. Cursor FOR loop

   e. LOOP index

5. Which one of the following is *not* true about exceptions?

   a. Exceptions raised within the declaration section are to be handled in the enclosing block, if you want to handle them.

   b. Statements in the execution section just after the statement responsible for raising exceptions are executed once the exception handler has finished execution.

   c. When the system raises exceptions and they are not handled by the programmer, all the committed changes made to database objects like tables by the execution section within which the exception occurred are not automatically rolled back by the system.

   d. Exceptions raised within a called procedure not handled by the procedure will roll back the changes made to IN OUT or OUT parameters by the procedure before the exception occurred.

   e. You can use your own exceptions for application-specific exception conditions that otherwise cannot be detected by the system or have no meaning for the system.

6. What is the main difference between a PL/SQL procedure and a function?

   a. A stored procedure is a defined set of actions written only using the SQL language, whereas a function uses the PL/SQL language.

   b. A stored procedure is a defined set of actions written using the PL/SQL language, whereas a function uses only the SQL language.

   c. A function is designed to return a value that can be used within a larger SQL statement.

   d. A stored procedure cannot be called directly from a SQL*Plus prompt.

   e. A stored procedure cannot execute SQL statements and manipulate data in tables.

7. Which of the following are valid system-defined exceptions? (Choose as many as apply.)

   a. INVALID_CURSOR

   b. NO_DATA_FOUND

   c. PROGRAM_ERROR

   d. TOO_MANY_ROWS

   e. TOO_MANY_COLUMNS

8. Which of the following statements are true regarding the declaration section of a PL/SQL block? (Choose four.)

   a. The declaration section is optional. All variable and constant declarations must come before any function or procedure declarations within the declaration section.

   b. A declaration tells PL/SQL to create a variable, constant, cursor, function, or procedure as specified in the declaration.

   c. When used, it begins after the header section and ends at the keyword BEGIN.

   d. When used, it begins after the execution section and ends at the keyword BEGIN.

   e. The declaration section contains the declarations for PL/SQL variables, constants, cursors, exceptions, functions, and procedures that will be used by the execution and exception sections of the block.

9. Which of the following statements are true regarding the execution section of a PL/SQL block? (Choose as many as apply.)

   a. The execution section starts with the keyword BEGIN and ends in one of two ways.

b. If no exception section is present, the execution section ends with the keyword END, followed optionally by the name of the function or procedure, and a semicolon.

c. The execution section tells PL/SQL to create a variable, constant, cursor, function, or procedure as specified in the declaration.

d. If there is an exception section, the execution section ends with the keyword EXCEPTION.

e. The execution section contains one or more PL/SQL statements that are executed when the block is run.

10. Which of the following statements are true regarding the exception section of a PL/SQL block? (Choose as many as apply.)

a. For each exception there is a WHEN *exception_name* statement that specifies what should be done when a specific exception occurs.

b. During the execution of PL/SQL statements in the execution section, an exception may be encountered that makes it impossible to proceed with the execution.

c. The exception section begins at the keyword EXCEPTION and ends at the end of the block.

d. All the statements between the statement that causes the exception and the exception section will be ignored.

e. The exception section contains one or more PL/SQL statements that are executed when the block is run.

11. Which of the following statements are true regarding cursors?

a. A cursor is opened using the command OPEN and rows can be fetched using the command FETCH.

b. The cursor stands for "current set of records."

c. Using a cursor, each row of the SQL statement associated with the cursor can be processed one at a time.

d. A cursor is a special PL/SQL element that has an associated SQL SELECT statement.

e. A cursor is declared in the exception section.

12. Which of the following statements are true regarding triggers? (Choose as many as apply.)

a. You can write triggers that fire when an INSERT, UPDATE, or DELETE statement is performed on a table.

b. You can write triggers that fire when a user logs on or off.

c. You cannot write triggers that fire when the database starts, encounters an error, or shuts down.

d. A trigger is a PL/SQL procedure that gets executed automatically whenever some event defined by the trigger—the triggering event—happens.

e. You can write triggers that fire when DDL statements are issued.

13. Which of the following statements are true regarding cursor FOR loops? (Choose three.)

a. You do not need to declare a cursor with a cursor FOR loop, as PL/SQL allows you to use a subquery.

b. A cursor FOR loop processes rows in an explicit cursor.

c. A cursor FOR loop allows you to apply updates and deletes to the row currently being addressed.

d. A cursor FOR loop is a shortcut; as the cursor is opened, rows are fetched one for each iteration in the loop and then the cursor is automatically closed when all the rows have been processed.

e. A cursor FOR loop allows you to change the logical flow of statements within a PL/SQL block with a number of control structures.

14. Which of the following statements are true regarding cursors? (Choose as many as apply.)

a. When opened, a cursor contains a set of records if the cursor's SELECT statement was successful and resulted in fetching selected rows from the database.

b. Explicit cursors are declared and named by the programmer.

c. You can use the OPEN, FETCH, and CLOSE statements to control the SQL cursor but you can't use cursor attributes to get information about the most recently executed SQL statement.

d. Each FETCH then removes a record from the open cursor and moves the record's contents into either a PL/SQL variable—of a record type that matches the record type of the cursor record—or into a different set of PL/SQL variables such that each variable in the list matches in type with the corresponding field in the cursor record.

e. Implicit cursors are declared for all DML and PL/SQL SELECT statements.

15. Which of the following statements are true regarding nested loops? (Choose as many as apply.)

a. You can nest loops to multiple levels.

b. Nested loops are loops of PL/SQL blocks placed inside each other.

c. Nested loops are restricted to 12 levels.

d. You can nest FOR, WHILE, and basic loops within one another.

e. The end of a nested loop does not end the enclosing loop unless an exception was raised.

■ Essay Quiz

1. What is the function of a PL/SQL procedure?

2. Describe the declaration section of a block.

3. Describe the function of variables.

4. How does a WHEN condition affect the result of a loop?

5. What is the purpose behind defining your own exceptions?

Lab Projects

• Lab Project 7.1

Case Study

John at the Clapham Specialty Store has asked you to create a statement that retrieves the employees from the EMPLOYEE table one by one until no more are left, and print out a list of those employees currently working with the job type of a delivery person.

You will need Oracle9*i* Database Server with the SQL*Plus tool. Then create the statement to John's specifications.

• Lab Project 7.2

Case Study

John at the Clapham Specialty Store has asked you to update rows in his EMPLOYEE table based on criteria that you provide from a cursor. He wants to increase the pay rate by 10 percent for each employee who works as a Register Clerk.

You will need the following materials:

■ Oracle9*i* Database Server with the SQL*Plus tool

■ Completion of Lab Exercise 5.2

Then do the following:

1. Create a cursor that selects the Employee Number, Full Name, and Pay_Rate from the EMPLOYEE table where the Job_Type is Register Clerk. Lock the rows of the table before you update the table in Step 2.

2. Using the cursor that you created in Step 1, create an UPDATE statement that takes the information from the cursor and loops through all employees (in the EMPLOYEE table) that are Register Clerks, increasing their salary by 10 percent.

Reading a Data Model

"No law or ordinance is mightier than understanding."
—PLATO (427 B.C.–347 B.C.)

In this chapter, you will learn how to

- **Describe the purpose and benefits of data model design**

- **Identify the types of data models and how each model type is used**

- **Read a data model**

- **Recognize and interpret data modeling notations**

I n previous chapters, you learned that databases are always designed to store specific types of information.

In this chapter, you will move a step further and look at reading and designing data models. A data model focuses on what data should be stored in the database and how the data should be organized. It shows the data's organization in a graphical representation reflecting both the company's data and its business concepts.

In this chapter, you will also examine the benefits and purposes of data models. You'll learn why it is so important to design an effective data model before you try to create database tables and fill them with data. You'll see the progression from one type of model to the next and the benefits you get at each step. You will learn how to read and interpret a data model. You'll also learn about the various types of data models and examine the components that comprise a data model.

■ Overview of Data Model Design

To prevent financial loss, engineers build models of cars, bridges, or highways to work out any design issues in advance. In the same way, software designers produce data models to investigate and specify the business process and needs of a client. **Data modeling** can be defined as the analysis of data objects that are used in a business and the identification of the relationships among these data objects. The data model focuses on what data objects (for example, products, customers, orders) should be stored in the database and then determines how the data objects relate to one another—such as the relationship between a customer, an order, and a product. Does every customer have an associated order? Do certain customers have multiple orders? Do the proper products exist for the orders? All of these questions have to be considered when creating a data model. Models are key ingredients to developing fine-tuned database systems.

Where to begin? Well, for starters, the designer must discuss the proposed system with the company owners, and review all policies and documentation from the current information system. Review the introduction to the Clapham Specialty Store case study in Chapter 1, before continuing with the chapter, to re-familiarize yourself with their information system.

Purpose and Benefits of Models

Why are data models so important? The purpose of data modeling is to create a representation of the data an organization needs to conduct its business. By depicting the organization's data in a clear, easy-to-understand way, a data model serves as a "discussion piece" that helps to focus discussion among the people tasked with creating or improving the organization's software application. The model is a primary means to improving the communication between all parties.

When you create a model, you create a standardized, simplified representation of what is happening in reality. Because the model is simplified, it is possible for a computer to help handle the problems; because the model is standardized, it is easy for many different people to understand. In the next few chapters, you will learn what these notations are and how to express the ideas and needs of the business (in this book, the case study).

The model needs to be accurate to the reality presented in the situation. The closer we can get to this reality, the easier it will be to use, extend, and modify the model as the business and its needs change.

Models help communicate the concepts in people's minds. A team leader may know exactly what he wants, but his greatest skill is communicating those ideas to his team and leading them to reach the goal. Good models provide a similar function. They can be used to investigate, specify, categorize, and analyze the client's business ideas. They express the ideas and concepts in the business in an unambiguous way. This helps a lot to make the communication between the people clear. The goal of a designer is to take the client's business ideas and produce a model that contains the necessary detail (products, customers, orders, and so on) for a developer to successfully build the database system, also ensuring that it is easy to understand and use. For example, let's take a look at Clapham Specialty Store. The basic operation of John's business requires that he organize different kinds of

Case Study

information in a database. A database will certainly help him keep track of this data and allow him to determine the profits by item in the store, but before we can store this data we need a structure in which to save it. This structure will help to ensure that we store only the data we need in an efficient manner. That's where data modeling comes in.

Relational Integrity: Quality Data

We call these models relational data models. What we are doing in the model is defining how each piece of the business in the case study relates to the other pieces. The relationships are central to the quality of the data that gets entered.

As an example, let's look at a spreadsheet of sales data:

	A	B	C	D	E	F	G
1	Product Sales for Customer						
2							
3	Line No	Date	Product	Qty	Price	Extended	Customer
4	1	3/2/2003	2# Hammer	10	$13.00	$ 130.00	Gordon Folkard
5	2	3/2/2003	# Hd. Screwdriver	2	$ 1.99	$ 3.98	Jeremy Chatwin
6	3	3/2/2003	1/2" wrench	1	$ 5.95	$ 5.95	Juan Hernandez
7	4	3/2/2003	Elec. Pliers	1	$14.56	$ 14.56	Jim Taylor
8	5	3/2/2003	2# hammer	2	$13.00	$ 26.00	Jere my Chatwin
9	6	3/2/2003	3" masking tape	20	$ 1.67	$ 33.40	Leslie thompson

• Flat file sales data

This lists the sales made to some customers of a hardware store. Look at the customers on lines 2 and 5. Are these really the same customer? It looks as though there's simply an extra space inserted in an otherwise regular name. If you let this quality of data get into a database, what are the consequences?

Say you want to search the database for all the sales for "Jeremy Chatwin." Your search would not retrieve the record showing a couple of 2# hammers being sold to Jeremy Chatwin. The computer software will be maddeningly literal in its search and will not recognize "Jere my Chatwin" as the same person. You can see this effect yourself when you search the Internet for some information. Misspelling your key word has disastrous results for the answers you get back.

In a relational database you must ensure the integrity (the "wholeness") of the data. You do this by relating the pieces of data to one another. So, in this example, you would relate the customers to the sales lines to ensure that you could only enter correct customer names that already existed in the customer table.

Cross Check

Looking for Relational Integrity

The exact format and spelling of the data is important to ensure that it can be found again.

What other pieces of data in this spreadsheet might cause a problem for integrity?

■ Types of Data Models

Three types of data models are used. Each one links to the next, and they follow the process you would go through to create a database design from the business' requirements. You start by listening to the people in the business and developing a conceptual model. This model can then be refined into a logical data model that expresses the business issues in a format more suited for storing data in a database. Finally, the detailed implementation takes place when you create a physical data model from the logical one.

Sometimes a designer will combine the conceptual and logical steps, since the conceptual step and logical step are closely related to the business needs. The conceptual model is the best way to feed back to the owner what you have understood about the business and clear up any misunderstandings because it expresses the issues of the business in the terms that the business owner is most used to.

Very few of the modeling tools available cover all three steps, and many use the terms conceptual and logical interchangeably. Fortunately, all agree on what a physical model is.

Conceptual Model

A conceptual model represents a picture of the information requirements of the entire organization. This model is expressed in terms the business is familiar with. You should not use words like "object," "table," "entity," or other computer-speak. The conceptual model may contain some process information or other concepts that cannot be expressed in a data model. The aim here is to understand the things, ideas, and concepts that the business uses. No assumptions are made about how you will implement the database system, or even if the system should be a database: it could be a handwritten list, a spreadsheet, or an Oracle database.

In this book, we will not cover the conceptual model in detail. The case study and the examples we use all assume that the conceptual model has been completed and that the people involved in creating the software application all know what the issues are.

The easiest way to create this model is to work through your interview notes (you did take notes, didn't you?). You'll find that nouns in the notes translate to entities and attributes—you'll find out later how to separate these—and the verbs translate into relationships between the entities. In this book the notes have been conveniently transcribed for you as the Clapham Specialty Store case study (see Chapter 1). In a conceptual model, these facts from the case would be diagrammed.

Case Study

There are a number of different notations for conceptual models, but a very common one is the Unified Modeling Language [1] (UML) class diagram—often called a domain model as it shows the extent (domain) of the business issues you are trying to deal with.

---

1   UML is a major subject in its own right. It is a comprehensive system of diagramming and designing software and business systems. You can pick up the basics from *UML Distilled: A Brief Guide to the Standard Object Modeling Language, Third Edition* by Martin Fowler.

This illustration refers to an individual named Dr. Chen; he will be introduced in detail in Chapter 9.

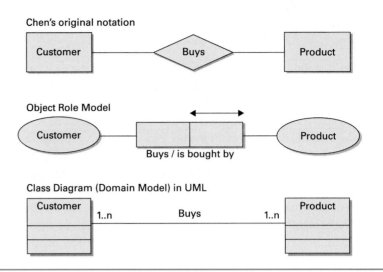

• Three common forms of conceptual model notation

Logical Data Model

A logical data model is a graphical representation of the information requirements of a business area (see Figure 8.1). It is not a database. A logical data model is independent of a data storage device. It is built using an Entity Relationship diagram (ERD). Logical data modeling assumes that you have chosen your database type, yet you may not have decided on a particular vendor's database server product. For example, you may have chosen to implement a relational database, but you may not have decided whether to use Oracle, Microsoft SQL Server, or any other database server. A logical data model is built to confirm the users' and analysts' understanding of the business requirements. It's extremely important to ensure that the system developed satisfies the needs of the business. The model includes all entities, relationships, attributes, and unique identifiers. While very few modeling tools can display a conceptual model, most can create and display logical data models. These models can then be transformed into physical designs, which in turn generate complete applications and databases.

Physical Data Model

The physical data model is the implementation of the logical data model for a particular database server (see Figure 8.2). It transforms the entities, attributes, and relations into tables, columns, and constraints. In the physical data model we start to look at the potential performance of the system and the physical arrangement of data on the hard disks. The database administrator or developer builds the physical

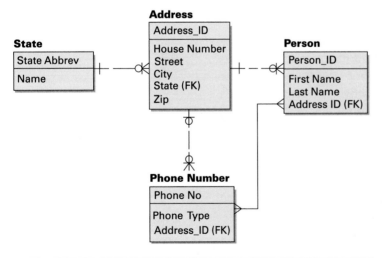

• **Figure 8.1** A logical data model

data model from the logical data model. During the physical design process, you convert the data entities gathered during the logical design phase into a description of the physical database structure.

The first step in transforming a logical data model into a physical data model is to perform a translation from logical terms to physical objects. The physical data modeling process consists of transforming the following:

- Entities into tables

- Attributes into columns

- Relationships to foreign key constraints or, sometimes, resolution tables

- Unique identifiers to unique key constraints

In working with databases, it is very rare that you can start your design with a blank sheet of paper and just imagine your way to the best solution. Usually there are bits and pieces of database in the form of spreadsheets, lists, or even a prototype relational database. When you work in such a situation, it is quite common to incorporate the original designs into your model. You will generally do this by **reverse engineering** the physical model from the actual tables and columns in the database. In other words the modeling software will connect to the system data dictionary, extract the table, column, and constraint definitions, and draw a model for you. However, such models will be missing a lot of the information and understanding you build up when you work through the design process from conceptual to physical models.

Table 8.1 compares some of the features of the three model types.

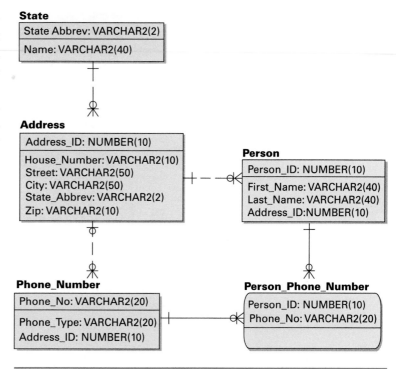

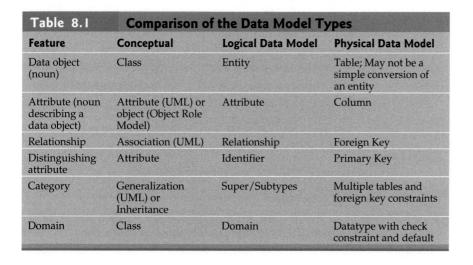

● Figure 8.2 Physical data model

Table 8.1	**Comparison of the Data Model Types**		
Feature	**Conceptual**	**Logical Data Model**	**Physical Data Model**
Data object (noun)	Class	Entity	Table; May not be a simple conversion of an entity
Attribute (noun describing a data object)	Attribute (UML) or object (Object Role Model)	Attribute	Column
Relationship	Association (UML)	Relationship	Foreign Key
Distinguishing attribute	Attribute	Identifier	Primary Key
Category	Generalization (UML) or Inheritance	Super/Subtypes	Multiple tables and foreign key constraints
Domain	Class	Domain	Datatype with check constraint and default

For additional information on conceptual, logical, and physical models, check out the Applied Information Science paper at `http://www.aisintl.com/case/CDM-PDM.html`.

Reading an Entity Relationship Diagram

An Entity Relationship (ER) diagram is a structure used to model systems for a database. It gives you a bird's-eye view of the major design constraints on your database tables. It assigns the components of a system into three categories: entities, their attributes, and relationships. There is no single standard for representing data objects and relationships in ER diagrams. Each modeling methodology uses its own notation. Today, there are a number of commonly used notations, including Bachman, crow's foot (IE), and IDEF1X. We examine these notations in more detail in Chapter 9.

Let's take a closer look at an ER diagram and see how we can read it. This is how you use the diagram to feed back to the business user what they told you and how you understood it.

In the diagram shown in Figure 8.2, the rectangles are the entities. These are the major components of the diagram. They are the holders or containers for the data. The names of the entities should match a single row or record within the entity. Thus the Address entity has one address on each row. The Person entity has the basic information for a single person on each row. Notice that there are two styles of entity rectangle—one with sharp corners, and one with radiused corners. The radiused corner entity has a dependency on its parent entity. It represents a data object that cannot exist without the parent entity or the entity at the other end of the relationship line.

Within the entity you list the attributes. These describe the entity. You put the data into separate attributes to help classify it and make it easier to find. Above the line are the primary key attributes that uniquely identify the row of the entity.

Now you come to the interesting part: the relationships that are drawn as lines between the entities. Notice that the line does not link particular attributes within the entity but the entity itself. The notations on the lines tell us more about the relationship and the role that each entity plays in it.

Entities

Hang on a minute: Until now we've been talking about tables, fields, records, and columns. What are entities?

An entity is simply a representation of a table. It looks like a table, it holds data like a table, but it is not quite the same thing. The term *entity* comes from the mathematics of the relational model. We use the term *entity* because it better fits the things and ideas that exist in the business user's world. As you reach the end of Chapter 10, you will see the subtle differences between tables and entities. For now it is enough to think of entities as tables.

An entity represents a thing or idea about which the business needs to store information.

A single entity occurrence will translate into a row of a table (for example, Tomato Ketchup is an instance, or occurrence, of a Product). You must not try to make Tomato Ketchup an entity.

There are certain design rules you should follow when indicating an entity in an ER diagram. The following conventions usually apply to entities:

- An entity is represented in an ER diagram using a box of any size or dimension.

- An entity name is always singular, unique, and usually displayed in mixed case and often with spaces.

- An entity should have an identifier . This is the attribute (or set of attributes) that uniquely identifies an instance of an entity. The identifier for State is the State Abbrev.

- An entity with identifier and attributes

Attributes

After you identify an entity, you describe it through its *attributes*. An attribute is any detail used to identify or describe the entity. Each entity can have an unlimited number of data attributes and each attribute can be required or optional. You should start questioning your design if you find entities with more than a handful of, say 20, attributes. When the attribute is required, a value must be present for every entity occurrence. When the attribute is optional, each entity occurrence may or may not have a value.

For an Employee entity, some common attributes might be: First Name, Last Name, Employee Identification Number, Employee Type, and Pay Rate. When designing your ER diagram, you may indicate that the Employee entity does not require each and every one of these attributes, but simply requires only the First Name and Last Name attributes. Which attributes should be optional, which mandatory? Ask yourself if every occurrence of the entity must have a value for the attribute. How about First Name? Is this mandatory? If it is, how would you enter "Sting" as the employee name? Here you would make Last Name mandatory and First Name optional, as shown in this illustration of an entity and its data.

Employee

Employee ID
Supervisor ID (FK)
Employee Type
First Name
Last Name
Social Security Number
Pay Rate

	A	B	C	D	E	F	G
1	Employee						
2							
3	Employee ID	Supervisor ID	Employee Type	First Name	Last Name	Social Security Number	Pay Rate
4	100		Owner	John	Balfour	123-45-6789	$ 30.00
5	101	100	Cashier	Susan	Saronnen	456-78-8912	$ 20.00
6	102	100	Cashier	Eric	La Sold	678-90-1234	$ 6.75
7	103	100	Storeman	Martin	Murphy	901-23-4567	$ 6.75
8	104	103	Delivery	Erica	Strange	234-56-7890	$ -
9	105	103	Delivery	Noah	Tamil	567-89-0123	$ -

- An entity with attributes and corresponding data

A unique identifier (UID) is an attribute or set of attributes that distinguishes individual occurrences of an entity. When searching for a particular instance of an entity, you need some means to ensure that you only get the one entity. That is, each instance of an entity must be distinctly identifiable from all other occurrences of that same type of entity. For example: Say you decide that the combination of first and last names makes a good unique identifier for Employee. What will happen when your company grows big enough to employ two John Smiths? To tell them apart in the database you give them an employee ID number that is guaranteed to be unique.

This requirement for uniqueness is why so many companies and organizations use ID numbers for people, credit cards, invoices, and all sorts of other items. While humans generally prefer names to numbers, humans can tolerate some ambiguity that computer systems cannot. So you number things when you design databases.

There are certain design rules to follow when indicating an attribute in an ER diagram. The following conventions may apply to attributes:

- An attribute is represented using a singular name in mixed case.

- An entity must have at least one attribute.

- One or more of the attributes must make the identifier for the entity.

- Required attributes may be identified by an asterisk: *

- Optional attributes may be identified with the letter *o*.

Case Study

When you define attributes, they should make sense to you and your business. Clapham Specialty Store found it necessary to assign a single mandatory ten-digit phone number attribute (for example, 201-555-1212) to every Customer entity, in order to contact a customer when a delivery is due. This number was not split down into area code, exchange, and number, but stored together in a single attribute.

However, the employees' names are split into two separate fields: First Name and Last Name. You do that because you often need to deal with each part of the name separately. For example: You need to sort the employees by last name, but you need to use both for their paychecks. You need only the last name when creating a memo to them, but you generally use first names in speech.

As with entities, you must distinguish between attributes and attribute occurrences. An attribute of an Employee entity could be "Address," and an occurrence of this attribute could be "123 Main Street."

Relationships

A relationship represents the interaction between two separate entities.

Just as you have relationships in your lives—Bill works for Clapham Specialty Store, Cathy manages a rock band, Brian teaches English—so must you indicate relationships in ER diagrams. The name of a relationship describes the association between the entities. You name a relationship using a descriptive phrase that makes sense to the interaction of the entities. For example, Customer "lives at" Address, Customer "places" Order.

Sometimes you'll find the roles are named in the diagram. A `role` is the description of how the entity is used in the relationship. It is usually a verb or verb phrase. You can read the relationship and its two entities as a simple fact-like sentence. The following illustration shows how to turn a typical relationship into English sentences. Often you have to guess at the verb to put in the sentence because the designer has left it out of the model.

Inside Information

Naming Entities and Attributes

The names you choose for the entities and attributes are very important. In fact, this is one of the most difficult—and most valuable—parts of the data modeling process. Listen closely to the description of the business and the issues they are trying to deal with; most names can be extracted directly from these conversations. Some will turn out to be ambiguous in that different people will mean different things while using the same word. Herein lies the art of the database designer! Choose names that are as self-explanatory as possible and would make sense to someone looking at the database for the first time.

Introduction to Relational Databases and SQL Programming

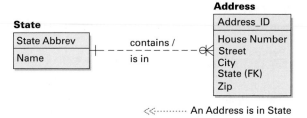

A State contains Address(es) ·······>>

State

State Abbrev
Name

contains /
is in

Address

Address_ID
House Number
Street
City
State (FK)
Zip

<<·········· An Address is in State

- Reading relationships

ERD relations are concerned with four basic things:

- The two (or more) entities that are related
- The number of entity occurrences, or instances, at each end of the relationship
- Whether the relationship is mandatory or optional
- Whether one entity is dependent on the other

Relations are drawn as a line from one entity to the other. You should be able to name the relationship with a phrase that includes a verb. Generally relationships are named for one direction down the line only.

Each entity has a role in the relationship. Each role is named using a verb or verb phrase and each role of the relationship contains a degree of cardinality. Cardinality asks the question "How many of these relate to how many of those?" For example, in a relationship between a State and an Address, cardinality answers the questions "How many States may an Address have?" and "How many Addresses may a State have?" To determine the cardinality for a relationship, you must determine how many instances of the second entity can relate to the first entity instance. In a relationship the "many" role is indicated with a crow's foot and the one role by a single line. In the preceding illustration, there can be many addresses in a state and an address can have only one state.

Each role of a relationship possesses not only a name, but also an indication of whether the entity is mandatory or optional in its role in the relationship. This is known as optionality. The optionality of an entity in the relationship is shown by a cross bar or open circle (in IE notation). You can think of optionality as a special case of cardinality: Instead of asking "How many?" you ask "How few?" or "Can you have zero entities at one end?" For example, in the State/Address you cannot have the State value missing in an address, so the State end is mandatory. Optional roles lead to optional attributes in the child entity. This allows the child entity to have data missing for that attribute.

When you look at the connecting line drawn from entity to entity, you will notice some are solid and some are dashed lines. In the version of IE notation that we are using in this book the solid line indicates an identifying relationship. An identifying relationship is one in which the entities are so closely coupled that the child entity cannot sensibly exist without the parent one. In the following illustration, the relationship between Person and Phone Call is an identifying relationship. What we mean is that the Person is such a vital part of the Phone Call that we must use the Person ID as part of the identifier of the call—it says that a Phone Call cannot exist without a Person. The call has several attributes used to identify it; one of these is the Person ID.

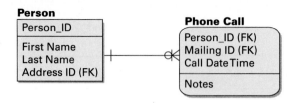

- An identifying relationship

Cross Check

Entity Relationship Diagram Basics

Now that you have been introduced to Entity Relationship diagrams and their components, check your knowledge by providing answers to the following questions:

1. What are the benefits of designing an Entity Relationship diagram?
2. List and describe the components of an ER diagram.
3. How are unique identifiers notated in an ER diagram?

Cardinality and Optionality Notations

Let us summarize the cardinality and optionality notations that you have seen so far in this chapter. Table 8.2 shows how each of these is represented in the various tools and standards that you might use. (The last two columns in the table refer to a commercial diagramming program named ERwin and an individual named James Martin; both will be introduced in detail in Chapter 9.)

In the full IE notation the cross bar serves a double purpose. The bar closest to the entity describes the cardinality. At the "many" end you should consider the bar as part of the crow's foot. The bar farther from the entity describes the optionality (bar indicates mandatory, circle indicates optional). James Martin's interpretation of IE is simpler but does not differentiate between identifying and nonidentifying relationships; they are all shown with solid lines.

Other differences between these notations are described in more detail in Chapter 9.

Table 8.2	Partial Set of Relationship Notations				
Cardinality	Optionality	IDEF1X	IE (full)	IE (ERwin)	IE (James Martin)
1	Mandatory				
1	Optional				
Many	Optional				
Many	Mandatory				
Many	Nonspecific				

Reading an Entity Relationship Diagram

In this exercise, you will practice reading information from a data model and transcribing it into lists. To complete this exercise, you will need the following:

- Blank paper
- A pencil
- A copy of Figure 8.1 to work from

Step 1

Examine the model shown earlier in Figure 8.1. This is the final result that you will work toward as you complete the exercises in this book. List all the entities shown.

Step 2

List the attributes in each entity, marking each one as

- Optional/Mandatory ("don't know" may be a satisfactory answer for some of these)
- Identifying/Describing attribute

Step 3

List each of the relationships shown. For each relationship fill in the following chart:

	From entity			To entity		
Relationship name	Role (verb phrase)	Optionality	Cardinality	Role (verb phrase)	Optionality	Cardinality

Test each of these by writing a sentence using the two entity names and the verb phrases.

Step 4

Make up a few rows of sample data to demonstrate these relationships. Usually only three or four rows from each entity will be sufficient.

Chapter 8 Review

■ Chapter Summary

After reading this chapter and completing the Step-by-Step tutorial and Cross Checks, you should understand the following facts about data models:

Describe the Purpose and Benefits of Data Model Design

- Data models develop an accurate representation of the client's information and business needs through a graphical design.

- Data models focus on what data objects should be stored in the database and how the data objects relate to one another.

- Data models help communicate the concepts in people's minds.

- Data models can be used to investigate, specify, categorize, and analyze the client's business ideas.

- They record information for the business in a clear, unambiguous, accurate format.

- Models provide an easy-to-read graphical design map.

Identify the Types of Data Models and How Each Model Type Is Used

- A conceptual model represents a picture of the information requirements of the entire organization in business terms. With conceptual modeling you make no commitment to whether the database will be relational, object-oriented, or even flat-file.

- Logical data modeling is the actual process of creating a diagram for a database that belongs to a database management system. Logical data models relate to business processes and display data entities and relationships.

- Physical data modeling is the creation of the database with SQL statements. Physical data models include database tables, columns, keys, datatypes, indexes, validation rules, triggers, stored procedures, views, and constraints.

Read a Data Model

- An entity represents an object or a collection of similar objects about which information needs to be known, such as a collection of departments, orders, events, or people.

- An attribute is any detail used to identify or describe the entity.

- Relationships are associations between entities.

- Relationships should be named and must have an indication of optionality and cardinality.

- Some relationships are identifying relationships in which the child attributes (copied from the identifying attributes of the parent) become part of the identifier of the child entity.

Recognize and Interpret Data Modeling Notations

- IDEF1X uses a solid circle to indicate the "many" role in a relationship.

- IDEF1X uses an open diamond to indicate an optional role of cardinality one.

- IE has a variety of different notations, though all use the "crow's foot" standard.

- The James Martin IE notation is the simplest, but lacks notation for identifying relationships.

- In this book the ERwin variety of IE notation is used.

■ Key Terms

attribute (237)
cardinality (239)
conceptual model (233)
data model (230)
data modeling (231)
dependency (236)
domain model (233)

entity (236)
entity occurrence (237)
Entity Relationship (ER) diagram (236)
identifier (237)
identifying relationship (239)
logical data model (234)

optionality (239)
physical data model (234)
reverse engineering (235)
role (238)
Unified Modeling Language (UML) (233)
unique identifier (237)

Key Term Quiz

Use the Key Terms list to complete the sentences that follow. Not all terms will be used.

1. A(n) _____ is an association between two entities.

2. The _____ is an attribute or a combination of attributes that uniquely identify an occurrence of an entity.

3. A(n) _____ creates a diagram for a database that belongs to a database management system and includes database tables, datatypes, and constraints.

4. A(n) _____ represents an object or a collection of similar objects about which information needs to be known.

5. The description of the part that an entity plays in a relationship is called a(n) _____.

Matching Definition Quiz

Relate each term on the left with the appropriate description on the right.

Term		Description	
1.	Optionality	a.	A detail used to identify or describe an entity
2.	Logical data model	b.	A design of the various entities in a business and the relationships between them
3.	Entity Relationship diagram	c.	Counts how many instances of one entity are related to a single instance of another entity
4.	Cardinality	d.	Indicates whether a relationship is mandatory or optional
5.	Attribute	e.	A graphical representation of the information requirements of a business area

Multiple-Choice Quiz

1. Which type of data model works primarily with entities and attributes?
   a. Entity Relationship diagram
   b. Logical data model
   c. Physical data model
   d. Conceptual model
   e. Relational data model

2. When translating a logical data model into a physical model, which element translates to a table?
   a. Entity
   b. Attribute
   c. Unique identifier
   d. Primary key
   e. Relationship

3. A relationship relates together two
   a. Tables
   b. Foreign key constraints
   c. Columns
   d. Entities
   e. Attributes

4. In an ER diagram, where would you see an attribute that is part of a unique identifier?
   a. In the lower part of the rectangle
   b. Alongside the relationship
   c. In the upper part of the rectangle
   d. Next to the rectangle
   e. Somewhere else

5. In an ER diagram, an optional role is identified by the following notation:
   a. A cross bar
   b. An open circle
   c. A crow's foot
   d. A solid line
   e. A dashed line

6. Dependency relationships are identified by this notation in an ER diagram:
   a. A cross bar
   b. An open circle
   c. A crow's foot
   d. A solid line
   e. A dashed line

7. How many attributes must an entity have?
   a. Zero
   b. At least one
   c. Two or more
   d. Lots
   e. Unlimited

8. What characters can be used for entity or attribute names?
   a. Uppercase only
   b. Any ASCII character
   c. Only letters and underscores
   d. Lowercase only with punctuation marks
   e. Mixed case with spaces

9. The following statements are benefits of an ER diagram. (Choose three.)
   a. It provides an easy-to-read graphical design map.
   b. It records information for the business in a clear, accurate format.
   c. It translates entities, attributes, and relationships into database tables.
   d. It is dependent on the selection of a database product.
   e. It offers an effective structure for communicating ideas.

10. An attribute that uniquely identifies an occurrence of an entity is known as a(n):
    a. Unique identifier
    b. Foreign key
    c. Required attribute
    d. Unique attribute
    e. Attribute occurrence

11. This element of a relationship counts how many instances of one entity are related to a single instance of another entity.
    a. Optionality
    b. Cardinality
    c. Uniqueness

    d. Role
    e. Foreign key

12. The notations in this illustration show which types of role? (Check all that apply.)

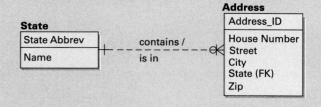

   • State/Address relationship

   a. Mandatory 1
   b. Optional 1
   c. Optional Many
   d. Mandatory Many
   e. Identifying

13. Optionality refers to
    a. The state of an attribute in an ER diagram
    b. The type of a relationship in an ER diagram
    c. The state of an entity in an ER diagram
    d. The state of a table in an ER diagram
    e. The number of instances of one entity that are related to a single instance of another entity

14. In an ER diagram, this element is always represented using a singular name:
    a. Entity
    b. Primary key
    c. Attribute
    d. Column
    e. Relationship

15. In an ER diagram, a dashed line represents
    a. An optional attribute
    b. A unique identifier
    c. A mandatory relationship
    d. A nonidentifying relationship
    e. An entity occurrence

■ Essay Quiz

1. Write a few sentences comparing the different types of data models and when you would create each type of model.

2. Why is it important to understand the optionality of a relationship?

3. What is the difference between optionality and cardinality in a relationship?

4. Describe the benefits of using data modeling software.

5. In the ERD of Clapham Specialty Store, the relationship between the Customer and Sale is optional. What reasons can you think of for making this an optional relationship?

Lab Projects

• Lab Project 8.1

You have been asked to develop a database for a hockey league. Another designer has developed the ER diagram and you must analyze this model before you can begin creating database tables.

You will need a pencil and paper.

View the Hockey League ER diagram in Figure 8.3 and then answer the following questions:

1. Identify all entities, attributes, and unique identifiers in the ER diagram.

2. What relationship exists between entities?

3. How many players can a team have? (Hint: Even if you know them, ignore the rules of hockey.)

4. How many positions can a player occupy in one team?

5. How many positions can a team have?

6. (Extra credit.) How would you improve this design?

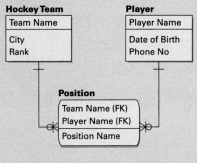

• **Figure 8.3** An ERD for hockey teams

• Lab Project 8.2

Case Study

Clapham Specialty Store has employee and register data. The original design of the conceptual model has been done. You need to "read" this design back to the business user (John Balfour) so that he understands the limits and possibilities of your design. For this lab you will write a commentary to go with the partial model shown in Figure 8.4.

You will need the following materials:

- A copy of the Partial ERD for Clapham Specialty Store (Figure 8.4)

- Pencil and paper

Then do the following:

1. List each of the entities with their attributes. For each entity write a brief (two-line?) description of the data this entity holds. Create four or five lines of sample data for each entity.

2. For each relationship write out the relations as sentences. You should create two sentences for each relationship, one for each direction along the line. Use the entity names and the roles (make them up if they do not show in the diagram!).

3. Describe the limits of cardinality and optionality for each relationship. Demonstrate this where you can from your sample data.

4. Do you think it is a good idea for the Location/ Product relationship to be optional? What will happen in the data arising from this?

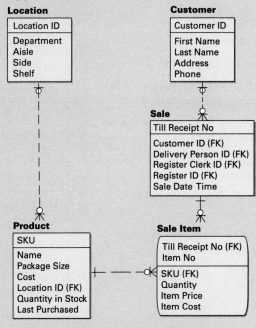

• **Figure 8.4** Partial ERD for Clapham Specialty Store

chapter 9

Basics of Designing a Database's Structure

"Always design a thing by considering it in its larger context—a chair in a room, a room in a house, a house in an environment, an environment in a city plan."

—Eliel Saarinen, *Time*, July 2, 1956

In this chapter, you will learn how to

- **Let the data tell you where it goes**
- **Select the grain for each subject area of the database**
- **Identify records uniquely with primary keys**
- **Compare common data modeling standards**
- **Identify the relationships in a model**
- **Model categories using supertypes and subtypes**

In the preceding chapter you learned about the different types of data models, as well as the reason for designing these models. You learned the basics of reading a model—a skill you will use in this and subsequent chapters as you learn how to build a model. Each model has its place in the process you go through to build a database. You saw some of the database design software that is available today.

In this chapter you will learn more about how to create a database structure to hold the data. You'll look at the various types of relationships between entities and how they work to ensure the data that is entered is accurate and consistent. As a more advanced topic, you'll learn about modeling categories of entities, or "inheritance" as the object modelers call it.

Finally, a note on terminology in this chapter: You will see the term "relationship" instead of the abbreviated "relation." The reason is that the mathematics of the Relational Model defines a relation very explicitly, and you do not want to start using a term loosely that you will see used strictly in other texts.

The Business Specification: Let the Data Tell You Where It Goes

When you develop a data model, you are really trying to solve a problem on the user's behalf. You are trying to design a way to store data that will help the user easily find the information they need.

In this sense, the early stages of designing a database are a voyage of discovery. As you interview the business subject-matter experts (usually the people working in the business), you will create a narrative or story about what data they want to store and how the different elements of the data work together and relate to each other. This is the stage when you create the conceptual model of the data.

You must take notes during this process—or if you are really lucky, you can get someone else to do this; in this book, it is done for you in the case study. From these notes you will discover the things that the business users are concerned about. These will be the nouns in the text. Each of these nouns will translate into an entity or an attribute for an entity. Later in this chapter, you will get some hints on how to tell the difference between an entity and an attribute. You will also determine the relationships between the things (the entities) from the verbs you used to describe the business.

This process will need a little educated guesswork on your part to put the correct names to all the entities, attributes, and relationships you discover. This is the art of the database designer.

When you have the beginnings of a model, you must take it back to the business users and explain it to them. What you are doing here is confirming to them that you really heard and understood what they said. With their help you will be able to refine the model, add new relationships, change the names of entities and attributes to better reflect the data they hold, add new entities, and remove unwanted ones. As you work through this chapter you will develop one model—the mailing list database. You will make some wrong decisions at times as you build the model. This is normal and demonstrates one of the key points of database design: database design is iterative; just do it again and again until it's good enough!

Selecting the Database's Grain

The grain of a database is the fundamental unit that is captured. This will determine just how much detail you capture in the data. If you get too much, the database grows to be huge and you cannot use it efficiently—you drown in information overload. If you do not get enough detail, you lose important information that would help you in the business.

It is important to remember that a database may cover several different subject areas and that each subject area may have a different grain.

If you have a database that records information about your bank account, what is the grain that you need? You would naturally record this check by check. Thus the check or, more generally, the transaction is the grain of the database. Think about this a little more. What happens when you go to the ATM and do several things all in one session? Say you deposit

a check, look at your balance, and withdraw some cash. Is this all one transaction? Take your clues from what you see on the ATM screen. It asks you "Another transaction or Exit?" Think about the bank statement. Do you really want to see all the detail of your deposit, balance, and withdrawal on one line of the statement? Each of these actions is a transaction and is a granular piece of data.

Another example: Amazon's web site. Here they record every click that the user makes, where she makes it, and what the result was. This is not hundreds but *tens of billions* of pieces of data. But they need this very fine level of granularity to be able to analyze how a user navigates through the site, finds things of interest, and then, maybe, purchases something. One of the things they are really interested in is the failed purchase: the user enters the store, browses around for a while, and then leaves. What Amazon needs is to find out what prevented the person from buying. So they cannot make their grain at the purchase level, or at the session (or login) level. The needs of the business drive the selection of the grain.

To summarize, grain defines the level of detail you need to save in the database. To decide this granularity, you need to know about what data is going to be recorded and what reports or information the user wants to get out of the database.

■ Entities and Attributes

So how do you tell entities and attributes apart? They both appear as nouns in the narrative. Two questions help:

1. Can this thing exist on its own or does it just describe another thing?

2. How important is it to the business?

Let's look at a database for storing data about people: their names, addresses, phone numbers, and so on. You want to be able to send mailings to the people in the database, but you need to select carefully so that you don't send special offers of refrigerators to people living in Alaska in the winter. You need to record their first and last names, their house number, street name, city, state, zip, and all their different phone numbers (home, work, cell, fax, and so on). Then you also have a call center where you receive telephone calls from the customers who respond to the mailing. You need to keep a record of when they call and some notes about the call, and you also need to know if they actually made a purchase as a result of the mailing and what exactly they bought.

So what are the entities here? List out the nouns or noun phrases:

```
People, name, address, phone number, mailing, database
special offer, refrigerator, Alaska, winter, first name,
```

```
last name, house number, street, city, state, zip, home phone,
work phone, fax number, cell phone, phone call, customer,
call record, notes, purchase
```

Look through these and try to pick out the more important ones. These will be the nouns that are significant to the business case and appear to encapsulate a concept. These seem to be:

```
People (person), mailing, name, address, state, phone number,
database, phone call, customer, purchase
```

Some items have different names but are essentially the same thing (for example, customer and person). Figure 9.1 shows these entities in a diagram. Notice that each item's name is singular in the diagram; for instance, "people" is shown as "person."

Which items cannot exist on their own or describe other items? (Remember, this question is relevant only within the context of this database, not generally.) These seem to be as follows:

```
1. First name and Last name both describe Name.

2. House number, street, city, state, and zip all describe an
address.

3. Home, work, cell, and fax each describe a type of phone number.

4. Special offer describes the mailing.

5. Notes describe more detail about a phone call.
```

Look at these lists carefully. All these describing things will become attributes. What about "database"? As you are trying to make a database, you should not put the *database* in the model; let's just say the database *is* the model. Notice that you have nothing to describe a purchase. Leave this for now; you will probably find some attributes when you work with the relationships. Remember you are not looking to finish this in one go!

Finally, you have a few nouns left over: refrigerator, winter, Alaska. These are not very general. Would you expect that *every* mailing is about refrigerators in winter in Alaska? This is a good type of question to help determine whether you have discovered an entity or just an occurrence of an entity. You should ask yourself if the noun you have heard describes every occurrence of its entity. Clearly refrigerator, winter, and Alaska don't.

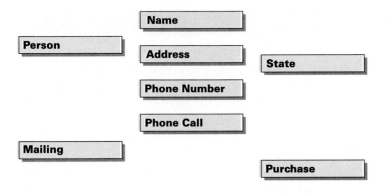

● **Figure 9.1**   Mailing database entities

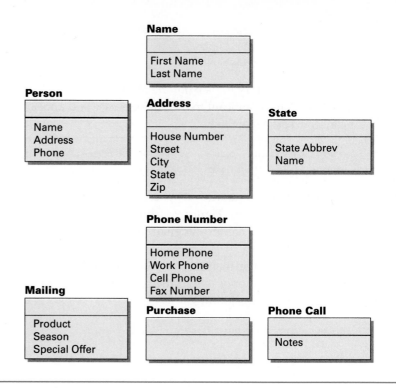

Figure 9.2 Entities with describing attributes

So you will use more general terms like product, season, and state. Adding these into the lists changes the description of a mailing:

```
4. Special offer, product, season describe the mailing.
```

Now you can add the attributes from the lists of describing nouns to make Figure 9.2.

After just a few simple steps you already have most of the structure of the database. The model has a few strange things going on, but these will be resolved as you progress. Part of the art of database design is not to try to do everything at once. By proceeding in simple steps, you can build up a complex model with a minimum of rework and also ensure you have the best possible understanding of the business and the problems you are trying to solve.

 Cross Check

Nouns in the Clapham Specialty Store

Case Study

As you start to analyze the case study, you will need to read carefully and make lists. This will allow you to then classify what you have read so that you can start designing.

1. Make a list of the nouns you can find in the Clapham Specialty Store case study (see Chapter 1).

2. Classify them into entities and attributes. For each entity make a list of describing attributes.

■ Identifying Records Reliably: Primary Keys

In this section you will learn one of the most fundamental and important pieces of information about designing a database: how to reliably identify the records you want.

Why Do You Need a Primary Key?

Why do you need a primary key? Well, what happens if you do not have a primary key? First, a reminder: An entity represents a list of records (see Chapter 1). Let's say you've managed to build the database for addresses without a primary key for the Name entity.

How many people are there called "John Smith"? How would you know which John Smith lives at which address? What you need is a unique identifier for the name or the person. The attribute or set of attributes that uniquely identify a record is known as an identifier. In the physical data model this identifier is known as a primary key .

In the State entity the unique identifier would be "State Abbrev." Fortunately the government and post office have already worked out a set of abbreviations that are unique and not likely to be changed. The entity is shown here.

State

State Abbrev
Name

- State entity

These identifiers, or keys, are vital to correct functioning of a database. Unfortunately SQL allows you to create tables without primary keys. You should make sure you do not let this happen in your databases. Most of the modeling tools will warn you if you try this.

Composite Primary Keys

The registration authority in a state can uniquely identify a car by the license plate.

The license plate is an obvious primary key. The data appears in one attribute only. What happens if you have a database of all vehicles in the U.S.? Is the license plate enough to identify the vehicle uniquely? What happens if two different states issue the same license plate? Now you need two pieces of data to uniquely identify the vehicle: the license plate and the state.

This is a composite key . It is an identifier made up from two or more attributes in the entity. An example is shown here:

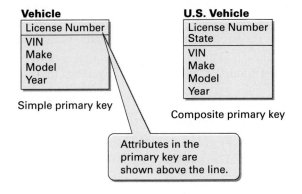

Vehicle

License Number
VIN
Make
Model
Year

Simple primary key

U.S. Vehicle

License Number State
VIN
Make
Model
Year

Composite primary key

Attributes in the primary key are shown above the line.

- Composite identifiers

Cross Check

Identifying Attributes for Employee

Case Study

Some of the nouns you listed out in the previous Cross Check were entities. Now you will use some of the remaining nouns to identify attributes.

1. What attributes would you pick for the Employee in Clapham Specialty Store to make an identifier?

2. Can you think of a set of data where the attributes you have chosen would not be enough to guarantee a unique Employee identifier?

Let's go back and consider the person example from earlier in this chapter.

What uniquely identifies a person? Is name enough? How about social security number, date of birth, place of birth, driver's license number, or credit card number? All these help to identify a person, but how much is really necessary?

- Name (first, last, and middle) is obviously not enough.

- Social security numbers are not unique (remember, they date from a pre-computer age when there were no primary keys!)

- Lots of people were born on any given day: date of birth won't do.

- Not everybody has a driver's license or a credit card.

Unique Person

| Last Name |
| First Name |
| Middle Name |
| SSN |
| DoB |

Person entity with large composite key

But in combination you can usually find enough data to identify a person from these. However, this gives us a composite key with, say, five columns (first, last, middle, SSN, date of birth). It is a valid identifier and you could use it, but it is somewhat impractical. Also, people change their names so this primary key is now being updated. When you read about relationships later in this chapter, you'll see why allowing updates is generally not a good idea. The large composite primary key for Person is shown here.

Natural Primary Keys vs. Surrogate Primary Keys

The problem of determining the primary key is very common. So far, in the preceding examples you have used attributes that come from the business domain. These are attributes that the business user would recognize and that you discovered from the interviews and notes. None of the attributes have been invented; they already existed and you merely discovered them. These identifiers are called natural keys .

Now it is time to learn about a made-up attribute called a surrogate key . This is an identifier that does not exist in the business domain; you create it to satisfy some of the needs of the database. Why would you need such a thing?

There are three conditions that demand the use of the surrogate key attribute:

1. The natural primary key (identifier) has become too big.

2. The users need to be able to edit the values in the primary key (see the Inside Information sidebar, "Updating Primary Keys").

3. One of the attributes of the primary key might have no value: the data is missing.

Introduction to Relational Databases and SQL Programming

If any one of these conditions is true, you add an additional attribute to the entity and fill it with a number. Usually the number is just an incremental number that increases every time you save a record. Oracle calls these **sequences**. You should use a number for such keys because they hold no meaning for the users, and (in some database engines) numbers are faster to search and index. Sometimes it is enough to say that the value in the primary key *might* be edited. It may be that you do not have control of the values and the people who do have control may decide to change them. Your database needs to be able to keep up with these changes as easily as possible.

For the Unique Person entity you would add a Person_ID attribute. Notice how the original identifying attributes have moved below the line and reverted to regular attributes.

Unique Person

| Last Name |
| First Name |
| Middle Name |
| SSN |
| DoB |
| |

Person entity with
large composite key

Unique Person 2

| Person_ID |
| Last Name |
| First Name |
| Middle Name |
| SSN |
| DoB |

Person entity with
surrogate primary key

• Person with composite key changed to surrogate key

To summarize, the two rules for establishing a primary key are

■ The values in the attributes making up the key must all be present (no nulls allowed).

■ The value of the key must be unique.

And a recommended guideline (see the Inside Information sidebar):

■ The user controls the value in the key, and it is not likely to change after it is entered.

Using these rules you can add the identifiers you need to the mailing database model as shown in Figure 9.3.

Cross Check

Natural vs. Surrogate Primary Keys

Using what you have learned in this section, you should be able to identify which keys or identifiers are not suitable for use as natural keys.

Case Study

1. Which of the primary keys in the Mailing model is a natural primary key?

2. How many entities in the Clapham Specialty Store have surrogate primary keys?

Inside Information

Updating Primary Keys

Are there situations when you might allow users to update a primary key value in an entity?

If the entity represents a **code table** *, it might be allowable for a database administrator (DBA) or programmer to update the value. Since the value in the code table and the meaning of that value are used in the code of the application (the user interface), it probably means that the purpose of the application has changed. In this situation the additional work and testing involved in changing the value is generally worthwhile. Code tables with natural primary keys can help when you create the application to make the code more readable and easier to understand.*

Updating the primary key has no adverse consequences and may be allowed if all of these circumstances apply:

■ *The table is a resolution table linking two or more tables.*

■ *The primary key of the resolution table is not used in a foreign key relationship.*

Typically you will find the "update" happens as a sequence of delete and insert, so updating is not an issue. In this situation you would not use a surrogate key since it just adds more data to store without any operational benefit.

Generally though, updating a primary key is not a good idea. If a column's values are likely to be updated after they are initially entered, that column is not a good candidate for use as a primary key—consider using a surrogate key instead.

Person

Person_ID
Name
Address
Phone

Name

First Name
Last Name

Address

Address_ID
House Number
Street
City
State
Zip

State

State_Abbrev
Name

Phone Number

Phone_Number_ID
Home Phone
Work Phone
Cell Phone
Fax Number

Mailing

Mailing_ID
Product
Season
Special Offer
Mailing Date

Purchase

Purchase Date
Product

Phone Call

Notes
Call Date Time

• **Figure 9.3**   Entities with identifiers in place

Relationships: Referring to Data in Other Tables

Now you have all the entities and attributes straight in your model. Next you must tackle the relationships between the entities. These relationships describe and, ultimately, limit how two entities can interact with each other. You go back to the original notes and descriptions that the business users gave you and this time look for the verbs. Unfortunately some of the verbs are somewhat implicit—they are assumed from our general knowledge of how the world works.

For these relationships to work correctly, you must have a primary key at one end of the relationship. For this reason, you should always have a primary key (identifier) in an entity. The entity at the other end of the relationship will have a set of attributes that match the primary key. These attributes have been "copied" from one entity to the other through the action of the relationship and are known as a `foreign key`. The entity at the primary key end of the relationship line is referred to as the `parent entity` and the one at the other end is the `child entity`. In the physical model these relationships are called foreign key constraints.

The verbs or adjectives in the business case description (see the section "Entities and Attributes" earlier in this chapter) are

```
Store, send, select, live(ing), record, respond, made.
```

You *send* a mailing to a person; a person *lives* at an address. *Store* and *record* mean the same thing. Both these and *select* are actions of the database which you specifically excluded from your model. The customer *responds* to a mailing and a purchase is *made* by a customer from a mailing. The other relationships you need are implicit ones such as "has/have," "belongs to," "is part of." Discovering relationships is the part of database design where you most often call on your general knowledge of the world.

The following relationships exist:

```
A. Person has a name

B. One or more people can live at an address

C. Person may have phone numbers

D. Phone number may belong to an address, and vice versa

E. Person is sent a mailing

F. Address is in a state

G. Customer makes a purchase
```

H. Person makes a phone call

I. Phone call is about a mailing

These relationships are shown as lines between the entities in Figure 9.4.

These lines have a lot more information on them that describe exactly how the relationship between the entities works. You will learn exactly what these symbols mean in the next section. For now let's just look at the lines and match each one to the relationships listed earlier.

Some of the lines have caused an attribute in the child entity to be marked with "(FK)". The values in these child attributes will be constrained by the database engine to match one of the primary key values. Take the State/Address relationship. If the State entity only contained the original 13 states, then the database would prevent us from adding addresses for any other state. By the same token, if an extra state were added, then you could enter addresses for this new state. This same constraint would prevent us from deleting a state if there were addresses for that state in the Address entity.

The collection of all these foreign key constraints for the database is known as referential integrity . This is how databases ensure that only valid and accurate data is maintained in the database.

Since primary keys can be composite, it follows that the child attributes in the child entity form a composite set of attributes. In fact, the child entity must contain all of the parent entity's primary-key attributes (although the attributes can have different names in the child entity, all the attributes must be represented). The relationship from Name to Person in Figure 9.4 reflects this.

■ Common Data Model Standards

As you learned in the preceding chapter, an Entity Relationship (ER) diagram is a structure used to model systems for a database. It assigns the components of a system into three categories: entities, their attributes, and relationships. There are several standard notations for representing data objects in ER diagrams. Each modeling methodology uses its own notation. Dr. Peter Chen originally proposed the ER approach in 1976. Today, a number of notations are used; among the more common are Bachman, IE ("crow's foot"), and IDEF1X. You will learn about IDEF1X and IE ("crow's foot") in this textbook.

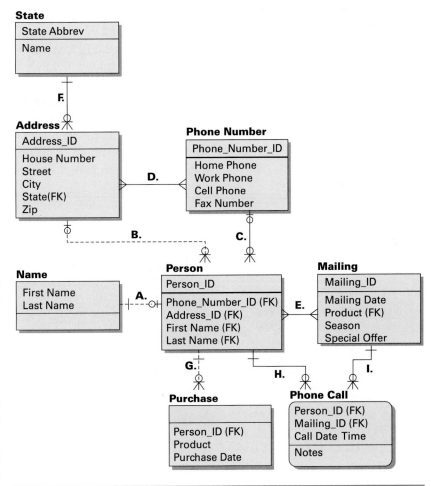

● **Figure 9.4**   Mailing database with relationships drawn in and lettered

Crow's Foot (IE)

A common standard is called IE, which stands for "Information Engineering." This standard, which is shown in most of the figures in this book, is often referred to as the "crow's foot" methodology because of the three-line "V" shape it uses to identify the "many" end of a one-to-many relationship.

The IE approach began with the work of Clive Finkelstein and is now one of the most popular notations for database design. Several different versions of IE exist and are supported by a variety of data modeling tools for implementation. The original IE notation introduced by Finkelstein in 1989 is simple and works well in enterprise data modeling.

Table 9.1 shows just a sample of the several design rules for the IE notation.

Be sure to take note of the notation used in this textbook's data model images. This book's diagrams have standardized, where possible, on the IE notation as used on ER/Studio and ERwin. Some of the modeling tools use a simplified version of IE, which uses only a single circle/cross-bar at each end of the relationship. The various components of IE notation are shown in Figure 9.5.

IDEF1X

A common modeling technique is IDEF developed in the late 1970s by Bob Brown at the Bank of America. IDEF was later extended into a set of standards including IDEF1X, which were adopted by the U.S. Air Force as the required methodology. IDEF1X is a method for designing relational databases used by data modeling software (ERwin, ER/Studio, and so on). The "IDEF" part of the name stands for "Integration DEFinition for Information Modeling," and the "1X" identifies which of the IDEF standards this is (there are other IDEF standards describing how other types of diagrams should look). The name "IDEF1X" stands for "IDEF standard 1 eXtended." IDEF1X focuses on logical data modeling, and you can see the major notations demonstrated in Figure 9.6.

Table 9.2 shows just a sample of the several design rules for the IDEF1X notation.

For a more in-depth look at the IDEF1X notation rules, check out the "IDEF1X Cheat Sheet" at `http://www.cio .gov.bc.ca/other/daf/ IDEF1X_Cheat_Sheet.pdf` or the Essential Strategies outline of IDEF1X at `http:// www.essentialstrategies .com/publications/ modeling/idef1x.htm.`

Table 9.1	Information Engineering (IE) Notation Rules
Item	**Notation Rule**
Entities	Square-cornered rectangles with a dividing line for attributes. The name of the entity is outside the rectangle.
Attributes	Describing attributes are shown below the entity dividing-line or above the line for identifying attributes.
Relationships	Cardinality is represented by a simple line with a bar or a crow's foot symbol. Optionality is represented by an open circle or bar.
Dependency	Identifying relationships are shown with a solid line, nonidentifying ones with a dashed line.

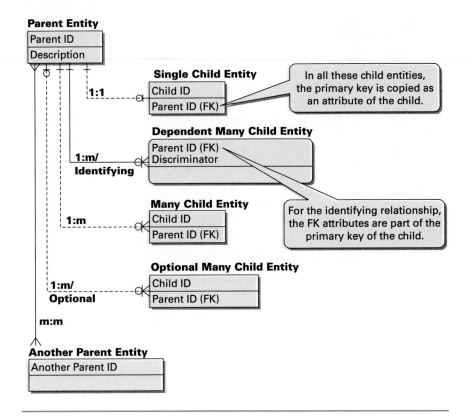

- **Figure 9.5** Example of IE notations

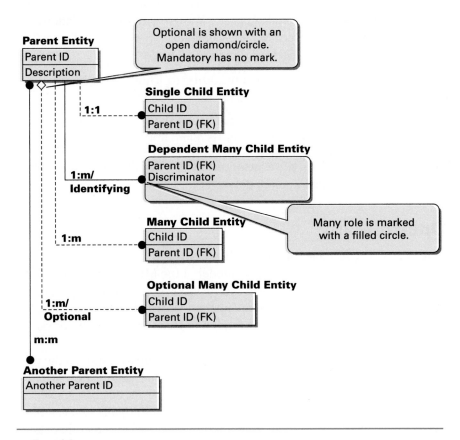

- **Figure 9.6** Example of IDEF1X notations

Table 9.2	IDEF1X Notation Rules
Item	**Notation Rule**
Entities	Square-cornered rectangles with a dividing line for identifying attributes. Round-cornered rectangles for dependent entities.
Identifier/ Primary Key	Indicated above entity dividing-line; names may include hyphens, underscores, or blanks.
Attributes	Indicated below entity dividing-line; names may include hyphens, underscores, or spaces.
Foreign Key Attributes	Indicated with the letters "FK."
Relationships	Combination of optionality and cardinality represented by a single dashed or solid line with a variety of symbols (a solid circle, small diamond, the letters P, Z, and the number 1).

■ Relationships: Cardinality and Optionality

Now let's look at the symbols at the ends of the relationship lines and ask what they mean. Cardinality is an expression of how many rows of one entity (the child) relate to how many rows of the other (the parent). Optionality is a special case of the "how many?" question that deals with zeros.

Each end of the relationship line must have cardinality and optionality defined. The ends of the relationships are known as roles. The relationship reads in both directions. In our Mailing Center example shown in Figure 9.4, you can say this about the State/Address relation:

- One state has zero, one, or many addresses. Thus the cardinality of the address role is "many" and the role is optional.

- One address must have one and only one state. The cardinality of the state role is "one" and the role is mandatory.

This is called a "mandatory 1:m" relationship. Each of the different possible cardinalities is explained in more detail here.

One-to-Many

One-to-many is the most common of the three types of cardinality. In the relationships shown in our discussion model of the Mailing database, six of the nine relationships are 1:m. The 1:m relationship introduces the idea of the relationship as a constraint. Remember you learned earlier that the relationships of an ERD translate into foreign key constraints in the physical model.

The database software will enforce the relationship as a limit on the values that can be inserted in the child table. For the State/Address relationship, this means that you can only have addresses in the database for which a state record exists. If the State entity only contained the original 13 states, then the database would prevent us from adding addresses for any other state.

By the same token this same constraint would prevent us from deleting a state if there were addresses for that state in the Address entity.

The "many" end of the relationship is marked with the "crow's foot;" the "one" end is just a cross bar. As you have only a tick or cross bar at the State end, this indicates that the state is mandatory in the address. The open circle at the address end means that the address is optional for a state. In other words, you can have states that have no addresses, but every address must have a state.

Let's look at another 1:m relationship in this model: Mailing to Phone Call. From the illustration you can read this relationship as two sentences using the roles or verb phrases from the model.

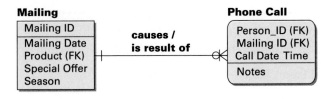

- A relationship with roles or verb phrases

Read this as:

A Mailing causes Phone Call(s)

A Phone Call is the result of a Mailing

In some models you will see that the role is used to name the attribute in the child table. Sometimes this helps to make the model clearer, especially when you have more than one relationship between the same two entities.

Let us consider this example. Say the Mailing is offering two different products: One is the primary product and the second is the bonus product; the free gift "just for purchasing this …". Here you have two relationships between a Product entity and the Mailing entity.

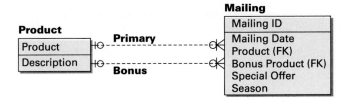

- Multiple relationships between entities

Each of these relationships specifies a role for the product. The role is used to distinguish the two child attributes that appear in the Mailing entity.

■ When you have two or more relationships between the same pair of entities, you *must* specify the roles.

Many-to-Many

The next cardinality for a relationship, many-to-many , only appears in a logical model. In fact, it is one of the sure clues that you are looking at a logical model rather than a physical one. The Mailing List example includes this many-to-many relationship:

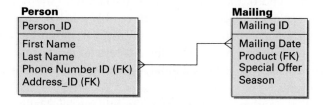

- Many-to-many relationship between entities

You discover a many-to-many relationship by asking the cardinality question "how many" for *both* roles of the relationship.

The Person to Mailing relationship cardinality is determined by asking:

- Can a Person receive many Mailings?

- Can a Mailing go to many People?

The answer to both of these is "yes," so you have a many-to-many relationship to deal with. In practice it turns out that the database software cannot directly handle a many-to-many relationship, so in the conversion to a physical model you must implement this using an additional table. This table is known as a link table, resolution table, or an intersection entity if it is expressed in the logical data model.

The usual implementation of this relationship calls for an identifying one-to-many foreign key from each original table to the new resolution table. In this way the model ensures that the new table has a primary key that prevents entering duplicates. With this primary key in place, a single mailing can only be sent to a person once. The physical tables for resolving the person/mailing many-to-many relationship are shown in this illustration:

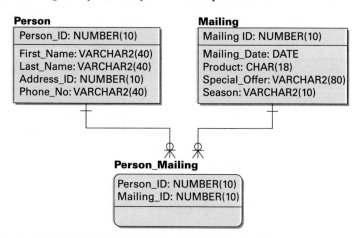

- Physical implementation of a many-to-many relationship using a resolution table

One-to-One

A one-to-one relationship exists where one row of a child entity must match one and only one row of the parent entity. In practice such relationships turn

Introduction to Relational Databases and SQL Programming

out to be very rare. The example mailing database contains an example of this, as shown in the following illustration.

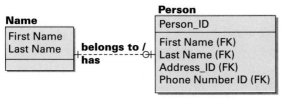

Name/person relationship before analysis

- A one-to-one relationship

Each Person has one and only one Name. Also a person cannot be un-named. This means the name is mandatory for the person.

Since the name is both mandatory and singular, you will move the attributes of name (First and Last) from Name into Person. This leaves Name with no attributes and so you drop it from the model like this:

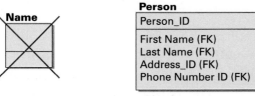

Name/person relationship after study
of the 1:1

- Getting rid of the one-to-one relationship

As you can see from the example, getting rid of the Name entity and the one-to-one relationship improves the capabilities of the database—you can now enter duplicate names in Person if needed (they are no longer the identifier of Name). It also simplifies the model by reducing the entities you have to manage. In general you will find that

■ Any one-to-one relationship can be removed from the logical model by combining the entities into one.

Optionality

When you refer to the optionality of the relationship, you are really referring to the role of the entity in the relationship. Since there are two entities involved,

One-to-One Relationships: When Should You Keep Them?

One-to-one relationships are sometimes necessary in the physical model when you implement the database structure. However, in the logical model they should always be examined closely in an effort to eliminate them. These are the conditions in which you might find one-to-one relationships used:

- ■ *If you are storing LOBs (Large Objects) in the database. The engine may perform faster if these are stored in a physically different location away from the rest of the columns of the table. This requires you to split the columns of a table into two tables with a 1:1 relationship between them.*

- ■ *If the data represents different categories of the entity. It may simplify the maintenance of the database to separate these categories into separate tables. Your physical model will end up with a key table and 1:1 relationships from that table to the several detail tables. This structure allows you to truncate and reload data for each category very quickly without disturbing the rest of the data in the table(s).*

- ■ *If you want to restrict access to some of the columns in a table. For instance, an EMPLOYEE table might contain Salary information that you do not want to display to everybody in the company. Since it is easy to control access (or security) for tables, you can split the confidential data off into a secondary table.*

Due to recent improvements in database technology, you will rarely find a reason to use a 1:1 relationship in a modern application. For instance, Oracle will let you separate the physical location of LOBs from the table without the need for another table. The ability to partition tables physically gives the DBA the same level of control for efficient loading and managing of tables. Any database will let you create views of a table (that is, virtual tables) that can hide columns from a set of users. Access permissions can be applied to the views to control which user sees what columns of data.

there are two specifications for optionality: one for each role of the relationship. You can find out the optionality by asking the question "Can you have *no* \<entity 1\> instance for an \<entity2\> instance?" If the answer to this is "yes," you have an optional role for \<entity 1\>.

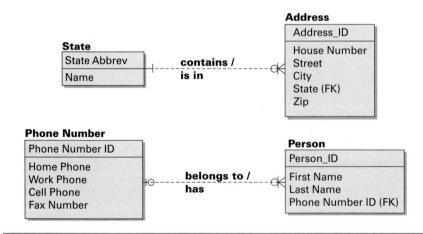

- • Optional and mandatory roles

- **Can State have no Address(es)?** Yes, this just means you haven't yet loaded an address for Hawaii, not that there are no addresses in Hawaii. So Address is optional.

- **Can Address have no State?** No, the mailing address is not very useful without a state. This makes State mandatory . You indicate this using the notation shown. Just a single bar on the line means State is mandatory; a circle on the crow's foot means the Address is optional.

- **Can Person have no Phone Number?** Yes, even in this day and age, there are people without phones!

- **Can Phone Number belong to no Person?** Yes, the phone could be in a college dorm or be a pay phone that does not belong to an individual. In both ends of the relationship you have optional roles. The only difference then between this and the previous relationship is that the "one" end has a circle on it to show optionality.

When you create a relationship in a modeling tool, you will notice that the identifier attribute(s) are copied across into the child entity. The optionality of the role at the parent end of the relationship determines whether missing data will be allowed in the child entity. If missing data is allowed, the attributes in the child entity must also be optional.

Dependency: Identifying Relationships

Sometimes the relationship between two entities is so close (this is referred to as "coupling") that the child entity cannot reasonably exist without the parent entity. In this illustration a Sale Item cannot exist without there being a Sale for it to be part of.

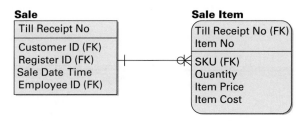

• An identifying relationship

The entity named Sale Item is a dependent entity for Sale. This type of identifying relationship is shown with a solid line and the child attribute, copied from the parent, becomes part of the identifier of the child. Thus you see that the Till Receipt No is the identifier for Sale, but also part of the identifier for Sale Item.

The most usual place to find such identifying relationships is when a many-to-many relationship is translated into a resolution table. The foreign key constraints in the physical model are both identifying relationships.

Recursive Relationship in Mailing Database

1. Can you find a recursive relationship in the Mailing database?

2. What is the sentence that describes the relationship?

3. Is it optional or mandatory? What is the cardinality?

Recursive vs. Binary

All the relationships you have seen so far have been between two different entities. These are known as binary relationships. There are occasions when the entities at the ends of a relationship are one and the same entity. This relationship is described as a recursive relationship.

Consider the Employee entity. Most employees have a manager or supervisor—everybody except the CEO or owner of the company. The supervisor will also be an employee. An employee will only have one supervisor, but a supervisor can have many employees reporting to her. The recursive relationship behaves exactly like the binary one, except that the child entity and parent entity are one and the same.

The rules for optionality and cardinality apply equally to recursive relationships as to binary ones. In this example the Supervisor ID is optional because there is at least one employee who has no supervisor: the owner or CEO.

Recursive relationships sometimes appear a little strange. Remember that an employee cannot be his/her own supervisor. The relationship links the *entity* back to the same entity; it does not link a row (occurrence) of an entity to itself. The relationship always links two different occurrences of the entity. If you look at the sample data in the following illustration, you will see that the supervisor is always different from the employee ID on the same row.

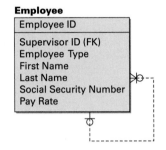

• Recursive relationship

	Employee ID	Supervisor ID	Employee Type	First Name	Last Name	Social Security Number	Pay Rate
1	Employee						
2							
3	**Employee ID**	**Supervisor ID**	**Employee Type**	**First Name**	**Last Name**	**Social Security Number**	**Pay Rate**
4	100		Owner	John	Balfour	123-45-6789	$ 30.00
5	101	100	Cashier	Susan	Saronnen	456-78-8912	$ 20.00
6	102	100	Cashier	Eric	La Sold	678-90-1234	$ 6.75
7	103	100	Storeman	Martin	Murphy	901-23-4567	$ 6.75
8	104	103	Delivery	Erica	Strange	234-56-7890	$ -
9	105	103	Delivery	Noah	Tamil	567-89-0123	$ -

• Sample data for a recursive relationship

■ Modeling Multiple Categories: Supertype and Subtypes

This special relationship is useful as a shorthand for showing an "is a" type of relationship. In the conceptual model it translates to an inheritance or generalization relationship. These terms come from the object-oriented programming world and represent powerful concepts used to design application programs.

Creating Basic Data Models

Now it is your opportunity to draw some basic data models. For each step, you will be given some business information with data and relationships that you will need to construct a model. Create data models for the situations listed in each step.

For this exercise, you will need a pencil, paper, and eraser (the eraser is important).

Step 1

A hospital has many rooms but each room is in only one hospital. Draw a data model showing a one-to-many relationship between the Hospital and Room entities, indicating the Hospital ID, Hospital Name, Room Number, and Number of Beds for each entity.

Step 2

A hospital has many doctors, but a doctor may not be employed by the hospital. To your first diagram add a Doctor entity with an optional one-to-many relationship from the Hospital to the Doctor. The identifier of Doctor is Doctor_ID and the entity has attributes of First_Name, Last_Name, and Specialty.

Step 3

There are many patients who come to the hospital. Each one is assigned to a room. A room may be a ward that has several beds and thus holds several patients. Add a Room_Type attribute to the Room entity. Add a Patient entity with attributes Patient_ID, Date_of_Admission, First_Name, and Last_Name to the diagram. Draw a one-to-many relationship from room to patient.

Step 4

A patient can have many doctors (for example, a surgeon, anesthetist, oncologist) and a doctor has many patients. Draw a many-to-many relationship between Patient and Doctor. Now redraw the many-to-many relationship as an intersection entity with an identifier made up of Patient_ID and Doctor_ID and two one-to-many relationships: one from Patient, one from Doctor, both going to the intersection entity. Finally add a Fee attribute to the intersection entity. This is optional and not part of the identifier.

Step 5

Get a clean piece of paper and draw the model out again. Try to ensure that the relationship lines don't cross each other and that the parent entity is always above and left of the child entity. The diagram layout makes a big difference as to how easy it is to read.

This relationship only exists in the logical model; when it is translated into a physical implementation using SQL, the tables, columns, and foreign key constraints appear just like other relationships. The power of super/subtype modeling is in the ability of the logical model to be implemented physically in several different ways. The implementations have a great deal of effect on the performance and ease of maintenance of the databases.

Categories, Supertypes, and Subtypes

As you develop an application, you may discover entities that seem to be very similar to one another. In fact, their only difference is the category they fall into. Let's look at the employee data again. When you read through the

Case Study

case study, you see that only two types of employee are mentioned: Register Clerk and Delivery Person. For each type of employee you have to keep the same basic data: last and first names, SSN, pay rate. Rather than repeating these attributes in two separate entities, why not have a "master" entity to hold the common attributes? This is shown in Figure 9.7.

Call the master entity with its common attributes a supertype. You can then draw a cluster symbol to show how the supertype relates to the subtypes, and you can remove the attributes in the subtype entities as they are no longer needed.

The cluster symbol shows how the subtypes cluster together to become the supertype. There are three things you can specify about this clustering.

- Is it complete or incomplete? A complete cluster means that you have every possible subtype shown in our model. An incomplete cluster means you have some, but not all possible, subtypes in our model. The employees cluster example is an incomplete one.

- Is it exclusive or inclusive? If the cluster is exclusive, then an object can only exist in one subtype. If it is inclusive, it might exist in more than one subtype. The employee cluster in our model is exclusive. One employee can only have one type. You could imagine a business in which the employees had multiple jobs; they could be both register clerk and delivery person. In this case the cluster would be inclusive. Sometimes you'll see the terms "disjoint" or "overlap" used in place of exclusive or inclusive.

- Depending on the specification of the cluster, you should choose a discriminator. This is an attribute from the supertype that allows you to know which subtype the record belongs to. In this example you would choose "Employee Type," or better yet "Job Type," as the discriminator. Figure 9.8 shows the Job Type attribute being used as the discriminator for the subtypes.

So why do all this extra complexity for something you could have modeled using the entities and relationships you have already learned?

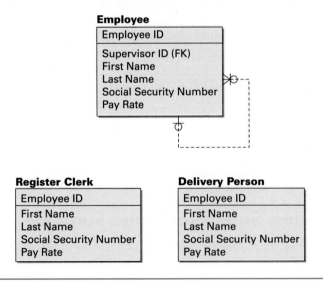

Employee

Employee ID
Supervisor ID (FK)
First Name
Last Name
Social Security Number
Pay Rate

Register Clerk

Employee ID
First Name
Last Name
Social Security Number
Pay Rate

Delivery Person

Employee ID
First Name
Last Name
Social Security Number
Pay Rate

● **Figure 9.7** Common attributes in a supertype

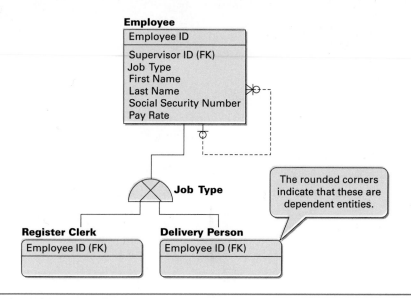

Employee

Employee ID
Supervisor ID (FK)
Job Type
First Name
Last Name
Social Security Number
Pay Rate

Job Type

Register Clerk

Employee ID (FK)

Delivery Person

Employee ID (FK)

The rounded corners indicate that these are dependent entities.

● **Figure 9.8** Super- and subtypes with a cluster

The reasons stem from the actions that the subtypes can perform. You saw earlier in this chapter that register clerks work with the registers and make sales to customers; delivery people take the sale items and deliver them to the customer. Each employee does a different job and has different relationships with the other entities in the business. By splitting the employee into subtypes, you can now make a relationship specific to that subtype.

If you put all the employees into one entity, then any relationship you create—for example, Employee to Sale—would work for both register clerks and delivery people. This clearly does not reflect the reality of the business where the delivery people may not be trained to operate the registers and so cannot act as register clerks.

Implementing Super/Subtypes in a Physical Model

The key things to remember about super- and subtypes are

- They are concerned with inheriting attributes.

- Different subtypes may have different relationships.

Since this modeling form only exists in the logical model, how do you implement it in the physical model? You need to translate the entities into tables and the attributes into columns. Incidentally, none of the modeling tools make a good job of this translation. You will have to learn to do it by hand or, at least, improve on the tool's translation.

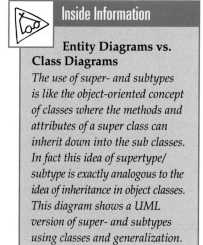

Inside Information

Entity Diagrams vs. Class Diagrams
The use of super- and subtypes is like the object-oriented concept of classes where the methods and attributes of a super class can inherit down into the sub classes. In fact this idea of supertype/subtype is exactly analogous to the idea of inheritance in object classes. This diagram shows a UML version of super- and subtypes using classes and generalization.

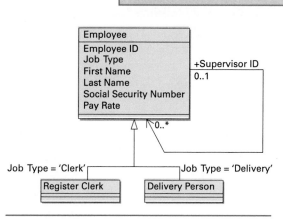

Employee

Employee ID
Job Type
First Name
Last Name
Social Security Number
Pay Rate

+Supervisor ID
0..1

0..*

Job Type = 'Clerk'

Register Clerk

Job Type = 'Delivery'

Delivery Person

● UML version of super/subtypes

Chapter 9 Review

■ Chapter Summary

After reading this chapter and completing the Step-by-Step tutorial and Cross Checks, you should understand the following facts about designing a database's structure:

Let the Data Tell You Where it Goes

- Data models develop an accurate representation of the client's information and business needs, through a graphical design.
- The nouns and verbs used by the business users will translate into entities, attributes, and relationships.
- Check your understanding by reading the model back to the users.

Select the Grain for Each Subject Area of the Database

- The grain of the database is the finest level of detail the database can store.
- A database may have more than one subject area. Each subject area will have its own grain.

Identify Records Uniquely with Primary Keys

- A unique identifier is needed for every entity.
- A unique identifier is an attribute or set of attributes that uniquely identifies a record.
- Identifiers are required for relationships to function correctly.

Compare Common Modeling Standards

- IE is the "crow's foot" notation. It exists in several versions.

- IDEF1X is another notation used for data models. It is used for government work.

Identify the Relationships in a Model

- Three types of cardinality exist: 1:1, 1:m, m:m.
- One-to-many relationships are the most common.
- Many-to-many relationships translate to two 1:m and a resolution table.
- One-to-one relationships should be avoided.
- Optionality defines the role of the entity in the relationship.
- A relationship has optionality and cardinality in both directions.
- An identifying relationship creates a dependent entity in which the child attribute is part of the child's identifier.

Model Categories Using Super- and Subtypes

- Some entities can be grouped together as categories of a common entity.
- Super/subtypes are not necessary for modeling, but add great convenience and descriptive power to the model.
- The entity with the common attributes is known as a supertype.
- The subtypes are entities for each category.
- Subtypes inherit the attributes of the supertype.
- The super/subtype entities can be translated several ways into a physical model.

■ Key Terms

binary relationship *(264)*
category *(265)*
child entity *(254)*
cluster *(266)*
code table *(253)*
composite key *(251)*
discriminator *(266)*
foreign key *(254)*

grain *(247)*
mandatory *(263)*
many-to-many *(259)*
natural key *(252)*
one-to-many *(258)*
one-to-one *(260)*
optional *(262)*
parent entity *(254)*

primary key *(251)*
recursive relationship *(264)*
referential integrity *(255)*
sequence *(253)*
subtype *(266)*
supertype *(266)*
surrogate key *(252)*

Key Term Quiz

Use the Key Terms list to complete the sentences that follow. Not all terms will be used.

1. A role is _____ if the entity must be present in the relationship.

2. A(n)_____ is a relationship in which a single table is associated with itself.

3. An identifying relationship means the child entity is a(n) _____.

4. The level of detail involved in an examination of objects is known as _____.

5. A(n) _____ is simply a primary key whose value is artificially derived.

Matching Definition Quiz

Relate each term on the left with the appropriate description on the right.

Term		Description
1.	Foreign key	a. The cardinality of a relationship between entities
2.	Unique identifier	b. A system of notation for ERDs
3.	Binary relationship	c. The child-table columns that contain primary-key values from a parent table
4.	IDEF1X	d. The attribute or set of attributes that uniquely identifies an occurrence of an entity
5.	Many-to-many	e. Relationship between two different entities

Multiple-Choice Quiz

1. To constrain an attribute's values in a relational database, its designer could use which of the following?

   a. Identifier

   b. Composite primary key

   c. Attribute

   d. Relationship

   e. Surrogate primary key

2. In this *relationship,* a record in Entity A has the potential to relate to zero, one, or many records in Entity B.

   a. Binary relationship

   b. Recursive relationship

   c. One-to-one relationship

   d. Many-to-many relationship

   e. One-to-many relationship

3. This verb phrase describes what an entity does in a relationship.

   a. Role

   b. Cardinality

   c. Unique attribute

   d. Optionality

   e. Relationship

4. If a relationship (in IE notation) shows a circle and a cross bar together next to the parent entity, what type of relationship could it be? (Choose two.)

   a. Grain

   b. Cardinality

   c. Identifying

   d. Optional

   e. One-to-many

5. A feature used by relational database systems that prevents users or applications from entering inconsistent data is

   a. Identifying relationship

   b. Cardinality

   c. Referential integrity

   d. Optionality

   e. Natural keys

6. An identifying relationship gives rise to?

   a. Recursive relationship

   b. Dependent entity

   c. Unique identifier

   d. Optional role

   e. Subtype

7. Which of the following are valid types of cardinality? (Choose three.)

    a. 1:m

    b. 1:1

    c. 0:1

    d. m:m

    e. 0,1:m

8. Which of the following are functions of an identifier? (Choose two.)

    a. Uniquely identify occurrences of an entity

    b. Identify the child attributes in other entities

    c. Generate unique values per attribute

    d. Establish attributes in an entity for use in a relationship

    e. Generate unique values per row

9. Which of the following are standard notations for representing data objects in ER diagrams? (Choose four.)

    a. Bachman

    b. Chong

    c. Chen

    d. IDEF1X

    e. Information Engineering

    f. IDEF

10. What concept has to do with the level of detail involved in an examination of objects?

    a. Generalization

    b. Granularity

    c. Business rules

    d. Data model notation

    e. Logical data modeling

11. In order for a relationship to exist between two entities, which of the following statements must be true? (Choose two.)

    a. There must be a parent-child relationship in which the parent is always dominant.

    b. All entities in the relationship must be equal.

    c. The parent entity must have an attribute (or set of attributes) that uniquely identifies every record it contains.

    d. The child entity must have an identical attribute (or set of attributes) to contain the values that uniquely identify the parent record.

    e. The parent entity must have an attribute (or set of attributes) that are generated by a sequence.

12. To qualify as an identifier for an entity, a set of attributes must meet the following criteria: (Choose two.)

    a. The values must not be artificially generated.

    b. The values can never be NULL.

    c. The values for each attribute must be unique.

    d. The values must be referenced by a unique identifier in another entity.

    e. The values for the set of attributes must be unique.

13. Which of the following symbols represent dependent entities in IDEF1X notation?

    a. Crow's foot

    b. Diamond

    c. Round-cornered rectangles

    d. Square-cornered rectangles

    e. Letter O

14. The verbs given to you in the business requirements by subject-matter experts can be translated to

    a. Entities

    b. Attributes

    c. Primary keys

    d. Relationships

    e. Foreign keys

15. How many entities are involved in a recursive relationship:

    a. 0

    b. 1

    c. 2

    d. 4

    e. many

■ Essay Quiz

1. Why aren't many-to-many relationships found in a physical relational database?

2. What is the difference between an identifying and a nonidentifying relationship?

3. What is the purpose of a foreign key?

4. Can one attribute of a composite identifier be NULL? Give reasons for your answer.

5. Briefly describe the concept of granularity.

Lab Projects

● Lab Project 9.1

Case Study

You have been asked to develop a logical data model for Clapham Specialty Store based on the information given to you by John and his staff. From the case study description, the analysis of the nouns and verbs gives you the following entity, attribute, and relationship information shown in Table 9.3.

You will need a pencil and paper; then do the following:

① Draw the entities with their attributes. You will need to invent surrogate keys where necessary.

② Indicate the relationships between the entities using IE notation. You will need to determine the cardinality and optionality for each direction of the relationships.

③ Add the roles to the relationships.

● Lab Project 9.2

You have been hired by *All-Sports Magazine* to create a simple data model that indicates the sports teams that exist in each city of the United States. *All-Sports Magazine* has asked you to show the city name, state, population, team name, sport, and stadium.

You will need a pencil and paper. Then do the following:

① Draw the entities with their attributes and indicate the relationships.

② What are the limits and benefits that the relationships impose on the data in the model?

Table 9.3	Entities, Attributes, and Relationships for Clapham Specialty Store	
Entity	**Attributes**	**Relationships**
Register Clerk	Last Name, First Name, Social Security Number, Pay Rate	Register Clerk logs in at a register, Clerk makes a Sale, Clerk is an Employee.
Delivery Person	Last Name, First Name, Social Security Number, Pay Rate	Delivery Person delivers a Sale, Delivery Person is an Employee.
Employee	Last Name, First Name, Social Security Number, Pay Rate, Job Type	Employee reports to a Supervisor.
Register	Department	
Register Log	Start Time, End Time	Register Log is for Register, Register Log records Register Clerk.
Location	Department, Aisle, Side, Shelf	Location displays Product.
Product	Stock Keeping Unit (SKU), Name, Package Size, Cost, Quantity in Stock, Last Purchased Date	Product is displayed at Location, Product is sold in Sale Item.
Sale	Till Receipt No, Sale Date-Time	Sale is made to Customer, Sale is made by Register Clerk, Sale is recorded on Register, Sale is made up of Sale Items.
Sale Item	Item No, SKU, Quantity Item Price, Item Cost	Sale Item is part of Sale, Sale Item is for Product.
Customer	First Name, Last Name, Address, Phone No	Customer receives Sale.

Normalization

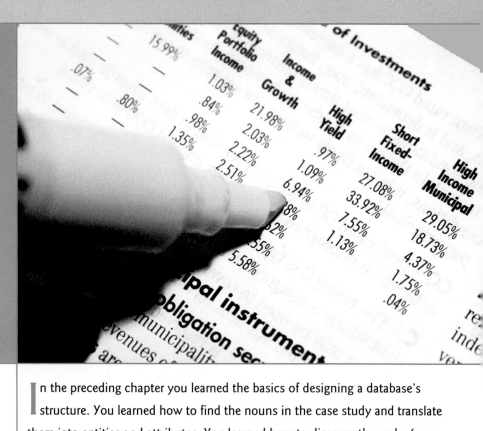

"A place for everything and everything in its place."

—Isabella Mary Beeton, *The Book of Household Management*, 1951

In this chapter, you will learn how to

- **Describe the benefits of normalizing a database**
- **Describe data dependency and determinacy**
- **Define the five normal forms of data**
- **Apply the normal forms to a database model**
- **Identify and correct data anomalies**
- **Convert a logical model to physical**

In the preceding chapter you learned the basics of designing a database's structure. You learned how to find the nouns in the case study and translate them into entities and attributes. You learned how to discover the verbs (even making up a few!) and translate them into relationships. You examined unique identifiers and how they contribute to the relationships. You learned how to specify a relationship—its cardinality and optionality. You then looked at identifying and recursive relationships.

In this chapter you will learn more about the semantics (or meaning) of the data and how this affects the data model. You will learn how to group attributes together and design relationships to satisfy each of the first three normal forms. You will examine the higher normal forms (fourth, fifth, and other) and learn when to apply these. You will work on the case study some more to enhance the design by normalizing the structure of entities, attributes, and relations.

Finally you will start the process of converting the logical model into a physical model. At last, you will be able to start implementing tables and columns and get away from paper and pencil.

■ The Process of Normalization

When you store data in a database, you need that data to be accurate and easy to manage. If you think of Amazon with their billions of rows of "click-stream" data, they have to be efficient about the storage of the data if they ever want to find it again. The difficulties of ensuring efficiency and accuracy really come to the fore when you have big databases. Dr. Codd's original papers about the relational model were specifically addressed to the storage of data in "large data banks." When you normalize a database, you are trying to make the storage of the data more accurate (less prone to error) and more efficient (simpler and faster to edit).

You ensure efficiency and accuracy in your database by

- Eliminating redundant data
- Keeping entities as independent of one another as possible

Normalization is the process of applying a set of rules to the data model to achieve one or more of the normal forms, which helps ensure that your database is efficient and accurate. Strictly speaking, normalization is only necessary if you are editing the data. If you have a read-only database—most data warehouses are designed to be read-only—you do not need to normalize. Just remember that even a read-only database has to be loaded at some time, and that means inserting data.

When designing a database, you must balance the editing needs with the reading needs. While normalization helps for data accuracy during editing, there is a price to pay in terms of performance when reading data. A good design will strike the correct balance with a little "denormalization" at the end of the design process.

You will find that applying these rules becomes easy if you follow the design process you have used so far—in fact, using the "noun" and "verb" principles, you will probably find that the normal form rules are only needed for a quick check of your model.

Obtaining the correct level of denormalization in a database design is something of a compromise. You should always get the model into a fully normalized form before attempting any denormalization.

■ Dependency

Much of the discussion in the remainder of the chapter has to do with the question of "closeness of coupling" between attributes. In formal database terminology this is known as dependency. Like most relationships this has two names, each associated with the role at the end of the relationship. The dependent is at one end, and the opposite end is the determinant.

Dependents and Determinants

We say that attribute B is dependent on attribute A if the value of B can be precisely and uniquely determined from the value of A. B is known as a dependent attribute. (Note that either "attribute" could represent a set of attributes.)

Consider the Product entity from the Clapham Specialty Store case study. In this case you can say that the Product Name is dependent on the SKU.

Case Study

It does not depend on the other attributes. You cannot determine the product name by knowing how many items are in stock

The converse of this is to describe SKU as the `determinant` of Product Name. The value in the SKU attribute determines the value of the Product Name attribute. You can think of the identifier as a determinant of *all* the other attributes in a properly normalized entity; however, the concept of determinant/dependent does not always involve the identifier or primary key, as you will see in the sections that cover normalization.

Transitive Dependency

We can also define a more indirect dependency: If B depends on A and C depends on B, we say that C is `transitively dependent` on A. This is a dependency that "transits" or passes through another entity or attribute.

Say the Product entity included a Location Description as shown in the illustration. The Location ID for the product depends on the SKU of the product. The Location Description really depends on the Location ID. Thus we can say that the Location Description is transitively dependent on the SKU. It is dependent, but one step removed from a direct dependency.

In the Product example the item in the middle of the list of attributes ("B," or Location ID) is another attribute and the dependencies are all between attributes within a single entity. There is another form of transitive dependency in which the middle item is another entity.

One of the most common forms of denormalization in a database is to include summary data in a parent entity. Say you needed to know how many of a Product (Product Name = "Baked Beans", SKU = "0134569027850") have been sold in total. What you could do is to simply count up the number of rows in the Sale Item entity where the SKU is "0134569027850". This is the dynamic method: you recalculate the count whenever necessary.

Clearly this takes a certain amount of computational effort every time you need the information. Maybe it would be faster and simpler for us to add an attribute to the Product entity and put the summary count in there as a piece of data, as shown in this illustration.

Product
SKU
Name
Package Size
Cost
Location ID (FK)
Location Description
Quantity in Stock
Last Purchased

- Product entity with description of location

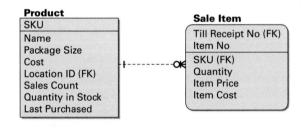

- Product data with an attribute for Sales Count

> When naming columns that contain counts, quantities, and sequence numbers, avoid using the word "number" or the abbreviation "no" in the name. For example, a column called Number Sales could refer to the sequence number of the sale or the number of sales (or count). Use count, quantity, and sequence to make the column name unambiguous.

What we have done is create a `transitive dependency` between the SKU attribute and the Sales Count attribute. The Sales Count attribute is dependent on the SKU attribute, but its value is dependent through the Sale Item entity. The number of rows in Sale Item can change at any time—whenever someone makes another sale—and the value of Sales Count must be updated at the same time to satisfy this dependency and ensure that the data in Sales Count is always accurate.

The Sales Count attribute is redundant. You do not need it for the database to be complete and accurate in its storage of the data. However, it may be useful in speeding up the querying of data.

The First Three Normal Forms

The rules for ensuring that databases are normalized are referred to as normal forms. These forms are numbered from first normal form (1NF) through fifth normal form (5NF). Each normal form has an increasing level of normalization. The first three normal forms are treated sequentially and build on one another. However, when you come to denormalize a database you will often find that you violate these normal forms independently—say breaking 2NF while leaving the requirements for 3NF in place.

In this section, you'll examine the standard normalization forms.

First Normal Form: Eliminate Repeating Groups

First normal form states: "Make a separate entity for each set of related attributes, with a unique identifier for each entity."

Let's have a look at the movie business. Figure 10.1 lists some of the Hollywood production companies or studios and some of their movies. Think of this as a little database. Think about searching it for all the movies made by "James Cameron." You would have to look up the director's name in two different columns, which is not very efficient.

What happens when Malpaso Pictures makes a third movie? You'll have to add more columns to this table. And then a fourth, fifth, and so on. Fortunately Clint Eastwood has only directed about 25 movies, so you only need 50 columns. How many movies has a big studio like Universal made?

Clearly this technique for listing movies is not very efficient. You need to apply the first normal form rule and separate each **repeating group** of attributes into another entity. This creates two entities: Movie and Studio with a many-to-many relationship between them.

The ERD is shown in the illustration which corresponds to the data in Figure 10.2 for each entity. You have resolved the relationship into a resolution entity with two one-to-many relationships for clarity. A many-to-many relationship is demanded by *Medicine Man,* which came from two studios.

Inside Information

History of Dr. E. F. Codd's Normalization Rules

Dr. E. F. Codd introduced normalization for relational databases in 1970 when he wrote a paper entitled Notes on a Data Sublanguage, *in which he introduced the idea of first normal form. Then, later in 1970, he wrote* The Second and Third Normal Forms for the Relational Model. *Finally, in 1972, he published* Further Normalization of the Data Base Relational Model *and* Normalized Data Base Structure *in which he addressed the fourth and fifth normal forms. Each of these papers is a mathematical treatise expanding on the set algebra that the relational model is based on. Other experts in the field have since expounded upon his initial normalization rules.*

The first three forms (1NF, 2NF, and 3NF) can be summarized as "Each attribute must be a fact about the key, the whole key, and nothing but the key," to which some irreverently add "so help me, Codd"!

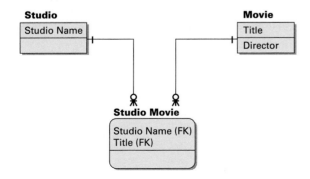

• Model for first normal form

	A	B	C	D	E
1	Studio Movie				
2	Studio	Movie 1	Director 1	Movie 2	Director 2
3	Artisan Entertainment	Twin Peaks	David Lynch	Terminator 2	James Cameron
4	Carolco	Rocky	John Avildsen	Rocky 2	Sylvestor Stallone
5	Cinergi	Tombstone	George Cosmatos	Medicine Man	John McTiernan
6	Malpaso Pictures	Absolute Powe	Clint Eastwood	Garden of Good and Evil	Clint Eastwood
7	MGM.UA Studios	Terminator	James Cameron		
8	Hollywood Pictures	Medicine Man	John McTiernan	Color of Night	Richard Rush
9	Warner Bros	Unforgiven	Clint Eastwood	Play Misty for Me	Clint Eastwood

• **Figure 10.1**   Studios, movies, and directors

	A	B	C	D	E	F	G
11							
12	Studio		Studio Movie			Movie	
13	Studio		Studio	Title		Title	Director
14	Artisan Entertainment		Artisan Entertainment	Terminator 2		Absolute Power	Clint Eastwood
15	Carolco		Artisan Entertainment	Twin Peaks		Color of Night	Richard Rush
16	Cinergi		Carolco	Rocky		Garden of Good and Evil	Clint Eastwood
17	Malpaso Pictures		Carolco	Rocky 2		Medicine Man	John McTiernan
18	MGM.UA Studios		Cinergi	Medicine Man		Play Misty for Me	Clint Eastwood
19	Hollywood Pictures		Cinergi	Tombstone		Rocky	John Avildsen
20	Warner Bros		Hollywood Pictures	Color of Night		Rocky 2	Sylvestor Stallone
21			Hollywood Pictures	Medicine Man		Terminator	James Cameron
22			Malpaso Pictures	Absolute Power		Terminator 2	James Cameron
23			Malpaso Pictures	Garden of Good and Evil		Tombstone	George Cosmatos
24			MGM.UA Studios	Terminator		The Doors	Oliver Stone
25			Warner Bros	Play Misty for Me		Unforgiven	Clint Eastwood
26			Warner Bros	Unforgiven			

• **Figure 10.2**   Data for first normal form

Now try the searches again. Finding all the movies directed by Cameron is easy; only one column to look at in our little database. You can add an unlimited number of movies for Malpaso; Clint can go on making movies for a hundred years and you'll still be able to list them all.

Just a couple more things about repeating groups: A group can be just one column or attribute—sometimes called a multivalued attribute; and repeating groups often hide from you. Look at the data in the following illustration for class events:

	A	B	C	D	E	F
1	Class events					
2	Class/Semester	Start date	End date	Midterm exam date	Final exam date	Labs completed date
3	SQL 101-Win03	1/4/2003	3/16/2003	2/8/2003	3/16/2003	3/21/2003
4	Java 101-Win03	1/5/2003	3/17/2003	2/9/2003	3/16/2003	3/21/2003
5	C++ 102-Win03	1/6/2003	3/23/2003	2/13/2003	3/25/2003	3/30/2003
6	Data bases-Spr03	3/6/2003	5/30/2003	4/17/2003	5/29/2003	6/3/2003

• Class events data

It does not look as though there are repeating groups. Each column has a different name and there are no tell-tale number suffixes. But think what would happen if you wanted to record another date for each class, say, "Results Ready Date." This would require another column. This is behaving just like the repeating groups of Movie/Director.

In fact, these *are* repeating groups. What hid them from our analysis was the column name. The information contained in the column name is what you need to separate out the data and normalize it. The column name is really an Event Type and should be converted to an attribute to realize first normal form as shown in this illustration.

	A	B	C
8	Class Events		
9	Class/Semester	Event Date	Event Type
10	C++ 102-Win03	1/4/2003	Start
11	C++ 102-Win03	3/16/2003	End
12	C++ 102-Win03	2/8/2003	Midterm exam
13	C++ 102-Win03	3/16/2003	Final exam
14	C++ 102-Win03	3/21/2003	Labs completed
15	Data bases-Spr03	1/5/2003	Start
16	Data bases-Spr03	2/9/2003	Midterm exam
17	Data bases-Spr03	3/16/2003	Final exam
18	Data bases-Spr03	3/17/2003	End
19	Data bases-Spr03	3/21/2003	Labs completed
20	Java 101-Win03	1/6/2003	Start
21	Java 101-Win03	3/23/2003	End
22	Java 101-Win03	2/13/2003	Midterm exam
23	Java 101-Win03	3/25/2003	Final exam
24	Java 101-Win03	3/30/2003	Labs completed
25	SQL 101-Win03	3/6/2003	Start
26	SQL 101-Win03	5/30/2003	End
27	SQL 101-Win03	4/17/2003	Midterm exam
28	SQL 101-Win03	5/29/2003	Final exam
29	SQL 101-Win03	6/3/2003	Labs completed

- Revised data with class events in first normal form

Now adding another type of date is easy—just add extra rows to the data.

Second Normal Form: Eliminate Redundant Data

Second normal form states: "If an attribute depends on only part of a multi-valued key, remove it to a separate entity."

Let's add some more information to our studio/movie database (shown in Figure 10.3).

Earlier we had the Male Lead Actor added to the Studio Movie entity. Suppose you decide the lead for *Medicine Man* was incorrect and you need to change it. You have to find *both* records in this entity and update two rows. As with the first normal form, this has potential for errors (it would be easy to update just one of them) and it's just plain inefficient. Clearly the Male Lead is more closely associated with the Movie than with the Studio Movie entity.

	A	B	C
29	Studio Movie		
30	Studio	Title	Male Lead
31	Artisan Entertainment	Terminator 2	Arnold Schwarzenegger
32	Artisan Entertainment	The Doors	Val Kilmer
33	Carolco	Rocky	Syvester Stallone
34	Carolco	Rocky 2	Syvester Stallone
35	Cinergi	Medicine Man	Sean Connery
36	Cinergi	Tombstone	Kurt Russell
37	Hollywood Pictures	Color of Night	Bruce Willis
38	Hollywood Pictures	Medicine Man	Sean Connery
39	Malpaso Pictures	Absolute Power	Clint Eastwood
40	Malpaso Pictures	Garden of Good and Evil	Kevin Spacey
41	MGM.UA Studios	Terminator	Arnold Schwarzenegger
42	Warner Bros	Play Misty for Me	Clint Eastwood
43	Warner Bros	Unforgiven	Clint Eastwood

- **Figure 10.3**   Studio and Movie with Male Lead

In other words, the Male Lead attribute depends on only part of the studio movie identifier (Studio, Title). You should move the Male Lead to the Movie entity. Now the lead only appears once for each Movie, so any update to *Medicine Man* occurs in only one row.

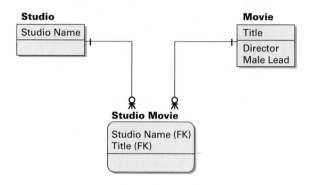

- Studio/Movie database in second normal form

Third Normal Form: Eliminate Attributes Not Dependent on the Primary Key

Third normal form states: "If attributes do not add to the description of the identifier, remove them to another entity."

All the movie stars have agents working for them to negotiate deals and get all that paperwork about movie making handled. Here you have added the Male Lead Agency attribute to the Movie entity. Remember that Movie has a single part identifier, so second normal form has not been violated and there are no repeating groups here, so first normal form is valid. But it is clear that you have repeated the Agency data a lot. In fact the Agency data is repeated in lock-step with the Male Lead. The Male Lead Agency does not help describe the Movie; it is really a descriptor of the actor. This data is shown in Figure 10.4.

	A	B	C	D
46	**Movie**			
47	**Title**	**Director**	**Male Lead**	**Male Lead Agency**
48	Absolute Power	Clint Eastwood	Clint Eastwood	CAA
49	Color of Night	Richard Rush	Bruce Willis	William Morris
50	Garden of Good and E	Clint Eastwood	Kevin Spacey	CAA
51	Medicine Man	John McTiernan	Sean Connery	ICM
52	Play Misty for Me	Clint Eastwood	Clint Eastwood	CAA
53	Rocky	John Avildsen	Syvester Stallone	MTM
54	Rocky 2	Sylvestor Stallone	Syvester Stallone	MTM
55	Terminator	James Cameron	Arnold Schwarzenegger	ICM
56	Terminator 2	James Cameron	Arnold Schwarzenegger	ICM
57	Tombstone	George Cosmatos	Kurt Russell	William Morris
58	The Doors	Oliver Stone	Val Kilmer	CAA
59	Unforgiven	Clint Eastwood	Clint Eastwood	CAA

- Figure 10.4   Movie entity with added data for agency

This leads us to apply third normal form and move the actor and his agency out into another entity. The new model is shown here.

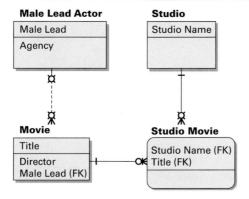

- Studio/Movie database in third normal form

■ Apply the Normal Forms to a Database Model

You have seen how to apply the first three normal forms to a simple database. The rules can be neatly summarized as "Each attribute must be a fact about the key, the whole key, and nothing but the key." In fact, if you think of the normal forms as expressing a *closeness of coupling* between the entity and attribute, or ask the question "which entity does this attribute most closely belong to?" you will find these first three rules are actually easy to apply. Normalization is a formal method for checking and determining the relationships between the attributes of an entity—each attribute should have a one-to-one relationship with the identifier of the entity. The process for designing a data model that you learned in Chapters 8 and 9 will take you a long way toward satisfying the basics of normalization without having to worry too hard about the rules.

■ The Fourth and Fifth Normal Forms

The last two rules are more abstract and few database designers

Cross Check

Applying Normal Form

In the mailing database the entity with phone numbers needs a little work to clean up the design. The Phone Number entity holds several different phone numbers and the set of numbers is associated with an Address. Each set of phone numbers is associated with a Person.

Some of the issues around phone numbers have not been modeled well. For instance, does a cell phone have an address? For this database, where the numbers are used for contacting people, the beauty of the cell phone is that it works in any location within its range. If a phone number is shared by several people, but they each have a separate cell phone (as might happen in a college dorm), the data has to be repeated.

The current data model is shown in Figure 10.5.

The entity for Phone Number needs to be normalized.

1. Which normal form is violated here?

2. Design a new entity to replace this.

3. Adjust the relationships to Address and Person to reflect the new structure of the Phone Number entity.

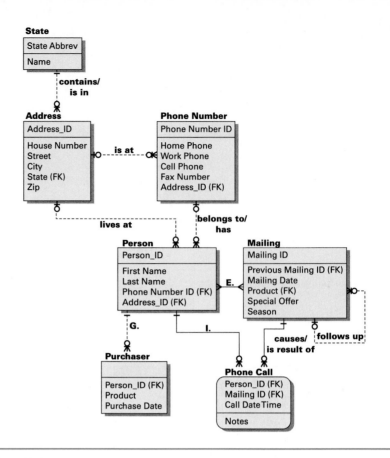

• **Figure 10.5**   Mailing database with Phone Number entity

consciously try to enforce them, but you do need to know them and recognize them because they can be a serious cause of performance problems in large databases. For both of these normal forms, the business rules must require their use. In other words, the conditions for implementing them may exist, but you may choose not to because the business needs of the database do not require it.

Fourth Normal Form: Isolate Independent Multiple Relationships

Fourth normal form states: "No entity may contain two or more 1:m or m:m relationships that are not logically related."

Let's extend our example a little more.

In the movie business the distribution rights for each movie are sold in a marketing region. A region can be a group of countries or simply a single country. Say your first attempt at modeling this data gave an ERD as shown in Figure 10.6.

There are really two relationships supported in this resolution entity: Title is sold in Region; Region is made up of Country. The first is a m:m, the second a 1:m. When you examine the data you will see that the country data has been inserted repeatedly and that the relationship between the North

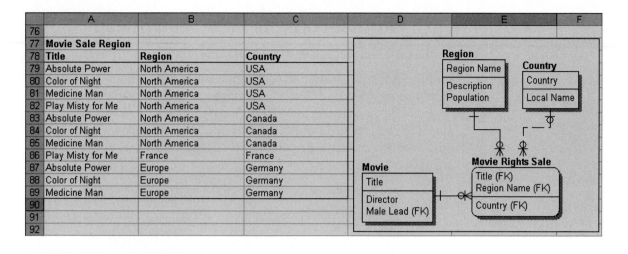

	A	B	C	D	E	F
76						
77	Movie Sale Region					
78	Title	Region	Country			
79	Absolute Power	North America	USA			
80	Color of Night	North America	USA			
81	Medicine Man	North America	USA			
82	Play Misty for Me	North America	USA			
83	Absolute Power	North America	Canada			
84	Color of Night	North America	Canada			
85	Medicine Man	North America	Canada			
86	Play Misty for Me	France	France			
87	Absolute Power	Europe	Germany			
88	Color of Night	Europe	Germany			
89	Medicine Man	Europe	Germany			
90						
91						
92						

• **Figure 10.6**   Movie rights sales ERD and sample data

America region and the four movies is in the data twice. There is more data here than you need to support the two relationships. In fact, you could say that the two relationships are *not* logically related. A title is sold into a region, but it is irrelevant to the title/region relationship what makes up the region. It does not change the title/region relationship if the region is a continent or a county in California. This is what we mean by logically independent. Thus, applying fourth normal form, they should not be represented in the same resolution entity. You should split the relationships to keep the 1:m and m:m separate, as shown in the following illustration:

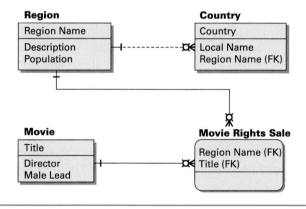

• Revised Movie data model to enforce fourth normal form

Fifth Normal Form: Isolate Semantically Related Multiple Relationships

Fifth normal form states: "Logically related many-to-many relationships should be separated if practical constraints on the information require it."

In the movie business the distribution rights for each movie are sold in a marketing region according to the medium. Typical media include Theatrical, Video (Purchase), Video (Rental), Satellite, Cable TV, DVD. The following illustration is the data for a few of the movies from our example.

	A	B	C
81	**Movie Rights Sale**		
82	**Title**	**Region**	**Medium**
83	Absolute Power	North America	Cable TV
84	Absolute Power	North America	Video (Purchase)
85	Absolute Power	North America	Theatrical
86	Color of Night	North America	Network TV
87	Color of Night	North America	Video (Purchase)
88	Color of Night	North America	Theatrical
89	Medicine Man	France	Satellite
90	Medicine Man	France	Video (Rental)
91	Play Misty for Me	France	Satellite
92	Play Misty for Me	France	Theatrical

• Movie Rights data with Medium added

This does not look suspicious; it is simply a resolution table between three entities. If you like, it represents a three-way m:m:m relationship. The ERD for this looks a little like a star with the resolution entity in the middle and others at the points of the star.

The movie industry is famous for making up new ways of doing business, and one of the rights sales companies determined that it was much more efficient—in business terms, that is—to sell a package of rights. They would bundle together Cable, Network, Satellite, Video Purchase, and Rental all in one deal. This means that for every title/region you would have to insert 5 rows of data in this resolution table. For the four titles and two regions you have in the illustration, this means 40 rows of data to insert ($4 \times 2 = 8$ title/region combinations $\times$ 5 media).

> When designing a database, keep in mind how many rows a table might contain. The number of rows will determine which are the core or major tables and which are look-up or code tables.

There is a better way. Though these relationships are logically related, they could be separated into three m:m relations. These three relationships contain the same information as the previous one, but now, to sell packages of rights, you need only insert 20 rows in the Movie Medium resolution entity, 8 rows in the Movie Region entity, and 10 rows in the Region Medium entity. This is a total of 38 inserts, which saves us two insert operations over the three-way resolution table that you started with. Though it doesn't seem like much, this can represent a major saving in processor time, disk accesses, and other practical issues in a large database.

How you draw the diagram is quite important in enabling you to recognize this situation. If you draw it correctly, showing the symmetry that exists in the data structure, you'll see a transformation from a star to a delta layout of entities and relationships.

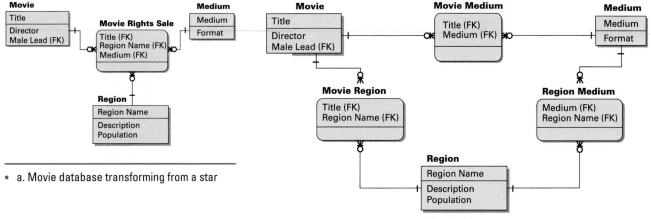

- a. Movie database transforming from a star

- b. Movie database transforming to a delta

What you have done here is to change the logical ERD to satisfy a need for improved performance in the physical implementation of the database. This change to satisfy fifth normal form is only of benefit in a few limited situations, primarily those where a very high proportion of the possible object relationships will be recorded. In this case the change of business practice—selling rights in packages—led to the change of the model. If the three-way resolution entity only contains a small fraction of the possible rows, then the three-way resolution entity is liable to be more efficient.

The fifth normal form is very rarely used—we've only seen it used in one case in 12 years of designing databases.

■ The Rules You Really Need

In the previous sections you learned about the five normal forms for relational data. You've seen that the last two only occur rarely. The natural question is "which rules can I break and get away with it?" Like all lawbreaking, this depends on how much of a penalty you are prepared to pay.

To keep the risks of bad data and inefficiencies to a minimum, you must follow the first three normal form rules when you design your database. After you have levered and twisted your design into third normal form, you may consider bending one or more of the rules to enhance the application performance. Experienced designers will often denormalize a design, *but only after it has been properly normalized.* Do not think you can take a shortcut and just go straight to the semi-normalized design. Every time we have done this in a design, we have had to come back and correct a major flaw that was missed in the original.

■ Anomalies in the Data

Normalizing is like obeying the law: You know things will go smoothly if you obey the law and there are penalties if you break the rules. One of the worst penalties you pay for not normalizing your design is that you risk anomalies in the data. An anomaly occurs when two different pieces of data can be found describing the same record or when a piece of data exists in

Normalizing the Data

Case Study

You are asked to normalize the Clapham Store's till receipts in their database. Currently they have the following information in a single database table: Till_Receipt_No, Customer_ID, First_Name, Last_Name, Address, Sale_Date_Time, Product_SKU1, Product_Name1, Quantity1, Item_Price1, Product_SKU2, Product_Name2, Quantity2, Item_Price2, Product_SKU3, Product_Name3, Quantity3, Item_Price3.

For this exercise, you will need a pencil and paper.

Step 1

Given the Clapham Store data, place the database in first normal form (1NF) by eliminating the repeating groups of data. Break the entity into two entities: Sale and Sale_Item. Include the Till_Receipt_No, Sale_Date_Time, and customer information in the Sale entity. Designate the Till_Receipt_No attribute as the primary key for the Sale entity. Take the repeating group of Product_SKU1, Product_Name1, Quantity1, and Item_Price1 and put them in the Sale_Item entity (remove the final "1" from the attribute names). Designate Till_Receipt_No and Product_SKU as the primary key for the Sale_Item entity. Draw a 1:m identifying relationship from Sale to Sale_Item since the item cannot exist without the sale.

Step 2

Place the database in second normal form (2NF) by ensuring that every non-key attribute depends on the entire primary key. As the Product_Name attribute is dependent only on the Product_SKU, not on the whole primary key of Sale_Item, create a new entity labeled Product. Move the Product_SKU and Product_Name attributes into the Product entity. Since the "Product_" part of the name is now redundant, reduce the attribute names to SKU and Name. Draw a 1:m identifying relationship from Product to Sale_Item. Incidentally, did you notice that this primary key only allows a product to be in a particular Sale once? You cannot have three tins of cat food as quantity 1 on each of three separate lines; you must enter it as quantity 3.

Step 3

Place the database in third normal form (3NF) by ensuring that no non-key attribute can depend on another non-key attribute. Currently, the customer attributes are not dependent on the Till_Receipt_No in the Sale entity; rather, they are dependent on the Customer_ID attribute. Create a new Customer entity that contains the Customer_ID attribute as the primary key, and First_Name, Last_Name, and Address as attributes. Update the Sale entity to contain only the Customer_ID, Till_Receipt_No, and Sale_Date_Time attributes. Draw a 1:m nonidentifying, optional relationship from Customer to Sale. The relationship is optional to allow a Sale to be made to a person who is not in the customer list.

You should now have successfully normalized the Clapham Specialty Store sales receipts database to third normal form (3NF).

one place in the database but a corresponding piece that should be there is missing. There are three types of anomaly: insert, delete, and update anomalies. Most anomalies can be prevented by applying the first, second, and third normal form.

Anomalies usually have to be caught and corrected in the software application that uses the database. Developers must put a lot more effort into making code that protects your database from the anomalies that your design will let through. You will not be popular with the application developers!

Insert

Insert anomalies are the result of inserting incomplete data into a database. Some anomalies arise from incorrect use of optional relationships and attributes; some arise from redundant data. If the database is not fully normalized (at least to 3NF), then there are opportunities for the insertion of data to be incomplete. For example, if the data is supposed to be in two different columns, it would be simple to insert data into one and miss the other.

Delete

Delete anomalies are the result of deleting data in such a way that other data is also lost.

In the Studio Movie data you saw in Figure 10.1, you might delete the Hollywood Pictures row. Unfortunately this would also delete the directors as well as their movies. In this case you are losing not only the studio data but also the movie titles and the directors. While the first deletion is intentional, probably the others are not.

If the database is normalized, then any attempt to delete the "Hollywood Pictures" Studio would be prevented by the foreign key constraint between Studio and Studio Movie.

Update

Update anomalies , however, can happen even when you have relational integrity active in the database. Update anomalies generally occur when you have redundant data; that is, data that is represented twice in the database.

Look at the data in the first example:

	A	B	C	D	E
1	Studio Movie				
2	Studio	Movie 1	Director 1	Movie 2	Director 2
3	Artisan Entertainment	Twin Peaks	David Lynch	Terminator 2	James Cameron
4	Carolco	Rocky	John Avildsen	Rocky 2	Sylvestor Stallone
5	Cinergi	Tombstone	George Cosmatos	Medicine Man	John McTiernan
6	Malpaso Pictures	Absolute Pow	Clint Eastwood	Garden of Good and Evil	Clint Eastwood
7	MGM.UA Studios	Terminator	James Cameron		
8	Hollywood Pictures	Medicine Man	John McTiernan	Color of Night	Richard Rush
9	Warner Bros	Unforgiven	Clint Eastwood	Play Misty for Me	Clint Eastwood

• Studio Movie data

If you want to change the Director of *Medicine Man*, it would be simple to find *Medicine Man* in the Movie 1 attribute and set the Director 1 on the same row to John Huston.

Now you have an update anomaly in which line 5 says John McTiernan is the director and line 8 says John Huston is the director of *Medicine Man*.

Clearly they cannot both be correct. These two versions of the truth represent an anomaly.

A Tax on Being Law-Abiding

A final point: There is a tax to pay for following the rules. When you separate the attribute of an entity to normalize the database, you have to use SQL joins to put them back together when you query. This takes computational time, and may lead to slower performance than you would like. For this reason, database designs are often partially denormalized in a practical real-world situation. By replicating some data and *creating new redundancies*, it may be possible to reduce the computation effort and query the database more quickly.

This is part of the art of database design: balancing the needs of accuracy and efficiency of updating with the speed and simplicity of querying.

■ Moving from Logical to Physical Models

In the previous sections we discussed some situations where you change the design of the logical model to satisfy the needs of the physical implementation. It is appropriate at this time to examine the translation from logical to physical model and some of the consequences of design choices.

Choosing Your Engine

The major reason for logical modeling is that you can design a database that is independent of the database engine you choose. In this way you can postpone the decision of which vendor's engine to use until you have all the details necessary to make a good, informed choice.

This is great theory but, in practice, you will nearly always find that the engine has been chosen long before the project started. The choice usually depends on the following criteria:

- **What is the company standard?** "We have to use Oracle because we've already purchased unlimited licenses from Oracle Corporation."

- **What are the available skills of the people?** "Nobody in the company knows SQL Server, so we always go with Oracle."

- **How big is this database going to be?** 10MB, 1GB, 100GB, 10TB …

If you do not have a decision forced on you, the last criterion is often the deciding factor: "Anything less than 10MB we can do with MS Access; bigger than that and we switch to Oracle."

These may not be very scientific reasons for the database system choice, but they involve the biggest argument of all: *money!* In terms of the capabilities of the different databases, there is little to choose between them, particularly with SQL as a common denominator. In this book we assume the database is big enough to warrant the use of Oracle and that the company standards do not prohibit its use.

Changing Terminology

The biggest change that you have to cope with from the logical to physical models is a change of terminology. Table 10.1 lists the basic translations that convert a logical model to a physical one.

Fortunately these translations are sufficiently mechanical that the database modeling tools can do a good job of executing them for us. Some relationships require multiple constraints to implement them correctly (for example, a one-to-one relationship needs both a foreign key and a unique constraint on the foreign key for physical implementation), so you will need to check the validity and accuracy of your physical data model.

In the following chapters you will deal mainly with the physical terminology.

Translating Super and Subtypes

The conversion of super and subtype entities and the cluster relationship is somewhat more complex because of the wide variety of choices to be made when creating the physical data model. The various translations necessary are listed in Table 10.2.

Table 10.1	General Transformations from Logical to Physical Models	
Logical Model	**Physical Model**	**Comment**
Entity	Table	Usually this is just a simple one-to-one translation. Some types of relationships change the translation (see Super/Subtype).
Attribute	Column	Most commonly this is a simple one-to-one translation. Most modeling tools will convert the generic datatype of the attribute into a specific datatype of the database engine.
Identifier	Primary Key	A table can only have one primary key, though it can have other unique indexes.
Relationship, Identifying	Foreign Key	The foreign key columns will be part of the primary key of the child table.
Relationship, Mandatory Role	Foreign Key	The columns in the child table will be mandatory or "NOT NULL" columns.
Relationship, Optional Role	Foreign Key	The columns in the foreign key can have NULL values.
Relationship, Many-to-many	Resolution table, two identifying foreign keys	This translation is more complex and involves the conversion of the relationship to a table.
Domain	Datatype and check constraint	This is a constraint on the values that can be entered in a column. Domains, datatypes, and check constraints are explained in more detail in Chapter 11, where we look at ensuring data quality.
Super/Subtype cluster	Multiple entities and foreign keys	This is a complex translation explained in more detail in Table 10.2.

	All Tables	**Supertype Tables Only**	**Subtype Tables Only**
	Table 10.2	**Translation of Super/Subtypes from Logical to Physical Models**	
Super Entity	Super table	Columns for all attributes from both super- and subtypes.	Copy the attributes into all of the subtype tables.
Sub Entity	One sub table for each sub entity	Copy the extra attributes as columns into the super table. Do not make sub tables.	Columns for all attributes from this subtype and the supertype. Each subtype table may have a different column set.
Relations	1:1 foreign keys from super to sub	The relationships from subtypes should be implemented as triggers.	Each subtype table has its own foreign key relations.
Discriminator Attribute	Not required, though you might use one.	Mandatory. If the cluster is inclusive, the discriminator attribute must be part of the primary key.	Do not use a discriminator. The discriminator information becomes part of the table name.
Comments	Rarely is this an optimal solution. You should try to avoid 1:1 relationships.	If the cluster is incomplete, it is easy to add another subtype later without changing the data model (you just add another value in the discriminator). The relationships to other entities can become complex to manage.	Implementing an exclusive cluster requires that the sub tables check each other's contents to ensure no duplicates appear in other subtype tables. This must be implemented with triggers.
Conclusion	Not recommended	One table but potentially complex relationships using triggers.	Multiple tables and simpler relationships.

Chapter 10 Review

Chapter Summary

After reading this chapter and completing the Step-by-Step tutorial and Cross Check, you should understand the following facts about database normalization:

Describe the Benefits of Normalizing a Database

- Database normalization is a technique that helps to improve the efficiency and accuracy of a database by removing redundant data and clarifying relationships.

- Guidelines for ensuring that databases are normalized are referred to as normal forms.

- Normalization may cause increased use of computer resources. A trade-off between update efficiency and querying performance affects the level of denormalization required.

Describe Data Dependency and Determinacy

- Dependent attributes are ones where the value can be determined from one or more other attributes.

- A determinant is a set of attributes that can uniquely identify the value in another attribute.

- A transitive dependency exists when an attribute is indirectly dependent on another attribute through a third attribute or another entity.

Define the Five Normal Forms of Data

- Normal forms are numbered from first normal form or (1NF) through fifth normal form (5NF).

- When a table has no repeating groups of data, it is said to be in first normal form (1NF).

- A table is in second normal form (2NF) if every non-key column depends on the entire primary key—eliminating partial dependencies.

- Third normal form (3NF) requires that no non-key column can depend on another non-key column—eliminating transitive dependencies.

- Fourth normal form (4NF) forbids logically independent relationships represented in one resolution entity.

- Fifth normal form (5NF) isolates logically related relationships into separate resolution entities.

- The first three normal forms (1NF, 2NF, and 3NF) will satisfy the database normalization requirements for the majority of databases.

Apply the Normal Forms to a Database Model

- Using good design practices during the early database design stages reduces the need for corrective action by normalization.

- Normalization is a response to the "closeness of coupling" between attributes in an entity.

Identify and Correct Data Anomalies

- Anomalies in the data are inconsistent data items. They are classified as insert, delete, and update anomalies.

- Insert and delete anomalies occur because of lack of implementation of foreign key constraints.

- Update anomalies occur because of redundant data.

Convert a Logical Model to Physical

- Translation for logical model to physical model is a deterministic process (can be accomplished by a machine).

- Optimization (including some denormalization) of the model may be necessary for good overall performance.

Key Terms

first normal form *(275)*

second normal form *(277)*

third normal form *(278)*

fourth normal form *(280)*

fifth normal form *(282)*

anomaly *(283)*

delete anomaly *(285)*

denormalize *(283)*

dependency *(273)*

dependent attribute *(273)*

determinant *(274)*

discriminator *(288)*

flat file *(277)*

insert anomaly *(285)*

normalization *(273)*

repeating group *(275)*

transitive dependency *(274)*

transitively dependent *(274)*

update anomaly *(285)*

Key Term Quiz

Use the Key Terms list to complete the sentences that follow. Not all terms will be used.

1. A table is in _____ if every non-key column depends on the entire primary key.

2. _____ is the process of ensuring that a database is most accurate and efficient in its storage of data.

3. An identifier in a logical model converts to a(n) _____.

4. _____ are caused by poor database design and result when information is inserted, deleted, or updated causing the information to be lost unexpectedly.

5. When a table has no repeating groups of data, it is said to be in _____.

Matching Definition Quiz

Relate each term on the left with the appropriate description on the right.

Term		Description	
1.	Update anomaly	a.	Breaks up logically independent relationships
2.	Third normal form (3NF)	b.	An attribute whose value is indirectly derived from a determinant attribute
3.	Transitive dependency	c.	Occurs when the database must make multiple changes to reflect a single value change
4.	Repeating groups	d.	Requires that no non-key column can depend on another non-key column
5.	Fourth normal form (4NF)	e.	A set of attributes that appear more than once in an entity

Multiple-Choice Quiz

1. An entity that has violated first normal form has
   a. Missing primary key
   b. No attributes
   c. Repeating groups
   d. A resolution table
   e. No determinants

2. What is the minimum number of attributes you can have in a repeating group?
   a. None
   b. 1
   c. 2
   d. 3
   e. Number of groups less 1

3. An identifier in the logical model translates to a
   a. Table
   b. Attribute
   c. Column
   d. Primary key
   e. Foreign key

4. A resolution table is the physical implementation of a
   a. Dependent relationship
   b. Identifier
   c. Many-to-many relationship
   d. Entity
   e. Foreign key

5. When not all data is available a problem may occur when a row cannot be added to a table. This problem is known as a(n)
   a. Insert anomaly
   b. Delete anomaly
   c. Determinant
   d. Primary key
   e. Update anomaly

6. A table for a sale contains Product_ID, Customer_ID, the customer name and address. Which normal form has been violated?

   a. First

   b. Second

   c. Third

   d. Fourth

   e. Fifth

7. To satisfy fourth normal form, you should separate relationships in an entity that are

   a. Logically dependent

   b. Logically independent

   c. One-to-one

   d. Identifying

   e. Recursive

8. A one-to-many relationship translates to

   a. Primary key

   b. Identifier

   c. Resolution table

   d. Column

   e. Foreign key constraint

9. When attribute B depends on attribute A and attribute C depends on attribute B, then the relation between A and C is known as a(n)

   a. Identifier

   b. Logical relationship

   c. Foreign key

   d. Transitive dependency

   e. Mandatory relationship

10. The process of ensuring that a database is most efficient and accurate is known as

    a. Normalization

    b. Fifth normal form

    c. Physical data model

    d. An anomaly

    e. Denormalization

11. When the non-key columns of a table are dependent only on the whole primary key, which normal form(s) is it in?

    a. First normal form

    b. Second normal form

    c. Third normal form

    d. First and second normal form

    e. First, second, and third normal form

12. The set of attributes that uniquely define the value of another attribute is

    a. Determinant

    b. Normalized

    c. Identifier

    d. Primary key

    e. Foreign key

13. Which normal forms do most designers skip when designing databases? (Select more than one.)

    a. Fifth

    b. Fourth

    c. Third

    d. Second

    e. First

14. Who first devised the normal forms of a database model?

    a. C. J. Date

    b. James Martin

    c. Clive Finkelstein

    d. Dr. E. F. Codd

    e. Simon Chatwin

15. To satisfy second normal form, the attributes in an entity must depend on

    a. The whole primary key

    b. Part of the primary key

    c. A determinant

    d. A dependent entity

    e. Only the primary key

Essay Quiz

1. What problems may occur with a database that is not normalized?

2. What are the trade-offs that are typically made in normalizing a database?

3. What is the difference between a determinant and a dependent attribute? Give two examples.

4. When were the normal forms first introduced, and by whom?

5. Why do most databases implement just the first, second, and third normal forms?

Lab Projects

• Lab Project 10.1

You have been asked to normalize a database for the New Brunswick Figure Skating Association. The data that is to be stored in this database relates to figure skaters, skating schools and locations, skating skills, and skill levels. You will need a pencil and paper.

　You have been given the data from the NB Figure Skating Association in a large flat file with the following columns:

Skater Number
Skater Name
School Number
School Name
School Location
Skill Number 1
Skill Number 2
Skill Number 3

Skill Name 1
Skill Name 2
Skill Name 3
Skill Location 1 (where the skill was learned)
Skill Location 2
Skill Location 3
Skill Level 1
Skill Level 2
Skill Level 3

Then do the following:

1. Normalize the database to first normal form (1NF).

2. Normalize the database to second normal form (2NF).

3. Normalize the database to third normal form (3NF).

• Lab Project 10.2

Case Study

Using the Clapham Specialty Store case study, John would like to find out how the product's location in the store affects sales. To do this, you must record the product's particular location and compare that with the rate of sales at different time periods. The ERD for the Product and Location is shown in Figure 10.7.

　You should extend the existing Product entity to add attributes for the location and the time in that location. Draw the revised ERD.

1. Which normal form is being violated?

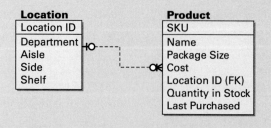

• **Figure 10.7** Product and Location for Clapham Specialty Store

2. Redesign the entity to bring it into normalization. (Ensure you leave the relationship between Product and Location in place.)

3. Explain what your model means:

   - Can a product be in more than one location at a time?

   - Can a product be put back into a previous location?

   - What does this Location ID in Product entity refer to?

4. Change the identifier of Product Location to allow a product to be displayed in several locations simultaneously.

5. By having Location relate directly to Product, and Location relate to Product via the Product Location, you have some redundant data. Which normal form has been violated here?

6. Remove a relationship to correct the violation.

Analyzing Data Quality Issues

"Facts are stubborn.
Statistics are more pliable."
—MARK TWAIN

In this chapter, you will learn how to

- **Define datatypes and enforce mandatory columns**
- **Describe a data domain**
- **Implement column and table constraints on data values**
- **Use unique indexes to limit primary key values**
- **Convert relationships into foreign key constraints**
- **Describe the benefits and limits of declarative relational integrity**
- **Create names for various database constraints**

ntil now you have been learning the theory behind creating data models and databases. You've learned what elements are found in a database and how to design models of databases to suit your business needs. You've learned the basics of designing a database's structure and the need for normalization. This chapter is going to be a lot more fun, because you're going to step out of the realm of theory and start getting your hands dirty. In this chapter you will learn about the physical data model and how to ensure the quality of the data stored in a database. You'll do this with a number of practical exercises starting with creating a table and dealing with datatypes and missing values or NULLs. Then you will see how to limit the data values in each column and implement constraints on the data. As you go through these exercises you'll see a number of different Oracle errors and we'll show you how to make them more meaningful. You'll learn about indexes and some of the ways they can help improve the data quality. Finally you'll do a couple of exercises that show some of the benefits and limitations of declarative relational integrity.

■ Datatypes and Missing Data: Quality Basics

In the previous chapters on design, we have talked at length about optional attributes and optional roles in relationships. When you convert these from the logical to the physical data model, you end up with columns that allow missing data. In the logical data model, you did not deal with datatypes. Datatypes are your first line of defense against the ravening hordes of bad data out there.

Handling Missing Values

Sometimes data is missing because there simply is no data to go there; sometimes it's missing because the value is just not known yet—there's a time delay before we can add the data. All large modern database engines support a special value that we use for missing or unknown values. This is `NULL` . NULL exists for all datatypes.

Beware of what NULL is *not*: It is not zero (0) or infinity or any other magic number. It is not a special date, 01/01/01 or 09/09/99. It is not a string full of spaces or "white text." NULL has some interesting properties too. If you compare two values and one of them is NULL, what would you expect the answer to be?

```
IF first_name = NULL
THEN
...
END IF;
```

Since NULL means unknown, this If expression will always evaluate to False. Even if First_Name holds this NULL value, we still evaluate this to False.

When a column in a table is declared to be optional, we are really saying it can hold NULL values. Conversely a mandatory column is said to be NOT NULL. If you try to insert a row into a table and do not have a value to insert in a `NOT NULL` column, the database will refuse to save the row and give you a missing data error.

When you design your database you should consider carefully whether you really need the column to be NULL. In many cases you can convert the column to be NOT NULL and use a default value to replace the NULLs. This has some performance advantages as NULLs do not appear in indexes. In large databases with complex requirements, some of the queries used for reporting the data can be greatly simplified if you do not have to handle NULLs in the query.

What do you get if you have an expression 34 × NULL? The NULL overrides and the answer is NULL. For all the math operators in the database, NULL will override any result. `Null propagation` is one of the unfortunate features of using NULLs to represent missing values.

Apples and Oranges: Defining Datatypes

Let's look at another comparison expression:

```
IF pay_rate = 'Simon'
THEN
...
END IF;
```

Does this make any sense to you? Would you stay in a job that paid you at 'Simon' per hour? Would you prefer to be paid at 'Chris' per hour? Neither makes any sense, because neither is a numeric value. To prevent these sorts of weird confusions in a database, you must assign a datatype to each column. You can do this in the logical data model, but it is absolutely required in the physical data model. The datatype will be enforced by the database engine to ensure that you cannot enter a string ('Simon') into a numerical column (Pay_Rate).

Oracle offers us these basic datatypes, from which all the other datatypes we might need can be created:

- NUMBER
- CHAR
- VARCHAR2
- DATE
- LOB

NUMBER

- **NUMBER** A signed numerical value

You can determine both the **precision** of the number (total number of significant digits) and the **scale** (number of decimal places). Precision must be larger than scale as it counts all digits, not just those to the left of the decimal place. The biggest number Oracle can handle accurately is 38 significant digits. It can save bigger numbers but only as a floating-point type (in the range 1×10^{-130} to $9.99...9 \times 10^{125}$). Examples include the following:

Datatype	Scale	Precision	Examples	Not Saved as Entered
NUMBER (10)	10 digits	0 dec. places	1, null, -52, 9013467234	'Three', 13.2 (stored as 13)
NUMBER (8, 2)	8 digits	2 dec. places	0, -256, 13.23, 901346.72, null	90134.672 (stored as 90134.67), 'Forty Two', 90134678.2 (too many digits)

CHAR

- **CHAR** A fixed-length string (padded with spaces at the end)

You can specify the string length up to 2000 characters (a single-spaced 8.5 × 11 page holds about 1000 characters). These must be ASCII characters. The biggest drawback to this datatype is that Oracle automatically adds spaces to the end of any string you input to make it up to the required length. This can be a major nuisance when you need to search for data. When searching for data, you use a WHERE clause that compares two values:

```
WHERE first_name = my_name
```

If My_Name is a VARCHAR2 and First_Name is a CHAR, then Oracle will do a quick datatype conversion on First_Name to cast it into a VARCHAR2 (Oracle always casts the left side of a WHERE clause if datatypes do not match) and will include all the spaces in the name. So, for a particular row of data you get the following:

```
WHERE 'Simon     ' = 'Simon'
```

The database, quite correctly, says these are not equal and does not display the row. However, this was probably not what you intended. You can correct this by trimming the spaces from the CHAR:

```
WHERE RTRIM(first_name) = my_name
```

Datatype	Constant Size	Examples	Not Allowed
CHAR(4)	4 characters	'.PDF', '2 ', 'Yes', '', null	'Madison'

VARCHAR2

- **VARCHAR2** A variable length string

This is the most commonly used string datatype. Since it is variable length, it only uses the occupied space of the string to save it to disk. If you save 'George' into a VARCHAR2(20) column, only six characters will be stored on the disk. This not only saves disk space but also improves performance since fewer characters have to be read to and from the disk. A limit of 4000 characters is imposed by Oracle. If you want to store something bigger than this, you must use a large object.

For all the string datatypes, apostrophes are a problem. Since single quotes are used to delimit a string, having an apostrophe in the middle of a string is often interpreted as the end of the string. Oracle requires you to double up the apostrophe in the string to get it entered correctly.

Datatype	Max. Size	Examples	Not Allowed
VARCHAR2(20)	20 characters	'.PDF', '2', 'Affirmative', '', null, 'O''Connor'	'Madison Square Gardens'

Inside Information

VARCHAR and VARCHAR2

Why VARCHAR2? Why not just plain VARCHAR? This is a peculiarity unique to Oracle. While they do have a VARCHAR datatype, they do not recommend using it and have been threatening to change the way the VARCHAR type works for many years. There is no apparent difference from the database user's perspective, though the internal coding of Oracle's engine may treat them differently. You should always use VARCHAR2 in Oracle.

DATE

- **DATE**   A representation of a date and time

Dates and times are stored in a single datatype in Oracle. Some other databases separate Date, Time, and Timestamp—a combination date/time datatype—as different datatypes. In Oracle dates are stored in an internal 7-byte datatype with each byte corresponding to century, year, month, day, hour, minute, and second respectively. This representation allows an Oracle database to easily deal with leap years and other anomalies in the calendar (such as the adjustment made in 1582 A.D. when 10 days were removed from that year to reset the calendar). When using dates in calculations, you can assume that the date is measured in days and decimal parts of a day so that '05-JAN-1953' + 5 = '10-JAN-1953'. Most of the issues around dates come in trying to enter them or read them from the database when you have to format the date to or from a string. The default format for dates is usually DD-MON-YY as shown in these examples:

Datatype	Scale	Formatted	Stored As
DATE	7 bytes	21-FEB-2003	20-03-02-21-00-00-00
		12:56:34 AM	00-00-00-00-56-34
		10-JAN-2003	(= 0.0392824 days)
		17:29:45	20-03-01-10-17-29-45

LOB

- **LOB**   A Large OBject

LOBs come in two main forms in Oracle: BLOB and CLOB, which are binary and character LOBs respectively. We will not be using LOBs in this book. In Oracle they can be binary or ASCII objects up to 4GB in size. Their storage and handling is very different from the regular datatypes and they cannot easily be used for searching.

Choosing a Datatype

In most cases the choice of datatype is clear. Anything that is a number and has arithmetic done on it should be a number; dates are easily identified and then all the rest are strings!

Okay, here's a question then: How would you store a telephone number? It is clearly all digits so could easily be a number. You should ask yourself three leading questions to determine if a number is really a number:

- Do you do math with it? For phone numbers the answer is no. If "no," you should strongly consider a string datatype; if "yes," you must use a numerical datatype.

- Can you ignore leading zeros? For SKU barcode numbers: "0012345678912" is a valid barcode. If it's stored as a number it will be shortened to "12345678912" when you retrieve it from the database. If "no," you must use a string datatype; if "yes," you could use a numerical datatype.

- If you were to sort a result set according to the values in the column, do you want the result in numerical order or alphabetical order? Should the order be 1,2,3,4,10,11 or 1,10,11,2,3,4? If numerical order is important, a numerical datatype is preferable; if alphabetical order is okay, you can use a string datatype.

Choosing the length and precision for the datatype requires more careful thought. You should try to get enough length for the longest value, but don't overestimate as you'll pay for it in unused disk space and slightly reduced performance. For money (accounting systems), you should usually pick just two decimal places. Rounding errors are the bane of the accounting computer person's life—there have been several tales of computer fraud where the rounded-off fractions from each transaction were transferred to one person's account. That account became worth several hundred thousand dollars within a very short time and no one noticed because the rounding was happening just as normal in all the transactions.

Step-by-Step 11.01

Creating a Table and Inserting Data

Let's experiment a bit with creating a table and entering some data using different datatypes.

For this exercise, you will need Oracle9*i* Database Server with the SQL*Plus tool.

Step 1

Open your copy of SQL*Plus and log in to the database. You should see the SQL> prompt. You are going to create the PERSON table with datatypes and optionality shown in the diagram and insert a few rows of data. Watch carefully for the messages that SQL*Plus gives you after you press the ENTER key each time.

Person

Person_ID: NUMBER(10) NOT NULL
First_Name: VARCHAR2(40) NULL
Last_Name: VARCHAR2(40) NOT NULL
Address_ID: NUMBER(10) NULL

Step 2

At the prompt type this:

```
DROP TABLE person;
CREATE TABLE person
(person_id     NUMBER(10)    NOT NULL,
 first_name    VARCHAR2(40)  NULL,
 last_name     VARCHAR2(40)  NOT NULL,
 address_id    NUMBER(10)    NULL );
```

Step 3

After the last line, press ENTER; Oracle should confirm your action by telling you "Table Created." If you see a different message, you will need to correct your typing and try again.

Step 4

As a quick check that the table really was created as you expected, type

```
DESC person
```

You should see this screen of SQL*Plus commands and confirmations:

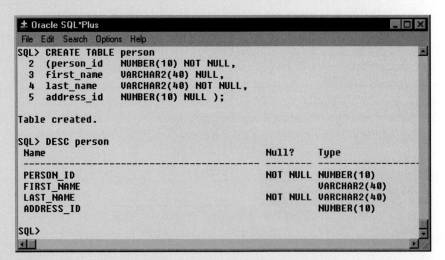

```
Oracle SQL*Plus                                              _ □ ✕
File  Edit  Search  Options  Help
SQL> CREATE TABLE person
  2  (person_id    NUMBER(10) NOT NULL,
  3  first_name    VARCHAR2(40) NULL,
  4  last_name     VARCHAR2(40) NOT NULL,
  5  address_id    NUMBER(10) NULL );

Table created.

SQL> DESC person
 Name                                        Null?     Type
 ---------------------------------------- --------- ------------------
 PERSON_ID                                NOT NULL  NUMBER(10)
 FIRST_NAME                                         VARCHAR2(40)
 LAST_NAME                                NOT NULL  VARCHAR2(40)
 ADDRESS_ID                                         NUMBER(10)

SQL>
```

Step 5

Now you can enter some data. Each of these lines will give either a confirmation or an error message:

```
INSERT INTO person VALUES(1, 'Simon', 'Chatwin', null);
INSERT INTO person VALUES(2, 'Sting', null, null);
INSERT INTO person VALUES(2, '', 'Sting', null);
INSERT INTO person VALUES('Three', 'Chris', 'Allen', '13');
INSERT INTO person VALUES(3, 'Chris', 'Allen', '13');
INSERT INTO person VALUES(4, 'Catherine', 46, null);
```

After inserting values into Person, the summary of the database responses should be like this:

```
Oracle SQL*Plus                                              _ □ ✕
File  Edit  Search  Options  Help
SQL> INSERT INTO person VALUES(1, 'Simon', 'Chatwin', null);

1 row created.

SQL> INSERT INTO person VALUES(2, 'Sting', null, null);
INSERT INTO person VALUES(2, 'Sting', null, null)
*
ERROR at line 1:
ORA-01400: cannot insert NULL into ("MAILING"."PERSON"."LAST_NAME")


SQL> INSERT INTO person VALUES(2, '', 'Sting', null);

1 row created.

SQL> INSERT INTO person VALUES('Three', 'Chris', 'Allen', '13');
INSERT INTO person VALUES('Three', 'Chris', 'Allen', '13')
                          *
ERROR at line 1:
ORA-01722: invalid number


SQL> INSERT INTO person VALUES(3, 'Chris', 'Allen', '13');

1 row created.

SQL> INSERT INTO person VALUES(4, 'Catherine', 46, null);

1 row created.

SQL> |
```

A few things you should notice about the preceding Step-by-Step:

- The SQL commands are case-insensitive, but the data is case-sensitive. You will see this if you compare the table creation command you typed against the description that Oracle returned to you.

- The last insert treated the number 46 as a string and accepted it without question.

- Oracle cannot tell that 'Three' represents a number!

- Oracle treats both the word "NULL" and a pair of single quotes (an empty string) as NULL values.

Converting Datatypes: Weak and Strong Typing

The Step-by-Step exercise showed you that Oracle didn't really care what the datatype was except in one circumstance. So much for datatyping as a way to help you distinguish numbers from strings! SQL is a weakly typed language. Like early versions of Basic, Visual Basic, Perl, and others, it performs implicit datatype conversions when necessary to make an expression work. Only if these type conversions fail do you get an error message.

Oracle could not convert the string 'Three' to the digit 3, so it issued an "invalid number" error. However, it could convert the number 46 to a string '46' without any problem. It could also convert the string '13' to a number 13 without raising an error.

A strongly typed language would force an explicit declaration of datatype and not do any automatic datatype conversions for you. With this sort of language, the compiler will catch any strange use of a datatype; with a weakly typed language, it's up to you as the designer to ensure that the datatypes and values are accurate enough for the program to work.

■ Data Domains: Sanity Checks

The datatypes available are very basic—for instance, specifying that the Pay_Rate column is a NUMBER datatype will ensure that only numbers are entered, but it will not guarantee that *useful* numbers are entered. You would not want a negative pay rate; you might want to limit the pay rate to a maximum of $200/hr; you might want to enter pay rates that were all exact multiples of $10. In other words, you have a set of particular values that you will allow to be used. This is known as a domain .

Domains as Sets of Values

Domains may be defined in a number of different ways:

- By setting a range of maximum and minimum values
- By a formula that must evaluate to true
- By checking the value against a list of allowed values

Case Study

In the Clapham Specialty Store case study, we defined an EMPLOYEE table with a column for the Pay_Rate as shown here:

Employee

Employee_ID: NUMBER(10) NOT NULL

Supervisor_ID: NUMBER(10) NULL
Job_Type: VARCHAR2(20) NOT NULL
First_Name: VARCHAR2(20) NULL
Last_Name: VARCHAR2(20) NOT NULL
Social_Security_Number: CHAR(11) NOT NULL
Pay_Rate: NUMBER(8,2) NULL

• EMPLOYEE table design

The Pay_Rate domain would be defined by these formulas:

```
(pay_rate > 0)
 and (mod(pay_rate, 10) = 0)
 and (pay_rate <= 200)
```

If these expressions evaluate to true, the Pay_Rate number can be saved in the database. If not, an error is raised and the insertion fails. (This constraint is not checked if the Pay_Rate value is NULL.)

The Job_Type column also needs a more restrictive domain than just the VARCHAR2(20) datatype. The only values that would be useful for this business are: Owner, Delivery, and Register Clerk. You can implement this domain by checking that the value is in the list like so:

```
job_type in ('Owner', 'Delivery', 'Register Clerk')
```

Since Job_Type is a NOT NULL column, you must have a separate constraint on the column to enforce the "NOT NULL" rule.

To summarize, a domain consists of

- A datatype with length and, if appropriate, precision and scale

- NULL or NOT NULL restriction

- Limits on the values by formula or list

■ Column and Table Constraints

How do you implement the rules that have been expressed in the domains? Domains essentially limit the values that can be stored in the database. Or you can say they *constrain* the values. Many different constraints are implemented throughout the database to ensure the quality of the data that is stored there. These constraints are an expression of the operating rules of the business. They come from the conceptual model as told to you by the business owner and were further expressed in the logical data model.

Constraints exist in a relational database at four different levels:

- Column level

- Table level across columns

- Table level down columns (between values on rows)

- Intertable level

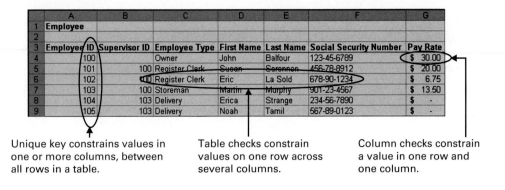

	A	B	C	D	E	F	G
1	Employee						
2							
3	Employee ID	Supervisor ID	Employee Type	First Name	Last Name	Social Security Number	Pay Rate
4	100		Owner	John	Balfour	123-45-6789	$ 30.00
5	101	100	Register Clerk	Susan	Sorennon	456-78-8912	$ 20.00
6	102	100	Register Clerk	Eric	La Sold	678-90-1234	$ 6.75
7	103	100	Storeman	Martin	Murphy	901-23-4567	$ 13.50
8	104	103	Delivery	Erica	Strange	234-56-7890	$ -
9	105	103	Delivery	Noah	Tamil	567-89-0123	$ -

Unique key constrains values in one or more columns, between all rows in a table.

Table checks constrain values on one row across several columns.

Column checks constrain a value in one row and one column.

• **Figure 11.1**   Different types of constraints on table data

The last of these is what you know as foreign key constraints deriving from the relationships. The scope of constraint types 1 through 3 are shown diagrammatically in Figure 11.1.

Column Constraints

Column constraints are the main way in which you implement domains. They provide a place to check the value entered against a limiting formula or expression.

Scope

How far a field (sorry about the pun!) can you go to find data to compare the column's value? A column constraint works only on the column the data is going into and only for that one row. You cannot compare values between different rows in a column constraint. This would be the task of a recursive foreign key constraint—see Chapter 9 for more details on this.

Rules

You can use any of Oracle's regular operators (+, *, -, OR, AND, and so on), any of the simple functions (MOD, INSTR, SUBSTR, DECODE, and so on), and also the Oracle system variables such as USER and SYSDATE. You've looked at the constraint for Pay_Rate and Job_Type in the preceding sections.

Actually, in the database, it is not easy to determine which are column constraints and which are table constraints since there is no flag or other attribute to tell you. You have to look at the expression that is enforced in the constraint to be able to tell if it's a column or a table constraint.

Let's try creating the table from Figure 11.1 complete with the constraints for Job_Type and Pay_Rate. In case you have a copy of the table from a previous chapter, we'll start by dropping any existing version of the table, along with any constraints that refer to it.

```
DROP TABLE employee CASCADE CONSTRAINTS;
CREATE TABLE employee (
        employee_id           NUMBER(10)   NOT NULL,
        supervisor_id         NUMBER(10)   NULL,
        first_name            VARCHAR2(20) NULL,
```

```
last_name                    VARCHAR2(20) NOT NULL,
social_security_number CHAR(11)      NOT NULL,
pay_rate                     NUMBER(8,2)  NULL,
job_type                     VARCHAR2(20) NOT NULL
);
```

When you declare a column as "NOT NULL" in the table specification you are really adding a check constraint to the column. You are saying to the database engine, "Values in this column must not be NULL."

So you could create a table without specifying the NULL/ NOT NULL option and then add individual check constraints afterwards by using the ALTER TABLE command:

```
ALTER TABLE employee
    ADD CONSTRAINT
    ck_employee_ssn_
    nt_null
    CHECK (social_security_
    number IS NOT NULL);
```

Actually, that is exactly how Oracle implements a NOT NULL column but since you don't specify a constraint name in the table definition, Oracle gives it one of the system default names like "SYS_012345." The shorthand of declaring the column NULL or NOT NULL is much simpler and more convenient.

You can add the constraints as separate statements by typing these:

```
ALTER TABLE employee
    ADD CONSTRAINT ck_employee_job_type_dmn
    CHECK (job_type in ('Owner', 'Delivery', 'Register Clerk')
        );
ALTER TABLE employee
    ADD CONSTRAINT ck_employee_pay_rate_dmn
    CHECK ((pay_rate > 0)
        and
        (mod(pay_rate, 10) = 0)
        and
        (pay_rate <= 200)
        );
```

You should see this as a screen confirmation:

```
Oracle SQL*Plus
File  Edit  Search  Options  Help

SQL> CREATE TABLE Employee (
  2         Employee_ID          NUMBER(10) NOT NULL,
  3         Supervisor_ID        NUMBER(10) NULL,
  4         First_Name           VARCHAR2(20) NULL,
  5         Last_Name            VARCHAR2(20) NOT NULL,
  6         Social_Security_Number CHAR(11) NOT NULL,
  7         Pay_Rate             NUMBER(8,2) NULL,
  8         Job_Type             VARCHAR2(20) NOT NULL
  9  );

Table created.

SQL> ALTER TABLE employee
  2         ADD CONSTRAINT ck_employee_job_type_dmn
  3         CHECK (job_type in ('Owner', 'Delivery', 'Register Clerk')
  4             );

Table altered.

SQL> ALTER TABLE employee
  2         ADD CONSTRAINT ck_employee_pay_rate_dmn
  3         CHECK (((pay_rate > 0)
  4                 and (mod(pay_rate, 10) = 0)
  5                 and (pay_rate <= 200)
  6             );

Table altered.

SQL> |
```

• Creating EMPLOYEE table with constraints

If you type **ED** ENTER at the SQL> prompt, you will open a Notepad or text editor window. This is much easier to use than the SQL*Plus line editor. When you have typed in the command correctly, close the window (ALT-F4) to return to SQL*Plus and type in a **/** (forward slash) followed by ENTER to execute the command.

Now try adding some values:

```
INSERT INTO employee VALUES
    (100, null, 'John', 'Balfour', '123-45-6789', 30, 'Owner');
INSERT INTO employee VALUES
    (101, 100, 'Susan', 'Saronnen', '456-78-8912', 20, 'Register Clerk');
```

```
INSERT INTO employee VALUES
    (102, 100, 'Eric', 'La Sold', '678-90-1234', 6.75, 'Register Clerk');
INSERT INTO employee VALUES
    (103, 100, 'Martin', 'Murphy', '901-23-4567', 13.5, 'Storeman');
INSERT INTO employee VALUES
    (104, 103, 'Erica', 'Strange', '234-56-7890', null, 'Delivery');
INSERT INTO employee VALUES
    (105, 103, 'Noah', 'Tamil', '567-89-0123', null, 'Delivery');
```

Running these commands will give you the confirmations and errors shown in Figure 11.2.

The error messages that Oracle generates can be pretty hard to understand. What makes them easier to understand is the name of the constraint that was violated. This is the name you typed in when you generated the constraint. If you had not bothered to type the name, Oracle would have generated a system name that looks something like "SYS_000870234," which is particularly unhelpful in determining what went wrong.

When designing a database, you should name all the constraints to simplify later troubleshooting.

Each row is treated separately when it comes to executing the constraint statements. You can see how some rows were correctly inserted and some not.

Table Constraints

Often we need to check the value being inserted against other values in the same row of data in the same table. This requirement exceeds the scope of

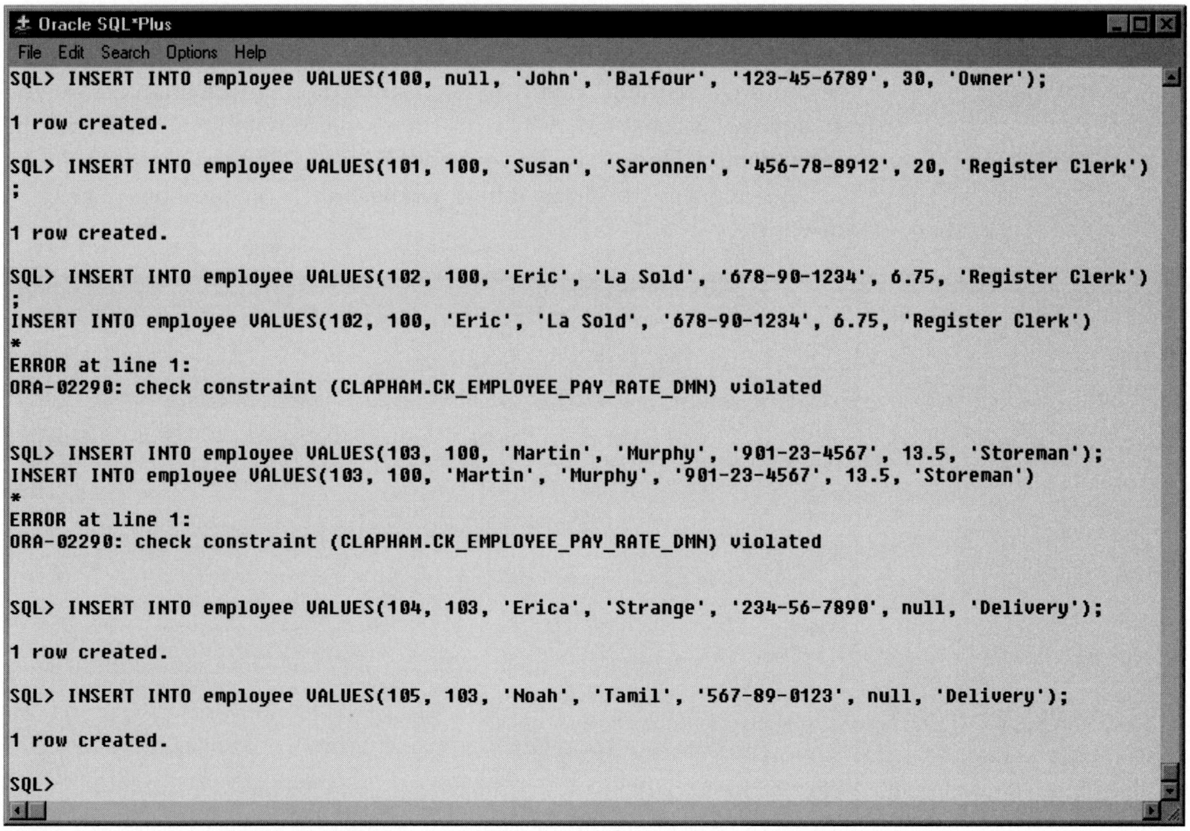

• **Figure 11.2**   Errors generated from inserting EMPLOYEE records

the column constraint, which cannot look outside the column. This is the second level of constraint: a **table constraint** .

Scope

In the mailing database we had a Mailing entity. The table design for MAILING looks like this:

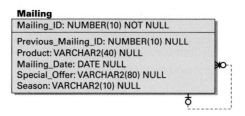

- The MAILING table

Let's say we had a new business rule added that a mailing must go out to the customers no later than 30 days into the season. This constraint requires the use of two columns from the table: Mailing_Date and Season. We should also add that if the season is unknown, this constraint should not apply.

You do not need any data from other tables to enforce this constraint, and all the data for the constraint is available on the same row of the table. The scope of the constraint is within the row of the table.

Intercolumn Constraints

The format and syntax for table-level constraints are exactly the same as for the column constraint. First, you need some more information before you can define this constraint. When does a season start and end? What are the season names? How early can you send a mailing? In this example a simple business request translates into a whole bunch of questions that need answering!

 Cross Check

Adding Check Constraints

You've seen how to add constraints to a table—both column-level and table-level check constraints. Now you can alter these constraints on the EMPLOYEE table to better fit the data.

1. Remove the existing Pay_Rate constraint using this syntax:

   ```
   ALTER TABLE employee DROP CONSTRAINT
   ck_employee_pay_rate_dmn;
   ```

2. Edit the Pay_Rate constraint to remove the requirement that all pay rates be an exact multiple of $10.

3. Add the new constraint back by altering the table again.

4. Check that the constraint is working by trying to insert the two rows that failed previously.

5. Describe how you would correct the remaining error.

	A	B	C
67	Season Dates		
68	Season	From	To
69	Spring	1-Apr	14-Jun
70	Summer	15-Jun	14-Oct
71	Fall	15-Oct	20-Dec
72	Winter	21-Dec	31-Mar

- Season start and end dates

Let's assume some of the answers and code a constraint as follows:

```
(season = 'Spring' AND mailing_date BETWEEN '21-DEC' AND '01-MAY') OR
(season = 'Summer' AND mailing_date BETWEEN '01-APR' AND '15-JUL') OR
(season = 'Fall' AND mailing_date BETWEEN '15-JUN' AND '15-NOV') OR
(season = 'Winter' AND mailing_date BETWEEN '15-OCT' AND '21-JAN')
```

Actually this particular constraint is quite difficult to format and code correctly. What is shown here is just the starting point. You should include the current year in the limits or, better yet, include the year number in the season. As you can see, this check constraint is starting to get complex and hard to understand, so you might find the design works better if you code these limits in the UI application rather than in the database.

■ Primary Key Constraints and Indexes

The last of the table-level constraints is the primary key or unique constraint. This constraint differs from the previous ones in that it handles multiple rows of data rather than a single row.

Uniqueness and How to Enforce It

The primary key is used to ensure that the values for the identifying attributes (or columns as we are now talking about a physical data model) are unique. Since every relationship or foreign key constraint must have a primary key to reference, primary keys are very important to the correct functioning of the database.

When you create a primary key, Oracle actually creates a `unique index` to enforce the constraint. A unique index only allows one entry for each value. Also remember that a primary key cannot contain any optional or NULL columns. Let's try creating a primary key for the STATE table in our mailing database.

Type this to create the basic table:

```
DROP TABLE state CASCADE CONSTRAINTS;
CREATE TABLE state
(state_abbrev VARCHAR2(2)  NOT NULL,
 name         VARCHAR2(40) NULL
);
```

Now you can add the primary key in the same way as the other constraints:

```
ALTER TABLE state
    ADD CONSTRAINT pk_state
    PRIMARY KEY (state_abbrev);
```

Oracle keeps a data dictionary about all the tables and other things you have created in the database. Two of the tables in the data dictionary are "ALL_INDEXES" and "ALL_CONSTRAINTS." You can check that both an index and a constraint were created by typing these queries:

```
SELECT table_name, index_name, uniqueness
FROM all_indexes
WHERE index_name = 'PK_STATE';

SELECT table_name, constraint_name, constraint_type, index_name
FROM all_constraints
WHERE constraint_name = 'PK_STATE';
```

The first of these queries lists a unique index on the table state and the second lists a primary key constraint on the same table using the PK_STATE index as shown here:

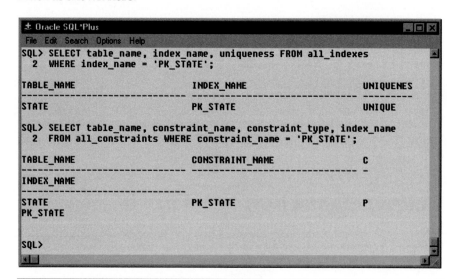

• Confirmation of index and constraint on STATE table

Now we have a table with its primary key constraint. Let's add some values:

```
INSERT INTO state VALUES ('AL', 'Alaska');
INSERT INTO state VALUES ('CA', 'California');
INSERT INTO state VALUES ('NY', 'New York');
INSERT INTO state VALUES ('AR', 'Arkansas');
```

```
INSERT INTO state VALUES ('TX', 'Texas');
INSERT INTO state VALUES ('AL', 'Alabama');
```

You should see this as SQL*Plus's confirmation:

• Confirmation and error from a unique constraint violation

The last insert failed due to our **unique constraint**. You know the primary key is on the State_Abbrev column so it must be the "AL" that was duplicated. However, the program is not smart enough to tell you which row has the already existing "AL" and it definitely cannot tell you which one is wrong!

Fortunately, correcting the mistake is easy at this stage. You delete the offending row and reinsert the correct values:

```
DELETE FROM state WHERE state_abbrev = 'AL';
INSERT INTO state VALUES ('AK', 'Alaska');
INSERT INTO state VALUES ('AL', 'Alabama');
```

Or just use the UPDATE command:

```
UPDATE state SET state_abbrev = 'AK'
WHERE state_abbrev = 'AL';
```

Because you know that State_Abbrev is unique—Oracle has guaranteed it!—you can be absolutely certain that the DELETE command will only delete the one row you need to get rid of.

```
Oracle SQL*Plus                                            _ □ X
File  Edit  Search  Options  Help
SQL> DELETE FROM state WHERE state_abbrev = 'AL';

1 row deleted.

SQL> INSERT INTO state VALUES ('AK', 'Alaska');

1 row created.

SQL> INSERT INTO state VALUES ('AL', 'Alabama');

1 row created.

SQL>
```

- SQL*Plus responses to correcting the STATE data

Primary keys are the first defense against bad data by ensuring that rows in the table are unique.

Alternate Keys

 A surrogate key is a sequential number used if the natural primary key is too complex or is liable to be updated often.

You can apply unique indexes to any columns in a table; they don't have to be the primary key columns. This is often done when the table uses a surrogate primary key.

Non-primary-key unique indexes have one difference from the primary-key unique indexes: They can have NULL values in the columns. This unique index can be the basis for an **alternate key**. An alternate key is a unique key that is not the primary key. Not every table has one.

Let's take another look at the PERSON table you created earlier and add a primary key and an alternate key:

```
DESC person

ALTER TABLE person
    ADD CONSTRAINT pk_person
    PRIMARY KEY (person_id);

ALTER TABLE person
    ADD CONSTRAINT ak_person_all_cols
    UNIQUE (last_name, first_name, address_id);
```

What does this new constraint mean to the business? How are you going to explain this to the owner of the mailing database? This constraint ensures that you can only have one person with a given name residing at an address. Think a moment about when this might be a nuisance. What happens if the son of the house is a "Junior"? With this constraint in place he would have to have a different first name or maybe a "Jr" appended to the last name. Only the business owner can tell you if this is acceptable.

Alternative Syntaxes for Table Creation

Oracle offers many alternative ways to write the code that creates a table. One that you will often see is where all the constraints are included in the table creation. This contrasts with the method in the main body of this book where you add constraints by using the ALTER TABLE command. For instance, you could create the EMPLOYEE table with all its constraints like this:

```
DROP TABLE employee;

CREATE TABLE employee (
        employee_id             NUMBER(10)   NOT NULL,
        supervisor_id           NUMBER(10)   NULL,
        first_name              VARCHAR2(20) NULL,
        last_name               VARCHAR2(20) NOT NULL,
        social_security_number  CHAR(11)     NOT NULL,
        pay_rate                NUMBER(8,2)  NULL,
        job_type                VARCHAR2(20) NOT NULL,
CONSTRAINT pk_employee PRIMARY KEY (employee_id),
CONSTRAINT ck_employee_job_type_dmn CHECK
        (job_type in ('Owner', 'Delivery', 'Register Clerk')),
CONSTRAINT ck_employee_pay_rate_dmn CHECK
        ((pay_rate > 0)
         and (mod(pay_rate, 10) = 0)
         and (pay_rate <= 200)
         )
);
```

This works well but has a couple of disadvantages. The statement is getting long and unwieldy, and if you make a typo in the middle, you have a lot of retyping to correct the statement. Graphical SQL tools can reduce this burden, but Oracle's own SQL*Plus has only a line editor. Also, by separating the creation of the table and using ALTER TABLE statements you get simpler troubleshooting. As in other computer languages, short, succinct, separate commands make code that is easier to follow.

Note that if you ran the SQL code above, you will need to re-insert the records shown just before Figure 11.2.

Other Indexes

As you can see, unique indexes are very helpful to ensure the quality of the data we store. What about the non-unique indexes?

All the non-unique indexes in a database are there for performance reasons—more speed!

Designers will usually add a `non-unique index` to support each foreign key constraint (more on these in the next section). Not only does this make the database's work of enforcing the constraint faster, but it also provides an index to support the most commonly used joins. A *join* is a type of query that gets its data from more than one table. The data in these two tables has to be joined using the primary key and foreign key columns. Oracle can support this join much more efficiently if it can use indexes rather than accessing the whole table.

In terms of the logical data model the indexes are pretty much irrelevant and we don't consider them at all. In the physical data model, performance should be considered more closely and you should create and assign indexes wherever necessary. The two major reasons for having non-unique indexes are

- To support a foreign key
- To support a query WHERE clause

■ Foreign Key Constraints: Values from Other Tables

So far you've just dealt with values within a single table. Now you get to implement the most important part of the database: the relational integrity. Here you will create foreign keys, which relate to primary keys in other tables.

Each of these foreign keys derives from a relationship you specified in your logical data model. Some of the relationships (for example, the many-to-many) have been resolved into a table and more foreign keys. The optionality of the roles will translate to NULL columns, and you will deal with identifying relationships by incorporating the foreign key columns into the primary key of the table. Figure 11.3 shows the full relational model for the mailing database. In the text and exercises for this chapter you will create tables and constraints to implement this model.

Adding the Constraint

Foreign key constraints are added to the table definition in the same way as the check and primary key constraints. The difference this time is that the primary key and the parent table must exist in the database. If the parent and child tables have values, those values must satisfy the foreign key constraint.

You already have a STATE table from the previous exercises with a suitable primary key. You should type in the following code to create an ADDRESS table with its own primary key:

```
DROP TABLE address;
CREATE TABLE address (
      address_id     NUMBER(10) NOT NULL,
      house_number   VARCHAR2(10) NULL,
      street         VARCHAR2(50) NULL,
      city           VARCHAR2(50) NULL,
      state          VARCHAR2(2) NOT NULL,
      zip            VARCHAR2(10) NULL
);
ALTER TABLE address
      ADD CONSTRAINT pk_address
      PRIMARY KEY (address_id);
```

Adding a foreign key constraint is just like a check constraint except that it references another table:

```
ALTER TABLE address
   ADD CONSTRAINT fk_address_r_state
   FOREIGN KEY (state)
   REFERENCES state(state_abbrev);
```

Note the syntax here: The constraint references a column in a parent table; it does not reference the primary key explicitly. Oracle will check to

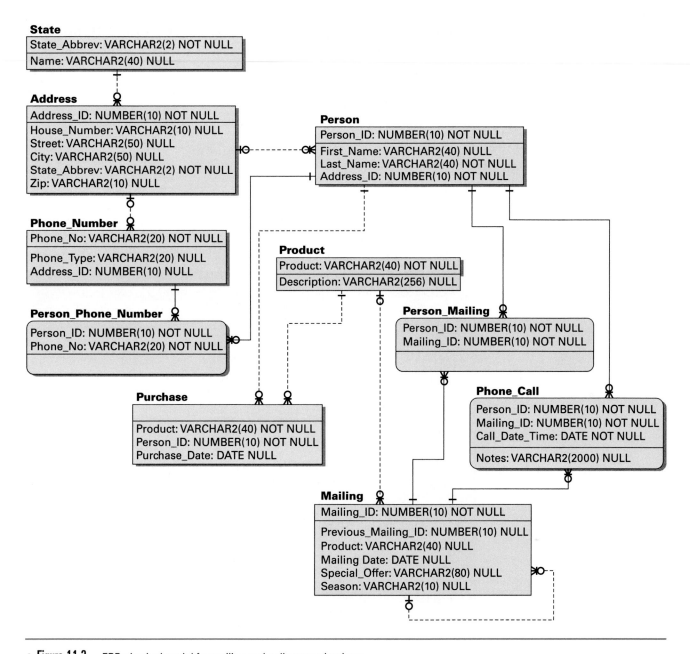

State

| State_Abbrev: VARCHAR2(2) NOT NULL |
| Name: VARCHAR2(40) NULL |

Address

| Address_ID: NUMBER(10) NOT NULL |
| House_Number: VARCHAR2(10) NULL |
| Street: VARCHAR2(50) NULL |
| City: VARCHAR2(50) NULL |
| State_Abbrev: VARCHAR2(2) NOT NULL |
| Zip: VARCHAR2(10) NULL |

Person

| Person_ID: NUMBER(10) NOT NULL |
| First_Name: VARCHAR2(40) NULL |
| Last_Name: VARCHAR2(40) NOT NULL |
| Address_ID: NUMBER(10) NOT NULL |

Phone_Number

| Phone_No: VARCHAR2(20) NOT NULL |
| Phone_Type: VARCHAR2(20) NULL |
| Address_ID: NUMBER(10) NULL |

Product

| Product: VARCHAR2(40) NOT NULL |
| Description: VARCHAR2(256) NULL |

Person_Phone_Number

| Person_ID: NUMBER(10) NOT NULL |
| Phone_No: VARCHAR2(20) NOT NULL |

Person_Mailing

| Person_ID: NUMBER(10) NOT NULL |
| Mailing_ID: NUMBER(10) NOT NULL |

Purchase

| Product: VARCHAR2(40) NOT NULL |
| Person_ID: NUMBER(10) NOT NULL |
| Purchase_Date: DATE NULL |

Phone_Call

| Person_ID: NUMBER(10) NOT NULL |
| Mailing_ID: NUMBER(10) NOT NULL |
| Call_Date_Time: DATE NOT NULL |
| Notes: VARCHAR2(2000) NULL |

Mailing

| Mailing_ID: NUMBER(10) NOT NULL |
| Previous_Mailing_ID: NUMBER(10) NULL |
| Product: VARCHAR2(40) NULL |
| Mailing Date: DATE NULL |
| Special_Offer: VARCHAR2(80) NULL |
| Season: VARCHAR2(10) NULL |

● **Figure 11.3** ERD physical model for mailing and call center database

ensure that there is either a primary key or an alternate key on specified columns in the STATE table. If you perform a check by querying the data dictionary for this constraint, you'll see this:

Notice that this foreign key constraint is only implemented in one direction. All it does is limit the values that might be inserted

```
± Oracle SQL*Plus
File  Edit  Search  Options  Help

SQL> SELECT table_name, constraint_name, constraint_type, r_constraint_name
  2  FROM all_constraints
  3  WHERE constraint_name = 'FK_ADDRESS_R_STATE'
  4  /

TABLE_NAME                      CONSTRAINT_NAME                 C
------------------------------- ------------------------------- -
R_CONSTRAINT_NAME
-------------------------------
ADDRESS                         FK_ADDRESS_R_STATE              R
PK_STATE

SQL> |
```

● Constraint details from the data dictionary

into the ADDRESS table. It has no limit on what might be entered in the parent (STATE) table.

```
INSERT INTO address VALUES(
        100, '7107', 'Sunset Blvd.', 'Los Angeles', 'CA', '90049');
INSERT INTO address VALUES(
        101, '', 'PO. Box 4109', 'Hoboken', 'NJ', '10024');
INSERT INTO address VALUES(
        102, '62', 'St Louis Dr.', 'Austen', 'TX', '70468');
INSERT INTO address VALUES(
        103, '15578', 'Pacific Coast Highway', 'Malibu', 'CA', '91320');
INSERT INTO address VALUES(
        104, '1445', 'Mountain Bear Rd.', 'Sitka', 'AK', '98004');
```

The results are shown here, in which the second row failed because "integrity constraint fk_address_r_state violated - parent key not found."

```
+ Oracle SQL*Plus                                                    _ |□|×
 File Edit Search Options Help
SQL> INSERT INTO address VALUES(100, '7107', 'Sunset Blvd.',
  2 'Los Angeles', 'CA', '90049');

1 row created.

SQL> INSERT INTO address VALUES(101, '', 'PO. Box 4109',
  2 'Hoboken', 'NJ', '10024');
INSERT INTO address VALUES(101, '', 'PO. Box 4109',
*
ERROR at line 1:
ORA-02291: integrity constraint (MAILING.FK_ADDRESS_R_STATE) violated - parent
key not found

SQL> INSERT INTO address VALUES(102, '62', 'St Louis Dr.',
  2 'Austen', 'TX', '70468');

1 row created.

SQL> INSERT INTO address VALUES(103, '15578', 'Pacific Coast Highway',
  2 'Malibu', 'CA', '91320');

1 row created.

SQL> INSERT INTO address VALUES(104, '1445', 'Mountain Bear Rd.',
  2 'Sitka', 'AK', '98004');

1 row created.

SQL> |
```

- SQL*Plus script showing foreign key violation

Again, you should note that the name of the constraint is important to how easily you can interpret this error message. The name was constructed as 'FK_' **child table** '_R_' **parent table** and should be read as "foreign key on **child table** relates to **parent table**." For most relationships this is sufficient to identify what has been violated. We'll talk more about naming conventions later in this chapter.

Implementing Cardinality and Optionality

The constraint you implemented in the previous section is concerned only with the basic relationship between state and address. There does not appear to be any mention of cardinality or optionality in the declaration. Where did they go?

We discussed optionality in Chapters 8 and 9 in terms of the NULL or NOT NULL feature of the column. If the parent table has an optional role in the relationship, then the migrated columns (in the child table) will, in turn, be optional or NULL.

The cardinality of a declared foreign key like this is assumed to be 1:m. The primary key columns from the parent are copied to the child table. How many values can we put in these foreign key columns in a row of the child table? Only one! Thus the child row can only refer to one parent row. However, a single parent row can clearly have values in many of the child table's rows. So the cardinality is restrained by the copying of the columns from the parent to the child tables.

In practice this means that an optional 1:1 relationship is generally implemented as a 1:m. To ensure 1:1 you would have to use a unique constraint on the foreign key in the child table.

Case Study

Say you have employees (from the Clapham Specialty Store) and they each have a parking space. Each employee can only occupy one space, though a space may be empty. You can implement this optional one-to-one relationship by using a foreign key and a unique constraint. You cannot use the Employee_ID in the child table as a primary key because it must be able to hold NULLs.

Check that your table is still in the database and add the PARKING_SPACE table:

```
DESC employee;

DROP TABLE parking_space;
CREATE TABLE parking_space
    (space_id    number(10) not null,
     employee_id number(10) null,
     CONSTRAINT pk_parking_space
     PRIMARY KEY (space_id)
);
```

Notice how this code has lumped the primary key in with the CREATE TABLE statement. The effect is identical to using ALTER TABLE—it just uses fewer characters!

Now add the foreign key and the unique constraint:

```
ALTER TABLE parking_space
    ADD CONSTRAINT fk_parking_space_r_employee
    FOREIGN KEY (employee_id)
    REFERENCES employee(employee_id);
ALTER TABLE parking_space
    ADD CONSTRAINT ak_parking_space_employee
    UNIQUE (employee_id);
```

And finally some data for each employee:

```
INSERT INTO parking_space VALUES(10, 100);
INSERT INTO parking_space VALUES(20, 102);
INSERT INTO parking_space VALUES(30, 101);
INSERT INTO parking_space VALUES(40, 105);
INSERT INTO parking_space VALUES(50, 100);
```

Whoops! You can see in the screen shot of the errors that now the owner (ID = 100) is only allowed to have one parking space for both his BMW and

Jaguar. Either he has to choose which car to bring to work or this unique constraint on the Employee_ID in PARKING_SPACE has to go!

```
Oracle SQL*Plus                                                    _ □ ✕
 File  Edit  Search  Options  Help
SQL> INSERT INTO parking_space VALUES(10, 100);

1 row created.

SQL> INSERT INTO parking_space VALUES(20, 102);

1 row created.

SQL> INSERT INTO parking_space VALUES(30, 101);

1 row created.

SQL> INSERT INTO parking_space VALUES(40, 105);

1 row created.

SQL> INSERT INTO parking_space VALUES(50, 100);
INSERT INTO parking_space VALUES(50, 100)
*
ERROR at line 1:
ORA-00001: unique constraint (CLAPHAM.AK_PARKING_SPACE_EMPLOYEE) violated

SQL>
```

• Violating the 1:1 relationship for parking spaces

As he's the owner, the constraint is removed:

```
ALTER TABLE parking_space DROP CONSTRAINT ak_parking_space_employee;
```

And now everybody can bring multiple cars to work. At least the database is fair!

Cascading Effects

So far we've only dealt with inserting records and ensuring that the data in these records is as accurate as possible. Relational integrity, and the data quality that comes from it, involves much more than just inserting new records. The database has to retain its integrity even if records are deleted or updated.

Let's try deleting one of the states from your beginning mailing database:

```
DELETE FROM state WHERE state_abbrev = 'AK';
```

This should be the result—depending on exactly what addresses you inserted into the ADDRESS table:

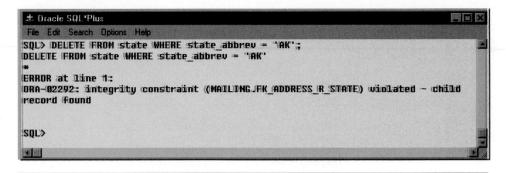

```
± Oracle SQL*Plus                                          _ □ ×
File  Edit  Search  Options  Help
SQL> DELETE FROM state WHERE state_abbrev = 'AK';
DELETE FROM state WHERE state_abbrev = 'AK'
*
ERROR at line 1:
ORA-02292: integrity constraint (MAILING.FK_ADDRESS_R_STATE) violated - child
record found


SQL>
```

- Result of attempting a deletion from STATE

The deletion has been restricted by the foreign key constraint because it has found at least one address for Alaska. This delete restrict is the default action for a foreign key constraint.

When you declare a foreign key constraint you can also declare, as part of the constraint, the cascade effects you want. For each possible action (insert, delete, update) at both child and parent tables, there are various possible cascading effects as shown in Table 11.1. You should note that these effects are not specified in the logical data model, just in the physical data model.

You now have all sorts of options available to enhance the foreign key and help keep your data quality at its best. When should you use these? First, note that in all cases shown in Table 11.1, restrict is the default option. The database will fail any action that attempts to break the parent-to-child foreign key relationship.

The cascade option, both for delete and update, is most useful where you have tight coupling between the rows of the two tables, and this is most

Table 11.1	Cascade Actions for Insert, Delete, and Update	
	Parent Table	**Child Table**
Insert into	No action on the child table.	Restrict if key values not found in parent (default). Set foreign key NULL if key values not found in parent.
Delete from	Restrict if rows found in the child (default). Set foreign key columns to NULL if found in the child. Cascade delete the corresponding rows from the child table.	No action on the parent table.
Update key values	Restrict if old value exists in the child (default). Cascade update the corresponding values in the foreign key in the child. Set the foreign key to NULL in the child.	Restrict if the new value does not exist in the parent (default). Set foreign key to NULL if the new value does not exist in the parent.

Case Study

often shown by an *identifying relationship*. In the Clapham Specialty Store the relationship shown here between the SALE and SALE_ITEM is an identifying relationship.

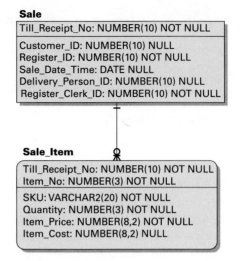

Sale

Till_Receipt_No: NUMBER(10) NOT NULL
Customer_ID: NUMBER(10) NULL
Register_ID: NUMBER(10) NOT NULL
Sale_Date_Time: DATE NULL
Delivery_Person_ID: NUMBER(10) NULL
Register_Clerk_ID: NUMBER(10) NOT NULL

Sale_Item

Till_Receipt_No: NUMBER(10) NOT NULL
Item_No: NUMBER(3) NOT NULL
SKU: VARCHAR2(20) NOT NULL
Quantity: NUMBER(3) NOT NULL
Item_Price: NUMBER(8,2) NOT NULL
Item_Cost: NUMBER(8,2) NULL

• Identifying relationship between SALE and SALE_ITEM

Since the sale item cannot exist without the sale record, it makes sense to delete any sales items if the master sale record is deleted. Would you also do a cascade update if the Till_Receipt_No was changed or updated? You should now start asking awkward questions of the owner such as "Why would you change the number that has already been printed on the receipt?" As with many of these design decisions, you need to refer back to the people who are going to be using the database. You create the cascade delete this way:

```
DROP TABLE sale CASCADE CONSTRAINTS;
CREATE TABLE sale (
        till_receipt_no         NUMBER(10) NOT NULL,
        customer_id             NUMBER(10) NULL,
        register_id             NUMBER(10) NOT NULL,
        sale_date_time          DATE NULL,
        register_clerk_id       NUMBER(10) NOT NULL,
        delivery_person_id      NUMBER(10) NULL
);
ALTER TABLE sale
        ADD CONSTRAINT pk_sale PRIMARY KEY
        (till_receipt_no);

DROP TABLE sale_item;
CREATE TABLE sale_item (
        till_receipt_no         NUMBER(10) NOT NULL,
        item_no                 NUMBER(3) NOT NULL,
        sku                     VARCHAR2(20) NOT NULL,
        quantity                NUMBER(3) DEFAULT 1 NOT NULL,
        item_price              NUMBER(8,2) NOT NULL,
        item_cost               NUMBER(8,2) NULL
);
```

```
ALTER TABLE sale_item
      ADD CONSTRAINT pk_sale_item PRIMARY KEY
      (till_receipt_no, item_no);
ALTER TABLE sale_item
      ADD CONSTRAINT fk_sale_item_r_sales FOREIGN KEY
      (till_receipt_no) REFERENCES sale(till_receipt_no )
      ON DELETE CASCADE;
```

You can also try specifying ON UPDATE CASCADE, but unfortunately Oracle cannot implement this using a declarative constraint such as the ones you have used so far. This more complex type of cascade must be implemented with some procedural code in a trigger. This is discussed in more detail in Chapter 7.

Cascade Delete on a Recursive Relationship

Case Study

Cascade delete appears to be a really powerful capability. The trouble with powerful capabilities is that they are also dangerous. In the EMPLOYEE table for the Clapham Specialty Store database, we used a recursive relationship for the employee's supervisor. Say we decided to add a cascade delete clause to the foreign key constraint:

```
ALTER TABLE employee
    ADD CONSTRAINT fk_employee_r_employee FOREIGN KEY
    (supervisor_id) REFERENCES employee(employee_id)
    ON DELETE CASCADE;
```

Unfortunately this returns an error that says there are Supervisor_ID values that cannot be found in the Employee_ID column. This demonstrates an important point about modifying existing databases: Oracle will check that every row in the table satisfies the constraint before allowing it to be imposed. This is particularly helpful if you already have data in the tables.

You can see immediately which supervisors are "bad" by querying the EMPLOYEE table:

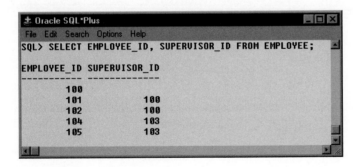

• Employees with invalid supervisor IDs

There are two ways to correct this situation: One is to add "Storeman" to the list of Job_Types and insert employee 103. The other is to change the supervisors for 104 and 105 to be employee 102. You should change the constraint and add the missing value like this:

```
ALTER TABLE employee
    DROP CONSTRAINT ck_employee_job_type_dmn;
```

```
ALTER TABLE employee
    ADD CONSTRAINT ck_employee_job_type_dmn CHECK
    (job_type IN ('Delivery', 'Owner', 'Storeman', 'Register Clerk')
    );
```

Now try inserting the record for the Storeman again:

```
INSERT INTO employee VALUES(
103, 100, 'Martin', 'Murphy', '901-23-4567', 20, 'Storeman'
);
```

 Cross Check

Replacing Unwieldy Check Constraints

Sometimes you will find that a check constraint such as the one on EMPLOYEE_Job_Type becomes longer and longer. As the age of the database grows, you find yourself continually having to come back and alter the constraint to add yet another value.

1. How would you change the logical data model to constrain the values in Job_Type using a different method? (Hint: Use another table.)

2. Write the SQL commands necessary to implement your change including statements to enter the data.

And, finally, try again to get the recursive foreign key into place. Now you have a powerful but dangerous tool in hand. What will happen if you try to delete Martin Murphy, the Storeman? The cascade delete will kick in and also delete the two Delivery people. More dangerous yet: What happens if you have to delete John Balfour, the Owner? John goes, the three who report to him get cascade deleted, and their deletion in turn forces the two Delivery people to be deleted. How many are now left in the company?

```
SELECT COUNT(*) FROM employee;
DELETE FROM employee WHERE EMPLOYEE_ID = 100;
SELECT COUNT(*) FROM employee;
```

The SQL shows an interesting result:

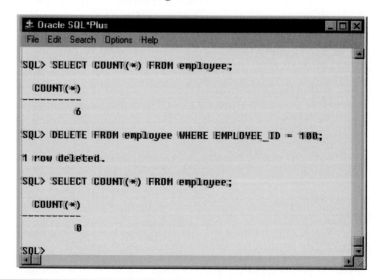

- Effects of over-zealous cascade deletion

Introduction to Relational Databases and SQL Programming

Oracle reports it has only deleted 1 row from employee yet everybody has gone! Fortunately the database engine provides us with a command to undo the damage:

```
Rollback;
```

You should get rid of this experimental constraint with the cascade delete before any more damage is done:

```
ALTER TABLE employee DROP CONSTRAINT fk_employee_r_employee;
ALTER TABLE employee
    ADD CONSTRAINT fk_employee_r_employee FOREIGN KEY
    (supervisor_id) REFERENCES employee(employee_id);
```

Be careful of cascade delete; it can get you in a whole host of trouble. You should stick to using it only when you originally specified an identifying relationship in the logical data model—and often not even then.

The Cascades That Don't

Let's say that the federal and state governments got together and decided to change the abbreviation for Alaska from AK to AA. What would happen in our database if we just tried to update the State_Abbrev column in the STATE table? For this situation you would need a cascade update clause in the foreign key constraint.

Oracle and most of the other database vendors do not allow you to implement a cascade update declaratively. Sorry, the easy way of adding "ON UPDATE CASCADE" is just not available. To implement this type of constraint, you will have to write some procedural code in the form of a trigger. A trigger is simply code that the database will execute every time a certain event happens. Triggers and procedural code are discussed in Chapter 7.

Cross Check

Relating Values from Other Tables

Case Study

The database's main tool for data integrity is the relational foreign key constraint. You will need a copy of the Clapham Specialty Store data model (refer to Figure 11.4 on the next page) and an open copy of SQL*Plus.

1. Create the table PHONE_NUMBER.

2. Add a primary key to the PHONE_NUMBER table.

3. Add a foreign key constraint on this table to reference the ADDRESS table.

4. Create a resolution table PERSON_PHONE_NUMBER with a suitable primary key.

5. Add two foreign key constraints on PERSON_PHONE_NUMBER, one to Person, one to Phone_Number.

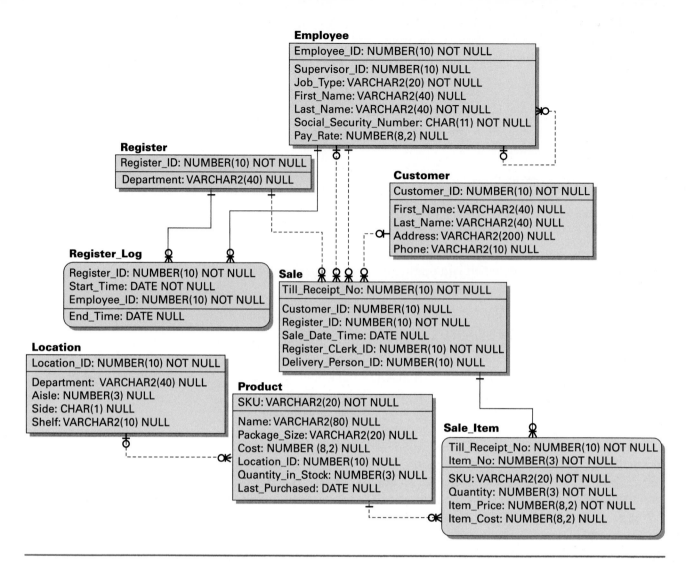

Employee

Employee_ID: NUMBER(10) NOT NULL
Supervisor_ID: NUMBER(10) NULL
Job_Type: VARCHAR2(20) NOT NULL
First_Name: VARCHAR2(40) NULL
Last_Name: VARCHAR2(40) NOT NULL
Social_Security_Number: CHAR(11) NOT NULL
Pay_Rate: NUMBER(8,2) NULL

Register

Register_ID: NUMBER(10) NOT NULL
Department: VARCHAR2(40) NULL

Customer

Customer_ID: NUMBER(10) NOT NULL
First_Name: VARCHAR2(40) NULL
Last_Name: VARCHAR2(40) NULL
Address: VARCHAR2(200) NULL
Phone: VARCHAR2(10) NULL

Register_Log

Register_ID: NUMBER(10) NOT NULL
Start_Time: DATE NOT NULL
Employee_ID: NUMBER(10) NOT NULL
End_Time: DATE NULL

Sale

Till_Receipt_No: NUMBER(10) NOT NULL
Customer_ID: NUMBER(10) NULL
Register_ID: NUMBER(10) NOT NULL
Sale_Date_Time: DATE NULL
Register_CLerk_ID: NUMBER(10) NOT NULL
Delivery_Person_ID: NUMBER(10) NULL

Location

Location_ID: NUMBER(10) NOT NULL
Department: VARCHAR2(40) NULL
Aisle: NUMBER(3) NULL
Side: CHAR(1) NULL
Shelf: VARCHAR2(10) NULL

Product

SKU: VARCHAR2(20) NOT NULL
Name: VARCHAR2(80) NULL
Package_Size: VARCHAR2(20) NULL
Cost: NUMBER (8,2) NULL
Location_ID: NUMBER(10) NULL
Quantity_in_Stock: NUMBER(3) NULL
Last_Purchased: DATE NULL

Sale_Item

Till_Receipt_No: NUMBER(10) NOT NULL
Item_No: NUMBER(3) NOT NULL
SKU: VARCHAR2(20) NOT NULL
Quantity: NUMBER(3) NOT NULL
Item_Price: NUMBER(8,2) NOT NULL
Item_Cost: NUMBER(8,2) NULL

● **Figure 11.4** Clapham Specialty Store data model

Step-by-Step 11.02

Creating the Movie Database

In this step-by-step tutorial, you will create the Movie database that was discussed in Chapter 10 and fill it with values from the data examples. If you receive errors from your entries, you should endeavor to correct them before moving on to the next step. Typos and spelling errors will not be tolerated! The database with relational integrity in place is a much stricter evaluator of accuracy than any instructor.

Step 1

Log on to Oracle using SQL*Plus and create the tables:

```
DROP TABLE country CASCADE CONSTRAINTS;
DROP TABLE male_lead_actor CASCADE CONSTRAINTS;
```

```
DROP TABLE medium CASCADE CONSTRAINTS;
DROP TABLE movie CASCADE CONSTRAINTS;
DROP TABLE movie_medium CASCADE CONSTRAINTS;
DROP TABLE movie_region CASCADE CONSTRAINTS;
DROP TABLE region CASCADE CONSTRAINTS;
DROP TABLE region_medium CASCADE CONSTRAINTS;
DROP TABLE studio CASCADE CONSTRAINTS;
DROP TABLE studio_movie CASCADE CONSTRAINTS;

CREATE TABLE country (
      country               VARCHAR2(20) NOT NULL,
      local_name            VARCHAR2(40) NULL,
      region_name           VARCHAR2(40) NOT NULL);
CREATE TABLE male_lead_actor (
      male_lead             VARCHAR2(80) NOT NULL,
      agency                VARCHAR2(20) NOT NULL,
      lead_id               NUMBER(10)   NOT NULL);
CREATE TABLE medium (
      medium                VARCHAR2(20) NOT NULL,
      format                VARCHAR2(20) NULL);
CREATE TABLE movie (
      title                 VARCHAR2(80) NOT NULL,
      director              VARCHAR2(80) NOT NULL,
      lead_id               NUMBER(10)   NULL);
CREATE TABLE movie_medium (
      title                 VARCHAR2(80) NOT NULL,
      medium                VARCHAR2(20) NOT NULL);
CREATE TABLE movie_region (
      title                 VARCHAR2(80) NOT NULL,
      region_name           VARCHAR2(40) NOT NULL);
CREATE TABLE region (
      region_name           VARCHAR2(40)  NOT NULL,
      description           VARCHAR2(256) NULL,
      population            NUMBER(8,1)   NULL);
CREATE TABLE region_medium (
      region_name           VARCHAR2(40) NOT NULL,
      medium                VARCHAR2(20) NOT NULL);
CREATE TABLE studio (
      studio_name           VARCHAR2(40) NOT NULL,
      movie_count           NUMBER(5)    NULL);
CREATE TABLE studio_movie (
      studio_name           VARCHAR2(40) NOT NULL,
      title                 VARCHAR2(80) NOT NULL);
```

Step 2

For each table add a primary key. Where required, add column-level check constraints.

```
ALTER TABLE country
   ADD CONSTRAINT pk_country PRIMARY KEY
   (country);
ALTER TABLE male_lead_actor
```

```
                    ADD CONSTRAINT pk_male_lead_actor PRIMARY KEY
                    (lead_id);
        ALTER TABLE medium
                    ADD CONSTRAINT pk_medium PRIMARY KEY
                    (medium);
        ALTER TABLE movie
                    ADD CONSTRAINT pk_movie PRIMARY KEY
                    (title);
        ALTER TABLE movie_medium
                    ADD CONSTRAINT pk_movie_medium PRIMARY KEY
                    (title, medium);
        ALTER TABLE movie_region
                    ADD CONSTRAINT pk_movie_region PRIMARY KEY
                    (title, region_name);
        ALTER TABLE region
                    ADD CONSTRAINT pk_region PRIMARY KEY
                    (region_name);
        ALTER TABLE region_medium
                    ADD CONSTRAINT pk_region_medium PRIMARY KEY
                    (medium, region_name);
        ALTER TABLE studio
                    ADD CONSTRAINT pk_studio PRIMARY KEY
                    (studio_name);
        ALTER TABLE studio_movie
                    ADD CONSTRAINT pk_studio_movie PRIMARY KEY
                    (studio_name, title);
```

Step 3

For each table add the foreign key constraints:

```
ALTER TABLE country
        ADD CONSTRAINT fk_country_r_region FOREIGN KEY
        (region_name) REFERENCES region(region_name);
ALTER TABLE movie
        ADD CONSTRAINT fk_movie_r_male_lead_actor FOREIGN KEY
        (lead_id) REFERENCES male_lead_actor(lead_id);
ALTER TABLE movie_medium
        ADD CONSTRAINT fk_movie_medium_r_medium FOREIGN KEY
        (medium) REFERENCES medium(medium);
ALTER TABLE movie_medium
        ADD CONSTRAINT fk_movie_medium_r_movie FOREIGN KEY
        (title) REFERENCES movie(title);
ALTER TABLE movie_region
      ADD CONSTRAINT fk_movie_region_r_region FOREIGN KEY
      (region_name) REFERENCES region(region_name);
ALTER TABLE movie_region
        ADD CONSTRAINT fk_movie_region_r_movie FOREIGN KEY
        (title) REFERENCES movie(title);
ALTER TABLE region_medium
        ADD CONSTRAINT fk_region_medium_r_region FOREIGN KEY
        (region_name) REFERENCES region(region_name);
ALTER TABLE region_medium
        ADD CONSTRAINT fk_region_medium_r_movie FOREIGN KEY
        (medium) REFERENCES medium(medium);
ALTER TABLE studio_movie
```

```
                        ADD CONSTRAINT fk_studio_movie_r_movie FOREIGN KEY
                        (title) REFERENCES movie(title);
                ALTER TABLE studio_movie
                        ADD CONSTRAINT fk_studio_movie_r_studio FOREIGN KEY
                        (studio_name) REFERENCES studio(studio_name);
```

Step 4

For each table insert some data rows. Notice that the order in which you fill the tables matters. If the data is not in the relevant primary key when you try to fill the foreign key columns, you'll get errors.

```
INSERT INTO male_lead_actor VALUES('Clint Eastwood', 'CAA', 10);
INSERT INTO male_lead_actor VALUES('Bruce Willis', 'William Morris', 11);
INSERT INTO male_lead_actor VALUES('Kevin Spacey', 'CAA', 12);
INSERT INTO male_lead_actor VALUES('Sean Connery', 'ICM', 13);
INSERT INTO male_lead_actor VALUES('Sylvester Stallone', 'MTM', 14);
INSERT INTO male_lead_actor VALUES('Arnold Schwarzenegger', 'ICM', 15);
INSERT INTO male_lead_actor VALUES('Kurt Russell', 'William Morris', 16);
INSERT INTO male_lead_actor VALUES('Val Kilmer', 'CAA', 17);
INSERT INTO movie VALUES('Absolute Power', 'Clint Eastwood', 10);
INSERT INTO movie VALUES('Color of Night', 'Richard Rush', 11);
INSERT INTO movie VALUES('Garden of Good and Evil', 'Clint Eastwood', 12);
INSERT INTO movie VALUES('Medicine Man', 'John McTiernan', 13);
INSERT INTO movie VALUES('Play Misty for Me', 'Clint Eastwood', 10);
INSERT INTO movie VALUES('Rocky', 'John Avildsen', 14);
INSERT INTO movie VALUES('Rocky 2', 'Sylvester Stallone', 14);
INSERT INTO movie VALUES('Terminator', 'James Cameron', 15);
INSERT INTO movie VALUES('Terminator 2', 'James Cameron', 15);
INSERT INTO movie VALUES('Tombstone', 'George Cosmatos', 15);
INSERT INTO movie VALUES('The Doors', 'Oliver Stone', 15);
INSERT INTO movie VALUES('Unforgiven', 'Clint Eastwood', 10);
INSERT INTO studio VALUES('Artisan Entertainment', 2);
INSERT INTO studio VALUES('Carolco', 2);
INSERT INTO studio VALUES('Cinergi', 2);
INSERT INTO studio VALUES('Malpaso Pictures', 3);
INSERT INTO studio VALUES('MGM.UA Studios', 1);
INSERT INTO studio VALUES('Hollywood Pictures', 2);
INSERT INTO studio VALUES('Warner Bros', 2);
INSERT INTO medium VALUES('Network TV', 'NTSC');
INSERT INTO medium VALUES('Cable TV', 'Letterbox');
INSERT INTO medium VALUES('Satellite', 'PAL (Digital)');
INSERT INTO medium VALUES('Theatrical', 'Film');
INSERT INTO medium VALUES('Video (Purchase)', 'VHS');
INSERT INTO medium VALUES('Video (Rental)', 'VHS');
INSERT INTO medium VALUES('DVD', 'NTSC');
INSERT INTO region VALUES('North America', '', 312.5);
INSERT INTO region VALUES('France', '', 56.6);
INSERT INTO region VALUES('Europe', '', 377.8);
INSERT INTO country VALUES ('USA', 'America', 'North America');
INSERT INTO country VALUES ('Canada', 'Canada', 'North America');
INSERT INTO country VALUES ('France', 'France', 'France');
INSERT INTO country VALUES ('Germany', 'Deutschland', 'Europe');
INSERT INTO movie_region VALUES ('Absolute Power', 'North America');
INSERT INTO movie_region VALUES ('Color of Night', 'North America');
INSERT INTO movie_region VALUES ('Medicine Man', 'North America');
```

```
INSERT INTO movie_region VALUES ('Play Misty for Me', 'North America');
INSERT INTO movie_region VALUES ('Play Misty for Me', 'France');
INSERT INTO movie_region VALUES ('Absolute Power', 'Europe');
INSERT INTO movie_region VALUES ('Color of Night', 'Europe');
INSERT INTO movie_region VALUES ('Medicine Man', 'Europe');
INSERT INTO region_medium VALUES('North America', 'Cable TV');
INSERT INTO region_medium VALUES('North America', 'Video (Purchase)');
INSERT INTO region_medium VALUES('North America', 'Theatrical');
INSERT INTO region_medium VALUES('North America', 'Network TV');
INSERT INTO region_medium VALUES('France', 'Satellite');
INSERT INTO region_medium VALUES('France', 'Video (Rental)');
INSERT INTO region_medium VALUES('France', 'Theatrical');
INSERT INTO studio_movie VALUES('Artisan Entertainment', 'Terminator 2');
INSERT INTO studio_movie VALUES('Carolco', 'Rocky');
INSERT INTO studio_movie VALUES('Carolco', 'Rocky 2');
INSERT INTO studio_movie VALUES('Cinergi', 'Medicine Man');
INSERT INTO studio_movie VALUES('Cinergi', 'Tombstone');
INSERT INTO studio_movie VALUES('Hollywood Pictures', 'Color of Night');
INSERT INTO studio_movie VALUES('Hollywood Pictures', 'Medicine Man');
INSERT INTO studio_movie VALUES('Malpaso Pictures', 'Absolute Power');
INSERT INTO studio_movie VALUES('Malpaso Pictures', 'Garden of Good and Evil');
INSERT INTO studio_movie VALUES('MGM.UA Studios', 'Terminator');
INSERT INTO studio_movie VALUES('Warner Bros', 'Play Misty for Me');
INSERT INTO studio_movie VALUES('Warner Bros', 'Unforgiven');
```

Step 5

Run this SELECT statement to retrieve the data in one set and check that it was entered correctly:

```
SELECT  sm.studio_name,
        sm.title,
        m.director,
        mla.male_lead,
        mla.agency
FROM    studio_movie    sm,
        male_lead_actor mla,
        movie           m
WHERE   sm.title = m.title
        AND
        m.lead_id = mla.lead_id
;
```

■ Declarative Relational Integrity: Pros and Cons

There are limits to the practical utility of declarative relational constraints. You have seen in the previous section that the database engine will not let you handle cascade updates. There are many other situations that are best handled with a trigger and some procedural code.

Declaring Foreign Key Constraints

You should use declarative constraints if they are available. In Oracle they execute much more quickly than triggers. They are reliable: Oracle has had a large number of developers and users testing them in every conceivable way for many years, whereas trigger code that you write has to be carefully and extensively tested to ensure that it does exactly what you intended. Declarative constraints are simple and easy to transfer from one database engine to another; the syntax is part of the ANSI SQL standard.

Triggers and Procedural Code

For the constraints that you cannot specify declaratively, you will need to write code in the form of triggers. A trigger is a small piece of procedural or PL/SQL code that the database invokes in response to an event in the database. Here are some examples of situations where you might want to enforce data integrity using such triggers. You should note that Oracle will not let you have both declarative and trigger-enforced foreign key constraints running in parallel between the same two tables. In virtually every case, you will find that the constraint and the trigger can be installed correctly, but every time the trigger code is executed you get a "mutating table" error. The exact causes for this are beyond the scope of this book; suffice it to say that triggers and declarative relational integrity cannot be combined.

The last two of these situations require the use of triggers to enforce the relationship *from the child to the parent*. Most of the scenarios we've discussed so far have been about enforcing the parent-to-child relationship.

Cascade Update

If you need a cascade update, then it is highly likely that you should have used a surrogate primary key. One of the purposes of the surrogate key is to allow the natural key to be edited. This allows the surrogate key to be left alone and never updated, hence removing the need for the cascade update. You will find that some designers insist that every table has a surrogate key so as to avoid this problem. This has disadvantages in terms of readability of the code and ease of querying the database. Also surrogate keys add extra processing requirements and storage needs and require the use of an alternate key in the same table if the natural key is to remain unique. You can find a discussion of this in Chapter 9 of this book.

Last One Out, Turn Off the Lights

Let's look at the SALE to SALE_ITEM constraint. It does not make much sense to have a SALE with no SALE_ITEM attached to it. In a regular UI program you would not save the SALE record until you knew you had a SALE_ITEM record to save immediately after it.

Now say you have a Sale #1204 with two items like so:

	A	B	C	D	E	F
1	Sale					
2	Till_Receipt_No	Customer_ID	Register_ID	Sale_Date_Time	Register_Clerk_ID	Delivery_Person_ID
3	1203	3211	2	3/15/2003 15:55	102	null
4	1204	4105	2	3/15/2003 15:59	102	105
5						
6						
7	Sale_Item					
8	Till_Receipt_No	Item_No	SKU	Quantity	Item_Price	Item_Cost
9	1203	1	001234567890	1	0.54	null
10	1203	2	5098765432011	2	1.25	null
11	1203	3	430980000125	1	10.99	null
12	1204	1	9876543210211	1	2.97	null
13	1204	2	0156789123455	3	3.59	null

- SALE and SALE_ITEM data

The customer suddenly decides not to buy the items, so you delete the last one (Item_No = 2), then you delete the first one (Item_No = 1). It would be useful if the database then deleted the corresponding SALE record since it now has no sale items attached to it. You would do this as a trigger that works on deletion from the SALE_ITEM table. This would query the remaining count of items belonging to the Till_Receipt_No and if this were zero, would then delete the SALE record.

In effect what you are doing here is enforcing a mandatory many role in the relationship. While this technique is not commonly used, it is useful for your design toolbox.

Summary Data in the Parent Table

When discussing normal forms in Chapter 10, we talked about a transitive dependency in which summary data was kept in a parent table as shown in this logical data model:

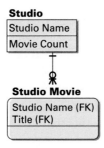

- Studio with Movie_Count attribute

While this did break third normal form, since the Movie_Count column has redundant data in it—it could be computed on the fly every time a query is run—it is a useful performance enhancement. The Movie_Count column could be updated with a trigger working from the STUDIO_MOVIE table that updated the count every time the STUDIO_MOVIE table was edited.

You should notice that this will slow down the performance of the inserts, updates, and deletes while speeding up the SELECT or query. As is so often the case with performance improvements, we have just moved the bottleneck from one place to another and, hopefully, to a place where the users will not notice it so much.

Naming Constraints: Make It Easy for the Programmers

All through this chapter you've created constraints with specific names. You can make the application programmers and database administrators very happy if you name all the constraints and indexes in a standard, easy-to-understand way. They will see these constraint names in the error message Oracle presents when it refuses to accept a data change—and it's much faster to diagnose the data problem when the constraint name helps you understand what the constraint is looking for.

There are no universal `naming conventions` for objects in a database. The important point to remember is this: it is more important that a standard is used than what the standard itself is. Anyone can learn a new standard quickly and proceed to be productive; what wastes time is constantly having to decode the meaning of something because it is named differently than other items in the same group. Keep it clear, keep it simple, and keep it consistent!

The Inside Information sidebar suggests a naming convention. It seems to be simple enough for people to understand quickly and they do not have to look up any reference documents to read the names and make a good guess at what the constraints are doing.

 Inside Information

Abbreviations

Don't abbreviate object names at all if you don't have to. Abbreviating will never make an object's name easier to understand—it can only make it harder to understand. So if a fully spelled out name for the object fits within the name-length limits of the environment you are working in, there is little reason to abbreviate at all. (Oracle limits object names to 30 characters.) Remember that the most expensive part of any application is the time invested by the people who build, maintain, and use it…so if you make your database object names as clear and self-explanatory as possible, you reduce the amount of time other people will have to spend investigating those objects just to find out what they contain.

If you must abbreviate, one approach to consider is the one recommended by Steve McConnell in Code Complete: A Practical Handbook of Software Construction *(Microsoft Press). He suggests removing all vowels from the name (except in the case of the name's first letter—if it is a vowel, leave it alone). Generally this works well in databases. Here are some examples:*

Studio_movie	reduces to	STD_MV
Employee	reduces to	EMPLY
Person_phone_number	reduces to	PRSN_PHN_NMBR

Naming Tables and Columns

You should choose names that will be meaningful to someone who is not familiar with the database, but who might know the business. The names should be meaningful to the end users of the database who do not understand computer terminology. These two suggestions generally mean that the best names will come out of the conceptual model at the beginning of the design process.

Since SQL ignores case on object names—and since Oracle stores all object names as uppercase—the best way to create space between words in an object name is with an underscore, for example:

- FIRST_NAME
- HOME_PHONE
- LAST_PROMOTION_DATE

Naming Check Constraints

For check constraints, the constraint name should include the following components: the name of the table and column the constraint is attached to, the type of value it accepts, and an indication that it is a check constraint. You can assemble these components in the order that makes the most sense to you—just be sure to use the same order consistently.

For example, you might start your check constraint names with "CK_ (to indicate "check"), followed by the table name, then either column name(s) or a description of the constraint. For example:

- CK_EMPLOYEE_Hire_Date
- CK_SALES_ITEM_ Price_Positive

Or you might assemble the naming components so that every object's name starts with the name of the table the object is related to, like this:

- EMPLOYEE_CK_Hire_Date
- SALES_ITEM_CK_Price_Positive

Naming Foreign Key Constraints

For foreign key constraints, the constraint name should include the name of the child table (the one the constraint is attached to) as well as the parent table (the one that is referenced). One approach could be to use FK as a prefix and _R_ to separate the table names, like this:

- FK_EMPLOYEE_R_DEPARTMENT
- FK_SALE_ITEM_R_PRODUCT

Or you might keep the child table name at the front, like this:

- EMPLOYEE_FK_DEPARTMENT
- SALE_ITEM_FK_PRODUCT

Occasionally you will have two separate relationships between the same pair of tables. In this case, use the relationships' role names to identify which is which, like this:

- FK_MAILING_MAIN_R_PRODUCT
- FK_MAILING_BONUS_R_PRODUCT

Or:

- MAILING_FK_PRODUCT_MAIN
- MAILING_FK_PRODUCT_BONUS

You can also give a name to each NOT NULL constraint in a database. However, you may find that it isn't worth your time to do so, because simply requiring data to be present is a common requirement.

Naming Indexes

Name the indexes to match the constraint they support. Thus primary key indexes might be named like this:

- PK_EMPLOYEE
- FK_MAILING_MAIN_PRODUCT

Or like this:

- EMPLOYEE_NDX_PK
- MAILING_NDX_PRODUCT_MAIN

Indexes used for general-purpose querying could be named for the table and the columns they cover and use the prefix SI (for Secondary Index), like this:

- SI_EMPLOYEE_Last_First_Names

Or you could keep the name of the related table in the front, use "NDX" followed by the columns in the index, and trust that the programmer understands what columns are within the table and what columns must be a foreign key to another table, like this:

- EMPLOYEE_NDX_First_Last_Names

As you can see, there are many ways to name constraints and indexes. The important thing to keep in mind is that your approach to naming must be applied consistently, and must be as self-explanatory as possible.

Chapter 11 Review

■ Chapter Summary

After reading this chapter and completing the Step-by-Step tutorials and Cross Checks, you should understand the following about ensuring quality data in your database:

Define Datatypes and Enforce Mandatory Columns

- Oracle uses five basic datatypes: NUMBER, CHAR, VARCHAR2, DATE, and LOB.

- NUMBER may have scale and precision declared; CHAR and VARCHAR2 have maximum length declared.

- A mandatory column is enforced using a "NOT NULL" constraint.

- Nulls propagate and override regular values when used in functions and with math operators.

- SQL uses weakly typed variables in which implicit datatype conversions are performed.

Describe a Data Domain

- A data domain is defined by a datatype, NULL/ NOT NULL constraint, and limits on the values.

- The check constraint must evaluate to true for the data to be accepted by the database.

Implement Column and Table Constraints on Data Values

- Column constraints work on one row in a column.

- Table constraints work on one row in a table.

- A column constraint is an effective way of implementing a domain.

- Column constraints can use math operators, basic Oracle functions, and Oracle system variables (USER, SYSDATE).

Use Unique Indexes to Limit Primary Key Values

- Primary key constraints work on all rows of the table, but only the columns assigned to the key.

- Primary keys are supported by unique indexes.

- Alternate keys are unique indexes that are not primary keys.

- Indexes are also used to improve performance of foreign key constraints and select queries.

Convert Relationships into Foreign Key Constraints

- A foreign key constraint is only declared for the child end of a relationship.

- Foreign key constraints only enforce the presence of matching values between the foreign key columns and the referenced primary key.

- Optional roles in relationships convert to NULL columns in the child table.

- Cascade delete may be defined on a foreign key constraint to enhance the relationship. These features are defined in the physical data model only.

- Identifying relationships may be good candidates for cascade delete constraints.

- Oracle does not implement all the possible forms of cascade effect directly, in particular cascade update and set NULL. You must code procedural triggers for this.

- Triggers may be used for enforcing other features of the relationship; for example, a mandatory many role.

Describe the Benefits and Limits of Declarative Relational Integrity

- Declarative RI is easier to transfer between different database vendors.

- Declarative RI executes faster than triggers.

- Several constraint declarations may be necessary to implement a relationship as defined in the logical data model.

Create Names for Various Database Constraints

- Constraint names assist programmers in troubleshooting when errors occur.

- A consistent naming convention is important for understandability.

Key Terms

alternate key *(310)*	domain *(301)*	precision *(296)*
cascade delete *(317)*	LOB *(298)*	scale *(296)*
cascade update *(317)*	naming convention *(329)*	strongly typed *(301)*
CHAR *(297)*	non-unique index *(311)*	table constraint *(306)*
column constraint *(303)*	NOT NULL *(295)*	unique constraint *(309)*
DATE *(298)*	NULL *(295)*	unique index *(307)*
declarative constraint *(327)*	null propagation *(295)*	VARCHAR2 *(297)*
delete restrict *(317)*	NUMBER *(296)*	weakly typed *(301)*

Key Term Quiz

Use the Key Terms list to complete the sentences that follow. Not all terms will be used.

1. A number datatype uses _____ to indicate the number of decimal places.

2. An identifying relationship may use _____ to ensure that the rows in the child table are automatically removed when the parent entry is deleted.

3. A(n) _____ is used to support an alternate key constraint.

4. A fixed-length string has a datatype of _____.

5. A(n) _____ is used to limit values in a domain.

Matching Definition Quiz

Relate each term on the left with the appropriate description on the right.

Term		Description	
1.	Naming convention	a.	A column in which missing values are allowed
2.	Strongly typed	b.	The default type of cascading for foreign key constraints
3.	NULL	c.	A sorted list of the values in a column
4.	Restrict	d.	A system for defining consistent names for constraints
5.	Non-unique index	e.	A language in which values must be explicitly converted for comparisons

Multiple-Choice Quiz

1. A naming convention is
   a. A place where movie moguls meet
   b. A system for creating standardized names
   c. A birthday gathering
   d. A place in the database where table names are stored
   e. A column constraint

2. A column that is used to store money values would use the following datatype:
   a. MONEY
   b. VARCHAR2(12,2)
   c. NUMBER (12,2)
   d. NUMBER
   e. LOB

3. What is the largest number of characters that a VARCHAR2 can hold?

   a. 2

   b. 2,000

   c. 4,000

   d. 2,000,000,000

   e. 2,147,483,647

4. What type of index would be used in a primary key? (Choose two.)

   a. Binary tree

   b. Non-unique index

   c. NULL

   d. Unique index

   e. Strongly typed

5. Which two constraints must be used to enforce an optional 1:1 relationship?

   a. Primary key

   b. Foreign key

   c. Table constraint

   d. Unique constraint

   e. Column constraint

6. Why should constraints be named?

   a. It makes them easier to find.

   b. To make them work.

   c. It standardizes the database.

   d. To make them understandable.

   e. So that troubleshooting by the programmers is easier.

7. In a table PURCHASE, you have a column Total_Amount. The purchase items are in a related table. How would you ensure that the Total_Amount is always correct?

   a. Use a trigger on Purchase_Item to update the column.

   b. Use a cascade update foreign key constraint.

   c. Relate the primary key of Purchase_Item back to the PURCHASE table.

   d. Use a set NULL foreign key constraint.

   e. Use a trigger on PURCHASE to update the column.

8. The model shows an identifying relationship between Person_Mailing and Phone_Call. What is the correct syntax for the foreign key?

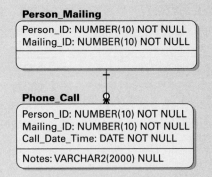

Person_Mailing

Person_ID: NUMBER(10) NOT NULL
Mailing_ID: NUMBER(10) NOT NULL

Phone_Call

Person_ID: NUMBER(10) NOT NULL
Mailing_ID: NUMBER(10) NOT NULL
Call_Date_Time: DATE NOT NULL

Notes: VARCHAR2(2000) NULL

- Person_Mailing to Phone_Call relationship

   a. ALTER TABLE person_mailing ADD CONSTRAINT fk_pm_r_pc FOREIGN KEY (person_id, mailing_id) REFERENCES phone_call(person_id, mailing_id)

   b. ALTER TABLE phone_call ADD CONSTRAINT fk_pc_r_pm FOREIGN KEY (person_id, mailing_id) REFERENCES person_mailing(person_id, mailing_id)

   c. ALTER TABLE phone_call ADD CONSTRAINT fk_pc_r_pm FOREIGN KEY (person_id) REFERENCES person_mailing(person_id)

   d. ALTER TABLE phone_call ADD CONSTRAINT fk_pc_r_pm FOREIGN KEY (person_id, mailing_id) REFERENCES person_mailing(mailing_id)

   e. ALTER TABLE phone_call ADD CONSTRAINT fk_pc_r_pm FOREIGN KEY (person_id, mailing_id, call_date_time) REFERENCES person_mailing(person_id, mailing_id)

9. A computer language that requires the programmer to check the datatypes is called

   a. Relational integrity

   b. Weakly typed

   c. Weakly written

   d. Strongly typed

   e. Restricted

10. A NUMBER datatype is defined by which two of these features?

   a. Optionality

   b. Length

   c. Cardinality

   d. Precision

   e. Scale

11. A table constraint limits values by comparing

   a. The values across several columns

   b. The values in a single column

   c. The value in field with a formula

   d. The unique values in an identifier

   e. The values in another table

12. A domain for a mandatory string column is a combination of three of the following:

   a. A NOT NULL constraint

   b. A single column expression that evaluates to true

   c. A datatype

   d. A datatype with length

   e. A multicolumn expression that must evaluate to true

13. To enforce a one-to-one relationship, what must you add to the table with the foreign key constraint?

   a. A non-unique index

   b. A NOT NULL constraint

   c. A primary key

   d. A domain

   e. A unique constraint on the foreign key columns

14. When you implement an identifying relationship, which type of cascade action would you *not* use?

   a. ON DELETE CASCADE

   b. ON UPDATE CASCADE

   c. ON DELETE SET NULL

   d. ON DELETE RESTRICT

   e. ON UPDATE RESTRICT

15. What is the result of an expression 100 / x where x is NULL?

   a. 100%

   b. 0

   c. Infinity

   d. Null

   e. $\sqrt{-1}$

■ Essay Quiz

1. Explain what a "cascade update" foreign key is and when you might use it.

2. Why is a primary key necessary for a foreign key constraint to function correctly?

3. What is the difference between a column constraint and a table constraint?

4. Describe a domain for storing telephone numbers.

5. When you have a recursive relationship, the role at the parent end is nearly always optional. Explain why you would not use a mandatory role in this situation. (Hint: Consider what happens at the top of a hierarchy.)

Lab Projects

• Lab Project 11.1

Case Study

Figure 11.5 shows the logical data model for the Clapham Specialty Store. Use this model and your best judgment and refer back to the original case study description to determine the domain for each attribute. Pay particular attention to any check constraints you might need.

① For each attribute decide on a datatype.

② For each attribute decide on a length, scale, and precision as appropriate.

③ For each attribute decide whether you can allow missing values.

④ For the following attributes add suitable limits to the values as either column or table constraints:

REGISTER_LOG.End_Time
SALE_ITEM.Quantity
LOCATION.Side
EMPLOYEE.Job_Type
EMPLOYEE.Social_Security_Number

⑤ Are there any unique constraints in addition to the primary keys that you should add? If so, which ones?

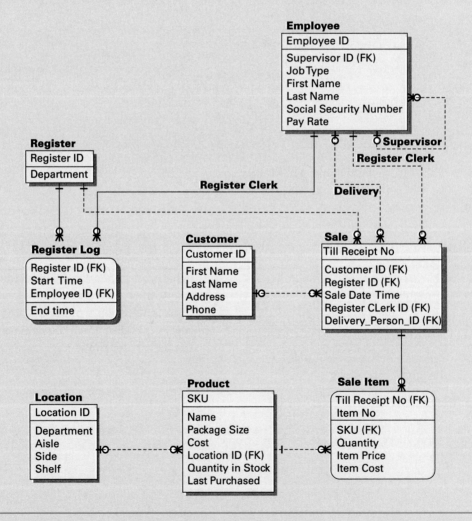

• **Figure 11.5**   Logical ERD for the Clapham Store

Case Study

Once again using the model shown in Figure 11.5, answer the following:

① Write a SQL script to create all the tables and implement the primary keys and foreign keys.

To prove your script works, you should show the SQL*Plus log.

② How would you ensure that the values used for Register_Clerk_Id and Delivery_Person_Id referenced employees who had the correct Job_Type?

Other Useful Oracle Techniques

"If the only tool you have is a hammer, you tend to see every problem as a nail."

—ABRAHAM MASLOW

In this chapter, you will learn how to

- **Transfer data between tables**
- **Rename tables**
- **Alter a table's structure**
- **Explore views**
- **Examine sequences and synonyms**

In the previous chapter you examined the physical data model and how to ensure the quality of the data that is saved. You created a table and dealt with datatypes and missing values or NULLs. Then you looked at limits to the data values in each column and implemented constraints on the data. You also learned about indexes and some of the ways they help improve data quality. Finally you completed exercises that showed some of the benefits and limitations of declarative relational integrity.

This chapter is a "catch-all" that presents a variety of tips and tools that will round out your knowledge of Oracle from a SQL standpoint. In it, you will learn how to transfer data between tables; rename tables and change their structure; and create and use views, sequences, and synonyms. Once you know the information in this chapter, you will be well equipped to start work as a beginning data modeler.

■ Transferring Data Between Tables

If you have not done the examples from the previous chapters, enter the following code to create the tables and data used in this chapter. (If you already have these tables and data, skip over the following code listing and continue reading.)

```
DROP TABLE test_purchase;
DROP TABLE test_product;
DROP TABLE test_person;
DROP TABLE test_old_item;
DROP TABLE test_purchase_archive;

CREATE TABLE test_person (
     person_code VARCHAR2(3) PRIMARY KEY,
     first_name  VARCHAR2(15),
     last_name   VARCHAR2(20),
     hire_date   DATE
     )
;
CREATE INDEX test_person_name_index
ON test_person(last_name, first_name);

INSERT INTO test_person VALUES
     ('CA', 'Charlene', 'Atlas', '01-FEB-2002');
INSERT INTO test_person VALUES
     ('GA', 'Gary', 'Anderson', '15-FEB-2002');
INSERT INTO test_person VALUES
     ('BB', 'Bobby', 'Barkenhagen', '28-FEB-2002');
INSERT INTO test_person VALUES
     ('LB', 'Laren', 'Baxter', '01-MAR-2002');

CREATE TABLE test_product (
     product_name     VARCHAR2(25),
     product_price    NUMBER(4,2),
     quantity_on_hand NUMBER(5,0),
     last_stock_date  DATE
     )
;
INSERT INTO test_product VALUES
     ('Small Widget', 99, 1, '15-JAN-2003');
INSERT INTO test_product VALUES
     ('Medium Wodget', 75, 1000, '15-JAN-2002');
INSERT INTO test_product VALUES
     ('Chrome Phoobar', 50, 100, '15-JAN-2003');
INSERT INTO test_product VALUES
     ('Round Chrome Snaphoo', 25, 10000, null);
INSERT INTO test_product VALUES
     ('Extra Huge Mega Phoobar +',9.95,1234,'15-JAN-2004');
INSERT INTO test_product VALUES ('Square Zinculator',
     45, 1, TO_DATE('December 31, 2002, 11:30 P.M.',
                    'Month dd, YYYY, HH:MI P.M.')
```

```
                                )
                        ;

                        CREATE TABLE test_purchase (
                             product_name  VARCHAR2(25),
                             salesperson   VARCHAR2(3),
                             purchase_date DATE,
                             quantity      NUMBER(4,2)
                             )
                        ;
                        CREATE INDEX test_purchase_product
                        ON test_purchase(product_name);
                        CREATE INDEX test_purchase_salesperson
                        ON test_purchase(salesperson);
                        INSERT INTO test_purchase VALUES
                             ('Small Widget', 'CA', '14-JUL-2003', 1);
                        INSERT INTO test_purchase VALUES
                             ('Medium Wodget', 'BB', '14-JUL-2003', 75);
                        INSERT INTO test_purchase VALUES
                             ('Chrome Phoobar', 'GA', '14-JUL-2003', 2);
                        INSERT INTO test_purchase VALUES
                             ('Small Widget', 'GA', '15-JUL-2003', 8);
                        INSERT INTO test_purchase VALUES
                             ('Medium Wodget', 'LB', '15-JUL-2003', 20);
                        INSERT INTO test_purchase VALUES
                             ('Round Chrome Snaphoo', 'CA', '16-JUL-2003', 5);

                        UPDATE test_product
                        SET    product_price = product_price * .9
                        WHERE  product_name NOT IN (
                               SELECT DISTINCT product_name
                               FROM   test_purchase
                               )
                        ;
                        CREATE TABLE test_old_item (
                             item_id   CHAR(20),
                             item_desc CHAR(25)
                             )
                        ;
                        INSERT INTO test_old_item VALUES
                             ('LA-101', 'Can, Small');
                        INSERT INTO test_old_item VALUES
                             ('LA-102', 'Can, Large');
                        INSERT INTO test_old_item VALUES
                             ('LA-103', 'Bottle, Small');
                        INSERT INTO test_old_item VALUES
                             ('LA-104', 'Bottle, Large');
                        INSERT INTO test_old_item VALUES
                             ('NY-101', 'Box, Small');
                        INSERT INTO test_old_item VALUES
                             ('NY-102', 'Box, Large');
                        INSERT INTO test_old_item VALUES
                             ('NY-103', 'Shipping Carton, Small');
                        INSERT INTO test_old_item VALUES
```

```
      ('NY-104', 'Shipping Carton, Large');
CREATE TABLE test_purchase_archive (
      product_name   VARCHAR2(25),
      salesperson    VARCHAR2(3),
      purchase_date DATE,
      quantity       NUMBER(4,2)
      )
;
INSERT INTO test_purchase_archive VALUES
      ('Round Snaphoo', 'BB', '21-JUN-2001', 10);
INSERT INTO test_purchase_archive VALUES
      ('Large Harflinger', 'GA', '22-JUN-2001', 50);
INSERT INTO test_purchase_archive VALUES
      ('Medium Wodget', 'LB', '23-JUN-2001', 20);
INSERT INTO test_purchase_archive VALUES
      ('Small Widget', 'ZZ', '24-JUN-2002', 80);
INSERT INTO test_purchase_archive VALUES
      ('Chrome Phoobar', 'CA', '25-JUN-2002', 2);
INSERT INTO test_purchase_archive VALUES
      ('Small Widget', 'JT', '26-JUN-2002', 50);
```

Now that you have learned how to use all of the basic DML commands, you are ready to put them to use performing a fundamental, and very necessary, function: copying records from one table to another. Being able to do this is important for a number of reasons:

- **Importing data from a legacy system** A regular part of SQL activities is transferring data from an existing system into a new system. Sometimes the existing system is being replaced by the new system. Other times the data has been purchased from an external source, and needs to be mapped and transferred into your own system. Often, the original data must be modified on its way to the new tables, which can involve using functions such as UPPER, LOWER, LTRIM, RTRIM, SUBSTR, INSTR, TO_CHAR, and DECODE.

- **Loading summaries into a data warehouse** The basic function of a data warehouse is to respond to queries about data—the kind of questions that can be answered with SUM, COUNT, AVG, MIN, and MAX functions along with GROUP BY clauses. These answers are often stored in a separate set of tables in which the aggregates have been precalculated to give really fast performance, and that set of tables is often populated using SQL queries.

- **Copying relational data into flat files for faster access** Relational databases are the most efficient way to store data, but retrieving data out of relational tables can take longer because the tables need to be joined, and table joins can be time-consuming. In some applications, it makes sense to place a copy of related data from multiple tables into a single flat-file table where the joins have already been done. The flat-file table is a form of denormalization that improves query performance by reducing the computational effort of joining tables at the expense of more complex updating of the data.

If you are dealing with a data warehouse (which is essentially a read-only source of data), you will find there are many Oracle optimizations that can be implemented to improve the database's ability to execute a select statement very quickly with huge amounts (more than 1 billion rows) of data.

Transferring Data Using INSERT

This popular technique utilizes an INSERT command with a subquery that causes the inserted data to come from another table. To give yourself a destination for this technique, enter the following command:

```
CREATE TABLE test_purchase_log (
     purchase_date     DATE,
     product_name      VARCHAR2(25),
     product_price     NUMBER(4,2),
     quantity          NUMBER(4,2),
     sales_first_name  VARCHAR2(15),
     sales_last_name   VARCHAR2(20)
     )
;
```

The TEST_PURCHASE_LOG table is a flat-file representation of the important information from each purchase: date, product name and price, quantity purchased, and full name of salesperson. A table like this serves well as the basis for queries to answer business questions such as "Who sold the largest and smallest quantities of the Red Snaphoo?" Placing a complete compilation of the information necessary to answer these queries into a single table allows the answers to be produced more quickly, and it helps ensure that access for users who are executing individual transactions (making sales in this case) is not slowed down by questions from people who need to analyze those transactions as a group.

Now that you have a flat-file table suitable for storing records to be analyzed, it's time to populate that table with data. You will do that using an INSERT INTO command that joins records from the PERSON, PRODUCT, and PURCHASE tables. The syntax for the command is as follows:

```
INSERT INTO table_name
     SELECT statement;
```

The SELECT statement portion of the syntax example will be whatever SELECT command will produce the data you want in a structure that matches that of the destination table. To see how this works, enter the following command, and check your results with those shown in Figure 12.1:

```
INSERT INTO test_purchase_log
     SELECT purc.purchase_date,
            prod.product_name,
            prod.product_price,
            purc.quantity,
            pers.first_name,
            pers.last_name
     FROM   test_product  prod,
            test_person    pers,
            test_purchase purc
     WHERE  prod.product_name = purc.product_name
            AND
            pers.person_code = purc.salesperson;

set lines 200
SELECT * FROM test_purchase_log;
```

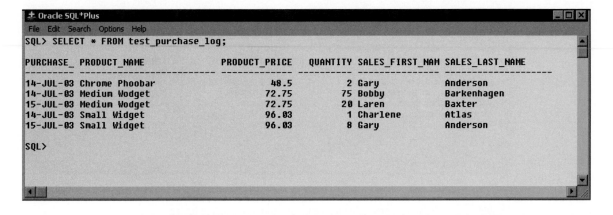

```
Oracle SQL*Plus                                                    _ □ X
File  Edit  Search  Options  Help
SQL> SELECT * FROM test_purchase_log;

PURCHASE_ PRODUCT_NAME           PRODUCT_PRICE   QUANTITY SALES_FIRST_NAM SALES_LAST_NAME
--------- ---------------------- ------------- ---------- --------------- ---------------
14-JUL-03 Chrome Phoobar                 48.5           2 Gary            Anderson
14-JUL-03 Medium Wodget                 72.75          75 Bobby           Barkenhagen
15-JUL-03 Medium Wodget                 72.75          20 Laren           Baxter
14-JUL-03 Small Widget                  96.03           1 Charlene        Atlas
15-JUL-03 Small Widget                  96.03           8 Gary            Anderson

SQL>
```

● **Figure 12.1**   Copying records from one table to another

As you can see, the TEST_PURCHASE_LOG table contains an easy-to-use collection of information about each transaction in the TEST_PURCHASE table.

Creating a New Table Based on an Existing One

The method you just learned for copying data from one table to another assumes that the destination table already exists. That's appropriate for day-to-day additions to the destination table—but there's a way to make the creation of that table easier, too. It's a variation on the CREATE TABLE command. The syntax is as follows:

```
CREATE TABLE new_table_name
AS
     SELECT statement
;
```

In this case, the SELECT statement portion of the command will be the same SELECT statement you used to populate the first destination table a moment ago. Enter the following code to create a second destination table with this technique, and compare your results with those shown in Figure 12.2:

```
CREATE TABLE test_purchase_log2
AS
     SELECT purc.purchase_date,
            prod.product_name,
            prod.product_price,
            purc.quantity,
            pers.first_name,
            pers.last_name
     FROM   test_product  prod,
            test_person    pers,
            test_purchase purc
     WHERE  prod.product_name = purc.product_name
       AND  pers.person_code = purc.salesperson
;

SELECT * FROM test_purchase_log2;
```

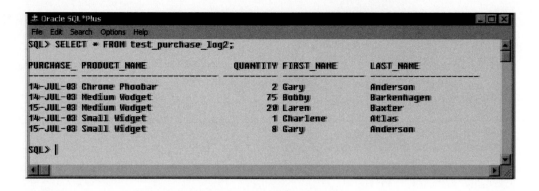

• **Figure 12.2**   Creating a new table based on one or more existing tables

Case Study

If we look at our case study example of the Clapham Specialty Store, we can see an example of when John might use this feature to create tables for his database. John currently has a PRODUCT table and a SALE_ITEM table in his database. The SALE_ITEM table contains some of the same data from the original PRODUCT table, which makes sense because items that are sold at the store get added to this table. The SALE_ITEM table is used when products are discounted for a special sale. Therefore, John could have chosen to create the SALE_ITEM table from the original PRODUCT table.

■ Renaming Tables

From time to time you will be called on to change the names of existing tables. It's very easy to do. The syntax is as follows:

```
RENAME old_table_name TO new_table_name;
```

Apply this to your own tables now by entering the following RENAME command:

```
RENAME test_purchase_log2 TO test_log;
```

This syntax for changing the names of tables also works for any other Oracle object. An Oracle object is any part of a structure in a database. Examples include the following:

- Tables
- Views
- Indexes
- Stored procedures
- Synonyms
- Sequences

Cross Check

Transferring Data

Now that you've been introduced to the concept of transferring data between tables, take a moment to check your knowledge by answering the following questions:

1. How is the INSERT command used in transferring data between tables?

2. How can you create a new table based on an existing table?

Introduction to Relational Databases and SQL Programming

■ Altering a Table's Structure

As a database evolves, the business needs that it must satisfy can change. This often creates reasons to change the structure of tables the database already contains. Fortunately, certain types of changes are simple to make: adding new columns, changing the datatypes of existing columns, and changing whether columns allow NULL values.

Adding Columns

You can add columns to a table at any time. New columns are appended to the end of the table's structure after all the existing columns. The syntax to do this is as follows:

```
ALTER TABLE table_name
ADD new_column_name datatype [NOT NULL]
;
```

Try out the `ALTER TABLE` command by adding a new column to the TEST_LOG table with the following code. Compare the results you get with those shown in Figure 12.3.

```
set lines 100
DESC test_log

ALTER TABLE test_log ADD data_load_date VARCHAR2(8);

DESC test_log
```

 Remember that all DDL commands—since they change the structure of the database—have an implicit COMMIT. This means that you cannot change your mind and simply issue a ROLLBACK command to undo the change.

Notice that here you added a NULL column, which makes sense as there will be no data for the new column. You can also add a NOT NULL column to a table. If you add a NOT NULL column, you will usually want to specify a default value for the column. Here is an example showing how to do this. In this example, you add an auditing column that stores the user's Oracle login ID each time a new record is inserted.

```
ALTER TABLE
    ADD data_loaded_by VARCHAR2(20) DEFAULT USER NOT NULL;
```

This uses Oracle's built-in variable USER to insert the account name (or user ID) into the column if the value is not specified by the INSERT statement.

Changing Column Datatypes

You may have wondered why the column you just added is a text column when its name suggests it is supposed to contain dates. The answer: so you can change the new column's datatype to one that is more appropriate.

The syntax to change the datatype of an existing column is as follows:

```
ALTER TABLE table_name
MODIFY column_name new_datatype
;
```

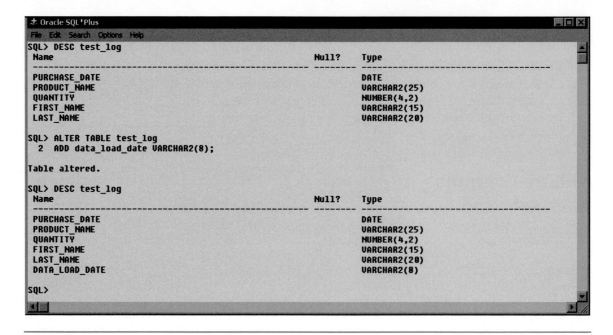

```
 Oracle SQL *Plus
File  Edit  Search  Options  Help
SQL> DESC test_log
 Name                                             Null?    Type
 ----------------------------------------------- -------- ------------------------
 PURCHASE_DATE                                             DATE
 PRODUCT_NAME                                              VARCHAR2(25)
 QUANTITY                                                  NUMBER(4,2)
 FIRST_NAME                                                VARCHAR2(15)
 LAST_NAME                                                 VARCHAR2(20)

SQL> ALTER TABLE test_log
  2   ADD data_load_date VARCHAR2(8);

Table altered.

SQL> DESC test_log
 Name                                             Null?    Type
 ----------------------------------------------- -------- ------------------------
 PURCHASE_DATE                                             DATE
 PRODUCT_NAME                                              VARCHAR2(25)
 QUANTITY                                                  NUMBER(4,2)
 FIRST_NAME                                                VARCHAR2(15)
 LAST_NAME                                                 VARCHAR2(20)
 DATA_LOAD_DATE                                            VARCHAR2(8)

SQL>
```

● **Figure 12.3**   Adding a column to an existing table

To apply this to your TEST_LOG table, enter the following code. Compare your results with those shown in Figure 12.4.

```
DESC test_log

ALTER TABLE test_log
MODIFY data_load_date DATE;

DESC test_log
```

There are a couple things you should beware of here. Oracle has a set of rules about when you can change a column and how you can change it. Often you will find that your MODIFY command is prohibited by these rules. They include the following:

- If the column contains data, its type cannot be changed.
- If the column contains data, a VARCHAR2 cannot be shortened, only lengthened.
- If a column contains a NULL, you cannot make the column NOT NULL.

Changing NULL Options

Often when a database is being designed, the users are not yet sure which columns will be required and which will not. Hopefully database designs that you create will not have this issue, because you will have followed the

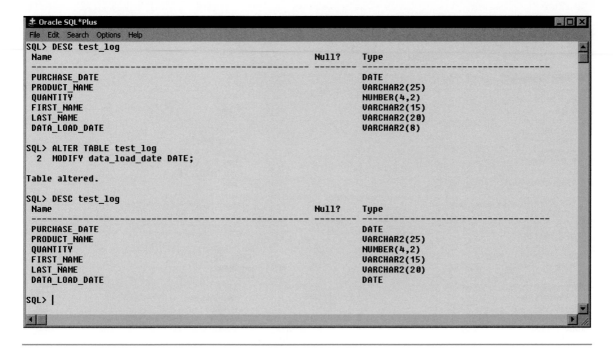

```
± Oracle SQL*Plus                                                        _□X
 File  Edit  Search  Options  Help
SQL> DESC test_log
  Name                                          Null?      Type
  ----------------------------------------- --------  --------------------
  PURCHASE_DATE                                          DATE
  PRODUCT_NAME                                           VARCHAR2(25)
  QUANTITY                                               NUMBER(4,2)
  FIRST_NAME                                             VARCHAR2(15)
  LAST_NAME                                              VARCHAR2(20)
  DATA_LOAD_DATE                                         VARCHAR2(8)

SQL> ALTER TABLE test_log
  2   MODIFY data_load_date DATE;

Table altered.

SQL> DESC test_log
  Name                                          Null?      Type
  ----------------------------------------- --------  --------------------
  PURCHASE_DATE                                          DATE
  PRODUCT_NAME                                           VARCHAR2(25)
  QUANTITY                                               NUMBER(4,2)
  FIRST_NAME                                             VARCHAR2(15)
  LAST_NAME                                              VARCHAR2(20)
  DATA_LOAD_DATE                                         DATE

SQL> |
```

• **Figure 12.4**   Changing the datatype of an existing column

guidelines in Chapters 8 and 9 and know what optionality to apply to the column! If you are unsure about the optionality, it's common to initially create the columns so they allow NULL values, and then later change them so they do not. (You can change NOT NULL columns to NULL too, of course.) The syntax to do this is as follows:

```
ALTER TABLE table_name
MODIFY column_name NOT NULL
;
```

Before you can modify your new column so it requires data, you must fill that column in the table's existing records. The following set of commands accomplishes this and then modifies the column so it will no longer accept NULL values. Enter the commands and compare their results with those shown in Figure 12.5.

```
UPDATE test_log SET data_load_date = '15-DEC-2003';

DESC test_log

ALTER TABLE test_log MODIFY data_load_date NOT NULL;

DESC test_log
```

```
± Oracle SQL*Plus                                                        _ □ ✕
File  Edit  Search  Options  Help
SQL> UPDATE test_log
  2   SET data_load_date = '15-DEC-2003';

5 rows updated.

SQL> DESC test_log
 Name                                                   Null?    Type
 ------------------------------------------------------ -------- ----------------------
 PURCHASE_DATE                                                   DATE
 PRODUCT_NAME                                                    VARCHAR2(25)
 QUANTITY                                                        NUMBER(4,2)
 FIRST_NAME                                                      VARCHAR2(15)
 LAST_NAME                                                       VARCHAR2(20)
 DATA_LOAD_DATE                                                  DATE

SQL> ALTER TABLE test_log
  2   MODIFY data_load_date NOT NULL;

Table altered.

SQL> DESC test_log
 Name                                                   Null?    Type
 ------------------------------------------------------ -------- ----------------------
 PURCHASE_DATE                                                   DATE
 PRODUCT_NAME                                                    VARCHAR2(25)
 QUANTITY                                                        NUMBER(4,2)
 FIRST_NAME                                                      VARCHAR2(15)
 LAST_NAME                                                       VARCHAR2(20)
 DATA_LOAD_DATE                                         NOT NULL DATE

SQL> |
```

● **Figure 12.5**   Changing the NULL option of an existing column

■ Views

The concept of a view is simple: Define a query that is going to be used frequently, store it in the Oracle database, and allow users to call it by name, as they would a table. When users select records from the view, Oracle runs the view's stored query, organizes the resulting records in whatever way is specified by the view, and presents them to the user. From the user's point of view, the view looks and behaves exactly like a table: Data appears to be retrieved from it. In reality, the data is actually coming *through* the view, from one or more other sources. Some views act so much like tables that you can insert and update or delete data through the view.

Why are views useful? A variety of reasons. One very common use for a view is to join data from two or more tables and present it to users in one easy-to-read list. By simplifying the record-retrieval process so that users don't have to understand how to join tables, you make the data available to a larger number of people.

Views are also useful for enforcing security, because they allow you to limit the columns and rows returned to the user. If you don't want them to see a personnel table's salary column, just don't include that column when defining the view. As far as the user of the view is concerned, the column will not exist. The same is true for limiting rows: Just include a WHERE clause when defining the view, and the records returned will be filtered in whatever way you want.

Finally, views can provide a convenience factor for you and other users. Certainly you would never design a table whose columns have hard-to-understand names or are in a bizarre order—but other people do, and sooner or later you will have to use their tables. Because a view is just a stored query, you can utilize a query's ability to change the names assigned to columns, as well as change the order in which the columns are displayed. For instance, recently we had the task of analyzing an existing database with hundreds of columns with names like ID101, ID205, ID3322, and so on. There was a reference guide explaining what each column contained, but continually referring to that reference would have wasted a lot of time, and users who didn't have the reference would have been out of luck. For each table in the database, a view was created that presented that table's columns using clear, easy-to-understand names. As a result, nobody tries retrieving data directly from the tables; everyone is retrieving from the views instead, because when they look at the column names, they understand what they're getting.

Creating a View

The method for creating a view is simplicity itself. Essentially, you specify the name of the view, and then the SELECT statement that the view will execute. The syntax is as follows:

```
CREATE OR REPLACE VIEW view_name AS
SELECT statement
;
```

Note that this **CREATE OR REPLACE VIEW** command has a new component: OR REPLACE. This addition allows the command to create a new view even if a view with the same name already exists. (The existing view gets overwritten in this case, of course.)

Let's take a look at our case study company, the Clapham Specialty Store. John may want his employees to only be available to see certain columns of database tables. Therefore he could execute the CREATE OR REPLACE VIEW command and create a view on a table or tables that would restrict users from seeing all columns of tables and only show them the columns that they require.

Case Study

To see a view in action, enter the following commands and compare your results with those shown in Figure 12.6:

```
SELECT * FROM test_purchase;

CREATE OR REPLACE VIEW test_sales_by_atlas_v AS
SELECT *
FROM    test_purchase
WHERE   salesperson = 'CA'
;

SELECT * FROM test_sales_by_atlas_v;
```

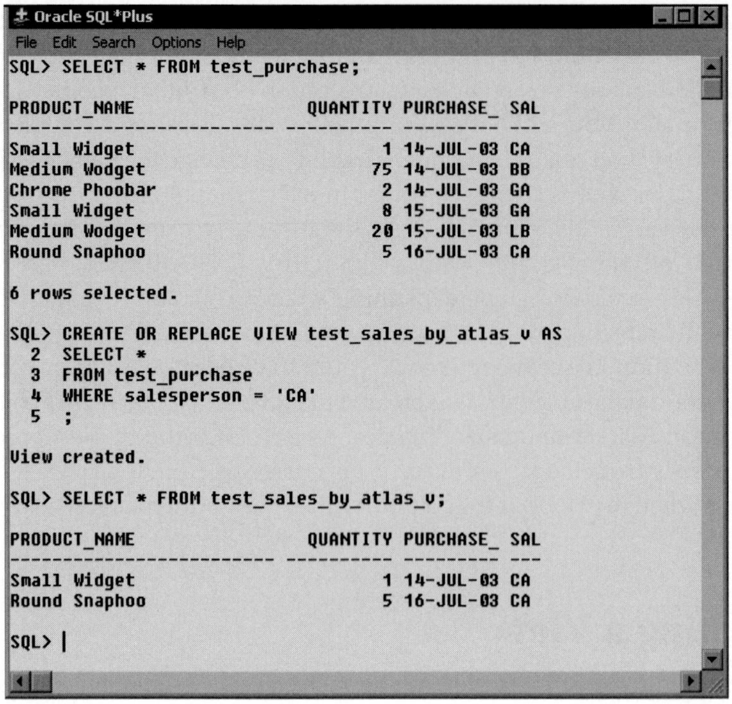

● **Figure 12.6** Creating a simple filtering view

To see how to create a view that presents data from joined tables, enter the following commands:

```
CREATE OR REPLACE VIEW test_sales_per_person_v AS
SELECT  pers.first_name || ' ' || pers.last_name SALESPERSON,
        purc.product_name,
        purc.purchase_date,
        purc.quantity
FROM    test_person    pers,
        test_purchase purc
WHERE   pers.person_code = purc.salesperson (+)
;

SELECT * FROM test_sales_per_person_v
ORDER BY salesperson, product_name, purchase_date;
```

Updateable Views

Some views are sufficiently simple that they can act exactly like tables and allow the users to execute INSERT, UPDATE, or DELETE statements. How do you know when you have such a view? The basic criteria are listed here:

■ The database engine must be able to uniquely identify the row of data from the underlying table you are working on.

■ *All* required (NOT NULL) columns are present in the view.

The example includes an ORDER BY clause in the SELECT statement that retrieves data *from* the view, but there is no ORDER BY clause within the view-creation statement itself. Up until Oracle8*i*, views could not include an ORDER BY clause. In 8*i* and subsequent versions, you can cause the view to sort the records it shows by including the ORDER BY clause right after the WHERE clause, just as you would in a standard SELECT statement.

- The value in the source column can be precisely computed from the value in the view column.

Say you create the TEST_LOG as a view rather than a table:

```
CREATE VIEW test_log_v AS
    SELECT purc.purchase_date,
           prod.product_name,
           prod.product_price,
           purc.quantity,
           pers.first_name,
           pers.last_name
    FROM   test_product  prod,
           test_person   pers,
           test_purchase purc
    WHERE  prod.product_name = purc.product_name
      AND  pers.person_code = purc.salesperson;

select * from test_log_v;
```

The SELECT statement shows you that this view contains exactly the same data as the flat-file table you made earlier. Can you insert a new record through this view? Because this view contains a join, the database cannot determine which row in which of the underlying tables to update. Since the view does not contain all the NOT NULL columns of the underlying tables, the INSERT would generate an error.

As the first two criteria have been violated, this view is not updateable and any attempt to insert or update records will generate an Oracle error.

A simple filtering view, such as the one in Figure 12.6, is updateable, however. It contains all the columns; it only references one table (no JOIN or UNION clauses); it has no functions applied to the columns. What would happen if you tried to insert this row of data?

```
INSERT INTO test_sales_by_atlas_v
VALUES ('Shaving Foam', 'SC', '12-MAR-2003', 2);

SELECT * FROM test_sales_by_atlas_v;
```

The insert works and your data is saved, but you cannot see the data through the view because the salesperson was SC instead of CA. This is known as a blind write (or more dramatically a "write-only" table!) and will cause concern for a user who will not believe that his precious data has been saved correctly. Oracle can help here with the CHECK OPTION applied to the view. If the view is created WITH CHECK OPTION, Oracle tests the data *against the WHERE clause* before allowing the INSERT. In the preceding example, the row would be failed as it does not pass the WHERE clause test and cannot be seen through the view.

Dropping Views

Dropping a view is as easy as dropping a table (but less destructive—since a view doesn't contain any data, the worst that can happen if you accidentally drop a view is having to re-create it). The syntax to drop a view is as follows:

```
DROP VIEW view_name;
```

Try the DROP VIEW command now by using it to drop the view you just created. The command to do this is

```
DROP VIEW test_sales_per_person_v;
```

Top N Analysis

Once you see how to make SQL show you the top 1, 10, or 100 records matching whatever criteria and sorting you specify, the technique is so easy you may prefer to simply use the technique manually, rather than creating a view that encapsulates it. Doing it for other users can score you big points, though, and increased user satisfaction equals increased job security and higher pay. Okay, maybe this technique won't get you a raise, but it might get you a free beverage of your choosing.

This technique leverages the fact that Oracle dynamically assigns row numbers to every row returned by each query it processes. This means that no matter where a row resides in its table, if it is the first (or only) row returned by a SELECT statement, it would have a row number of 1 within that query. You can refer to these row numbers in a SELECT statement's WHERE clause. If you write your SELECT statement to sort its results in a way you care about, you can get Oracle to show you the 5, 50, or 500 most important records by including a WHERE clause statement that restricts the row number to the number of records you want.

The syntax to perform this is as follows:

```
SELECT *
FROM    (SELECT column_name_1[, column_name_2...]
          FROM    table_name
          ORDER BY column_with_value_you_care_about
          )
WHERE ROWNUM <= number of records you want;
```

ROWNUM can be a tricky variable to use. It's important to understand at what point in the execution of the query Oracle generates and applies the ROWNUM: ROWNUM is added to the column list *before* any ORDER BY, GROUP BY, or DISTINCT clauses are executed. In the example in this section, we fool Oracle into applying ROWNUMs in a specific order by forcing it to order the rows in a subquery before the main query sees (and numbers) them. This is one of the useful features of allowing ORDER BY clauses in views.

Applying this to the small number of records contained in your sample tables for this book won't produce impressive results, but it will demonstrate how the technique works. The following command shows how to create a view that shows the three products whose stock quantities are the highest:

```
CREATE OR REPLACE VIEW test_overstocked_items AS
SELECT *
FROM    (SELECT product_name, quantity_on_hand
          FROM    test_product
          ORDER BY quantity_on_hand DESC
          )
WHERE ROWNUM <= 3;

SELECT * FROM test_overstocked_items;
```

Cross Check

Views

Now that you've been introduced to the concept of views, take a moment to check your knowledge by answering the following questions:

1. What are the reasons for using views?

2. How can you alter a view's definition?

Step-by-Step 12.01

Creating a View on a Table

Case Study

John at the Clapham Specialty Store has asked you to create several views on tables so that his users are only able to see the data from the tables that he wants them to see.

For this exercise, you will need the following materials:

- Oracle9*i* Database Server with the SQL*Plus tool

- Creation of the PRODUCT, CUSTOMER, SALE and SALE_ITEM tables for the Clapham Specialty Store

Step 1

If you have not yet created the tables for the Clapham Specialty Store, execute the following SQL code before proceeding to the text. If you have already created the tables, skip to Step 2.

```
DROP TABLE customer CASCADE CONSTRAINTS;
DROP TABLE employee CASCADE CONSTRAINTS;
DROP TABLE location CASCADE CONSTRAINTS;
DROP TABLE product CASCADE CONSTRAINTS;
DROP TABLE register CASCADE CONSTRAINTS;
DROP TABLE register_log CASCADE CONSTRAINTS;
DROP TABLE sale CASCADE CONSTRAINTS;
DROP TABLE sale_item CASCADE CONSTRAINTS;

CREATE TABLE customer (
        customer_id          NUMBER(10) NOT NULL,
        first_name           VARCHAR2(40),
        last_name            VARCHAR2(40),
        address              VARCHAR2(200),
        phone                VARCHAR2(10)
        );
ALTER TABLE customer
        ADD CONSTRAINT pk_customer
        PRIMARY KEY (customer_id);

CREATE TABLE employee (
        employee_id          NUMBER(10) NOT NULL,
```

```
                    supervisor_id          NUMBER(10),
                    first_name             VARCHAR2(40),
                    last_name              VARCHAR2(40) NOT NULL,
                    social_security_number CHAR(11) NOT NULL,
                    pay_rate               NUMBER(8,2),
                    job_type               VARCHAR2(20) NOT NULL
                    );
          CREATE INDEX fk_employee_r_employee
                    ON employee(supervisor_id);
          ALTER TABLE employee
                    ADD CONSTRAINT pk_employee
                    PRIMARY KEY (employee_id);

          CREATE TABLE location (
                    location_id            NUMBER(10) NOT NULL,
                    department             VARCHAR2(40),
                    aisle                  NUMBER(3),
                    side                   CHAR(1),
                    shelf                  VARCHAR2(10)
                    );
          ALTER TABLE location
                    ADD CONSTRAINT pk_location
                    PRIMARY KEY (location_id);

          CREATE TABLE product (
                    sku                    VARCHAR2(20) NOT NULL,
                    name                   VARCHAR2(80),
                    package_size           VARCHAR2(20),
                    cost                   NUMBER(8,2),
                    location_id            NUMBER(10),
                    quantity_in_stock      NUMBER(3),
                    last_purchased         DATE
                    );
           ALTER TABLE product
                    ADD CONSTRAINT pk_product
                    PRIMARY KEY (sku);
          CREATE INDEX fk_product_r_location ON Product(location_id);

          CREATE TABLE register (
                    register_id            NUMBER(10) NOT NULL,
                    department             VARCHAR2(40)
                    );
          ALTER TABLE register
                    ADD CONSTRAINT pk_register
                    PRIMARY KEY (register_id);

           CREATE TABLE sale (
                    till_receipt_no        NUMBER(10) NOT NULL,
                    customer_id            NUMBER(10),
                    register_id            NUMBER(10) NOT NULL,
                    sale_date_time         DATE,
                    register_clerk_id      NUMBER(10) NOT NULL,
                    delivery_person_id     NUMBER(10)
                    );
```

```
                    ALTER TABLE sale
                        ADD CONSTRAINT pk_sale
                        PRIMARY KEY (till_receipt_no);
            CREATE INDEX fk_sale_r_customer ON sale(customer_id);
            CREATE INDEX fk_sale_r_register ON sale(register_id);
            CREATE INDEX fk_sale_reg_clrk_r_employee ON sale(register_clerk_id);
            CREATE INDEX fk_sale_dlrvry_prsn_r_employee ON sale(delivery_person_id);

            CREATE TABLE sale_item (
                        till_receipt_no      NUMBER(10) NOT NULL,
                        item_no              NUMBER(3) NOT NULL,
                        sku                  VARCHAR2(20) NOT NULL,
                        quantity             NUMBER(3) DEFAULT 1 NOT NULL,
                        item_price           NUMBER(8,2) NOT NULL,
                        item_cost            NUMBER(8,2)
                        );
            ALTER TABLE sale_item
                        ADD CONSTRAINT pk_sale_item
                        PRIMARY KEY (till_receipt_no, item_no);
            CREATE INDEX fk_sale_item_r_sale ON sale_item(till_receipt_no);
            CREATE INDEX fk_sale_item_r_product ON sale_item(sku);

            ALTER TABLE employee
                        ADD CONSTRAINT fk_employee_r_employee
                        FOREIGN KEY (supervisor_id)
                        REFERENCES employee(employee_id);

            ALTER TABLE product
                        ADD CONSTRAINT fk_product_r_location
                        FOREIGN KEY (location_id)
                        REFERENCES location(location_id);

             ALTER TABLE sale
                        ADD CONSTRAINT fk_sale_dlvry_r_employee
                        FOREIGN KEY (delivery_person_id)
                        REFERENCES employee(employee_id);
            ALTER TABLE sale
                        ADD CONSTRAINT fk_sale_rgstr_clrk_r_employee
                        FOREIGN KEY (register_clerk_id)
                        REFERENCES employee(employee_id);
            ALTER TABLE sale
                        ADD CONSTRAINT fk_sale_r_register
                        FOREIGN KEY (register_id)
                        REFERENCES register(register_id);
            ALTER TABLE sale
                        ADD CONSTRAINT fk_sale_r_customer
                        FOREIGN KEY (customer_id)
                        REFERENCES customer(customer_id);

            ALTER TABLE sale_item
                        ADD CONSTRAINT fk_sale_item_r_product
                        FOREIGN KEY (sku)
                        REFERENCES product(sku);
```

```
ALTER TABLE sale_item
        ADD CONSTRAINT fk_sale_item_r_sale
        FOREIGN KEY (till_receipt_no)
        REFERENCES sale(till_receipt_no);
```

Step 2

To insert records into the LOCATION and PRODUCT tables and view the current contents of the PRODUCT table, execute the following commands:

```
INSERT INTO location VALUES (400, 'produce', 1, 'R', 'single');
INSERT INTO location VALUES (402, 'produce', 1, 'L', 'upper');
INSERT INTO location VALUES (405, 'produce', 1, 'L', 'single');
INSERT INTO location VALUES (300, 'dairy', 2, 'L', 'middle');
INSERT INTO location VALUES (310, 'dairy', 2, 'L', 'lower');
INSERT INTO location VALUES (350, 'dairy', 2, 'R', 'upper');
INSERT INTO product VALUES
('2340588D', 'Milk', '1 quart', 1.00, 300, 240, '03-AUG-2003');
INSERT INTO product VALUES
('2340548D', 'Butter', '1 lb pack', 1.25, 300, 240, '04-AUG-2003');
INSERT INTO product VALUES
('2340878P', 'Romaine Lettuce', 'Each', 0.50, 400, 241, '09-AUG-2003');
INSERT INTO product VALUES
('2340392P', 'Iceberg Lettuce', 'Each', .30, 400, 241, '08-AUG-2003');
INSERT INTO product VALUES
('2340244P', 'Red Lettuce', 'Each', 0.60, 400, 242, '07-AUG-2003');
INSERT INTO product VALUES
('2340313P', 'Turnips', 'Loose', 0.65, 402, 241, '08-AUG-2003');
INSERT INTO product VALUES
('2340922P', 'Eggplant', 'Loose', 0.60, 402, 241, '07-AUG-2003');
INSERT INTO product VALUES
('2340399P', 'Red Peppers', 'Each', 0.28, 405, 241, '05-AUG-2003');
INSERT INTO product VALUES
('2340993P', 'Green Peppers', 'Each', 0.25, 405, 241, '04-AUG-2003');
INSERT INTO product VALUES
('2340235P', 'Lemons', 'Each', 0.10, 405, 241, '04-AUG-2003');
COMMIT;

SELECT * FROM product;
```

Step 3

Insert the following records into the CUSTOMER and EMPLOYEE tables:

```
INSERT INTO customer VALUES
(1001, 'Jessica', 'Simpson', '124 Johnson Avenue', '2015551111');
INSERT INTO customer VALUES
(1002, 'Jon', 'Hirsch', '125 Johnson Avenue', '2015551122');
INSERT INTO customer VALUES
(1003, 'Kathy', 'Gleason', '333 Highland Avenue', '2015551229');
INSERT INTO employee VALUES
(100, null, 'John', 'Balfour', '123-45-6789', 30, 'Owner');
INSERT INTO employee VALUES
(101, 100, 'Susan', 'Saronnen', '456-78-8912', 20, 'Register Clerk');
INSERT INTO employee VALUES
(102, 100, 'Eric', 'La Sold', '678-90-1234', 6.75, 'Register Clerk');
INSERT INTO employee VALUES
```

```
(103, 100, 'Martin', 'Murphy', '901-23-4567', 13.5, 'Storeman');
INSERT INTO employee VALUES
(104, 103, 'Erica', 'Strange', '234-56-7890', null, 'Delivery');
INSERT INTO employee VALUES
(105, 103, 'Noah', 'Tamil', '567-89-0123', null, 'Delivery');

COMMIT;
SELECT * FROM customer;
SELECT * FROM employee;
```

Step 4

Insert the following records into the REGISTER and SALE tables:

```
INSERT INTO register VALUES (1, 'Deli');
INSERT INTO register VALUES (2, 'Dairy');
INSERT INTO register VALUES (3, 'Grocery');
INSERT INTO sale VALUES (5345, 1001, 2, '10-JUL-2003', 103, NULL);
INSERT INTO sale VALUES (5346, NULL, 2, '10-JUL-2003', 103, NULL);
INSERT INTO sale VALUES (5347, 1002, 3, '11-JUL-2003', 103, 105);
INSERT INTO sale VALUES (5348, 1003, 3, '11-JUL-2003', 103, NULL);

COMMIT;
SELECT * FROM sale;
```

Step 5

Insert the following records into the SALE_ITEM table:

```
INSERT INTO sale_item VALUES (5345, 1, '2340588D', 1, 1.1, 1);
INSERT INTO sale_item VALUES (5345, 2, '2340548D', 2, 1.5625, 1.25);
INSERT INTO sale_item VALUES (5345, 3, '2340878P', 1, 0.525, 0.5);
INSERT INTO sale_item VALUES (5346, 1, '2340313P', 6, 0.819, 0.65);
INSERT INTO sale_item VALUES (5346, 2, '2340922P', 6, 0.69, 0.6);
INSERT INTO sale_item VALUES (5346, 3, '2340399P', 1, 0.308, 0.28);
INSERT INTO sale_item VALUES (5347, 1, '2340993P', 2, 0.2625, 0.25);
INSERT INTO sale_item VALUES (5348, 1, '2340235P', 3, 0.109, 0.1);
INSERT INTO sale_item VALUES (5348, 2, '2340244P', 4, 0.81, 0.6);
INSERT INTO sale_item VALUES (5348, 3, '2340548D', 5, 1.5625, 1.25);
INSERT INTO sale_item VALUES (5348, 4, '2340878P', 1, 0.525, 0.5);
INSERT INTO sale_item VALUES (5348, 5, '2340313P', 1, 0.819, 0.65);
INSERT INTO sale_item VALUES (5348, 6, '2340993P', 2, 0.2625, 0.25);
INSERT INTO sale_item VALUES (5348, 7, '2340235P', 3, 0.109, 0.1);

COMMIT;
```

Step 6

To create a view on the PRODUCT table, execute the following command:

```
CREATE OR REPLACE VIEW product_v AS
     SELECT *
     FROM   product
     WHERE  cost > 0.60
;
```

Step 7

To see the result of the view you created, execute the following command:

```
SELECT * FROM product_v;
```

To create a view based on data from the SALE, SALE_ITEM, PRODUCT, and CUSTOMER tables, execute the following command:

```
CREATE OR REPLACE VIEW customer_summary_sale_v AS
SELECT cust.first_name || ' ' || cust.last_name customer,
       cust.customer_id,
       count(distinct sale.till_receipt_no) qty_visits,
       count(distinct prod.name) qty_products,
       sum(quantity) qty_of_items,
       sum(quantity * item_price) total_sale,
       sum(quantity * (item_price - item_cost)) total_profit
FROM   customer   CUST,
       product     PROD,
       sale,
       sale_item
WHERE  cust.customer_id = sale.customer_id
  AND  sale_item.till_receipt_no = sale.till_receipt_no
  AND  prod.sku = sale_item.sku
GROUP BY cust.first_name || ' ' || cust.last_name,
         cust.customer_id
;
```

To see the results of the view you created, execute the following command:

```
SELECT * FROM customer_summary_sale_v
ORDER BY customer_id
;
```

To drop the views you created, type

```
DROP VIEW customer_summary_sale_v;
DROP VIEW product_v;
```

You should have successfully created and dropped views according to John's requirements for the Clapham Specialty Store. If you refer back to the original statement of the case study in Chapter 1, you will find that this was the data that John really needed. He wanted to know how profitable each sale was and what the characteristics of the sale were.

■ Other Database Objects

The final section of this chapter covers an assortment of techniques that you could end up using every day. In the pages that follow, you will learn how to use sequences, synonyms, and the Oracle data dictionary.

Sequences

Databases are all about saving information accurately so that it is easy to find again. You will often use surrogate primary keys in your database design, and these are usually filled by a series of sequential numbers. Oracle allows you to create counters called sequences that increment each time they are used. By referring to the sequence when inserting records, you can ensure that a new unique number is assigned to each record inserted.

Sequences are unusual in the database world because they work outside the control of the transaction. You cannot commit or rollback a number pulled from a sequence. Even if your insert fails, the number you pulled from the sequence is used up, thrown away, and cannot be re-used.

Creating a Sequence

The syntax to create a sequence is as follows:

```
CREATE SEQUENCE sequence_name;
```

The CREATE SEQUENCE command creates a sequence that starts at 1 and increments by 1 each time it is used. This is often all you will require from a sequence. However, there are many optional parameters you can use when defining a sequence. Take a look at the following syntax to see some of the more useful parameters:

```
CREATE SEQUENCE sequence_name
[INCREMENT BY increment_quantity]
[START WITH starting_value]
[MAXVALUE highest_value]
[MINVALUE lowest_value]
[CYCLE]
[NOCACHE]
;
```

The INCREMENT BY parameter allows you to create sequences that jump in intervals other than 1. The values for this parameter can have up to 28 digits (although there won't be many opportunities to use an increment like that!). If you specify a negative value here, the sequence will decrement in value each time it is used.

The START WITH parameter enables you to create a sequence whose first value is something other than 1. This can be handy when you are creating a sequence for a table that already contains records: You can tell the sequence to start at the next value after the highest existing record ID.

The MAXVALUE and MINVALUE parameters allow you to define limits for the numbers the sequence generates. If you use these in conjunction with the CYCLE parameter, you can create a sequence that loops repeatedly through a set of values you define.

By far, the most common sequences increment by 1 and have no limit on their values. Execute the following command to create such a sequence, and then proceed to the next topic to put it to use:

```
CREATE SEQUENCE test_test_seq;
```

Using a Sequence

To get values from a sequence, you must refer to it like a table. Sequences contain two "pseudocolumns" named CURRVAL and NEXTVAL that return the sequence's current and next value, respectively. Selecting from the NEXTVAL column causes the sequence to automatically increment to its

Most programmers use a 32-bit signed integer variable for ID numbers (such as used in surrogate primary keys). The biggest number this variable type can handle is $2^{31}-1 =$ 2,147,483,647. If the number goes beyond this, it will inadvertently cycle and 2,147,483,648 will be read in the code as -2,147,483,647. Set the MAXVALUE unless you are sure the code in the application can handle a bigger number.

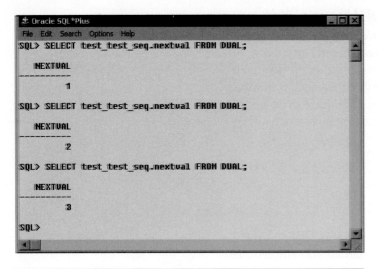

next number; selecting CURRVAL will get the current number, without incrementing the sequence.

To see this in action, enter the following commands and compare your results with those shown in Figure 12.7:

```
SELECT test_test_seq.nextval FROM DUAL;
SELECT test_test_seq.nextval FROM DUAL;
SELECT test_test_seq.currval FROM DUAL;
```

● **Figure 12.7**   Using a sequence from the command line

Now that you have seen how a sequence operates, it is time to learn the method for populating a table's column from a sequence. You can accomplish this by including a reference to the sequence as a value in the INSERT statement. To see how this works, enter the following commands and compare the results you see with those in Figure 12.8:

```
CREATE TABLE test_test (
    record_id    NUMBER(18,0),
    record_text VARCHAR2(10)
);

INSERT INTO test_test VALUES (
    test_test_seq.nextval,
    'Record A'
);

INSERT INTO test_test VALUES (
    test_test_seq.nextval,
    'Record B'
);

SELECT * FROM test_test;
```

While a sequence is often designed to be used by one table, there is no restriction in Oracle that requires this. A sequence is an independent object. It can be used by one table, many tables, or no tables at all.

CURRVAL deserves a special mention as it is only valid within a single user session and *after* a NEXTVAL call. In other words, any attempt to use CURRVAL before you have made a call using NEXTVAL will return an exception "ORA-08002: sequence <sequence name>.CURRVAL is not yet defined in this session." CURRVAL calls are most often seen in PL/SQL stored procedures.

Modifying an Existing Sequence

Once a sequence has been created, you can modify it in a number of ways. You can alter the increment value, adjust or remove minimum and maximum values, or change whether it loops when it reaches its limits, among other things.

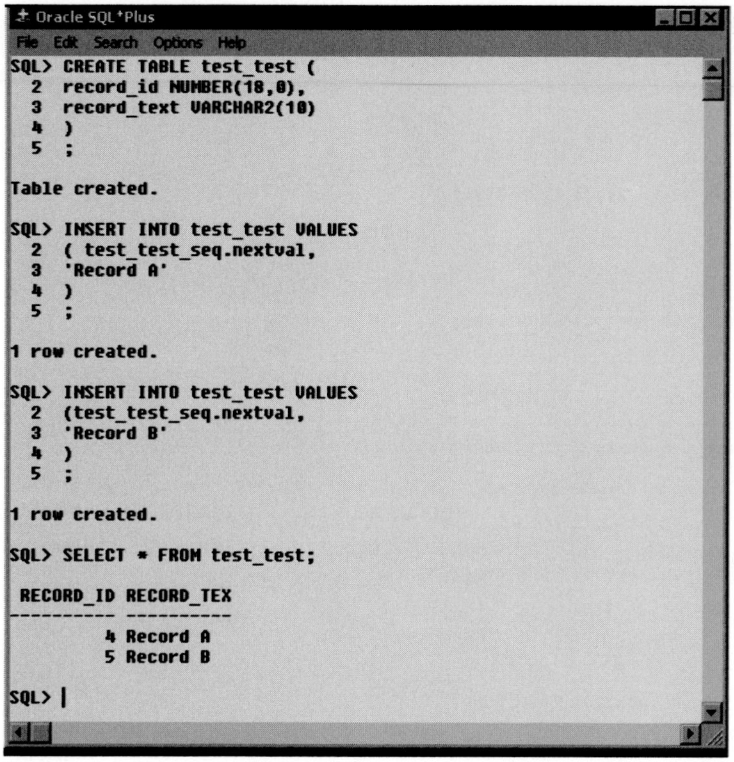

● **Figure 12.8**   Using a sequence to populate a table's column

The syntax for making these changes to an existing sequence is very similar to what you used to create the sequence in the first place. The syntax is as follows:

```
ALTER SEQUENCE sequence_name
[INCREMENT BY increment_quantity]
[MAXVALUE highest_value | NOMAXVALUE]
[MINVALUE lowest_value | NOMINVALUE]
[CYCLE | NOCYCLE]
;
```

Notice that you cannot alter the START WITH parameter. To see this in action, compare Figure 12.9 with the results you get from entering the following commands:

```
ALTER SEQUENCE test_test_seq
MAXVALUE 10
;

SELECT test_test_seq.nextval FROM DUAL;
SELECT test_test_seq.nextval FROM DUAL;
SELECT test_test_seq.nextval FROM DUAL;
SELECT test_test_seq.nextval FROM DUAL;
SELECT test_test_seq.nextval FROM DUAL;
SELECT test_test_seq.nextval FROM DUAL;
```

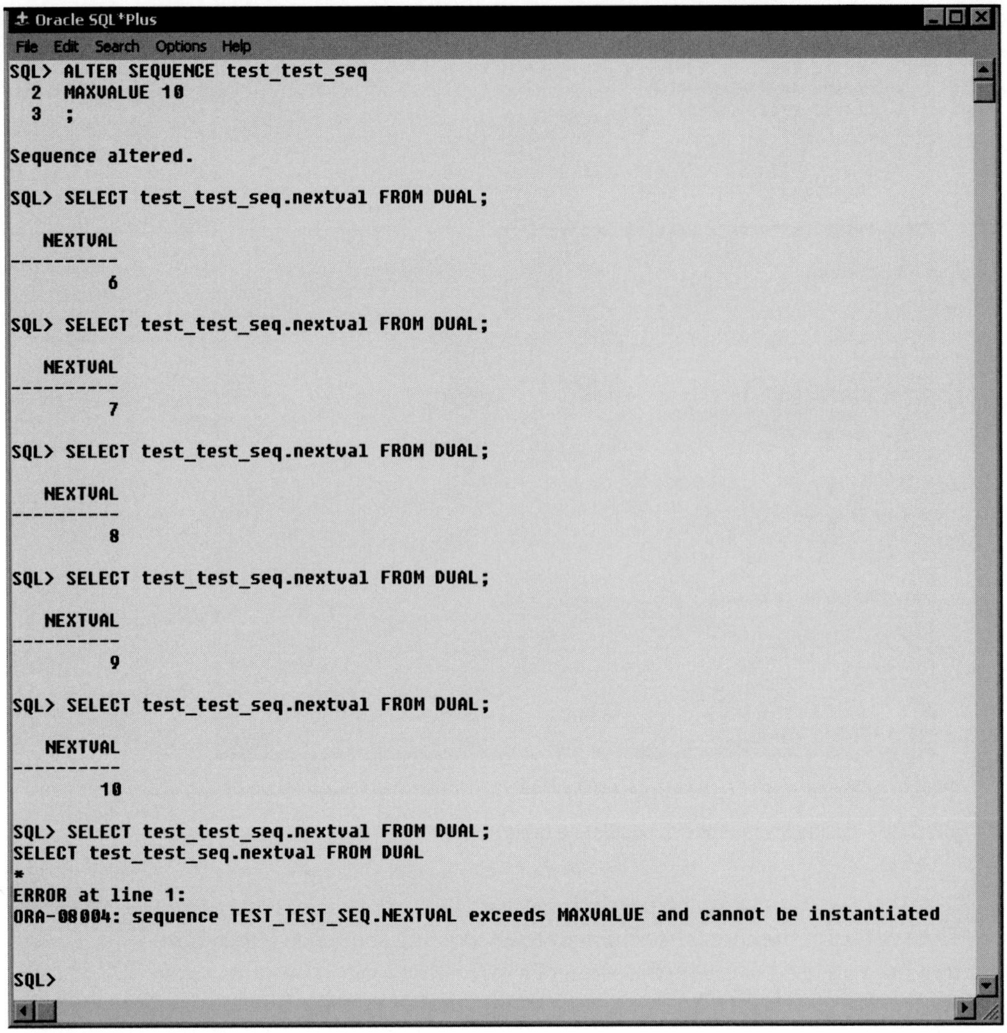

```
± Oracle SQL*Plus                                                    _ □ ×
 File  Edit  Search  Options  Help
SQL> ALTER SEQUENCE test_test_seq
  2   MAXVALUE 10
  3   ;

Sequence altered.

SQL> SELECT test_test_seq.nextval FROM DUAL;

   NEXTVAL
----------
         6

SQL> SELECT test_test_seq.nextval FROM DUAL;

   NEXTVAL
----------
         7

SQL> SELECT test_test_seq.nextval FROM DUAL;

   NEXTVAL
----------
         8

SQL> SELECT test_test_seq.nextval FROM DUAL;

   NEXTVAL
----------
         9

SQL> SELECT test_test_seq.nextval FROM DUAL;

   NEXTVAL
----------
        10

SQL> SELECT test_test_seq.nextval FROM DUAL;
SELECT test_test_seq.nextval FROM DUAL
       *
ERROR at line 1:
ORA-08004: sequence TEST_TEST_SEQ.NEXTVAL exceeds MAXVALUE and cannot be instantiated

SQL>
```

• **Figure 12.9**   Altering an existing sequence

Synonyms

A synonym allows you to refer to an Oracle object by a name other than its
actual name. You can apply synonyms to a table, view, or sequence, as well
as to objects you saw earlier in this book, such as functions, procedures, and
packages. The rest of this discussion will talk about synonyms as they relate
to tables, but the information also applies to synonyms assigned to other
objects.

Why would you want to create a synonym for something? The main reason is convenience: Synonyms can make it easier for other people to access
your data. Tables are organized by the Oracle user ID of the person who created them, and if another user wants to reference a table you have created,
they generally have to place your username in front of the name of the table,
as demonstrated here:

```
SELECT * FROM your_user_name.your_table_name;
```

This can get tedious, and if the table is moved to a different user, then any existing code referencing the table must be changed. Synonyms have an option enabling the table to be "visible" to anyone even if its owner's name is not specified. This allows you to write SQL statements that will continue to work even if the tables they refer to move to another user.

> Synonyms and their use extend into the access control of objects. You should refer to the Oracle manuals for more details on this powerful concept.

Creating a Synonym

The syntax to create a synonym is as follows:

```
CREATE [PUBLIC] SYNONYM synonym_name
FOR object_name
;
```

To see how a synonym works, issue the following commands. Figure 12.10 shows the results you should see.

```
SELECT * FROM test_product;

SELECT * FROM prod;

CREATE SYNONYM prod FOR test_product;

SELECT * FROM prod;
```

If you simply want to make a table available to other users, you can create a public synonym that has the same name as the table. An example of this type of command follows:

```
CREATE PUBLIC SYNONYM test_product FOR test_product;
```

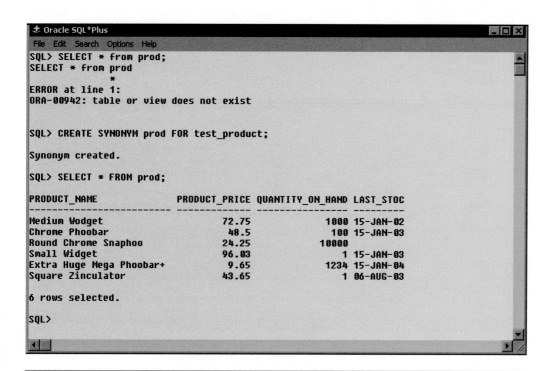

● Figure 12.10   Creating a synonym for a table

Synonyms continue to exist even after the underlying object has been dropped. The underlying table that the synonym points to can be dropped and re-created and the original synonym will still find the table (assuming it has the same owner and name, or course).

Modifying an Existing Synonym

Because a synonym is so simple, Oracle does not offer any means of altering one. Instead, you simply drop the old synonym and create a new one. The syntax is

```
DROP [PUBLIC] SYNONYM synonym_name;
```

To drop the first synonym you created enabling the TEST_PRODUCT table to be referred to as PROD, execute this command:

```
DROP SYNONYM prod;
```

To drop the public synonym you created, issue this command:

```
DROP PUBLIC SYNONYM test_product;
```

You can rename a synonym as this illustration shows:

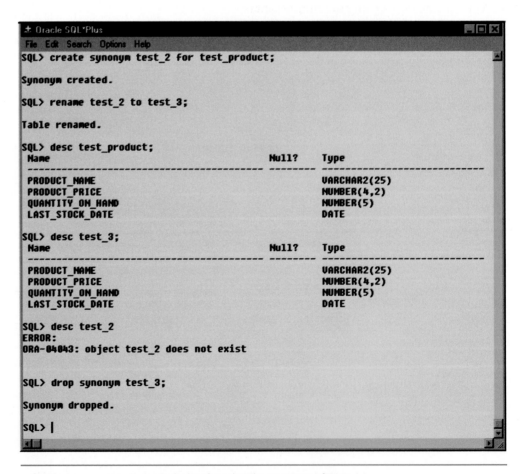

• Create a synonym and rename it showing what the synonym refers to.

Chapter 12 Review

■ Chapter Summary

After reading this chapter and completing the Step-by-Step tutorial and Cross Checks, you should understand the following facts about useful Oracle techniques:

Transfer Data Between Tables

- You transfer data between tables using an INSERT statement that has a SELECT statement where you would normally place the values to be inserted.

- You can also transfer data by executing a CREATE TABLE statement whose column definitions are replaced by a SELECT statement.

Rename Tables

- You rename tables using the simple syntax

  ```
  RENAME old_table_name TO new_table_name;
  ```

Alter a Table's Structure

- You can alter a table's structure by adding new columns, changing the datatypes of existing columns, and changing whether columns accept null values. You can add columns to a table at any time with this statement:

  ```
  ALTER TABLE table_name ADD new_column_name
  datatype [NOT NULL];
  ```

- The syntax to change the datatype of an existing column is

  ```
  ALTER TABLE table_name MODIFY column_name
  new_datatype;
  ```

- The syntax to change the NULL options of an existing column is

  ```
  ALTER TABLE table_name MODIFY column_name
  [NOT] NULL;
  ```

- Oracle has several restrictions on changing column properties including: datatype changes can only be made to empty columns; and columns must contain data for NOT NULL conversions.

Explore Views

- Views are essentially stored queries.

- Some simple views can be updateable if the view has all NOT NULL columns present, and does not contain a JOIN or a UNION or use a function.

- Views allow you to write the command to create a customized result from one or more tables and store that command so it can easily be used over and over.

- One very common use for a view is to join data from two or more tables and present it to users in one easy-to-read list. By simplifying the record-retrieval process so that users don't have to understand how to join tables, you make the data available to a larger number of people.

- Views are also useful for enforcing security, because they allow you to limit the columns and rows returned to the user.

- The syntax for creating a view is

  ```
  CREATE OR REPLACE VIEW view_name AS SELECT
  statement;
  ```

- Dropping a view is as easy as dropping a table but less destructive—since a view doesn't contain any data, the worst that can happen if you accidentally drop a view is having to re-create it.

- The only way to change a view is drop it and re-create it using the CREATE OR REPLACE syntax.

- Oracle dynamically assigns row numbers to every row returned by each query it processes. This means that no matter where a row resides in its table, if it is the first (or only) row returned by a SELECT statement, it would have a row number of 1 within that query. You can refer to these row numbers in a SELECT statement's WHERE clause.

- The ROWNUM is assigned before any ORDER BY or GROUP BY clause within the SELECT statement.

Examine Sequences and Synonyms

- Sequences are Oracle's mechanism for generating sequential numbers for use as record IDs and other counting operations.

- The CREATE SEQUENCE command allows you to specify parameters such as the starting value, lowest and highest values, increment quantity, and whether the sequence loops back to its beginning value once it reaches its limit.

- You can incorporate a sequence's value into an INSERT statement by including a reference to *sequence_name*.NEXTVAL in the values to be inserted.

- Synonyms allow you to refer to an Oracle object by a name other than its actual name.

- Synonyms also enable you to make a table or other object available to all users of a database without them needing to know who owns the table.

■ Key Terms

ALTER TABLE *(345)*	**INCREMENT BY** *(359)*	**sequences** *(359)*
CREATE OR REPLACE VIEW *(349)*	**MAXVALUE** *(359)*	**START WITH** *(359)*
CREATE SEQUENCE *(359)*	**MINVALUE** *(359)*	**synonym** *(362)*
CURRVAL *(359)*	**NEXTVAL** *(359)*	**view** *(348)*
CYCLE *(359)*	**public synonym** *(363)*	**WITH CHECK OPTION** *(351)*
DROP VIEW *(352)*	**RENAME** *(344)*	

■ Key Term Quiz

Use the Key Terms list to complete the sentences that follow. Not all terms will be used.

1. The _____ command creates a sequence that starts at 1 and increments by 1 each time it is used.

2. The _____ parameter allows you to define the top limit for the numbers the sequence generates.

3. The _____ in a CREATE VIEW command ensures that only rows that are selected via the view can be inserted through the view.

4. A _____ allows any user to refer to a stored procedure without using the name of the procedure's owner.

5. You can add columns to a table at any time by using the _____ command.

■ Matching Definition Quiz

Relate each term on the left with the appropriate description on the right.

Term		Description
1. Sequence	a.	This parameter allows you to create sequences that jump in intervals other than 1.
2. View	b.	A query stored in the database and given a name.
3. Synonym	c.	This parameter enables you to specify the first value of a sequence.
4. INCREMENT BY	d.	Oracle allows you to create these counters that increment each time they are used.
5. START WITH	e.	This allows you to refer to an Oracle object by a name other than its actual name.

1. Which of the following commands would transfer data from a table named PRODUCT to an existing table named PRODUCT_ARCHIVE?

   a. INSERT INTO product
      SELECT *
      FROM product_archive
      ;

   b. COPY * FROM product TO product_archive;

   c. CREATE TABLE product_archive AS
      SELECT * FROM product;

   d. INSERT INTO product_archive SELECT *
      FROM product;

2. Which of the following commands will rename a table?

   a. RENAME *table_name new_table_name*;

   b. RENAME *table_name* TO *new_table_name*;

   c. RENAME TABLE *table_name new_table_name*;

   d. RENAME TABLE *table_name* TO
      new_table_name;

3. Which of the following commands will add a required text column named New_Column to a table named TAB1?

   a. ALTER TABLE tab1
      ADD new_column VARCHAR2(10) NULL;

   b. ADD new_column VARCHAR2(10) NULL
      TO tab1;

   c. ALTER tab1
      ADD new_column VARCHAR2(10) NOT
      NULL;

   d. ADD new_column VARCHAR2(10) NOT
      NULL
      TO TABLE tab1;

4. Which of the following is *not* a benefit offered by views?

   a. Can rename columns to more readable names than those used in the underlying table

   b. Can join information from multiple tables

   c. Can filter data so only certain rows or columns are displayed

   d. Can speed up data access by referring directly to the columns needed

5. Which of the following commands would *not* result in the creation of a sequence? (Choose two.)

   a. CREATE SEQUENCE new_seq1
      NOMAXVALUE;

   b. CREATE SEQUENCE 2new_seq START
      WITH 2;

   c. CREATE SEQUENCE new3_seq MIN 1
      MAX 100 CYCLE;

   d. CREATE SEQUENCE new_4seq
      INCREMENT BY -1;

6. Which of the following are benefits of using table synonyms? (Choose two.)

   a. Can increase data throughput speed

   b. Allows column to be referred to by a different name

   c. Allows table to be referred to by a different name

   d. Enables other users to reference a table without knowing its owner

7. Which of the following optional sequence parameters enables you to create a sequence that loops repeatedly through a set of values you define?

   a. MAXVAL

   b. MINVAL

   c. INCREMENT BY

   d. CYCLE

   e. NOMINVALUE

8. What are the names of Oracle sequence "pseudocolumns" that return sequence values? (Choose two.)

   a. MAXVAL

   b. MINVAL

   c. CURRVAL

   d. NEXTVAL

   e. CYCLE

9. How many digits can the values for the INCREMENT BY optional sequence parameter contain?

   a. 12
   b. 16
   c. 20
   d. 28
   e. 32

10. What is the result if you specify a negative value for the INCREMENT BY optional sequence parameter?

    a. You will get an error message.
    b. The sequence will decrement in value each time it is used.
    c. The sequence will increment by the value specified.
    d. The sequence will reach its MAXVALUE and then decrement in value each time it is used.
    e. The sequence will fail to be created.

11. How can you write a SELECT statement to sort its results and then show you the 50 smallest values from a column?

    a. By including a WHERE clause statement that restricts the row number to the number of records you want
    b. By including a MAXVALUE of 50
    c. By indicating MAXVALUE < 51
    d. By indicating a TOP number of 50

12. Which optional sequence parameter enables you to create a sequence whose first value is something other than 1?

    a. FIRSTVAL
    b. NEXTVAL
    c. INCREMENT BY
    d. START WITH
    e. CURRVAL

13. What term is used to make a synonym available to all users beyond the current schema?

    a. CREATE SYNONYM
    b. START WITH
    c. SHARE SYNONYM
    d. MAKE PUBLIC
    e. PUBLIC

14. What two terms could be used with the ALTER TABLE command to alter a table's structure?

    a. ADD
    b. CURRVAL
    c. PUBLIC
    d. MODIFY
    e. START WITH

15. What three tasks can be done with the ALTER TABLE statement?

    a. Add NULL options to a column
    b. Add a column to a table
    c. Add a synonym to the table
    d. Add rows to the table
    e. Change the datatype of an empty column

■ Essay Quiz

1. How can you use the ORDER BY clause in a view?

2. Describe why you would want to create a synonym for a database object.

3. Describe the function of sequences in a database.

4. Explain why it's important to be able to copy records from one table to another.

5. How do you obtain values from a sequence?

Lab Projects

• Lab Project 12.1

Case Study

John at the Clapham Specialty Store has asked you to create a sequence named Customer_ID to be used with the Customer_ID primary key column of the CUSTOMER table so that customer identification numbers will increase by increments of 10. The

sequence should start at 1000 and have a maximum value of 2147483647. You will need Oracle9*i* Database Server with the SQL*Plus tool.

Create the sequence according to John's requirements.

• Lab Project 12.2

Case Study

John at the Clapham Specialty Store has asked you to create a view based on data from the PRODUCT and LOCATION tables so that he can easily see how many different products are in each location. He wants the view to include the indicated data from both tables that share the same Location_ID column.

You will need Oracle9*i* Database Server with the SQL*Plus tool.

Then create a view called PROD_LOCATION_V based on the product SKU, name of the product, department, aisle, shelf, and side. Label the columns in the view Stock_Keeping_Unit, Product_Name, Department, Aisle, Shelf_Number, and Side respectively.

On the CD-ROMs

■ About Oracle 9*i* Standard Edition for Windows

In this textbook you will find a three CD-ROM set from which you can install a trial version of Oracle 9*i* Standard Edition. The installation process is relatively easy, but here are some tips to make the installation of Oracle 9*i* even easier.

System Requirements

To install Oracle 9*i*, you will need the following components:

- A personal computer with at least a Pentium 166 processor (Pentium 266 or higher recommended)
- Windows NT\2000 or Windows XP operating system
- 2.8 gigabytes of hard disk space
- 128 Megabytes of Random Access Memory (256MB recommended)
- 200 megabytes of virtual memory (Initial Size 200MB, Maximum Size 400MB)

- 256 color video adapter

- An Internet connection and one of the following: Netscape Navigator 4.76 or higher, Microsoft Internet Explorer 5.0 or higher, or Microsoft Internet Explorer 6.0 (required with Windows XP)

Registering with the Oracle Technology Network

Before you can install Oracle 9*i*, you must first register with the Oracle Technology Network (OTN). At the end of the registration process, you will be sent an email with a registration key that will unlock your version of Oracle 9*i*. Registration is free and so is the trial software, but you won't be able to install the software unless you register with OTN and receive a registration key.

OTN is an online community where you can download the latest development programs and sample code, find documentation about Oracle software, get security alerts and other updates, and join user groups.

To begin the OTN registration process, follow these steps:

> ⚠️ When you join OTN, you agree that Oracle may contact you for marketing purposes. You also agree that any information you provide Oracle may be used for marketing purposes.

1. Insert CD-ROM 1 of 3 into your computer's CD-ROM drive. The CD installation program should begin automatically. If the CD-ROM installation does not start automatically, browse to you computer's CD-ROM drive, find the **setup.exe** file in the root directory and double-click on it.

2. When the Oracle Universal Installer Welcome screen appears, click the Next button located at the bottom right of the screen.

3. At the Product Registration screen, click the Register button. Your Web browser should launch automatically and take you to `http://otn.oracle.com/books`. If this does not happen automatically, simply launch the browser yourself, type **http://otn.oracle.com/books** into the address window and press ENTER.

4. When the first registration screen appears, click on the Oracle 9*i* Database link.

5. Next, sign into the Oracle Technology Network. Unless you are already a member of OTN, sign in as a new user. Enter your email address and create a unique password. Your password should be 6–8 letters and/or numbers.

6. Complete the registration form by entering your name, address, phone, and other information. Red stars indicate required fields. When you're done, click the Continue button at the bottom of the screen.

7. Another screen will appear thanking you for your time and requesting three more pieces of information: the publisher of the book you are using, the title of the book, and the book's ISBN. Enter the following information:

   - Publisher: **McGraw-Hill**

   - Book title: **Introduction to Relational Databases and SQL Programming**

- ISBN: **0072229241**

  Check the Agree box at the bottom of the page and then click Continue.

8. An email will be automatically sent to you with the registration key. You'll then be ready to install Oracle 9*i*.

Installing Oracle 9*i* Standard Edition

The Oracle 9*i* installation process is automated, so it should proceed rather easily. Here's how you can get started:

1. Once you've received your registration key, return to the Product Registration Screen and enter the registration key in the box provided. Click Next.

2. The next screen is called File Locations. Under Destination… you'll find two boxes. The first is for the Oracle Home name and the other is for the file path where the program will be installed. Unless your instructor tells you to do otherwise, use the default Oracle Home name and file path. Click Next.

3. When prompted, select Oracle 9*i* Database Standard Edition and General Purpose from the list of available products.

4. At the Database Identification screen, enter a Global Database name in the box provided. Typically, the form of the name is *name.domain*. Unless your teacher instructs you to do otherwise, create a name that is easy to remember. You can also create your own Oracle System Identifier (SID). Click Next.

5. When the Database File Location screen appears, it will suggest you store the database files and program files on separate disks. Unless your instructor tells you otherwise, accept the default database location by clicking Next.

6. When the Database Character Set screen appears, select Use The Default Character Set button and click Next.

7. A Summary Screen will appear, providing you with a list of all of the components that will be installed. Click Install.

8. After that, the software installation is automatic. The installation will take some time and will require use of all three installation discs. The installation will prompt you when the next installation disc should be inserted into your computer's CD-ROM drive.

ACCEPT A command that, when executed, allows you to define any prompt in SQL*Plus that you want. (4)

actual parameter Actual variables or constants that are usually copied to the formal parameters of a function or procedure when a call is made. There are ways to specify that the actual parameters will not be copied, but those techniques are not covered in this book. (7)

ADD_MONTHS A SQL function that returns a date that has the same day of the month as the original date it was provided, but is a specified number of months in the future (or the past). (5)

ALTER TABLE A SQL command used to change a table's definition. (12)

alternate key A column or set of columns that can be used to uniquely identify a row of the table. While generally similar to primary keys, unique constraints can contain NULL values. (11)

AND This operator is used to select records containing both of two specified values—for instance, every product that is both *square* and *blue*. The AND operator requires both conditions in the statement to be true for any record to be selected. (3)

anomaly An anomaly occurs when the same piece of data is represented in more than one way in the database and the representations are different. In other words, the database is contradicting itself! (10)

anonymous block A PL/SQL basic block without any name or specification. The header section is empty. (7)

AS The AS keyword is used before the column alias name to indicate that an alias name will be used. (2)

attribute A descriptor of an entity. An attribute contains part of the information about an entity. (8)

attributes of the cursor Indicators that show a cursor's state, for example, FOUND, ISOPEN, NOTFOUND. (7)

AVG A SQL function that returns the average of the values in the column you specify. If this function encounters a NULL value, it ignores the NULL. (5)

basic block A PL/SQL basic block is made up of four sections: the header section, an optional declaration section, the execution section, and the optional exception section. (7)

BETWEEN This clause is used to define a range of acceptable values between two criteria. (3)

binary relationship A relationship between two different entities. (9)

bitmap index An Oracle index suited for a column that contains only a few unique values. (6)

branch block In a B-tree index, the non-leaf block that does not contain any actual records but only values for indexed fields in records to help reach the leaf blocks in as few steps as possible. (6)

B-tree index Index structure that organizes record pointers into hierarchical groups known as "branch" and "leaf" blocks. Using a B-tree index enables a computer to quickly locate records containing a specified value. (6)

buffer width   A SQL*Plus setting that determines how many characters of each line will be stored in memory for later retrieval. (4)

cardinality   The quantity of objects that a role in a relationship may apply to. Usually expressed as a range: one to many (1:m), zero to one (0:1), one (1). (8)

Cartesian product   A join without a WHERE clause that results in combining each record from one table with every record in the other. (6)

cascade delete   A characteristic of a foreign key relationship in which deletion of the parent row causes deletion of the corresponding child rows. (11)

cascade update   A characteristic of a foreign key relationship in which an update or change of the parent key value causes a corresponding update or change of the child key values. In Oracle this must be executed using a trigger. (11)

category   When describing supertypes and subtypes, the category is the attribute that distinguishes objects in the different subtype entities. (9)

CHANGE   A command that allows you to replace any text string in a command with any other string. CHANGE is not a SQL command; it works only within the SQL*Plus program. (4)

CHAR   A basic Oracle datatype for fixed-length strings. The maximum length of a string is 2000 characters and the value inserted is always padded with spaces to fill the entire variable. (11)

character function   Oracle functions for manipulating text strings. (5)

child entity   The entity at the dependent or "many" end of a parent-child relationship. (9)

cluster   The symbol that links supertype entities to subtype entities. It describes the rules for the subtypes: exclusive/inclusive, complete/ incomplete. (9)

code table   A table with only a few rows in which the values in the table are used in the code of the application for determining program flow. (9)

column   A collection of one type of information stored in a table (for instance, all of the phone numbers or all of the last names). (1)

COLUMN   Affects the way your own copy of SQL*Plus displays information in regards to column headings, alignment, and so on. The COLUMN command does not get sent to the Oracle database. (4)

column alias   A surrogate name assigned to a column in SQL commands. (2)

column constraint   A constraint that acts only on a single column of a table. (11)

COMMIT   To control transactions, SQL provides this command to save recent DML changes to the database. (3)

composite index   An index based on more than one column in a table. (6)

composite key   A key made up of several columns. *See also* composite index. (9)

concatenated index   An index based on concatenated values from more than one column. *See also* composite index. (6)

concatenation   The operation of joining two pieces of text to make a single piece of text. (2)

conceptual model   The model of a business that describes the issues and their context, which the database and its software application are intended to address. (8)

conditional processing   In an IF clause, a WHEN clause, or a LOOP, the processing of a set of commands on the basis of whether the conditions specified in the command have been met. (7)

constant   A fixed value used in a formula or program. (2)

constraint   Characteristic that must be true about the data in order for it to be accepted by the database. (1)

correlated subquery   A nested SELECT statement that refers to a column from the SELECT statement it is nested within. (6)

COUNT   A SQL function that counts records or values in a column. (5)

CREATE OR REPLACE VIEW   A SQL command used to create or change a view. Privileges and other dependent Oracle objects remain in place when you use OR REPLACE. (12)

CREATE SEQUENCE   A SQL command used to create a sequence. (12)

CREATE TABLE   A SQL command used to create tables in a database. (2)

CURRVAL   A sequence "pseudocolumn" that returns the current value. It is only valid *after* a NEXTVAL has been used. (12)

cursor   An abbreviation for CURrent Set Of Records. A cursor is used within an Oracle PL/SQL procedure as a memory array to hold data pulled into the procedure via a SQL SELECT statement. You then use the FETCH command to process individual records from the cursor set. (7)

CYCLE   A sequence parameter that forces a sequence to loop repeatedly through a set of values you define. (12)

Data Control Language (DCL)   Commands that control who can do what within the database, with object privileges controlling access to individual database objects and system privileges providing global privileges across the entire database. DCL commands include GRANT and REVOKE. (3)

data conversion   The operation of converting information from one datatype to another—usually between text and dates, times, or numbers. (5)

Data Definition Language (DDL)   Commands that are used to define the structure of the data to be stored; these commands include CREATE, ALTER, DROP, RENAME, and TRUNCATE. (3)

Data Manipulation Language (DML)   Commands that enable you to work with your data; they include INSERT, UPDATE, and DELETE. (3)

data model   *See* Entity Relationship Diagram. (8)

data modeling   The analysis of data objects that are used in a business and the identification of the relationships among these data objects. (8)

database   A collection of related tables. (1)

datatype   Type of data—for example, NUMBER, CHAR, and so on. (2)

DATE   A basic Oracle datatype for storing dates and times. These are stored as 7-byte values with a byte each for century, year, month, day, hour, minute, and second. (11)

date math   Arithmetic operations with dates—for example, finding the number of days between two dates. (2)

declarative constraint   A foreign key constraint that is enforced by declaring the relationship. This is different from a relationship enforced by the procedural code of a trigger. (11)

delete anomaly   An anomaly that occurs as the result of a deletion. (10)

delete restrict   A characteristic of a foreign key relationship in which deletion of the parent row is prevented by the presence of the corresponding child rows. This is the default behavior for a foreign key constraint. (11)

denormalize   The process of copying redundant data columns into tables to improve performance. (10)

dependency   1. An entity that is dependent on another entity is so closely coupled that the dependent entity cannot exist without the presence of the parent entity. 2. An attribute is dependent on another attribute if the value of the first can be determined from the second. (8, 10)

dependent attribute   An attribute whose value can be determined from another attribute. (10)

determinant   A determinant is a column or set of columns that functionally determines another column. Determinant and dependent are the two roles in a dependency relationship. (10)

discriminator   In a supertype or subtype relationship, this is the attribute that differentiates between the multiple subtypes. (9, 10)

DISTINCT This modifier can be added to a SELECT statement to select unique values from a table. (3)

domain A described set of values that can be stored in a column. A domain consists of a datatype, an optionality clause, and a check constraint. (11)

domain model A type of conceptual model using Unified Modeling Language notation. (8)

DROP The SQL command used to delete objects from a database. *See also* DROP INDEX, DROP TABLE, and DROP VIEW. (2)

DROP INDEX The SQL command used to delete an index from a database. (6)

DROP TABLE Tables can be removed from the database with the SQL command DROP TABLE. (3)

DROP VIEW The SQL command used to drop or delete a view definition. Dropping a view does not delete any data. (12)

DUAL A virtual table automatically created by Oracle along with the data dictionary. It has one column, DUMMY, defined to be VARCHAR2(1), and contains one row with a value 'X'. (3)

EDIT A SQL*Plus command that can be used to start your system's default text editor to create a new script file. (4)

enclosing basic block An outer block of code surrounding the block in which the exception was raised. (7)

entity A thing, object, or concept that you want to store data about. (8)

entity occurrence A specific example of an entity. John Smith is an occurrence of the Person entity. (8)

Entity Relationship (ER) Diagram A diagram showing how data is organized in a database. Often abbreviated as ERD, an entity relationship diagram generally shows database tables as rectangles called "entities." Each entity contains one or more "attributes" that represent columns within the table. A database's logical data design is reflected in the ERD; its physical design is reflected in the data model; for instance, the ERD may show a

many-to-many relationship as a single line between two independent entities, while the data model will show the dependent junction table connecting the two independent tables, with two relationship lines going to it—one from each independent table. (8)

exception An error condition at runtime that prevents the application or program from executing any further in its normal flow of execution. If the exception is not handled, the application exits. (7)

exception handler Executable statements in the exception section of a PL/SQL program unit that do something when the exception occurs. They may print out an error message or try to rectify the exception. (7)

exception handling If a PL/SQL block has an exception block, exception handling is the processing that occurs in that block. If it does not occur, the exception is passed up to the enclosing block where it may or may not be handled. (7)

explicit cursors Cursors declared by a programmer explicitly using CURSOR ... IS syntax. A cursor is the go-between structure used by PL/SQL to contain and manage SQL statement execution. (7)

expression A method of specifying a value as a formula or reference, rather than as a literal "hard coded" value. When used in a command or program, an expression is interpreted at the time of execution, returning one or more values. For example, 3 + 4 is an expression, as is Sales_Tax / Product. (2)

FETCH A PL/SQL command that brings the next row of data into a cursor and moves the record's contents into either a PL/SQL record variable— that matches the record type of the cursor—or into a set of variables such that each variable in the list matches in type with the corresponding field in the cursor record. (7)

field The junction of a row and a column in a table containing a single piece of information about something. (1)

fifth normal form Fifth normal form isolates relationships that are logically dependent but need to be separate to satisfy the business needs of the database. (10)

first normal form First normal form eliminates repeating groups of columns by moving them to another table. (10)

flat file A single large table that stores information without using relationships, repeating the information as many times as needed. For example, a SALES_ORDER flat-file table will repeat all the fields for a particular product for every row for that product. (1, 5)

FOR loop A fixed-duration LOOP. In contrast to a WHILE loop, the exit condition in a LOOP is only evaluated once at the entry to the loop instead of at every passage through the loop. FOR loops can use a simple counter or can step through the rows of a cursor. (7)

foreign key The child table column(s) that contains the primary-key values from the parent table. (6, 9)

formal parameter The list of names and datatypes for variables a function or procedure accepts from the caller that act like variables local to the function or procedure. (7)

FOUND A cursor attribute that checks whether there is a record in the cursor. (7)

fourth normal form Fourth normal form isolates relationships that are not logically dependent on one another. (10)

function Functions return values when called by commands. For instance, the Oracle function ROUND() returns the value you give it, rounded to the number of decimal places you specify. Oracle has many built-in functions for common data and programming tasks, and it also allows you to write your own functions. (5)

function-based index An Oracle index by which you can index the function on a column, precompute the product of the function (this can be an arithmetic expression, or an expression that contains a SQL or PL/SQL function), and store that value in the index—rather than the original column data. (6)

grain The smallest unit of data that is to be recorded in a table or database. (9)

GROUP BY A clause used to create groups. After the GROUP BY clause, you simply state what columns contain the values you want the groups to be based on. (5)

group function Oracle functions that work on groups of records—for example, SUM, AVG, MIN, MAX, and so on. Also known as aggregate functions. (5)

group separator A character that separates hundreds, thousands, and so on, within a number. Typically a comma. (4)

hard-coded Information or values explicitly written into scripts or programs. *See also* literal. (4)

HAVING This clause works with the GROUP BY clause and filters groups based on group values. (5)

identifier An attribute or set of attributes that uniquely identifies a row or occurrence of an entity. (8)

identifying relationship A relationship in which the child entity is dependent on the parent entity. The identifier of the parent entity is transferred to become part of the identifier of the child entity. (8)

IF Used for directing the process flow in a PL/SQL block, the IF command branches depending on the evaluation of a Boolean expression. (7)

implicit cursor A hidden cursor that Oracle declares internally, used for SQL statements within PL/SQL. (7)

INCREMENT BY A sequence parameter used to specify the step used in the issuing of sequence numbers. The parameter may be negative. If not specified, the default is 1. (12)

INITCAP A SQL function that capitalizes the first character of each word of the text you indicate. (5)

inner join A join between tables that is created when the values in the columns from both tables in the join are equal. An inner join excludes missing values from the result set. (6)

INSERT Rows are added to tables by using the SQL command INSERT. (2, 3)

insert anomaly   An anomaly that occurs as the result of inserting data. (10)

INSTR   A SQL function that searches for the text you specify and returns a number identifying the starting position of that text within a string. (5)

INTERSECT   A SQL set operator that returns only the values that are present in *both* result sets from two SELECT statements. (6)

iteration   A repetition of a loop. (7)

iterative operation   An operation that is repeated in a loop. (7)

join   Writing a command that combines data from more than one table into a single list is called creating a join. (6)

JOIN   New in Oracle 9*i*, the JOIN keyword provides an alternate method for specifying a join between tables. (6)

Julian dates   A calendar system that counts the number of days starting from a specific day. For example, Oracle uses January 1, 4712 B.C. as the starting day. Time of day is treated as a fractional part of the date, for example, 54321.5 means noon of the 54,322nd day starting from January 1, 4712 B.C. (2)

LAST_DAY   A SQL function that returns the last day of whatever month is included in the date that was given to the function. (5)

leaf block   When building a B-tree index, Oracle analyzes the columns of the table and then splits the tables into storage units called "blocks" with each block containing the same number of records. This block is called a "leaf block" in the index. (6)

LENGTH   A SQL function that determines the character count of data stored in a database column. (5)

linesize   Sets the maximum width SQL*Plus will provide for each line before wrapping. (4)

literal   Fixed text in a command or program that does not change and is interpreted literally, instead of as a name for a variable. (2)

LOB (Large OBject)   Oracle provides this datatype to handle values that may be longer than 4,000 characters. A LOB can be up to 2GB in size. Typical large objects might be a word document, a music file, or a video recording. (11)

logical data model   A logical data model is a graphical representation of the information requirements of a business area. A logical data model is independent of a data storage device. It is built using an Entity Relationship Diagram (ERD). (8)

LOOP   A PL/SQL command enabling a section of PL/SQL code to be repeated until a condition (specified by the programmer) is met. (7)

loop index   The variable used in a FOR loop as the loop counter. It occurs between the FOR and IN parts of the FOR statement. (7)

LOWER   A SQL function that changes the case of the text to lowercase. (5)

LPAD   A SQL function that will right-justify your output by adding spaces or characters to the left of data in order to fill the void between data and the column width specified by the user. (5)

LTRIM   A SQL function that removes spaces from the beginning of a string. (5)

mandatory   An entity that has a mandatory role in a relationship must be present. (9)

many-to-many   In a many-to-many relationship, a single row in the first table links to many rows in the second table and a single row in the second table links to many rows in the first table. (9)

MAX   A SQL function that returns the largest value found in the column specified in its argument. (5)

MAXVALUE   A sequence parameter that allows you to define a maximum limit for the numbers the sequence generates. (12)

MIN   A SQL function that returns the smallest value found in the column specified in its argument. (5)

MINUS   A SQL set operator that shows you records from one result set that are *not* in another similarly formed result set. (6)

MINVALUE   A sequence parameter that allows you to define a minimum limit for the numbers the sequence generates—useful for sequences that have a negative INCREMENT BY parameter. (12)

MONTHS_BETWEEN   A SQL function that returns the number of months between any two dates. (5)

multirow subquery   A subquery that may return more than one row or record. (6)

named notation   A way of calling a procedure or function such that each actual parameter is matched to its formal parameter by using *formal_name =>*
actual_name notation. This allows for default-valued formal parameters to be anywhere in the list, not just at the end of the list of formal parameters. (7)

naming convention   A systematic method for generating names for database objects. The exact makeup of a convention is less important than whether you follow it consistently. (11)

natural key   Attributes that form an identifier where the attributes have real-world significance. *See also* surrogate key. (9)

nested loops   Loops placed one inside another. For a single iteration of the outer loop, the entire inner loop is executed. (7)

nesting   Placing one function or statement within another. (5)

NEXTVAL   A sequence "pseudocolumn" that returns the value and increments the sequence. (12)

non-unique index   An index that allows duplicate values. This is the default type of Oracle index. (11)

normalization   The process of applying the rules of normal form. Normalization reduces the redundancy of the data and improves its accuracy and the efficiency of handling the data. (10)

NOT NULL   A constraint on a column that enforces the mandatory optionality. (11)

NOTFOUND   A cursor attribute that checks if the cursor is empty (has no row in it). (7)

NULL   An indicator that data does not exist. Not to be confused with zero or blank space, which are valid data values. NULL means the value is not known or is missing. (2, 11)

null propagation   In math operations and many functions, using a NULL value forces the result to be NULL irrespective of the other values. In this sense the NULL is propagated through the operation. (11)

NUMBER   A basic Oracle datatype. Maximum precision (number of digits) is 38. The range of numbers that Oracle can handle is 1×10^{-130} to $9.99...9 \times 10^{125}$. (11)

NVL   A SQL function that, whenever presented with a value that is NULL, returns a value of your choosing instead. (5)

object privilege   Privilege for a specific database object like a table, sequence, and so on. An example of an object privilege would be the ability to INSERT records into an EMPLOYEE table. (1, 3)

ON   Used in many SQL commands, ON precedes the name of the table the command should affect. (6)

one-to-many   A relationship in which one row of the parent table refers to many rows of the child table. (9)

one-to-one   A relationship in which one row of the parent table refers to only one row of the child table. (9)

operator precedence   The order in which different operations are performed in an expression with more than one operator. For example, 3 – 4 / 2 will first perform 4 / 2, which is 2, and then 3 – 2, giving the final value of 1. (2)

operators   The technical name for mathematical operation symbols, such as the plus sign and minus sign. (2)

optional   A role of a relationship in which the entity is not required. Optional roles lead to NULL columns in the physical model. (9)

optionality   Each role of a relationship possesses an indication of whether the entity is mandatory or optional in the relationship. (8)

OR   This operator is used to select records containing any of a group of values—for instance, every product whose color is either red *or* green *or* white. The OR operator requires either condition in the statement to be true for any record to be selected. (3)

ORDER BY   A clause added to a SELECT statement that allows you to identify one or more columns that Oracle should sort the records by. (3)

outer join   A type of join between SQL tables in Oracle in which rows that would be excluded by an inner join due to missing data values are included in the result set. There are left, right, and full outer joins. (6)

pagesize   Controls how many lines of data SQL*Plus will display in response to a SELECT command before it repeats the column headings. (4)

parent entity   The entity with the lower cardinality in a relationship. In a one-to-many relationship, the parent entity is the one at the "one" end of the relationship. (9)

physical data model   The physical data model is the implementation of the logical model for a particular database server. It transforms the entities, attributes, and relations into tables, columns, and constraints. (8)

PL/SQL   Procedural Language for SQL. A programming language provided by Oracle to extend SQL by adding variables, flow of control, and other structures. (7)

PL/SQL function   *See* function. (7)

PL/SQL identifier   The name assigned by a PL/SQL programmer to any named object within the PL/SQL code (for example, the name of a variable or constant). (7)

PL/SQL package   PL/SQL program units that can contain procedures, functions, and type and variable declarations. Packages expose only the interface or specification to its contents for use by other program units. (7)

PL/SQL stored procedure   PL/SQL pieces of code made up of one or more PL/SQL basic blocks that perform sets of well-defined actions when called and that may accept a set of inputs and outputs called "formal parameters." (7)

populated   When a valid data value is stored in an attribute or a field, that attribute is said to be populated. (2)

positional notation   A way of calling a procedure or function where the actual parameters are matched to formal parameters by their respective positions in the list of formal parameters. If formal parameters with default values are to be used as optional parameters, they must be the last ones in the list. (7)

precision   The number of significant digits that a NUMBER variable can store. Maximum is 38. (11)

primary key   A column or set of columns that uniquely identifies each row in a table. Primary keys are essential for the operation of *relational integrity*. *See also* identifier. (6, 9)

privilege   A right or action that can be granted to a user for a database action or on an object. (1, 3)

Procedural Language/Structured Query Language
See PL/SQL. (7)

procedure body   The body of a stored procedure. This is the code that does the computational work. The header section of the body and the specification of the procedure must match exactly. (7)

procedure specification   The specification for a PL/SQL procedure made up of the name of the procedure and the list of its formal parameters. (7)

program flow   The ability to do conditional and iterative processing to control the flow of execution. (7)

public synonym   A SQL command used to create a public synonym. Public synonyms must be unique through the database. Objects with public synonyms do not need an owner when referring to them in SQL statements. (12)

raised   An error that is activated is considered "raised." (7)

raising an exception   Forcing an exception to be generated. This exception must then be handled in the EXCEPTION block or it will cause the procedure to terminate execution. (7)

range scan   A database scan that looks up a range of values in an index. (6)

record   Data contained in a table row. (1)

recursive relationship   A relationship in which one entity references itself. (9)

referential integrity   The system of relationships that enforce integrity in the data and make up a relational database. (9)

relational database   A database that organizes data in the form of tables and relationships among those tables. (1)

relationship   An association between two or more tables made up of the columns of the table. For example, the items in the Product_ID column of a SALES_ORDER table must come from the values in the Product_ID column of the PRODUCT_CATALOG table. This relationship between the two tables is established by making the Product_ID column in the SALES_ORDER table a foreign key referring to the Product_ID column in the PRODUCT_CATALOG table. (1)

RENAME   The SQL command that allows you to rename an object. (12)

repeating group   A set of columns in a table that are repeated. (10)

reverse engineering   The process of building and drawing a physical model from the actual database implementation. (8)

role   A set of privileges. Roles are a shorthand way of granting the same set of privileges to multiple users. (1, 8)

ROLLBACK   A SQL command that can be executed to undo changes to a database. (3)

ROUND   A SQL function that rounds numbers to whatever scale (number of decimal places) you specify. (5)

row   One line in a table. (1)

RPAD   A SQL function that will left-justify your output by adding spaces or characters to the right in order to fill the void between data and column width. (5)

RTRIM   This function removes spaces from the end of a string. (5)

SAVEPOINT   To be able to undo to intermediate points, you have to mark those points by issuing this command at whatever point you want to be able to roll back to. (3)

scale   Number of decimal places a NUMBER variable can store. Must be less than the precision. (11)

scope   A portion of a PL/SQL block that starts at the beginning of the block's declaration section and ends at the end of its exception section. The scope defines the context within which the variables are valid. (7)

script file   A plain text file of SQL commands. You can use the SQL*Plus EDIT command to start your system's default text editor to create a new script file. (4)

second normal form   Second normal form eliminates columns not dependent on the whole primary key to another table. It is only violated in the presence of a composite primary key. (10)

SELECT   The SQL command SELECT retrieves data from a database. (2)

self-join   The process of joining a table to itself. You must use table aliases in a self-join. (6)

sequence   An Oracle database object that issues sequential numbers. These numbers are often used for the values of a surrogate key. (9)

sequences   A database counter that automatically increments or decrements when you select a value from it and can be configured to start and stop at limiting values chosen. You can also configure it to recycle values when it reaches its limits. (12)

SET ECHO   Commands that control whether commands in the script file are shown to the user. (4)

set operator   Operator for combining results from two SQL queries (SELECT statements) in various ways—for example, UNION, MINUS, INTERSECT, and UNION ALL. (6)

SET VERIFY Commands that can be added to a script to help improve its appearance when the script is run. (4)

single-row function SQL functions that operate on one row of the data at a time. They include the categories: System Variables, Number, Character (text), Date, and Data Conversion. *See also* group function. (5)

single-row subquery A subquery that returns at most a single row or record. (6)

SPOOL The process of writing information out to a file on a disk. The SPOOL command opens a file and starts copying data from SQL*Plus into the file. (4)

spooling The process of writing information out to a file on a disk. (4)

START WITH A sequence parameter that specifies what the first value to be taken from the sequence will be. (12)

STORE A command that instructs SQL*Plus to save all of your current environment settings into a disk file. (4)

stored procedure A defined set of actions written using the PL/SQL language. When a procedure is called, it performs the actions it contains. A stored procedure can execute SQL statements and manipulate data in tables. *See also* PL/SQL stored procedure. (7)

string Text. (2)

strongly typed In a strongly typed language, the compiler checks the datatypes of all expressions, functions, and procedures. No automatic conversion of datatypes is allowed. *See also* weakly typed. (11)

Structured Query Language (SQL) A standard language use to manipulate data in a database. The standard is maintained and updated by the International Standards Organization (www.iso.org). (1)

subquery A standard SELECT query that is nested within a SELECT, UPDATE, or DELETE command. It can be used in either the SELECT (column) or WHERE clauses of a SELECT statement. In the FROM clause, a subquery is known as an "inline view." (6)

SUBSTR A SQL function used to cut strings up into substrings. (5)

substring A part of a string. (5)

subtype An entity that contains objects that group together in a certain category. The subtype entity has attributes that differentiate between the categories. (9)

SUM A SQL function that adds numeric values and returns the total value. (5)

supertype The entity that holds the common attributes in a supertype/subtype relationship. (9)

surrogate key A primary key that is composed of a unique number that has no interpretable meaning to the users. This number is usually generated from an Oracle sequence. (9)

synonym A database synonym is another name given to an existing database object. (12)

syntax The valid way of writing a command or language construct. Only those commands and language constructs that are correct and complete in syntax can be successful. (2, 12)

SYS_CONTEXT A SQL function that returns session attributes. (5)

SYSDATE A SQL function that returns the current date and time from the Oracle server's point of view, so if the server happens to be in another time zone, that time for that zone will be returned. (5)

system privilege Privileges for actions anywhere in the database—for example, inserting into any table. (1, 3)

system variable Variables maintained by Oracle to provide you with information about the environment in which the database is running. (5)

table A collection of rows and columns all of which store information about one type of thing (for instance, people or products). (1)

table alias A shorthand name that may be assigned to a table name within SQL statements and that then can be used to refer to the table throughout the rest of the statement. (6)

table constraint   A constraint that uses values from multiple columns of a row of a table. For example, on the EMPLOYEE table a constraint might be "(job_title LIKE 'Manager%' and SALARY > 100000) OR (job_title NOT LIKE 'Manager%')". (11)

third normal form   Third normal form eliminates columns whose values are only indirectly dependent on the primary key. (10)

TO_CHAR   This SQL function converts dates, times, or numbers to text. Its primary use is to format values for display purposes; the fact that they are text is irrelevant when they are scrolling across a SQL*Plus screen. (5)

TO_DATE   This SQL function converts text that looks like a date (and/or time) into an actual Oracle date/time value. (5)

transitive dependency   A transitive dependency exists when an attribute is indirectly dependent on another attribute through a third attribute or another entity. (10)

transitively dependent   *See* transitive dependency. (10)

trigger   A PL/SQL block that gets executed automatically if the event specified in it ("triggering event") happens. (7)

triggering event   An event, such as an INSERT, UPDATE, or DELETE statement, that may be used to cause execution of a trigger. (7)

trimming   The process of removing extra spaces from the beginning or end of a text string. (5)

TRUNC   *See* TRUNCATE. (5)

TRUNCATE (same as TRUNC)   This function truncates the decimal places from a number. Compare this with ROUND. TRUNCATE on a datetime variable removes the time part of a date. (3)

Unified Modeling Language (UML)   A methodology for creating diagrams that depict business processes and technical architecture. (8)

UNION   A SQL set operator that performs the useful task of combining data from multiple result sets into a single list, excluding duplicates. (6)

UNION ALL   A SQL set operator that functions similarly to the UNION set operator, except that UNION ALL causes every row to be returned, instead of just one distinct row for each unique value. (6)

UNIQUE   *See* distinct. (3)

unique constraint   A constraint on a column or set of columns to ensure that all values are unique. Unique constraint columns can have NULL values. (11)

unique identifier   *See* identifier. (8)

unique index   An index in which all the values are unique. Unique indexes are used for enforcing unique constraints and primary keys. (11)

UPDATE   A SQL command employed to identify the table to be updated, state what value should be assigned to what column, and then specify what condition a record must meet in order to receive the update. (3)

update anomaly   An anomaly that occurs as the result of updating data. (10)

UPPER   A SQL function that changes the case of the text to uppercase. (5)

USER   A SQL function that returns the Oracle user ID of the person who issued the command containing the USER function. (5)

USERENV   A SQL function that can return a variety of different facts about the computer environment of the person who issued the command containing the USERENV function. (5)

VARCHAR2   A basic Oracle datatype for variable-length strings. The maximum length of a string is 4,000 characters. (11)

variable   Used in formulas and programs, variables store values that can change. *See also* constant. (4)

view   A query stored in the database and given a name. (12)

weakly typed In a weakly typed language, the developer or code writer must check the datatypes of all expressions, functions, and procedures. Automatic conversion of datatypes is performed. *See also* strongly typed. (11)

WHERE A clause used to filter table records. You follow the WHERE clause with a statement of whatever conditions must be true about records in order for them to be shown. (3)

WHERE CURRENT OF *cursor* A special WHERE clause of an UPDATE or DELETE statement that refers to the row of data currently held in the cursor. (7)

WHILE loop A loop suited for situations when the number of loop iterations is not known in advance, but rather is determined by some external factor. Every time, before entering the loop, the condition for the WHILE is evaluated and must be true. (7)

wildcard A method for specific text that can vary in a search. In Oracle, a single-character wildcard is represented by _, and a group of wildcard characters is represented by %. (3)

WITH CHECK OPTION Optional parameter when creating a view; causes Oracle to require that inserted data contain values matching the view's WHERE clause. (12)

, (comma), 63–64, 92
:= (assignment operator), 198
* (asterisk), 19, 39, 83
 (at sign), 96
| | (concatenation operator), 41–42
$ (dollar sign), 91–92
= (equal sign), 56
> (greater-than sign), 56–57
< (less-than sign), 56–57
( ) parenthesis, 59
% (percent sign), 60
+ (plus sign), 39, 168–169
" (quotation marks), 42–43
' (quote marks), 26, 37, 59, 69, 297
_ (underscore), 60, 330
| (vertical bar), 41–43, 93
< > (angle brackets), 92
- (minus sign), 39, 92
/ (slash), 39, 83, 97, 200
-- (comment), 137, 215
/** / command, 137–139, 215
!= operator, 57
<> operator, 57
1NF (first normal form), 275–277, 284, 377
2NF (second normal form), 277–278, 284, 381
3NF (third normal form), 278–279, 284

A

abbreviations, 329
ACCEPT command, 96, 98, 373
access control, 53–54
ADD_MONTHS function, 123, 373
aliases
        column names, 42–43
        tables, 166–167, 382–383
alignment, decimal, 90–91
ALTER TABLE command, 345–346, 373
ALTER TABLE statements, 311

alternate keys, 310–311, 373
American National Standards Institute (ANSI), 10, 26
AND operator, 56–59, 373
angle brackets < >, 92
anomalies, 283–286, 373
anonymous blocks, 196–197, 373
ANSI (American National Standards Institute), 10, 26
ANSI SQL Standard, 10
apostrophe ('), 26, 37, 59, 69, 297
applications
        database, 1
        exceptions, 220
        transferring data between, 114–118
arguments, 194–195
AS keyword, 43, 373
ASCII files, 26
ASCII standard, 26
assignment operator (:=), 198
asterisk (*), 19, 39, 83
at sign (), 96
attributes
        conventions, 238
        cursors, 211–212, 373
        dependency, 273–275
        described, 31, 237–238, 373
        eliminating, 278–279
        entities, 236–238
        IDEF1X notation rules, 258
        identifying, 249–250, 252
        IE notation rules, 256
        multivalued, 276
        names, 238
        optional, 238
        populated, 380
        primary keys and, 278–279
        repeating groups, 275
        required, 238
        vs. entities, 248–250
averaging values, 141
AVG function, 141, 373

B

B-tree indexes, 157–160, 373
basic blocks, 196–199, 373, 376
BCNF (Boyce-Codd Normal Form), 280
BEGIN keyword, 198
BETWEEN clause, 57, 61, 373
binary large objects (BLOBs), 298
binary relationships, 264, 373
bitmap indexes, 159–160, 373
BLOBs (binary large objects), 298
blocks
        anonymous, 196–197, 373
        basic, 196–199, 373, 376
        branch, 158, 373–374
        leaf, 158, 378
        nested, 197
        PL/SQL, 196–199
Boyce-Codd Normal Form (BCNF), 280
branch blocks, 158, 373–374
Brown, Bob, 256
buffers
        length, 88
        scrollback, 87–88
        SQL*Plus, 87–88
        width, 88, 374
business analysis, 8
business specifications, 247

C

C language, 8
C++ language, 8
calculations, 39–41, 298
cardinality
        columns, 159–160
        described, 374
        implementing, 314–316
        relationships, 239, 258–261
cardinality notation, 240
Cartesian products, 165, 374

cascade delete clause, 319–321
cascade deletes, 317–321, 374
cascade updates, 317–322, 327, 374
cascading effects, 316–319
case, text, 110–112
case-sensitivity, 60
categories, 264–267, 374
CD-ROM content, 370–372
CHANGE command, 83–85, 374
CHAR datatype, 25–26, 118, 374
character functions, 110, 374
character large objects
    (CLOBs), 298
characters
        comment, 137, 215
        maximum number
            stored, 297
        in strings. *See* strings
        wildcard, 60
check constraints, 320, 330
Chen, Dr. Peter, 258
child entities, 254, 374
child records, 164
child tables, 162–164
Clapham Specialty Store, 6
class diagrams, 267
CLOBs (character large
    objects), 298
CLOSE cursor, 213
cluster symbol, 266
clusters, 266–267, 374
COBOL language, 8
Codd, Dr. Edgar F., 9, 275
code
        blocks of. *See* blocks
        hard-coded data, 96, 377
        indenting, 117
        procedural, 327–329
code tables, 253, 374
COLUMN command, 90–94, 374
columns
        adding to tables, 345–346
        aliases, 42–43, 374
        aligning decimals, 90–91
        altering, 345
        attributes, 31
        cardinality, 159–160
        changing datatypes, 345–346
        concatenating, 41–42
        constraints, 302–307, 374
        described, 2–3, 374
        formatting, 90–94
        group separator, 91

headings, 42–43, 92–94
largest items in, 142
length, 25
line breaks, 93
multicolumn subqueries, 180
names, 21–24, 30, 42–43,
    274, 330
NOT NULL, 304
NULL, 31–32, 295, 304
number, 24, 27, 157
order of, 38
restricting access to, 262
selection, 38
separating data in, 113–114
smallest items in, 141
sorting on, 63–64
text, 24–26
unique values in, 64–66
wrapping text in, 91–92
comma (,), 63–64, 92
commands. *See also specific*
    commands
        copying, 85–87
        customizing with, 89
        displaying, 96
        editing, 81–85
        executing, 83, 95–96
        pasting, 85–87
        in script files. *See* script files
        syntax, 25
comment characters (--), 137, 215
comments
        inserting in SQL scripts,
            137–139
        multiple line, 137–139
        PL/SQL, 215
        single-line, 137–138
        types of, 137
COMMIT command, 54,
    71–73, 374
composite indexes, 157, 374
composite keys, 251–252, 255, 374
computer name, 108
concatenated indexes, 157, 374
concatenation, 41–42, 374
concatenation operator (| |), 41–42
conceptual models, 233–235, 374
conditional processing,
    205–217, 374
conditions, 58–59
constants
        described, 40, 374
        PL/SQL, 202–203

constraints
        check, 320, 330
        column, 302–307, 374
        data, 6
        database, 6
        declarative, 327–329, 375
        described, 374
        enforcing, 307–310
        errors, 305, 309, 319, 329
        foreign key, 254–255,
            312–326, 330–331
        intercolumn, 306–307
        names, 305, 314, 329–331
        NOT NULL, 202, 331, 379
        primary key, 307–313
        quality and, 6
        relational, 326–329
        table, 303, 305–307, 383
        triggers and, 327–329
        types of, 302–303
        unique, 307–310, 383
control structures, 205–217
COPY command, 86
copying commands, 85–87
correlated subqueries,
    181–182, 375
COUNT function, 140–141, 375
counter variables, 209–210
coupling, 263
CREATE INDEX command,
    156–157
CREATE OR REPLACE VIEW
    command, 349–350, 375
CREATE SEQUENCE command,
    359, 375
CREATE SYNONYM command,
    363–364
CREATE TABLE command, 17,
    32, 343, 375
cross bar, 240
"crow's foot" methodology,
    256, 259
currency symbol, 91–92
CURRVAL column, 359–360
CURRVAL sequence, 375
cursor-based records, 212
cursor FOR loop, 213
CURSOR_ALREADY_OPEN
    exception, 218
cursors
        attributes, 211–212, 373
        closing, 211, 213
        declaring, 211–212

described, 375
empty, 213
error messages, 213, 218
explicit, 211
FETCH, 213
fetching rows, 213
implicit, 211, 377
invalid, 213, 218
opening, 211, 213
PL/SQL, 210–217
WHERE CURRENT OF,
213–215, 384
customization
with commands, 89
saving configurations, 89–90
SQL*Plus, 87–90
CYCLE parameter, 359
CYCLE sequence, 375

■ D

data
adding to tables, 53
adding values, 140–141
analyzing, 8
anomalies, 283–286, 373
committing changes to,
71–73
conceptual model of, 247
constraints, 6
controlling access to, 53–54
described, 4
displaying, 164–167
in functions, 104
grouping, 142–144
hard-coded, 96, 377
importing, 341
inserting. See inserting data
integrity, 232, 326–329
joins. See joins
justifying, 136–137
length, 112–113
making available, 72
math operations on, 39–41
missing values, 295
modifying in tables, 67
from multiple tables,
164–167
NULL. See NULL values
padding, 118–120
parsing, 114–118
quality, 6, 295–301
raw, 4

redundant, 277–278, 285–286
removing from tables, 53
retrieval of, 54
return points, 70–72
rolling back changes to,
70–72
separating into substrings,
113–114
spaces in, 118–120
spreadsheet, 277
transferring between
applications, 114–118
transferring between tables,
339–344
types of, 24
updating, 53, 67
working with, 52–79
data blocks. See blocks
Data Control Language. See DDL
data conversion, 126–133, 375
Data Definition Language.
See DDL
data dictionary, 308
Data Manipulation Language.
See DML
data modeling software, 256
data models. See also ERD
basic, 265
benefits of, 231–232
conceptual, 233–235
creating, 265
described, 230
design, 231–232
development of, 247
logical, 234–235
overview, 231–232
physical, 234–236
purpose of, 231
reading, 230–245
relational, 232
standards for, 255–258
types of, 233–236
data warehouses, 341
database administrator (DBA), 8
database engines, 286–287
database objects, 53
database platforms, 53
database programs, 1
databases
access to, 53–54
administration of, 8
advantages of, 8

constraints, 6
described, 375
designing, 7, 246–271
grain, 247–248
initializing, 160
integrity, 232, 326–329
on the Internet, 1, 3
large, 5
Mailing database, 254–263
normalizing. See
normalization
overview, 1–3
relational, 1–15, 381
search engines, 1
security. See security
uses for, 1, 9
vs. spreadsheets, 3–7
datatypes. See also specific datatypes
changing in columns,
345–346
CHAR, 118
choosing, 298–301
converting, 301
defining, 296–298
described, 24, 375
errors, 301
length, 299
PL/SQL, 200, 202
precision, 299
procedure parameters, 195
strong typing, 301
VARCHAR, 297
VARCHAR2, 25–26, 118,
297, 383
weak typing, 301, 384
DATE datatype, 29–30, 298, 375
date functions, 121–126
date math, 29–30, 375
dates
in calculations, 298
comparing, 125–126
converting to Oracle values,
131–133
converting to text, 127–130
default format for, 298
filtering records based on,
60–62
formatting, 127–134
four-digit, 40
inserting, 106–107, 131–133
Julian, 29–30
manipulating, 106–107
nesting, 125–126

returning, 106–107
returning last day of month, 124–125, 378
returning months between two dates, 125–126
returning past/future months, 123, 373
spelling out, 129
storage of, 28–30, 298
truncating, 121–122
two-digit, 40
working with, 121–126
days
returning last day of month, 124–125, 378
spelling out, 129
DBS directory, 90
DCL (Data Control Language), 375
DDL (Data Definition Language), 53, 375
DDL commands, 73, 345
decimal indicator, 90, 92
decimal point, 90–92, 108–110
declaration, cursor, 211–212
declaration section, PL/SQL blocks, 197–198
declarative constraints, 327–329, 375
declarative languages, 189
declarative relational integrity, 326–329
delete anomalies, 285, 375
DELETE command, 53, 68–69
delete restricts, 317, 375
DELETE statement, 179
deleting
extra spaces, 118–120
records, 53, 68–69
rows, 68–69
delta schema, 282–283
denormalization, 273, 283, 375
dependencies, 273–275
described, 273, 375
IE notation rules, 256
relationships, 263
transitive, 274–275
dependent attributes, 273–274, 375
dependent entities, 263
dependents, 273–275
DESC command, 30
determinants, 273–275, 375
directories, Oracle home, 89
discriminators, 266, 375

disk, spooling to, 94–95
DISTINCT modifier, 65–66, 376
DML (Data Manipulation Language), 53, 375
DML operations, 161–162
DML statement, 106
DML transactions, 54, 69–73
dollar sign ($), 91–92
domain model, 233, 376
domains, 301–302, 376
DROP command, 18–20, 376
DROP INDEX command, 376
DROP TABLE command, 73, 376
DROP VIEW command, 352, 376
dropping items
synonyms, 364
tables, 18–20, 73, 376
views, 351–352, 376
DUAL table, 66–67, 376
DUP_VAL_ON_INDEX exception, 218

■ E

ED text editor, 83
EDIT command, 81–83, 95, 376
editing
line-level, 83–85
with mouse, 86–87
SQL commands, 81–85
END keyword, 198
entities
attributes, 236–238, 248–250
categories, 262
child, 254, 374
conventions, 237
defining, 248–250
dependent, 263
described, 236–237, 376
IDEF1X notation rules, 258
IE notation rules, 256
names, 237–238
parent, 254, 380
primary keys. See primary keys
relationships, 238–240, 254–255, 281
resolution, 275
roles, 261–263
subtype, 382
vs. attributes, 248–250
entity diagrams, 267
entity occurrences, 237, 376

Entity Relationship Diagram. See ERD
Environment dialog box, 87–89
environment settings, 89–90
equal sign (=), 56
ER/Studio software, 256
ERD (Entity Relationship Diagram)
data model standards, 255
described, 236, 376
fifth normal form, 282–283
first normal form, 275
logical data model, 234
reading, 236–241
relationships, 239, 258, 281
error handling, 217
errors
constraints, 305, 309, 319, 329
cursors, 213, 218
datatypes, 301
dropped tables and, 19–20
invalid cursor, 213, 218
invalid number, 301
mutating table, 327
ORA, 218–219
PL/SQL, 198–199, 217
raised, 380
rounding, 299
type conversions, 301
ERwin software, 256
events, 195, 383
exception handlers, 217–218, 376
exception handling, 199, 376
EXCEPTION keyword, 198
exceptions. See also specific exceptions
application-specific, 220
described, 217, 376
PL/SQL, 198–199, 217–218
programmer-defined, 220–222
raising, 199, 380
system-defined, 218–219
explicit cursors, 211, 376
explicit transactions, 73
expressions, 40–41, 376
extensions, 94

■ F

FETCH command, 376
FETCH cursor, 213
fields, 2–3, 376

fifth normal form, 279–280, 376
file extensions, 94
files
    ASCII, 26
    flat, 6, 277, 341, 377
    script. *See* script files
    spool, 94
filtering
    based on dates, 60–62
    based on text, 59–60
    groups, 143–144
    records, 143–144
    views, 349–350
    with wildcards, 59–60
Finkelstein, Clive, 256
first normal form (1NF), 275–277,
    284, 377
FK. *See* foreign keys
flat-file tables, 341
flat files, 6, 277, 341, 377
FOR loop, 209–210, 213, 377
FOR UPDATE clause, 212
foreign keys (FK)
    constraints, 254–255,
        312–326, 330–331
    described, 254, 377
    IDEF1X notation rules, 258
    one-to-many, 260
formal parameters, 377
formatting
    columns, 90–94
    dates, 127–134
    numbers, 90–91, 130–131
    numbers in SQL*Plus, 90–94
    text, 91–92
    time, 127–134
Forms Developer product, 8
FOUND attribute, 213, 377
fourth normal form, 279–281, 377
function-based indexes,
    160–161, 377
functions. *See also specific functions*
    calling, 200–201
    character, 110, 374
    data in, 104
    date, 121–126
    date conversion, 126–133
    described, 104, 377
    group, 139–142, 145–146, 377
    nesting, 116
    number, 108–110
    Oracle built-in, 104–151
    PL/SQL, 193, 200–201

    single-row, 104–139
    stored, 195
    text, 110–120

■ G

glossary, 373–384
grain, database, 247–248, 377
GRANT command, 54
greater-than sign (>), 56–57
GROUP BY clause, 142–144, 377
group functions
    described, 139, 377
    example, 145–146
    implementing, 139–142
group separator, 91–92, 377
grouping data, 142–144
groups
    excluding, 143–144
    filtering, 143–144
    including, 143–144
    privileges, 5
    repeated, 275–277
GUI environment, 8

■ H

hard-coded data, 96, 377
HAVING clause, 143–144, 377
headings, column, 42–43, 92–94

■ I

IDEF (Integration Definition), 256
IDEF1X (Integration Definition for
    Information Modeling), 256–258
identifiers. *See also* primary keys
    described, 251–252, 377
    PL/SQL, 202, 380
    rules/guidelines, 253
    unique, 237–238
    uses for, 251
identifying relationships,
    239–240, 377
IE (Information Engineering), 256
IE notation, 240, 256
IF command, 206–208, 377
implicit cursors, 211, 377
implicit transactions, 73
importing data, 341
IN function, 58, 179
IN keyword, 195
INCREMENT BY parameter,
    359, 377

indexes, 155–163
    B-tree, 157–160, 373
    bitmap, 159–160, 373
    composite, 157, 374
    concatenated, 157, 374
    cost of, 156
    creating, 156–157, 163
    function-based, 160–161, 377
    loop, 209, 378
    names, 331
    non-unique, 311–312, 379
    overview, 155–156
    performance and, 155–156,
        160–162
    synchronized, 156
    types of, 157–161
    unique, 307–310, 383
    uses for, 155–156, 161–162
    WHERE clause and, 157
Information Engineering (IE),
    240, 256
INITCAP function, 110–112, 377
initializing databases, 160
inner joins, 167–168, 377
insert anomalies, 285, 378
INSERT command
    adding data, 18, 53
    described, 377
    single quotes and, 26
    transferring data, 342–343
INSERT statement
    inserting dates, 106–107
    NULL values and, 32–35
inserting data
    apostrophes and, 37
    with INSERT command,
        18, 53
    NULL values and, 32–36
    procedure for, 299–301
installing Oracle 9*i* software,
    370–372
INSTR function, 114–118, 378
Integration Definition (IDEF), 256
Integration Definition for
    Information Modeling (IDEF1X),
    256–258
integrity
    data, 232
    database, 232
    declarative, 326–329
    referential, 255, 381
    relational, 232, 326–329
Internet, 1, 3

INTERSECT operator, 174, 176, 378
invalid cursor message, 213, 218
invalid number error, 301
INVALID_CURSOR exception, 218
IS NOT NULL parameter, 61–62
IS NULL parameter, 61–62
ISO currency symbol, 92
iteration, 378
iteration constructs, 208–210
iterative operations, 206, 378

J

Java language, 8
JOIN keyword, 171–173, 378
joins
    described, 164–165, 311, 378
    inner, 167–168, 377
    JOIN keyword, 171–173
    outer, 168–170, 380
    SELECT statement, 164–173
    self, 170–171, 381
    types of, 167–173
    WHERE clause and, 165–169
Julian dates, 29–30, 378
justifying data, 136–137

K

keys
    alternate, 310–311, 373
    composite, 251–252, 255, 374
    foreign. See foreign keys
    natural, 252–253, 379
    primary. See primary keys
    surrogate, 252–253, 310, 327, 358–359, 376

L

languages
    C, 8
    C++, 8
    COBOL, 8
    DCL, 375
    DDL, 53, 375
    declarative, 189
    DML, 53, 375
    Java, 8
    procedural, 189
    SEQUEL, 9

SQL. See SQL
    strong typing, 301, 382
    UML, 233–234, 383
    weak typing, 301, 384
large objects. See LOBs
LAST_DAY function, 124–125, 378
leaf blocks, 158, 378
LENGTH function, 112–113, 378
less-than sign (<), 56–57
line breaks, 93
linesize option, 88–89
linesizing, 378
literals, 42, 378
LOB datatype, 298
LOBs (large objects), 262, 298, 378
logical models
    described, 234, 378
    many-to-many relationships, 259–260
    moving to physical models, 286–288
    one-to-one relationships, 261–262
    super/subtypes, 264–267
    vs. physical models, 234
login.sql file, 89–90
LONG datatype, 26
LOOP command, 378
LOOP construct, 208–209
loop index, 209, 378
loops
    FOR, 209–210, 213, 377
    iteration of, 208–210
    nested, 215–217, 379
    PL/SQL, 208–210, 213, 215–217
    WHILE, 209, 384
LOWER function, 110, 378
LPAD function, 137, 378
.lst extension, 94
LTRIM function, 118–119, 378

M

Mailing database, 254–263
mandatory role, 378
Martin, James, 256
math operations, 39–41, 298
math operators, 39–41
MAX function, 142, 378
MAXVALUE parameter, 359, 378
memory buffers, 87–88
MIN function, 141, 378

MINUS operator, 174, 176, 378
minus sign (-), 39, 92
MINVALUE parameter, 359, 379
MODIFY command, 346
money, 299
months
    returning between two dates, 125–126, 379
    returning last day of, 124–125
    returning past/future, 123
    separating from dates, 129–130
MONTHS_BETWEEN function, 125–126, 379
movie database, 322–326
multicolumn subqueries, 180
multirow subqueries, 179–180, 379

N

named notation, 201, 379
naming conventions, 329–331, 379
natural keys, 252–253, 379
negative values, 92
nested items
    blocks, 197
    dates, 125–126
    described, 379
    functions, 116
    loops, 215–217, 379
    SELECT statements, 181–182
NEXTVAL column, 359–360
NEXTVAL sequence, 379
NO_DATA_FOUND exception, 218
non-unique indexes, 311–312, 379
normal forms, 275–286, 376–377, 381, 383
normalization, 272–293
    data anomalies, 283–286
    denormalization, 273, 283
    dependency, 273–275
    described, 273, 379
    moving from logical to physical models, 286–288
    normal forms, 275–286
    process for, 283–284
NOT clause, 61
NOT modifier, 57
NOT NULL columns, 295, 304
NOT NULL constraints, 202, 331, 379

NOT NULL keyword, 31–34, 36
Notepad, 83
NOTFOUND attribute, 213, 379
NULL columns, 304
NULL indicator, 379
NULL keyword, 31–33
null propagation, 295, 379
NULL values
        averaging and, 141
        changing options for,
            346–348
        in columns, 31–32
        data insertion and, 32–36
        described, 31
        domains and, 302
        filling automatically,
            132–136
        handling, 295
        in records, 32–36
        search conditions, 61–62
        selecting records based on,
            61–62
number columns, 24, 27
NUMBER datatype, 27, 296, 379
number functions, 108–110
numbers
        aligning decimals, 90–91
        analyzing, 298
        averaging, 141
        decimal points, 108–110
        displaying zeros, 92
        formatting, 130–131
        formatting in SQL*Plus,
            90–91
        group separator, 91
        limits, 296
        money and, 299
        precision, 296
        returning largest value, 142
        returning smallest value, 141
        Roman numerals, 92
        rounding, 108–109, 299
        scale, 296
        sorting, 298
        standardizing display of,
            130–131
        storage of, 27
        in text columns, 24
        top number analysis, 352
        truncating, 109–110
        zeros, 92, 218, 298
NVL function, 132–136, 379

■ O

objects
        database, 53
        names, 329–330
        privileges, 4, 53, 379
        synonyms, 362–364
ON indicator, 379
ON keyword, 171–173
OPEN cursor, 213
operators. *See also specific operators*
        described, 379
        math, 39–41
        precedence, 41, 58–59, 379
        set, 173–176, 381
optionality
        described, 379
        implementing, 314–316
        relationships, 239, 258,
            261–263
optionality notations, 240
OR clause, 57
OR operator, 58–59, 379–380
ORA errors, 218–219
Oracle 9i Standard Edition,
    installing, 370–372
Oracle Corporation, 9
Oracle home, 89
Oracle reserved words, 21–23
Oracle Technology Network
    (OTN), 371–372
ORDER BY clause, 63, 176, 350,
    352, 380
OTHER exception, 218
OTN (Oracle Technology
    Network), 371–372
OUT keyword, 195
outer joins, 168–170, 380

■ P

pagesize option, 88–89, 380
parameters
        actual, 194–195, 373
        formal, 194–195, 377
        PL/SQL, 200–201
        procedure, 195
parent/child relationships, 164
parent entities, 254, 380
parent records, 164
parent tables, 162–164, 328–329
parenthesis ( ), 59
parsing strings, 114–118

PASTE command, 86
pasting commands, 85–87
paths, 94–95
percent sign (%), 60
performance
        bitmap indexes, 160
        indexes and, 155–156,
            161–162
        triggers and, 328–329
physical models, 234–236,
    286–288, 380
PL/SQL, 188–229
        block structure, 196–199
        calling functions, 200–201
        calling procedures, 200–201
        comments, 215
        conditional processing,
            205–217
        constants, 202–203
        control structures, 205–217
        creating simple procedure,
            199–201
        cursors, 210–217
        datatypes, 200, 202
        described, 189, 192–193, 380
        errors, 198–199, 217
        exception handling, 217–218
        exceptions, 217–218
        functions, 193
        IF statement, 206–208
        loops, 208–210, 213, 215–217
        parameters, 200–201
        SQL and, 193–194
        SQL*Plus and, 193–194
        stored functions, 195
        stored procedures, 193–195
        triggers, 195–196
        variables, 201–205
PL/SQL blocks, 196–199
PL/SQL functions, 380
PL/SQL identifiers, 202, 380
PL/SQL packages, 380
PL/SQL records, 212
PL/SQL stored procedures, 380
plus sign (+), 39, 168–169
positional notation, 201, 380
precedence, 41, 58–59, 379
precision, 296, 299, 380
primary keys
        attributes and, 278–279
        composite, 251–252, 255
        constraints, 307–313
        described, 162, 164, 380

examples of, 162
IDEF1X notation rules, 258
identifying, 251–255
natural, 252–253
purpose of, 251
relationships, 254
rules/guidelines for, 253
sequences and, 358–359
surrogate, 252–253, 310, 327, 358–359, 376
updating, 253
privileges
assigning, 54
described, 380
groups, 5
object, 4, 53, 379
removing, 54
system, 4, 53
users, 4–5
.prn extension, 94
procedural code, 327–329
Procedural Language/Structured Query Language. See PL/SQL
procedural languages, 189
procedure body, 195, 380
procedure specifications, 194–195, 380
procedures
calling, 200–201
PL/SQL, 200–201
program flow, 206, 380
PROGRAM_ERROR exception, 218
programmer-defined exceptions, 220–222
programmer-defined records, 212
programming languages. See languages
public synonym, 363–364, 380

■ Q

quality, 6, 295–301
queries. See subqueries
quotation marks ("), 42–43
quote marks ('), 26, 37, 59, 69, 297

■ R

range scan, 159, 380
raw data, 4
records
adding values, 140–141
apostrophes in, 37

child, 164
counting, 140–141
cursor-based, 212
deleting, 53, 68–69
described, 1, 381
excluding, 57
filtering, 59–62, 143–144
grouping, 142–144
identifying, 251–255
inserting, 18, 32–37
limiting, 54–62
NULL values in, 32–37
order of, 62–64
parent, 164
PL/SQL, 212
programmer-defined, 212
removing from tables, 68–69
returning largest value, 142
returning smallest value, 141
selecting, 18, 55–58
sorting. See sorting
subset of, 54–62
table-based, 212
tracking activity of, 107–108
truncating, 68–69
values in, 55–58
viewing, 62–64
recursive relationships, 264, 319–321, 381
redundancy, 285–286
relational data models, 232
relational databases, 1–15, 381. See also databases
relational integrity, 232, 326–329
Relational Model, 281
Relational Software Inc. (RSI). See Oracle Corporation
relationship notations, 240
relationships
binary, 264, 373
cardinality, 239, 258–261
common, 254–255
coupling, 263
data in other tables, 254–255
dependency, 263, 273–275
described, 238–240, 381
entities, 236–241, 254–255, 281
IDEF1X notation rules, 258
identifying, 239–240, 377
IE notation rules, 256
isolating, 280–283
logically independent, 281

mandatory, 258
many-to-many, 259–260, 275–276, 378
one-to-many, 258–259, 275, 379
one-to-one, 260–261, 379
optionality, 258, 261–263, 379
parent/child, 164
primary keys, 254
recursive, 264, 319–321, 381
roles, 238–239, 258–263
separating, 282–283
splitting, 281
subtypes, 264–267
supertypes, 264–267
tables, 5–6, 162–176
vs. relations, 246
RENAME command, 344, 381
repeating groups, 381
reserved words, 21–23
resolution entity, 275
REVERSE command, 210
reverse engineering, 235, 381
REVOKE command, 54
roles
described, 5, 238–239, 258, 381
entities, 261–263
mandatory, 262
optional, 262
relationships, 238–239, 258–263
security and, 4–5
ROLLBACK command, 54, 70–72, 381
Roman numerals, 92
ROUND function, 108–109, 381
rounding errors, 299
rounding numbers, 108–109, 381
ROWIDs, 155–156
ROWNUM variable, 352
rows
deleting, 68–69
described, 1, 381
excluding, 143–144
including, 143–144
locking/unlocking, 211–212
multiple, 3
multirow subqueries, 179–180
number of, 282
returning, 173–176
unique, 310

RPAD function, 136, 381
RTRIM function, 118–120, 381

■ S

Save As command, 95
SAVEPOINT command, 54,
    70–72, 381
savepoints, 70–72
scale, 296, 381
schemas, 282–283
scope, 381
screen, 87
script files. *See also* SQL scripts
    comments in, 137–139
    creating, 95–96
    described, 95, 381
    running, 96
    SQL*Plus, 94–98
    variables in, 96–98
search engines, 1
second normal form (2NF),
    277–278, 284, 381
security
    databases, 4–5
    overview, 4–5
    roles. *See* roles
    user access, 4–5
    views and, 348
SELECT command
    data retrieval, 54
    described, 381
    DUAL table selections, 66–67
    inserting records, 18–20
    limiting record selection,
        54–62
    record order, 62–64
    showing unique values, 64–66
    table creation, 343–344
    transferring data, 342–343
SELECT statement
    column order, 38
    column selection, 38
    concatenation, 41–42
    displaying data, 164–167
    joins and, 164–173
    math operations, 39–41
    multiple group functions in,
        143–144
    nested, 181–182
    parenthesis and, 59
    top number analysis, 352
self-joins, 170–171, 381

SEQUEL (Structured English
    Query Language), 9
sequences, 253, 358–362, 381
SET ECHO command, 96, 98, 381
set operators, 173–176, 381
SET SCAN OFF command, 37
SET VERIFY command, 97, 382
single-row functions, 104–139, 382
single-row subquery, 382
slash (/), 39, 83, 97, 200
software development, 8
sorting
    on individual columns, 63
    on multiple columns, 63–64
    numbers, 298
    unique values, 64–66
spaces
    concatenation and, 42
    removing extra, 118–120
    strings, 297
    in table/column names, 21
    between words, 330
SPOOL command, 94, 382
spooling, 94–95, 382
spreadsheets, 1–7, 277
SQL (Structured Query Language)
    advantages of, 8
    ANSI SQL Standard, 10
    described, 382
    history, 9–10
    importance of, 8
    PL/SQL and, 193–194
SQL commands. *See* commands
.sql extension, 94
SQL*Plus, 80–103
    clearing screen, 87
    customizing, 87–90
    editing prior commands,
        81–85
    environment settings, 89–90
    formatting in, 90–94
    group separator, 91
    improving output of, 90–93
    PL/SQL and, 193–194
    script files, 94–98
    scrollback buffer, 87–88
    text editors, 81–85
SQL*Plus menu, 87–89
SQL scripts. *See also* script files
    described, 381
    inserting comments in,
        137–139
    stored procedures and, 196

SQLCODE command, 218–219
SQLERRM command, 218–219
star schema, 282–283
START WITH parameter, 359, 361
START WITH sequence, 382
STORAGE_ERROR exception, 218
STORE command, 89–90, 382
stored functions, 195
stored procedures, 193–196, 382
strings
    changing case, 110–112
    described, 26, 382
    dividing, 114–118
    length, 112–113, 297
    matching, 59
    parsing, 114–118
    quote marks and, 37, 59
    spaces in, 297
    substrings, 113–114, 382
    trimming, 118–120
    variable length, 297
strongly typed languages, 301, 382
Structured English Query
    Language (SEQUEL), 9
Structured Query Language.
    See SQL
subqueries, 177–182
    correlated, 181–182
    described, 177, 382
    multicolumn, 180
    multirow, 179–180
    single-row, 177–179
    uses for, 177
substitution variables, 96–97
SUBSTR function, 113–114, 382
substrings, 113–114, 382
subtype entities, 382
subtypes, 264–267, 287–288
SUM function, 140, 382
summary data, 328–329
supertypes
    described, 382
    relationships, 264–267
    translating, 287–288
surrogate keys, 252–253, 310, 327,
    358–359, 382
synonyms, 362–364, 382
syntax, 25, 382
SYS_CONTEXT function, 108, 382
SYSDATE function, 106–107,
    121–122, 382
system-defined exceptions,
    218–219

system privileges, 4, 53, 382
system requirements, 370–371
system variables, 106–108, 382

■ T

table-based records, 212
table creation
    alternative syntax for, 311
    based on existing table,
      343–344
    complex tables, 24–30
    with CREATE TABLE
      command, 17, 375
    example, 35–36
    guidelines, 20–21
    naming tables, 21–24
    table structure, 30
    test tables, 153–155
tables
    adding columns to, 345–346
    adding data to, 53
    aliases, 166–167, 382–383
    altering structure of, 345–348
    based on existing tables,
      343–344
    child, 162–164
    code, 253
    combining data from,
      174–176
    committing changes to,
      71–73
    complex, 24–30
    constraints, 303, 305–307, 383
    creating. See table creation
    data in other tables, 254–255
    described, 1, 382
    displaying data from,
      164–167
    dropping, 18–20, 73, 376
    DUAL, 66–67
    flat-file, 341
    inserting records, 18, 32–37
    joining. See joins
    making available to
      users, 363
    modifying data in, 67
    multiple, 164–167
    names, 21–24, 330, 344
    parent, 162–164, 328–329
    populating, 18, 32–37
    relationships, 5–6, 162–176

removing data from, 53,
    68–69
structure of, 30–31
test, 153–155
tracking activity on, 107–108
transferring data between,
    339–344
truncating, 69
updating data in, 53, 67
uses for, 1
viewing contents, 37–44
terms, glossary of, 373–384
test tables, 153–155
text
    changing case of, 110–112
    connecting pieces of, 41–42
    converting dates to, 127–130
    converting times to, 127–130
    filtering records based on,
      59–60
    formatting in SQL*Plus,
      91–92
    storage of, 24–27
    wrapping, 91–92
text columns, 24–26
text editors, 81–85
text functions, 110–120
text strings. See strings
third normal form (3NF), 278–279,
    284, 383
time
    converting to Oracle values,
      131–133
    converting to text, 127–130
    formatting, 127–134
    inserting, 131–133
    returning, 106–107
    storage of, 298
TIME_OUT_ON_RESOURCE
    exception, 218
TO_CHAR function, 127–132, 383
TO_DATE function, 131–132, 383
TOO_MANY_ROWS
    exception, 218
top number analysis, 352
transactions, 54, 69–73
transitive dependency,
    274–275, 383
triggering events, 195, 383
triggers
    cascades and, 321
    constraints and, 327–329

described, 383
performance and, 328–329
PL/SQL, 195–196
trimming, 119, 383
TRUE value, 56–58
TRUNCATE command, 68–69
TRUNCATE function, 109–110,
    121–122, 383
truncating records, 68–69
truncating tables, 69
.txt extension, 94
type conversions, 301

■ U

UIDs (unique identifiers), 237–238.
    See also identifiers
UML (Unified Modeling
    Language), 233–234, 383
underscore (_), 60, 330
undo facility, 54, 69–73
Unified Modeling Language
    (UML), 233–234, 383
UNION ALL operator,
    174–176, 383
UNION operator, 174–175, 383
UNIQUE modifier, 66. See also
    DISTINCT modifier
unique constraints, 307–310, 383
unique identifiers (UIDs), 237–238.
    See also identifiers
unique index, 307–310, 383
UNIQUE modifier, 66
uniqueness, 307–310
Unix systems, 94–95
UPDATE command, 53, 67, 383
UPDATE statement, 179–180
updates
    anomalies, 285–286, 383
    cascade, 317–322, 327, 374
    primary keys, 253
UPPER function, 110–112, 383
USER function, 107, 383
USERENV function, 108, 383
USERENV namespace, 108
users
    making tables available
      to, 363
    multiple, 4
    privileges, 4–5
    roles. See roles
    security and, 4–5

■ V

VALUE_ERROR exception, 218
values
    acceptable, 58
    adding, 140–141
    averaging, 141
    domains as, 301–302
    grouping, 142–144
    from multiple tables,
        312–326
    negative, 92
    NULL. *See* NULL values
    ranges, 56–57
    records based on, 55–58
    returning largest, 142
    returning smallest, 141
    from single tables, 307–310
    unique, 64–66
VARCHAR datatype, 297
VARCHAR2 datatype, 25–26, 118,
    297, 383
variables
    counter, 209–210
    described, 96, 383
PL/SQL, 201–205
    in script files, 96–98
    substitution, 96–97
    system, 106–108, 382
vertical bar (|), 41–43, 93
VI text editor, 83
views, 348–358
    changes to, 43–44
    creating, 349–350, 353–358
    described, 348, 383
    dropping, 351–352, 376
    filtering, 349–350
    security and, 348
    table, 37–44
    updates to, 350–351
    uses for, 348–349

■ W

Web pages, 1
Web sites, 1, 3, 10
WHEN condition, 208–209

WHERE clause
    described, 384
    filtering records, 54–55,
        59, 144
    indexes and, 157
    joins and, 165–169
WHERE condition, 67
WHERE CURRENT OF cursor,
    213–215, 384
WHILE loop, 209, 384
wildcards, 59–60, 384
WITH CHECK OPTION
    parameter, 351, 384
wrapping text, 91–92

■ Z

ZERO_DIVIDE exception, 218
zeros, 92, 218, 298

INTERNATIONAL CONTACT INFORMATION

AUSTRALIA
McGraw-Hill Book Company
Australia Pty. Ltd.
TEL +61-2-9900-1800
FAX +61-2-9878-8881
http://www.mcgraw-hill.com.au
books-it_sydney@mcgraw-hill.com

CANADA
McGraw-Hill Ryerson Ltd.
TEL +905-430-5000
FAX +905-430-5020
http://www.mcgraw-hill.ca

GREECE, MIDDLE EAST, & AFRICA
(Excluding South Africa)
McGraw-Hill Hellas
TEL +30-210-6560-990
TEL +30-210-6560-993
TEL +30-210-6560-994
FAX +30-210-6545-525

MEXICO (Also serving Latin America)
McGraw-Hill Interamericana Editores
S.A. de C.V.
TEL +525-1500-5108
FAX +525-117-1589
http://www.mcgraw-hill.com.mx
carlos_ruiz@mcgraw-hill.com

SINGAPORE (Serving Asia)
McGraw-Hill Book Company
TEL +65-6863-1580
FAX +65-6862-3354
http://www.mcgraw-hill.com.sg
mghasia@mcgraw-hill.com

SOUTH AFRICA
McGraw-Hill South Africa
TEL +27-11-622-7512
FAX +27-11-622-9045
robyn_swanepoel@mcgraw-hill.com

SPAIN
McGraw-Hill/
Interamericana de España, S.A.U.
TEL +34-91-180-3000
FAX +34-91-372-8513
http://www.mcgraw-hill.es
professional@mcgraw-hill.es

UNITED KINGDOM, NORTHERN,
EASTERN, & CENTRAL EUROPE
McGraw-Hill Education Europe
TEL +44-1-628-502500
FAX +44-1-628-770224
http://www.mcgraw-hill.co.uk
emea_queries@mcgraw-hill.com

ALL OTHER INQUIRIES Contact:
McGraw-Hill Technology Education
TEL +1-630-789-4000
FAX +1-630-789-5226
omg_international@mcgraw-hill.com

ORACLE SOFTWARE LICENSE AGREEMENT

YOU SHOULD CAREFULLY READ THE FOLLOWING TERMS AND CONDITIONS BEFORE BREAKING THE SEAL ON THE DISC ENVELOPE. AMONG OTHER THINGS, THIS AGREEMENT LICENSES THE ENCLOSED SOFTWARE TO YOU AND CONTAINS WARRANTY AND LIABILITY DISCLAIMERS. BY USING THE DISC AND/OR INSTALLING THE SOFTWARE, YOU ARE ACCEPTING AND AGREEING TO THE TERMS AND CONDITIONS OF THIS AGREEMENT. IF YOU DO NOT AGREE TO THE TERMS OF THIS AGREEMENT, DO NOT BREAK THE SEAL OR USE THE DISC. YOU SHOULD PROMPTLY RETURN THE PACKAGE UNOPENED.

LICENSE: ORACLE CORPORATION ("ORACLE") GRANTS END USER ("YOU" OR "YOUR") A NON-EXCLUSIVE, NON-TRANSFERABLE DEVELOPMENT ONLY LIMITED USE LICENSE TO USE THE ENCLOSED SOFTWARE AND DOCUMENTATION ("SOFTWARE") SUBJECT TO THE TERMS AND CONDITIONS, INCLUDING USE RESTRICTIONS, SPECIFIED BELOW.

You shall have the right to use the Software (a) only in object code form, (b) for development purposes only in the indicated operating environment for a single developer (one person) on a single computer, (c) solely with the publication with which the Software is included, and (d) solely for Your personal use and as a single user.

You are prohibited from and shall not (a) transfer, sell, sublicense, assign or otherwise convey the Software, (b) timeshare, rent or market the Software, (c) use the Software for or as part of a service bureau, and/or (d) distribute the Software in whole or in part. Any attempt to transfer, sell, sublicense, assign or otherwise convey any of the rights, duties or obligations hereunder is void. You are prohibited from and shall not use the Software for internal data processing operations, processing data of a third party or for any commercial or production use. If You desire to use the Software for any use other than the development use allowed under this Agreement, You must contact Oracle, or an authorized Oracle reseller, to obtain the appropriate licenses. You are prohibited from and shall not cause or permit the reverse engineering, disassembly, decompilation, modification or creation of derivative works based on the Software. You are prohibited from and shall not copy or duplicate the Software except as follows: You may make one copy of the Software in machine readable form solely for back-up purposes. No other copies shall be made without Oracle's prior written consent. You are prohibited from and shall not: (a) remove any product identification, copyright notices, or other notices or proprietary restrictions from the Software, or (b) run any benchmark tests with or of the Software. This Agreement does not authorize You to use any Oracle name, trademark or logo.

COPYRIGHT/OWNERSHIP OF SOFTWARE: The Software is the confidential and proprietary product of Oracle and is protected by copyright and other intellectual property laws. You acquire only the right to use the Software and do not acquire any rights, express or implied, in the Software or media containing the Software other than those specified in this Agreement. Oracle, or its licensor, shall at all times, including but not limited to after termination of this Agreement, retain all rights, title, interest, including intellectual property rights, in the Software and media.

WARRANTY DISCLAIMER: THE SOFTWARE IS PROVIDED "AS IS" AND ORACLE SPECIFICALLY DISCLAIMS ALL WARRANTIES OF ANY KIND, EITHER EXPRESS OR IMPLIED, INCLUDING, BUT NOT LIMITED TO, THE IMPLIED WARRANTIES OF MERCHANTABILITY, SATISFACTORY QUALITY AND FITNESS FOR A PARTICULAR PURPOSE. ORACLE DOES NOT WARRANT, GUARANTEE OR MAKE ANY REPRESENTATIONS REGARDING THE USE, OR THE RESULTS OF THE USE, OF THE SOFTWARE IN TERMS OF CORRECTNESS, ACCURACY, RELIABILITY, CURRENTNESS OR OTHERWISE, AND DOES NOT WARRANT THAT THE OPERATION OF THE SOFTWARE WILL BE UNINTERRUPTED OR ERROR FREE. ORACLE EXPRESSLY DISCLAIMS ALL WARRANTIES NOT STATED HEREIN, NO ORAL OR WRITTEN INFORMATION OR ADVICE GIVEN BY ORACLE OR OTHERS SHALL CREATE A WARRANTY OR IN ANY WAY INCREASE THE SCOPE OF THIS LICENSE, AND YOU MAY NOT RELY ON ANY SUCH INFORMATION OR ADVICE.

LIMITATION OF LIABILITY: IN NO EVENT SHALL ORACLE OR ITS LICENSORS BE LIABLE FOR ANY DIRECT, INDIRECT, INCIDENTAL, SPECIAL OR CONSEQUENTIAL DAMAGES, OR DAMAGES FOR LOSS OF PROFITS, REVENUE, DATA OR DATA USE, INCURRED BY YOU OR ANY THIRD PARTY, WHETHER IN AN ACTION IN CONTRACT OR TORT, EVEN IF ORACLE AND/OR ITS LICENSORS HAVE BEEN ADVISED OF THE POSSIBILITY OF SUCH DAMAGES. SOME JURISDICTIONS DO NOT ALLOW THE EXCLUSION OF IMPLIED WARRANTIES OR LIMITATION OR EXCLUSION OF LIABILITY FOR INCIDENTAL OR CONSEQUENTIAL DAMAGES SO THE ABOVE EXCLUSIONS AND LIMITATION MAY NOT APPLY TO YOU.

TERMINATION: You may terminate this license at any time by discontinuing use of and destroying the Software together with any copies in any form. This license will also terminate if You fail to comply with any term or condition of this Agreement. Upon termination of the license, You agree to discontinue use of and destroy the Software together with any copies in any form. The Warranty Disclaimer, Limitation of Liability, and Export Administration sections of this Agreement shall survive termination of this Agreement.

NO TECHNICAL SUPPORT: Oracle is not obligated to provide and this Agreement does not entitle You to any updates or up-grades to, or any technical support or phone support for, the Software.

EXPORT ADMINISTRATION: You acknowledge that the Software, including technical data, is subject to United States export control laws, including the United States Export Administration Act and its associated regulations, and may be subject to export or import regulations in other countries. You agree to comply fully with all laws and regulations of the United States and other countries ("Export Laws") to assure that neither the Software, nor any direct products thereof, are (a) exported, directly or indirectly, in violation of Export Laws, either to countries or nationals that are subject to United States export restrictions or to any end user who has been prohibited from participating in the Unites States export transactions by any federal agency of the United States government; or (b) intended to be used for any purposes prohibited by the Export Laws, including, without limitation, nuclear, chemical or biological weapons proliferation. You acknowledge that the Software may include technical data subject to export and re-export restrictions imposed by United States law.

RESTRICTED RIGHTS: The Software is provided with Restricted Rights. Use, duplication or disclosure of the Software by the United State government is subject to the restrictions set forth in the Rights in Technical Data and Computer Software Clauses in DFARS 252.227-7013(c)(1)(ii) and FAR 52.227-19(c)(2) as applicable. Manufacturer is Oracle Corporation, 500 Oracle Parkway, Redwood City, CA 94065.

MISCELLANEOUS: This Agreement and all related actions thereto shall be governed by California law. Oracle may audit Your use of the Software. If any provision of this Agreement is held to be invalid or unenforceable, the remaining provisions of this Agreement will remain in full force.

YOU ACKNOWLEDGE THAT YOU HAVE READ THIS AGREEMENT, UNDERSTAND IT, AND AGREE TO BE BOUND BY ITS TERMS AND CONDITIONS. YOU FURTHER AGREE THAT IT IS THE COMPLETE AND EXCLUSIVE STATEMENT OF THE AGREEMENT BETWEEN ORACLE AND YOU.

Oracle is a registered trademark of Oracle Corporation.

Register for the *Oracle Technology Network* (OTN)

Oracle Technology Network ("OTN") is the primary technical source for developers building Oracle-based applications. As an OTN member, you will be part of an online community with access to technical papers, code samples, product documentation, self-service technical support, free software, OTN-sponsored Internet developer conferences, and discussion groups on up-to-date Oracle technology. Membership is FREE! Register for OTN on the World Wide Web at

```
http://otn.oracle.com/books
```